The LEA Guide to Composition

JAMES D. WILLIAMS

LEA
2001

LAWRENCE ERLBAUM ASSOCIATES, PUBLISHERS
Mahwah, New Jersey   London

Lawrence Erlbaum Associates, Inc., Publishers
10 Industrial Avenue
Mahwah, NJ 07430

Cover design by Kathryn Houghtaling Lacey

Library of Congress Cataloging-in-Publication Data

Williams, James D. (James Dale), 1949–
The LEA guide to composition / James D. Williams.

                                                  p.   cm.
    Includes index.
ISBN 0-8058-3137-1 (cloth : alk. paper)
1. English language—Rhetoric. 2. Report writing—Problems, exercises,
    etc. 3. English language—Textbooks for foreign speakers.
    4. College readers.   I. Title: Guide to composition.   II. Title.
PE1408 .W594   2001
808'.042 —dc21   00-052833
                                                                         CIP

Books published by Lawrence Erlbaum Associates are printed on
acid-free paper, and their bindings are chosen for strength and dura-
bility.

Printed in the United States of America
10 9 8 7 6 5 4 3 2 1

BRIEF CONTENTS

Chapter 1   Personal Writing   1

Chapter 2   Building Bridges   29

Chapter 3   Writing as a Process   59

Chapter 4   Reporting Events   87

Chapter 5   Reporting Information   125

Chapter 6   Interpreting Events   165

Chapter 7   Interpreting Information   207

Chapter 8   Evaluating Events   241

Chapter 9   Evaluating Information   271

Chapter 10   Argumentation   295

Chapter 11   Persuasion   329

Chapter 12   Interpreting Short Fiction   349

Handbook   **383**

DETAILED CONTENTS*

Chapter 1   *Personal Writing*   *1*

Conventions   *1*
Personal Reflection   *2*
   ❖ Journal Entry   *2*
Features of Personal Writing   *2*
   Personal Writing Entertains and Teaches   *3*
      ❖ Linked Assignment: Sharing an Experience   *3*
   Two Methods for Conveying a Lesson: Direct and Indirect   *4*
      ❖ Diverse Voices   *4*
      • Michael Nava, "Gardenland, Sacramento, California"   *5*
      ❖ Writing Assignment: A Personal Experience   *10*
   Student Paper   *10*
      • Leslie, "My First Job"   *12*
      ❖ Applying Key Ideas: Identifying the Lesson in Personal Writing   *15*
      ❖ Writing Assignment: Personal Writing with Analysis   *15*
      • Richard Selzer, "Imelda"   *16*
      ❖ Applying Key Ideas: A Chronicle of Change   *24*
Readings   *25*
      • Kate Scannell, "Skills and Pills"   *25*
      ❖ Critical Reading Guide   *27*
      ❖ Writing Assignment: Personal Writing Using the Indirect Method   *27*
      ❖ Group Activities: Personal Writing Using the Indirect Method   *28*

Chapter 2   *Building Bridges*   *29*

Language and Groups: Insiders and Outsiders   *29*
   Conventional Reality   *30*
Writing and Groups   *30*
   Analysis   *31*
   Reasons for Writing   *31*
Interpreting   *31*
   Interpreting Is a Social Action   *32*
   Interpretations Are Linked to Argument   *32*
   Interpretations Are Linked to Who You Are   *32*
      ❖ Applying Key Ideas: Who Are You?   *33*

---

*The symbol ❖ indicates a pedagogical feature of the text.

Insiders and Outsiders *33*

Audience and Rhetorical Stance *33*

Conventions and Audience *34*

❖ Diverse Voices *34*

Subject Matter *34*

❖ Applying Key Ideas: Your Role as an Insider *35*

Standards of Proof *35*

❖ Applying Key Ideas: Wanting to Join a Group *36*

Insiders Writing for Insiders *37*

Insiders or Outsiders Writing for Outsiders *37*

❖ Linked Assignment: Insiders and Outsiders: Your School's
Mission Statement *38*

❖ Writing Assignment: Exploring the Language of Inclusion
& Exclusion *39*

The Teacher as Audience *39*

Subject Areas, Subject, Topic, and Thesis *39*

Subject Areas *40*

Subjects *40*

Topics *41*

Thesis *41*

❖ Applying Key Ideas: Differences Between Topics and Theses *41*

Developing a Thesis *42*

❖ Journal Entry *43*

Premises *43*

When Your Audience Doesn't Accept Your Premises *44*

❖ Applying Key Ideas: Identifying Premises *44*

Have a Thesis in Advance *44*

Evaluating Your Claim *45*

❖ Journal Entry *45*

Rhetorical Purpose *46*

A Model of Traditional Rhetorical Purpose *46*

• Morris Bishop, "The Middle Ages" *47*

A Model of Innovative Rhetorical Purposes *50*

• Bonnie Anderson & Judith Zinsser, "The Townswoman's Daily
Life: The Twelfth to the Seventeenth Centuries" *51*

A Model of Confrontational Rhetorical Purpose *54*

• Shulamith Shahar, "Townswomen" *54*

❖ Critical Reading Guide *56*

❖ Applying Key Ideas: Recognizing Rhetorical Purposes
in Your Own Writing *58*

❖ Writing Assignment: Writing a Mission Statement for Your School *58*

Chapter 3   *Writing as a Process*   *59*

Stages of Writing *59*

❖ Linked Assignment: Understanding Your Writing Process *60*

Invention *61*

Discussion *61*

Outlining *62*

❖ Applying Key Ideas: Outlining for Content *62*

Freewriting *62*

- Jennifer, Freewriting Sample *63*
- ❖ Linked Assignment: Freewriting *63*

Journals *64*
- Chris, Journal Sample *64*
- ❖ Journal Entry *65*

Talk–Write *65*
- ❖ Applying Key Ideas: Creating an Oral Composition *65*

Metaphor *65*
- ❖ Applying Key Ideas: Generating Metaphors *66*
- ❖ Diverse Voices *67*

Planning *67*
Drafting *68*
Revising *68*
- Karen, "The Decision," Draft 1 *69*
- Karen, "The Decision," Draft 2 *73*
- Karen, "The Decision," Draft 3 *76*
- Karen, "Deciding to Go to College," Final Draft *80*

Writing as Problem Solving *81*
Private Writing *81*
- ❖ Journal Entry *82*

Editing *82*
- ❖ Applying Key Ideas: Varying Sentences *82*
- ❖ Writing Assignment: Is College Worth the Sacrifice? *83*
- ❖ Group Activities: Is College Worth the Sacrifice? *83*
- ❖ Writing Assignment: Characterizing Your Writing Process *84*
- ❖ Writing Guide: Characterizing Your Writing Process *84*

Chapter 4 *Reporting Events* *87*

Title, Introduction, Body, and Conclusion *87*

Title *88*
Introduction 88
Finding a Familiar Starting Place as a Point of Reference *88*
- ❖ Linked Assignment: Campus Events *89*

Moving from the Known to the Unknown *89*
Cultural Factors: Building on Shared Experiences *89*
- ❖ Diverse Voices *90*

Shared Experiences in Writing for Outsiders *90*
- Passage 1: Marco Polo (Daniel Boorstin) *90*
- Passage 2: Pasteur and Rabies (Peter Radetsky) *91*
- Passage 3: Civil War Terms of Enlistment (James M. McPherson) *91*

The Richly Detailed Body *92*
- Passage 4: Marco Polo's Voyage Home (Daniel Boorstin) *92*

Closing the Scene: The Conclusion *93*
Conclusions Linked to the End of the Event *94*
- Passage 5: The Retreat at Bull Run (James M. McPherson) *94*

Conclusions That Look Forward or Outward Through a Generalization *95*
- Passage 6: Riots in Watts (Robert Weisbrot) *95*
- ❖ Writing Assignment: Reporting a Campus or Community Event *97*

The Interpretive Report   *97*

Beyond Surface Appearances   *97*

Knowledge Specific to a Particular Audience   *98*

- Passage 7: The Bookshop Fire (Amanda)   *98*
- Passage 8: Campus Attack (Karen)   *99*
- ❖ Linked Assignment: Interpreting What You See   *100*

Setting the Scene When You Are an Insider Writing to Insiders   *100*

- Passage 9: Testing Memory (M. Masson and J. Miller)   *101*
- Passage 10: Shopping Mall Survey (Amy)   *101*

Reason as a Means of Support   *102*

Cause and Effect   *102*

Definition   *102*

Comparison and Contrast   *102*

Character as a Means of Support   *103*

- ❖ Journal Entry   *103*

Reason and Character Combined   *104*

- Passage 11: A Japanese Child Learns English (Kenji Hakuta)   *104*
- ❖ Diverse Voices   *106*
- ❖ Journal Entry   *106*

Readings   *106*

- Peter Radetsky, "Viruses"   *107*
- ❖ Critical Reading Guide   *108*
- James M. McPherson, "Farewell to the Ninety Days' War"   *109*
- ❖ Critical Reading Guide   *112*
- Robert Weisbrot, "Freedom Bound: A History of America's Civil Rights Movement"   *112*
- ❖ Critical Reading Guide   *114*
- Daniel Boorstin, "The Discoverers"   *115*
- ❖ Critical Reading Guide   *118*
- Craig, "Observations of the Locomotion, Grooming, and Reproductive Behavior of *Acheta Domesticus*" (student sample report of an event)   *119*
- ❖ Critical Reading Guide   *121*
- ❖ Writing Assignment: Writing an Interpretive Report of Events   *122*
- ❖ Writing Guide: Writing an Interpretive Report   *122*
- ❖ Group Activities: Writing an Interpretive Report   *124*

Chapter 5   *Reporting Information*   *125*

Facts Are What We Agree They Are   *126*

Facts and Group Membership   *127*

- ❖ Diverse Voices   *128*
- ❖ Journal Entry   *129*
- ❖ Applying Key Ideas: Agreeing on Facts   *129*

Presenting Facts in a Report   *129*

Sources of Facts   *129*

Identifying the Aim of Your Report   *130*

Summarizing Information   *130*

- Passage 1: Alternating Between Summary and Detail within a Sentence (Jill)   *130*

- Passage 2: Alternating Between Summary and Detail within a Paragraph (Sarah W. Freedman) *131*
- Passage 3: Alternating Between Summary and Detail Across Paragraphs (Scott) *131*
- ❖ Applying Key Ideas: Recognizing Shifts Between Summary and Factual Detail *132*
- ❖ Diverse Voices *132*

Deciding What to Summarize *133*

Reports of Information That Aim to Teach 133

Summary Reports: Outsiders to Insiders *133*
- Passage 4: Summary Report of a Book (Hiro) *134*
- Passage 5: Summary Report of a Poem (Amy) *135*

Summary Reports: Outsiders and Insiders to Outsiders *136*
- Passage 6: Fractal Geometry (James Gleick) *136*
- ❖ Writing Assignment: Summarizing Information *140*
- ❖ Group Activities: Summarizing Information *143*

Reports of Information That Lead to Action 143
- Passage 7: The Changing Demographics of San Jose (Scott) *144*
- Passage 8: The Best Way to Fix Medicare (Michael Kinsley) *145*

Readings 147
- Patrick L. Courts, "Literacy and Empowerment: The Meanings Makers" *147*
- ❖ Critical Reading Guide *149*
- ❖ Journal Entry *149*
- John L. Casti, "Paradigms Lost" *150*
- ❖ Critical Reading Guide *152*
- Deborah Tannen, "You Just Don't Understand: Women and Men in Conversation" *152*
- ❖ Writing Assignment: Summarizing What You Have Read *154*
- ❖ Writing Guide: Summarizing What You Have Read *154*
- ❖ Writing Assignment: Reporting and Interpreting What You Have Read *156*
- Nan Hentoff, "When Nice People Burn Books" *157*
- ❖ Writing Guide: Reporting and Interpreting What You Have Read *160*

Chapter 6   *Interpreting Events*   *165*

- ❖ Diverse Voices *165*

Interpretations of Events Have Aims 166

Explaining What an Event *Is* *166*
- ❖ Journal Entry *167*

Explaining What an Event Is Through Comparison and Contrast *167*
- Passage 1: The Growing Distrust of Government (Miguel) *168*

Explaining What an Event Is Through Analysis *170*
- Passage 2: The System Doesn't Work (Mary) *170*

Explaining What an Event Is Through Definition *173*
- Passage 3: The Case of Clarence Thomas and Anita Hill (Sandra L. Bloom) *173*
- ❖ Applying Key Ideas: Using Metaphor *176*
- ❖ Writing Assignment: Explaining What an Event Is *176*
- ❖ Diverse Voices *176*

Explaining Underlying Causes *177*
- • Passage 4: When Will People Help? (John Darley and Bibb Latané) *177*
- ❖ Applying Key Ideas: Reporting Events and Interpreting Causality *180*

Looking for Fresh Perspectives *180*
- • Passage 5: Innocent Victim or Intolerant Invader? (Patricia N. Limerick) *181*
- ❖ Linked Assignment: Considering Causes of Events *184*
- ❖ Writing Assignment: Interpreting an Event *184*

Predicting the Future *185*
- • Passage 6: The Crisis of Meaning in American Cities (Bill Bradley) *185*
- • Passage 7: Causes, Root Causes, and Cures (Charles Murray) *189*
- ❖ Writing Assignment: Providing an Interpretation That Predicts the Future *193*
- ❖ Group Activities: Providing an Interpretation That Predicts the Future *193*

Readings *194*
- • Peter Brown, "Person and Group in Judaism and Early Christianity" *194*
- ❖ Critical Reading Guide *198*
- • Michael Williams, "China and the World After Tian An Men" *199*
- ❖ Critical Reading Guide *200*
- ❖ Writing Assignment: Japanese-Americans in U.S. Concentration Camps *201*
- ❖ Writing Guide: Japanese-Americans in U.S. Concentration Camps *202*
- ❖ Group Activities: Japanese-Americans in U.S. Concentration Camps *204*

Chapter 7   *Interpreting Information*   *207*

Analysis and Synthesis *207*
- • Passage 1: Analysis by Classification (Russell Baker) *208*
- • Passage 2: Fitting a Piece into a Whole (Verlyn Klinkenborg) *208*

Organization *209*

Thesis and Antithesis *209*
- • Passage 3: Overturning a Thesis with an Antithesis (Gerald Gunderson) *209*
- ❖ Journal Entry *210*

The Structure of Interpretation *210*
- • Passage 4: Political vs. Spiritual Love (Ako) *211*
- ❖ Group Activities: Asking Questions about Analysis and Interpretation *214*
- ❖ Diverse Voices *214*

Building Your Interpretation *215*
- ❖ Writing Assignment: Interpreting a Text *215*
- ❖ Group Activities: Interpreting a Text *217*

Readings *218*
- • Paul E. Peterson, "Give Kids the Vote" *219*
- ❖ Critical Reading Guide *221*

DETAILED CONTENTS

- Daniel J. Singal, "The Other Crisis in American Education"   *222*
- ❖ Critical Reading Guide   *227*
- ❖ Writing Assignment: Interpreting "The Other Crisis in American Education"   *228*
- Lauren B. Resnick, "Literacy in School and Out"   *228*
- ❖ Critical Reading Guide   *237*
- ❖ Writing Assignment: Interpreting the Literacy Crisis   *237*
- ❖ Writing Guide: Interpreting the Literacy Crisis   *237*

Chapter 8   *Evaluating Events*   *241*

- Passage 1: Pearl Harbor (Phuong)   *242*

Discourse Communities and Your Evaluation   244
- ❖ Journal Entry   *244*
- ❖ Diverse Voices   *244*

Selecting an Event for Evaluation   245
Avoiding the Commonplace   *245*
- ❖ Linked Assignment: Selecting an Event for Evaluation   *246*

Provide a Background for the Event   247
- Passage 2: Why College Tuitions Are So High (Elliot Negin)   *247*
- ❖ Linked Assignment: Creating a Background   *248*

Interpreting the Event   248
- Passage 3: Why College Tuitions Are So High (Elliot Negin)   *249*

Evaluating the Event   250
- Passage 4: Why College Tuitions Are So High (Elliot Negin)   *250*

Placing the Event in a Broader Context   250
- Passage 5: Why College Tuitions Are So High (Elliot Negin)   *251*
- ❖ Writing Assignment: Evaluating a Campus Event   *251*

Readings   251
- Stephen Jay Gould, "Bully for Brontosaurus: Reflections in Natural History"   *252*
- ❖ Critical Reading Guide   *255*
- Susan Faludi, "Backlash"   *256*
- ❖ Critical Reading Guide   *260*
- ❖ Writing Assignment: Evaluating an Abstract Event   *261*
- Elliot Negin, "Why College Tuitions Are So High"   *261*
- ❖ Writing Guide: Evaluating an Abstract Event   *267*
- ❖ Group Activities: Evaluating an Abstract Event   *268*

Chapter 9   *Evaluating Information*   *271*

Evaluations of Data   272
- Passage 1: The Great Disruption (Francis Fukuyama)   *272*
- ❖ Applying Key Ideas: When Evaluation and Interpretation Overlap   *275*

Reviews of Articles and Books   275
- Passage 2: A Review of *Gaining Ground in College Writing* (Robert Brooke)   *275*
- ❖ Journal Entry   *278*
- ❖ Writing Assignment: Reviewing a Textbook   *279*

Evaluating Interpretations   *279*
- Passage 3: Frequency in Errors (Gary Sloan)   *279*

- Passage 4: The Education of a Torturer (Janice Gibson and Mika Haritos-Fatouros) *280*
- Passage 5: And God Created . . . From Fish to Gish (John L. Casti) *281*
- ❖ Diverse Voices *284*

Readings *284*
- James D. Williams, "Preparing to Teach Writing" *284*
- ❖ Critical Reading Guide *286*
- Cammie, "Saint Augustine and Platonic Thought" *287*
- ❖ Critical Reading Guide *288*
- ❖ Writing Assignment: A Short Evaluation of an Interpretation *289*
- ❖ Writing Guide: A Short Evaluation of an Interpretation *291*
- ❖ Group Activities: A Short Evaluation of an Interpretation *293*

Chapter 10 *Argumentation* *295*

The Structure of Arguments *295*
- Passage 1: The Child in the Supermarket *296*
- ❖ Applying Key Ideas: Differentiating Arguments *297*

Starting with a Problem *299*
- ❖ Linked Assignment: Identifying Problems in Your Community *299*

Premises *299*
- Passage 2: The Rock-n-Roll Star *300*

People Don't Always Agree on Premises *301*
- ❖ Applying Key Ideas: Identifying Premises *301*
- ❖ Diverse Voices *301*
- ❖ Journal Entry *302*

Proposals and Claims *302*

Argumentation and Persuasion *302*

What Makes a Claim Argumentative? *302*

Where Should You Put Your Claim? *303*
- Passage 3: A Claim Near the Beginning of an Argumentation (Susan E. Davis) *303*

Minor Claims *304*
- Susan E. Davis, "Natural Restoration: When Humans Walk Away" *304*

Support *309*

Logical Proof *309*

Character as Proof *311*

Emotional Proof *312*

Presenting Evidence *312*

Using Examples *313*

Recognizing Contrary Views *313*
- ❖ Applying Key Ideas: Including Contrary Views in an Argument *315*

Thesis and Antithesis *315*
- Passage 4: Genes and Crime (Gilberto) *316*

Conclusions *317*
- Passage 5: An Outward Looking Conclusion (Susan E. Davis) *318*
- ❖ Writing Assignment: Scofflaws *318*
- ❖ Writing Assignment: Problems on Campus *319*

Common Flaws in Arguments *319*

  Faulty Causality *319*

  Faulty Generalization *320*

  Slippery Slope *320*

  Attacking the Person *320*

    ❖ Journal Entry *321*

  Either/Or Fallacy *321*

Readings *321*

  • Albert Shanker, "Value Free?" *322*

  ❖ Critical Reading Guide *323*

  • Henry Louis Gates, Jr., "Whose Culture Is It Anyway?" *323*

  ❖ Critical Reading Guide *324*

  ❖ Writing Assignment: Arguing Diversity *325*

  ❖ Writing Guide: Arguing Diversity *325*

Chapter 11 *Persuasion* *329*

Persuasive Essays *330*

  • Passage 1: Teach by the Values You Preach (Jane Tompkins) *331*

  ❖ Writing Assignment: Your Ideal Classroom *334*

  Supplying Information in the Persuasive Essay *335*

  ❖ Journal Entry *335*

  • Passage 2: Why I Hate "Family Values" (Let Me Count the Ways) (Katha Pollitt) *335*

  ❖ Linked Assignment: Values and Persuasion *340*

  ❖ Writing Assignment: Calling for an Action *340*

Advertising *341*

  ❖ Diverse Voices *341*

  ❖ Applying Key Ideas: Analyzing Persuasive Appeals in Print Ads *341*

  ❖ Writing Assignment: Producing an Ad *342*

Political Speeches *342*

  • John F. Kennedy, "Campaign Speech, Houston, Texas, September 12, 1960" *343*

  ❖ Linked Assignment: Preparing for a Political Campaign *346*

  ❖ Writing Assignment: A Political Speech *347*

  ❖ Group Activities: A Political Speech *347*

Chapter 12 *Interpreting Short Fiction* *349*

  • John Steinbeck, "The Chrysanthemums" *350*

Key Elements of Fiction *356*

  Setting *356*

  Characters *358*

  ❖ Linked Assignment: Analyzing Character *359*

  Plot *359*

  Theme and Message *360*

    Group Membership and Meaning *360*

    Interpreting Literature for Your Place and Time *361*

    ❖ Linked Assignment: Theme and Message *362*

  Point of View *362*

    Omniscient *362*

      Limited Omniscient *362*

      First Person *363*

      Dramatic *363*

      ❖ Linked Assignment: Point of View *363*

    Irony *363*

      ❖ Diverse Voices *364*

      ❖ Writing Assignment: Interpreting "The Chrysanthemums" *364*

      ❖ Writing Guide: Interpreting "The Chrysanthemums" *364*

      • Maria, "Sexual Repression in 'The Chrysanthemums'" *366*

The Response Paper **368**

      ❖ Journal Entry *368*

      • T. C. Boyle, "The Descent of Man" *368*

      • Connie, Response Paper to "The Descent of Man" *375*

Readings **376**

      • Shirley Jackson, "The Lottery" *377*

      ❖ Critical Reading Guide *381*

      ❖ Writing Assignment: "The Lottery" *381*

      ❖ Group Activities: "The Lottery" *382*

The Handbook   *383*

Part One: Form and Function *385*

Sentence Structure **386**

    Subjects and Predicates *387*

    Clauses and Phrases *387*

Summary **388**

      ❖ Applying Key Ideas *388*

    Objects *389*

    Nouns *389*

    Pronouns *392*

Summary **392**

    Personal Pronouns *393*

    Case *393*

      ❖ Applying Key Ideas *394*

    Demonstrative Pronouns *394*

Summary **395**

    Reciprocal Pronouns *396*

    Possessive Pronouns *396*

Summary **397**

    Indefinite Pronouns *397*

Summary **399**

      ❖ Applying Key Ideas *399*

    He and She—His and Her *400*

Summary **400**

    Either *401*

    Few and Less *401*

Summary **401**

    Neither *402*

    None *402*

                                           DETAILED CONTENTS

Summary *402*

Reflexive Pronouns *402*

Summary *403*

Relative Pronouns *403*

Relative Clauses *403*

That and Which *404*

Summary *404*

Who and Whom *404*

Summary *405*

That and Who *405*

❖ Applying Key Ideas *405*

Verbs *406*

Transitive and Intransitive Verbs *406*

Linking Verbs *407*

Tense *408*

Number *408*

Subject–Verb Agreement *409*

Verb Forms *409*

Progressive Verb Form *409*

Perfect Verb Form *410*

Perfect Progressive Verb Form *410*

❖ Applying Key Ideas *410*

Modifiers: Adjectivals and Adverbials *411*

Adjectivals *411*

Adverbials *412*

More on Linking Verbs *412*

Good and Well *412*

Bad and Badly *413*

Summary *414*

❖ Applying Key Ideas *414*

Conjunctions *414*

Coordination *415*

Summary *416*

Summary *416*

Subordination *416*

Because *417*

Since, While, Because, and Whereas *417*

Summary *418*

❖ Applying Key Ideas *418*

Prepositional Phrases *419*

Number of Prepositions *420*

At the End of Sentences *420*

Like *420*

Summary *421*

❖ Applying Key Ideas *421*

Restrictive and Nonrestrictive Clauses *422*

Summary *422*

Summary *423*

Punctuation *423*

   Periods *423*

   Commas *423*

   Semicolon *424*

   Colon *425*

   Parentheses and the Dash *425*

   Salutations *426*

   Quotation Marks *426*

    ❖ Applying Key Ideas *427*

Word Choice *427*

   Commonly Confused Words *429*

Sentence Variety *434*

Paragraph Development *436*

   Coherence and Unity *436*

Part Two: Academic Writing *439*

Introduction *439*

Documentation *440*

   Paraphrasing *441*

    Original *441*

    Unacceptable Paraphrase *441*

    Acceptable Paraphrase *441*

   Rhetorical Factors *442*

   Common Knowledge *442*

   Using Quotations *443*

    Ellipses *444*

Writing in the Humanities *444*

The MLA Documentation Style *445*

   In-Text Citation *446*

Works Cited *447*

   Books *447*

   Dissertations *450*

   Articles *450*

   Electronic Sources *451*

   Film and Television Programs *464*

    • Craig, Sample Paper: "Observations of the Locomotion, Grooming, and Reproductive Behavior of the *Acheta domesticus*" *465*

Writing in Science *470*

Scientific Documentation Style *470*

   In-Text Citation *471*

References *472*

   Books *472*

   Dissertations *474*

   Articles *474*

   Electronic Sources *475*

    • Nancy, Sample Paper: "Perpetual Motion" *476*

Index *482*

Selection Credits *490*

GUIDE TO READINGS AND WRITING ASSIGNMENTS*

Chapter 1 *Personal Writing* 1

Readings
- Michael Nava, "Gardenland, Sacramento, California" 5
- Leslie, "My First Job" 12
- Richard Selzer, "Imelda" 16
- Kate Scannell, "Skills and Pills" 25
- ❖ Critical Reading Guide 27

Writing Assignments
- A Personal Experience 10
- Personal Writing with Analysis 15
- Personal Writing Using the Indirect Method 27

Chapter 2 *Building Bridges* 29

Readings
- Morris Bishop, "The Middle Ages" 47
- Bonnie Anderson & Judith Zinsser, "The Townswoman's Daily Life: The Twelfth to the Seventeenth Centuries" 51
- Shulamith Shahar, "Townswomen" 54
- ❖ Critical Reading Guide 56

Writing Assignments
- Exploring the Language of Inclusion & Exclusion 39
- Writing a Mission Statement for Your School 58

Chapter 3 *Writing as a Process* 59

Readings
- Jennifer, Freewriting Sample 63
- Chris, Journal Sample 64
- Karen, "The Decision," Draft 1 69
- Karen, "The Decision," Draft 2 73
- Karen, "The Decision," Draft 3 76
- Karen, "Deciding to Go to College," Final Draft 80

*The symbol ❖ indicates a pedagogical feature of the text.

Writing Assignments
- Is College Worth the Sacrifice? *83*
- Characterizing Your Writing Process *84*

Chapter 4   *Reporting Events*   *87*

Readings
- Passage 1: Marco Polo (Daniel Boorstin) *90*
- Passage 2: Pasteur and Rabies (Peter Radetsky) *91*
- Passage 3: Civil War Terms of Enlistment (James M. McPherson) *91*
- Passage 4: Marco Polo's Voyage Home (Daniel Boorstin) *92*
- Passage 5: The Retreat at Bull Run (James M. McPherson) *94*
- Passage 6: Riots in Watts (Robert Weisbrot) *95*
- Passage 7: The Bookshop Fire (Amanda) *98*
- Passage 8: Campus Attack (Karen) *99*
- Passage 9: Testing Memory (M. Masson and J. Miller) *101*
- Passage 10: Shopping Mall Survey (Amy) *101*
- Passage 11: A Japanese Child Learns English (Kenji Hakuta) *104*
- Peter Radetsky, "Viruses" *107*
- ❖ Critical Reading Guide *108*
- James M. McPherson, "Farewell to the Ninety Days' War" *109*
- ❖ Critical Reading Guide *112*
- Robert Weisbrot, "Freedom Bound: A History of America's Civil Rights Movement" *112*
- ❖ Critical Reading Guide *114*
- Daniel Boorstin, "The Discoverers" *115*
- ❖ Critical Reading Guide *118*
- Craig, "Observations of the Locomotion, Grooming, and Reproductive Behavior of *Acheta Domesticus*" *119*
- ❖ Critical Reading Guide *121*

Writing Assignments
- Reporting a Campus or Community Event *97*
- Writing an Interpretive Report of Events *122*

Chapter 5   *Reporting Information*   *125*

Readings
- Passage 1: Alternating Between Summary and Detail within a Sentence (Jill) *130*
- Passage 2: Alternating Between Summary and Detail within a Paragraph (Sarah W. Freedman) *131*
- Passage 3: Alternating Between Summary and Detail Across Paragraphs (Scott) *131*
- Passage 4: Summary Report of a Book (Hiro) *134*
- Passage 5: Summary Report of a Poem (Amy) *135*
- Passage 6: Fractal Geometry (James Gleick) *136*
- Passage 7: The Changing Demographics of San Jose (Scott) *144*
- Passage 8: The Best Way to Fix Medicare (Michael Kinsley) *145*
- Patrick L. Courts, "Literacy and Empowerment: The Meaning Makers" *147*

GUIDE TO READINGS AND WRITING ASSIGNMENTS

- ❖ Critical Reading Guide *149*
- • John L. Casti, "Paradigms Lost" *150*
- ❖ Critical Reading Guide *152*
- • Deborah Tannen, "You Just Don't Understand: Women and Men in Conversation" *152*

Writing Assignments
- • Summarizing Information *140*
- • Summarizing What You Have Read *154*
- • Reporting and Interpreting What You Have Read *156*

Chapter 6   *Interpreting Events*   *165*

Readings
- • Passage 1: The Growing Distrust of Government (Miguel) *168*
- • Passage 2: The System Doesn't Work (Mary) *170*
- • Passage 3: The Case of Clarence Thomas and Anita Hill (Sandra L. Bloom) *173*
- • Passage 4: When Will People Help? (John Darley and Bibb Latané) *177*
- • Passage 5: Innocent Victim or Intolerant Invader? (Patricia N. Limerick) *181*
- • Passage 6: The Crisis of Meaning in American Cities (Bill Bradley) *185*
- • Passage 7: Causes, Root Causes, and Cures (Charles Murray) *189*
- • Peter Brown, "Person and Group in Judaism and Early Christianity" *194*
- ❖ Critical Reading Guide *198*
- • Michael Williams, "China and the World After Tian An Men" *199*
- ❖ Critical Reading Guide *200*

Writing Assignments
- • Explaining What an Event Is *176*
- • Interpreting an Event *184*
- • Providing an Interpretation That Predicts the Future *193*
- • Japanese-Americans in U.S. Concentration Camps *201*

Chapter 7   *Interpreting Information*   *207*

Readings
- • Passage 1: Analysis by Classification (Russell Baker) *208*
- • Passage 2: Fitting a Piece into a Whole (Verlyn Klinkenborg) *208*
- • Passage 3: Overturning a Thesis with an Antithesis (Gerald Gunderson) *209*
- • Passage 4: Political vs. Spiritual Love (Ako) *211*
- • Paul E. Peterson, "Give Kids the Vote" *219*
- ❖ Critical Reading Guide *221*
- • Daniel J. Singal, "The Other Crisis in American Education" *222*
- ❖ Critical Reading Guide *227*
- • Lauren B. Resnick, "Literacy in School and Out" *228*
- ❖ Critical Reading Guide *237*

Writing Assignments
- • Interpreting a Text *215*
- • Interpreting "The Other Crisis in American Education" *228*
- • Interpreting the Literacy Crisis *237*

| Chapter 8 | *Evaluating Events* | *241* |

Readings
- Passage 1: Pearl Harbor (Phuong) *242*
- Passage 2: Why College Tuitions Are So High (Elliot Negin) *247*
- Passage 3: Why College Tuitions Are So High (Elliot Negin) *249*
- Passage 4: Why College Tuitions Are So High (Elliot Negin) *250*
- Passage 5: Why College Tuitions Are So High (Elliot Negin) *251*
- Stephen Jay Gould, "Bully for Brontosaurus: Reflections in Natural History" *252*
- ❖ Critical Reading Guide *255*
- Susan Faludi, "Backlash" *256*
- ❖ Critical Reading Guide *260*
- Elliot Negin, "Why College Tuitions Are So High" *261*

Writing Assignments
- Evaluating a Campus Event *251*
- Evaluating an Abstract Event *261*

| Chapter 9 | *Evaluating Information* | *271* |

Readings
- Passage 1: The Great Disruption (Francis Fukuyama) *272*
- Passage 2: A Review of *Gaining Ground in College Writing* (Robert Brooke) *275*
- Passage 3: Frequency in Errors (Gary Sloan) *279*
- Passage 4: The Education of a Torturer (Janice Gibson and Mika Haritos-Fatouros) *280*
- Passage 5: And God Created . . . From Fish to Gish (John L. Casti) *281*
- James D. Williams, "Preparing to Teach Writing" *284*
- ❖ Critical Reading Guide *286*
- Cammie, "Saint Augustine and Platonic Thought" *287*
- ❖ Critical Reading Guide *288*

Writing Assignments
- Reviewing a Textbook *279*
- A Short Evaluation of an Interpretation *289*

| Chapter 10 | *Argumentation* | *295* |

Readings
- Passage 1: The Child in the Supermarket *296*
- Passage 2: The Rock-n-Roll Star *300*
- Passage 3: A Claim Near the Beginning of an Argumentation (Susan E. Davis) *303*
- Susan E. Davis, "Natural Restoration: When Humans Walk Away" *304*
- Passage 4: Genes and Crime (Gilberto) *316*
- Passage 5: An Outward Looking Conclusion (Susan E. Davis) *318*
- Albert Shanker, "Value Free?" *322*
- ❖ Critical Reading Guide *323*

• Henry Louis Gates, Jr., "Whose Culture Is It Anyway?" *323*
❖ Critical Reading Guide *324*

Writing Assignments
• Scofflaws *318*
• Problems on Campus *319*
• Arguing Diversity *325*

Chapter 11   *Persuasion*   *329*

Readings
• Passage 1: Teach by the Values You Preach (Jane Tompkins) *331*
• Passage 2: Why I Hate "Family Values" (Let Me Count the Ways)
  (Katha Pollitt) *335*
• John F. Kennedy, "Campaign Speech, Houston, Texas,
  September 12, 1960" *343*

Writing Assignments
• Your Ideal Classroom *334*
• Calling for an Action *340*
• Producing an Ad *342*
• A Political Speech *347*

Chapter 12   *Interpreting Short Fiction*   *349*

Readings
• John Steinbeck, "The Chrysanthemums" *350*
• Maria, "Sexual Repression in 'The Chrysanthemums'" *366*
• T. C. Boyle, "The Descent of Man" *368*
• Connie, Response Paper to "The Descent of Man" *375*
• Shirley Jackson, "The Lottery" *377*
❖ Critical Reading Guide *381*

Writing Assignments
• Interpreting "The Chrysanthemums" *364*
• Interpreting "The Lottery" *381*

PREFACE

The LEA Guide to Composition is not just about the act of writing, although this is, of course, its primary focus. It is about using writing as a vehicle for learning—learning about the world, about the academy, about oneself. *The LEA Guide* explores, for example, ways of knowing, standards of proof, the role of reflection in writing, as well as the various conventions that govern writing in the undergraduate curriculum and beyond. It challenges students to rise above their own expectations and to look more deeply at themselves and what it means to be an educated person.

The LEA Guide is based on the idea that effective writing connects people through shared ideas, experiences, and beliefs. More than a social action, writing is a means of building community. *The LEA Guide* recognizes, however, that *community* is a broad concept and that everyone is a member of some communities but not of others. From the perspective of college composition and undergraduate writing, students are in the position of seeking entry to communities—generally represented by their majors or career goals—that have barriers to admittance. Consequently, they must engage in a process that involves mastering content-area information, using their diverse experiences as a bridge to the academy and defining who they are with respect to discrete academic communities and the wider world.

Underlying *The LEA Guide* is a simple premise: Writing is fundamentally argumentative. When we write, we commonly are interpreting an event or information and asking readers to accept that interpretation. Other types of writing naturally have different aims. Reports of events and information seek to convey information, whereas evaluations judge the worth of whatever the subject happens to be. But even in these instances, we can see that a report of an event, for example, is argumentative insofar as it gets readers to accept the representation of reality inherent in the report as being accurate. *The LEA Guide to Composition* considers a wide range of writing genres, yet the argumentative focus is constant throughout.

PEDAGOGICAL FEATURES

The theoretical framework of any textbook is meaningful only if it is supported by a well-known and effective pedagogical apparatus. *The LEA Guide* draws on the most significant strategies and techniques in composition studies. Moreover, *The LEA Guide* was **classroom tested** at various universities over a 4-year period to refine and improve the pedagogical apparatus. Although it suggests ways of instruction that are congruent with what we know about how people most easily learn how to become competent writers, *The LEA Guide* allows for numerous approaches to teaching composition.

Reading–Writing Connection

The connection between reading and writing is now well understood and widely accepted. Good writers are people who not only read regularly but who also read a variety of material, which allows them to internalize models and acquire appropriate genre familiarity. *The LEA Guide* therefore provides an extensive selection of fresh, thought-provoking, professional work. Because students gain a great deal from seeing how other students have responded to real writing tasks similar to those they must face, *The LEA Guide* also offers many student papers. Selections include personal experience essays, reports of events, reports of information, evaluations, arguments, and persuasive essays. In all instances, the readings engage students in topics that encourage reflection and thought.

Critical Reading and Thinking

Part of the undergraduate experience involves learning how to look beyond the surface of texts and get at ideas and messages that defy superficial analysis. In other words, it involves learning how to read and think critically. Although many texts claim to enhance critical-thinking skills, few provide the tools necessary to do so. *The LEA Guide,* however, fully embraces the premise that effective writing emerges out of critical thinking. Consequently, numerous reading selections are thoroughly analyzed to provide students with models of close, critical reading. Many others are linked to **Critical Reading Guides** that draw students into the reading selections by asking rhetorical questions that develop critical thinking skills and better understanding of how the authors' produced key effects.

Writing Activities

Because composition teachers have many different needs and goals, the key to providing effective writing activities is to offer a high degree of flexibility. *The LEA Guide* therefore offers **approximately 60 writing activities** of various types, suitable to students with a range of writing experience. Many of these activities are short writing assignments that are **linked** to longer ones, which allows students to build their skills sequentially, adding new skills as old ones are practiced and mastered.

Writing Guides

Composition research has shown that the most effective instruction occurs one on one, with the teacher acting as a guide through the writing process. The experience of composition teaching, however, rarely affords such individualized instruction: Students often work on papers at home alone, and class sizes make individualized instruction difficult. *The LEA Guide* provides the best possible substitute through its **Writing Guides,** which provide detailed information about how to succeed on selected assignments in each chapter. These guides offer concrete, practical advice based on years of teaching experience.

Group Activities

Composition teachers nationwide have for many years recognized the advantages in collaborative workshop activities, and for this reason *The LEA Guide* offers **Group Activities** in each chapter for selected writing assignments. These guides help students organize their workshops and prompt them to engage in a variety of group efforts that enhance the writing process. As a result, group work progresses with a clear purpose and well-defined goals, leading to more student involvement and, ultimately, better writing.

Application of Key Ideas

A vital key to better writing is practice. *The LEA Guide to Composition* therefore complements writing assignments, Writing Guides, and Critical Reading Guides with **Applying Key Ideas,** activities that allow students to practice using important concepts discussed in the text before they begin an actual writing assignment. Many of these activities involve writing tasks that help students understand how to use a rhetorical technique or that engage them in a reflective exercise that will inform an upcoming writing assignment.

Journal Entries

We now understand that journal writing is important because it increases the amount of writing students do and that it significantly enhances reflection and critical thinking. *The LEA Guide* applies this understanding by providing **Journal Entry** prompts throughout. These prompts encourage students to reflect not only on the material presented in the text but also on their lives as undergraduates. They serve as an effective means of helping students make connections between college and their lives outside of class.

Diverse Voices

Large numbers of composition classes today are highly diverse in terms of language, culture, ethnicity, age, and sexual orientation. In recognition of the enriching potential of this diversity, *The LEA Guide* provides specially designed writing activities that encourage students whose home language is one other than English and who come from nonmainstream cultural backgrounds to share their unique perspectives with the entire class. These classroom-tested activities develop an atmosphere of inclusion that makes diversity meaningful on a daily basis.

Handbook

The rhetorical discussions in *The LEA Guide to Composition* are complemented by the **Handbook,** which appears at the end of the text. The Handbook provides basic information about the form and function of language, but, more important, it focuses on the usage conventions that are a crucial part of academic writing. In addition, it discusses differences and similarities in the more specific conventions that govern writing in the humanities, social sciences, and science. The documentation formats for these three major divisions of the undergraduate curriculum are described in detail, with full-length student papers to illustrate the formats in context.

ACKNOWLEDGMENTS

This book took several years to complete, and it benefitted from the help of many people. Indeed, the list of those who contributed in one way or another is quite long. Some, however, merit special recognition. Therefore, I offer special thanks to the numerous students in North Carolina, Illinois, and California who used the book in draft form to help me refine each chapter. I am also grateful to the dozens of anonymous reviewers who devoted much time and thought in their written comments to me about how to make the book better. My editor at Lawrence Erlbaum Associates, Naomi Silverman, gave me the support and encouragement I frequently needed; I am glad that she has been my friend for many years. I never could have completed *The LEA Guide* without the help of my student assistants, Glenn Blalock, D'Ann Pletcher, Chris Morris, Michelle Mouton, Jim Baxley, Michelle Kelly, and Jennifer Olds. Finally, I offer thanks to my wife, Ako, for her loving support throughout the years I devoted to this book.

—*James D. Williams*

Personal Writing

The LEA Guide to Composition is not just about the act of writing, although this is, of course, its primary focus. It is about using writing as a vehicle for learning— learning about the world, about the academy, about oneself.

CHAPTER ONE

Personal Writing

Language is paramount. We use it to define who we are and to shape our place in life. We use it to learn, to socialize, to dream, to think. Throughout history, language has served as a bond to bring people together into single societies and to preserve their customs, culture, laws, and stories. In fact, some people argue that we could not even have society without language.

We also use language to get things done. For this reason, we can say that language in general and writing in particular are social actions. The way people use language depends on their *goals and intentions*, but it also depends on *situation*, which is inevitably social. For example, the language you use when talking with friends is less formal than the language you use when talking to a professor.

Most of us don't have to think about adjusting our level of formality from one situation to the next—it is an awareness that we acquired when we were children. With writing, however, we usually *do* have to think about how we use language, perhaps because the level of formality is so much greater in writing than in speech. Much of this book is designed to help you better understand the goals and intentions that influence how we use language, but it also aims to help you explore the situation-specific factors that govern what and how we write.

CONVENTIONS

If there were rules for writing, composition would be easy. You simply would learn the rules and apply them whenever you had to write. Unfortunately, there aren't any rules. Instead, *social conventions* govern language use. *Conventions are expectations that people around you have regarding the way you use language.* For example, these conventions dictate that we speak softly in a library, that we offer condolences when we learn that a friend has suffered a loss, and so on.

Conventions also govern how people use *written language*. Because most of your writing will be in response to *social demands* at school or on the job, the situations that prompt your writing will determine which conventions you will use. These conventions consist of expectations that the audience has regarding subject matter, format, standards of proof, tone, word choice, and a host of other factors. Thus, if you have to write a psychology paper, your teacher will expect you not only to write about a topic in psychology but also to use the conventions associated with writing in the social sciences in general and psychology in particular. Of course, if you don't know what those conventions are, you have a problem.

Writing conventions are different from social conventions in that many of them are the result of conscious decisions that people have made about the way texts should appear. Psychologists, for instance, decided as a group that writing in their field should have certain distinctive characteristics. After agreeing on what those characteristics would be, they published a guide for anyone writing psychology texts, titled the *Publication Manual of the American Psychological Association*. (This publication usually is referred to simply as the *APA Guide*.) This guide proved so popular that is was adopted by nearly everyone working in the social sciences. People in other areas have produced their own guides. Those working in literature developed the *MLA (Modern Language Association) Handbook for Writers of Research Papers*, which is widely used by those working in the humanities. Personal writing, unlike academic and business writing, applies a set of more general conventions that are not in a special guide.

PERSONAL REFLECTION

Centuries ago, the Greek philosopher Socrates exhorted his students to know themselves if they wished to attain true knowledge. Education hasn't changed all that much since the days when Socrates loitered in the Athenian agora urging young people to look inward. Teachers today encourage students to reflect on their experiences and to use them as a bridge to the world of academia.

Success requires an investment of time to figure out what one's personal experiences mean. Writing about personal experiences is understood to be one of the better ways of reflecting on life because putting words on paper or a computer screen is slow and ponderous—the time it takes provides ample opportunity to think.

Successful personal writing is challenging. It is also an invaluable part of becoming a better writer. Periodically throughout this book, you will find prompts intended to encourage you to keep a journal in which you can reflect on your experiences. Reflection of this sort can help you find meaning in a busy life, and it also can help you become a better, more thoughtful writer.

Journal Entry

Reflect on how you change your language on the basis of situation. What are some factors that influence the changes you make? Also consider your writing. Have you consciously thought about how different writing tasks call for different conventions? If so, how have the tasks you've performed and their associated writing conventions differed?

FEATURES OF PERSONAL WRITING

Good personal writing is like fiction—except the events are real. For example, both kinds of writing do far more than simply narrate events. They present problems that the people or characters involved must solve. On a deeper level, they allow readers to share experiences that, one way or another, give them insight into their own lives.

Both kinds of writing also have a similar structure. The beginning of a short story and the beginning of a piece of personal writing set the scenes for readers. The middle portion of personal writing describes how the writer overcame or failed to overcome the problem. (Not every piece of personal writing is about success in solving a problem.) In many instances, the middle will develop themes that wind their way through the work. It also may provide a chronicle of inner changes that give the writer new and deeper insight. The ending not only concludes the experience but also offers a message to readers. It may link the writer's inner change and insight to the message offered readers.

Still, the idea of a problem is very important. Personal writing without a problem can be fun, but it may not strike readers as particularly meaningful, which is why the writers of the samples below generally deal with hardship of one type or another. I elected to include samples that reflect individual struggles with life because such writing shows the strength of the human spirit and offers powerful lessons for us all. Personal writing without a problem may be interesting and entertaining, but rarely is it edifying.

Personal Writing Entertains and Teaches

Personal writing involves an important assumption—that people read it because they want to, not because they have to. Personal writing, therefore, is challenging in part because of the need to be interesting and entertaining. There is no question that much of the appeal of personal writing lies in its ability to give readers glimpses into the private lives of others. But it also teaches. Readers can recognize in the stories of people's lives important lessons that they can apply to themselves. Writers can recognize in their work the bonds that tie them to others. We are all much the same. Indeed, the most meaningful lessons seem to be those that remind readers of their common humanity. The teaching function of personal writing therefore means that your work must be generalizable to readers. It should allow them to see something of themselves in your work.

Identifying personal experiences that others can relate to is a fundamental requirement for success. Simply sharing something about life is not sufficient. For example, if I wrote a short paper merely about a trip to the market and how I bought a carton of milk, I would be sharing an experience, but not one that means anything. Anyone reading my paper would ask the question that is deadly for any piece of writing: "So what?" In addition, really good personal writing does something more, something hard to define and even harder to teach: Readers will find it inspirational, moving. Touching readers' emotions is the most powerful and worthwhile goal of personal (as well as fictional) writing.

Linked Assignment

SHARING AN EXPERIENCE

This activity gives you an opportunity to begin planning for a shared experience. It is linked to the writing assignment on page 10. Consider the experiences in your life that are special to you. Select two or three and write a short summary for each. Then respond to the following questions for each experience, discussing them with students in your class, if possible: (1) What happened in the experience? (2) What did I learn? (3) Why do I consider it to be special? (4) Why would anyone else find this experience interesting? (5) What is meaningful about the experience? You'll use these experiences later in the chapter for other exercises and writing assignments.

Two Methods For Conveying A Lesson: Direct and Indirect

Even people who have thought long and hard about their experiences find it difficult to convey to readers the lessons they've learned without sounding pedantic, like a little professor. They know that the lessons must be linked to the narrative, but how? There is always the temptation simply to tack a moral to the end, but that approach is not effective. Many writers rely on two methods to convey their lessons. The first I call *direct*. Writers describe their experience, outline their problem, how they overcame or failed to overcome the problem, and what they learned. Writers may state something as simple as "I learned . . . ." The passage presented here written by Michael Nava uses this approach.

The second method is what I call *indirect*. Writers *tell* readers very little; instead, the lesson emerges from the narrative. Stated another way, the writers *show* rather than tell. The second passage, written by Richard Selzer, uses this approach. The indirect method makes personal writing seem more like fiction because fiction also shows rather than tells. I admit to being partial to the second method. It seems that in the very best personal writing, the lessons emerge out of narratives about shared experiences. Some writers, of course, combine both methods in their work.

As you read the passages that follow, pay close attention to how the writers convey their lessons. Many writers stumble when they reach the edifying part of their work, and the passages below serve as effective models that you can use for your own work.

Diverse Voices

Not all cultures place the same value on the ability to write well. Even within a given culture, writing ability is often viewed in different ways. In the United States, for example, members of the working class generally value writing ability differently from members of the professional class. What value does your culture place on writing ability? Does it differ from what you have experienced in the United States?

Michael Nava

Michael Nava received a law degree from Stanford in 1981 and went on to work as an attorney for the City of Los Angeles before turning to writing full time. He has published several mystery novels, including *The Little Death, Goldenboy*, and *How Town*. The following passage describes part of his childhood in Sacramento, California, during the 1950s and 1960s.

GARDENLAND, SACRAMENTO, CALIFORNIA

1   I grew up in a neighborhood of Sacramento called Gardenland, a poor community, almost entirely Mexican, where my maternal family, the Acunas, had lived since the 1920s. Sacramento's only distinction used to be that it was the state capital. Today, because it frequently appears on lists of the country's most livable cities, weary big-town urbanites have turned it into a boomtown rapidly becoming unlivable. But when I was a child, in the late fifties and early sixties, the only people who lived in Sacramento were the people who'd been born there.

2   Downtown the wide residential neighborhoods were lined with oaks shading turreted, run-down Victorian mansions, some partitioned into apartments, others still of a piece, but all of them exuding a shadowy small-town melancholy. The commercial district was block after block of shabby brick buildings housing small businesses. The city's skyline was dominated by the gold-domed capitol, a confectioner's spun-sugar dream of a building. It was set in a shady park whose grass seemed always to glisten magically, as if hidden under each blade of grass were an Easter egg.

3   Sacramento's only other landmarks of note were its two rivers, the American and the Sacramento. They came together in muddy confluence beneath the slender iron joints of railroad bridges. Broad and shallow, the rivers passed as slowly as thought between the thick and tumble of their banks.

4   A system of levees fed into the rivers. One of these tributaries was called the Bannon Slough. Gardenland was a series of streets carved out of farmland backed up against the slough. It flowed south, curving east behind a street called Columbus Avenue, creating Gardenland's southern and eastern boundaries. The northern boundary was a street called El Camino. Beyond El Camino was middle-class tract housing. To the west, beyond Bowman Street, were fields and then another neighborhood that may just as well have existed on another planet for all I knew of it.

5   What I knew were the nine streets of Gardenland: Columbus, Jefferson, Harding, Cleveland, El Camino, Peralta, Wilson, Haggin, and Bowman; an explorer, an odd lot of presidents, an unimaginative Spanish phrase, and three inexplicable proper names, one in Spanish, two in English. It was as if the streets had been named out of a haphazard perusal of a child's history text. There were two other significant facts about the streets in Gardenland; they all dead-ended into the levee and their names were not continued across El Camino Boulevard into the Anglo suburb, called Northgate. Gardenland's streets led, literally, nowhere.

6   Unlike El Camino, where little square houses sat on little square lots, Gardenland had not been subdivided to maximum utility. Broad uncultivated fields stretched between and behind the ramshackle houses. Someone's "front yard" might consist of a quarter acre of tall grass and the remnants of an almond orchard. The fields were littered with abandoned farming implements and the foundations of long-gone houses. For a dreamy boy like me, these artifacts were magical. Finding my own world often harsh, I could imagine from these rusted pieces of metal and fragments of walls a world in which I would have been a prince.

7   But princes were hard to come by in Gardenland. Almost everyone was poor, and most residents continued to farm after a fashion, keeping vegetable gardens and flocks of chickens. There were neither sidewalks nor streetlights, and the roads, cheaply paved, were always crumbling and narrow as country lanes. At night, the streets and fields were lit by moonlight and the stars burned with millennial intensity above the low roofs of our houses.

8   The best way to think of Gardenland is not as an American suburb at all, but rather as a Mexican village, transported perhaps from Guanajuato,

where my grandmother's family originated, and set down lock, stock, and chicken coop in the middle of California.

9   My cousin Josephine Robles had divided her tiny house in half and ran a beauty shop from one side. Above her porch was a wooden sign that said in big blue letters GARDENLAND and, in smaller print below, BEAUTY SALON. Over the years the weather took its toll and the bottom half faded completely, leaving only the word GARDEN-LAND in that celestial blue, like a road sign to a cut-rate Eden.

10   By the time I was born, in 1954, my family had lived in Gardenland for at least twenty-five years. Virtually all I know of my grandfather's family, the Acunas, was that they were Yaqui Indians living in northern Mexico near the American border at Yuma, Arizona. My grandmother's family, the Trujillos, had come out of central Mexico in 1920, escaping the displacements caused by the Mexican Revolution of 1910. I have dim memories of my great-grandparents, Ygnacio and Phillipa Trujillo, doll-like, white-haired figures living in a big, dark two-story house in east Sacramento.

11   My grandparents settled on Haggin Avenue in a house they built themselves. My cousins, the Robles, lived two doors down. My family also eventually lived on Haggin Avenue, next door to my grandparents. Our house was the pastel plaster box that became standard suburban architecture in California in the fifties and sixties but it was the exception in Gardenland.

12   Most houses seemed to have begun as shacks to which rooms were added to accommodate expanding families. They were not built with privacy in mind but simply as shelter. We lived in a series of such houses until our final move to Haggin Avenue. In one of them, the living room was separated from the kitchen by the narrow rectangular bedroom in which my brothers and sisters and I slept. Adults were always walking through it while we were trying to sleep. This made for jittery children, but no one had patience for our complaints. It was enough that we had a place to live.

13   By the standards of these places, my grandparents' house was luxurious. It was a four-bedroom, L-shaped building that they had built themselves. My grandmother put up the original three rooms while my grandfather was in the navy during World War II. My aunt Socorro told me that my grandmother measured the rooms by having her children lie head to toe across a plot of ground. She bought the cement for the foundations, mixed and troweled it, and even installed pipes for plumbing. Later, when my grandfather returned, they added a series of long, narrow rooms paneled in slats of dark-stained pine, solid and thick walled.

14   Massive, dusty couches upholstered in a heavy maroon fabric, oversize beds soft as sponges, and a leather-topped dining room table furnished the house. Like the rusted combines in the field, these things seemed magical in their antiquity. I would slip into the house while my grandparents were both at work and wander through it, opening drawers and inspecting whatever presented itself to my attention. It was in this fashion that I opened a little-used closet and found it full of men's clothes that obviously were not my grandfather's. Later I learned that they had belonged to my uncle Raymond who had been killed in a car accident. In a subsequent exploration I found pictures of his funeral, including a picture taken of him in his casket, a smooth-faced, dark-skinned, pretty boy of fifteen.

15   Another time, I found a voluminous red petticoat in a cedar chest. Without much hesitation, I put it on and went into my grandmother's bedroom where I took out her face powder and lipstick. I applied these in the careful manner of my grandmother, transforming myself in the dressing mirror beneath the grim gaze of a crucified Christ. Looking back, I don't think I was trying to transform myself into a girl, but only emulating the one adult in my family who loved me without condition. Because she was the soul of kindness, it never occurred to me, as a child, that my grandmother might be unhappy. Only looking back do I see it.

16   She and my grandfather slept in separate rooms at opposite ends of their house. In the evening, my grandfather would sit on a couch in front of the television quietly drinking himself into a stupor while my grandmother did needlework at the kitchen table. They barely spoke. I would sit with my grandmother, looking at pictures in the *Encyclopedia Americana*, comfortable with the silence, which, to her, must have been a deafening indictment of a failed marriage.

17   In my parents' house, the marriage of my mother and stepfather was as noisily unhappy as my grandparents' was quietly miserable. In each shab-

by house where we lived I would be awakened by their fights. I learned to turn myself into a stone, or become part of the bed or the walls so as to abate the terror I felt. No one ever spoke of it. There was only one house in which my family lived together peaceably but it only existed as a blueprint that had come somehow into my stepfather's possession.

18   In the evening, he would take it down from a shelf and unroll it on the kitchen table. Together we would study it, laying claim to rooms, planning alterations. At the time, we lived in a tiny one-bedroom cinder-block house. My brother and I slept on a bunk bed in an alcove off the kitchen. At night, I could hear mice scampering across the cement floor, terrifying me when I woke up having to pee and pick my way through the darkness to the bathroom.

19   When we finally moved from the cinder-block house, it was to another, bigger version of that house rather than to the dream house of the blueprint. One night, my mother's screaming woke me. I hurried into the bedroom she and my stepfather occupied and found him beating her. When I tried to stop him, he threw me across the room. The next morning my mother told me he was sorry, but it was too late. Where I lived no longer mattered to me because I learned to live completely within myself in rooms of rage and grief. Now I think these rooms were not so different from the rooms we all occupied, my unhappy family and I.

20 Although not literally cut off from the outside world, Gardenland was little touched by it. We were tribal in our outlook and our practices. Anglos were generically called "paddies," whether or not they were Irish. All fair-skinned people were mysterious but also alike. Even TV, that great equalizer, only emphasized our isolation since we never saw anyone who looked remotely like us, or lived as we did, on any of the popular shows of the day. At school, the same homogeneity prevailed. Until I was nine I attended a neighborhood grade school where virtually every other child was like me, dark eyed and dark skinned, answering to names like Juarez, Delgadillo, Robles, Martinez. My own name, Michael Angel, was but an Anglicized version of Miguel Angel, a name I shared with at least three other of my classmates.

21   I had a remarkable amount of freedom as a child. As I said, we eventually lived on the same street as other members of my maternal family and I roamed their houses as unself-consciously as a Bedouin child might move among the tents of his people. I ate in whatever house I found myself at mealtime and the meals were the same in each of my relatives' houses—rice, beans, lettuce and tomato salad, stewed or fried meat, tortillas, salsa. My grandparents did not lock their doors at night—who did? what was there to steal?—so that I could slip into their house quietly and make my bed on their sofa when my parents were fighting.

But most of the time I spent outdoors, alone or 22 with my friends. In spring, the field behind my house was overrun with thistles. We neighborhood kids put in long days cutting trails through them and hacking out clearings that became our forts. Tiring of the fields, we'd lurk in abandoned houses, empty barns, and chicken coops. When all other amusements failed, there was always Bannon Slough, a muddy brown creek that flowed between thickly wooded banks. It was too filthy to swim in. Instead, in the steep shadows of bridges and railroad trestles we taught each other how to smoke and to swear.

Just as often I would be off by myself. Early on, 23 I looked for ways to escape my family. I found it in the stillness of the grass and the slap of the slough's brown water against the shore. There I discovered my own capacity for stillness. Lying on the slope of the levee, I could hear my own breath in the wind and feel my skin in the warm blades of grass that pressed against my neck. In those moments, Gardenland *was* Eden, and I felt the wonder and loneliness of the first being.

For, like Adam, I was lonely. Being everyone's 24 child, I was no one's child. I could disappear in the morning and stay out until dusk and my absence went unnoticed. Children barely counted as humans in our tribe. We were more like livestock and our parents' main concern was that the head count at night matched the head count in the morning.

My loneliness became as much a part of me as 25 my brown hair and the mole above my lip, something unremarkable. When I came out, I missed that sense of joining a community of others like me that so many of my friends describe. My habits of secrecy and loneliness were too deeply ingrained. I had become like my grandfather, who, in a rare moment of self-revelation, told me he was a "lone wolf"; the most unsociable of an unsociable tribe. Though I've changed as I've grown older, I still sometimes wonder if one reason I write is because I am filled with all the words I never spoke as a child.

26 Two things opened up for me the narrow passage through which I finally escaped Gardenland for good. The first was books. I learned to read early and, once started, could not get enough of books. In this affinity, I was neither encouraged nor discouraged by my family. Education beyond its most basic functions, learning how to read and write, to do sums, had absolutely no interest for them. My love of reading became simply another secret part of me.

27 There wasn't a library in Gardenland. Instead, a big white van pulled up to the corner of Wilson and El Camino, the city Bookmobile. Inside, patrons squeezed into a narrow passageway between tall shelves of books. The children's books occupied the bottom shelves. At the exit, a woman checked out books from a standing desk. The Bookmobile came once a week and I was a regular customer, always taking my limit of books.

28 Everything about the process pleased me. I was proud of my library card, a yellow piece of cardboard with my name typed on it, which I carried in a cowhide wallet that was otherwise empty. I liked taking books from the shelves, noting their heft and volume, the kind of type, whether they were illustrated, and I studied the record of their circulation, the checkout dates stamped in blue on stiff white cards in paper pockets on the inside covers. I loved the books as much as I loved reading. To me, they were organic things, as alive in their way as I was.

29 Like so many other bright children growing up in the inarticulate world of the poor, books fueled my imagination, answered my questions, led me to new ones, and helped me conceive of a world in which I would not feel so set apart. Yet I do not believe that my brains alone, even aided by my bookish fantasies, would have been enough to escape Gardenland. For this, I needed the kind of courage that arises out of desperation.

30 I found this courage in my homosexuality. Early on, I acquired a taste for reading history, particularly ancient history. I suppose that pictures of ruined Greek cities reminded me of the crumbling, abandoned houses in the fields of Gardenland. But I was also fascinated by pictures of the nude male statues. There was something about the smooth, headless torsos, the irisless eyes of ephebes that made me stop my idle flipping through pages and touch the paper where these things were depicted. By the time I was twelve I understood that my fascination was rooted in my sexual nature. One day, walking to school, clutching my books to my chest, girl-style, I heard myself say, "I'm a queer."

31 It was absolutely clear to me that Gardenland could not accommodate this revelation. Gardenland provided the barest of existences for its people. What made it palatable was the knowledge that everyone was about the same, united in ethnicity and poverty and passivity. The only rituals were the rituals of family, and family was everything there. But I knew that I was not the same as everyone else. And I was certain that my family, already puzzled by my silent devotion to books, would reject me entirely if it became known exactly what thoughts occupied my silence.

32 Had I been a different child I would have run away from home. Instead, I ran away without leaving home. I escaped to books, to sexual fantasy, to painful, unrequited crushes on male classmates. No one ever knew. I turned myself into an outsider, someone at the margins of a community that was itself outcast. Paradoxically, by doing this, I learned the peasant virtues of my hometown, endurance and survival. As a member of yet another embattled community, those virtues I absorbed as a child continue to serve me.

Nava begins by setting the scene. He describes the Sacramento of his childhood, a small town whose only distinction was being the capitol of California. Look at the details Nava provides. He writes about the oak trees shading the "turreted, run-down Victorian mansions" that exuded "a shadowy small-town melancholy." The commercial district downtown was "block after block of shabby brick buildings housing small businesses."

Two questions are important regarding the introduction: Why does Nava provide details, and why does he provide these particular details? The details are necessary to make the scene real, to enable readers to visualize the place of the narrative. In fact, Nava uses details throughout the narrative to help with visualization. Because actions are intimately linked to location, readers need details to understand the narrative. The specific details Nava uses in the introduction serve to generate an atmosphere that helps explain his sense of dreary, sad isolation. Other details that follow reinforce the atmosphere. Together, these details develop themes for the passage: isolation and loneliness. In this case, the themes also define the problem that Nava has to overcome.

Without these details, the passage would not have the same effect on readers. For example, consider this alternative to the first two paragraphs:

> *I grew up in Sacramento. It was a pretty boring place because not much happened there. In fact, its only claim to fame was being the state capitol. The residential areas were shady because there were lots of trees. The business district was full of brick buildings.*

This paraphrase has so few details that it does not allow readers to visualize the scene very well. Moreover, it is boring. The lesson here is that you must stay away from generalities unless you support them with concrete details, a technique that is examined here.

After setting the general scene, Nava becomes more specific, describing his neighborhood and some of the people in it to give readers more insight into his life. Greater specificity sharpens the themes. Notice that Nava has not yet moved toward a resolution of his problem, nor has he addressed his lesson. The details again are important; they help Nava develop a context for his narrative. The technique he uses is worthy of attention. In paragraph 7, Nava says that "almost everyone was poor." This statement by itself does not have much impact. Nava therefore provides details to make the statement more tangible: "Most residents continued to farm after a fashion, keeping vegetable gardens and flocks of chickens. There were neither sidewalks nor streetlights, and the roads, cheaply paved, were always crumbling and narrow as country lanes." These images are effective because they indicate that the residents had to keep gardens and chickens so they would have enough food on their tables. They give substance to the initial observation that "almost everyone was poor." When providing details, you always should move from the general to the specific. Indeed, this is one of the more important lessons about writing well.

With the necessary background information in place, Nava shifts in paragraph 10 to his own life. He further develops the theme of isolation. His family members did not speak to one another much because they were either "noisily unhappy" or "quietly miserable." It is not surprising to learn that Nava spent much of his time outdoors, and you may be tempted to conclude that his own life was "quietly miserable." The details of paragraphs 12–25 serve to heighten the sense of Nava's isolation and loneliness. Particularly powerful is this sentence from paragraph 19: "Where I lived no longer mattered to me because I learned to live completely within myself in rooms of rage and grief."

This sentence is important for another reason: It reflects a feature of the passage that is characteristic of much personal writing. Nava describes his life and the lives of those around him, and he tells readers about the lessons he learned, lessons that are valuable for everyone. But he offers few analytical comments in the process. He leaves it to readers to draw their own conclusions. For example,

Nava does not attempt to analyze what caused his stepfather to abuse his mother; he does not attempt to explain the pervasive unhappiness of his family. If Nava had provided such analysis, commentary, and explanation, of course, he would have produced a quite different work. The passage would have been more overtly instructional, more pedantic.

Nava instead relies primarily on the example of his own life to convey the lessons in this passage. The first lesson is that education was central to his ability to leave Gardenland. Initially, when Nava begins describing his experience with books, he appears to be providing just one more detail about his boyhood. Paragraph 29, however, indicates that this experience was particularly meaningful. He states that books "helped me conceive of a world in which I would not feel so set apart." Books, in other words, helped him begin to solve the problem of his isolation, his difference. They were a form of escape. Nava states this lesson directly. But in an interesting twist, Nava states that neither books nor education was sufficient for an escape—metaphorical as well as physical—from Gardenland. In his words, "For this, I needed the kind of courage that arises out of desperation." Facing fear and finding inner courage comprise Nava's second lesson.

Nava is telling rather than showing when presenting these lessons. The intellectual and spiritual poverty, as well as the financial, were powerful motivators to seek something better, but they also were mighty obstacles that could not be overcome easily. Nava suggests that with knowledge and courage anyone can face change and move on to new circumstances. Both lessons are important, and both are generalizable.

The direct method of conveying lessons in personal writing is effective in Nava's hands. It does not place many demands on readers. It also allows him to explore the details associated with the lessons, understanding that his readers can place them in a clear context. Nava lets readers know that he successfully escaped Gardenland and acknowledged his homosexuality. The point now is to share the details of the journey.

Writing Assignment

A PERSONAL EXPERIENCE

Use an experience that you developed for the linked assignment on page 3 as the basis for a personal experience paper. You should use the direct method for conveying your lesson, and you should follow Nava's example insofar as avoiding commentary and analysis. Be certain to provide rich details throughout.

Student Paper

The sample paper presented here was written by Leslie, a first-year student enrolled in a composition course. Leslie wrote this paper after drawing up a list of experiences similar to the one you produced in your personal experience. You should look at her preliminary work before reading her paper. The comments Leslie's groupmate made in response to the list of experiences are shown in the margins.

Preliminary List:

1. My father's funeral.

From the open casket, my father's face looked white and unreal. The church was full of people: friends, relatives, people from my dad's company. I never realized how many people knew and liked my father. I had always thought that my dad would live forever, so I guess I took him for granted. As a result, we weren't as close as I now wish we had been. The lesson I learned that day was that we need to cherish and appreciate those we love while we can, because we never know when they will be gone forever.

I don't know whether this would be a good idea. Some people might think it is too grim. Sorry.

2. My first day at college.

I walked into the gym and was swallowed in a sea of people, other students trying to sign up for classes. The walls of the gym were lined with tables for every department on campus, and the people behind the tables were handing out registration cards. I had never got around to visiting my advisor, so I didn't have a clue as to what I was supposed to do; I didn't even know what courses I should sign up for. I had worked out a schedule based on classes that looked interesting, but after standing in line after line, watching the time tick away before finally reaching a table, I discovered that most of the courses that looked interesting were upper level or graduate courses that I couldn't take. After 4 hours of this frustration, I simply sat down in the middle of the gym floor and started to cry. The lesson I learned was that I need to plan better before jumping into an unknown situation.

Well, this is something that we all could relate to. But maybe that's the problem. Is it too common to be interesting?

3. My senior prom.

Mike and I had been dating for about 6 months by the time of the prom, so I thought I knew him pretty well. But about an hour into the prom I was shocked when Mike followed some of his friends into a dark corner of the gym where several of the guys pulled out flasks. Mike took long drinks each time a flask came his way. When he came back to where I was standing with a couple of my friends, he smelled of alcohol and his voice was slurred. He told me he wanted to dance, but I was angry with him and said no. He said fine and walked away, disappearing into the crowd. I thought he would come back in a few minutes, but when he didn't, I went to look for him. I found him outside with Gina, one of my friends, and they were kissing. The lessons I learned from this were that sometimes we may think we know someone far better than we actually do and that 6 months isn't much time at all when it comes to learning about someone's true nature.

Now this sounds really cool. People like to read about romance and scandal, so it could work. It could turn out to be really interesting!

4. My first job.

My first job was in a clothing boutique that carried expensive clothes for older women. I didn't receive any training. I was just told to be polite to the customers and to help them as much as possible. I was assigned to work with another girl, Vicki, who was a couple of years older than me. The first couple of days, I didn't sell anything, but I watched Vicki and tried to learn. What I saw made me feel uncomfortable. Vicki would watch customers put on hideous outfits that made them look like clowns or mutants (I couldn't decide which), and then she would tell them that they looked gorgeous. Flattered, the women bought the outfits. I decided I couldn't be dishonest with customers the way Vicki was but would try to help customers find clothes that really made them look good. My plan didn't work very well. After a week on the job, I hadn't sold a single item. The owner called me into her office and told me that if I didn't improve, she would have to let me go. The second

Yes, this sounds like it could work really well. Not many people will have had the experience of working in a clothing store, which means that we can learn something from your paper.

week I sold only one scarf, and I was fired. The lesson I learned from this was that most people prefer flattery to honesty, at least as far as their looks are concerned.

5. The night my mother started dating after my father died.

No, this just seems too personal to write about. It seems as though you have some unresolved issues here that you need to work out, and I don't think a paper is the place to do it.

My father had been dead for about 4 months the night I noticed that my mom was getting all primped up. I saw a new dress laid out on the bed, that she'd had her hair done, and had gone for a manicure. Curious, I asked her what the special occasion was. She actually blushed. But then she said that she had met a very nice man a few weeks ago and that he had asked her out for dinner. I suppose I must have looked as shocked as I felt, because my mom said quickly that it was no big deal, it was just dinner; then she went back to her makeup. I walked back to my room stunned. I couldn't believe that my mom would even think about going out with another man so soon after my dad's death. I heard her return from her date just after 2 a.m. The lesson I learned from this experience was that maybe my parent's marriage hadn't been as good as it had always seemed to me and that maybe my mom was happier now that dad was gone.

Final List:

1. My father's funeral.
2. My first job.

I selected these two events as being the best for my personal paper because of the comments I received from my group. My groupmate, as well as a couple of others in the group who looked at my first list, felt that these topics had the most potential. Personally, I wanted to write about my senior prom or my mom's dating. I felt I could do a better job on these because the feelings were pretty intense. But my groupmate said that that was the problem. I was too close to the emotions to write effectively; instead, I would just produce what our teacher calls "psychological venting." I still don't know which topic I'll choose when it comes time to write the paper.

My First Job
Leslie

1   With high school graduation behind me and college tuition waiting for me in the fall, I suddenly discovered the value of money last summer. It isn't that I was oblivious to money before that summer—it's just that I'd never before faced the panic associated with really needing more of it than I had. Tuition, books, food, dorm contract—they added up to more per year than what my car cost, and I don't drive a cheap car. So I examined my options and decided to get a job.

2   This wasn't an easy decision because I'd never worked before. Babysitting doesn't count, right? I didn't have a clue as to how I should go about getting a job, and I knew even less about what I would do if I could get one. My mom suggested that I look through the Help Wanted ads in the newspaper. Boy, was that a depressing experience. I realized after a few minutes that engineers and radiology technicians are in very short supply. I also realized that I was what you might call "underqualified."

3   Thoroughly depressed, I did what every red-blooded American 18-year-old girl does: I called my friend Amy and suggested we go to the mall. As soon as we walked through the doors and into the stale, recirculated, over-conditioned atmosphere of the mall, my spirits brightened.

4   "I'm really down today," I told Amy, "so let's just try on clothes at the most expensive shops." Away we went, eager to try on outfit after outfit that we had neither the intention nor the means to buy.

5   But as we were walking toward the first store, we passed a shop with a sign in the window that read "Help Wanted" in bright orange letters. Now this wasn't just any old shop. It was Mondevado's, a boutique that carried exclusive clothes for older women who thought nothing of spending $2,000 for a designer dress. Although I knew nothing about working, I sure knew clothes, and everybody told me I had great taste in fashion. This job seemed perfect for me.

6   "Amy, stop!" I said. "I'm going to go in and try to get this job."

7   Amy said she'd meet up with me later at the Food Corral, and I walked into the shop. A woman just a couple years older than me walked up immediately and asked if she could help me with anything. I told her I was interested in the job advertised in the window. She smiled and asked me to follow her to the rear of the boutique where there was a door marked "Private." The girl knocked lightly, and a voice inside called out, "Come in."

8   The carpeting inside the office was plush cobalt blue. The walls were covered with velvet, aquamarine wallpaper. The desk was glass and polished steel, ultra-modern, ultra-chic. And behind the desk sat a beautiful, dark-haired woman of about 40 wearing an impeccable Dior silk suit and Ferragamo pumps that together equaled at least my first semester's tuition.

9   "Ms. Valdez, this young lady is here to inquire about our opening," the sales-girl said. She ushered me into the office and closed the door behind me. The interview went quickly. Ms. Valdez didn't seem to mind that I had no experience; she seemed more interested in my knowledge of fashion. She asked me lots of questions about various designers and their lines of clothes. I was suddenly very grateful for subscribing to *Vogue*, *Elle*, and *Allure*. Still, I was surprised when Ms. Valdez asked me when I could start. "Tomorrow would be fine," I told her. "Fine. Tomorrow it is, then. Wear a dress and pumps. Vicki will show you everything else you need to know. Be here at 9."

10   When I walked out of the store, I could hardly believe that I had my first job. I felt dizzy. I rushed over to the Food Corral and found Amy. She could tell by my expression that I had good news, and when I got to her we did a lot of jumping up and down and squealing.

11   I was so eager the next morning that I got to the mall at 8:30, only to find all the doors locked. A security guard opened the mall entrance just before 9, and I hurried over to the boutique. I didn't want to be late. Vicki was just unlocking the steel gate that covered the boutique when it was closed, and a motor lifted it up into the ceiling out of sight. "Hi, Leslie," she said as I walked up to her. Then she unlocked the front door and started punching buttons on the security system on the nearby wall. "We don't open until 10," she said, "so I have time to show you around and explain how everything works."

12   Quickly, Vicki showed me how to work the register, how to remove security tags from garments, and how to use the credit-card authorization system. She showed me the stockroom and explained the difference between European and American sizing systems, which are entirely different. Then she told me about taking breaks, lunch, and straightening the stock after the store closed. At some point, I realized that I didn't even know how much I'd be making, so I decided to ask, even though I was a bit embarrassed to do so. "Oh," Vicki said, "Ms. Valdez said you would start at $5.50 an hour plus commission." "How much is the com-

mission?" I asked, and Vicki said, "Ten percent." My quick tour of the boutique had included prices, so I did some rapid calculations and figured that I'd probably make about $10,000 that summer. The thought gave me goose bumps. "Because we work essentially on commission," Vicki continued, "we have to focus on the sale. You can watch me at first, but then it's up to you. Ms. Valdez expects us to move a lot of merchandise, so you have to convince customers that they can't live without what we sell."

13 When the first customers began to arrive, I watched Vicki carefully. She was so smooth, so polished. A woman would see an outfit she liked and try it on. When she came out of the dressing room, Vicki would act as though she were dazzled by the effect. Then she quickly would begin accessorizing. What had started out as a single purchase turned into a purchase of half a dozen items. It seemed to me, though, that Vicki often flattered women after they had put on outfits that were totally unsuited to them. For example, a woman came in later that morning with bright, orange-red hair. She picked out an orange dress, and when she came out of the dressing room she looked like a carrot. Vicki told her that it looked perfect on her and ended up with the sale.

14 Just before lunch, a woman came in while Vicki was busy with another customer. I decided it was time to plunge in. I gave her my best smile and asked if I could help her. She told me she just wanted to browse a bit, so I stepped back and invited her to look around. She took her time but eventually picked out a plaid de la Renta skirt and jacket and a black Dior cocktail dress.

15 I suppose I should mention that this woman was almost 60 and that the cocktail dress was short, very short. When she came out of the dressing room with it on, I knew that it was hopeless. If she had been even 20 years younger, the dress might have worked, but even with black stockings her legs would look like two gnarled sausages.

16 "What do you think, deary?" she asked.

17 "It's a beautiful dress," I said, "but we have another one that would be much more flattering. Here, let me get it." I rushed over to the rack and pulled off an elegant black gown. I held it up to her so she could get a sense of how it would look immediately.

18 "Oh, no. That's not what I'm looking for at all. Let me try on the plaid," she said. She changed into the de la Renta and stepped out looking like a table cloth.

19 "What do you think, deary?" she asked.

20 "Well," I said, "is this for a special occasion?"

21 "Oh, I'm thinking about having a few friends over for a casual dinner party and want something new."

22 Casual dinner party to me brought up images of something pastel, so I quickly pulled a soft cream dress off the rack and held it up. "Even a casual party is a time to be elegant," I said. "This dress would flatter you and bring out the color of your eyes."

23 The woman looked at me and sighed. "Oh, never mind." She went back into the dressing room, put her clothes back on, and left. It went like that all the rest of the week. Customers would come in, put on something totally wrong for them, listen to me make suggestions for something more flattering, and leave without buying anything. "You've got to push the sale," Vicki kept saying, but I just couldn't bring myself to tell these women that they looked great in an outfit that made them look hideous. With so many nice outfits to choose from, it didn't make sense

to me to let them buy something inappropriate. I wanted to help them look better, not worse.

24   On Friday, Ms. Valdez called me into her office. It wasn't a pleasant meeting. So far, I hadn't made a single sale. She told me that I'd have to improve quickly or she would let me go. I knew what that meant. Fired.

25   My second week, I tried to be more dishonest, but I couldn't. Even when I said a dress looked great on a woman, there just wasn't enough conviction in my voice, and I guess it turned customers off. "Listen," Vicki told me one afternoon, "you have to realize that when most people put their clothes on and look at themselves in the mirror, they think 'Damn, I look good!' To make a sale, you have to reinforce the image people have of themselves. Our customers are successful and egotistical. Challenging their choices doesn't make the sale."

26   I knew Vicki was right, but I couldn't do it. No matter how much I tried, my flattery always sounded as false as it was. I felt really depressed, even though I did manage somehow to sell a scarf. But it wasn't enough. At the end of the week, Ms. Valdez called me into her office again. She handed me my paycheck and fired me without so much as blinking an eye.

27   A couple weeks later, after I had found a job waiting tables at a local restaurant, I'd had time to think about my first job. Maybe Vicki was wrong about what she said about people. Maybe they don't think they look so great in the mirror. Maybe they are insecure about the way they look, and maybe they want a salesgirl to reassure them that they are indeed attractive. It occurred to me that people need flattery more than honesty whenever their appearance is concerned. It also occurred to me that maybe I was wrong, too. It really wouldn't have cost me so much to flatter those customers, to make them feel better about themselves. It would have been such a small act of kindness.

Applying Key Ideas

IDENTIFYING THE LESSON IN PERSONAL WRITING

This activity is intended to give you practice in applying some of the ideas we've discussed regarding personal writing. What is the lesson that Leslie wants to communicate in this piece? Why might readers judge it to be meaningful? How does Leslie convey this lesson?

Writing Assignment

PERSONAL WRITING WITH ANALYSIS

Return to the experiences you listed for the activity on page 3. Select one that you did *not* use and develop it. Use the direct method of conveying your lesson but provide analysis and commentary throughout, following the model provided by Michael Nava passage.

Richard Selzer

Our final passage comes from Richard Selzer, a surgeon for 25 years who served as a professor of surgery at Yale University until 1985. He did not begin writing until he was in his 40s, and then he did it part time, rising in the middle of the night, writing for a couple of hours, then going back to sleep before getting up a 6 a.m. to begin practicing medicine. The passage below was published in 1982 and describes an important event in Selzer's life when he was a medical student.

The Selzer passage illustrates the second way of conveying a lesson, the indirect method. As you read, pay careful attention to how Selzer uses the interactions of people to communicate his underlying messages. You also should note that this passage is as much about Selzer's mentor, Dr. Hugh Franciscus, as it is about himself. Selzer's personal lesson is linked to something that Franciscus learns, something that may or may not be generalizable but that nevertheless is moving. In its use of the indirect method, its narrative technique, and its message, this passage goes significantly beyond what you saw in the previous examples.

IMELDA

1   I heard the other day that Hugh Franciscus had died. I knew him once. He was the Chief of Plastic Surgery when I was a medical student at Albany Medical College. Dr. Franciscus was the archetype of the professor of surgery—tall, vigorous, muscular, as precise in his technique as he was impeccable in his dress. Each day a clean lab coat monkishly starched, that sort of thing. I doubt that he ever read books. One book only, that of the human body, took the place of all others. He never raised his eyes from it. He read it like a printed page as though he knew that in the calligraphy there just beneath the skin were all the secrets of the world. Long before it became visible to anyone else, he could detect the first sign of granulation at the base of a wound, the first blue line of new epithelium at the periphery that would tell him that a wound would heal, or the barest hint of necrosis that presaged failure. This gave him the appearance of a prophet. "This skin graft will take," he would say, and you must believe beyond all cyanosis, exudation and inflammation that it would.

2   He had enemies, of course, who said he was arrogant, that he exalted activity for its own sake.

Perhaps. But perhaps it was no more than the honesty of one who knows his own worth. Just look at a scalpel, after all. What a feeling of sovereignty, megalomania even, when you know that it is you and you alone who will make certain use of it. It was said, too, that he was a ladies' man. I don't know about that. It was all rumor. Besides, I think he had other things in mind than mere living. Hugh Franciscus was a zealous hunter. Every fall during the season he drove upstate to hunt deer. There was a glass-front case in his office where he showed his guns. How could he shoot a deer? we asked. But he knew better. To us medical students he was someone heroic, someone made up of several gods, beheld at a distance, and always from a lesser height. If he had grown accustomed to his miracles, we had not. He had no close friends on the staff. There was something a little sad in that. As though once long ago he had been flayed by friendship and now the slightest breeze would hurt. Confidences resulted in dishonor. Perhaps the person in whom one confided would scorn him, betray. Even though he spent his days among those less fortunate, weaker than he—the sick, after all—Franciscus seemed aware of an air of personal harshness in his environment to which he reacted by keeping his own counsel, by a certain remoteness. It was what gave him the appearance of being haughty. With the patients he was forthright. All the facts laid out, every question anticipated and answered with specific information. He delivered good news and bad with the same dispassion.

3 I was a third-year student, just turned onto the wards for the first time, and clerking on Surgery. Everything—the operating room, the morgue, the emergency room, the patients, professors, even the nurses—was terrifying. One picked one's way among the mines and booby traps of the hospital, hoping only to avoid the hemorrhage and perforation of disgrace. The opportunity for humiliation was everywhere.

4 It all began on Ward Rounds. Dr. Franciscus was demonstrating a cross-leg flap graft he had constructed to cover a large fleshy defect in the leg of a merchant seaman who had injured himself in a fall. The man was from Spain and spoke no English. There had been a comminuted fracture of the femur, much soft tissue damage, necrosis. After weeks of debridement and dressings, the wound had been made ready for grafting. Now the patient was in his fifth postoperative day. What we saw was a thick web of pale blue flesh arising from the man's left thigh, and which had been sutured to the open wound on the right thigh. When the surgeon pressed the pedicle with his finger, it blanched; when he let up, there was a slow return of the violaceous color.

5 "The circulation is good," Franciscus announced. "It will get better." In several weeks, we were told, he would divide the tube of flesh at its site of origin, and tailor it to fit the defect to which, by then, it would have grown more solidly. All at once, the webbed man in the bed reached out, and gripping Franciscus by the arm, began to speak rapidly, pointing to his groin and hip. Franciscus stepped back at once to disengage his arm from the patient's grasp.

6 "Anyone here know Spanish? I didn't get a word of that."

7 "The cast is digging into him up above," I said. "The edges of the plaster are rough. When he moves, they hurt."

8 Without acknowledging my assistance, Dr. Franciscus took a plaster shears from the dressing cart and with several large snips cut away the rough edges of the cast.

9 "*Gracias, gracias.*" The man in the bed smiled. But Franciscus had already moved on to the next bed. He seemed to me a man of immense strength and ability, yet without affection for the patients. He did not want to be touched by them. It was less kindness that he showed them than a reassurance that he would never give up, that he would bend every effort. If anyone could, he would solve the problems of their flesh.

10 Ward Rounds had disbanded and I was halfway down the corridor when I heard Dr. Franciscus's voice behind me.

11 "You speak Spanish." It seemed a command.

12 "I lived in Spain for two years," I told him.

13 "I'm taking a surgical team to Honduras next week to operate on the natives down there. I do it every year for three weeks, somewhere. This year, Honduras. I can arrange the time away from your duties here if you'd like to come along. You will act as interpreter. I'll show you how to use the clinical camera. What you'd see would make it worthwhile."

14 So it was that, a week later, the envy of my classmates, I joined the mobile surgical unit—surgeons, anesthetists, nurses and equipment—aboard a Military Air Transport plane to spend three weeks performing plastic surgery on people who had been previously selected by an advance team. Honduras. I don't suppose I shall ever see it again. Nor do I especially want to. From the plane it seemed a country made of clay—burnt umber, raw sienna, dry. It had a dead-weight quality, as though the ground had no buoyancy, no air sacs through which a breeze might wander. Our destination was Comayagua, a town in the Central Highlands. The town itself was situated on the edge of one of the flatlands that were linked in a network between the granite mountains. Above, all was brown, with only an occasional Spanish cedar tree; below, patches of luxuriant tropical growth. It was a day's bus ride from the airport. For hours, the town kept appearing and disappearing with the convolutions of the road. At last, there it lay before us, panting and exhausted at the bottom of the mountain.

15 That was all I was to see of the countryside. From then on, there was only the derelict hospital of Comayagua, with the smell of spoiling bananas and the accumulated odors of everyone who had

been sick there for the last hundred years. Of the two, I much preferred the frank smell of the sick. The heat of the place was incendiary. So hot that, as we stepped from the bus, our own words did not carry through the air, but hung limply at our lips and chins. Just in front of the hospital was a thirsty courtyard where mobs of waiting people squatted or lay in the meager shade, and where, on dry days, a fine dust rose through which untethered goats shouldered. Against the walls of this courtyard, gaunt, dejected men stood, their faces, like their country, preternaturally solemn, leaden. Here no one looked up at the sky. Every head was bent beneath a wide-brimmed straw hat. In the days that followed, from the doorway of the dispensary, I would watch the brown mountains sliding about, drinking the hospital into their shadow as the afternoon grew later and later, flattening us by their very altitude.

16   The people were mestizos, of mixed Spanish and Indian blood. They had flat, broad, dumb museum feet. At first they seemed to me indistinguishable the one from the other, without animation. All the vitality, the hidden sexuality, was in their black hair. Soon I was to know them by the fissures with which each face was graven. But, even so, compared to us, they were masked, shut away. My job was to follow Dr. Franciscus around, photograph the patients before and after surgery, interpret and generally act as aide-de-camp. It was exhilarating. Within days I had decided that I was not just useful, but essential. Despite that we spent all day in each other's company, there were no overtures of friendship from Dr. Franciscus. He knew my place, and I knew it, too. In the afternoon he examined the patients scheduled for the next day's surgery. I would call out a name from the doorway to the examining room. In the courtyard someone would rise. I would usher the patient in, and nudge him to the examining table where Franciscus stood, always, I thought, on the verge of irritability. I would read aloud the case history, then wait while he carried out his examination. While I took the "before" photographs, Dr. Franciscus would dictate into a tape recorder:

17   "Ulcerating basal cell carcinoma of the right orbit—six by eight centimeters—involving the right eye and extending into the floor of the orbit. Operative plan: wide excision with enucleation of the eye. Later, bone and skin grafting." The next morning we would be in the operating room where the procedure would be carried out.

We were more than two weeks into our tour of   18 duty—a few days to go—when it happened. Earlier in the day I had caught sight of her through the window of the dispensary. A thin, dark Indian girl about fourteen years old. A figurine, orange-brown, terra-cotta, and still attached to the unshaped clay from which she had been carved. An older, sun-weathered woman stood behind and somewhat to the left of the girl. The mother was short and dumpy. She wore a broad-brimmed hat with a high crown, and a shapeless dress like a cassock. The girl had long, loose black hair. There were tiny gold hoops in her ears. The dress she wore could have been her mother's. Far too big, it hung from her thin shoulders at some risk of slipping down her arms. Even with her in it, the dress was empty, something hanging on the back of a door. Her breasts made only the smallest imprint in the cloth, her hips none at all. All the while, she pressed to her mouth a filthy, pink, balled-up rag as though to stanch a flow or buttress against pain. I knew that what she had come to show us, what we were there to see, was hidden beneath that pink cloth. As I watched, the woman handed down to her a gourd from which the girl drank, lapping like a dog. She was the last patient of the day. They had been waiting in the courtyard for hours.

"Imelda Valdez," I called out. Slowly she rose   19 to her feet, the cloth never leaving her mouth, and followed her mother to the examining-room door. I shooed them in.

"You sit up there on the table," I told her.   20 "Mother, you stand over there, please." I read from the chart:

"This is a fourteen-year-old girl with a com-   21 plete, unilateral, left-sided cleft lip and cleft palate. No other diseases or congenital defects. Laboratory tests, chest X-ray—negative."

"Tell her to take the rag away," said Dr. Fran-   22 ciscus. I did, and the girl shrank back, pressing the cloth all the more firmly.

"Listen, this is silly," said Franciscus. "Tell her   23 I've got to see it. Either she behaves, or send her away."

"Please give me the cloth," I said to the girl as   24 gently as possible. She did not. She could not. Just then, Franciscus reached up and, taking the hand that held the rag, pulled it away with a hard jerk. For an instant the girl's head followed the cloth as it left her face, one arm still upflung against showing. Against all hope, she would hide herself. A moment later, she relaxed and sat still. She seemed to me then like an animal that looks outward at the infinite, at death, without fear, with recognition only.

25 Set as it was in the center of the girl's face, the defect was utterly hideous—a nude rubbery insect that had fastened there. The upper lip was widely split all the way to the nose. One white tooth perched upon the protruding upper jaw projecting through the hole. Some of the bone seemed to have been gnawed away as well. Above the thing, clear almond eyes and long black hair reflected the light. Below, a slender neck where the pulse trilled visibly. Under our gaze the girl's eyes fell to her lap where her hands lay palms upward, half open. She was a beautiful bird with a crushed beak. And tense with the expectation of more shame.

26 "Open your mouth," said the surgeon. I translated. She did so, and the surgeon tipped back her head to see inside.

27 "The palate, too. Complete," he said. There was a long silence. At last he spoke.

28 "What is your name?" The margins of the wound melted until she herself was being sucked into it.

29 "Imelda." The syllables leaked through the hole with a slosh and a whistle.

30 "Tomorrow," said the surgeon, "I will fix your lip. *Mañana*."

31 It seemed to me that Hugh Franciscus, in spite of his years of experience, in spite of all the dreadful things he had seen, must have been awed by the sight of this girl. I could see it flit across his face for an instant. Perhaps it was her small act of concealment, that he had had to demand that she show him the lip, that he had had to force her to show it to him. Perhaps it was her resistance that intensified the disfigurement. Had she brought her mouth to him willingly, without shame, she would have been for him neither more nor less than any other patient.

32 He measured the defect with calipers, studied it from different angles, turning her head with a finger at her chin.

33 "How can it ever be put back together?" I asked.

34 "Take her picture," he said. And to her, "Look straight ahead." Through the eye of the camera she seemed more pitiful than ever, her humiliation more complete.

35 "Wait!" The surgeon stopped me. I lowered the camera. A strand of her hair had fallen across her face and found its way to her mouth, becoming stuck there by saliva. He removed the hair and secured it behind her ear.

36 "Go ahead," he ordered. There was the click of the camera. The girl winced.

37 "Take three more, just in case."

38 When the girl and her mother had left, he took paper and pen and with a few lines drew a remarkable likeness of the girl's face.

39 "Look," he said. "If this dot is A, and this one B, this, C, and this, D, the incisions are made A to B, then C to D. CD must equal AB. It is all equilateral triangles." All well and good, but then came X and Y and rotation flaps and the rest.

40 "Do you see?" he asked.

41 "It is confusing," I told him.

42 "It is simply a matter of dropping the upper lip into a normal position, then crossing the gap with two triangular flaps. It is geometry," he said.

43 "Yes," I said. "Geometry." And relinquished all hope of becoming a plastic surgeon.

44 In the operating room the next morning the anesthesia had already been administered when we arrived from Ward Rounds. The tube emerging from the girl's mouth was pressed against her lower lip to be kept out of the field of surgery. Already, a nurse was scrubbing the face which swam in a reddish-brown lather. The tiny gold earrings were included in the scrub. Now and then, one of them gave a brave flash. The face was washed for the last time, and dried. Green towels were placed over the face to hide everything but the mouth and nose. The drapes were applied.

45 "Calipers!" The surgeon measured, locating the peak of the distorted Cupid's bow.

46 "Marking pen!" He placed the first blue dot at the apex of the bow. The nasal sills were dotted; next, the inferior philtral dimple, the vermilion line. The A flap and the B flap were outlined. On he worked, peppering the lip and nose, making sense of chaos, realizing the lip that lay waiting in that deep essential pink, that only he could see. The last dot and line were placed. He was ready.

47 "Scalpel!" He held the knife above the girl's mouth.

48 "O.K. to go ahead?" he asked the anesthetist.

49 "Yes."

50 He lowered the knife.

51 "No! Wait!" The anesthetist's voice was tense, staccato. "Hold it!"

52 The surgeon's hand was motionless.

53 "What's the matter?"

54 "Something's wrong. I'm not sure. God, she's hot as a pistol. Blood pressure is way up. Pulse one eighty. Get a rectal temperature." A nurse fumbled beneath the drapes. We waited. The nurse retrieved the thermometer.

55 "One hundred seven . . . no . . . eight." There was disbelief in her voice.

56 "Malignant hyperthermia," said the anesthetist. "Ice! Ice! Get lots of ice!" I raced out the door, accosted the first nurse I saw.

57 "Ice!" I shouted. "*Hielo!*"[1] Quickly! *Hielo!*" The woman's expression was blank. I ran to another. "*Hielo! Hielo!* For the love of God, ice."

58 "*Hielo?*" She shrugged. "*Nada.*"[2] I ran back to the operating room.

59 "There isn't any ice." I reported. Dr. Franciscus had ripped off his rubber gloves and was feeling the skin of the girl's abdomen. Above the mask his eyes were the eyes of a horse in battle.

60 "The EKG is wild. . ."

61 "I can't get a pulse. . ."

62 "What the hell. . ."

63 The surgeon reached for the girl's groin. No femoral pulse.

64 "EKG flat. My God! She's dead!"

65 "She can't be."

66 "She is."

67 The surgeon's fingers pressed the groin where there was no pulse to be felt, only his own pulse hammering at the girl's flesh to be let in.

68 It was noon, four hours later, when we left the operating room. It was a day so hot and humid I felt steamed open like an envelope. The woman was sitting on a bench in the courtyard in her dress like a cassock. In one hand she held the piece of cloth the girl had used to conceal her mouth. As we watched, she folded it once neatly, and then again, smoothing it, cleaning the cloth which might have been the head of the girl in her lap that she stroked and consoled.

[1]Ice. [Eds.]
[2]Nothing. [Eds.]

"I'll do the talking here," he said. He would tell 69 her himself, in whatever Spanish he could find. Only if she did not understand was I to speak for him. I watched him brace himself, set his shoulders. How could he tell her? I wondered. What? But I knew he would tell her everything, exactly as it had happened. As much for himself as for her, he needed to explain. But suppose she screamed, fell to the ground, attacked him, even? All that hope of love . . . gone. Even in his discomfort I knew that he was teaching me. The way to do it was professionally. Now he was standing above her. When the woman saw that he did not speak, she lifted her eyes and saw what he held crammed in his mouth to tell her. She knew, and rose to her feet.

"*Señora*," he began, "I am sorry." All at once he 70 seemed to me shorter than he was, scarcely taller than she. There was a place at the crown of his head where the hair had grown thin. His lips were stones. He could hardly move them. The voice dry, dusty.

"No one could have known. Some bad reaction 71 to the medicine for sleeping. It poisoned her. High fever. She did not wake up." The last, a whisper. The woman studied his lips as though she were deaf. He tried, but could not control a twitching at the corner of his mouth. He raised a thumb and forefinger to press something back into his eyes.

"*Muerte*,"[3] the woman announced to herself. 72 Her eyes were human, deadly.

"*Sí, muerte.*" At that moment he was like some- 73 one cast, still alive, as an effigy for his own tomb. He closed his eyes. Nor did he open them until he felt the touch of the woman's hand on his arm, a touch from which he did not withdraw. Then he looked and saw the grief corroding her face, breaking it down, melting the features so that eyes, nose, mouth ran together in a distortion, like the girl's. For a long time they stood in silence. It seemed to me that minutes passed. At last her face cleared, the features rearranged themselves. She spoke, the words coming slowly to make certain that he understood her. She would go home now. The next day her sons would come for the girl, to take her home for burial. The doctor must not be sad. God has decided. And she was happy now that the harelip had been fixed so that her daughter might go to Heaven without it. Her bare feet

[3]Dead. [Eds.]

retreating were the felted pads of a great bereft animal.

74   The next morning I did not go to the wards, but stood at the gate leading from the courtyard to the road outside. Two young men in striped ponchos lifted the girl's body wrapped in a straw mat onto the back of a wooden cart. A donkey waited. I had been drawn to this place as one is drawn, inexplicably, to certain scenes of desolation—executions, battlefields. All at once, the woman looked up and saw me. She had taken off her hat. The heavy-hanging coil of her hair made her head seem larger, darker, noble. I pressed some money into her hand.

75   "For flowers," I said. "A priest." Her cheeks shook as though minutes ago a stone had been dropped into her navel and the ripples were just now reaching her head. I regretted having come to that place.

76   "Sí, sí," The woman said. Her own face was stitched with flies. "The doctor is one of the angels. He has finished the work of God. My daughter is beautiful."

77   What could she mean! The lip had not been fixed. The girl had died before he would have done it.

78   "Only a fine line that God will erase in time," she said.

79   I reached into the cart and lifted a corner of the mat in which the girl had been rolled. Where the cleft had been there was now a fresh line of tiny sutures. The Cupid's bow was delicately shaped, the vermilion border aligned. The flattened nostril had now the same rounded shape as the other one. I let the mat fall over the face of the dead girl, but not before I had seen the touching place where the finest black hairs sprang from the temple.

80   "Adiós, adiós. . . ." And the cart creaked away to the sound of hooves, a tinkling bell.

81   There are events in a doctor's life that seem to mark the boundary between youth and age, seeing and perceiving. Like certain dreams, they illuminate a whole lifetime of past behavior. After such an event, a doctor is not the same as he was before. It had seemed to me then to have been the act of someone demented, or at least insanely arrogant. An attempt to reorder events. Her death had come to him out of order. It should have come after the lip had been repaired, not before. He could have told the mother that, no, the lip had not been fixed. But

he did not. He said nothing. It had been an act of omission, one of those strange lapses to which all of us are subject and which we live to regret. It must have been then, at that moment, that the knowledge of what he would do appeared to him. The words of the mother had not consoled him; they had hunted him down. He had not done it for her. The dire necessity was his. He would not accept that Imelda had died before he could repair her lip. People who do such things break free from society. They follow their own lonely path. They have a secret which they can never reveal. I must never let on that I knew.

82   How often I have imagined it. Ten o'clock at night. The hospital of Comayagua is all but dark. Here and there lanterns tilt and skitter up and down the corridors. One of these lamps breaks free from the others and descends the stone steps to the underground room that is the morgue of the hospital. This room wears the expression as if it had waited all night for someone to come. No silence so deep as this place with its cargo of newly dead. Only the slow drip of water over stone. The door closes gassily and clicks shut. The lock is turned. There are four tables, each with a body encased in a paper shroud. There is no mistaking her. She is the smallest. The surgeon takes a knife from his pocket and slits open the paper shroud, that part in which the girl's head is enclosed. The wound seems to be living on long after she has died. Waves of heat emanate from it, blurring his vision. All at once, he turns to peer over his shoulder. He sees nothing, only a wooden crucifix on the wall.

83   He removes a package of instruments from a satchel and arranges them on a tray. Scalpel, scissors, forceps, needle holder. Sutures and gauze sponges are produced. Stealthy, hunched, engaged, he begins. The dots of blue dye are still there upon her mouth. He raises the scalpel, pauses. A second glance into the darkness. From the wall a small lizard watches and accepts. The first cut is made. A sluggish flow of dark blood appears. He wipes it away with a sponge. No new blood comes to take its place. Again and again he cuts, connecting each of the blue dots until the whole of the zigzag slice is made, first on one side of the cleft, then on the other. Now the edges of the cleft are lined with fresh tissue. He sets down the scalpel and takes up scissors and forceps, undermining the little flaps until each triangle is attached only at one side. He rotates

each flap into its new position. He must be certain that they can be swung without tension. They can. He is ready to suture. He fits the tiny curved needle into the jaws of the needle holder. Each suture is placed precisely the same number of millimeters from the cut edge, and the same distance apart. He ties each knot down until the edges are apposed. Not too tightly. These are the most meticulous sutures of his life. He cuts each thread close to the knot. It goes well. The vermilion border with its white skin roll is exactly aligned. One more stitch and the Cupid's bow appears as if by magic. The man's face shines with moisture. Now the nostril is incised around the margin, released, and sutured into a round shape to match its mate. He wipes the blood from the face of the girl with gauze that he has dipped in water. Crumbs of light are scattered on the girl's face. The shroud is folded once more about her. The instruments are handed into the satchel. In a moment the morgue is dark and a lone lantern ascends the stairs and is extinguished.

84   Six weeks later I was in the darkened amphitheater of the Medical School. Tiers of seats rose in a semicircle above the small stage where Hugh Franciscus stood presenting the case material he had encountered in Honduras. It was the highlight of the year. The hall was filled. The night before he had arranged the slides in the order in which they were to be shown. I was at the controls of the slide projector.

85   "Next slide!" he would order from time to time in that military voice which had called forth blind obedience from generations of medical students, interns, residents and patients.

86   "This is a fifty-seven-year-old man with a severe burn contracture of the neck. You will notice the rigid webbing that has fused the chin to the presternal tissues. No motion of the head on the torso is possible. . . . Next slide!"

87   "Click," went the projector.

88   "Here he is after the excision of the scar tissue and with the head in full extension for the first time. The defect was then covered. . . . Next slide!"

89   "Click."

90   ". . . with full-thickness drums of skin taken from the abdomen with the Padgett dermatome. Next slide!"

91   "Click."

92   And suddenly there she was, extracted from the shadows, suspended above and beyond all of us like a resurrection. There was the oval face, the long black hair unbraided, the tiny gold hoops in her ears. And that luminous gnawed mouth. The whole of her life seemed to have been summed up in this photograph. A long silence followed that was the surgeon's alone to break. Almost at once, like the anesthetist in the operating room in Comayagua, I knew that something was wrong. It was not that the man would not speak as that he could not. The audience of doctors, nurses and students seemed to have been infected by the black, limitless silence. My own pulse doubled. It was hard to breathe. Why did he not call out for the next slide? Why did he not save himself? Why had he not removed this slide from the ones to be shown? All at once I knew that he had used his camera on her again. I could see the long black shadows of her hair flowing into the darker shadows of the morgue. The sudden blinding flash . . . The next slide would be the one taken in the morgue. He would be exposed.

93   In the dim light reflected from the slide, I saw him gazing up at her, seeing not the colored photograph, I thought, but the negative of it where the ghost of the girl was. For me, the amphitheater had become Honduras. I saw again that courtyard littered with patients. I could see the dust in the beam of light from the projector. It was then that I knew that she was his measure of perfection and pain—the one lost, the other gained. He, too, had heard the click of the camera, had seen her wince and felt his mercy enlarge. At last he spoke.

94   "Imelda." It was the one word he had heard her say. At the sound of his voice I removed the next slide from the projector. "Click" . . . and she was gone. "Click" again, and in her place the man with the orbital cancer. For a long moment Franciscus looked up in my direction, on his face an expression that I have given up trying to interpret. Gratitude? Sorrow? It made me think of the gaze of the girl when at last she understood that she must hand over to him the evidence of her body.

95   "This is a sixty-two-year-old man with a basal cell carcinoma of the temple eroding into the bony orbit . . ." he began as though nothing had happened.

96   At the end of the hour, even before the lights went on, there was loud applause. I hurried to find him among the departing crowd. I could not. Some weeks went by before I caught sight of him. He seemed vaguely convalescent, as though a fever had taken its toll before burning out.

Hugh Franciscus continued to teach for fifteen years, although he operated a good deal less, then gave it up entirely. It was as though he had grown tired of blood, of always having to be involved with blood, of having to draw it, spill it, wipe it away, stanch it. He was a quieter, softer man, I heard, the ferocity diminished. There were no more expeditions to Honduras or anywhere else.

I, too, have not been entirely free of her. Now and then, in the years that have passed, I see that donkey-cart cortège, or his face bent over hers in the morgue. I would like to have told him what I now know, that his unrealistic act was one of goodness, one of those small, persevering acts done, perhaps, to ward off madness. Like lighting a lamp, boiling water for tea, washing a shirt. But, of course, it's too late now.

The description of Franciscus is central to everything in Selzer's experience, and it is important on at least two levels. It shows the doctor to be an aloof, precise, perhaps even arrogant man. This characterization is not surprising because it fits the image that many people have of physicians. Therefore, it seems to act as a kind of metaphor for the medical profession, populated by clinical, dispassionate, arrogant demigods who have no time for the common folk. Selzer reinforces this image in paragraph 2, where he states that he and his fellow medical students saw in Franciscus "someone heroic, someone made up of several gods, beheld at a distance, and always from a lesser height." On the second level, the description serves to tell us quite a bit about Selzer. In retrospect, for example, the second sentence of the first paragraph is highly ironic: "I knew him once." The truth is that Selzer knew his teacher reasonably well, in one sense, because he had worked as Franciscus' aide; he knew him intimately, in another sense, because the experience in Honduras let Selzer look directly into his mentor's soul, where he saw his own face staring back at him. The ironic understatement, "I knew him once," suggests that Selzer's education was effective, for he has some of the same distance and dispassion that characterized his mentor.

More is at work in the description than what surface appearances indicate. Selzer skillfully suggests that Franciscus was a highly complex person with a depth that was hard to calculate. The fact that Franciscus had no close friends leads Selzer to comment on the sadness of it and to speculate that his mentor had once been so hurt by a friend that friendship was a luxury he no longer afforded himself. This kind of sensitivity is at odds with the image of an arrogant archetype. Selzer suggests (showing and not telling) that his mentor's remoteness is not motivated by harshness but rather its opposite. It is weakness that makes Franciscus aloof: He understands that he is vulnerable to the pain his patients experience; he understands that he must protect himself from feelings if he is to do his job. For this reason, Franciscus "delivered good news and bad with the same dispassion." For this reason, Franciscus cuts the irritating rough edges off the cast in paragraph 8 and goes on to the next bed without waiting to hear his patient tell him "Gracias." Selzer suggests that his mentor is a man of stark contrasts, of extreme tenderness masked by fierce dispassion, of great sensitivity masked by professional arrogance.

After setting the context for the narrative, Selzer goes on to set the scene, which is the village of Comayagua. He needs only two paragraphs, 15 and 16, to capture the atmosphere of the place: It is a Third World country sunk in heat and dejection. Selzer and his group are there to do battle against the misery of the place, and he describes those first 2 weeks as a "tour of duty."

Then Selzer becomes more specific. He describes Imelda, "a beautiful bird with a crushed beak," and begins to reveal his mentor's true nature more fully.

Paragraph 31 does an effective job of telling readers about how Franciscus was moved by the young girl, but the action in paragraph 35 is far more powerful. Seeing a strand of Imelda's hair stuck to her mouth, Franciscus stops Selzer from taking her picture long enough for him to reach out and straighten the girl's hair for the photograph. This single act of kindness speaks volumes and is itself quite moving. It is made more so by the doctor's attempt to hide the moment: In paragraph 42 he reduces Imelda to a matter of geometry, which prompts Selzer to relinquish "all hope of becoming a plastic surgeon." These paragraphs, you'll notice, are quite different from the approach Michael Nava used. They are more moving. I would suggest, however, that emotions are more important in Selzer's piece than they were in Nava's. Consequently, in this case it is more effective to use actions to reveal character than to use summary. Many experts on writing have expressed the point thus: "Show, don't tell."

Selzer describes Imelda's death in just a few hurried sentences, as though to tell readers that it sometimes happens like that. The lesson Selzer wants to convey comes in paragraphs 69–73, when Franciscus tells the mother that her daughter is dead. The two dozen paragraphs that finish the narrative elaborate the lesson, but they add nothing to it. The lesson is that all of us are human. It does not seem particularly profound and probably is not intended to be. But this simple lesson is powerful. The arrogant demigod is brought low by a little girl who dies unexpectedly on the operating table. There is no real explanation for why this girl touched Franciscus; clearly the doctor had lost patients in the past. Nevertheless, the experience fractures his carefully constructed control, causes him to try to "press something" that appears to be tears "back into his eyes." Meanwhile, Selzer's view of his mentor changes significantly: "All at once he seemed to me shorter than he was, scarcely taller than she [the mother]. There was a place at the crown of his head where the hair had grown thin. His lips were stones. He could hardly move them. The voice dry, dusty." The student saw the teacher as a man for the first time, and men always are smaller than the heroes others wish them to be.

Selzer did not grasp the lesson in this transformation immediately, nor did he grasp the reason why Franciscus repaired the girl's deformed lip after she was dead. Initially, the surgery struck Selzer as being a supreme act of arrogance, as though his mentor refused to allow death to prevent him from helping Imelda. Only later, after the incident with the slide projector, did he begin to understand that the doctor's act had been one of kindness. In paragraph 81, Selzer states a second lesson when he writes that "There are events in a doctor's life that seem to mark the boundary between youth and age, seeing and perceiving." This is his personal lesson, because the experience with Imelda marked a boundary for him. It allowed him to grow from seeing to "perceiving," which we would like to believe is "understanding."

Applying Key Ideas

A CHRONICLE OF CHANGE

In each of our models, you have seen how the writers changed over time and how that change helped them solve a problem or gain insight that made them more complete people. Consider your experiences again and the lessons you have learned, but this time make a list of five people who have taught you something important about yourself and life. At least two of these people should be outside your family. Next to each name, write a brief statement of the lesson you learned. Then answer the following questions: Why are the people you selected important? Why are the lessons they helped you learn important? Why are the lessons generalizable? Why would readers find your account of this experience with this person interesting? Finally, write a brief chronology of your experience with one of these people that describes the inner changes you underwent that enhanced your insight.

READINGS

Kate Scannell

Kate Scannell is a physician what has spent years working in the fight against AIDS. In addition to her medical practice, she has taught medicine at the University of California at San Francisco.

KATE SCANNELL

SKILLS AND PILLS

1 *Doctors are trained to heal people, but what can a doctor do when there is no cure and the patient's illness is fatal? In this personal testimony, Kate Scannell (b. 1953) describes her own "retraining" in the wake of the AIDS epidemic. Learning that sometimes the Hippocratic oath has to be adjusted in the face of suffering for which there is no release but in death, Scannell shares the private thoughts of a physician fighting against a vicious killer in a battle in which she has been given no effective weapons save compassion. Kate Scannell is a clinical immunologist who has practiced at San Francisco General Hospital and taught medicine at the University of California, San Francisco.*

2 When I originally set foot in this Bay Area county hospital, I had no intention to work primarily with AIDS patients. Fresh out of university-based medical practice as an internal medicine resident, rheumatology fellow, and bench researcher, I had decided to forgo academic medicine and practice community-based general medicine in my favorite setting, a county hospital. By now, I have been working for more than two years in this county hospital's AIDS ward.

3 Shortly after my arrival in the hospital, I discovered that a number of beds were taken by AIDS patients. Most of them were about my age, and many were dying. Several of them had arrived in the county health care system through tragic personal circumstances attending their AIDS diagnosis, which had cost them their jobs and sometimes their health insurance. I was overwhelmed by their illness, their very complex medical problems, their awesome psychological and emotional needs, and their dying. I was frightened by the desperation of many who wanted to be made well again or to survive that which could not be survived.

4 I felt all I really had to offer these patients were the tools in my doctor's bag and this head stuffed with information. So it became imperative that this small offering from me be the best and biggest it could.

5 During the first few months of my work, I began my hospital rounds with the non-AIDS patients because so much time was involved in the AIDS ward routine. I stayed late hours without meals nearly every day so I could figure out the fever sources, treat the pneumonias, push the chemotherapy, perform the lumbar punctures, and

counsel the lovers and families. Like a very weary but ever-ready gunfighter, I stalked the hallways ready for surprise developments and acute medical problems to present themselves; I would shoot them down with my skills and pills. The diseases that would not respond favorably to my treatments and the patients who would die were all my failures, fought to the end. No patient who wanted treatment died because they did not receive aggressive full-service care from me. I became such a sharpshooter for AIDS-related medical problems that the patients with AIDS were soon gravitating to my medical service.

6   Some patients were so emaciated by profound wasting that I could not shake disquieting memories of photographs I had seen as a little girl which depicted Auschwitz and Buchenwald prisoners. There were young men on the ward who were grossly disfigured by masses of purple skin tumors. One of these men, who had one eye bulging forward and the other closed tight because of his tumors, caused me to have a recurring nightmare about the Hunchback of Notre Dame.

7   There were so many sad stories and unhappy events on the ward. I barely spoke of these to my closest friends, and I avoided telling them how I was being personally affected by all the tragedy and death. I was hesitant to be so serious with my friends, and I really didn't even know how to verbalize what it was I was seeing, hearing, and experiencing in the first place.

8   Months elapsed in this way. One day Raphael, a twenty-two-year-old man, was admitted to the ward. He was a large, bloated, purple, knobby mass with eyes so swollen shut that he could not see. His dense, purple tumors had insinuated themselves into multiple lymph nodes and into the roof of his mouth. One imposing tender tumor mass extended from the bottom of his right foot so that he could not walk. His breathing was made difficult by the massive amount of fluid surrounding and compressing his lungs. Tears literally squeezed out from the cracks between his eyelids. He asked me to help him. I heard the voices of my old teachers who prodded me through my years of medical training—I heard them telling me to fix this man's breathing disfunction, instructing me how to decipher and treat his anemia, reviewing with me how to relieve his body swelling with medications while correcting his electrolyte disturbances. I heard these voices reviewing with me the latest therapies for Kaposi's sarcoma. Raphael asked me to help him. I stuck needles into his veins and arteries to get more information about him. I stuck an intravenous line into one of the few spots on his arm that wasn't thickened by firm swelling or hard purple tumors.

He asked for more help. I stuck a plastic can-   9 nula into his nose to give him more oxygen. I gave him potassium in his IV line. I told him his problems were being corrected and we could discuss chemotherapy options in the morning. After I left the hospital that night, feeling exhausted but confident I'd given "my all," another physician on duty was called to see my patient. Raphael asked the physician to help him. The physician stopped the intravenous fluid and potassium, cancelled the blood testing and the transfusion, and simply gave Raphael some morphine. I was told Raphael smiled and thanked the doctor for helping him, and then expired later that evening.

I think of Raphael often now and I ask him for   10 his forgiveness during my frequent meditations. I also tell him that I have never practiced medicine the same way since his death; that my eyes focus differently now, and that my ears hear more clearly the speaker behind the words. Like the vision of Raphael's spirit rising free from his disease-racked corpse in death, the clothing fashioned for me by years of traditional Western medical training fell off me like tattered rags. I began to hear my own voices and compassionate sensibilities once again, louder and clearer than the chorus of voices of my old mentors. Nowadays, as in an archaeological expedition, I sometimes try to uncover how I had become so lost in the first place. I envision that I got crushed under mounds of rubble that collected over the years of my intense and all-consuming medical training, during which I strove so hard, twenty-four hours a day, to become a physician in the mode of traditional Western medicine. Some of the rubble I can identify as parts of this structure: the trend towards increasing technological interventions; the overriding philosophy that competent physicians save lives, not "lose" them; the blatant chastisement of physicians who use their "sensors" and intuitive insights when interacting with patients; the taboo against using compassion as a diagnostic and therapeutic medical skill.

11 Shortly after Raphael's death, I assumed the position of clinical director of AIDS services at this county hospital. Subsequently, the targets for my diagnostic sharpshooting abilities became fewer and smaller. I am no longer frightened by this awesome disease and I no longer have nightmares. I cry often and stand the bedside deathwatch frequently. I have been able to communicate with patients now, when I know that I am hearing and seeing them with tremendous clarity, and when I am able to speak clearly to them with the truths I know in my heart as well as my mind. I have substituted ice cream or local bakery products as primary or sole therapy for some AIDS patients with "complex medical disease." I have officially prescribed sunshine, a trip to Macy's, and massages for some patients who had no need for my traditional skills and pills.

12 On daily rounds, I have visited a demented AIDS patient whose intermittent cerebral flailings sometimes made him think he was back on his Texas ranch tending the pigs and chickens. For days we had discussed the problems a few of the pigs were posing and the most lucrative way to sell eggs; once we made plans to invite the neighbors (other patients on the ward) over for a farm-style breakfast. He never saw my stethoscope or a needle in his arms; I believe he was peaceful and pain-free when he died. As each AIDS patient experiences stages of understanding and accepting of his own disease and death in the Kübler–Ross scheme, I feel I have passed through similar stages as a physician in response to the entire specter of AIDS.

13 I am currently waddling between grief and acceptance of this disease. I am learning how to temper hope with reality. Through a long period of unhappiness responding to all the death I was seeing, I have been able to find some peace, walking comfortably, day to day, alongside the promise of my own death. And I am grateful to hear my own voices and feel the strength of my compassionate sensibilities once again. I think of Raphael often.

Critical Reading Guide

1. The beginning of this passage provides important background information. What are two crucial pieces of information, and why are they important to the piece as a whole?

2. When asked to identify the problem that Scannell presents in this passage, many readers suggest that it is AIDS. They are wrong. What is the real problem, and how does Scannell solve it?

3. What is the lesson that Scannell conveys? Does she use the direct or indirect method to present her lesson?

4. Some readers argue that Scannell's personal experience is not generalizable because so few people are physicians and even fewer treat AIDS patients. How would you respond to this argument?

5. What role did Raphael play in helping Scannell learn the lesson in this work?

Writing Assignment

PERSONAL WRITING USING THE INDIRECT METHOD

This assignment asks you to apply all that you've learned about personal writing. From your work on the activity on pages 24–25, write a personal experience paper that focuses on the person who taught you something important. Your paper should be about five pages long. Keep in mind the structural features in the models above. For example, your introduction should set the scene for the narrative. The details you provide should make the scene vivid, should enable readers to "see" the scene as well as you and the person who is part of your experience. For this assignment, you should use the indirect technique you saw in Selzer's passage.

GROUP ACTIVITIES: PERSONAL WRITING USING THE INDIRECT METHOD

1. For 5 minutes, write about the person you intend to include in your personal writing. Don't worry about organization or structure—concentrate on getting ideas down. For another 5 minutes, write about the scene and the narrative. Finally, write for 5 minutes about your lesson and how it is linked to the narrative and the person in your personal writing. Do you see any controlling ideas that might help you develop the narrative and the lesson?

2. Team up with one or two of your groupmates. Each person should read his or her writing; the groupmates should brainstorm to generate additional details and information for the three parts while the writer takes notes.

3. Use your notes to produce a first draft of the paper. Exchange your draft with a groupmate so that you may check each other's papers for details, clarity, and effectiveness. Questions you might ask yourself are: Can I visualize the people and the setting? Is the narrative easy to follow? Are the events interesting? Is the lesson generalizable? Provide the writer with written suggestions for ways to improve the paper.

4. Exchange revised papers across groups. Read the paper and then summarize the lesson it conveys. List three elements of the personal writing that you believe were particularly well done. List three elements that you believe could be improved and offer suggestions for each.

5. After your paper has been returned, share the comments with your groupmates, who should help you decide which suggestions to follow and which to ignore.

Building Bridges

Attending college is about learning new things, but that learning is made meaningful by the knowledge and experiences people bring to their studies.

CHAPTER TWO

Building Bridges

Attending college is about learning new things, but that learning is made meaningful by the knowledge and experiences people bring to their studies. Selecting a major, for example, commonly is influenced by family and friends: An engineering major may have a family member who already is an engineer; a business major may have accumulated work experience in the business world, and so forth. It is also important to recognize that how we understand the knowledge college offers depends on past experience. Interpretation, for example, often hinges on personal factors that color our determination of what something means. From this perspective, personal experience forms the basis for building bridges to your academic work.

LANGUAGE AND GROUPS: INSIDERS AND OUTSIDERS

Infants and toddlers use language primarily to do things, such as get a drink or a piggyback ride from Mommy or Daddy. As they become older, however, language becomes an important means of joining groups, or *communities*. Children who move to the West Coast from the South, for example, quickly lose their southern accent so they will fit in with their peers at school. Slang is another way young people, particularly teenagers, use language to join groups: It easily identifies who belongs to the group and who doesn't. In high school, you may have been part of a group of friends who deliberately invented expressions for certain actions or things, expressions that had meaning only for you and the others in the group. Your language differentiated *insiders* from *outsiders*. Adults also use language in this way, and their special terms are called *jargon*.

To a significant degree, mastering the language of a given group is a basic requirement for admission. If you want to become an attorney, you will have to be able to use the language of law. If you want to become a psychologist, you will have to be able to use the language of psychology. Obviously, more is involved than merely knowing which terms to use. You have to understand the core knowledge of the discipline. You have to grasp the way members of the discipline view reality. But these factors are intimately related to language, which is why such groups usually are referred to as *discourse communities*.

College is a place where you find out more about yourself, about who you are, what you like, who you want to be. Much of what you learn comes through your experiences in classes that introduce you to the discourse communities, or *disciplines*, of the academy: history, geography, English literature, psychology, and so forth. The process involves building connections between what you already know and what you are learning. When you make these connections, you are actively involved in an apprenticeship with your teachers and the discipline as a whole. You are participating in the discourse community. Over time, with motivation and study, you change until your language, your way of looking at the world, and what you know are defined largely by a given community. When this change occurs, you no longer are on the outside looking in. *You are an insider.*

Conventional Reality

Some things are facts. They can be demonstrated to be true in such a way that no one doubts or disagrees with them. Many other things are not facts. They are merely perceptions that people accept as true. Experiences and associations with others influence these perceptions so strongly that many scholars have suggested that they are "constructed" by a group mentality. *A conventional reality is based primarily on perceptions rather than facts.*

Money is a good example of a conventional reality. There is nothing inherent in the pieces of paper we use as $20 bills that gives them value. However, as a society, we have agreed that pieces of paper with certain markings on them count as $20 bills. In this analysis, money is a social construct and a social fact; the value of $20 bills therefore is a conventional reality.

Although we agree that a $20 bill is worth $20, the different perceptions people have regarding money cause different views of the *personal value* of $20. For some, $20 is a great deal of money, whereas for other it isn't. People see the world differently. The point here is straightforward: Groups have a significant effect on the way their members perceive reality. At the same time, however, individual members have the potential to exert an influence on the group. People commonly use writing for this purpose. In fact, an important goal of writing is to express a particular view of reality.

WRITING AND GROUPS

Writing is similar to speech in many respects, but I want to stress that the most important similarity is its social nature. People use writing to get things done and to interact with others. They write in response to social demands. The result is a reciprocal relationship in which both writers and those they write for change, usually in miniscule—but sometimes in profound—ways.

People also use writing to form groups that differentiate insiders from outsiders. As already mentioned, these groups have adopted conventions that govern the writing their members produce. Biologists, for instance, have specific conventions for the sort of writing biologists do. A biology lab report therefore always has at least four parts: an introduction, a statement of methods, a statement of results, and a statement of conclusions. On a broader scale, consider that the sciences and social sciences expect writers to use the past tense when making references to published information. The humanities, on the other hand, expect the present tense. If you wrote a psychology paper for an audience of psychologists and used the present tense rather than the past, readers would conclude that you had violated accepted conventions. Perhaps more important, they would recognize that you do not belong to the group defined by psychology—you would signal that you are an outsider.

Analysis

Analysis is a central part of reading and writing. When you analyze, you divide a whole into its constituent parts for close examination. For example, when examining an essay, you might analyze it in terms of its thesis, or claim, the evidence it offers in support of the thesis, and the conclusion; or you might analyze it in terms of its aims and the reasons the writer had for producing it. You have many possibilities.

The first step in any analysis consists of determining what something is. An essay may be a "piece of writing," but you normally have to be more specific and determine what kind of essay it is—descriptive, narrative, persuasive, argumentative, and so forth. Successful analysis generally involves asking—and then answering—various questions about an experience you have had, a text you have read, or data you have collected. In addition, it seldom stands alone as a particular kind of writing but rather supports a claim you make about an experience, a text, or data.

Reasons for Writing

The social factors associated with writing are powerful, but I do not want to suggest that people are writing robots responding to the orders of those around them. People have personal as well as social reasons for writing. They also have the freedom to reject the social demands that commonly prompt writing. For example, no one forces you to complete the writing assignments your teachers give you. You complete them, in part, because you want to get good grades and earn your degree.

The freedom to reject social demands also extends to writing conventions. The conventions that govern the *how* and *what* of writing are not rules. They are simply guidelines that readers expect you to follow. At some point after you have mastered the conventions of writing in a given discipline, you have the authority to violate them. You may choose to do so as part of a creative effort or out of disagreement with the established form. Keep in mind, however, that there usually is a price to pay for flaunting writing conventions, just as there is one to pay for flaunting social ones.

INTERPRETING

College is a community made up of smaller communities—the disciplines that comprise the undergraduate and, at some schools, graduate programs. When your school sent you your admission notice, it invited you to join the community of the college, which in many respects is quite different from any experience you've had before. One practical consequence of being in this new community is that the language skills that served you well in the past may not meet the standards or expectations of college faculty.

A college education may be viewed as a process of developing knowledge and relationships. College is a place where you can acquire knowledge that will allow you to exercise greater degrees of power over your life and in your community. Historically, colleges and universities have prepared people to shape their societies, to be leaders more than followers. This mission provides a compelling reason for taking composition. Effective writers have the power to demonstrate their knowledge in ways that influence their communities, and one of their more important contributions consists of interpreting what facts mean.

Interpreting Is a Social Action

Interpreting is a social action. People interpret for others as well as for themselves, and they commonly share their views rather than keep them private. Moreover, people interpret facts as well as experiences daily, and the vital part interpretation plays in life is evident everywhere. When you go to the movies with your friends, there is not going to be any disagreement regarding who directed the picture or who starred in it, but there may well be disagreement regarding what the movie was about. Interpretation allows you and your friends to sort through the possibilities.

Interpretations Are Linked to Argument

Interpretation rarely occurs as an isolated action. For example, suppose that you and your friends watched a movie and that afterward you offered your interpretation of it. Your interpretation represents what you believe the movie means or what it is about. When you voice your belief, you are making a claim: "I believe that *The Lion King* was about the important role fathers play in family life," or "I believe that *Titanic* was about our fear of being alone in the world."

As soon as someone asks you *why* you believe the movie means what you said it does, you are pretty much expected to support your view. In doing so, you are engaging in argument. It is important to stress that the term *argument* is not being used here in its popular sense—a noisy disagreement or fight. Also, you should not think of argument as an attempt to prove a point or to establish the "truth." Instead, intellectual arguments are linked to getting others to *accept an interpretation as being reasonable.*

Interpretations Are Linked to Who You Are

Intellectual life at college is complex by its very nature and offers exciting challenges. One goal is to examine life's more difficult questions because the easy ones have been answered already. Knowledge is the principal resource in this endeavor, and writing is the principal tool. The majority of the writing assignments in college fall into two broad categories. The first consists of *writing as a form of examination*. In this kind of writing, you have to show that you have mastered the knowledge of a book, a unit, or a course. The focus is on presenting information. The second category consists of *writing as a means of learning*. In this kind of writing, you have to show that you understand something (such as course material or your personal experiences) so well that you can explain what it means.

Your teachers therefore have important reasons for asking you to write in college. Most believe that having a head full of information is not particularly valuable if you cannot make sense of it. At the same time, they recognize that writing helps you learn more about the subjects they teach. It helps you develop crucial interpretive skills so that you can understand and explain what you know. *And it helps you define who you are and who you want to be.*

Writing instructors are especially interested in helping students develop their ability to interpret the world around them. They understand that those who can successfully interpret how we experience the world shape the realities we all live by. They see the lessons to be learned in the way Karl Marx's writing affected the lives of hundreds of millions and in the way Thomas Paine's writing helped form a new nation. Writing teachers recognize that they play an important role in helping students develop the ability to lead rather than follow.

Applying Key Ideas

WHO ARE YOU?

The question of self-definition is problematic for a number of reasons. Many people take it for granted that their "personhood" is already fixed, that they defined who they are long ago. Others may believe that they redefine who they are for different contexts—mother by day, college student by night; part-time security guard on weekends, studious criminology student during the week, and so on. Or they may believe that who they are always is evolving over time. Each of these possibilities is real; there doesn't appear to be any "right" or "wrong" answer to the question of self-definition. Nevertheless, each implicitly recognizes that at any given moment people have a definition of themselves that they project to others.

This activity is intended to give you an opportunity to reflect on the discussion above and relate it to your perception of yourself. In about a page, define who you are.

INSIDERS AND OUTSIDERS

The idea that writing is a social action is at odds with the popular view that writing is something a person does in complete isolation: in a log cabin out in the woods or in a dark, damp attic, hammering out words of lonely inspiration that come from the soul. The social perspective suggests that the first requirement for good writing involves recognizing that *what you produce is intended for someone else.*

Audience and Rhetorical Stance

The someone else you write for—your reader or readers—is your audience. If your audience belongs to an identifiable group, you will be writing for *insiders*. If your audience does not belong to such a group, you will be writing for *outsiders*.

Now consider something a bit more complex. Your reasons for writing will determine your own status vis-à-vis your audience. You may write as an insider or outsider for insiders or outsiders. Your relationship to your audience, whether it is composed of insiders or outsiders, is what is called your *rhetorical stance*.

One of the difficulties college students face is that, almost by definition, they are outsiders working to become insiders. As an undergraduate, you are not part of the community associated with an academic discipline, and those who are members (such as your teachers) are not going to let you in until you have proven yourself. *Nevertheless, you often will be asked to write in a way that approximates the voice of the insider.* Such assignments are valuable apprenticeship experiences that *prepare you to become a member of a given group.*

Conventions and Audience

In real writing situations, your audience and your rhetorical stance influence all other features of your writing. They determine, for example, the content of a paper and which conventions you will use. If your audience consists of psychologists, your paper probably will be about psychology, and it will use the conventions associated with the social sciences in general and psychology in particular. If your audience does not consist of psychologists, the content of your paper still may deal with psychology, but you will use a different set of conventions, a point that is discussed when considering writing for outsiders.

Diverse Voices

In the United States, formal education plays perhaps the most important role in becoming an insider. Other countries, however, have other mechanisms. Does your culture have other mechanisms? If so, what are they?

Subject Matter

Mastering a discipline or becoming a member of a group involves understanding, even adopting, a certain view of reality. An old proverb captures this idea well: "When in Rome, do as the Romans do." A more thorough exploration returns us to conventional reality—people commonly view and react to the world around them on the basis of who they are and what groups they belong to. For example, attorneys have a tendency to process daily experiences in terms of liability and potential litigation. Accountants, on the other hand, have a tendency to view the world in terms of tax exemptions, investments, and dividends. Because you are a student, you may tend to measure your weeks by the classes you take, the papers you have due, and the exams you must prepare for.

It should not be surprising that the subject matter of the papers the attorneys produce is law, whereas the subject matter of those the accountants produce is money. In addition, attorneys do not write motions because they think it is fun; they write them because they want a judge to make a ruling for their clients. Likewise, the subject matter of the papers you produce will be related to the courses you take. If you have an astronomy class and your teacher asks for a paper, you will write about astronomy, not U.S. history. Two questions you have to answer before producing the paper are these:

- What is my rhetorical stance?
- What do I want my paper to do?

Thus, your audience determines to a very large extent the subject matter of your writing. However, no sort of universal mind set is a work in professional communities. Members disagree with one another regularly, and every time they do they are likely to disagree on individual interpretations of law or finance, the subject matter at hand. They do not disagree about the conventions that govern the writing they produce.

Applying Key Ideas

YOUR ROLE AS AN INSIDER

Although it may seem that as a college student you are perpetually an outsider, in truth most people are insiders in some situations and outsiders in others. If you have ever taught a younger brother or sister how to skate, play baseball, bake cookies, or if you have ever given directions to someone who was lost, you spoke from the perspective of an insider, one who knows what to do and how to do it. If you belonged to any clubs in high school or simply were part of the "in" group, you were in the role of an insider.

This activity is intended to give you an opportunity to reflect on the concepts of insider and outsider discussed previously. In addition, it asks you to consider how your status influenced your language in the past.

Make a list of several situations in which you have been an insider. Look for patterns in your language, behavior, and attitude that are common to each situation. Then select one situation and write a paragraph or two that describe how you interacted with those outsiders who wanted to be insiders. You might consider, for example, how the insider status affected your language—Did you make it more complex or less complex? Did you speak more slowly or more quickly? Try to explain why this happened in each case.

Standards of Proof

Interpretation is linked to argument, and whenever you make a claim and attempt to support it, you are engaged in argument. Taking this position a step further, it is reasonable to propose that all writing is argumentative.

At first glance, this view may be hard to accept. Novels and poems hardly seem argumentative. They do not involve supporting a thesis. They don't try to prove anything, and they are not particularly concerned with truth. However, the goal of argument is not to "prove" anything, and it certainly is not linked in any absolute way to "truth." Instead, the goal is to get readers to accept an interpretation of reality as being *reasonable*.

Chapter 10 examines this notion more extensively, but here it is possible to see that, in this account, even novels and poems will be argumentative. Successful works manage to get readers to accept their interpretations of reality as being reasonable. For example, the reasonableness of the universe it creates is a significant factor in distinguishing good science fiction from bad. Similarly, because most people do not believe in vampires, anyone writing a horror novel must take special care to make a vampire story reasonable; otherwise the tale turns quickly into comedy.

The key question for writers is: *What makes an audience accept an argument as being reasonable?* The answer is this: *the support they provide for their claim.* In a very broad sense, such support is called "proof," and chapter 10 examines three categories of proof: *reason, emotion*, and *character*. At this point, however, it is more important that you understand that different discourse communities expect different kinds of proof. They have different standards for what counts as proof. For example, the standard of proof in science and social science is related to observations of natural or social phenomena. The standard of proof in the humanities is related to texts.

These standards exist on a continuum in every instance. As a result, some proof in any discipline may be rigorous and compelling, whereas other proof may be just the opposite. There are numerous gradations in between. Standards of proof vary largely on the basis of rhetorical stance. If you are writing as an insider for fellow insiders, you will need to provide a fairly high standard of proof or readers will dismiss your claim. However, all other rhetorical stances allow for lower standards of proof, which can work to your advantage. If you are writing as an insider for outsiders, the audience actually will appreciate an argument that spares them support that is technical and specialized. If you are writing as an outsider for insiders, the audience will be inclined to expect less in the way of proof owing to the fact that you are an outsider. You should note, of course, that your chances of gaining entry into that group may be jeopardized unless, over time, you are able to shift to a higher standard of proof.

Applying Key Ideas

WANTING TO JOIN A GROUP

People generally are social and enjoy belonging to groups. The character of those groups is in certain respects a reflection of who people are and who they want to be. This activity is designed to help you explore your goals and ambitions, and it asks you to reflect on some of the ideas discussed so far in the chapter.

Make a list of several groups you would like to belong to. Take one of these communities and explain in at least two paragraphs why you want to belong, then describe what you would have to do to become a member.

Insiders Writing for Insiders

Insider-to-insider writing is produced by members of a given discourse community for fellow members. It is governed by the conventions accepted in that community. One result is that the language, concepts, interpretations, and conclusions tend to *exclude outsiders*. For example, a paper written by a psychologist for publication in a psychology journal will use the language of psychology as well as the structural format specified by the *APA Guide*. If the paper reports research findings, it will be governed by accepted procedures for experimental designs, data collection, statistical analysis, and interpretation. The paper will be about psychology, of course, but more specifically it will be about a feature of human behavior that is currently the focus of study and questioning in the field.

Insiders write for fellow insiders for several reasons. A common one is professional advancement. No matter what the profession, those who write clear, readable prose tend to move up the ladder. Another reason is status in the group. Such texts usually are published to ensure wide distribution, and those who publish regularly gain status. And yet a third reason is to contribute to the group by providing new knowledge or new understanding of a subject. Contributions of this sort influence the community; they define and shape it in quite tangible ways.

Insiders or Outsiders Writing for Outsiders

A text produced for outsiders is similar to one produced for insiders in some respects, but there are several important differences. Using the psychology example again, such a text might use the APA format for listing references in its bibliography, but it probably would not adhere to the guidelines for overall organization. It most likely would address a topic that is currently the focus of study in the field, but it would *summarize* the work of others without making its own contribution.

Insiders often write for outsiders so as to reach a broader audience. Scholars such as E. O. Wilson and Stephen Gould, for example, appear to love their fields so much that they want nonscientists to be able to experience some of the joy and excitement that they feel when working on complex questions in biology and geology, respectively. Outsiders often write for other outsiders because they have the ability to explain complex subjects to people who lack any expertise. Technical writers fall into this category: They usually are not scientists or engineers, but they understand enough about these fields to make difficult information accessible to people with a need or desire to know.

Characteristically, outsiders are limited by the level of expertise they can bring to the subject. Vocabulary, sentence structure, technical information, and standards of proof therefore must match the audience and so are quite different from what you would find in something written for insiders. Overall, these differences are so great that the writing conventions that govern texts for outsiders are "journalistic" in the broadest sense of the word—*even when they are produced by insiders*. An important consequence is that texts produced for outsiders are *inclusive* rather than *exclusive*.

INSIDERS AND OUTSIDERS: WRITERS AND AUDIENCES

Rhetorical Stance	*Characteristics*
Insiders Writing for Insiders	• Uses the language conventions of the community, such as specialized terms and a specified format. These conventions tend to exclude outsiders. • Relies on the audience's expertise in the field, thus avoiding the need to explain basic concepts, problems, and questions. • Rhetorical purpose is to argue for an interpretation. • Reasons for writing include making a contribution to the community, gaining status and recognition, furthering career. • Has the potential to influence the community of insiders.
Insiders and Outsiders Writing for Outsiders	• Uses journalistic language conventions that are inclusive rather than exclusive. That is, the text avoids specialized language; where such language is unavoidable, the writer makes efforts to define or explain the terms. • Abstract concepts are presented in a simple manner that usually includes an analogy or comparison to some everyday event. • Recognizes that the audience lacks expertise in the field. • Rhetorical purpose is to inform the audience by making specialized knowledge accessible. • Reasons for writing include a desire to reach a broader audience or a need to make complex information accessible to readers who lack expertise. • Has the potential to influence policy and decision makers in some instances.

Linked Assignment

INSIDERS AND OUTSIDERS: YOUR SCHOOL'S MISSION STATEMENT

This assignment gives you an opportunity to apply what you have learned so far about insiders and outsiders, and it is linked to the writing assignment on page 39. Most college bulletins, the books that schools use to describe themselves, their degree programs, and their course offerings, contain a statement by the president or some other top administrator about the school's mission. Get a copy of your college bulletin, turn to this mission statement, and determine the rhetorical stance the writer adopts. Is it insider to insider? Insider to outsider? Or outsider to outsider?

In one page, identify three features of the statement that reflect this stance and then describe how the writer's relationship to the audience has shaped the piece of writing as a whole.

Writing Assignment

EXPLORING THE LANGUAGE
OF INCLUSION & EXCLUSION

Being able to read a text and recognize its inclusive or exclusive nature is an important step toward improving your own writing. It can help you match your language to your rhetorical stance. This writing assignment asks you to examine a piece of writing and determine what makes it inclusive or exclusive. It gives you an opportunity to apply more substantively what you have learned about rhetorical stance.

First, find two published pieces of writing that reflect different rhetorical stances. One should use language of exclusion, the other language of inclusion. (Federal tax-return booklets, Supreme Court decisions, and newspaper editorials are just three examples of texts you can use.)

Second, write a two-page paper to fellow students that explains how these texts exclude and include readers. Is it the language? The subject matter? The sentence structure? What evidence from the texts supports your explanation?

The Teacher as Audience

One of your tasks as a student writer is to accumulate the knowledge necessary to bring yourself to the threshold that separates outsiders from insiders. You must study and then master the conventions that govern professional writing in a given community or communities and apply them when required. As a result, you must engage in a certain degree of *role-playing*. You frequently must assume the role of an insider writing for your "professional peers." One difficulty you face, however, is the natural temptation to write to your teachers, who not only set most assignments but who also constitute an immediate, tangible audience. But to the extent that you write to your teacher, your work will be by an outsider for an insider. Some kinds of writing nearly always entail this relationship, such as essay exams and research papers. Writing as a form of examination can be an important part of your training to be an insider, but it represents just a single facet of this training.

Essay exams and research papers that show only that you have mastered the course material are not characteristic of the kind of writing you would produce if you were a member of a given community. Such texts have little if any influence on the field. Many writing assignments will invite you to participate as an insider. Those that do usually ask you to make connections between what you know and an important topic in the discipline.

SUBJECT AREAS, SUBJECT,
TOPIC, AND THESIS

A hierarchy based on focus provides a useful way of looking at academic and professional writing:

- Subject area
- Subject
- Topic
- Thesis

The subject comes out of a subject area; a topic comes out of a subject, and a thesis comes out of a topic.

FOUR FACTORS ASSOCIATED WITH WRITING

Subject area

↓

Subject

↓

Topic

↓

Thesis

Subject Areas

As noted earlier, texts are linked to communities. In college, these communities consist of the academic disciplines that make up the undergraduate curriculum. Outside of college, they consist of groups such at attorneys, psychologists, accountants, and so on.

Communities, however, is a fairly broad term. Although attorneys deal with the law, there are discrete categories of law, and many attorneys specialize. As a result, an attorney who practices family law will produce a motion that is different from one produced by an attorney who practices tax law, if for no other reason than that the contents address different matters.

Professional communities generally are divided into categories of specialization, and I call these categories *subject areas*. Subject areas are not fixed; group members often establish new categories or divide old ones to further differentiate their various interests. The community of English literature scholars, for example, has established the broad subject areas of American and British literature, which in turn have been further divided into narrower subject areas.

Subjects

Subjects are the artifacts and ideas that make up a subject area, and there are vast numbers of them. Consider this simple example: In college, you declare a major in a *subject area* such as math, history, or English literature. For your major, the courses you take focus on more narrow *subjects*, such as calculus, U.S. history, and Shakespeare's plays.

Topics

Topics are the material you use for interpretation. They arise out of subjects. In a literature class examining Shakespeare's plays, for example, you might write about Hamlet's "indecision" because this is an important part of the play and thus is a significant topic. Note that the topic comes out of the subject, one of Shakespeare's plays, but it is linked to the broader subject area of Renaissance English literature, where those who talk and write about such topics form an identifiable community.

Thesis

In its most basic form, an interpretation is a claim.[1] A paper about *Hamlet* might have a claim resembling the following: "Hamlet's indecision is the result of . . ." You would fill in the blank with your interpretation. *A thesis, or claim, is the interpretive assertion you want readers to accept as reasonable when they are finished with your paper.*

How people arrive at a thesis is a complex question. A wide range of factors appears to be involved, everything from knowledge of the subject to political orientation, religious affiliation, personal philosophy or world view, and interpersonal skills. To a large extent, a thesis will reflect your understanding of a topic and how it relates to subject and subject area. Formulating a thesis therefore requires that you have something to say about the topic, but a thesis also is an important bridge between your personal experiences and knowledge and the discourse community.

A word of caution. The categories of subject and topic are not rigid. For example, ozone depletion easily could be (and on many occasions is) the subject of a more specific topic: chemical mechanisms in the atmosphere that lead to the destruction of ozone. Tax liability of the middle class could easily supply another topic: the shrinking middle class. At issue is the level of detail you can (and want to) address. Thus, use the distinctions above as a guide rather than as a set of rules.

Applying Key Ideas

DIFFERENCES BETWEEN TOPICS AND THESES

Although the distinctions between subject areas and subjects are clear, those between topics and theses sometimes are confusing. This activity will help you begin to recognize those distinctions and see them more clearly.

Using the examples above as a guide, generate some topics associated with classes you currently are taking. From these topics, produce some associated the-

---

[1]*Thesis* and *claim* mean the same thing. Some writing teachers have come to prefer *claim* because it seems a bit clearer. Throughout this book, the terms are used interchangeably.

EXAMPLES OF SUBJECT AREA, SUBJECT, TOPIC, AND THESIS

Subject Area	Subject	Topic	Thesis
Renaissance literature	Shakespeare's plays (*Hamlet*)	Hamlet's indecision	Hamlet cannot easily decide to kill his stepfather because he cannot easily accept that he really spoke to his dead father's ghost.
Chemistry	Environmental chemistry	Ozone depletion	The Western world's efforts to reduce significantly the rate of ozone depletion have been largely unsuccessful.
Economics	Taxation	Tax liability of the middle class	High taxes are eliminating the middle class.
U.S. politics	Politics and the media	The effect of TV on voting	Television encourages people to vote for the candidates who project the better image rather than for those who have the better agenda.

ses. See what pattern emerges that characterizes the relationship between topics and theses. Try to describe the pattern in a paragraph or two.

DEVELOPING A THESIS

In most situations, a key to finding something worthwhile to say about a topic lies in having some ideas or opinions about it in advance. You should not rely on what you have heard others say about it, however. Instead, you should use that information to complement what you can see for yourself and what you already know. If you merely try to repeat what you have heard, from your teacher, say, you are immediately at a disadvantage. You know much less than your teachers when it comes to academic subjects. Also, most teachers are not particularly interested in having you repeat what they have told you. They are more interested in seeing how you can use that information, how it is reflected in your own thoughts. *What matters most is not so much what you know but what you understand.*

The next chapter considers several techniques that can help you explore topics before you begin writing. These techniques are usually referred to as *invention activities*. Talking with your teacher and your classmates is one kind of invention activity; doing some background reading in the library is another. These activities engage you in thinking about what you will write. They can help you discover what you already know about topics, and they provide the means to learn more about them. Thus, a second key to finding something worthwhile to say about a topic lies in being able to generate ideas and to clarify your thoughts.

As noted earlier, one of the more useful writing tools is the journal, a notebook in which you record your life experiences but more importantly your thoughts about those experiences. Your journal also can provide a useful place to jot down responses to reading assignments in your classes. Such responses can form the foundation for later classroom discussions of the reading; they can offer a handy reference when reviewing for exams; and they can provide a valuable starting point for any papers you may have to write. Your journal can offer a handy starting point for a well-written paper. I encourage you to keep a journal as part of your work for this class. In fact, some of the writing assignments later in this book assume that you are keeping a journal.

Journal Entry

Record your impressions of college. What do you think of your classes, teachers, and fellow students? Does the experience match your expectations?

Premises

Premises are the building blocks of most writing. They are a kind of belief system that writers and readers must share if a paper is to develop a claim successfully. (Some teachers use the term *warrants* rather than *premises* when talking about argument; others use the term *assumptions*. The terms mean the same thing, however.)

Consider how this text has stressed the role of interpretation and argument in writing. Consider also that intellectual arguments aim to get your audience to accept your interpretation as being reasonable. If you suspect that the focus on acceptance suggests that agreement is more important than disagreement, you are right. Reasonable disagreements cannot move forward without preliminary agreement on certain assumptions, values, and so forth. Intellectual arguments depend on acceptance throughout, and premises are where this acceptance starts. Moreover, for any given paper, you can have multiple premises. They can deal with assumptions of what is factual and true, or they can deal with what is preferable.

Determining what is factual and true is not easy, but fortunately writers do not have to make that determination when working with this category of premise. What matters is that the audience and writer *share the perception* that something is indeed factual and true. Many facts, for example, are anything but facts; they are falsehoods that have been repeated so many times that they are believed by almost everyone and so often have the force of facts. For example, huge numbers of people believe mistakenly that Albert Einstein failed algebra in high school; many others believe that Cleopatra was black, even though historical documents show that she was a direct descendant of one of Alexander the Great's generals and therefore Greek. It is common for people to use such falsehoods to support an argument. When they do, they are arguing from ignorance.

Premises dealing with what is preferable most often are concerned with values and hierarchies. Again, writers don't have to distinguish between the valuable and the worthless, because what is important is sharing the perception of what is valuable with the audience. Let's make this idea more concrete by considering *Hamlet*. Box 2.3 presents a claim for the topic of "Hamlet's indecision": "Hamlet cannot easily decide to kill his stepfather because he cannot easily accept that he really spoke to his dead father's ghost."

Listed here are some of the premises underlying this claim. Before an audience can accept the claim, it must accept most, if not all, of these premises:

- Human life is valuable.
- Ghosts don't exist.
- Murder is wrong.
- A son has an obligation to obey his father.
- Criminals should be brought to justice.

When Your Audience Doesn't Accept Your Premises

Intellectual arguments cannot proceed if there is disagreement on premises. In fact, some scholars have suggested that disagreement on premises can lead to conflicts in everyday life. Several historians, for example, have argued that the Civil War was the result of a conflict between the different premises of government held by the North and the South. The North's premise maintained that state government was subordinate to federal authority. The South's premise, on the other hand, maintained that the federal government received its authority from the individual states and that it therefore was subordinate to them. You might want to review the premises that were listed as underlying our claim about Hamlet. Do you disagree with any of them?

Various controversial subjects that may be interesting to write about are not suited to intellectual argument because of the difficulty associated with agreement on premises. Abortion, gun control, capital punishment, and euthanasia are four such subjects. Many teachers actually prohibit students from writing on these subjects because there is no place for intellectual argument. The sides are so polarized that neither accepts the premises of the other.

Applying Key Ideas

IDENTIFYING PREMISES

Being able to recognize premises can help you become a better writer, and the goal of this activity is to give you some practice. Return to the theses in the box on page 42 and see how many premises you can identify for each.

Have a Thesis in Advance

At the end of the first *Star Trek* movie, Captain Kirk tells Lieutenant Sulu, "Ahead warp factor 2." Sulu asks for a heading, a direction, a destination. Kirk smiles wanly, waves in the general direction of space as seen through the viewer, and says, "That way. Let's just see what's out there."

The idea of just setting out without a destination appeals to the romantic in us all. Unfortunately, it does not work very well when you are writing a paper. You really need to know what your thesis is before you start writing; otherwise, you're likely to make so many false starts that you will never meet your deadline.

It is important to recognize a distinction, however. I am not suggesting that you already should know what you are going to say when you approach a *topic*. The invention activities in chapter 3 will help you learn more about a topic, and they also will help you reach conclusions about the topic. Both are central to successful composing. Furthermore, invention activities frequently will help you discover a thesis. But after you have completed these activities, you need a clear sense of direction before you put that first word on paper.

From time to time, students discover after writing a few pages that they no longer agree with their own claim. For example, you might start out with the view that all freshmen should be required to take a physical education class, only to realize that there are more reasons for opposing the requirement than for endorsing it. The intellectual processes that led to this new point of view are valuable, but in most circumstances you should not expect readers to participate in your own voyage of discovery. If you change your mind about your claim after you have started writing, you should consider that effort to be an early draft necessary to help you get your ideas straight. You should then start over, revising the paper to reflect your new point of view.

Evaluating Your Claim

Successful writers generally have to adopt the role of readers and ask themselves whether what they have to say is something they would want to read. Does the claim have the potential to inform readers, or is it an idea that is already well known among educated people, or even worse, is it a self-evident truth (what is termed a *truism*)? The well-known and truisms *bore readers*.

Admittedly, outsiders often may not know enough about a subject or a topic to recognize a widely accepted claim. The writer Gabriel García Márquez describes this situation beautifully in the novel *One Hundred Years of Solitude*. Amid the banana plantations and rain forests of Columbia in the late 1800s, the character José Arcadio Buendía spends months charting the movement of the stars, becoming more and more pensive, finally falling into a depression. Then, unable to bear the weight of his discovery any longer, he announces to his startled family: "The earth is round, like an orange."

The task of outsiders who want to become insiders is to interact with members of the community and with one another, sharing ideas, their growing knowledge, and insights. Such interaction is an important part of learning. It would have helped poor José Arcadio Buendía recognize that his discovery had been made long before.

Journal Entry

Recall a time when you talked with a friend or relative and disagreed on premises. What was the outcome?

RHETORICAL PURPOSE

People write for a reason. They write in the workplace because they must produce a report that conveys information, a business letter that acknowledges an order, a memo that communicates a new policy, or a proposal that aims to bring in new business. Likewise, students write because they must demonstrate that they have learned course material, that they can interpret information using what they have learned in class, or that they can work independently or in a group.

Underlying each instance is an individual reason for writing. This reason is called *rhetorical purpose*. It includes personal goals for producing a text. Rhetorical purpose, however, is not the same as the principal aim of a text, which may be to inform, argue, or persuade. Rhetorical purpose is about you, the writer, whereas the aim of a text is about the audience, about the effect a paper should have on readers.

The range of individual purposes is broad but not limitless. Within professional groups, there are three categories of rhetorical purpose: *traditional, innovative,* and *confrontational*. It is common to think of scientists, for example, as people who typically write to disseminate new facts. Some do, and they have an innovative rhetorical purpose. However, scientists also replicate experiments to validate work others have performed. When they publish their findings, these writers have a traditional rhetorical purpose, to the extent that their research confirms established conclusions, a very valuable purpose in every field. Scientists who attempt to overturn established conclusions may have a confrontational rhetorical purpose.

THREE CATEGORIES OF RHETORICAL PURPOSE

Traditional: To maintain the accepted point of view or facts of a group.

Innovative: To share new knowledge or a view of reality.

Confrontational: To overturn an established point of view, using confrontational language; writers are insiders, but they often distance themselves from the group to attack it.

A Model of Traditional Rhetorical Purpose

Since about the early 1980s, some scholars have suggested that history has focused on the activities of men to such an extent that readers of history have only a fuzzy notion of what women did in the past. The community of historians has responded to this suggestion, but slowly. The majority of historical writing continues in about the same vein that has dominated the field for a long time. Consider the reading selection below, for example. It was written by Morris Bishop, a well-known medieval scholar. Although the writing is informative, it is hard to view it as innovative, particularly in regard to the question of women's roles in history. As you read his account of medieval towns, try to find references to women and their activities.

1   Paris, the natural commercial center of France, boomed. It was not, however, a free city, nor was it totally given to business, being dominated by the royal government, the church, and the university. In England all roads led to London. Its population is estimated at about 30,000 at a time when Venice, Milan, and Paris had over 100,000. In Spain Barcelona became very important, controlling inland trade and sending its fleets throughout the Mediterranean.

2   The case of Germany was special. Most of its large cities became self-governing in the twelfth century. But instead of competing fiercely among themselves as the Italian cities did, they eventually united in leagues, of which the most famous are the Hanseatic and the Swabian. The Hanse merchants of Lübeck and other northern seaboard cities developed overland routes to Italy, but the Hanse's chief business was water-borne. By around 1400 it had offices in one hundred sixty towns, and factories or compounds, with their own docks and warehouses, in London, Bruges, Bergen, and Novgorod. The league held a monopoly on the Norwegian fish trade, exploited Sweden's mineral and agricultural resources, and brought timber, tar, grain, butter, cheese, and bacon to Flanders and England. It dealt in everything, being, like the Hudson's Bay Company or the Dutch East Indies Company of later days, limited only by territory and not by type of merchandise. The league seldom used force to maintain its supremacy. It employed, instead, embargoes, boycotts, and commercial pressures, with which recalcitrant cities and even kings could be subdued. It did go to war, however, with King Waldemar of Denmark in the middle of the fourteenth century, capturing Copenhagen, and with it the monopoly of the Baltic fish trade. The Hanseatic cities loved monopolies, particularly the one that controlled the transport of Flemish cloth to Russia in exchange for furs. This trade promoted a steady infiltration of Russia by German traders and settlers, who penetrated even into the deep interior.

3   In the West most of the towns developed from episcopal or other church centers, or from burghs or bourgs, walled fortresses. The inhabitants therefore were called burghers or bourgeois. Other towns had their origins in trading settlements situated advantageously where roads met or rivers could be forded or crossed by ferry. These towns began to appear around the millennium, and two centuries later they abounded. Since the feudal system made little provision for trade and industry, the towns had to make their own place in society. Purchasing charters and freedoms from the landholders, they gained territorial immunity and became "legal islands" and sanctuaries. They did obeisance only to the king, and that with qualifications. Avignon, in a treaty of 1208, declared that it obeyed no one but God. The towns raised their own militia and spent about eighty percent of their revenues for defense—walls, moats, armaments. When night fell the burghers locked their gates and slept secure.

4   Kings and nobles came to recognize the profits in city real-estate development and founded "New Towns" in their own territories, and especially in the wild borderlands of eastern Germany. They tempted settlers with promises of freedoms, tax exemptions, cheap land, and low rents. Their recruiting methods resemble exactly those of the big operators who, in the nineteenth century, transported whole provincial populations from Europe to the American West. These new towns, *villes neuves* or *bastides*, fascinate modern city planners, being laid out rationally, with streets on a gridiron plan, like Philadelphia, like any New City from Texas to Siberia.

5   Off the main traffic routes many medieval towns persist today, their spires and fortress towers rising above weedy walls. Unlike modern cities, they take naturally poses of beauty, show colors dimmed to nature's harmony. They rejoice the artist, from the medieval miniaturist to Maxfield Parrish. Apologetic for disturbing old ghosts, we

walk the cobbled streets, gaze at the faded pride of their decrepit, nearly empty churches, at the merchants' mansions now serving as rickety inns or garages, at the pathetic pomp of fallen fortunes.

6   The typical town was a series of concentric rings, each marking a stage of growth. The innermost ring was the original stronghold; the outermost, the defensive walls. Intervening rings showed where walls had once stood, before being dismantled and replaced by boulevards. The plan of Paris today clearly shows the development. When the citizens decided to expand the town and build new walls, they left enough space to accommodate gardens, orchards, and vineyards, as a precaution against siege.

7   The market square was the town center. Here stood the great church, the town hall, the clock, and the market cross, which reminded the citizens that God was watching to punish any malefactor who might disturb the market's peace. Here too stood often the pillory, stocks, cucking stool for scolding women, gallows, and gibbet. (The Paris gibbet accommodated twenty-four; when a new occupant arrived, an old skeleton was thrown into a nearby charnel pit.) In the square the troops drilled, wandering actors performed, young men played a kind of mass football. This was the business center. Round about was the shopping area, often arcaded. In many towns, especially in Germany, a quarter was walled off for the Jews. This segregation was intended as much to protect as to humiliate them; often it was the rabbi who held the keys.

8   Each trade might have its separate street—Shoe Lane, Leather Lane—as it still does in Athens and the East. The shops were marked, not by lettered signboards, but by symbols—a barber's basin, a gilded boot, or for a tavern, a bush, though good wine needs no bush. The shops were narrow and deep, with a frontage that might be only six feet wide. Here the workmen plied their trades, where the light was best, where their work could be inspected and admired, and where they could exchange pleasantries with the passersby. (Window workers are now extinct; the last to go were the cigar rollers.) Artisans usually kept no stock; they worked only on orders. They would have been shocked by ready-made shoes and clothes.

9   The streets, except in the new towns, were narrow, irregular, with unexpected angles that record a householder's successful fight with the munici-

pality. The street level was likely to rise above the house floors, for street repairs were made by dumping sand and gravel on old bases. Hence in many towns one steps down from the street to visit old churches. The streets were made chiefly for pedestrians, not for wheeled traffic. Paving was paid for by tolls imposed on carts entering the town; the tolls were graduated according to the weight and type of vehicle and its presumed injury to pavements, as our motorcar registration fees are. The highest rate was paid by carts with iron-rimmed or nail-studded wheels. The parking problem on market days was acute.

10   Houses were built flush with the street or overhanging it, marking the triumph of the owner over the general good. Building styles varied with local materials and conventions. In England and the north, houses were mostly of wood, with thatched roofs that were very flammable. The frequent fires in London led, in time, to reconstruction, with tiled roofs and stone party-walls. Every burgher was enjoined to keep tubs of water ready. The city supplied hooks to pull burning thatch into the street, hence our hook-and-ladder companies. A common cause of fire was the custom of sleeping on straw mattresses beside the hearth. On the other hand, the times were spared the hazards of cigarettes and electrical wiring.

11   In the early centuries the houses had considerable yard and garden space in the rear, enough for maintaining a cow and a few pigs. But as the cities grew within their constricting walls, this open space was much encroached upon. The houses lacked air, light, and *confort moderne*; but people had little taste for privacy. They lived most of their lives on the streets, noisy indeed by day with pounding hammers, screaming saws, clattering wooden shoes, street cries of vendors of goods and services, and the hand bells of pietists summoning all to pray for the souls of the dead.

12   But at night reigned a blessed silence, broken only by the watchman rattling his iron-shod staff and crying, "All's well!" Nightwalking was prohibited after curfew, at about nine o'clock, as presumptive of ill-doing. There were, of course, no street lights or illuminated shop fronts.

13   Men met in taverns; women had their social hour when they fetched water from the public fountains, which, as in Perugia, could be the city's pride. All progressive cities had a municipal water

system, but it was advisable not to drink the water straight. City water fed public bathhouses, which included sweat baths.

14 Efforts toward municipal hygiene could not prevail against old custom, which ruled that the street before a man's house was part of his domain. (A relic of this custom is the sidewalk café, which in Mediterranean lands may expand halfway across the road.) The medieval streets were unquestionably foul. Butchers slaughtered animals at their shop fronts and let the blood run into the gutters. Poulterers flung chicken heads and feathers into the streets. Dyers released noisome waters from their vats. City officials in Italy would throw the fishmonger's unsold fish into the street for the poor, to make sure it would not sicken honest purchasers. Pigs ran free as scavengers, and in London "genteel dogs," though not commoners' dogs, were allowed to roam at will. Flies settled down in clouds to their banquets, but few, besides Petrarch, complained. The walker, perhaps with a perfumed handkerchief to his nose, picked his way carefully, dodging the black mud thrown up by the squash of horses' hooves. And there was always a menace from overhead. Louis IX of France, Saint Louis, received the contents of a dumped chamber pot on his royal cloak. He dismounted and ran to the culprit's lair, finding him to be a student who had risen early to study. The king gave him a scholarship. (The king, of course, was a saint.)

15 Sewage disposal was an impossible problem. Only the big cities had sewers, which emptied into rivers below the laundry area. At Strasbourg malefactors were ducked where the sewer joined the river. Pollution of the streams became a serious concern; everyone agreed that something should be done about it. Street cleaning and the removal of wastes to rural dumps were usually left to individual householders, who were apt to toss their refuse over the city walls or abandon it just outside the gates. On the other hand, in a well-policed city like Paris the garbage man, "Maistre Fifi," called regularly. In *The City in History* Lewis Mumford points out that in the early Middle Ages, with a good deal of open land behind the houses and privies in the gardens, conditions could be as cleanly as in the idyllic American small town of the 1890s. The wastes were mostly organic matter, not tin cans, glass, and plastic; they decomposed, and enriched the soil. Mr. Mumford, who frowns upon moderni-

ty, even celebrates the remembered smells of horse and cow dung. "Is the reek of gasoline exhaust, the sour smell of a subway crowd, the pervasive odor of a garbage dump, the sulphurous fumes of a chemical works, the carbolated rankness of a public lavatory, for that matter the chlorinated exudation from a glass of ordinary drinking water more gratifying? Even in the matter of smells, sweetness is not entirely on the side of the modern town; but since the smells are *our* smells, many of us blandly fail to notice them." True, but we should certainly have disliked *their* smells, and there is overwhelming evidence that they disliked them too. Some used a deodorizing charcoal in the privies. Edward III of England said that the York stink was worse than that of any other town he had smelled. Henry III's asthmatic Queen Eleanor was driven from Nottingham by coal fumes. In Westminster Palace the garbage was carried out from the royal kitchen through the palace halls. It made the courtiers sick; and in 1260 an outlet was built in the kitchen.

16 The cities, fair or foul, were the natural habitat of the bourgeoisie. Merchants or sons of merchants, an oligarchy of competence, they were forced to organize their agglomerations. They created from nothing a system of municipal administration for free men living crowded together. They elected their own town officials, mayor, and aldermen. (Aldermen are "elder men." They met at a dinner table, a board; hence the board of aldermen.) The educated bourgeoisie infiltrated the officeholding class, providing many lawyers, notaries, and accountants. Their power and abilities were recognized by kings, whom they entertained at dinner. In 1190 Philip Augustus of France took the unprecedented step of appointing six bourgeois to the council of regency during his absence on crusade. The bourgeois had a strong civic sentiment, which could expand, in time, to become a national sentiment, or patriotism. They had their own moral code of behavior, exalting both personal and business virtue. The idea gained ground that ability is measured by wealth, that the rich are the best and wisest men, and the poor are the worst.

17 The chief organization of medieval economy was the guild. The origins of the guild have been traced back to primitive Germanic and religious brotherhoods. The word first appears in Charle-

magne's decrees. In Anglo-Saxon England the guilds, religious associations of men with similar mercantile interests, were established to provide mutual aid, protection, and good times.

18   At first there was one guild to a town, but as population grew and interests diverged, the guilds divided vertically and horizontally. Vertically they divided into the merchant-owners and the workers, employers and employees, rich and poor. Horizontally the original guild divided into craft guilds, each representing a particular trade. The craft guilds tended to subdivide. In England it took three craftsmen to make a knife: a bladesmith, a cutler for the handle and fitments, and a sheather. The purpose of the craft guild, like any trade union, was to promote the economic welfare of its members and guarantee full employment at high wages by restricting membership. It held a local monopoly of its product, discouraged competition among guildsmen, and suppressed scab labor. It regulated work procedures and hours of labor. It set wages, but maximum, not minimum wages. It standardized the quality and price of the product and opposed innovation. It forbade price cutting, overtime work, public advertising, overenergetic salesmanship, the introduction of new tools, the employment of one's wife or underage children. The guild's aim was regularization, the preservation of the status quo. Hence it failed to adjust to technological progress, which took place outside the guilds.

    The craft guilds promoted discipline and solidarity among their members. Guilds owned property, had their own chapels in churches, contributed stained-glass windows to cathedrals. They cared for destitute members and for widows and orphans. They presented mystery plays; the plasterers staged the building of the ark; the wine dealers, the marriage at Cana; the fishmongers, Jonah and the whale and the miraculous draft of fishes; the bakers, the Last Supper. Even thieves, beggars, and vagabonds formed trade association in imitation of the guilds. 19

A Model of Innovative Rhetorical Purpose

Bonnie Anderson and Judith Zinsser are historians who recognized that historians had failed to provide adequate discussions of the roles women played in history. Their rhetorical purpose, however, was not to confront their fellow group members in an effort to point out their shortcomings. Instead, it was to educate. Consequently, Anderson and Zinsser used the conventions associated with mainstream historical scholarship, which was an important decision because it made their audience view the argument as being reasonable and acceptable.

    The following sample comes from *A History of Their Own: Women in Europe from Prehistory to the Present*. In their introduction, Anderson and Zinsser write: "This book arose from perceptions of . . . the disparity between our own growing knowledge of women and their activities both past and present, and the almost total absence of women from the pages of history books."

THE TOWNSWOMAN'S DAILY LIFE: THE TWELFTH TO THE SEVENTEENTH CENTURIES

Alleyways, Streets, and Squares

1   The European towns of the twelfth to the seventeenth centuries bore little relation to modern urban metropolises, in appearance, size of population, and the activities of the inhabitants. There was less contrast with the countryside; the poor worked the fields just outside the walls, the wealthy had orchards and household gardens around their houses. Though the towns were crowded, the numbers of inhabitants never reached the millions of the eighteenth, nineteenth, and twentieth centuries. Cologne, fifteenth-century Germany's largest town, had a population of about 20,000. Fourteenth-century Florence began to incorporate surrounding communes into its orbit, so that by the fifteenth century 40,000 women and men lived inside the walls or just outside. By the beginning of the 1600s, Genoa, Milan, Venice, Naples, Seville, and Paris had populations from 60,000 to 100,000. A very large town like London created new parishes, forty-seven inside the walls in 1695 and fifty-four outside to accommodate its over 400,000 inhabitants.

2   Even the most populous urban centers provided smaller, more rural, and more controlled environments than would the sprawling neighborhoods and masses of humanity that filled the modern cities. Daily tasks familiar to a countrywoman, small-scale manufacturing and retailing guild protections and restrictions characterized the occupations of the townspeople. A late fifteenth-century engraving of Cologne shows the roads coming from the mountains and along the River Rhine. The tiled rooftops and the spires of the churches rise just above the crenelated walls and towers. The country noblewoman in her covered cart, the young peasant girl and her mother from a nearby manor would have waited just outside the gates, with other women and men come to buy and sell goods or to find a few hours labor.

3   All of this scene was familiar to the townswoman who lived inside the walls. With cockcrow, with first light, the bells of the town cathedral rang, and the gates opened to herald the beginning of another market day. The streets, alleyways, and squares filled with wagons, animals, and people. Contemporaries described the carts pouring into fifteenth-century Vienna, carrying flour, eggs, bread, meat, crayfish, and poultry. At the time of the harvest 1,200 horses a day brought in the casks of new wine. Gondolas carrying goods filled the Grand Canal of Venice in the early sixteenth century; there were twenty-five sailboats bringing nothing but melons. Venice's bridge, the Rialto, was like a market unto itself, a bustling thoroughfare lined with shops and warehouses.

4   The biggest towns, like London, had many markets, each specializing in one kind of produce or another: fish at Billingsgate, leather near Leaden Hall. The townswomen pushed by each other with baskets full of cabbages, of oranges, of secondhand clothing mended and patched to be sold again: the merchant's wife on her way to early mass; the laundress and the brick carrier on their way to the day's work; the herbalist returned from gathering her medicinal plants at sunrise; the silk spinner's apprentice on an errand for her mistress; street sellers like the baker's wife with her meat and cheese pies calling out the goods and the prices from the stalls set all around and across the square.

5   Away from the busy market squares, the town was a crowded, noisy, dark world in comparison to the light and space of the fields and countryside around it. Though townspeople represented only about 10 percent of the overall population of Europe, from the twelfth to the eighteenth centuries, in the oldest sections of towns like London and Paris as many as three to five hundred would be crowded together in one hectare (2.74 acres).

Because of the towns, sometimes whole regions took on an urban character. In Tuscany in northern Italy 26.3 percent of the local population had moved to ten of its towns by the beginning of the fourteenth century. So many had come to Florence and its environs in the 1300s that the population density was greater than in the twentieth century (85 per square kilometer).

6 The poorest women lived in the oldest, most crowded neighborhoods. By the end of the fourteenth century, the alleyways were cobbled and so less muddy, but no less dirty. Waste and refuge [sic] went out the door or the window of the wooden dwellings that lined the narrow streets. Into the fifteenth century in towns like Nuremberg, pigs and other animals scavenged freely just as they did in the manor forests in the fall.

7 In London in the fifteenth and sixteenth centuries, a pieceworker or a day laborer and her family lived in a single rented room, perhaps six feet by ten feet in size, fronting on the alleyway. In 1580 new building had been prohibited by the town council to try to ease the crowding, but the poorest women and men continued to piece shelters together out of whatever materials they could find. In the campaign of 1381–82 Froissart, the chronicler of the Hundred Years War, described one of these dwellings in Bruges in Belgium, where the Count of Flanders had fled to hide: a "poor grimy hovel, blackened by the smoke of the peat fire." "An old sheet of smoke-stained cloth" shielded the fire; "a ladder with seven rungs" led to a "cramped little loft" overhead where the children slept. The woman nursed her baby by the open fire. In Madrid the women day laborers lived outside the walls near the orchards and fields they worked, in one-story dwellings they and their families had built out of mud.

8 When towns counted their inhabitants, these women would be too poor to appear on any tallies of household hearths. Not so with all women, however. Those who had become associated with the crafts and their guilds, either by marriage or in their own right, appear in the historical record. For they would be listed among the town's elite, members of those families that paid taxes: the 135 grocers, 150 goldsmiths, 170 skinners on the tax rolls of London in the last quarter of the fourteenth century; the 169 bakers, 75 fishsellers, 110 barber-surgeons of Antwerp listed in the second half of the sixteenth century.

9 Craftswomen's houses were in newer sections of the town, substantial two- and three-story buildings with ten to twelve feet fronting on the street, twenty feet deep with a household garden at the back. Most of their houses would be constructed of wood; in Rouen most were made of half-timbered stucco, in Amsterdam, brick. The second story was commonly built to overhang the street by a few feet. As this was the principal living space for the family, the extension gave more room for sleeping, cooking, and eating. Curtains or walls divided off areas inside. Here the artisan or craftsman's wife performed her household duties, making the meals over the central stone hearth. In German and Dutch towns an earthenware stove, in southern France braziers, heated the rooms in the winter. A third floor in a prosperous artisan's family meant private space for the mistress and master, who could then send the apprentices and servants to the top floor. The workshop took up the whole of the ground floor. Shutters on the front of the building opened; the top served as an awning, the bottom as a counter from which the wife could sell the products made in the household.

10 The richest townswomen, members of the families of the governing elite of merchant and banker guilds, lived in a still more prosperous neighborhood and enjoyed differences of scale and comfort way beyond women in other parts of the town. In fourteenth-century Genoa, the family of the merchant, Andrea Doria, lived together with their kin in the section known as San Matteo. It was a compound with shared houses grouped about their own square with a family-endowed church to service their religious needs. Initially, in the twelfth and thirteenth centuries in towns like Genoa, the houses were fortified with towers and thick outer walls, similar to the castles and manors in the countryside. Families warred for power and built their houses as protected refuges. When the warring ceased, in Venice in the fourteenth century, then in Florence in the fifteenth century, and gradually across Europe in Bourges, Nuremberg, London, Paris, Madrid, the winning families built the grand private houses still associated with their names.

11 Order and prosperity meant the luxury of houses with business and living space on different

floors, with interior rooms giving privacy for different branches of the family and the public and private activities of the wife and her husband. In Prato, Italy, when the wool merchant, Francesco Datini, built a new home for his wife and himself late in the fourteenth century, he put the warehouse at the end of the garden, separating it from their living space. Palazzos of fourteenth- and fifteenth-century Florence, like that of Cosimo de' Medici, were on an even grander scale. The ground floor still consisted of offices and storerooms, but rooms above were designed for beauty and comfort, with high ceilings and frescoed walls. The Medici Palazzo had a row of large glass windows facing the garden.

12 Elite merchant-banker families in other towns made the same changes. The Runtinger family of Regensburg, Germany, in the late 1370s took three adjacent buildings on Keplerstrasse (its twentieth-century name) and remodeled them so that the office and kitchen were on the ground floor, the public rooms on the second, the family area and special rooms for the women on the third. Instead of warehouses at one end of a courtyard, the fourth and fifth floors were used for storage, much as they were in the merchant houses of Amsterdam, where the overhang for the pulleys used to raise goods from the street still exists. The house of banker Jacques Coeur in Bourges, France, built in the 1440s, perhaps in deference to the old styles had one side much like a fortress, but the other was of soft stone carefully carved and decorated. Designed around a central courtyard to insure light for the rooms that did not front on the street, the interior design combined the public and private with fourteen large rooms, each with a series of small rooms clustered around it for dressing and for antechambers. By the beginning of the seventeenth century, the well-to-do of Madrid in Spain had given up all pretense of defense and had balconies along the third story so that the family could sit out and watch the public events staged in the Plaza Mayor.

13 These walled towns created a vital new world for women. Young country girls, the daughters of peasants, immigrated in large numbers. Young men came to the town from far away, day laborers looking for any work, journeymen seeking to finish out their training before becoming masters of their craft. Young women tended to come from closer by, from the neighboring villages. A study of seventeenth-century Weissenburg in Bavaria, Germany, showed that two thirds of the female immigrants came from within a forty-mile radius.

14 Perhaps they had first come to the town as little girls on their fathers' cart, fulfilling one of the tasks of his manorial contract. Once they came, the women stayed. They did not leave even when widowed in the last decades of their lives. In the towns women could find work, they could acquire possessions, even access to property, perhaps membership in a guild. Some could hope to make their own way without being dependent on a husband or father.

15 The tax records of towns like Florence in the early fifteenth century show that women could become almost independent, "masterless" in the language of German town ordinances. In Florence in 1427, 15.6 percent of all households were headed by women. Records of parishes for London, in the early fifteenth and late seventeenth centuries, show the same possibilities for single and widowed women, women of substance listed as heads of households, as freeholders (owners of property in their own right). More women came, more stayed, and created a pattern unique to European history: in the towns of the fourteenth, fifteenth, sixteenth, and seventeenth centuries, overall, there were from 20–30 percent more women than men. For example, in Bologna in 1395 the ratio of females to males was 100:95.6 and in Nuremberg in 1419 100:84. The Florentine figures for the same century show that the imbalances occurred especially in different age groups. Women outnumbered men from thirteen to seventeen, suggesting the greater immigration of young women, and again from the late forties to late fifties. This latter statistic also suggests earlier death for men and longer life for women once they had passed their childbearing years.

16 The walled towns of Europe offered unique opportunities to the young woman brave enough to take the risk. As early as the thirteenth century in England, leaving the manor and running away to the nearby town could break the tie of serfdom imposed by her birth. If she could survive a year in a royal, chartered borough, she would become a free woman in the eyes of the law. In 1303 Matilda Siggeword and Alice White lived in Lin-

colnshire on the manor of Ingoldmalls. The lord's records tell of their escape but not of their return. Like other young peasant women they probably went to the nearest municipality, hoping for a more prosperous life than was offered in the countryside. There they would work, marry, and remain, providing the labor and the skills that fostered the economic transformation of Europe from a predominantly rural to a predominantly urban environment.

A Model of Confrontational Rhetorical Purpose

The slow pace of change in many communities has caused some members to become frustrated and to challenge established perceptions. Such writing illustrates a confrontational rhetorical purpose because it is often rebellious, challenging, and impatient. You can get a sense of this kind of writing by reading the sample written by Shulamith Shahar, a feminist historian. Like the previous sample, it deals with towns in the middle ages, and it uses many of the same facts. Shahar's goal, however, is to describe the ways in which men excluded women from participating fully in society, thereby highlighting a significant gap in traditional treatments of the subject. Shahar's piece reflects a tone that some historians have deemed "abrasive." If you compare it to Bishop, you should begin to see some important differences. As you read, consider how intellectual arguments aim to get an audience to accept their claims as reasonable and acceptable.

SHULAMITH SHAHAR

TOWNSWOMEN

1 Urban society was new in several senses and woman's role in it can be understood only against the background of its unique economic, social and cultural structure. But it is important to emphasize at the outset that women's rights continued to be restricted within the new structure of urban life, although this was no longer a warrior society like the nobility, or a partially unfree society like the peasantry. The town was a place of peace (*locus pacificus*). Peace was essential to its development and its economic activity, which was based on artisanship, commerce and money affairs. It evolved its own ethos, which differed from that of the feudal nobility. Though urban society was a class society from the outset, it abolished the distinctions between freemen and serfs and, legally speaking (in contrast to rural areas), all townspeople were free.

2 The town arose as a secular corporation, like the guilds which grew up within it and were also secular corporations (excluding the universities), and a stratum of lay officials, notaries and judges developed. A lay society which was not a society of warriors and whose members enjoyed free competition might have been expected to expand women's political rights, but this did not occur. This appears to substantiate the evaluation (based on comparative study of the history of women and their status in society) that woman's status in general and political status in particular in a specific society cannot always be explained on the basis of the economic structure of that society or the degree to which it is

democratic. One need only recall democratic Athens in its heyday, where women's rights were restricted even according to the criteria of ancient Greece.

3   The restriction of the rights of urban women was reflected primarily in the fact that women played no part in running the town. Different forms of government evolved in different towns, some oligarchical, others aristocratic or semi-democratic. But in none, whatever their regimes, did women play a part in government. They were not elected to municipal councils, did not hold positions of authority, and only in exceptional cases did they take part in town assemblies. In this respect the townswoman's lot was no better than that of the peasant woman. However, though women could not fulfil [sic] functions in manors and village communities, spinsters and widows in rural areas did attend village assemblies, whereas in town no woman, whatever her marital status, attended such assemblies. The increase in the number of male officiaries and wielders of authority in towns did not bring about a corresponding increase in the number of women who played a part in government. The opposite is true, in fact, so much so that within the framework of the history of women in urban society there is no room for discussion of town government.

4   In contrast women played an important part in the urban economy. One could scarcely envisage production in the medieval town or its internal commerce without the activities of women. Their role in labour—and there are those who regard it as one of the manifestations of the new urban ethos—was particularly prominent, and won them some place in the guilds of artisans and petty merchants, despite the restrictions imposed on them. The guild which became an ecclesiastical corporation—the university—was closed to them.

WOMEN AS CITIZENS

5   Women were considered to be citizens of towns, and became such by force of urban property (*burgagia*, as it was called in some towns) which they held either by right of inheritance, through purchase, by right of membership of a guild (in some towns membership of a guild was not only a precondition for permission to work but also for qualification for citizenship), or because they were married to citizens of the town. A man who became a citizen was obliged to pay a certain sum to the community, and sometimes also to the lord of the town, and to take an oath of loyalty to the town. But a female citizen enjoyed only part of the urban privileges. She was entitled to engage in commerce and was answerable only to the municipal courts applying municipal law, at which town judges presided (if the town enjoyed maximal legal autonomy). On the other hand, she did not have the right to elect or be elected to the institutions of government in the town, and in a town which sent representatives to the local or national representative assembly, she was not eligible to elect or represent.

6   An exception was the participation of women in the mid-fourteenth-century referendum in Provins in the Champagne. In this referendum, which encompassed citizens of the town and the surrounding villages, the population were asked whether they wished to continue to live under the rule of the local officials (*scabini*) of the commune or to become directly subject to the king. Some 1741 town voters and 960 from rural areas, 2700 in all, took part in the referendum, and 350 of them, or 13 per cent, were women. The women voters included widows, married women and apparently spinsters as well. In some cases their occupations were listed beside their names: baker; tavern-keeper, seamstress and cloth-dyer. In several towns, women also took part in the election of representatives to the assembly summoned by Philip IV in Tours in 1308. There were almost certainly other exceptions which are unknown to us, but generally speaking women played no part in urban assemblies and councils.

7   The rights of a female citizen are comparable to those of the son of a citizen while still dependent on his father. But whereas the standing of the dependent son was temporary, the woman's was permanent. The status of a woman who fulfilled the financial requirements of citizenship was superior to that of the poor townsman who could not become a citizen because he did not own urban property, was not a member of a guild or could not pay the necessary fee for citizenship. But in principle at least, the possibility existed that he might some day become a citizen with full rights.

8   The laws of inheritance of urban property varied from region to region and even from town to town,

but as in the case of the fief and the peasant estate, the rights of sons almost always took precedence over those of daughters, and those of daughters over those of males of collateral lines. In most English towns where the principle of primogeniture of sons prevailed, recognition was given to the right of the other sons and daughters to enjoy urban liberties. If there were no sons, the daughter inherited, and the registers reveal numerous cases of daughters who inherited shops, the rent of urban properties, and land near towns. Sometimes an arrangement was made (as was customary in some rural areas) by which the father transferred his property to his daughter in his lifetime and she guaranteed to support him and supply all his needs as befitted his station. Brothers too sometimes bequeathed property to their sisters, and husbands to their wives in addition to what they received by right of dower. Girls enjoyed inheritance rights very similar to those of sons in most towns in Flanders: Aire, Arras, Douai, Lille, Bruges, Ypres, Saint Omer and also in Verdun, and in Cuenca and Sepúlveda in Spain.

The most drastic curtailment of female inheritance rights was in Italian towns and in Avignon: daughters who wed and were given a dowry received no part of their father's legacy, while in most Western European towns the dowry was merely deducted from their inheritance (just as property which sons received on marriage was deducted from their future legacy). Not all daughters were destined for marriage and some were sent to nunneries to which a smaller dowry was paid than a bridegroom would have received. This curtailment of the inheritance rights of daughters in Italian towns derived not only from fear of dispersal of the family property but also from fear that the property might end up in alien hands in the event that the daughter married a man from outside the town (*propter nuptias extra territoriam*). In Florence it was explicitly stipulated in the contract of sale of a part of a fortress that it must not, through inheritance, come into the hands of a woman. If no male heir could be found it should be sold.

Critical Reading Guide

1. One of the more frequent comments teachers make about student writing is that it could benefit from more details that enable readers to see or understand what a paper is trying to convey. Look at paragraphs 2–4 in Anderson and Zinsser's chapter and examine the details and examples they provide. How do these details help you understand the writing?

2. Anderson and Zinsser use an effective way of organizing their information when they talk about the living quarters of women in medieval towns. What is their organization, and why do you think it's effective?

3. Morris Bishop writes that streets in medieval towns were "narrow, irregular, with unexpected angles that record a householder's successful fight with the municipality." The tolls on carts and wagons were "graduated according to the weight and type of vehicle and its presumed injury to pavements, as our motorcar registration fees are." These examples are designed to give readers a better understanding of what life in such towns was like. Study these examples to see what pattern you can detect that characterizes Bishop's writing. What does he do to make his examples effective? Can you find some other examples in this sample that illustrate the technique?

4. Bishop says that medieval building styles "varied with local materials and conventions. In England and the north, houses were mostly of wood, with

thatched roofs that were very flammable. The frequent fires in London led, in time, to reconstruction, with tiled roofs and stone party-walls." He also says that medieval people "had little taste for privacy. They lived most of their lives on the streets, noisy indeed by day with pounding hammers, screaming saws, clattering wooden shoes, street cries of vendors. . . . But at night reigned a blessed silence, broken only by the watchman rattling his iron-shod staff." In which of these quotations is Bishop reporting facts, and in which is he interpreting? Can you find some other examples of facts and interpretation?

5. Shahar's excerpt illustrates an outsider-to-insider rhetorical stance. Can you find some examples of language in her text that reflect this stance?

6. Shahar periodically uses Latin terms that most students will not understand because few study Latin in school. Who *would* understand those terms? Why did she included them in her text?

7. Anderson and Zinsser's writing can be characterized as inclusive, whereas Shahar's writing can be characterized as exclusive. How do the texts reflect these different orientations? Look for examples of language as well as organization that reflect inclusion and exclusion in these two professional samples.

8. The professional samples present three different views of medieval towns, even though many of their facts are the same. Which presents the most positive view of town life? Which presents the most negative? Can you identify features of the writing in each choice that develop this view?

9. Some people view writing as problem solving. Skim through the three professional samples and then write a description of the problems the authors are trying to solve. (Try to limit yourself to about 10 minutes so that you don't produce more than you can discuss efficiently as a group.) How do their problems, as well as their solutions, differ? Exchange descriptions and discuss how perceptions in the group vary, if at all.

10. Role-playing is an important part of your apprenticeship at college, and this activity gives you an opportunity to improve your skill. Two people in your group should assume the role of Anderson and Zinsser, who have been invited to make a presentation of their work on medieval townswomen to a group of feminist scholars. They know that they will have to make some changes to their chapter, but they aren't sure exactly what those changes should be, so they ask some friends and colleagues—the other members of the group—for advice. Talk to Anderson and Zinsser about recommended changes, and give them the opportunity to write down your recommendations. (Again, you should limit your time for this activity; try to keep it at about 15 minutes.)

11. After the role-playing, rewrite the first two paragraphs of Anderson and Zinsser's chapter as a group. Then share your revisions with the whole class. You won't have much time left, so you'll need to watch the clock here. Try to you use no more than 20 minutes.

12. Audience is important for any writing task. For this activity, change the audience for the role-playing to a group of conservative male historians. Assume that Shahar has been asked to address them and doesn't want to provoke them. Rewrite the first three paragraphs of her chapter as a group, and then share your revisions with the whole class. Keeping this activity to about 20 minutes will allow ample time afterwards for discussion.

Applying Key Ideas

RECOGNIZING RHETORICAL
PURPOSES IN YOUR OWN WRITING

This activity is intended to help you recognize the rhetorical purpose in your own writing. It also is intended to help you recognize the functional nature of writing, how it gets things done. The first step is to make a list of some of the things you wrote over the past year. You do not have to limit yourself to papers or reports. You may want to include letters, memos, or shopping lists. Next, provide a brief description of each item and explain what it did and why you wrote it. Be sure to include who it was written for and what outcome, if any, you achieved. For example, if you wrote a letter to your parents telling them you needed more money to buy books for your classes, did they send it?

After you have finished, group tasks by category, such as business letter, shopping list, analytical essay, book report, or diary entry. Then write two pages that examine how you went about completing each task. Did you approach writing each item in the same way?

Writing Assignment

WRITING A MISSION STATEMENT
FOR YOUR SCHOOL

The linked assignment on page 38 asked you to evaluate the rhetorical stance of the mission statement in your college bulletin. This assignment asks you to build on that activity so that you can begin applying your understanding of rhetorical stance in your writing.

Write your own mission statement for your college, keeping it about the same length as the original. However, develop a rhetorical stance that is different from the one in the college bulletin. For example, if the original is insider to outsider, you might make yours insider to insider.

Writing as a Process

Successful writers do a great deal of planning before they start writing. They usually have information at hand about their topic because they have spent time researching, thinking, and talking about it. They also benefit from reflection—time spent in quiet contemplation about the topic, its complexities, and its implications.

CHAPTER THREE

Writing as a Process

A key to composing lies in following the processes that good writers use, such as *planning, reading, revising*, and *attending to audience needs*. Successful writers do a great deal of planning before they start writing. They usually have information at hand about their topic because they have spent time researching, thinking, and talking about it. They also benefit from reflection—time spent in quiet contemplation about the topic, its complexities, and its implications.

Reflection occurs throughout, but it can be especially important at the beginning of a project because it enables writers to develop a fairly flexible initial plan for the text. Reflection and planning during actual composing often occurs during the pauses successful writers take as they compose. During these pauses, they read the text and compare it mentally to their initial plan. They assess how well the words on the page match the plan, and on the basis of this assessment they change the plan or the direction the draft is taking. *They revise both the plan and the text as they work.*

STAGES OF WRITING

No two people write in exactly the same way. Nevertheless, it is possible to describe the composing processes that successful writers tend to use. These processes usually are categorized and described in terms of "stages of writing." This expression makes it easier to analyze and talk about what writers do at various points during their work. Table 3.1 lists some of the more important stages in a successful composing process, which the next sections discuss in more detail.

Please note that the term *stages*, as well as the table, gives the impression that the actions that lead to successful writing are distinct, but they aren't at all. The amount of overlap is considerable, and the boundaries that separate them are remarkably fuzzy. Also, consider this important point: Writers do not always take their work through every stage that this chapter considers. They respond to circumstances and goals that influence their composing process. Some situations, for example, make formal revising unfeasible. However, to the extent possible, successful writers generally address each stage.

TABLE 3.1
Stages of Writing

Writing Process	Definition	Description
Invention	Generating ideas, strategies, and information for a given writing task.	Invention activities take place before starting on the first draft of a paper. They include *discussion, outlining, freewriting, journals, talk–write,* and *metaphor.*
Planning	Reflecting on the material produced during invention to develop a plan to achieve the aim of the paper.	Planning involves considering your rhetorical stance, rhetorical purpose, the principal aim of the text, how these factors are interrelated, and how they are connected to the information generated during invention. Planning also involves selecting support for your claim and blocking out at least a rough organizational structure.
Drafting	Producing words on a computer or on paper that match (more or less) the initial plan for the work.	Drafting occurs over time. Successful writers seldom try to produce an entire text in one sitting or even in one day.
Pausing	Moments when you aren't writing but instead are reflecting on what you have produced and how well it matches your plan. Usually includes reading.	Pausing occurs among successful and unsuccessful writers, but they use it in different ways. Successful writers consider "global" factors: how well the text matches the plan, how well it is meeting audience needs, and overall organization.
Reading	Moments during pausing when you read what you've written and compare it to your plan.	Reading and writing are interrelated activities. Good readers are good writers and vise versa. The reading that takes place during writing is crucial to the reflection process during pausing.
Revising	Literally "re-seeing" the text with the goal of making large-scale changes so that text and plan match.	Revising occurs after you've finished your first draft. It involves making changes that enhance the match between plan and text. Factors to consider usually are the same as those you considered during planning: rhetorical stance, rhetorical purpose, and so on. *Serious revising almost always includes getting suggestions from friends or colleagues on how to improve the writing.*
Editing	Focusing on sentence-level concerns, such as punctuation, sentence length, spelling, agreement of subjects and predicates, and style.	Editing occurs after revising. The goal is to give your paper a professional appearance.
Publishing	Sharing your finished text with its intended audience.	Publishing isn't limited to getting a text printed in a journal. It includes turing a paper in to a teacher, a boss, or an agency.

Linked Assignment

UNDERSTANDING YOUR WRITING PROCESS

A goal of the discussion above is to motivate you to consider your own writing process. What strategies and techniques do you use? Another goal, one that forms the rationale for this chapter, is to help you change the way you write so that your strategies and techniques more closely resemble those successful writers use, if they don't already. Toward these ends, look closely at Table 3.1. Spend some time reflecting on your own writing process; afterward, identify *which* of the listed processes you use regularly when you write. Jot down a sentence or two that describes *how* you use each process.

Invention

Invention activities help writers generate ideas, strategies, information, and approaches for a given writing task. They are processes that engage the writer's mind with the writing task at hand. From this perspective, invention, in its broadest sense, is the *thinking* writers do before they start composing.

The sections that follow describe some of the more effective ways to stimulate your thinking about a topic. Note that there is not one best way to go about invention. What works well for some people does not work so well for others; what works well for one assignment will not work well for another. Some writers use various combinations of invention activities, whereas others are committed to only one. You should experiment to determine what works best for you.

Discussion

Perhaps the oldest invention activity, discussion provides multiple points of view on a given topic. The Discussion Checklist provides questions that can help stimulate and guide your discussions. (In fact, you may find these questions useful whenever you face a writing task.) You should not assume, however, that these questions are comprehensive; they simply illustrate the kinds of questions involved in an effective discussion. Listening to what others have to say will help you determine if your preliminary plan is a good one.

DISCUSSION CHECKLIST

√ Who is the audience for this paper?

√ What am I trying to do in this assignment? Interpret? Explain? Analyze? Compare and contrast? Am I writing a term paper that reflects everything I learned during the semester? Am I writing a paper that applies a single principle studied during class? Am I writing a research paper that demonstrates my ability to identify and interpret leading work in the field?

√ What effect am I trying to produce in those who read my paper? Am I writing as an insider or an outsider? Do I want to show the audience that I understand the topic? Do I want the audience to understand the topic better? Do I want the audience to accept my point of view?

√ What point or message do I want to convey?

√ How should I begin?

√ Where will I get information about my topic? Through library research? Through experience? Through background reading?

√ When explaining a point in the paper, what kind of examples should I use? How will the examples work to make my paper more readable, informative, or convincing?

√ If I make a claim in the paper, how do I support it? On the basis of experience? By citing authorities? On the basis of reason? On the basis of emotion?

√ What's the most effective way to organize the paper, to make sure that the various arts fit together well?

√ What should the conclusion do?

Outlining

Almost everyone has been asked to produce an outline at one time or another. Outlines can be very beneficial if used properly. Too often, however, the focus is on the *structural details* of the outline rather than its content. That is, students spend much effort deciding whether an *A* must have a *B*; whether a primary heading begins with a Roman numeral or an uppercase letter; whether a secondary heading begins with a lowercase letter, a lowercase Roman numeral, an Arabic numeral, and so on.

Outlines begin when you list the major points you want to address in your paper, without worrying much about their order. They become more useful when they acquire more features, especially secondary ones that are related to the major points. In other words, outlines start with *general* points and shift to *specific* ones. It is worth noting, however, that *outlines appear to work best when writers use them to generate ideas about topics and theses that they have already decided on.*

Applying Key Ideas

OUTLINING FOR CONTENT

An effective way to practice focusing on the content of an outline rather than the structure is to outline a completed text, especially when it is someone else's. This activity, therefore, is intended to give you that practice. However, it also gives you an opportunity to make connections between reading and analyzing texts and improving your writing.

First, you and your classmates should exchange papers that you completed for another class; they even can be from high school. Read one person's paper and create an outline for it. Afterward, confer with the writer to talk about how well each of you identified the key parts of the paper in your outlines. During this discussion, you may want to mention ways the writer could have made the paper better. You also should consider whether you agree with the writer about such things as how well the paper supported a thesis and whether the rhetorical stance was clear.

For the second part of this activity, use *another* paper that you have written for a class. Write an outline for it, then exchange both the paper and the outline with a classmate. Evaluate how well the paper and the outline match. As you were producing your outline, did you think of any new ideas that could have been in the paper but weren't? If so, share them with the writer and discuss whether they would have enhanced the paper and why.

Freewriting

Freewriting draws on the perception that, when present too early, concerns about audience, aims, organization, and structure can keep writers from fully exploring potential ideas and meanings for topics. Freewriting is intended to force writers to set such concerns aside while they consider potential ideas. The main goal is to discover things to say about a topic rather than to plan the paper.

This technique involves writing nonstop for 5, 10, or 15 minutes. During this period, you keep generating words, even if you can't think of anything meaningful to say. The rationale is that, eventually, you will begin producing ideas that you can develop later into an effective paper. Sometimes freewriting is combined with an activity called *looping*, in which you stop freewriting after 5 minutes and reread what you've produced. If you have a good idea, you use it as the basis for another freewriting period, repeating the process for about 15 minutes.

An example of freewriting is presented here. It was produced by Jennifer, a student in a composition class:

Freewriting Sample

Jennifer

1   I have to write a paper about my major, but I don't know much about my major yet. I'm only a freshman so how am I supposed to know anything about it? But the teacher says I have to write the paper and that I can find out information about my major—pharmacy—by talking to one of my professors, but all my classes except one are taught by TAs, except for this one of course and I'm afraid to talk to my biochem professor. I don't even think he knows who I am the class is so large there must be 300 people in there but the teacher says that setting up an appointment will be a good way to get to know my professor, good way for him to get to know me. I know a little about him already, like that he's doing research on new drugs to control diabetes. He's working with a couple of doctors in the med school. He's supposed to be really well known in the field, so I guess he would be a good person to get information from. He's also worked at Glaxo[1] and still serves as a consultant there, so he has knowledge of university as well as private company research into new drugs. I wonder how much he knows about genetic research. It seems that everyday there's something in the news about how one person or another has found a gene responsible for some disease, and it makes me wonder if some time in the future we won't use drugs to treat illness the way we do now but will treat people through genetic engineering.

2   That might make for an interesting paper, though. It would be really something if pharmacology was replaced by genetic engineering. And that reminds me of something I read a few weeks ago, about how companies like Glaxo are working on drugs that target viruses like HIV. They identify the protein sheath surrounding each cell and destroy it without harming healthy cells. Maybe I could do something about the future of pharmacy and pharmacology, how drugs will become more and more specific. I'll have to do some reading on this.

Linked Assignment

FREEWRITING

The writing assignment on page 83 asks you to consider that many high school graduates don't go on to college but instead go to work or start a family. Over the last decade or so, the number of these people who decide to return to school for a college degree has been increasing. This decision is difficult in most instances

---

[1]Glaxo is a large, multinational pharmaceutical company.

because of the responsibilities such students carry: Many have full-time jobs, mortgages, children, civic obligations, and so on. The writing assignment asks you to role-play by pretending that the editor of your local newspaper asked you to write an article that encourages people in this situation to return to school for a degree.

This activity is designed to get you started on the upcoming writing assignment, and it gives you an opportunity to practice freewriting. Freewrite for about 15 minutes to generate ideas for the newspaper article just described.

Journals

Journals, like diaries, have a way of helping you reflect on your experiences. They are places where you can filter and process ideas in private. Such reflection is an important part of good writing.

One of the more effective ways to plan writing tasks is to keep a reading journal, in which you record your reactions to all the reading you do, assessing texts, summarizing their main points, linking them to one another and to the ideas you are encountering in your composition class. When you receive a writing assignment, your journal can serve as an effective starting place, because it will contain not only a wealth of information but also your reactions to and interpretations of this information, which are central to your success as a writer. Sometimes you may find striking connections among your texts that can help you explore topics in fresh and insightful ways, an important characteristic of good writing.

Below is an excerpt from a journal that a student kept for a grammar course. The journal notes refer to a chapter dealing with certain ungrammatical structures:

Journal Sample

Chris

1   Ok, I'm not sure I understand this chapter, particularly these examples:
2   a. Someone wrote Woody Allen's <u>Stardust Memories</u> in 1980.
3   b. Woody Allen's <u>Stardust Memories</u> was written in 1980.
4   The text says that "a" is the underlying structure of "b" because "a" is active and "b" is passive. The problem is that the underlying structure of a passive has to be grammatical. I'm not even sure that "a" is grammatical because Woody Allen wrote <u>Stardust Memories</u> and is known to have written <u>Stardust Memories</u>. I just don't see how, in this case, we can use "someone" as a filler subject for the underlying form. The subject has to be "Woody Allen," not "someone"! At the very least, "a" is meaningless, which isn't a good status for an underlying structure for the passive. Actives and passives have to be able to coexist as grammatical, meaningful sentences. These don't.
5   Then there are these other sentences that don't make sense:
6   c. The umpire flipped the coin.
7   d. *The Patricia flipped the coin.
8   Now, "d" is ungrammatical. The chapter says that count nouns like "umpire" can follow "the" but that a proper noun like "Rita" can't. Hmmm. Well what about "The elder Rita flipped the coin"? That seems perfectly grammatical to me. Am I missing something here, or did the author?

Talk–Write

Another invention activity is based on the perception that speaking, listening, reading, writing, and thinking are intimately related and mutually reinforcing. It also is based on the idea that if you can explain a concept or an operation to someone you probably understand it pretty well.

Talk–write involves constructing a plan mentally and then delivering an oral composition, either to your teacher or to classmates. Your goal is to make your plan as complete as possible, with minimal reliance on writing. Generally, you have a relatively short time for planning—at least 20 minutes but seldom more than a full class period. You may jot down a few notes initially, but when you deliver your oral composition, you must do so without using any notes. After you finish, your teacher and/or your classmates provide suggestions and comments designed to help you improve and elaborate your plan. The next step is to begin writing, using what you learned from your presentation to develop a first draft of the assignment.

Applying Key Ideas

CREATING AN ORAL COMPOSITION

The linked assignment on page 63 gave you an opportunity to do some freewriting about an upcoming writing assignment: writing an article that encourages people who have not gone to college to do so. The freewriting has started a writing process that involves thinking about things to say on the topic. Now consider the topic a bit more. Construct a mental plan for the topic and develop an oral composition on it. Use writing sparingly.

When you've finished, deliver your oral composition to your group or to the whole class. After making your presentation, reflect on the experience. What sorts of things did you learn from it?

Metaphor

Metaphor, the last invention activity discussed in this section, is one that many people never consider. *Metaphor is a description in which one thing is compare to another.* Here are some simple metaphors that illustrate how the comparison works:

1. The car was a lemon.
2. The party was a bomb.

3. Fred was a real animal.

4. The outgoing governor was a lame duck.

5. Rita sure is a hothead.

Many discussions of metaphor suggest that it is merely a figurative use of language that helps writers create special images. In this view, metaphor is a feature of style. The perception here is a little broader. Metaphor is a powerful model-building device that can help you generate ideas and information. In this account, metaphor includes comparisons such as those just listed, but it also includes *metaphorical language*—that is, statements that use imagery without the formal comparison associated with true metaphors. For example, consider the following sentences:

1. The day I came home from my vacation, several science projects greeted me when I opened the refrigerator.

2. It was raining cats and dogs.

3. Fritz insisted that he wasn't thin, really, but when he stripped to his swim trunks at Rita's pool party, I decided that *Webster's Dictionary* needed to add a new entry under the definition of "toothpick."

4. Historians have described American Indians in one of two ways—as noble tribesmen living in harmony with nature on the one hand, or as vicious brutes caught up in perpetual warfare with their neighbors and then the white settlers on the other—and neither is quite correct. In reality, American Indians were examples of evolution in action, people driven to the brink of extinction when faced with social and technological changes that they couldn't understand, couldn't even grasp.

You can use metaphor as a way of discovering things to say about a topic. The models you can create with metaphors help you hold information, organization, or purpose in memory while you compose. Consider, for example, how the metaphor of America as a "melting pot" has provided an influential model of our society and has shaped many essays over the years. Consider how the Reverend Jesse Jackson used the metaphor of the "rainbow coalition" as the cornerstone of his political endeavors.

 *Applying Key Ideas*

GENERATING METAPHORS

Metaphor can be a powerful tool. A movie called *Il Postino* (*The Postman*), expresses this idea well. Frustrated by his attempt to become a poet, Mario, the main character, turns to his famous friend, Pablo Neruda, one afternoon and asks: "Do you mean to say that everything around us—the mountains, the sea, the sky, the stars—are simply metaphors for something else?" Mario's failure as a poet was rooted in his inability to find meaning (or to recognize metaphor) in the world around him, which made his writing sound like an insurance report.

This activity is intended to give you an opportunity to practice creating metaphors and, more important, metaphorical language that develops an idea or a model of some facet of reality. Stating that "The car was a lemon" is easy, but it is not very original. In fact, this metaphor has been used so many times that it has become worn out, a cliché. More difficult is this metaphor from García Márquez: "Macondo was . . . built on the bank of a river of clear water that ran along a bed of polished stones, which were white and enormous, like prehistoric eggs." A more famous metaphor comes from astronomy—*black holes*, which certainly aren't holes and aren't really black because they can't even be seen.

For this activity, create some metaphors that describe the world immediately around you. Notice the stress on the word "create"—you don't want to include any clichés. Afterward, try the more challenging task: Create a metaphor or metaphorical language that describes something less tangible, such as an idea, a social condition, or a human experience.

Diverse Voices

Metaphor is an important part of all languages, and they include technical metaphors—"All the world's a stage"—and metaphorical language. Proverbs generally are good examples of metaphorical language. A popular Mexican proverb tells us that *El que anda con lobos, aullar aprende* ("Run with wolves, and you'll learn how to howl"). A well-known English proverb tells us that "A bird in the hand is worth two in the bush." And a Japanese proverb states that *Buta-mo odatereba ki ni noboru* ("Flattery will make even a pig climb a tree").

Metaphors have a way of shaping our visions of ourselves and the world around us. For example, it has become popular in America to compare the human brain to a computer, even though brains and computers work on significantly different principles. Before the development of computers, other metaphors were popular. The Industrial Revolution made machines (particularly clocks) a popular metaphor for the universe as well as people.

Can you provide some examples of metaphorical language from your home culture? What are some metaphors that your home culture provides for people, life, or the universe? Write down a couple and then write a paragraph for each, explaining the nature of the metaphor.

Planning

Planning is one of the more rewarding, yet challenging, features of effective writing. It involves considering your rhetorical stance (are you an insider or an outsider with respect to the audience and the topic?), your rhetorical purpose (why are you writing the paper?), and your aim (what do you want the paper to do?) In addition, planning involves some consideration of organization, an appropriate introduction, a satisfying conclusion, minor claims that will appear throughout the paper, evidence to support claims, and the need (or not) for research.

Drafting

After you have generated some ideas about your topic and developed a working plan, the next step is to begin writing. Several factors influence a successful drafting process. You must be able to budget your time and plan ahead. Don't wait until the last minute to begin work. The downfall of many writers is their belief that their first draft should be perfect; they spend far too much time fiddling with sentences and punctuation when they should be concentrating on getting their ideas on paper. Some writers, in fact, will get a good idea while writing a draft and will worry so much about how to express the idea that it slips away or becomes strangely less appealing as the frustration level mounts.

A first draft simply should chart the territory of your topic. It should be like a road map, marking the general direction you intend to take and waiting for details and elaboration to come later.

Most teachers strongly encourage you to use a computer for all your writing, including drafts. Computers make drafting easier for several reasons. Most people can type faster than they can write by hand, and the work is easier to read, too. Moreover, computers can check for spelling errors, so writers are freed from the worry of whether they've spelled something incorrectly. Having a typed draft is particularly important if your class is divided into work groups. People read more intelligently and efficiently when they have a typed paper. As a result, they are able to give better feedback about what works and what doesn't. Perhaps the greatest benefit, however, is that computers allow writers to move text around at will, cutting, pasting, and rewriting with ease.

In the first century BC, a Greek author named Longinus recommended that writers who were serious about their work should set a draft aside for 9 years before going back to it and making changes. His idea was that the passage of time would allow writers to see their writing more clearly and to determine whether it was worth improving. Longinus was a bit extreme in recommending a wait of 9 years, but the principle he advocated was right on target. After you finish a draft, you should allow some time to pass before you read it again to make changes. You will see it more clearly and will be able to make better decisions about how to improve it.

How many drafts should you produce before you can consider a text finished? There is no answer to this question. Every paper is different; every paper has its own context and requirements that you have to consider as you are writing. Sometimes, such as when you are writing a letter or a memo, you will be able to write a single draft, and it will not need any changes. Other times, you may have to go through 5, 6, or even 10 drafts before your text does what you want it to.

Revising

Revising is an important part of writing well, yet some people have an unclear perception of what revising is about. They may concentrate on correcting spelling, changing individual words, or reorganizing sentences. Actually, revising occurs on different levels and at different times. The level just described, fiddling with sentences and punctuation, perhaps more accurately should be called *editing*, which is considered toward the end of this chapter. Editing deals with the surface features of writing and is generally performed *after* a paper does what you want it to do. Revising is more properly what you do to your writing *before* a paper does what you want it to do.

Successful revising requires that you consider your role and that of your readers as insiders and outsiders in regard to the topic. In addition, it depends on having knowledge about your audience's motivation for reading what you have to share. It requires that you be a critical reader. You need to be able to look at writing that has taken you much time and effort to produce and see it as it is, not as you wish it to be. You must be willing to cut sentences and paragraphs that do not work. You must be willing to shift sections from one place to another to enhance the overall organization of the composition. Revising and drafting are not the same, so one revision does not equal one draft. You may revise a draft many times before you consider it a new draft.

Because revising is so important, a sample student paper follows that illustrates how revising takes place and how it changes a text. It also illustrates the connection between reading and writing. Karen, who wrote the piece, was a first-year student responding to the following assignment:

> *Many high school graduates don't go on to college, which is causing some of our country's leaders to worry that in the future we may not have a sufficiently well-educated populace to run a technology-driven society. You obviously made the decision to attend college, and you now know something about what it's like. Suppose the high school principal were to ask you to write an article for your former high school newspaper that tries to persuade students to go to college after graduation. What would you say?*

Deletions appear as crossed-out text; additions appear in boldface type. The comments in the margins were made by a student in Karen's work group, whose suggestions were supposed to help Karen improve the paper.

Draft 1

The Decision
by Karen

This first sentence seems a bit trite.

I don't think you can say that anyone who doesn't go to college will end up as a beggar.

1 College: to go or not to go, that is the question, is a major idea that every **high school** graduate has to make a decision about. It is a ~~decision~~ choice that could make or break ~~you~~ **the rest of your life**, believe it or not! Do you want to spend the rest of your life selling shoes, driving a taxi, or begging for handouts on the street? Not many people do. I sure don't. So what can you do about it? Go to college.

This is a good point, but is it true? It seems too simple.

What's wrong with selling shoes? It's a honest job!

2   Any education past ~~high school~~ **the secondary level** is a good deal. It will aid you in gaining career opportunities that is meaningful and pays well, a job makes you become a well-rounded individual, both intellectually and socially, and shows you the burden or happiness of responsibility, more than it would if you didn't attend college and ended up sleeping in the street.

3   Most companies today that are looking for people to fill executive positions take a person's resume and look to see if he/she graduated from college. If they don't see that, they will **automatically** disqualify the person because the person won't be qualified. You can't be the president of IBM if you don't know something beyond what you learned in **high** school, if anything. the next thing they look at is the person's final grade point average and/or the highest degree they attained (i. e. BA or MA). This can also determine the salary he gets.

4   If you attend college, **the intellectual stimulation** you can acquire is as good as you make it. College gives you the ~~chance~~ opportunity to learn and to better yourself. If you don't attend this type of institution, you are left behind with a high school background, which we know isn't very good. All the surveys show that high school graduates can't find the state they live in when they look at a map of the ~~U. S.~~ United States and that they can't make change and all that. The social aspect of college is also a necessity for a well-balanced ~~person~~ individual. Having to deal with all the people around you, whether it be in a class or where you reside, is good for every person to experience. The world is getting more and more crowded, so we have to deal with it. If you decide not to got to college right after high school, but do make the decision to get a job, you may be dealing with different customers, but you will be working with the same people day in and day out. Not being able to meet new people can hinder your social abilities. You won't be able to interact and you'll end up being alone. Nobody wants that.

5   If you don't go to college, what will you do? Some ideas come to mind. Travel, get married, or get a job come to mind. Traveling is a great cultural experience and will show you the ways and customs of the world, but you won't learn anything else; you can't learn math, develop your scientific abilities, or enhance your English. Plus, where's the money coming from? Getting married right after high school is a cop out. It is as if you are saying that you have nothing better to do with your life so you're going to live with one person for the rest of your life and stay around the house. BORING! (As a statistical fact, most teenage marriages end in divorce anyhow. Teenagers can't earn enough money, which puts huge amounts of stress on the marriage, and most teenagers are curious to experiment with many sexual part-

I don't think this part is relevant.

ners and eventually don't want to be tied down to one partner, which also puts huge amounts of stress on the partners to sneak around or to allow an open marriage or to bring other partners into their marriage bed in some kind of menage.) And as for getting a job, as I've said before, there aren't too many place that will accept someone who only has a high school diploma. Unless it's McDonald's or Burger King. But how far will $5 an hour get you?

This is a good point, but your tone suggests people who don't go to college are stupid. I don't think you should do that.

6   All of the things that I have mentioned can be done while you attend college. Colleges have a mix of many people with different **ethnic** backgrounds. This could add to your culture and to your days, but there are other things, such as a semester at sea. This is a program that allows the student to travel while getting a college education. Instead of getting married, ~~you could~~ why don't you try out living with someone? This shows you if you are truly compatable while living with someone. Also, in place of a serious commitment, why not go to college. You are given the opportunity of making new friends and meeting people to go out and have fun with. And finally, if you want to work, no problema! Get a job while you're in school. Colleges have many opportunities for students to work and earn money while they are receiving a good education.

You may want to mention that working while going to school isn't easy.

7   Now you're probably saying, you don't have enough money to attend a college/university. My answer to that is, yes, you do. First of all, a college education is worth any amount of money. There are many state schools that are government funded. These are usually fairly inexpensive. But just because it is inexpensive doesn't mean that it is any worse than a more expensive education. There are also private universities. These have a higher tuition. This shouldn't stop you from thinking about this school as one of your possibilities. There are many grants, scholarships, and loans that are available to every college student. Even you. If you indeed need money for school, then you will most likely get it. If you're smart, you can even get scholarships!

You make this all seem pretty easy, but financial aid is not that easy to get.

8   Attending a college **or university** is something that everyone should do. It is a socially and intellectually stimulating experience. There is no reason for not at least trying it out. Continuing ~~with school~~ **your education** is the best thing you could do for yourself. Maybe if you start with this decision you can show yourself that you really can make important choices. If you don't go to college, you'll never know what you are missing.

There is no way to present accurately Karen's revising activities in this text because revising is dynamic, whereas your book is static. After the first draft, we cannot differentiate between the revising she performed during pauses as she was writing and the revising she performed after the first draft of the paper was completed. Still, her paper can give you some insight into how to revise your own work.

In Karen's mind, the decision to go to school initially seems to resemble the sort of internal debate Shakespeare's Hamlet has when faced with a difficult choice. The opening paragraph reflects the connection she sees, but it also sets a pretty negative tone for the paper. She tells her audience of high school students that they are not going to have a very bright future if they don't go to college. The marginal comments indicate that Karen's groupmate did not like the first paragraph much, but as the subsequent drafts show, Karen was reluctant to make any serious changes immediately. Instead, she worked on editing, really—making changes in word choice. Such reluctance is not unusual in writers, even experienced ones, because writing is hard work and most people would prefer to get it right the first time. When they hear that they haven't got it right, they are not happy about having to invest more effort. The lesson here is that you should take it for granted that your first attempt will require revising.

In the second paragraph, Karen continues with her negative tone, implying that readers will end up sleeping in the street if they do not go to college. The problem here is twofold. First, some readers might sense that Karen is suggesting that they are stupid if they do not go to college. Two assumptions are at work: that everyone has the ability to go to college and that no one wants to sleep on the street. These assumptions may or may not be correct, but it is usually incorrect for writers to suggest that they think readers are not very bright. The second problem is that Karen sets up what is called a *false dichotomy*, an either/or situation that is unrealistic. Either high school students go to college, or they will end up sleeping in the street. This false dichotomy ignores the fact that almost 30% of high school students drop out before graduation—they aren't all sleeping in the street.

People use false dichotomies frequently to simplify reality, to dramatize it, or to pressure others into doing things they do not really want to do. On more than one occasion you may have received phone calls from solicitors asking for money. Many of the causes they are working for are legitimate and worthy, but many people do not have the time, and they seldom have the money, to help them out. If you hesitate to contribute, their typical response is to ask: "You support world peace, don't you?" The simplistic (and guilt-inducing) implication is that you can't be concerned about world peace if you don't contribute. As it turns out, reality resists simplification, particularly the sort characteristic of either/or scenarios. Critical readers tend to dismiss false dichotomies and to conclude that a writer who uses them is not addressing the complexities of issues.

Karen's tendency to oversimplify in this first draft also is evident in paragraph 3, where she tells readers that they cannot be president of IBM if they do not have an education beyond high school. The suggestion is that the presidency of IBM is primarily the result of going to college, even though far more is involved. Karen would have been more successful if she had used a different approach. Effective writers use concrete details to support generalizations. Karen therefore should have said that most of the top executives in U.S. companies have a college education, and then she could have used IBM as an example to illustrate her point, providing she could describe the educational background of the current president of IBM.

These first three paragraphs are not particularly effective for another reason: Karen does not supply readers with much new information. Most high school students—her audience, remember—hear about the economic benefits of a college education on a regular basis. Large numbers choose to ignore this message, refuse to believe it, or find the rewards of a full-time job, even if it is serving up burgers at McDonalds for $5 an hour, more immediate than the promise of higher earnings years into the future. Nationwide, about 65% of high school graduates go on to college.

But in paragraph 4, Karen begins to deal with other benefits. She states that college provides intellectual stimulation and helps people become well-balanced and more fulfilled. These reasons for going to school are not likely to appeal to everyone, but they probably will not be any less effective than the monetary ones. Also, the course of study leading to a bachelor's degree is not intended to prepare students to become captains of industry. Instead, it focuses on a liberal arts education that provides intellectual stimulation and intends to help students become well-balanced adults who can lead interesting, productive lives. So Karen is getting at real reasons for going to college. In this first draft, however, these reasons are overpowered by her negative view of anyone who does not go to college ("high school graduates can't find the state they live in when they look at a map") and by some confusion regarding what becoming a well-balanced person is all about.

Paragraph 5 is like paragraph 4 in that it has a couple of good ideas that are submerged beneath an array of unfruitful ones. It is the case that most unskilled jobs are filled by people without an education, which is an undeveloped idea in this paragraph. And teenagers today probably have fewer options in regard to a desirable future than teenagers of just two or three generations ago. The wrong choice can make life difficult. But Karen is not at a point in her planning that allows her to develop these ideas, so she gets sidetracked and begins writing about teen marriages, which may be easier to discuss but which are not sufficiently relevant to warrant the amount of space she gives them.

In paragraphs 6 and 7, Karen demonstrates an effective rhetorical strategy: She anticipates potential objections to her argument. College can be a place to have fun and prepare for a career at the same time, she tells her readers as she adopts language that resembles what you might expect to see in a recruitment brochure. These paragraphs aren't sufficiently focused yet. In paragraph 6, for example, it isn't clear how a mix of people can add to "your days." Moreover, as her groupmate pointed out, Karen makes financing a college education seem easy. Your own experience in this regard may indicate that paying for tuition, books, housing, food, and so on is difficult for most students and their families.

The final paragraph is interesting because it so well illustrates the problem of an unsupported conclusion, something that occurs often in the work of inexperienced writers—particularly in their first drafts. Notice that the first three sentences are indeed concluding sentences, but do they reflect anything that Karen has actually demonstrated? That is, has she demonstrated in this paper that attending college is something everyone should do? Has she demonstrated that college is a stimulating experience? Has she demonstrated that her readers have no reason for not trying it out? In each instance, the answer is no.

Draft 2

<u>The Decision</u>
by Karen

1 College: to go or not to go, that is the question, is a major idea that e-Every high school graduate has to make a decision **about this question**. It is a choice that could make or break the rest of you life, believe it or not! Do you want to spend the rest of your life selling shoes or driving a taxi, or

Maybe you could provide more background here. Some people might not know what the question is.

begging for handouts on the street? Not many people do. I sure don't. So what can you do about it? Go to college.

2   Any education past the secondary level is ~~a~~ good ~~deal~~. It will **provide you** ~~aid you in gaining~~ a career ~~opportuni-ties~~ that is meaningful and pays well, a job makes you become a well-rounded individual, both intellectually and socially~~, and shows you the burden or happiness of respon-sibility, more than it would if you didn't attend college and ended up sleeping in the street~~.

Why is this important?

3   Most companies today that are looking for people to fill executive positions take a person's resume and look to see if he/she graduated from college. If they don't see that, they will automatically disqualify the person ~~because the person won't be qualified~~. You can't be the president of IBM if you don't know something beyond what you learned in high school~~, if anything~~. The next thing they look at is the person's final grade point average and/or the highest degree they attained (i. e. BA or MA). This can also determine the salary he gets.

I think you're being too negative here.

4   If you attend college, the intellectual stimulation you can acquire is as good as you make it. College gives you the opportunity to learn and to better yourself. If you don't attend this type of institution, you are left behind with a high school background, which we know isn't very good. All the surveys show that high school graduates can't find the state they live in when they look at a map of the Unit-ed States and that they can't make change and all that. The social aspect of college is also a necessity for a well-bal-anced individual. Having to deal with all the people around you, whether it be in a class or where you reside, is good for every person to experience. ~~The world is getting more and more crowded, so we have to deal with it.~~ If you decide not to got to college right after high school, but do make the decision to get a job, your social options are limited. ~~you may be dealing with different customers, but you will be working with the same people day in and day out. Not being able to meet new people can hinder your social abil-ities.~~ You won't be able to interact and you'll end up being alone. ~~Nobody wants that.~~

I don't understand what you mean.

This seems too simple to me.

You seem to think that people who don't go to college are stupid. Some readers might be put off by this. Besides, didn't Bill Gates drop out of Harvard? He may not have a college degree, but he's successful, and he seems pretty smart.

5   If you don't go to college, what will you do? Some ideas come to mind. Travel, get married, or get a job ~~come to mind~~. Traveling is a great cultural experience and will show you the ways and customs of the world, but you won't learn anything else; you can't learn math, develop your scientific abilities, or enhance your English. Plus, where's the money coming from? Getting married right after high school is a cop out. It is as if you are saying that you have nothing bet-ter to do ~~with your life~~ so you're going to live with one per-son for the rest of your life and stay around the house. BOR-

Marriage might be ok for some people, but I agree that teenagers probably should wait.

I don't see how this is an argument for going to college.

I don't think you need to talk about this.

ING! (As a statistical fact, most teenage marriages end in divorce anyhow. Teenagers can't earn enough money, which puts huge amounts of stress on the marriage, and most teenagers are curious to experiment with many sexual partners and eventually don't want to be tied down to one partner, which also puts huge amounts of stress on the partners to sneak around or to allow an open marriage or to bring other partners into their marriage bed in some kind of menage.) And as for getting a job, as I've said before, there aren't too many places that will accept someone who only has a high school diploma. Unless it's McDonalds or Burger King. But how far will $5 an hour get you?

6   All of the things that I have mentioned can be done while you attend college. Colleges have a mix of many people with different ethnic backgrounds. This could add to your culture and to your days, but there are other things, such as a semester at sea. This is a program that allows the student to travel while getting a college education. Instead of getting married, why don't you try out living with someone? This shows you if you are truly compatable while living with someone. Also, in place of a serious commitment, why not go to college. You are given the opportunity of making new friends and meeting people to go out and have fun with. And finally, if you want to work, ~~no problema! Get~~ you can get a job while you're in school. Colleges have many opportunities for students to work and earn money while they are receiving a good education.

7   Now you're probably saying, you don't have enough money to attend a college/university. My answer to that is, yes, you do. First of all, a college education is worth any amount of money. There are many state schools that are government funded, **so the tuition is low.** ~~These are usually fairly inexpensive~~. But just because it is inexpensive doesn't mean that it is**n't as good as a** ~~any worse than a~~ more expensive education. There are also private universities. These have a higher tuition. This shouldn't stop you from thinking about such schools ~~this school as one of your possibilities~~. There are many grants, scholarships, and loans that are available to every college student. Even you. If you indeed need money for school, then you will most likely get it. If you're smart, you can even get scholarships!

This is a good point!

8   Attending a college or university is something that everyone should do. It is a socially and intellectually stimulating experience. There is no reason for not at least trying it out. Continuing your education is the best thing you could do for yourself. Maybe if you start with this decision you can show yourself that you really can make important choices. If you don't go to college, you'll never know what you are missing.

The conclusion is good!

Karen's second draft indicates that she is having a problem understanding the suggestions she received on draft 1 from her groupmate as well as those she received orally from her teacher. She has a vague mental plan of what the paper should be, but the suggestions do not appear to fit it. Consequently, her second draft reflects only a few changes.

Notice how Karen begins the first paragraph. Sentence 1 suggests that she is trying to sort out for herself what her argument should be, because it assumes that the reader already knows what the question is. It also indicates that Karen is still engaged with the topic, thinking about what she wants to say and how she should say it, still invention and planning. Were she to stop at this point, her paper would be unsuccessful.

Karen adds very little to her second draft. Most of her revising consists of deletions—*which is quite important*. Because she had so much irrelevant and unfocused material in draft 1, deletion is what she needs to do. After Karen gets rid of the excess ideas, she can see more clearly what her important points are. It is a pruning process that may be painful but that is necessary. The substance of the paper remains the same, however. As noted earlier, Karen seems reluctant to make the large-scale changes she needs to produce a good paper. We should give her the benefit of the doubt, of course, because Karen is still planning, still mentally constructing a model that reflects the suggestions she received, what she wants to say, and the requirements of the assignment. In fact, when we get to draft 3, Karen seems to have synthesized a new model for the paper, because her revisions are extensive. That is why it is important to recognize that planing is not an isolated stage that occurs only at the beginning of the composing process.

Draft 3

<u>The Decision</u>
by Karen

1   ~~College: to go or not to go, that is the question, is a major idea that e~~ **E**~~very high school graduate has to make a decision~~ **about this question.** ~~It is a choice that could make or break the rest of you life, believe it or not! Do you want to spend the rest of your life selling shoes, or driving a taxi, or begging for handouts on the street? Not many people do. I sure don't. So what can you do about it? Go to college.~~ **You've heard it all before. You owe it to yourself to go to college. College graduates earn two or three times more money over their lifetimes than high school graduates. And you're still not convinced. Well, I'm saying you should be—and I'm not a parent or a teacher. I'm someone who just a few months ago was in exactly the place you are in, faced with the same decision. Going to college or not is a choice that really will affect the rest of your life.**

I like this introduction. It seems real, and it gets readers interested.

This is good.

2   ~~Any education past the secondary level is a good deal. It will~~ **provide you** ~~aid you in gaining a career opportunities that is meaningful and pays well, a job makes you become a well-rounded individual, both intellectually and~~

Can you explain the difference between a job and a career without offending people who have a job?

socially, and shows you the burden or happiness of responsibility, more than it would if you didn't attend college and ended up sleeping in the street. **You have to understand that education won't just get you a job. It will prepare you for a career. The difference is pretty big. On the one hand you have a boring 9–5 that you do—on the other you have something that your are. A career will be linked to your becoming a well-rounded individual, satisfied intellectually and socially.**

3   Most companies today that are looking for people to fill executive positions take a person's resume and look to see if he/she graduated from college. If they don't see that, they will automatically disqualify the person because the person won't be qualified. You can't be the president of IBM if you don't know something beyond what you learned in high school, if anything. The next thing they look at is the person's final grade point average and/or the highest degree they attained (i. e. BA or MA). This can also determine the salary he gets. **Being well-rounded is part of what college is about. It gives you the opportunity to learn and to better yourself. The classes you take make you think about the world and who you are. Having to interact with people from all over the world, with different backgrounds and cultures, forces you to see the world through their eyes. You come to realize that your views aren't the only way, and that makes you a better person.**

4   If you attend college, the intellectual stimulation you can acquire is as good as you make it. College gives you the opportunity to learn and to better yourself. If you don't attend this type of institution, you are left behind with a high school background, which we know isn't very good. All the surveys show that high school graduates can't find the state they live in when they look at a map of the United States and that they can't make change and all that. The social aspect of college is also a necessity for a well balanced individual. Having to deal with all the people around you, whether it be in a class or where you reside, is good for every person to experience. The world is getting more and more crowded, so we have to deal with it. If you decide not to got to college right after high school, but do make the decision to get a job, your social options are limited. you may be dealing with different customers, but you will be working with the same people day in and day out. Not being able to meet new people can hinder your social abilities. You won't be able to interact and you'll end up being alone. Nobody wants that.

5   If you don't go to college, what will you do? Some ideas come to mind. Travel, get married, or get a job come to mind. Traveling is a great cultural experience and will show you the ways and customs of the world, but you won't

Can you explain the difference between a job and a career without offending people who have a job?

~~lean anything else; you can't learn math, develop your scientific abilities, or enhance your English. Plus, where's the money coming from? Getting married right after high school is a cop out. It is as if you are saying that you have nothing better to do with your life so you're going to live with one person for the rest of your life and stay around the house. BORING! (As a statistical fact, most teenage marriages end in divorce anyhow. Teenagers can't earn enough money, which puts huge amounts of stress on the marriage, and most teenagers are curious to experiment with many sexual partners and eventually don't want to be tied down to one partner, which also puts huge amounts of stress on the partners to sneak around or to allow an open marriage or to bring other partners into their marriage bed in some kind of menage.) And as for getting a job, as I've said before, there aren't too many places that will accept someone who only has a high school diploma. Unless it's McDonald's or Burger King. But how far will $5 an hour get you?~~ **There aren't many things you can do these days without a college education, and it's hard to make it in the world when you're 18. You can get a job turning burgers at McDonalds or cleaning houses, but how far will $5 an hour get you? That translates into $200 a week before taxes. Hard to live on that, considering how expensive everything is. As unfair as it may be, everything we do revolves around money in one way or another. Do you want to travel after high school? How will you pay for it? Do you want to marry your high school sweetheart? Where will you get the money for the rent?**

You make some really good points here. Most young people don't seem to think much about money. I know I didn't before I came to college!

6   ~~All of the things that I have mentioned can be done while you attend college. Colleges have a mix of many people with different ethnic backgrounds. This could add to your culture and to your days, but there are other things, such as a semester at sea. This is a program that allows the student to travel while getting a college education. Instead of getting married, why don't you try out living with someone? This shows you if you are truly compatable while living with someone. Also, in place of a serious commitment, why not go to college. You are given the opportunity of making new friends and meeting people to go out and have fun with. And finally, if you want to work, no problema! Get you can get a job while you're in school. Colleges have many opportunities for students to work and earn money while they are receiving a good education.~~

7   ~~Now you're probably saying, you don't have enough money to attend a college/university. My answer to that is, yes, you do. First of all, a college education is worth any amount of money. There are many state schools that are government funded, so~~ **the tuition is low.** ~~These are usual-~~

~~ly fairly inexpensive. But just because it is inexpensive doesn't mean that it is~~**n't as good as a** ~~any worse than a more expensive education. There are also private universities. These have a higher tuition. This shouldn't stop you from thinking about~~ ~~such schools~~ **this school** ~~as one of your possibilities. There are many grants, scholarships, and loans that are available to every college student. Even you. If you indeed need money for school, then you will most likely get it. If you're smart, you can even get scholarships!~~ **Fortunately, when it comes to college, money isn't a big problem. State schools are funded by the government, so the tuition is low. All schools offer financial aid through work–study programs that let you work on campus, through loans payable after you graduate and get a job, through grants, and through scholarships. The money is there—you simply have to get it.**

You need to explain this more.

8 ~~Attending a college or university is something that everyone should do. It is a socially and intellectually stimulating experience. There is no reason for not at least trying it out. Continuing your education is the best thing you could do for yourself. Maybe if you start with this decision you can show yourself that you really can make important choices. If you don't go to college, you'll never know what you are missing.~~ **I'm six weeks into my first semester of college. Yes, it's hard work. Yes, I keep long hours. But I've never had so much fun in my life. Every day I have a new experience. Every day I learn something new. I've never regreted my decision to go to college, and I urge you to make the same decision. You owe it to yourself.**

This is really good. You made some nice changes.

The first paragraph of draft 3 indicates that Karen reached a better understanding of the needs of her audience. She recognized, for example, that her designated readers are likely to have heard the economic argument for going to college and that they will have little motivation to hear it again. By telling these readers that she has much in common with them and indeed was in just their position a short time earlier, Karen very effectively identified herself with the audience, which creates a bond that will motivate readers at least to pay more attention to what she has to say.

Paragraph 2 also is entirely new, but it does not abandon the linkage between college and money. Instead, Karen shifts the ground of the argument, making a nice distinction between a job and a career. Some readers—her teacher, for instance—might want a more detailed analysis of the differences between the two, but what she offers seems sufficient when one considers that the paper is supposed to be printed in a school newspaper, where space is limited. This second paragraph also makes an important connection between career and being a satisfied, well-rounded person. In the earlier versions, monetary rewards and intellectual rewards seemed in conflict, and Karen appears wisely to have recognized that such need not be the case.

Karen deletes all of paragraph 4, which in the earlier drafts contained little useful information, and she finally drops the long, inappropriate section on marriage and sexual behavior in paragraph 5. She decides to focus instead on a point that was largely submerged before—how difficult it is for teenagers to make it in the world when they can't get the kind of jobs that will allow them to support themselves.

Paragraph 7 makes attending college an attractive alternative to the images developed in paragraph 6. Karen may still be oversimplifying in suggesting that money is not a problem for college students, but it is true that colleges have a variety of financial aid programs available to those who need assistance.

Karen's last paragraph continues in the same voice that she established in paragraph 1. She shifts the focus, however. Whereas before she identified with her readers, she now works to get readers to identify with her. It is easy to see the insider–outsider perspectives shift. Karen is straightforward about the hard work and long hours—she's careful not to suggest that college is all fun and games. But the challenge of college provides a level of stimulation and excitement that seems genuine, so readers can relate to Karen's experience.

This draft is not perfect, but it is a significant improvement over Karen's earlier efforts. She dropped the negative tone that suggested anyone who did not go to college was stupid, and she deleted extraneous material that really did not help her develop a convincing argument for attending college. With her paper clearly focused in terms of goals, audience, reasons, and organization, Karen was able to go on to editing, which is reflected in her final draft. The editing changes she made were designed to make the writing smoother by adding connections and transitions.

Final Draft

<u>Deciding to Go to College</u>
by Karen

1   OK. So you've heard it all before. How you owe it to yourself to go to college. How college graduates earn two or three times more money over their lifetimes than high school graduates. And you're still not convinced. Well, I'm saying you should be—and I'm not a parent or a teacher or a counselor. I'm someone who just a few months ago was in exactly the place you are in, faced with the same decision. Going to college or not is a choice that really will affect the rest of your life.

2   I suppose the first thing you have to understand is that a college education won't just get you a job. It will prepare you for a career. The difference is pretty big. On the one hand you have something that you do—on the other you have something that your are. A career will be linked to your becoming a well-rounded individual, satisfied intellectually and socially.

3   Being well-rounded is a major part of what college is about. It gives you the opportunity to learn and to better yourself. The classes you take make you think about the world, who you are, and how you fit in. Having to interact with people from all over the world, with different backgrounds and cultures, forces you to see the world through their eyes. You come to realize that your views aren't the only ones, and that makes you a better, more interesting person.

4   Realistically, there aren't many options these days for people without a college education, especially when they're only 18. You can get a job turning burgers at McDonalds or cleaning houses, but how far will $5 an hour get you? That trans-

lates into $200 a week before taxes. Hard to live on that, considering how expensive everything is. As unfair as it may be, everything we do revolves around money in one way or another. Do you want to travel after high school? How will you pay for the tickets? Do you want to marry your high school sweetheart? Where will the two of you get the money for the rent?

5   Fortunately, when it comes to college, money isn't a big problem. State schools are funded by the government, so the tuition is low. All schools offer financial aid through work–study programs that let you work on campus, through loans payable after you graduate and get a job, through grants, and through scholarships. The money is there—you simply have to apply for it.

6   I'm six weeks into my first semester of college. Yes, it's hard work. Yes, I keep long hours. But I've never had so much fun in my life. Every day I have a new experience. Every day I learn something about the world, about life, about myself. I've never regretted my decision to go to college, and I urge you to make the same decision. You owe it to yourself to become the best that you can be.

Writing as Problem Solving

There are certain advantages to thinking of writing as problem solving. It demystifies the act of writing, removing it from the realm of inspiration and placing it squarely in the realm of everyday practicality. It enables you to better understand the nature of the task, which consists fundamentally of coming up with something worthwhile to say and of expressing it in a way that matches your objectives while meeting the needs of your audience at the same time.

If we go back to Karen's first draft with this problem-solving perspective, it should be clear that she had not decided at that point what would count for high school students as good reasons for going to college. She puts too much emphasis on money, perhaps because she has heard parents and teachers offer it as a reason for attending college. Karen knows what she wants her paper to do, but she must discover how to get it to do what she wants. Initially, she takes the easiest approach and repeats a reason she has heard others give. Also, Karen is not sure how she should present her argument, even though she has probably read newspaper editorials and is familiar with their characteristics.

Private Writing

The role of private writing in composition is complex, in part because of its character. When you're writing for yourself rather than for others, you do not have to worry about how readers will respond to your work. You do not have to support interpretations because people usually do not challenge their own views without good reason. Some people use private writing as therapy. Other people use private writing to explore their feelings and thoughts about books they've read, places they've seen, and people they've met. The diary and journal are examples of private writing intended to record such explorations.

The writing required in school and business appears to be antithetical to private discourse. In these environments, writing is inherently public. However, *private writing often can be the beginning of public writing*. All the stages that come before revising are a form of private writing, even though they may benefit from the input of others. Revising on this account is the most important part of the writing process because it transforms private writing into public.

Journal Entry

What do you hope to get out of college? What do you hope to contribute?

Editing

As noted earlier, editing is different from revising. Editing is the last step in composing before you publish your paper. Most of your editing will focus on sentence-level concerns, such as punctuation, spelling, subject–verb agreement, and style. This section does not examine these activities because they are discussed in the handbook.

Style is in some respects one of the more interesting parts of the editing process. It involves not only word choice but also sentence length and variety. Successful writers vary the length of their sentences, using some that are short, medium, and long. Moreover, they try not to have too many sentences of the same length following one another, and they try to vary the structure of their sentences. Most sentences begin with the subject, but if every one were to start this way, it would be monotonous. A useful rule of thumb, therefore, is to begin most sentences with the subject but to start some with, say, an introductory phrase or clause.

Editing is a *conscious* process. Successful writers have devised a variety of methods to heighten their consciousness of structure. When editing for sentence type and length, they often underline all the sentences in two or three paragraphs that begin with the subject. When they have finished, they have a visual aid that helps them adjust sentence patterns. They may use other techniques for different structural concerns. For example, poor writing characteristically has too many prepositional phrases. Circling prepositions highlights the phrases and is a first step toward reducing them through editing. Admittedly, these techniques are time consuming. Fortunately, people internalize many of them after a short period of practice and application. Once internalized, editing goes faster.

Many students dismiss editing, arguing that all that matters in a text is content. The problem with this view is that it isn't very practical. The appearance of a text is important. It says a lot about the writer and the writer's relationship with readers. A finished paper is not a gift that writers give to readers. It is an invitation to share ideas, experiences, and feelings, usually with people writers want to impress. Successful writers want their texts to look good and to be free of errors. They know that readers assume that writers who don't care about how their work looks simply don't take it seriously.

 *Applying Key Ideas*

VARYING SENTENCES

The purpose of this activity is to help you become more aware of the patterns you use when you write sentences and to give you an opportunity to practice modifying them. For the first part of the activity, take a paper that you are working on or one that you've already finished. Select two or three consecutive paragraphs and underline all the sentences that begin with the subject. If 70% to 80% of your sentences do not begin with the subject, place the subject up front; otherwise, experiment with different ways of beginning and reconstructing them.

For the second part of this activity, count the number of words per sentence in two or three paragraphs of your paper. If the sentences are all a similar length, say 10 to 14 words, try joining some short sentences to form longer ones using words such as *and, but, for, yet, although, because, until*, and *whereas* (these words are called *conjunctions*). You should aim for an average sentence length of 20 words.

Writing Assignment

IS COLLEGE WORTH THE SACRIFICE?

The linked assignment on page 63 asked you to freewrite on the topic of encouraging people who did not attend college after high school to enter higher education and get a degree. The activity on page 65 then asked you to develop an oral composition on this topic. Now you have the opportunity to use these invention activities to develop a paper that allows you to apply the ideas you've encountered thus far. Using the sample assignment on page 69 and Karen's response to it as a foundation, respond to the following:

Many high school graduates do not go on to college but instead go to work or start a family. Increasing numbers of these people make the decision later in life to return to school to get a college degree. This decision is difficult for many because it entails sacrifice—going to school evenings while working during the day (or vice versa), arranging and paying for additional child care, and so on. Suppose the editor of your local newspaper were to ask you to write an article that tries to persuade people in this situation to return to school for a degree. What would you say?

GROUP ACTIVITIES: IS COLLEGE WORTH THE SACRIFICE?

1. Your work group is an important source of information and ideas for writing assignments. Before you begin this assignment, divide into two subgroups, ideally of two and three members. Your first activity will focus on invention, and it involves role playing. The smaller subgroup, following through on the aim of writing a newspaper article, should assume the role of interviewers. The larger subgroup should assume the role of interviewees and should put themselves in the position of the audience described in the assignment. Interviewees should develop a metaphor that captures the relationship between college and life, such as "College provides food for the mind, wings for the soul." They should try to use their metaphor to generate ideas for their papers. Interviewers should ask a range of questions designed to help interviewees produce a well-informed article. Wherever possible, they should help interviewees elaborate their metaphors and translate them into concrete ideas for the papers.

2. Exchange the first draft of the assignment with another member of your group, read it once, and then a second time, placing check marks next to those

places where the writer seems most effectively to be using the conventions of newspaper writing. (If you're unsure of what those conventions are, bring a newspaper to class so your group can analyze the writing.) On a separate piece of paper, describe the rhetorical stance the writer establishes with the audience. Is it insider to outsider, outsider to outsider, or something else? What should it be? On a separate sheet of paper, list three things you would like the writer to change in this first draft, then briefly explain why.

Writing Assignment

CHARACTERIZING YOUR WRITING PROCESS

You began characterizing your writing process by examining the Stages of Writing table on page 60. You now are in a better position to examine that process and to determine whether it has changed after your work with this chapter.

Write a paper about three pages long that examines your writing process for the assignment above. How many of the stages did you use? Are you more conscious of how you produce a text now? Has your process changed? If yes, in what ways? If no, why not? What can you do to modify your writing process to make it better match the way successful writers work?

WRITING GUIDE: CHARACTERIZING YOUR WRITING PROCESS

Invention

An important first step for this assignment is to return to the activity on page 60 and review what you produced. Then reflect on the process you used when writing your paper about returning to school to get a college degree. Make some notes about that process. Keep in mind that part of the goal here is to determine whether your process has changed as a result of working through the material in this chapter. Toward that end, consider the similarities and differences between the process you described for the activity on page 60 and the process you actually used to write the paper about returning to college. You may want to do some more freewriting to explore how your process has changed, or if it hasn't, to explore why. Would a chart help you visualize your writing process? Are there any useful metaphors that help capture the experience of process? Try to identify some details and examples that you can use to give substance to your paper. In addition, who is the audience for this paper? What do you want it to do?

Planning

The assignment asks several questions, which suggests that you should try to answer them in your paper. It therefore could be useful to identify those that you think are most important. The next step would be to decide how to organize your answers: Will you deal with the most important questions first or last? One effective way of organizing a paper is to deal with important questions first, go on to

CHAPTER 3

those of less importance, but finish with the single most important question. You will also need to plan how to begin and end the paper.

Details and examples are crucial to effective writing, yet they often are slighted in papers like this one. Details have layers that you can explore to give depth and insight to your writing. Give some thought to the details and examples you identified earlier and consider how you might use them to answer the questions that are part of the assignment.

Drafting

Introductions can cause even the best writers an inordinate amount of grief. If you have trouble with the introduction, set it aside and work on another part of the paper. For this assignment, you might find it more effective to begin drafting answers to the questions. Ideas for the introduction and the conclusion are likely to arise as you develop the middle part. If you came up with a metaphor to describe your writing process, you may want to elaborate it, see where it takes you in your examination of your process.

Pausing and Reading

As you write, you will pause periodically. Use this time to reflect on and read what you've written so far. Focus your attention on the questions raised under planning. As you read, you want to consider how well your draft is matching the goals you set for the paper, how well it fits your rhetorical stance, how well it meets the needs of the audience you have identified. Do not let your attention drift to things like punctuation and word choice. It is tempting to start working on these features early because they are concrete, and fixing them provides a comforting sense of accomplishment. However, this is not the right time.

Revising

Most drafts have holes that revising is intended to fill, but it can be hard to see those holes if revising follows drafting too soon. You should set your draft aside for at least a day before beginning your revising. Read through the draft and ask yourself key questions: Does my introduction state my thesis? Does the paper answer the questions raised in the assignment? Is my rhetorical stance clear and consistent? Have I provided details and examples to help readers understand my thesis? Are there better ways to organize my information?

Answering these questions is a large part of what revising is about. You will have to add new sentences and paragraphs and remove others. You may have to shift some sentences and paragraphs around. Return to Karen's paper and study the changes she made in her various drafts. These drafts can give you useful insight into how to revise your paper to make it more effective.

Editing

Your revised draft will have spelling and typing errors, lapses in punctuation, and a few words that could be replaced with others to make the writing more successful. After all, during drafting and revising, you should not focus much attention on these concerns. Now you can.

A hunt for prepositional phrases is a good way to start editing. Prepositions are words such as "of," "in," "above," "into," "beyond," and so forth. The handbook provides a longer list, and you may want to look at it before continuing. A good rule of thumb is that no sentence should have more than three prepositional phrases, so if you have more than three prepositions per sentence, you'll need to edit them out. Following is an example of how to do that:

1. The determination (of) the various factors associated (with) my writing process is an interesting task.
2. Determining the factors that are part of my writing process is an interesting task.

This edit eliminated one prepositional phrase, "of the various factors," by changing the structure and wording of the sentence. It still is not as good as it could be, probably. A little more tinkering could eliminate the second prepositional phrase as well. You may want to reflect on how to do that.

Sentence structure is important in successful writing, as indicated on page 82. You do not want all of your sentences to follow the same pattern. At this point, you might want to check sentence length by calculating the average number of words per sentence in a couple of paragraphs. If they are all about the same length, make some adjustments by combining short sentences into longer ones and by breaking long sentences into shorter ones.

Finally, check word choice, spelling, and punctuation. The handbook is a good resource here. It illustrates commonly misused words and provides a quick review of punctuation.

Publishing

You do not have to print your paper on high-quality bond, but you should not use cheap paper, either. Standard typing or photocopying paper works well. Be sure that your printer produces clean, crisp print. Most teachers appreciate a title page, but you should check with individual teachers about this. The same advice applies to format.

Reporting Events

Life is made up of events—the actions of people, animals, and nature. Walking to class is an event, as is taking a test, making chocolate chip cookies, a hurricane, and a baby's cry. The cumulative events of people's lives shape who they are and who they become.

CHAPTER FOUR

Reporting Events

Life is made up of events—the actions of people, animals, and nature. Walking to class is an event, as is taking a test, making chocolate chip cookies, a hurricane, and a baby's cry. The cumulative events of people's lives shape who they are and who they become. Lives are characterized by actions, by verbs. Events trigger both states of mind and states of emotion, but the states themselves cannot be classified as events. On this account, being happy isn't an event, whereas the birth of a child, which caused the happiness, is. The centrality of events in every facet of life is one reason people always have celebrated the telling of events. From pre-historical times, poets and bards were largely responsible for the telling. Often, fact and fiction became intertwined. In more recent times, poetry and song and the events they celebrate have become subordinate to prose and *reporting*, and there has been a corresponding effort to separate fact from fiction, although many argue that the effort has been largely unsuccessful.

Reporting is a slippery term because it does not mean the same thing to every-one. The different understandings of the word usually are the result of disagree-ments over the amount of *objectivity* or *subjectivity* writers can or should use in their reports. *Objective reports* are those that convey few of the reporter's per-sonal feelings, prejudices, and biases. *Subjective reports* have these personal fac-tors in abundance.

Regardless of orientation, written reports strive to teach. Some do so more explicitly than others, for they attempt to explain what an event means. Such reports often are referred to as *interpretive reports*.

TITLE, INTRODUCTION, BODY, AND CONCLUSION

Reports of events begin by setting the scene for readers in a way that lets them understand the sequence of actions about to unfold. Fairy tales and children's stories have developed a simple formula for setting the scene: "Once upon a time . . . ." This convention governs children's stories but not academic and professional writing. One of the more useful approaches for setting the scene comes from jour-nalism, where writers are asked to answer five questions:

1. Who?
2. What?
3. When?
4. Where?
5. How?

Title

Several factors help set the scene, such as the *title* of a report. Titles generate expectations in the audience, so they should be descriptive and informative, giving readers some insight into what the report is about. It can be useful to think of any title you come up with for your report as a *working title* only. After you have finished your report, you may discover a much better title, so you should be willing to consider alternatives. The working title, however, will serve a useful purpose, helping you focus your writing as you develop the first draft.

Introduction

When a report strives to create a word picture of an event without interpretation, there is no claim in the introduction, only focus, which sets the scene for readers. The five questions just listed can be valuable tools in this regard. Answering them can provide a context that gives readers important background information about the event. When a report is interpretive, however, the introduction will set the scene and provide a thesis.

Writing introductions can be frustratingly hard at times. On more than a few occasions, I have copied introductions from other papers I was writing and pasted them on the first page of the computer screen, just to know that *something* was there, even if it was entirely irrelevant to that text. Having a couple of paragraphs in place alleviates the worry of what one is going to say first so that it is easier get down to the business of writing the main part of the paper. Once a significant portion of the text is in draft, it is possible to return to the mock introduction and start on the real one. The difficulty writers face when working on an introduction is this: They have to conceptualize the whole paper and synthesize everything they know about the topic and what they hope to do with it—before they've done it.

Sometimes, introductions still don't gel until the first draft is finished. If you encounter this problem, try setting the introduction aside after blocking out a rough draft of it. Work more on the main part of the paper, revising and polishing, and then come back to the introduction later. Setting the introduction aside and working on other parts of a paper is a valuable incubation period. A portion of the brain is wrestling with the introduction, often unconsciously. After some time passes, you usually will be able to put a good introduction together with a measure of ease.

Finding a Familiar Starting Place as a Point of Reference

A text of completely new information is very difficult, perhaps even impossible, to understand. Thus, a goal of good writing is to combine new information with old by blending the known and the unknown so as to make the text more comprehensible. *Every reader therefore needs a familiar starting place as a point of reference.* Without this familiar starting place, a text will be hard to understand.

Linked Assignment

CAMPUS EVENTS

This activity gives you an opportunity to improve your powers of observation, and it also serves as an invention activity for the writing assignment on page 97.

Pretend you are a reporter for the campus paper who has been assigned to write an article about something happening on campus. Identify three events that you have observed and write a few paragraphs for each that answer the five questions listed on page 88: who, what, when, where, and how.

Moving from the Known to the Unknown

Successful writers have a tendency to use common experiences and general knowledge to establish a starting place for the audience. They move from the known to the unknown, which is a fundamental part of the role writing plays in teaching things to readers. "Relationships are like automobiles," a writer of a self-help book might propose, "because you always have to work on them to keep them going." In this country, just about everyone owns a car, and just about everyone knows how important proper maintenance is. The writer has drawn on this shared experience to make the analogy work and to make the book about maintaining human relationships easier to understand.

Cultural Factors: Building on Shared Experiences

Many starting places for writing are tied to common cultural experiences. Culture and history play an important part in comprehension of all types, but they are especially important in regard to texts. People lacking the necessary cultural context will not comprehend what they read. For example, a few years ago a friend who teaches history told me about the time a local paper asked him to write an article reporting events surrounding the Japanese-American experience in internment camps during World War II. He received many letters from concerned readers afterward. They said they could not figure out the article and did not know what the writer was trying to say. Some accused him of being un-American. Many stated that they did not know that the United States had fought Japan during the war. Many more by far did not know that the U.S. government had kept Japanese-Americans (nearly all U.S. citizens) in concentration camps for years.

A characteristic of effective writing, therefore, will be its recognition of the cultural contexts readers might bring, *or fail to bring*, to the text. Successful writers know how to use cultural knowledge to move from the known to the unknown.

A friend from Japan, although fluent in English, often has difficulty with American songs. She was listening to an "oldies" station, which plays popular music from the 1950s, 1960s, and 1970s, when a song came on by Don McLean called "American Pie." Afterward, she asked an American friend to explain what the song was about. The task was very difficult because the entire song consists of references to American popular culture.

For the first part of this activity, collect several popular texts whose meaning seems unclear, even though you understand the individual words. Such texts may be steeped in cultural factors. You may use song lyrics, jokes (which nearly always depend on cultural factors for their humor), dialogue from a movie, or a passage from a book or magazine article. Bring these texts to class and share them with your group. The group should discuss the cultural factors that give meaning to the text.

For the second part of this activity, collect several popular texts from your home culture that people raised in the United States might find difficult to understand, even if they were proficient in your language. Again, the group should discuss how the meaning of these texts is based on cultural factors. What conclusions, if any, can you draw about the relation between meaning and culture?

Shared Experiences
in Writing for Outsiders

When writing for outsiders, cultural knowledge is an important way to move from the known to the unknown. Consider, for example, the following paragraph, which comes from Daniel Boorstin's book *The Discoverers: A History of Man's Search to Know His World and Himself*. It begins a chapter titled "The Discovery of Asia" that reports European efforts to learn about the Orient. An insider writing for outsiders, Boorstin probably anticipated that few readers would know much about these efforts, so his rhetorical problem was to start with what he could reasonably expect people to know. Marco Polo turned out to be the solution to his problem. Just about everyone old enough to read a book like this could be expected to know something about Marco Polo, even if it were nothing more than the fact that he traveled to China on a long adventure. Audience familiarity with the adventures of Marco Polo therefore is crucial to this chapter. Polo is part of the necessary known that allows readers to access the unknown.

Passage 1: Marco Polo

Marco Polo excelled all other known Christian travelers in his experience, in his product, and in his influence. The Franciscans went to Mongolia and back in less than three years, and stayed in their roles as missionary-diplomats. Marco Polo's journey lasted twenty-four years. He reached farther than his predecessors, beyond Mongolia to the heart of Cathay. He traversed the whole of China all the way to the Ocean, and he played a variety of roles, becoming the confidant of Kublai Khan and governor of a great Chinese city. He was at home in the language, and immersed himself in the daily life and culture of Cathay. For generations of Europe, his copious, vivid, and factual account of Eastern ways was the discovery of Asia. (Boorstin, p. 134)

Whenever you are composing for outsiders, for what is often called a "general" audience, you can have only a vague notion of your readers. Whether your own role is that of insider or outsider, much of the writing you have to do in college involves an audience of outsiders, and cultural factors can provide you with an effective starting point because they consist of shared experiences. They can create a bond between you and your readers because they allow you to identify your concerns with their concerns. Successful reports of events appear to require this bond more than other types of writing; the reason is that readers want to accept reports of events as being factual and trustworthy. Without the bond, there is no trust. Consider how Boorstin solves the problem of moving readers from the known to the unknown in this passage. The solution provides a model that you can use in your own writing.

Passages 2 and 3 also illustrate this principle. The writers understand how cultural knowledge works to build shared experiences for reports of events. As you read, consider how they set the scene for readers.

Passage 2: Pasteur and Rabies

In 1880, when Pasteur turned his attention to the disease, only three things could be said about rabies with any certainty at all: whatever caused it was contained in the saliva of the rabid animal; it was transmitted by a bite that broke the skin; and after transmission it took anywhere from a few days to months before the symptoms appeared in its victim. Beyond that, all was mystery. Pasteur had his work cut out for him. (Radetsky, p. 51)

This passage very nicely moves the audience from the known to the unknown, and it provides another model that you can use in your own writing. Radetsky can reasonably expect readers to know something about rabies. After all, every pet owner must have cats and dogs vaccinated against the disease by law, and rabies outbreaks in one state or another are mentioned in the news regularly. But Radetsky cannot expect readers to know much about Pasteur. He therefore uses the known (rabies) to move to the unknown (Pasteur's work against the disease). The paragraphs following this introduction serve to teach; they report the events leading to Pasteur's discovery of a rabies vaccine.

Passage 3: Civil War Terms of Enlistment

General McDowell had good reason for his reluctance to march green troops "Forward to Richmond" in July 1861. Circumstances beyond his control plagued the campaign from its outset. Scheduled to begin July 8, the movement of McDowell's 30,000 men was delayed by shortages of supply wagons and by the necessity to organize late-arriving regiments into brigades and divisions. When the army finally began to move out on July 16, the terms of several ninety-day men were about to expire. Indeed, an infantry regiment and artillery battery went home on the eve of the ensuing battle. The longer enlistments of Confederate soldiers gave them a psychological advantage, for the recruit whose time was almost up seemed less motivated to fight. (McPherson, p. 339)

One of the outstanding characteristics of McPherson's book about the Civil War is the way it makes readers consider the small factors that influenced every facet of the conflict. Passage 3 offers an illustration. Perhaps you know something about the Civil War, and you probably know something about war in general. But before reading this passage, did you ever consider that the troops involved in the Civil War were enlistees? More important, did you ever consider that many of the terms of enlistment were only for 3 months? McPherson very skillfully takes readers from the known to the unknown, helping them see beyond the surface appearance of events to get at deeper layers of meaning and understanding. Like the other passages, McPherson's provides a model that you can use in your work. It is particularly relevant for seeing the teaching function of writing.

The Richly Detailed Body

Subject, topic, and thesis are connected in several ways. A thesis, for example, is supported by *details* that are associated with the subject area, the subject, and the topic. These details appear in the middle portion, or *body*, of a composition, and they are textured according to the focus of the text. More and finer details, in fact, provide the focus.

The following passage, taken from Boorstin's *The Discoverers*, illustrates this point. Here Boorstin describes the first stage of Marco Polo's difficult return to Venice from China after a sojourn of many years. It is an important part of Boorstin's report, so he provides more and richer details here than in other sections:

Passage 4: Marco Polo's Voyage Home

We do not know how Nicolò and Maffeo Polo spent their time at the court of the Khan, except that, at the end of the seventeen years, they had "acquired great wealth in jewels and gold." Every year Kublai Khan became more reluctant to lose Marco's services. But in 1292 an escort was required for a Tartar princess who was to become the bride of the Ilkahn of Persia. Envoys of the Ilkhan had already failed in their efforts to deliver the seventeen-year-old bride overland. Returned to the court of Kublai Khan, they hoped to secure sea passage. Just then Marco had come back from an assignment that had taken him on a long sea voyage to India. The Persian envoys, who knew the seafaring reputation of Venetians, persuaded Kublai Khan to allow the Polos to accompany them and the bride by sea. The Khan outfitted fourteen ships, with an entourage of six hundred persons and supplies for two years. After a treacherous sea voyage through the South China Sea to Sumatra and through the Sea of India from which only eighteen of the six hundred survived, the Tartar princess was safely delivered to the Persian court. She had become so attached to the Venetians that she wept at the parting. (Boorstin, p. 137)

Boorstin has two goals in this passage, but his focus is on illustrating that Marco Polo was a remarkable person. First, he wants readers to understand that Polo was important in the Imperial court. He was so important that only a diplomatic mission of great consequence and difficulty could persuade the Khan to part with him. The details of the mission, therefore, are important in realizing this goal and, in turn, in achieving the desired focus. Note that the first attempt to deliver the princess bride "had already failed." The Polos, however, were so famous that the envoys struck on the idea of an attempt by sea, with the Venetians heading the expedition.

The second goal is to illustrate the difficulty of the voyage, which enhances the remarkable character of Marco Polo. "The Khan outfitted fourteen ships, with an entourage of six hundred persons and supplies for two years." The details make the expedition sound more like preparation for a battle than a voyage. The trip was so treacherous that "only eighteen of the six hundred survived." This is truly amazing, and it suggests that Marco and the other Polos either were fantastically lucky or as strong as demigods. However, Boorstin appears to recognize that this detail may be too much for readers to accept as true, so he concludes with another that reveals Marco's human side. The princess "had become so attached to the Venetians that she wept at the parting." Throughout, this passage illustrates an excellent use of details.

THE INTRODUCTION AND BODY OF A PAPER

Introduction

The introduction should set the scene for a report. A useful guide is one taught in journalism classes: An introduction answers the questions *who? what? when? where?* and *how?*

In addition, a good introduction establishes a bond between the writer and the audience, often by finding a common ground of shared experiences. Sometimes, this common ground consists of cultural factors. Other times, however, it may consist of information or knowledge particular to the audience.

Finally, an introduction should let readers know what is to follow. It should give the audience insight into what the text is about.

Body

The body of a paper contains most of the content. There are exceptions, of course: Certain types of writing, such as lab reports, don't have a body as such, although they do contain a procedures section that presents a report of the events associated with the data collection.

The middle portion of a well-written report is richly detailed, creating what we call *presence*, which gives the audience the impression that the writer actually has witnessed the event. But the details in the body of an interpretive report do more: They provide support for the interpretation of the reported event you are reporting.

Two types of support are most common in college and business writing—*reason* and *character*.

Closing the Scene: The Conclusion

Conclusions often are slighted in discussions about writing. Sometimes they are dismissed as nothing more than a reworded repetition of the introduction, even though few successful papers end with such a repetition. Other times they are labeled as empty appendages that merely call for additional research or that provide a moral of some sort to let the audience know what it is supposed to learn from the event. Conclusions are more important than either view suggests.

Although effective writers use a variety of techniques for their conclusions, two of the more common involve:

1. Ending the paper with the end of the event.
2. Looking forward or outward through a generalization.

Conclusions Linked
to the End of the Event

The first approach to ending a paper is understood most easily by thinking about the end of a chronology: The battle is over, the journey is finished, or the experiment has run its course. Such endings sometimes are accompanied by reflective comments that serve to enforce the writer's thesis, but as often as not the details of the final events that the writer chooses to report achieve the same goal.

Passage 5 concludes the section from McPherson's book about the Civil War. As you read, try asking yourself how this conclusion serves as a suitable end of the chronology of the Battle of Bull Run:

Passage 5: The Retreat at Bull Run

Startled by this screaming counterattack, the discouraged and exhausted Yankee soldiers, their three-month term almost up, suddenly decided they had fought enough. They began to fall back, slowly and with scattered resistance at first, but with increasing panic as their officers lost control, men became separated from their companies, and the last shred of discipline disappeared. The retreat became a rout as men threw away guns, packs, and anything else that might slow them down in the wild scramble for the crossings of Bull Run. Some units of Sherman's brigade and several companies of regulars maintained their discipline and formed a rear guard that slowed the disorganized rebel pursuit. (McPherson, p. 344)

Perhaps the best way to examine the significant features of this conclusion is to compare it to the introduction.

Looking at the introduction and conclusion of this portion of McPherson's book shows how the two parts of a report of events differ. The introduction sets the scene for the event. No battle action has occurred yet, but McPherson provides revealing and ultimately important information about the "psychological advantage" of the Confederate troops. A Union infantry regiment and artillery battery had demobilized and left the field for home, their enlistments up. Those Union troops who remained on the field were on what is frequently referred to as "short time," and they "seemed less motivated to fight."

In this passage, McPherson has set the scene for the disaster the Union troops faced at Bull Run. Now look at the first sentence of the conclusion and observe how skillfully McPherson links the limited terms of enlistment on the Union side with the outcome of the battle. This sort of connection is characteristic of superior writing. Note that McPherson is not repeating the introduction; he is merely providing a verbal reminder of what appeared several pages earlier. The Confederate soldiers counterattacked, the Union troops decided they had fought enough, and they ran away. After they crossed Bull Run, the battle was over, and there was nothing left to report. At the same time, of course, McPherson is offering an interpretation of the Union rout, which he believes had its roots in the terms of enlistment of the Union troops.

INTRODUCTION: CIVIL WAR TERMS OF ENLISTMENT	CONCLUSION: RETREAT AT BULL RUN
General McDowell had good reason for his reluctance to march green troops "Forward to Richmond" in July 1861. Circumstances beyond his control plagued the campaign from its outset. Scheduled to begin July 8, the movement of McDowell's 30,000 men was delayed by shortages of supply wagons and by the necessity to organize late-arriving regiments into brigades and divisions. When the army finally began to move out on July 16, the terms of several ninety-day men were about to expire. Indeed, an infantry regiment and artillery battery went home on the eve of the ensuing battle. The longer enlistments of Confederate soldiers gave them a psychological advantage, for the recruit whose time was almost up seemed less motivated to fight.	Startled by this screaming counterattack, the discouraged and exhausted Yankee soldiers, their three-month term almost up, suddenly decided they had fought enough. They began to fall back, slowly and with scattered resistance at first, but with increasing panic as their officers lost control, men became separated from their companies, and the last shred of discipline disappeared. The retreat became a rout as men threw away guns, packs, and anything else that might slow them down in the wild scramble for the crossings of Bull Run. Some units of Sherman's brigade and several companies of regulars maintained their discipline and formed a rear guard that slowed the disorganized rebel pursuit.

Conclusions That Look Forward or Outward Through a Generalization

Although many reports of events conclude with the end of the event, many others, especially interpretive reports, commonly do something more—they offer a generalization that looks forward or outward, generalizing from the reported event not only to life in general but also to the readers' experiences.

Passage 6 illustrates this type of conclusion:

Passage 6: Riots in Watts

King and his companions ruefully confessed that the carnage pointed not only to the failures of the wider society but also to the limits of their own movement. It seemed more than grim coincidence that Watts exploded five days after black leaders had jubilantly hailed the passage of voting rights legislation. Residents of Watts, Harlem, or Chicago's West Side slums could read about Southern Negro triumphs in their local papers and watch Lyndon Johnson declaim about new laws against discrimination. Yet their own lives remained as bleak as before the Greensboro sit-in. (Weisbrot, p. 159)

Again, it may be illuminating to look simultaneously at the introduction and the conclusion of this piece. The introductory paragraph included in the next box comes from Robert Weisbrot's passage on the Watts riots, which appears on page 112.

INTRODUCTION: RIOTS IN WATTS

Marquette Frye, a twenty-one-year-old black, was driving down a busy Los Angeles street, indifferently sampling parts of each lane, when the police officer Lee Minikus waved him over to the side and asked for his driver's license. By all accounts, Minikus was unfailingly courteous, smiled at Frye's banter, but found the youth intoxicated and unable even to produce his license. The event diverted residents already gathered in the street, seeking relief from the heat wave in its fourth day. They watched the proceedings with some amusement and good-naturedly joked with Minikus and his suspect. Even Frye's mother, Rena, took the officer's side, scolding her son for driving drunk and urging him to go quietly and make it easy on himself. But in the ghetto, where policemen were viewed as intruders rather than as peace officers, the mood of the bystanders could turn suddenly.

CONCLUSION: RIOTS IN WATTS

King and his companions ruefully confessed that the damage pointed not only to the failures of the wider society but also to the limits of their own movement. It seemed more than grim coincidence that Watts exploded five days after black leaders had jubilantly hailed the passage of voting rights legislation. Residents of Watts, Harlem, or Chicago's West Side slums could read about Southern Negro triumphs in their local papers and watch Lyndon Johnson declaim about new laws against discrimination. Yet their own lives remained as bleak as before the Greensboro sit-in.

Weisbrot's introduction has all the characteristics of a simple report. It sets the scene for the event without attempting to interpret, and it is rich with details, such as Officer Minikus' courtesy and smile, Frye's inability to present his driver's license, and the appearance of Frye's mother. Weisbrot presents few personal comments, such as "the mood of bystanders could turn suddenly."

The conclusion, however, is thoughtful, reflective. It provides a revealing assessment of the Civil Rights Movement of the 1960s. It offers an observation that many people have not considered or have chosen to ignore: The Civil Rights Movement may have benefited black Americans in the South far more than it did their counterparts in the North. Astute readers cannot miss the irony. Northern liberals had played a significant role in desegregating the South while failing to note that the North was plagued by covert racism that was every bit as strong as the South's overt racism. This failure, the conclusion suggests, was at least in part responsible for the Watts riots.

Writing Assignment

REPORTING A CAMPUS OR COMMUNITY EVENT

Campus and community events are reported regularly in your school and local newspapers, but these sources cannot include all the events that are happening. Many events, for example, may not be deemed sufficiently newsworthy to merit publication.

This assignment gives you an opportunity to apply some of the techniques discussed in the previous pages. You should report an event that you witnessed or that you know about that has not appeared in the local papers. Your report should be about two pages.

THE INTERPRETIVE REPORT

An interpretive report goes beyond the actions of the event and offers an interpretation of what the event means. Generally, the event reported is interpreted as fitting into a larger pattern. In Passage 7, for example, the writer's report of a local bookstore fire allows her to report other, similar fires, which are linked to her claim that all commercial buildings need sprinkler systems. Interpretive reports therefore have claims that require support. Support comes from details of various types, but the three that are most relevant are *emotion*, *reason*, and *character*. For our purposes here, I limit the discussion to the latter two, in part because most of the writing you do in college and in the workplace will rely primarily on these categories.

Interpretive Reports

Interpretive reports describe the actions of an event and then provide an interpretation of what the event means. Many people believe that the meaning of an event is self-evident, but even a casual consideration of everyday reality indicates that such is not the case. Events have implications and meanings that often take years to figure out. Consider the assassination of President Kennedy and the collapse of the Soviet Union—events of significant magnitude. What did they mean when they happened, and what do they mean now? Interpretive reports of events attempt to answer such questions.

Beyond Surface Appearances

Some people differentiate *looking* from *seeing*. They suggest that being able to notice details of events is only part of being observant. From this perspective, seeing involves going beyond surface appearances to find meaning.

A simple example illustrates this point. Many years ago, I praised the film, *E.T., The Extraterrestrial*, at a Hollywood party. A great movie full of light-hearted entertainment. A friend in the group laughed and said I had to be kidding. She told me that the film projects themes that reinforce some of our worst inclinations. The director, Steven Spielberg, portrays adults in general and scientists in particular as hideous, heartless criminals willing to slay the ugly alien for the sake of "knowledge." In a world with few real villains but much complaisance, she said, a little scientist bashing may seem harmless enough, but it has a dark side. It reveals the sort of anti-intellectual, anti-technological message that young people just don't need. This friend had seen the film an a deeper level, obviously.

A significant part of what your teachers will ask you to do, and a significant part of what writing is about, involves looking beyond the obvious to see pattern and meaning. This ability is understood to be a hallmark of intelligence as well as good writing. Those who aren't able to see simply don't have much to say, particularly when trying to write an interpretive report of an event.

Learning how to see requires attending to details, questioning initial impressions, rejecting simple solutions, formulating hypotheses, and speculating repeatedly about alternative interpretations. In other words, seeing involves thinking about what events mean, and that is what differentiates *seeing* from *looking*.

Knowledge Specific to a Particular Audience

Although cultural factors are important in setting the scene, they are not the only means you have available. You also have experiences and knowledge that cannot be readily labeled "cultural" because they usually are specific and particular to an audience that is more narrow than the ones Boorstin, Radetsky, and McPherson targeted. Determining just how experiences and knowledge can connect to the audience, the event, and the scene may require some reflection.

Consider the following two examples. Amanda, a first-year student, wanted to write a report about fires. She wanted to use her report to argue that all public buildings, new and old alike, should have sprinkler systems. That is her claim. She began by briefly reporting about a fire in town that destroyed a bookstore that was a local landmark. This event was fresh in the minds of her readers and allowed Amanda to report on similar fires, all of which would have caused very little damage if the respective buildings had been equipped with sprinkler systems. By starting her report with the bookstore fire, Amanda effectively established a shared experience for readers.

Passage 7: The Bookshop Fire

The fire started at 6:30 p.m. against the back wall of the Intimate Bookshop, but the call to the fire department didn't go out until 6:55 p.m., and the first fire trucks didn't arrive until 7:05. By that time, the fire had eaten its way through the wall and found the books. And when they started to burn, the flames exploded through the roof. As the fire trucks pulled up outside, the flames were shooting 200 feet into the air and threatening surrounding buildings. The fire chief later reported that a sprinkler system would have stopped the fire as soon as it came through the wall.

When Amanda started working on this paper, the fire was a recent event for everyone in town. Students and community residents alike considered the Intimate Bookshop a landmark and a storehouse of shared experiences. People were greatly upset about the loss, particularly after the fire chief reported that a sprinkler system would have saved the place. This shared experience set the scene for Amanda's real goals in her report, which was to teach readers about the value of sprinkler systems and to suggest that laws requiring such systems should be enacted everywhere.

Another student, Karen, wanted to report on crimes around campus that seemed directly related to the lack of adequate lighting. Her interpretation of the attacks was that they argued strongly for improved lighting and increased security around the campus. She began her paper by reporting a recent attack on the head basketball coach's wife that left the woman hospitalized. The attack, which happened at night, shocked the whole community and was the focus of much discussion. Karen went on to report a variety of similar attacks, all of which occurred at night in areas without lighting. Everyone likely to read Karen's paper at the time could be expected to know about the incident because the audience was local people, and Karen used this particular knowledge effectively to set the scene for her report. The similar circumstances of the attacks she reported helped make her interpretation convincing.

Passage 8: Campus Attack

When Coach Smith's wife left the meeting at Wilson Library, it was 8 p.m. and already dark. She had to cross the quad between the library and the parking lot to get to her car. There are no lights anywhere in the quad, and the only illumination for the parking lot comes from a street light half a block away. The large trees throughout the area cast shadows that reduce visibility almost to zero, which allowed Mrs. Smith's attacker to lurk two feet away from her path without being seen. Even when he grabbed her and forced her to the ground, she couldn't really see him. He appeared simply as a moving shadow among other shadows. As he beat her unconscious, she later told police, she wished there had been just a glimmer of light so she could see his face. But there was no light then, and there is no light today, a full year after the attack.

The particular knowledge that Karen draws on extends beyond the attack; it also includes the audience's awareness of the lack of lighting on this campus. After all, she is writing for her fellow students. On her campus, walking from one building to another at night was like entering a black tunnel. In addition, the number of nighttime attacks on students—male as well as female—had led to many calls for administrative action to improve campus lighting. Given the crime situation on most college campuses, readers can follow the introduction even if they lack particular knowledge of this attack, the frequency of attacks on other campuses, and the poor state of campus lighting nationwide. However, readers *with* this knowledge are likely to find the report more compelling because it is part of their shared experience. Their bond with Karen is likely to be greater as a result.

This passage does more than illustrate how important shared knowledge is for setting the scene of a report of an event. It also shows how a successful writer uses her own knowledge and experiences to make connections with readers and the assignment.

Linked Assignment

INTERPRETING WHAT YOU SEE

The ways people use language are endlessly fascinating. Consider, for example, the distance people keep between themselves when having a conversation. People raised in the United States who don't know one another very well keep at least 24 inches apart. This distance shrinks, however, as the level of familiarity grows. In fact, it is possible to assess the level of intimacy between two people simply by examining the distance between them when they converse and by reading their "body language"—gestures and movements that send recognizable signals to the other party. A couple who have an intimate relationship, or who want to develop one, will lean toward each other when talking. When people are not receptive to what someone is saying, they physically close themselves off by crossing their arms or legs and by tilting their bodies away from the speaker.

This activity is intended to give you an opportunity to sharpen your powers of observation and to help you begin interpreting what you see. Go to a crowded place on or off campus and observe two or more people interacting. Although you can pick your subjects at random (the first you see in a given location), a better approach is to choose people who catch your attention for some reason. Perhaps they are laughing, crying, or arguing (you probably should avoid really obvious situations because the linked writing assignment on page 122 calls for an in-depth interpretation). Write down everything you observe the subjects doing. Afterward, describe any patterns of body language you observed and, in one or two paragraphs, interpret what the patterns tell you about the relationship between the people. Repeat this activity for at least two more situations.

Setting the Scene When You Are an Insider Writing to Insiders

Sometimes you may have to produce reports of events that reflect an insider-to-insider stance. Such tasks give you an opportunity to imitate the language and conventions of the discourse community so you can begin to master them—a necessary first step toward becoming an actual insider. Recognizing that you are engaged in an apprenticeship can be helpful when approaching insider-to-insider tasks because it reminds you that you must do a bit of role-playing as you adopt insider perspectives and language. Role-playing actually can be fun. To succeed, however, you need to know a bit about the discourse community and its conventions, which typically involves building on what you already know by, perhaps, talking with one of your teachers. Without this knowledge, it is easy for the role-playing to become an empty exercise that results in writing that is merely a caricature of what an insider would produce.

When a teacher asks you to produce insider-to-insider writing, you begin by selecting a topic appropriate to the subject area. In psychology it might be a topic dealing with human memory, whereas in business it might be a marketing survey. The next step is to study successful texts that can serve as a model for what you have to do on your assignment. You will discover that the act of setting the scene for readers differs by subject area. Consider, for example, the next two passages. The first comes from psychology, the second from business.

Passage 9: Testing Memory

Subjects were tested in a single group. In the first session they read the two passages on which explicit and inferential test statements were based. The passages contained a combined total of about 800 words, and all subjects finished reading them within 6 min[utes]. Then the letter span test was administered in which series of consonants were presented via slide projector with each item appearing for 1 sec[ond]. . . . Subjects were then given a typed list of the test statements taken from the stories read at the beginning of the session. They marked each as true or false based on their understanding of the relevant passage and assigned a confidence rating (using a three-point scale) to each decision. (Masson & Miller, pp. 314–318)

Unlike earlier passages, "Testing Memory" does not have much personal voice. In Boorstin's passage about Marco Polo and in Karen's passage about the campus attack, readers sense that the authors are distinct personalities, real people with feelings and opinions, even passion, for what they write. "Testing Memory," on the other hand, shows few signs of a distinct personality. Scientific writing strives to reduce personal voice as much as possible in an effort to project a greater sense of objectivity.

Nevertheless, the structure of this passage is similar to the others examined previously. The event occurs over time and is reported sequentially. The writers, Masson and Miller, provide important details to make the passage understandable. It is the manner in which they report the events that is different.

Many business reports include a section that discusses the events associated with the data collection. Passage 10 is the introduction to the procedures section of a business paper and is fairly typical. It was written by Amy, a student who used questionnaires to measure customer brand preferences in a shopping mall:

Passage 10: Shopping Mall Survey

I requested the participation of shoppers as they exited each of the three stores involved in the study. I collected 100 questionnaires at each store from customers who did not make a purchase as well as from those who did make a purchase. Before a customer filled out the questionnaire, I explained in general terms the nature of the study and stressed that its success depended on honest answers to each question. I also explained that I was not an employee of the store and that no one employed by the store would see their responses. I assured every participant that his or her questionnaire would remain confidential.

There are three features to consider in this passage. First, Amy reports the events in chronological order, providing the audience with an easy-to-follow sequence of actions. Second, she provides details about the events that enable readers to understand clearly what happened. In this respect, Amy's report is very similar to the others we've examined. The third feature is Amy's use of the personal pronoun, which usually is limited in business and social science writing. However, there have been calls for years to make such writing more personal, to recognize that real people produced the work, by using personal pronouns.

Reason as a Means of Support

As noted earlier, interpretive reports offer claims that must be supported, usually by reason and character. Support based on *reason* includes observation and experimentation. It also includes the ability to examine a complex event and interpret it in a manner that is *logical*. In both instances, the foundation of support by reason is the ability to analyze. Analysis involves looking at a whole in terms of its parts, but the process may involve examining the relationship between *cause and effect* in an event, *defining* the nature of an event, or *comparing and contrasting* similar events or elements within a single event. Each of the details related to cause and effect, for example, can serve to support the thesis.

Cause and Effect

People generally believe that all events have causes. Analysis based on cause and effect attempts to explain what caused a given event (or effect). It usually involves a causal thesis, which in the most simple form includes the word *because*: *Tuition is high because universities have adopted a designer-label approach to education; Sexuality in America is repressed because most of us hold fundamentalist notions of morality.*

Most types of writing, however, do not lend themselves to this formula but require a less explicit approach. The word *because* is implicit in the claim.

Definition

Definitions often play a central role in a report of an event, especially when the topic is controversial, which leads the writer to use a definition to establish premises. Thus, not every report of an event will require a definition, but successful writers are able to provide one when necessary. The first impulse is to quote a dictionary: "According to *Webster's Unabridged Dictionary*, 'life' is defined as . . . ." Try to resist this impulse. The dictionary is a fine place to start when you need a definition, but you do not want to use it for your writing. Dictionaries provide general definitions of words, and in most instances your writing will need a specific definition, one that reflects *your* perception and understanding of what a term means. So when you need a definition to help support your interpretation of an event, use your own, not someone else's. Keep in mind that you cannot decide that words mean whatever you want them to. Your definition has to be reasonable.

Comparison and Contrast

Comparison and contrast involves analyzing two things, ideas, or events in terms of their similarities and differences. Boorstin used comparison and contrast to open his discussion of Marco Polo in Passage 1 on page 90:

> Marco Polo excelled all other known Christian travelers in his experience, in his product, and in his influence. The Franciscans went to Mongolia and back in less than three years, and stayed in their roles as missionary-diplomats. Marco Polo's journey lasted twenty-four years.

In these three sentences, Boorstin states that Marco Polo was similar to other Christian travelers in that he journeyed to Asia, but he was different because his journey was much longer and because it "excelled" all others.

Comparison and contrast is particularly useful in reports of events because it can work so effectively to move readers from the known to the unknown. You have the opportunity to compare an unusual event or contrast it with an event that is well known to your audience.

Character as a Means of Support

Character refers to the persona (sometimes called *voice*) that writers develop in their work. Sometimes it is funny, sarcastic, or cynical, but in most academic writing the character reflects expertise or authority through a reasonable, sensible voice. Thus, character is a means of support. A note of caution: It is easy to start using big words that may sound pretty impressive at first blush but that commonly are not appropriate to the task. Most readers very easily can recognize when the voice in a paper doesn't seem real, when the character is phony. It is best to use a voice that feels comfortable without becoming conversational. Readers want to sense that a real person is communicating through the words on a page.

Insiders have an advantage because often they *are* experts and they are comfortable writing with authority. Their characters support their interpretations of events. Even so, it is common for experts to refer to the work of other experts, which enhances their character in a couple of ways. First, it lends authority to their character by linking what they have to say with the voices of other experts who agree with them. Second, it makes their characters appear knowledgeable and reasonable, willing to explore the ideas and interpretations of others.

In your writing, you must draw on your knowledge and experience to develop an appropriate character to support an interpretive report and to make connections with the discourse community. The most effective way to do this is to follow the lead of the insiders: Use references to authorities you have found through research who agree with your interpretation of the event.

The paraphrases and quotations you include in these papers provide important supporting details. Paraphrases are particularly valuable because they allow you to transfer the ideas and knowledge of experts into your own language. When you do, you are, in a sense, making those ideas and knowledge your own—not in any absolute sense, of course, because that runs the risk of plagiarism, but in the sense that you internalize them. The fact that the experts agree with your claims gives credibility to your work and to you as a writer-researcher, which in turn makes your claim more acceptable. This technique has the added advantage of increasing your knowledge, moving you closer to insider status.

Journal Entry

What kind of character, or voice, do you admire most? How successful have you been in imitating that character in your academic writing?

Reason and Character Combined

Academic writing involves using both reason and character as supporting details, so you should not exclude one or the other. Passage 11 illustrates how a successful writer combines reason and character in an interpretive report to support a thesis. Written by Kenji Hakuta, a leading scholar in bilingualism, it comes from a book called *Mirror of Language*. In this section, Hakuta reports the events surrounding a young Japanese girl's development of English language skills. He uses this report not only to teach his audience of outsiders (hoping to become insiders, perhaps) something about language but also to claim that children acquire second languages much in the way that they acquire their first language—that is, without any formal instruction but merely by being immersed in the language. The rhetorical stance allowed Hakuta to make the details of character implicit. His details of reason, however, are explicit. As you read, examine the rhetorical stance Hakuta has established with the audience, the specific details he selects to support his claim about language acquisition, and the effectiveness of the details.

Passage 11: A Japanese Child Learns English

1   In the early 1970s when I was an undergraduate, I met a visiting scholar from Japan. Mr. Tanaka (not his real name) invited me home to dinner to meet his family. The Tanakas had just moved into the first floor of a typical multifamily unit in a working-class, English-speaking neighborhood in Somerville, Massachusetts. Mr. Tanaka's spoken English was what might be described as "halting" (he was more comfortable with written English); his wife had studied English in college and was quite fluent. The family member who most interested me, however, was their five-year-old daughter. We will call her Uguisu ("nightingale" in Japanese).

2   When I first met Uguisu, she had just been enrolled in a neighborhood public kindergarten and had begun to make friends with children on her street. Since she was receiving no formal instruction in English at school, Uguisu made for a nice comparison with children who acquire English as their native language. That first evening, I tried unsuccessfully to get Uguisu to speak English. Apparently, her one English phrase was "not in particular," which she had picked up from her mother.

3   The next few months were difficult ones for Uguisu. Her parents reported that she complained of headaches and was generally cranky, which they attributed to the pains of being in a new environment and coping with an unfamiliar language. She played well, sharing toys with her friends, and she occasionally used a few English phrases—usually imitations of what her friends had just said. For example, she learned to say "I'm the leader," which her friends used to yell out as they stormed around the house, and she used it frequently in a variety of contexts, such as when she wanted to show her friends how to play with toys. When asked in Japanese what she thought that meant, she translated it as "I am the big sister," that is, a show of authority. It was not until almost seven months after her initial exposure to English that Uguisu's English really blossomed. Her parents felt that this flowering was triggered by a lengthy automobile trip that the family had taken. On the trip, they were accompanied by an American adult, with whom Uguisu got along well, and this may have given her the needed confidence to use the "data" that she had stored up over the months.

4   From that point on, her rate of development was awesome; a nightingale had been turned loose. During the next six months, English became her predominant language. She even started talking to her parents in English, which they did not actively discourage, although they usually responded in Japanese. And she used it

when playing on her own, such as in the bathtub with her toys. I suspect that within eighteen months after her initial exposure to English, only a trained ear would have been able to distinguish her from a native speaker. . . . At the end of two years, the family returned home to Japan. (Hakuta, pp. 107–108)

Let's look more closely at the information Hakuta supplied to make this section richly detailed. Doing so will give you a model for how to analyze texts like Hakuta's, and you can in turn apply this model to your own writing, analyzing it for strengths and weaknesses. In the second paragraph, Hakuta tells us that Uguisu:

1. Had begun to make friends with children on her street.
2. Was receiving no formal instruction in English at school.

These two points are important because they support Hakuta's claim that children acquire second languages in about the same way that they acquire their first—through a natural interaction with native speakers of the language. The first detail lets us know that Uguisu had English-speaking friends to play with; the second lets us know that she did not receive any formal instruction in English. These details are based on reason because they draw on the audience's ability to make connections between one set of behaviors (those associated with acquiring a first language) and another (those associated with acquiring a second language).

The third paragraph contains quite a bit of information, but only four supporting details:

1. Uguisu played well, sharing toys with her friends.

2. She occasionally used a few English phrases—usually imitations of what her friends had just said; for example, she learned to say "I'm the leader," which her friends used to yell out as they stormed around the house, and she used it frequently in a variety of contexts, such as when she wanted to show her friends how to play with toys.

3. When asked in Japanese what she thought "I'm the leader" meant, Uguisu translated it as "I am the big sister," that is, a show of authority.

4. It was not until almost seven months after her initial exposure to English that Uguisu's English really blossomed.

What do these details reveal? Uguisu got along well with other children, who were the principal source of her exposure to English. She started to use limited English phrases in the context of play with her friends. The phrases were imitations of expressions her friends used, a detail that stresses the role that immersion plays in second-language acquisition. More important, it shows that these phrases were linked to actions, such as playing with toys. Underlying this detail of reason is the important factor of Hakuta's character. Earlier in the book he cites research of his own and others that shows how children develop their first language on the basis of actions related to directions and explanations. This detail provides a crucial support for the claim.

Readers also learn that Uguisu was approximating a meaning for phrases such as "I'm the leader." Again, the support provided by character is established earlier in the book, where Hakuta refers to studies that suggest that children acquiring their first language make similar approximations, engaging in a kind of matching procedure over time until their approximation actually fits the meaning of an expression. The *comparison* between the events and their similarity, even though the languages are different, provides additional support for Hakuta's claim. When Hakuta mentions the time involved in Uguisu's English language development, he's providing support by reason, but it is based on support by character. Numerous studies, mentioned elsewhere in the book, indicate that language acquisition develops over time. Most children do not begin speaking until they are 12 to 18 months old, and scholars agree that the first year or so of life is a period in which children sort through the language patterns they experience. Then, at a certain point, they have enough information about the language to start using it. By suggesting that a similar process was at work in Uguisu, Hakuta effectively links himself to other scholars in the field and enhances his character, as well as his thesis.

Diverse Voices

How people learn a second language is a question that has generated huge amounts of research over the years. It's an important question not only in itself but also because answering it has great implications for teaching.

This activity has two parts, one for those who speak English as a second language and one for those who have studied a second language other than English. If you're in the first group, you should write a simple report about how you learned English. If you grew up bilingual and can't remember, talk to relatives about your process. Provide as many details as possible so that readers can visualize the process.

If you're in the other group, write a simple report about how you learned your second language. Provide as many details as possible so that readers can visualize the process. Afterward, share your reports in your group. I encourage you to spend some time discussing the differences and similarities in the two processes. What are some conclusions that you can draw from these reports? If your high school were modifying its second-language program, could you make any recommendations on the basis of these reports?

Journal Entry

What are some lessons that you've learned from observing or experiencing events that you think are important enough to want to share with others? How have you interpreted those lessons?

READINGS

Peter Radetsky

This first reading selection continues Passage 2 on page 91. It reports the events that led to Pasteur's discovery of a vaccine against rabies, which before Pasteur's research killed many thousands of people each year. The author, Peter Radetsky, is a journalist whose work focuses on medical topics. Before publishing *Invisible Invaders: The Story of the Emerging Age of Viruses*, the book that this selection came from, Radetsky had co-authored two other books with medical doctors.

PETER RADETSKY

VIRUSES

1   In 1880, when Pasteur turned his attention to the disease, only three things could be said about rabies with any certainty at all: whatever caused it was contained in the saliva of the rabid animal; it was transmitted by a bite that broke the skin; and after transmission it took anywhere from a few days to months before the symptoms appeared in its victims. Beyond that, all was mystery. Pasteur had his work cut out for him.

2   His first task was to try to isolate the cause, which he suspected to be a microbe. He tried directly inoculating animals with rabid saliva, which, of course, had to be collected by hand—a hazardous occupation. On one occasion, Pasteur himself drew saliva from a mad bulldog, which was dragged from its cage by a lasso around the neck, then held down on a table by two courageous attendants while the semiparalyzed Pasteur bent over the animal's foaming mouth and carefully sucked a few drops of the lethal saliva through a glass tube between his lips. One slip might have meant a fatal bite on the face.

3   But these inoculations proved to be inconclusive. Sometimes the rabbits, guinea pigs, and other animals came down with rabies, but all too often nothing would happen, or another disease would appear. And in any case, the rabies simply took too long to show up for the purposes of manageable laboratory study.

4   So Pasteur tried a different tack. He obtained mucus from the mouth of a five-year-old child who had died of rabies just four hours earlier. After mixing the mucus with water, he injected it into laboratory rabbits. This time all the animals died within thirty-six hours, and when blood from the dead rabbits was injected into other rabbits, they too died. It seemed possible that Pasteur had indeed found the virulent germ.

5   But what was it? Pasteur put some of the rabbit blood on a slide under the microscope. He saw something very interesting: "an extremely short rod, somewhat constricted in its center, in other words shaped like an 8." Pasteur cultivated the microbe in the laboratory, injected it into rabbits and dogs, and examined the blood of the dead animals to find the same microbe once again. Could this be the cause of rabies? For a time, he was tempted to think so. But then Pasteur began to find the same microbe in the saliva of healthy children, and children suffering other diseases, and healthy adults. No, it couldn't be the rabies germ. Refusing to be sidetracked, he began to search elsewhere—and so inadvertently passed by the cause of a far wider killer than rabies. Years later, it was determined that his figure-8 microbe was the pneumococcus bacterium, the cause of pneumonia. No wonder the rabbits had died quickly.

6   Pasteur pushed on. Having decided to look elsewhere than in saliva, he turned his attention to the nervous system. The early symptoms of rabies—the difficulty in swallowing, the creeping sensations on the skin—and the later paralysis all pointed to an involvement of the nerves. With the help of his assistant Emile Roux, Pasteur injected rabbits with a solution containing the ground-up tip of a rabid dog's spinal cord. This time a greater proportion of the rabbits contracted rabies than when injected with saliva, but again there were some that kept hopping as though nothing had happened. And again it simply took too long to see a result one way or another. Pasteur decided to inject the rabid nerve material directly into the brain of a laboratory dog.

7   That is, he decided that it should be done; he was entirely incapable of doing it himself. A prime target of antivivisectionists (in this, as in so many other ways, Pasteur's experience foreshadowed our own times), Pasteur was notoriously solicitous of his laboratory animals, preferring to leave the actual laying on of hands to others. So, Roux made the

injection, and in two weeks the dog began howling and snarling madly, attacked and destroyed its bed, then stiffened and in another five days died. When the researchers repeated the experiment on other dogs, they obtained much the same results. They had finally found a reliable means of transmitting the disease and ensuring a manageably short incubation period. But the next step, cultivating and studying the infective agent, as they had done with the chicken-cholera microbe, seemed insurmountable. Their usual method of growing the agent in a nutrient solution in the lab just wouldn't work, for they had no idea what that agent might be. Whatever it was, it didn't show up under the microscope. Perhaps it simply was too small to be seen. Yet it existed—there had to be a way to work with it.

8   "Since this unknown thing is living," Pasteur said, "we must cultivate it; failing an artificial medium, let us try the brain of living rabbits; it would indeed be an experimental feat!" The experiment was a great success. He passed the rabid solution from one rabbit brain to another, over and over, with the result that the agent actually became more virulent. It killed in a progressively shorter length of time, until by the hundredth passage incubation time was down to six days—and there it stayed. They now had a constant supply of a "fixed" infective agent, even if they didn't know what that agent was. They could cause rabies at will; now they could try to see if there was a way to prevent it.

9   The inspiration for the final breakthrough came from Emile Roux. While Pasteur was busy experimenting with passing the rabies infective agent from rabbit to rabbit, Roux was studying how long the agent could survive in the spinal cord. He had hung part of the infected spinal cord of a rabbit in a flask by suspending it from a stopper wedged in the upper opening. One day Pasteur happened to walk into the incubator where Roux had placed the flask. Another assistant, Adrien Loir, later described how Pasteur fell into a characteristically impenetrable spell of concentration. . . .

Critical Reading Guide

1. Look at how Radetsky organizes his first paragraph. What information does he supply that sets the scene for readers?

2. Radetsky probably had a wealth of material to choose from in narrating Pasteur's efforts to find a vaccine for rabies. For example, Radetsky could have told readers why the pneumonia bacterium appeared in the saliva of healthy children and adults, but he did not. Produce a list of potential information that could have been part of Radetsky's material, then list what he actually provides in paragraphs 2–5. What principle appears to govern Radetsky's choices?

3. In this excerpt, Radetsky provides two quotations from Pasteur (paragraphs 5 and 6). What effect do they have on readers? Is it a useful technique in reports?

4. Radetsky writes in paragraph 7: "A prime target of antivivisectionists (in this, as in so many other ways, Pasteur's experience foreshadowed our own times), Pasteur was notoriously solicitous of his laboratory animals." This sentence offers an interpretation that Radetsky makes for readers. Find two additional places in the text where Radetsky offers an interpretation. Characterize each interpretation in terms of length, placement in the report, and type of information provided. What pattern do you see? What purpose do these interpretations serve? What effect do they have on readers?

James McPherson

The Civil War has been studied extensively. Some estimates indicate that more than 60,000 books have been published about the conflict, making it one of the most written-about topics in the world. There are several reasons the war attracts such interest: the huge casualties on both sides, the severe deprivations the soldiers endured, the moral issues involved, and the way it fundamentally shifted the United States from an agrarian to an industrial society.

The next reading, a paragraph of which was examined on page 91, comes from James M. McPherson's book *Battle Cry of Freedom: The Civil War Era*. One of the nation's foremost historians, McPherson teaches history at Princeton University and has written extensively about the war. When *Battle Cry of Freedom* was published, it immediately received praise from scholars and popular critics alike. It was nominated for a National Book Award as well as a National Book Critics Circle Award and received the Pulitzer Prize for the best historical work of 1989. The excerpt included here reports one of the bloodier battles of the war.

JAMES M. McPHERSON

FAREWELL TO THE NINETY DAYS' WAR

1   General McDowell had good reason for his reluctance to march green troops "Forward to Richmond" in July 1861. Circumstances beyond his control plagued the campaign from its outset. Scheduled to begin July 8, the movement of McDowell's 30,000 men was delayed by shortages of supply wagons and by the necessity to organize late-arriving regiments into brigades and divisions. When the army finally began to move out on July 16, the terms of several ninety-day men were about to expire. Indeed, an infantry regiment and artillery battery went home on the eve of the ensuing battle. The longer enlistments of Confederate soldiers gave them a psychological advantage, for the recruit whose time was almost up seemed less motivated to fight.

2   Out in the Shenandoah Valley, General Robert Patterson likewise feared that the ninety-day recruits in his army of 15,000 would not stand fast in a real battle against Joseph E. Johnston's 11,000 Confederates. This was one of several reasons why Patterson failed in his task of pinning down Johnston in the Valley while McDowell attacked Beauregard at Manassas. Patterson was also confused by orders from Washington that left it unclear whether he should attack or merely maneuver against Johnston. Wrongly believing himself outnumbered by the enemy, Patterson chose the safer course of maneuver. Unfortunately, he maneuvered himself right out of the campaign. On July 18 and 19, Johnston's army gave him the slip, marched from Winchester to the railroad at Piedmont, and entrained for Manassas. With their arrival the Confederate forces at Manassas became equal in size to McDowell's invading army.

3   Beauregard had been forewarned of McDowell's advance by his espionage network in Washington, headed by Rose O'Neal Greenhow, a friend of several northern politicians but also a Confederate spy. In the best romantic tradition, coded messages carried by southern belles riding fast steeds brought word of Union plans. Even with this advance knowledge, Johnston could not have reinforced Beauregard in time if McDowell's army had moved faster than a snail's pace. At this stage of the war, soldiers without marching experience carrying fifty pounds of equipment took three days to cover a distance that road-wise veterans later slogged in one day. At every turn in the road, troops halted to clear away trees felled by rebel axemen or

to seek cover from rumored "masked batteries." Halts at the head of a column undulated accordion-like back to the rear, where men got tired of standing for hours in the July sun and wandered off to look for water or to pick blackberries. When the Yankees finally reached Centreville, three miles from the Confederate defenses behind Bull Run, they had eaten all their food and had to delay another day while more rations were brought up. Lacking trained cavalry, McDowell personally scouted enemy lines and discovered that rugged terrain and strong defenses on the Confederate right ruled out his original plan to turn that flank. Another day went by as he planned an attack on the left flank and scouted the roads in that direction. While this was going on, the overworked railroad was bringing Johnston's troops to Manassas. By the time McDowell launched his assault on the morning of July 21, three Valley brigades had arrived and the fourth was on its way.

4   Despite all the delays, McDowell's attack came within an ace of success. Beauregard had distributed his troops along the south bank of Bull Run, a sluggish, tree-choked river a few miles north of Manassas. Confederate regiments guarded the railroad bridge on the right, the Warrenton turnpike bridge six miles upstream on the left, and a half-dozen fords between the bridges. Expecting McDowell to attack toward the railroad, Beauregard placed nine of his ten and one-half brigades on that flank, from which he planned to anticipate the Yankees by launching his own surprise assault on the morning of July 21. Instead, the roar of artillery and crack of musketry several miles upstream shortly after sunrise indicated that McDowell had sprung his surprise first.

5   The Union attacking column, 10,000 strong, had roused itself at 2:00 a.m. and stumbled through the underbrush and ruts of a cart track on a six-mile flanking march while other regiments made a feint at the turnpike bridge. The flanking column forded Bull Run two miles upriver from the bridge, where no Confederates expected them. The commander of rebel forces at the bridge was Colonel Nathan "Shanks" Evans (so-called because of his spindly legs), a hard-bitten, hard-drinking South Carolinian. Recognizing the Union shelling of the bridge as a feint and seeing the dust cloud from the flanking column to his left, Evans took most of his troops to meet the first Yankee brigade pouring across the fields. Evans slowed the Union attack long enough for two brigades of Confederate reinforcements to come up.

6   For two hours 4,500 rebels gave ground grudgingly to 10,000 Yankees north of the turnpike. Never before under fire, the men on both sides fought surprisingly well. But lack of experience prevented northern officers from coordinating simultaneous assaults by different regiments. Nevertheless, the weight of numbers finally pushed the Confederates across the turnpike and up the slopes of Henry House Hill. Several southern regiments broke and fled to the rear; McDowell appeared to be on the verge of a smashing success. A multitude of northern reporters, congressmen, and other civilians had driven out from Washington to watch the battle. They could see little but smoke from their vantage point two miles from the fighting. But they cheered reports of Union victory, while telegrams to Washington raised high hopes in the White House.

7   The reports were premature. Johnston and Beauregard had sent additional reinforcements to the Confederate left and had arrived personally on the fighting front, where they helped rally broken Confederate units. For several hours during the afternoon, fierce but uncoordinated attacks and counterattacks surged back and forth across Henry House Hill (named for the home of Judith Henry, a bedridden widow who insisted on remaining in her house and was killed by a shell). Men whom the war would make famous were in the thick of the fighting: on the Union side Ambrose E. Burnside, William Tecumseh Sherman, and Oliver O. Howard, each of whom commanded a brigade and would command an army before the war was over; on the Confederate side Beauregard and Johnston, the former in field command and the latter in overall command; along with James E. B. ("Jeb") Stuart, the dashing, romantic, bearded, plumed, and deadly efficient colonel of a cavalry regiment that broke one Union infantry attack with a headlong charge; Wade Hampton, whose South Carolina legion suffered heavy casualties; and Thomas J. Jackson, a former professor at V.M.I. now commanding a brigade of Virginians from the Shenandoah Valley. Humorless, secretive, eccentric, a stern disciplinarian without tolerance for human weaknesses, a devout Presbyterian who ascribed Confederate successes to the Lord and likened Yankees to the devil, Jackson became one of the war's best generals, a legend in his own time.

8   The legend began there on Henry House Hill. As the Confederate regiments that had fought in the morning retreated across the hill at noon, Jackson brought his fresh troops into line just behind the crest. General Barnard Bee of South Carolina, trying to rally his broken brigade, pointed to Jackson's men and shouted something like: "There is Jackson standing like a stone wall! Rally behind the Virginians!" But at least one observer placed a different construction on Bee's remark, claiming that the South Carolinian gestured angrily at Jackson's troops standing immobile behind the crest, and said: "Look at Jackson standing there like a damned stone wall!" Whatever Bee said—he could not settle the question by his own testimony, for a bullet killed him soon afterward—Jackson's brigade stopped the Union assault and suffered more casualties than any other southern brigade this day. Ever after, Jackson was known as "Stonewall" and his men who had stood fast at Manassas became the Stonewall Brigade.

9   Much confusion of uniforms occurred during the battle. On numerous occasions regiments withheld their fire for fear of hitting friends, or fired on friends by mistake. The same problem arose with the national flags carried by each regiment. With eleven stars on a blue field set in the corner of a flag with two red and one white horizontal bars, the Confederate "stars and bars" could be mistaken for the stars and stripes in the smoke and haze of battle. Afterwards Beauregard designed a new battle flag, with white stars embedded in a blue St. Andrew's Cross on a red field, which became the familiar banner of the Confederacy.

10   One mixup in uniforms affected the outcome of the battle. At the height of the fighting for Henry House Hill, two Union artillery batteries were blasting gaps in the Confederate line. Suddenly a blue-clad regiment emerged from the woods seventy yards to the right of two of the guns. Thinking the regiment might be its requested infantry support, the artillery withheld fire for fatal minutes while the regiment, which turned out to be the 33rd Virginia of Jackson's brigade, leveled muskets and fired. The guns were wiped out and the Union attack lost cohesion in that sector of the battlefield.

Indeed, by midafternoon the northern army lost what little cohesion it had everywhere, as regiments 11 continued to fight in a disconnected manner, stragglers began melting to the rear, and McDowell failed to get two reserve brigades into the action. Johnston and Beauregard, by contrast, had brought up every unit within reach, including the last brigade from the Valley, just off the train and marching onto the field about 4:00 p.m. By that time the rebels had an equal number of men in the battle zone (about 18,000 were eventually engaged on each side) and a decisive superiority in fresh troops. Most of the Union regiments had been marching or fighting for the better part of fourteen hours with little food or water on a brutally hot, sultry day. Seeing Confederate reinforcements appear in front of them, some northern soldiers asked: "Where are *our* reserves?" At this moment, sensing his advantage, Beauregard ordered a counterattack all along the line. As Confederate units surged forward a strange, eerie scream rent the air. Soon to be known as the rebel yell, this unearthly wail struck fear into the hearts of the enemy, then and later. "There is nothing like it on this side of the infernal region," recalled a northern veteran after the war. "The peculiar corkscrew sensation that it sends down your backbone under these circumstances can never be told. You have to feel it."

Startled by this screaming counterattack the discouraged and exhausted Yankee soldiers, their 12 three-month term almost up, suddenly decided they had fought enough. They began to fall back, slowly and with scattered resistance at first, but with increasing panic as their officers lost control, men became separated from their companies, and the last shred of discipline disappeared. The retreat became a rout as men threw away guns, packs, and anything else that might slow them down in the wild scramble for the crossings of Bull Run. Some units of Sherman's brigade and several companies of regulars maintained their discipline and formed a rear guard that slowed the disorganized rebel pursuit.

1. McPherson's passage describes the Battle of Bull Run, which left thousands of troops dead and injured. Rather than begin by discussing the positioning of the armies or the strategies of the officers, McPherson opens with a paragraph that focuses on the 90-day tours of duty that were about to expire for large numbers of Union soldiers. But the passage itself is not about this topic, which really is not mentioned again until the final paragraph. Why do you think McPherson started the passage with this focus, and why do you think he moves quickly away from it? In addition, what purpose is served by returning to these 90-day tours in the final paragraph?

2. McPherson's writing is rich in details. Make a list of the details in paragraph 3. What effect do they have on readers?

3. A significant element of McPherson's analysis of the Civil War is his claim that the outcome was largely uncertain until toward the end of the conflict. Victory could have gone either way. What factors in the passage illustrate this interpretation?

Robert Weisbrot

Robert Weisbrot teaches history. Much of his writing has focused on questions of racial equality, and he has stated that his work attempts to understand how individual people have struggled to advance human rights. The following selection comes from his book *Freedom Bound: A History of America's Civil Rights Movement*. It offers an unromantic look at civil rights in the United States.

ROBERT WEISBROT

FREEDOM BOUND: A HISTORY OF AMERICA'S CIVIL RIGHTS MOVEMENT

1 Marquette Frye, a twenty-one-year-old black, was driving drunk down a busy Los Angeles street, indifferently sampling parts of each lane, when the police officer Lee Minikus waved him over to the side and asked for his driver's license. By all accounts Minikus was unfailingly courteous, smiled at Frye's banter, but found the youth intoxicated and unable even to produce his license. The event diverted residents already gathered in the street, seeking relief from a heat wave in its fourth day. They watched the proceedings with some amusement and good-naturedly joked with Minikus and his suspect. Even Frye's mother, Rena, took the officer's side, scolding her son for driving drunk and urging him to go quietly and make it easy on himself. But in the ghetto, where policemen were viewed as intruders rather than as peace officers, the mood of bystanders could turn suddenly.

2 Marquette Frye began to panic at the thought of jail. He pulled away from Minikus, then released his feelings in a stream of obscenities. Backup police and local residents multiplied on the street, the atmosphere souring amid muttered curses of the "blue-eyed" cops. Frye suddenly lunged for the nightstick Minikus carried, while his older brother Ronald, fearing a general police assault, remonstrated with an officer nearby. The newly arriving patrolman John Wilson surveyed the near chaos, decided that his brethren in blue needed rescue

from 150 angry blacks and charged straight on. One blow of his riot baton doubled over Ronald Frye, and two more sent Marquette to the ground. Rena Frye desperately clutched at Minikus to get him to stop the beatings but instead found herself herded, along with her sons, into police squad cars. An onlooker screamed, "We've got no rights at all—it's just like Selma!" Another black raised the stakes: "Come on, let's get them!"

3   Twenty-year-old Joyce Ann Gaines was standing a few yards from the line of police, bedecked with pink hair curlers and a hairdresser's smock, chatting with another young woman until she realized that this once amusing scene was getting out of hand. She began to walk away, just as a policeman felt a spray of saliva strike his neck and wheeled around to see Gaines fading into the crowd. He yanked on her left arm while a woman friend defiantly yanked back on her right. As Gaines struggled for balance, her curlers sailed into the crowd and her smock billowed in front of her, making her appear pregnant. Then she disappeared into yet another squad car. Within minutes the ghetto grapevine was embellishing the incident with ugly details that confirmed popular suspicions of the police force. In one version, a cop struck a pregnant woman in the belly with his club. In another, the cop pushed the woman against a patrol car and tried to choke her. Reaction was swift. Stones and bottles rained down on the officers as blacks avenged the woman of these imaginary tales, and a history of sullen submission to ghetto police.

4   Had this been a middle-class area like Striver's Row in Harlem, where lawyers, doctors, and businessmen upheld a "model neighborhood," rage might have melted away amid concern for property values. But this was Watts, a district fifty miles square that lay beneath the approaches to the city's international airport, a squalid human anthill where more than 250,000 Negroes were crammed into faded stucco buildings. Four times as many people per square block lived in Watts as in the rest of Los Angeles. Trash collection was a rare event, so a stroll along any street in Watts meant an encounter with broken glass, rusty cans, rotting food. Two-thirds of the residents were on welfare, unemployment among adult males was 34 percent, yet $20 million in federal antipoverty funds went unused while local politicians jockeyed for control. Complaints about racist police resounded throughout Watts, where the population was 98 percent black yet 200 of the 205 officers were white. These conditions afforded little incentive for "keeping cool" after the arrest of Marquette Frye. Instead residents went about the cathartic business of destroying their neighborhood.

5   Within two days of the first disturbance five thousand blacks were smashing everything in a 150-block area. Dick Gregory appealed to the higher sentiments of the crowd and was shot in the leg. Rioters hurled Molotov cocktails at buildings and sniped at firemen answering the alarms, killing one of them. Looters followed the light of a hundred fires to carry away guns, appliances, liquor, jewelry, and anything else of value from ghetto stores. Frantic merchants posted signs in their store windows declaring "Soul Brother," "Negro owned," "Owned by a Brother." But while looters often targeted white-owned shops, some seized the good life with a single-minded frenzy that did not admit distinctions of color, ownership, or law. The black writer Louis Lomax confronted one enterprising man carrying a sofa from a burning furniture store by balancing it on his head and shoulders. "Brother, brother," Lomax implored, "do you realize what you're doing?" "Don't bother me now," the man replied; "I've got to hurry back to get the matching chair."

6   Fourteen thousand national guardsmen and several thousand local police needed six days to stop the arson, rock throwing, theft, and sniping. The violence left thirty-four people dead, including a sheriff's deputy and a fireman who had been shot in the first days of the riot, before fire fighters were routinely issued bullet-proof vests. Nine hundred blacks suffered injuries, and four thousand were arrested for violence, vandalism, looting, loitering, or simply happening upon a policeman at an inopportune moment. Hundreds of families were left homeless, while businessmen found their stores charred and plundered. The damage, after inflated insurance claims were discounted, came to some $45 million. Amid the wreckage of Watts, civil rights leaders like Roy Wilkins left behind their hopes of ending "all the years of oppression" and instead realized that they "were just beginning a new ordeal."

7   Even after the riot had burned itself out, the embers of hostility continued to smolder. "The

riots will continue," a young black man said, "because I, as a Negro, am immediately considered to be a criminal by police and, if I have a pretty woman with me, she is a tramp even if she is my wife or mother." Los Angeles police chief William Parker set the tone for his officers by explaining the violence in Watts as simply the work of a "criminal element," ignoring the fact that the majority of those arrested had no police record and that residents widely approved the acts of defiance. At bottom Parker expressed the prevalent urban approach to race relations, which was to downplay black grievances and to pacify the ghettos chiefly through police vigilance.

8 Bayard Rustin, Andrew Young, and Martin Luther King, Jr., saw firsthand the desperation that had fueled this violence as they toured the ruins of Watts. When a group of youngsters told them joyously, "We won," the civil rights leaders asked, "How can you say you won when thirty-four Negroes are dead, your community is destroyed, and whites are using the riot as an excuse for inaction?" "We won," the youths insisted, "because we made them pay attention to us."

King and his companions ruefully confessed 9 that the carnage pointed not only to the failures of the wider society but also to the limits of their own movement. It seemed more than grim coincidence that Watts exploded five days after black leaders had jubilantly hailed the passage of voting rights legislation. Residents of Watts, Harlem, or Chicago's West Side slums could read about Southern Negro triumphs in their local papers and watch Lyndon Johnson declaim about new laws against discrimination. Yet their own lives remained as bleak as before the Greensboro sit-in.

Critical Reading Guide

1. The first five sentences in Weisbrot's introductory paragraph effectively set the scene for readers. What is the role of the last sentence in that paragraph?

2. Paragraph 3 does a good job of describing the confusion surrounding such an event and skillfully shows how easily "fact" and "fiction" can become intertwined. Now look at paragraphs 2 and 3 and make a list of the events they report. Do you get the impression that Weisbrot was at the riot? What problem does Weisbrot's report pose for readers?

3. Does Weisbrot seem to offer a "lesson" at the end of this selection? If so, what is it?

4. What cultural information does Weisbrot use to make this selection more readable? What cultural information does he use to help convey his message?

Daniel J. Boorstin

Daniel J. Boorstin has had a long, distinguished career as a scholar and writer. Although trained as an attorney, he is now considered to be one of the world's premier historians. Boorstin taught history at the University of Chicago from 1944 to 1969 and then went on to direct the National Museum of American History at the Smithsonian Institution from 1969 to 1973. He became chief librarian for the Library of Congress after being nominated by President Ford. His book *The Americans: The National Experience* won the Pulitzer Prize for history in 1974. In 1983, he published *The Discoverers: A History of Man's Search to Know His Work and Himself*, from which the following selection comes. For this book, the French government inducted Boorstin into the Legion of Honor.

The Discoverers offers a popular history of the world from the perspective of a writer who values the contributions of individuals and their accomplishments.

The work focuses on discoveries, such as the clock, that Boorstin believes have changed the world. The selection below, a portion of which was discussed earlier on page 102, describes the contributions of Marco Polo in opening lines of communication between Europe and Asia.

DANIEL BOORSTIN

THE DISCOVERERS

The Discovery of Asia

1 Marco Polo excelled all other known Christian travelers in his experience, in his product, and in his influence. The Franciscans went to Mongolia and back in less than three years, and stayed in their roles as missionary-diplomats. Marco Polo's journey lasted twenty-four years. He reached farther than his predecessors, beyond Mongolia to the heart of Cathay. He traversed the whole of China all the way to the Ocean, and he played a variety of roles, becoming the confidant of Kublai Khan and governor of a great Chinese city. He was at home in the language, and immersed himself in the daily life and culture of Cathay. For generations of Europe, his copious, vivid, and factual account of Eastern ways was the discovery of Asia.

2 Venice at the time was a great center for commerce in the Mediterranean and beyond. Marco Polo was just fifteen years of age in 1269, when his father, Nicolò, and his uncle Maffeo Polo returned to Venice from their nine-year journey to the East. Another of Marco's uncles, also named Marco Polo, had trading houses in Constantinople and at Soldaia in the Crimea, where Nicolò and Maffeo had joined him in 1260 in his trading ventures. Marco Polo opens his own book with an account of these earlier travels in which he had no part. Nicolò and Maffeo laid in a stock of jewels at Constantinople which they took by sea to Soldaia, then north and east along the Volga to the splendid court of Barka Khan, son of Genghis Khan. Barka Khan not only treated them courteously and with honor but, what was more to the point, bought their whole stock of jewels, as Marco Polo observes, "causing the Brothers to receive at least twice its value."

3 When a war between Barka Khan and a rival Tartar prince cut off the Polo brothers' return to Constantinople, they decided to take their trading ventures farther eastward. A seventeen-day journey across the desert took them to Bokhara, where they fell in with some Tartar envoys who were en route to the court of the Great Khan, Kublai Khan. These envoys persuaded the Polos that Kublai Khan, who had never before seen any Latins, intensely desired to see them, and would treat them with great honor and liberality. The envoys promised to guard them on the way. The Polo brothers took up this invitation, and after a full year's journey, "seeing many marvels of divers and sundry kinds," arrived at the court of Kublai Khan. The Great Khan, every bit as friendly as had been promised, proved to be a man of wide-ranging curiosity and alert intelligence, eager to learn everything about the West.

4 Finally he asked the two brothers to be his envoys to the Pope, requesting one hundred missionaries educated in all the Seven Arts to teach his people about Christianity and Western science. He also wanted some oil from the lamp at the Holy Sepulcher in Jerusalem. When Nicolò and Maffeo departed, they carried the Emperor's Tablet of Gold, his certificate of safe passage, ordering everybody en route to supply their needs. Arriving at Acre in April 1269, the two brothers learned that the Pope had died and his successor had not yet been named. They returned to Venice to await the result. When the new pope, Gregory X, was finally named, he did not offer the requested hundred missionaries, but instead only assigned two Dominican friars to accompany the Polos.

5 In 1271, when Nicolò and Maffeo Polo set out from Venice on their return journey to Kublai

Khan, they took with them Nicolò's seventeen-year-old son, Marco, who was destined to make their trip historic. At Lajazzo on the eastern Mediterranean the two Dominicans left in panic. The three Polos, now alone, proceeded to Baghdad, then on to Ormuz at the mouth of the Persian Gulf, where they might have taken ship for a long journey through the Sea of India. Instead they chose to go north and east overland through the Persian Desert of Kerman to the frigid mountains of Badakhshan, noted for its rubies and lapis lazuli, and its fine horses. There used to be horses here, Marco tells us, which were "directly descended from Alexander's horse Bucephalus out of mares that had conceived from him and they were all born like him with a horn on the forehead." There they stayed a year to allow Marco to recover from an illness by breathing the pure mountain air.

6 Then up still higher, across a land of glaciers, with many peaks over twenty thousand feet—Pamir, which the natives accurately called "The Roof of the World." "Wild game of every sort abounds. There are great quantities of wild sheep of huge size [now known as *ovis Poli*, though William of Rubruck had noted them before]. Their horns grow to as much as six palms in length and are never less than three or four. From these horns the shepherds make big bowls from which they feed, and also fences to keep in their flocks." "No birds fly here because of the height and the cold. And I assure you that, because of this great cold, fire is not so bright here nor of the same colour as elsewhere, and food does not cook well." They then took the old southern caravan route through northern Kashmir, where no European would be seen again till the nineteenth century, then eastward to the edge of the Gobi Desert.

7 The party rested at Lop, a town at the western edge of the desert, where travelers usually took supplies to strengthen them against the terror of the crossing.

8 Beasts and birds there are none, because they find nothing to eat. But I assure you that one thing is found here, and that a very strange one, which I will relate to you.

The truth is this. When a man is riding by night through this desert and something happens to make him loiter and lose touch with his companions, by dropping asleep or for some other reason, and afterwards he wants to rejoin them, then he hears spirits talking in such a way that they seem to be his companions. Sometimes, indeed, they even hail him by name. Often these voices make him stray from the path, so that he never finds it again. And in this way many travellers have been lost and have perished.

9 Across the desert they entered Tangut, in extreme northwestern China, traversed the Mongolian steppes and arrived in the court of the Great Khan after a trek of three and a half years.

10 Kublai Khan received the Venetians with great honor. Sensing the talents of the twenty-one-year-old Marco, the Khan at once enlisted him in his service, and sent him on an embassy to a country six months away. When we read Marco Polo's travels today, we all reap the fruits of the voracious curiosity of that thirteenth-century Mongol emperor.

11 Now he had taken note on several occasions that when the Prince's ambassadors returned from different parts of the world, they were able to tell him about nothing except the business on which they had gone, and that the Prince in consequence held them for no better than fools and dolts, and would say: "I had far liever hearken about the strange things, and the manners of the different countries you have seen, than hearing of the affairs of strange countries." Mark therefore, as he went and returned, took great pains to learn about all kinds of different matters in the countries which he visited, in order to be able to tell about them to the Great Khan. . . . Thereafter Messer Marco abode in the Khan's employment some seventeen years, continually going and coming, hither and thither, on the missions that were entrusted to him. . . . And, as he knew all the sovereign's ways, like a sensible man he always took much pains to gather knowledge of anything that would be likely to interest him, and then on his return to Court he would relate everything in regular order, and thus the Emperor came to hold him in great love and favour. . . . And thus it came about that Messer Marco Polo had knowledge of, or had actually visited, a greater number of the different countries of the World than any other man; the more that he was always giving his mind to get knowledge, and to spy out and enquire into everything in order to have matter to relate to the Lord.

It seemed, the Khan would exclaim, that only Marco Polo had learned to use his eyes!

12 We do not know how Nicolò and Maffeo Polo spent their time at the court of the Khan, except

that, at the end of the seventeen years, they had "acquired great wealth in jewels and gold." Every year Kublai Khan became more reluctant to lose Marco's services. But in 1292 an escort was required for a Tartar princess who was to become the bride of the Ilkhan of Persia. Envoys of the Ilkhan had already failed in their efforts to deliver the seventeen-year-old bride overland. Returned to the court of Kublai Khan, they hoped to secure sea passage. Just then Marco had come back from an assignment that had taken him on a long sea voyage to India. The Persian envoys, who knew the seafaring reputation of Venetians, persuaded Kublai Khan to allow the Polos to accompany them and the bride by sea. The Khan outfitted fourteen ships, with an entourage of six hundred persons and supplies for two years. After a treacherous sea voyage through the South China Sea to Sumatra and through the Sea of India from which only eighteen of the six hundred survived, the Tartar princess was safely delivered to the Persian court. She had become so attached to the Venetians that she wept at the parting.

13 The Polos, returning home overland by way of Tabriz in northern Persia, Trebizond on the south coast of the Black Sea, to Constantinople, finally reached Venice in the winter of 1295, after their absence of twenty-four years. The Polo family had long since given them up for dead. A plausible tradition reports that when these three shabby strangers appeared, looking more like Tartars than Venetians, their noble relatives would have nothing to do with them. But the relatives' memories were quickly jogged when the unkempt wanderers ripped open the seams of their sordid garments and produced their secret treasure—a shower of rubies, diamonds, and emeralds. The returned travelers were affectionately embraced, and then entertained at a luxurious banquet, where music and jollity were mixed with exotic reminiscence.

14 Those were years of bitter rivalry between Venice and Genoa for the Mediterranean seafaring trade. On September 6, 1298, a climactic sea battle between Venice and Genoa at Curzola off the Dalmatian coast left the Genoese victors, with seven thousand prisoners. Among these was a "gentleman commander" of a Venetian galley, Marco Polo. Brought back in chains to a prison in Genoa, he became friendly with another prisoner, relic of an earlier Genoese victory over the Pisans.

This Rustichello happened to be a writer of romances who already had a considerable reputation for his retelling of the tales of King Arthur and his Round Table. Not a literary genius, Rustichello still was master of his genre, industrious and persuasive. In Marco Polo's reminiscences he saw the raw material for a new kind of romance—"A Description of the World"—and he persuaded the Venetian to cooperate. Marco Polo must somehow have managed to secure his notes from home. Then, profiting from his enforced leisure and from their confinement together, the Venetian dictated a copious account of his travels to Rustichello, who wrote it all down.

15 If either Marco Polo or Rustichello had not fought in the wars against Genoa, we might have no record of Marco Polo's travels and might not even have heard his name. Luckily, Rustichello was a writer congenial to the great Venetian traveler, and he knew the makings of a romance to charm the world for seven hundred years. Of course he could not restrain himself from occasionally embellishing Marco Polo's facts with his own fancies. Some of the more colorful episodes are adapted from earlier writings by Rustichello or others. For example, the extravagant praise that Kublai Khan lavished on the young Marco when he first arrived at the court recalls what King Arthur said, according to Rustichello's own romance, when he received the young Tristan at Camelot. This was not the first or the last time a writer made the reputation of an adventurer. The formula, "as told to," which nowadays appears less often than it rightly should on title pages of books, has a surprisingly respectable history. Why did the energetic Venetian, who was literate in several languages, who must have written much to please Kublai Khan and extensive detailed notes for his own use, not write down for himself his personal adventures? Perhaps if promptly on his return to the commercial city of Venice in 1295 he had been tempted by a publisher's contract, he might have written his own book. But two centuries would pass before a publishing trade flourished.

16 Other great medieval travelers—Friar Odoric of Pordenone, Nicolo de' Conti, and Ibn Battuta—and the noted French chronicler and biographer of Saint Louis, Jean de Joinville (1224?–1317?), also dictated their books. The rewards of money or celebrity were not yet dangled before so many, nor

was literacy required to get or to hold political power. The opening sentence of the prologue of Marco Polo's book exhorts: "Emperors and kings, dukes and marquises, counts, knights, and towns-folk, and all people who wish to know the various races of men and the peculiarities of the various regions of the world, take this book, take this book *and have it read to you*."

Rustichello wrote Marco Polo's book in French, which in Western Europe in those days was current among the laity just as Latin was among the cler-gy. Before long it was translated into most Euro-pean languages, and numerous manuscripts sur-vive. Never before or since has a single book brought so much authentic new information, or so widened the vistas for a continent.

Critical Reading Guide

1. Boorstin uses a technique characteristic of adventure tales to engage read-ers: descriptions of strange places and people and references to fortunes in dia-monds, rubies, and gold. But he also uses another technique to keep the audi-ence's attention. Can you identify what it is?

2. Because of the relative ease of travel today, many people do not consider how difficult travel was in the past. Boorstin, however, mentions frequently the amount of time it took the Polos to travel from one place to another. Can you think of any reasons why Boorstin makes these references to time?

3. Although the Great Khan asked the Pope to send 100 missionaries "to teach his people about Christianity and Western science," the Pope sent only two, and they abandoned the expedition before it had left the eastern Mediterranean. This detail may seem insignificant, but I would suggest that Boorstin included it for a purpose. What do you think that purpose might have been? What does the detail add to the report?

4. Boorstin clearly recognizes Marco Polo as a significant contributor to Western knowledge, but he emphasizes that chance or fate played a large part in this contribution. Why do you think Boorstin considered chance to be important in this instance?

5. The last few paragraphs explain how Polo's adventures came to be record-ed. In fact, Boorstin devotes almost as much space to this part of the report as he does to the report of Marco's travels and experiences. Can you think of any rea-sons Boorstin gave so much emphasis to Rustichello's role in the production of Marco Polo's book and why he took time to explain that other medieval travelers had "also dictated their books"?

6. Can you identify some descriptive details that give this report presence? How does Boorstin integrate them into the report?

7. Does this report have a thesis? If so, what is it and how is it expressed?

OBSERVATIONS OF THE LOCOMOTION, GROOMING, AND REPRODUCTIVE BEHAVIOR OF ACHETA DOMESTICUS

Craig

1 **Introduction**

2 The laboratory exercises dealt with the locomotion, grooming, and reproduction of the house cricket, *Acheta domesticus*. The student teams attempted to observe the walking, jumping, and grooming behaviors in a group of selected crickets. The teams also attempted to observe reproductive behavior, examining male-female activities before, during, and after copulation.

3 **Methods**

4 The crickets used were grown on a Tennessee "Cricket Ranch" and belonged to the species *Acheta domesticus* (also called *Bryllus domesticus*). One large female cricket was used for the locomotion and grooming phases of the study; it was removed from the breeder just prior to the start of observations. One male cricket was used for the reproduction portion of the experiment. It had been isolated for 24 hours in half of the test terrarium. The terrarium was covered with sand, had a water dispenser, and a cricket "home" made out of a piece of egg carton. The terrarium was divided in half by two dividers fitted in its center. The females selected for the reproduction portion of the experiment had been isolated in individual coffee cans for an unknown length of time (presumably 24 hours).

5 Equipment included a terrarium, a length of string, and liquid paper in various colors. The string was used as a leash in the grooming and locomotion observations. The liquid paper was used to mark the female crickets for identical purposes in the reproduction portion of the experiment. The female cricket was leashed with a piece of string tied behind the first two pairs of legs. It was induced to jump by lightly prodding its posterior. The approximate length and height of each jump were measured and recorded. Then the cricket was suspended over the table and lowered to its top.

6 This cricket also was used in the walking portion of the experiment. To slow its movements, the cricket was induced to walk up a screen. Observation focused on sequence of leg movements, speed of movement, distance covered, and length of a stride interval.

7 To assess grooming behavior, alcohol was dabbed with a Q-tip on the antennae and legs of the female cricket.

8 The isolated male's reproductive behavior was observed by introducing four female crickets into the terrarium. The female used in the earlier portions of the experiment was not used in this portion. Each female had been isolated in coffee cans for approximately 24 hours. Each female was marked on the dorsal side of its thorax with a dab of liquid paper; each female was marked with a different color for identification.

9 Two female crickets were placed on each side of the terrarium. They were shifted randomly from one side to the other in an effort to induce mating with the single male.

Results

Jumping was preceded by a characteristic posture. The female cricket stood still with its body low and its legs close to the body. The cricket's rear jumping legs were pulled close to the body. During the jump, the legs were extended behind the abdomen and remained in this position for a moment after each jump.

The results of 10 consecutive jumps are shown in Table 1. The height of each jump was difficult to measure accurately; however, each jump was about 4 inches off the ground.

When the cricket was suspended over the table, it showed two types of behavior. It either froze in a jumping position or attempted to fly. When the cricket hit the table in a jumping position, it started to jump, whereas the flying cricket stopped all movement.

Figure 1 shows the stride pattern of the cricket. This pattern indicates that the cricket moved at about two inches a second on a flat porous surface and at approximately half an inch every second on a nearly vertical screen. The stride interval varied depending on where the cricket was walking, and the variation was too great to make any meaningful average. Consequently, no measure of its length or duration was recorded.

During the grooming portion of the experiment, the cricket cleaned itself constantly. It pulled the alcohol treated antennae down to its jaws with its prothoracic legs. The antennae was always groomed from the head to the tip. Leg grooming was similar to antennae grooming. The leg was moved up to the jaws, and the cricket worked from the body outward toward the claw.

When the first two marked females were introduced into the male's territory, they exhibited a great deal of activity. The females ran around the cage for approximately three minutes before they settled down. The male also as very active during this time.

The male made contact with one of the females by placing his antennae against hers. The male then turned to face away from the female's head. He then raised his body high on his hind legs with his wings buzzing quickly, making a soft, quick, chirping sound. The female made an attempt to mount the male, but another female jostled them and the mounting female moved away.

When this happened, the male chirped loudly twice and pivoted back and forth quickly with his body raised in the air. He then groomed his antennae and waved them around quickly when he was finished. The male then started to prowl the tank.

When the male made contact with either female in the tank, he would quickly turn around and chirp softly and quickly. The females, however, seemed uninterested in this display and wandered off soon after the male started. The remaining two females were added in the hope that they might mate with the male. Unfortunately, these females also would not mate with the male, even though he constantly put on a display for the females he came into contact with.

Discussion

The jumping behavior in crickets appears to be a standard flight mechanism. The crickets jump to get away from perceived danger, such as a hand attempting to grab them or a prod on their abdomens. The motionlessness before the jump is what Donald Broom (1981) called "exaggerating primary defense, e.g., a camouflaged animal remaining motionless," and the jump is another kind of defense Broom called "flight." If the cricket finds it has been discovered, it first tries to discourage predation by blending in with its surroundings. If this does not work, the animal leaps away. The cricket can get away quickly by making a series of leaps of approximately a foot long; it then remains motionless.

22   Walking in the cricket follows a stride pattern that gives the animal good footing on most surfaces. The cricket always has most of his legs supporting him. Furthermore, the legs on one side or the legs of a pair are not moved directly after each other because it might reduce traction.

23   Crickets seem to rely on their antennae for a good deal of their sensory information, which most likely is the reason that the crickets in this study groomed their antennae whenever the alcohol was dabbed on them. The legs, on the other hand, were groomed less often, perhaps because they are not used in perception.

24   After the male had determined that he was dealing with a female by making antennae contact, he went into his courtship behavior. The females for the most part failed to respond. The reason was that they might have been shook up from the handling or that the male might have been giving inappropriate signals. The latter seems more likely because many of the females in other tanks did mate with the males. If this was the case, the females were weeding out an unwanted behavioral trait by refusing to mate with a male that might pass the behavior on to offspring. The nature of this undesirable trait could not be identified.

25   By using both auditory and visual signals, the male cricket increases the chance to mate, and the female has a better chance of finding him. Presumably, this lends to the success of the species by allowing more offspring to be born to compatible adults. Reproductive success is particularly important for crickets because they live for only about two months.

26   All of the behaviors that were studied seem to have positive survival value. Jumping allows the cricket to escape and breed at a later time. Grooming keeps the cricket in working order, which also would be an aid in breeding. Finally, behavior during breeding can have very positive effects on the species' survival. If something is wrong with the male, either behaviorally or physically, the female will not breed with him, thereby stopping the abnormality before it can be passed on to offspring.

27   **References**

28   Broom, Donald M. *Biology of Behavior*. Cambridge University Press, New York, NY, 1981, pg. 158.

29   Laboratory Handout *Crickets: General Information*.

Critical Reading Guide

1. Unlike most professional reports of lab work, the introduction to Craig's paper is quite short. Can you think of some reasons why it is so brief?

2. What is the most important factor missing in the introduction?

3. The methods section is where we find Craig's report of events. Can you identify some details that give the writing presence? If you were working with Craig on this paper, what suggestions would you give him that might improve the quality of the report?

4. Is there an element of reporting in Craig's results section? An interesting exercise would be to use your library to find some professional examples of laboratory research that you can compare to Craig's results section. Would they be similar or different?

5. The discussion section of a lab report is supposed to generalize the research findings. Does Craig's discussion generalize his findings effectively? If you were

working with Craig on this paper, what suggestions would you give him that might improve this section?

6. Craig wrote this paper for a psychology class. Compare his references section to the recommended APA format for psychology papers. What would Craig need to do to this section to make it consistent with the APA format?

 *Writing Assignment*

WRITING AN INTERPRETIVE REPORT OF EVENTS

The linked assignment on page 100 asked you to observe people on or off campus and to write a few paragraphs interpreting the patterns of behavior that you saw. The goal of this assignment is to have you develop those initial observations and conclusions into an interpretive report, applying all the factors that you have learned in this chapter. You should set the scene and provide a thesis, use details of reason and character to support that thesis, and provide a generalizable conclusion.

WRITING GUIDE: WRITING AN INTERPRETIVE REPORT

Invention

You already know a great deal about human behavior and are adept at interpreting gestures and facial expressions, but before you begin writing, you should take the time to consider your possible choices, based on your observations for the linked assignment on page 100. You could report an argument and conclude that when people shout at one another, scowl, and use short, aggressive gestures they are angry. Or you could describe someone crying and conclude that tears and sobs are usually indicative of sadness. One problem is that these patterns of behavior and the associated conclusions are fairly obvious and aren't challenging. Review your notes and the finished paragraphs for the linked assignment. Expand them as much as possible, using an invention technique.

After you have decided what to report, you will need to decide again who you are writing for and what kind of rhetorical stance you intend to develop. If you want to write as an insider, you may want to include special information about human behavior. An introductory text on psychology will give you some of the basic terminology that an insider would be expected to have. If your audience consists of outsiders, which it most likely will, you cannot assume that readers will know what such terminology means, so you will need to plan on explaining it in each instance, perhaps providing definitions of key terms. Or you may want to compare and contrast behaviors.

Planning

After expanding your notes and paragraphs, you may have more information than you can use in your report. The next step, then, is to sort through your observations and highlight those events that lend themselves to interpretation. You can discard some actions as being irrelevant to your interpretation.

Consider how to set the scene for readers. There are two options. You can begin by describing the location and the actions, as Weisbrot does in the passage on page 100, or you can begin by making a few general remarks about the ways in which human behavior can reveal underlying patterns. Your report in this case becomes a single example illustrating the validity of your general remarks. What will your focus be? You may want to identify details that provide this focus and that also lend themselves to the conclusion.

Drafting

Describe the events you observed by drawing directly from your notes. After they are in place, go back through them and start elaborating. It is unlikely that you were able to record details for everything you observed, so it will be necessary to supplement your notes from memory. Try to recreate the events in a way that will enable readers to visualize the scene.

What is there in the events that allows you to interpret them? At what points in the report will your interpretation help readers understand the event? Highlight these points.

Pausing and Reading

During your pauses, read through the draft and ask yourself whether the words on the page create a verbal picture of the event. If you find places where they do not, make a note so that you can go back later and add or delete material. Also ask yourself whether the details in the body of the paper support your claim. What kind of details are you using for support? If they are not details of reason and character, make a note so that you can adjust them later. Is your rhetorical stance clear? Is your conclusion generalizable? Does it look forward or outward? Then, as you continue drafting, make adjustments to your focus so that you can answer these questions increasingly in the positive.

Revising

Read through your paper with your audience in mind at all times. Ask yourself what additional information, what additional details, would give your report greater presence. Look carefully at your interpretation and assess how well fits the behavior you observed. Is your rhetorical stance consistent? Is the tone you use appropriate? Is your claim easily recognizable?

After making any needed changes, read the paper again. Does the introduction set the scene and provide expectations that are met in the rest of the paper? Consider your conclusion: How does it end the report? Is the paper interesting? Are you pleased with what you have produced? If it is not interesting or if you are not pleased, why not? What can you do to improve the paper on this level?

Editing

Before you turn the report in, you should edit it. The editing techniques described in the handbook will prove useful. A report such as this one lends itself to what are called *existential verbs*, forms of "to be": *is, was, are*, and *were*. Try to make the writing crisper by periodically using other verbs. Be careful not to overdo it, however—you don't want your report to start sounding like fiction. Finally, you should ask someone to read your paper to assess the overall effect and to check your editing.

Publishing

Print your paper on quality paper, using 1-inch margins on all sides. Provide a title page. (Because the publishing criteria will not change for the rest of the assignments in this text, they will not be mentioned from this point on.)

GROUP ACTIVITIES: WRITING AN INTERPRETIVE REPORT

1. Talk with members of your work group about possible topics and tentative conclusions, then spend about 15 minutes making a list of possibilities. Select the two topics you find most interesting and discuss with your work group possible locations where you could make your observations.

2. You may want to team up with one or more people in your group for this assignment because it will be easier to record all the details of the behavior you will observe. If you decide to use this approach, spend about 15 minutes discussing how you will share the responsibilities for observation as well as for writing the report.

3. After discussing the assignment in your work group, write a paragraph outlining what you intend to do. Twenty minutes should be about right for this part of the assignment. At the end of this time, invite another work group to join yours so you can share ideas. Members of the two groups should read their paragraphs aloud, commenting on and offering suggestions for each outline. Feedback should address such questions as: (a) Does the outline focus on behavior that lends itself to an obvious conclusion? (b) Does the outline propose a feasible observation? (c) Is the connection between behavior and conclusion seem clear? (d) Is the finished report likely to be interesting and informative?

4. When you have finished your first draft, exchange it with one or more members of your work group. Read your group mate's draft and answer the following questions: (a) Has the writer described the observed behavior in sufficient detail? (b) Where would you like to see more detail? (c) Does the introduction set the scene? (d) Is the writer's interpretation an integral part of the report, or does it seem to be merely added on? (e) What did you learn from reading the report?

5. Exchange completed drafts with a member of your group and edit the paper for mechanical errors as well as style. Use the handbook for help with punctuation, word usage, and subject/verb agreement.

Reporting Information

It often seems as though the very concept of "information" changes according to a text's principal aim. The information in a report of events is different from the information in a report of information, an evaluation, an argument, and so on. The problem is that defining this difference is quite difficult.

CHAPTER FIVE

Reporting Information

It is possible to understand the world and all events in the world as signs. We read these signs and learn from them. What we learn can be characterized as *information*, or knowledge, that we gain through experience, observation, study, or instruction. Information, therefore, is inherent in everything around us and everything we do.

When people write, they learn more about subjects and topics, and they also teach their audience about those subjects and topics by moving readers from the known to the unknown, by giving them new knowledge. From this perspective, all writing is composed of signs, and all writing conveys information. As a result, there is overlap among writing tasks that blurs categories.

To orient themselves, those who study composing commonly differentiate types of writing on the basis of principal aims and other distinguishing characteristics. Consequently, reports of information are different from reports of events and other kinds of writing, even though all convey knowledge. A report of an event, for example, focuses on the actions that make up the event and the chronological sequence of those actions. Any analysis usually is related to an interpretation of the events. In addition, events frequently are about specific people and their activities, as in the case of Boorstin's report of Marco Polo's travels discussed in the previous chapter. In a report of information, on the other hand, actions seldom are the major factor. Instead, the focus is on transmitting knowledge indirectly related to actions. Analysis plays a more significant role, and human actions may not be involved at all. *When they are, the focus is not on individuals but on people in general*. A report of an event, for example, might focus on the assassination of Malcolm X, whereas a report of information might focus on how Malcolm X's views on race relations in America changed over time.

It often seems as though the very concept of "information" changes according to a text's principal aim. The information in a report of events is different from the information in a report of information, an evaluation, an argument, and so on. The problem is that defining this difference is quite difficult. Your textbooks are reports of information, but how is that information different from the information contained in a report of a football game? To simplify matters, we can say that reports of information deal primarily with facts and ideas.

Reports of information commonly condense a body of information into a coherent, detailed overview that presents and very often explains "facts" to readers. But the notion of what constitutes a "fact" is not always clear-cut. Some people would define a fact as anything that can be proved; others would say it is anything that can be measured; still others would say a fact is anything that is always "true."

Unfortunately, there are problems with these definitions. Let's take up each one in turn, starting with the idea that facts are things that can be proved. Every few months, the tabloids in the local supermarket run a headline that reads something like, "Proof that UFOs Exist!" Inside are photos of things that look like spaceships and things that look like space creatures. The photos, we are told, have been supplied by reputable people who report their encounters with aliens in elaborate detail. Many report their experiences under hypnosis, which the article insists confirms the truth of the encounter because people "can't lie" when they are in a hypnotic trance.

On the face of it, the combination of photographs and eyewitness reports should be convincing and should prove even to the most jaded skeptic that UFOs exist. The same combination linked to a bank holdup very likely would send somebody to jail because it would prove guilt beyond a reasonable doubt. Although surveys report that more than half the people in the country believe in UFOs, even hard-core believers refuse to accept the tabloid articles as anything more than entertainment. The question therefore is, what constitutes *acceptable* proof?

As the UFO example suggests, the answer depends on several factors, all of which are linked to social conventions associated with agreement. Conventions are formalized social "agreements" and codified "expectations." Acceptable proof therefore must rank high on four criteria that underlie expectations and agreement:

1. The claim must be reasonable and within the realm of physical possibility.

2. The person or people making the claim must have sufficient character to be believable.

3. The situation in which the claim is made must be open to scrutiny and should not lead to opportunities for self-aggrandizement.

4. Independent sources must be able to substantiate the claim by replicating the proof.

Let's consider how these criteria work by using a hypothetical example. Before his untimely death, Carl Sagan was a world-renowned astronomer dedicated to finding signs of extraterrestrial intelligence. With this information as a starting point, we can construct an imaginary scenario: Suppose Sagan and his research team—rather than workers at a tabloid newspaper—took a picture of an alien spaceship that they had viewed through a telescope at an observatory. Suppose also that when Sagan released the photograph he stated that it *appeared* to show an alien spaceship rather than stating that it *showed* an alien spaceship. The nature of the claim is muted; Sagan would not be insisting that UFOs exist, only that he had a photograph of something that *looked like* an alien spaceship. Sagan's high status as an expert in astronomy would have made it unlikely that he had asked an assistant to toss a Frisbee into the air for the camera. The photograph, in other words, could be characterized a part of a well-planned and well-documented search for extraterrestrial life.

As a result, people hearing or reading Sagan's account of the photograph would be less inclined to dismiss it than they would be if the account appeared in a tabloid. The photo, however, would not be *acceptable proof* unless other evidence from independent sources corroborated the existence of the spaceship. Criterion number four would have to be met before the proof was acceptable.

The idea that a fact is anything that can be measured seems like a good one—until we try to apply it. Many people have had the frustrating experience of expressing their love to a sweetheart, only to face the impossible question: "Oh, yeah? How much?" Does the inability to measure feelings make them any less real, any less "factual"? People encounter the same difficulty with a vast array of human behaviors, such as self-sacrifice, generosity, and loyalty. Even with physical objects that lend themselves to measurement it is not easy to decide on an appropriate measuring instrument. If a man says his foot is 12 inches long and that he can demonstrate it with a ruler, a friend could easily prove him wrong by measuring the length with a micrometer instead. The more accurate micrometer will show that the man's foot is not *exactly* 12 inches.

A recent book proposed that a fact is anything that is always true and illustrated this proposal through the use of some interesting examples:

- There are 365 days in a year.
- Water extinguishes fire.
- Helium is lighter than air.

These appear to offer, at last, a viable definition of "fact"—until you consider that leap years have 366 days, that water spreads electrical fires, and that helium is heavier than air when it is cooled below a certain temperature.

Facts and Group Membership

What, then, is a "fact"? The definition proposed here is based on the perception that societies tend to construct reality rather than receive it in a finished, predetermined form. Consequently, a "fact" is what a majority of people (as members of a given group) agree to call a "fact" *until they have some reason not to*. In everyday conversation, it suffices to say that the distance from San Francisco to New York City is 3,000 miles. Most people tacitly accept this as an accurate figure. Indeed, many of the accepted facts of a given group are based on tacit agreement. For a map maker, however, this measurement is not accurate enough, so he or she has reason to disagree with the proposal that the distance from San Francisco to New York City is 3,000 miles. For a map maker, this figure just is not a fact. By the same token, $3 + 4 = 7$ is a "fact," but only so long as people tacitly agree to work with a base-10 number system.

Just because facts are not always provable, measurable, or true doesn't mean that people can label whatever they want to a "fact." For example, opinions, omens, and conclusions are not facts. Why not?

Perhaps with the exception of polls, opinions are limited to individuals or small groups.[1] They also are personal views that usually cannot be substantiated by independent means. A person may think that her college basketball team is Number 1, but that doesn't mean it is. Another person may believe that hamburgers taste better than hot dogs, but individual taste is so variable that it can't be deemed a fact. Yet another person may believe that a boss, a politician, a criminal, or a bureaucrat is the meanest, most detestable person on earth, but chances are high that somewhere that person has a loving, devoted friend or relative.

Omens are not facts for pretty much the same reason: They are individual signs that are read differently by different people. I had a maternal grandmother, for example, who believed that the appearance of a crow in the front yard signaled that someone was going to die. Imagine my confusion (and dismay) when my paternal grandmother insisted that a crow in the front yard signaled that the house was blessed with good luck!

Individual conclusions generally are not facts either but rather interpretations of reality. For example, accountants often tell the following joke: If you ask the man or woman on the street how much 2 + 3 equals, the answer is always 5. If you ask an account, the answer is "How much do you want it to be?" Or consider that before the Copernican revolution a person might reasonably conclude that the heavens revolved around the earth. The lesson to be learned here is that just because you believe something is a fact doesn't make it so. Part of becoming a critical thinker involves having healthy skepticism about most things.

Diverse Voices

What counts as fact varies significantly from culture to culture. For example, large numbers of Japanese, perhaps a majority, believe in ghosts. Ghosts are facts for them. Consider some of the facts that are particular to your home culture. How are they different from American cultural facts? How are they similar? What is the basis for their factual nature?

Try writing a few paragraphs that describe one or more of your cultural facts. Share the writing with your groupmates to stimulate a discussion about how membership in a community can shape and influence what people label as facts and what they do not.

---

[1]Opinion polls might be described more accurately as attitude surveys. They generally measure the attitudes of people toward a political candidate or a consumer product, for example. It is important to keep in mind, however, that even national opinion polls are based on fewer than 2,000 people in nearly every instance. The poll takers then use statistical procedures to generalize from this small group to a larger one.

Applying Key Ideas

AGREEING ON FACTS

This activity gives you an opportunity to consider the characteristics of facts. Reporting information commonly requires a quick evaluation of *proposed* facts to determine whether they are or are not actually facts. This determination is based on the criteria listed on page 126.

For this activity, draw up a list of five things you consider "facts." Then team up with three or four classmates. Take turns reading each list aloud. After the last person is finished, read each list aloud once more. This time, however, the group should try to reach a consensus on every item. Which is actually a "fact"? Delete those items that the majority could not agree were "facts."

Next, write one or two paragraphs that explain what you learned from this activity.

Presenting Facts in a Report

Presenting facts is central to what reports of information are about, but writers cannot present facts the same way in every report. Different audiences impose different conventions. Also, the goals of a text and the writer's rhetorical stance as insider or outsider have a significant influence. For example, an insider-to-insider stance requires more facts than an insider- or outsider-to-outsider stance. A report of information for outsiders will rely on *summary* rather than on in-depth presentation of details.

Sources of Facts

The *source* of the facts in a report varies by discourse community. Writers in the sciences and social sciences, including business, obtain their facts from observation and experimentation as well as from published documents. Observations of children and their families, for instance, have shown that children develop language that is similar but not identical to their parents'. In psychology and linguistics, these observations constitute a fact. Marketing surveys have indicated that buyers from the low end of the socioeconomic scale have greater "brand loyalty" than buyers from the high end. In marketing, the results of these surveys are deemed to be fact. Writers in the humanities, however, obtain their facts almost exclusively from documents. In Mark Twain's *Huckleberry Finn*, Huck forges a strong friendship with the runaway slave, Jim, and in Herman Melville's *Moby Dick* Captain Ahab is obsessed with a certain white whale: These are facts.

IDENTIFYING THE AIM OF YOUR REPORT

Writing *does* something. It has aims that link the writer, the text, and the audience in important and interesting ways. Although any given text is likely to have multiple aims, we usually recognize that it has one *primary aim*, whether it be to inform, evaluate, argue, persuade, teach, or entertain. Two principal aims that we commonly see in reports of information are *teaching* and *action*.

Moving from the known to the unknown gives readers new knowledge, new information. This is the *teaching* aim. Reports of information also provide readers a foundation for making *a decision to do something or not to do something*. For example, an executive may use a sales report as the basis for modifying a company's advertising, or Congress may use an Environmental Protection Agency report on air quality to develop legislation regulating automobile emissions. The primary aim of such reports is *action*.

SUMMARIZING INFORMATION

Facts are particular and concrete; in a report they are *factual details*. But few reports of information consist exclusively of factual details. Those that do, such as some kinds of legal documents and financial statements, conform to quite specific conventions. In most writing situations, effective writers present some factual details and some *summary*, varying the two to make the work textured, more interesting, and easier to read.

The following excerpts illustrate the effective use of summary in conjunction with factual details. Passage 1 was written by Jill, a sophomore enrolled in a biology class. Students had been studying a unit on reproduction, and their lab work was intended to supplement readings and lectures about reproductive mechanisms. Jill's experiment was designed to study reproduction in sea urchins, and it focused on the effects of time on motility[2] and fertilization:

Passage 1: Alternating Between Summary and Detail within a Sentence

The fresh sperm samples examined under the microscope exhibited a high degree of motility; these active sperm combined with all of the fresh eggs in the field of view within 90 seconds.

---

[2]*Motility* is a term often used in biology; it means that an organism is capable of spontaneous, self-propelled motion.

The underlined part of the sentence summarizes information. Jill generalizes that the sperm "exhibited a high degree of motility," without specifying what a "high degree" is or how it was measured. The second part of the sentence, however, balances the summary with a specific fact that makes her general statement about motility concrete: The sperm were so motile that they combined with all eggs "within 90 seconds." (Note that the accuracy of Jill's measurement is not an issue here. Whether the time involved was actually 89, 90, or 91 seconds is irrelevant. What matters is that the specific time supports the general observation of "high degree of motility." If the time had been 3 hours, of course, the fact would not support the general statement.)

Passage 2 illustrates a similar technique. It comes from an article published in a professional journal. The author was investigating the kinds of comments ninth-grade students in English classes provide one another when involved in group activities. The passage deals with how students discussed the "substance" of their writing:

Passage 2: Alternating Between Summary and Detail within a Paragraph

Students also spent some of their time straightforwardly responding, discussing the substance of their writing as the sheets directed.[3] Given that both Glass and Peterson[4] designed the sheets to stimulate the students to spend their group time in this way, students devoted relatively few of the sampled episodes to this kind of discussion. As Table 3 reveals, only 24% of the episodes in Peterson's class and 18% in Glass's fell into this category. (Sarah W. Freedman, 71–107.)

Notice that the first sentence summarizes information, stating that students "spent some of their time" discussing substance, but the writer does not specify how much time. The second sentence also provides summary, informing the audience that students "devoted relatively" little of their discussion to substance. In the last sentence, however, the writer shifts from these generalizations to provide specific facts about the number of episodes related to substance: 24% in one class and 18% in the other.

The next passage illustrates how alternating between summary and factual details can extend across paragraphs. It comes from a friend, Scott, who used to write reports for a financial consulting firm.

Passage 3: Alternating Between Summary and Detail across Paragraphs

San Jose began shedding its agricultural economic base during the 1950s, and the result was an increase in the number of white-collar workers aged 25–35. The number of inhabitants over the age of 60 began to decline, and the number of inhabitants over 60 with annual incomes greater than $100,000 dropped sharply.

By 1965, the shift toward a computer-based economy had accelerated significantly. Donnelly Marketing reports that the median household income had risen from $9,000 a year in 1960 to $15,000 in 1965. Meanwhile, the average age continued to decline as the population grew by 35 percent over the same period. From 1955 to 1965, it fell from 37 to 28.

---

[3]These were response sheets that their teachers gave students to help guide the activity.
[4]Glass and Peterson were the two teachers involved in the study.

The first paragraph is summary, even though it presents some numbers. These numbers are not linked to concrete information. The first sentence, for example, tells us that the number of white-collar workers between the ages of 25 and 35 increased, but it does not tell us *how much* of an increase occurred. The same is true of the statement about the drop in the number of inhabitants over age 60 with incomes greater than $100,000. We do not have any specific information regarding the extent of this drop. The second paragraph, on the other hand, does present factual details, although the first sentence is summary. The next sentence tells us that household incomes rose from $9,000 to $15,000 between 1960 and 1965; these are factual details. Notice that the third sentence summarizes information that the last sentence makes specific—"From 1955 to 1965, it [the average age] fell from 37 to 28."

Being able to shift easily from summary to details, from the general to the specific and back again, is a hallmark of an effective writer. But before you apply this technique in your own writing, you may want to practice recognizing the difference between the two, which will help you understand how they are used together when reporting information.

Applying Key Ideas

RECOGNIZING SHIFTS BETWEEN SUMMARY AND FACTUAL DETAIL

This activity is intended to give you an opportunity to practice differentiating between summary and detail. It also gives you an opportunity to transfer to your own writing the skills you are developing from the analysis of models.

For the first part of the activity, select four published texts from different disciplines, such as articles from professional journals and textbooks for your classes. You may even use this textbook, if you like. Examine five consecutive paragraphs in each and identify summaries and details. Remember that summary is general, whereas detail is specific. How are summary and detail used differently in the various texts? Can you arrive at any useful generalizations? Here's a hint for the last question: Examine summary and detail in the context of what each selection is *trying to do*. Write a couple of paragraphs that describe the results of your examination.

For the second part of this activity, use two of your own papers. Identify the places where you provided summary and where you provided detail. How does your use differ from what you observed in the published texts? How would you characterize the factual details in your writing? Write a couple of paragraphs describing the results of your analysis.

Diverse Voices

Some cultures stress modesty and self-effacement. As a result, writers from these cultures tend to feel uncomfortable expressing their own views or interpretations, so they rely almost entirely on summary when writing a report of information. Adjusting to American expectations of a strong personal voice can be difficult.

Perhaps you have experienced this difficulty or know someone who has. This activity has two parts: First, in a few paragraphs, try to summarize your experience or that of a friend in adjusting to American expectations of a strong personal voice; second, explain what these different expectations mean for you as a student in a U.S. college.

Deciding What to Summarize

When deciding between summarizing information or reporting it in detail, keep in mind that information ought to be ranked in the order of its importance. Information of less importance should be summarized, whereas information of more importance should be presented in detail. But how do successful writers know which information is important and which isn't? Summary involves putting someone else's ideas or information into your own words. Any decisions related to summarizing must take into account not only what *you* consider important but also what *your readers* might consider important. Once again, draw on the connection between your experiences and knowledge and the community of insiders you want to join.

Effective writers regularly use cues to signal what is important. When reading a text that contains information you plan to report, you can use these cues to help you decide what to summarize. Of course, you also should use them in your writing to provide the same cues to readers. Some of the more visible cues are:

- Italicizing key words or points
- Setting key ideas off with numbers or bullets
- Providing subheadings to mark important divisions
- Using words such as *truly, actually, most important*, and so on to emphasize key concepts
- Telling readers, "This information is important"

REPORTS OF INFORMATION THAT AIM TO TEACH

Many reports aim to teach, and usually they involve providing information to outsiders. But in classroom assignments, the distinction between teaching and learning can be blurred. For example, professors may assign a report of information as a teaching tool; you write the report and learn something in the process. The audience (the teacher) is an insider, not an outsider. Thus, there can be an underlying aim that is implicit in the work but that is not figured into common rhetorical concerns.

Summary Reports: Outsiders to Insiders

Students frequently have to read a book or article and summarize the contents in two pages or less. The resulting reports require a rhetorical stance of outsider to insider because they have many of the features of a test. Although the writer's rhetorical aim may be to teach something about the material, the writer's underlying goal is to demonstrate to the teacher that he or she has read and understood the material. Teachers commonly use such reports as a means of judging who has the potential to join a given community.

This kind of report involves few detailed facts, and occasionally it does not involve any at all. Instead, it relies on summary, which is why it often is referred to as *summary report*. (Some teachers use the term *précis*.) A key to writing a successful summary report lies not only in skillful reading but also in being able to condense the information and present it in very few words. Listed here are some of the more important kinds of information that summary reports of books and essays include:

1. The title of the work and the name of the author
2. The topic
3. The author's rhetorical purpose
4. The thesis statement
5. Details that support the thesis
6. The author's conclusion

A summary report of a poem, a play, or a work of fiction, might include the following features:

7. Statement of the theme, or underlying message, of the work
8. Examples of language, images, dialogue, or narrative that illustrate the theme

The following examples illustrate these guidelines being applied. The first comes from Hiro, a first-year student who was asked to write a summary report about an excerpt from Martin Luther King Jr.'s book *Stride Toward Freedom*. As you read, notice how Hiro explicitly links King to the information he is summarizing.

Passage 4: Summary Report of a Book

In the excerpt from *Stride Toward Freedom*, Martin Luther King defines his view of nonviolent resistance. He states that his philosophy is based on six important points: 1) It is a form of spiritual resistance; 2) It doesn't seem to defeat but to gain understanding; 3) It does not direct its efforts against people but against institutions and evil; 4) It involves accepting punishment for resistance; 5) It is both physically and spiritually nonviolent; and 6) It maintains that good will always ultimately triumph over evil. In the process of defining his philosophy of nonviolence, King says that he also is developing a way of living. The principles of nonviolence, according to King, should be part of every day's activities, not simply part of resistance to racism.

This is a good summary because it includes several of the features listed above. In the first sentence, Hiro offers a thesis for *Stride Toward Freedom*: It defines King's "view of nonviolent resistance." Equally important, Hiro identifies the title of the book and the author, critical pieces of information for a summary report. He then succinctly lists six points that appear to summarize the position that King takes in the book. Notice that Hiro clearly attributes the points to King so that readers understand that these are King's ideas, not his. The last sentence in the paragraph provides a nice summary conclusion, for it provides a statement that is both informative (telling readers an important part of King's views) and moving—"the principles of nonviolence . . . should be part of every day's activities."

Some of the more challenging summary reports of information involve literature assignments. Unlike other types of writing, literature often conveys meaning implicitly rather than explicitly, requiring you to read carefully and to make an extra effort to see beyond surface appearances. Nevertheless, a summary report on a work of literature should include the features that were listed in the guide on page 134. The following passage offers an example. It comes from Amy, a sophomore whose teacher asked her to write a summary report of a poem, shown here, by Elizabeth Browning:

Passage 5: Summary Report of a Poem

How do I love thee? Let me count the ways.
I love thee to the depth and breadth and height
My soul can reach, when feeling out of sight
For the ends of Being and ideal Grace.
I love thee to the level of every day's   5
Most quiet need, by sun and candlelight.
I love thee freely, as men strive for Right;
I love thee purely, as they turn from Praise;
I love thee with the passion put to use
In my old griefs, and with my childhood's faith.   10
I love thee with a love I seemed to lose
With my lost saints—I love thee with the breath,
Smiles, tears of all my life!—and, if God choose,
I shall but love thee better after death.

This poem is about love, and it comes from Elizabeth Barrett Browning's *Sonnets from the Portuguese*. It provides a list of the various ways the poet feels love, and it strives to show that the emotion elevates the poet. For example, love is connected to noble ideas such as justice [line 7] and spiritual aspiration [lines 9–12]. At the same time, however, the poem links the feeling of love to simple pleasures and needs— the warmth of the sun by day and the comfort of candlelight by night [line 6]. The poem suggests that the love the poet feels will last forever. In fact, the last line suggests that the love will become stronger after death.

Notice that Amy's summary report is brief. This point is important because it allows us to make a simple distinction between a summary report and a literary interpretation. Literary interpretations, discussed in chapter 12, usually are longer than a paragraph or two, and they do more than summarize the basic features of a text. They analyze the features very closely and develop and support a thesis. A summary report may offer an interpretation, but it does not provide much detailed support.

Amy provides three critical pieces of information in her first sentence: the theme of the poem, the author's name, and the work in which it appears. She then refines them via an interpretation—the poem "strives to show that the emotion [of love] elevates the poet." Amy provides factual details from the poem to support her interpretation, details that are linked to the poem's theme, and she successfully focuses on the conclusion of the poem, stating that "love will become stronger after death." This part of the summary would have been stronger if Amy had mentioned the way the last line reinforces the spiritual nature of the poem as a whole. Nevertheless, Amy's summary report is well written and effective.

Summary Reports: Outsiders and Insiders to Outsiders

The less readers know about a subject, the harder it is for them to process facts. People writing for an audience of outsiders therefore tend to limit the quantity of facts they present. They rely significantly on summary, often synthesizing vast amounts of information to produce a text that people without expertise can read easily. An important characteristic of such reports is that they explicitly aim to help readers understand the subject or topic better.

Popular books and articles about specialized subjects—science, psychology, architecture, and so forth—are written for outsiders. They rely on summary reporting because the audience of outsiders cannot be expected to understand the intricate factual details of the subjects. The passage below illustrates this principle. It comes from a book called *Chaos*, by James Gleick. Chaos theory investigates turbulence. Highly mathematical, it owes much of its development to the study of special kinds of shapes called *fractals*. If, for example, you take an equilateral triangle and in the middle of each side attach an identical triangle one third the size of the original, and then repeat this process infinitely, you will have a fractal, shown in Fig. 5.1. Fractals, then, are shapes that duplicate an initial shape on a progressively smaller scale. (A curious characteristic of fractals is that, theoretically, they allow for a line of infinite length in a finite space.) The study of fractals is called *fractal geometry*, and it involves the study of scale. The following passage is a report on fractal geometry.

Passage 6: Fractal Geometry

James Gleick

1   *How big is it? How long does it last?* These are the most basic questions a scientist can ask about a thing. They are so basic to the way people conceptualize the world that it is not easy to see that they imply a certain bias. They suggest that size and duration, qualities that depend on scale, are qualities with meaning, qualities that can help describe an object or classify it. When a biologist describes a human being, or a physicist describes a quark, *how big* and *how long* are indeed appropriate questions. In their gross physical structure, animals are very much tied to a particular scale. Imagine a human being scaled up to twice its size, keeping all proportions the same, and you imagine a structure whose bones will collapse under its weight. Scale is important.

2   The physics of earthquake behavior is mostly independent of scale. A large earthquake is just a scaled-up version of a small earthquake. That distinguishes earthquakes from animals, for example—a ten-inch animal must be structured quite differently from a one-inch animal, and a hundred-inch animal needs a different architecture still, if its bones are not to snap under the increased mass. Clouds, on the other hand, are scaling phenomena like earthquakes. Their characteristic irregularity—describable in terms of fractal dimension—changes not at all as they are observed on different scales. That is why air travelers lose all perspective on how far away a cloud is. Without help from cues such as haziness, a cloud twenty feet away can be indistinguishable from two thousand feet away. Indeed, analysis of satellite pictures has shown an invariant fractal dimension in clouds observed from hundreds of miles away.

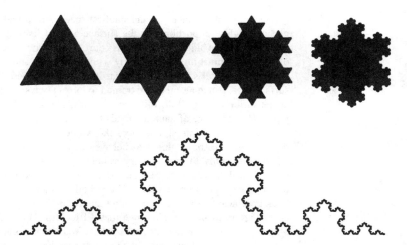

THE KOCH SNOWFLAKE. "A rough but vigorous model of a coastline," in Mandelbrot's words. To construct a Koch curve, begin with a triangle with sides of length 1. At the middle of each side, add a new triangle one-third the size; and so on. The length of the boundary is 3 x 4/3 x 4/3 x 4/3 . . .—infinity. Yet the area remains less than the area of a circle drawn around the original triangle. Thus an infinitely long line surrounds a finite area.

FIG. 5.1.   A simple fractal shape.

3   It is hard to break the habit of thinking of things in terms of how big they are and how long they last. But the claim of fractal geometry is that, for some elements of nature, looking for a characteristic scale becomes a distraction. *Hurricane*. By definition, it is a storm of a certain size. But the definition is imposed by people on nature. In reality, atmospheric scientists are realizing that tumult in the air forms a continuum, from the gusty swirling of litter on a city street corner to the vast cyclonic systems visible from space. Categories mislead. The ends of the continuum are of a piece with the middle.

4   It happens that the equations of fluid flow are in many contexts dimensionless, meaning that they apply without regard to scale. Scaled-down airplane wings and ship propellers can be tested in wind tunnels and laboratory basins. And, with some limitations, small storms act like large storms.

5   Blood vessels, from aorta to capillaries, form another kind of continuum. They branch and divide and branch again until they become so narrow that blood cells are forced to slide through single file. The nature of their branching is fractal. Their structure resembles one of the monstrous imaginary objects conceived by Mandelbrot's turn-of-the-century mathematicians. As a matter of physiological necessity, blood vessels must perform a bit of dimensional magic. Just as the Koch curve, for example, squeezes a line of infinite length into a small area, the circulatory system must squeeze a huge surface area into a limited volume. In terms of the body's resources, blood is expensive and space is at a premium. The fractal structure nature has devised works so efficiently that, in most tissue, no cell is ever more than three or four cells away from a blood vessel. Yet the vessels and blood take up little space, no more than about five percent of the body. It is, as Mandelbrot put it, the Merchant of Venice Syndrome—not only can't you take a pound of flesh without spilling blood, you can't take a milligram.

6   This exquisite structure—actually, two interwining trees of veins and arteries—is far from exceptional. The body is filled with such complexity. In the digestive tract, tissue reveals undulations within undulations. The lungs, too, need to pack the

greatest possible surface into the smallest space. An animal's ability to absorb oxygen is roughly proportional to the surface area of its lungs. Typical human lungs pack in a surface bigger than a tennis court. As an added complication, the labyrinth of windpipes must merge efficiently with the arteries and veins.

7   Every medical student knows that lungs are designed to accommodate a huge surface area. But anatomists are trained to look at one scale at a time—for example, at the millions of alveoli, microscopic sacs, that end the sequence of branching pipes. The language of anatomy tends to obscure the unity *across* scales. The fractal approach, by contrast, embraces the whole structure in terms of the branching that produces it, branching that behaves consistently from large scales to small. Anatomists study the vasculatory system by classifying blood vessels into categories based on size—arteries and arterioles, veins and venules. For some purposes, those categories prove useful. But for others they mislead. Sometimes the textbook approach seems to dance around the truth: "In the gradual transition from one type of artery to another it is sometimes difficult to classify the intermediate region. Some arteries of intermediate caliber have walls that suggest larger arteries, while some large arteries have walls like those of medium-sized arteries. The transitional regions . . . are often designated arteries of mixed type."

8   Not immediately, but a decade after Mandelbrot published his physiological speculations, some theoretical biologists began to find fractal organization controlling structures all through the body. The standard "exponential" description of bronchial branching proved to be quite wrong; a fractal description turned out to fit the data. The urinary collecting system proved fractal. The biliary duct in the liver. The network of special fibers in the heart that carry pulses of electric current to the contracting muscles. The last structure, known to heart specialists as the His-Purkinje network, inspired a particularly important line of research. Considerable work on healthy and abnormal hearts turned out to hinge on the details of how the muscle cells of the left and right pumping chambers all manage to coordinate their timing. Several chaos-minded cardiologists found that the frequency spectrum of heartbeat timing, like earthquakes and economic phenomena, followed fractal laws, and they argued that one key to understanding heartbeat timing was the fractal organization of the His-Purkinje network, a labyrinth of branching pathways organized to be self-similar on smaller and smaller scales.

9   How did nature manage to evolve such complicated architecture? Mandelbrot's point is that the complications exist only in the context of traditional Euclidean geometry. As fractals, branching structures can be described with transparent simplicity, with just a few bits of information. Perhaps the simple transformations that gave rise to the shapes devised by Koch, Peano, and Sierpiński have their analogue in the coded instructions of an organism's genes. DNA surely cannot specify the vast number of bronchi, bronchioles, and alveoli or the particular spatial structure of the resulting tree, but it can specify a repeating process of bifurcation and development. Such processes suit nature's purposes. When E. I. DuPont de Nemours & Company and the United States Army finally began to produce a synthetic match for goose down, it was by finally realizing that the phenomenal air-trapping ability of the natural product came from the fractal nodes and branches of down's key protein, keratin. Mandelbrot glided matter-of-factly from pulmonary and vascular trees to real botanical trees, trees that need to capture sun and resist wind, with fractal branches and fractal leaves. And theoretical biologists began to speculate that fractal scaling was not just common but universal in morphogenesis. They argued that understanding how such patterns were encoded and processed had become a major challenge to biology.

This passage is part of a larger work, so there is not much delineation of introduction, body, and conclusion. It has implicit connections to other parts of the book and is building on what has come before. References to Mandelbrot, a well-known mathematician, depend on earlier chapters. It is clear that the passage is intended to report information about a very complex topic in a way that people without mathematical knowledge can understand. We would expect great reliance on summary, and Gleick meets our expectations. The first three sentences of paragraph 1, for example, summarize scientific endeavor by condensing it to answering two basic questions.

Gleick also concentrates a great deal on *explaining* the information he presents. In the first paragraph, he writes that "size" and "duration" are important qualities in science because they are meaningful. He then offers an example to illustrate why they are meaningful: A human being twice the normal size would collapse under his or her own weight. This example offers an easy segue into the discussion of *scale*, which is the real focus of this section.

But note how Gleick continues in the same vein after beginning the discussion of scale. He uses summary in paragraph 2 to inform us that some phenomena are dependent on scale, whereas others are not. (If Gleick did not summarize here, he would have to make specific references to research on the subject.) Then he offers an example to help *explain* what this means in practical terms. Earthquakes and clouds are independent of scale, but animals are dependent (paragraph 2). As a result, the size of animals is related to their structure, but the size of a cloud is not related to its structure, which leads to a loss of perspective when flying.

The previous discussion emphasizes the goal of explaining for a reason. When you are writing a summary report of information for outsiders, the existing convention requires you to make a special effort to help the audience understand what the information means. Such reports have a strong interpretive purpose. Consequently, if you summarize the information but do not provide an interpretation, your readers are likely to feel that you have failed them. They will not be able to relate the information you present to their own lives, which is likely to affect their understanding. This point is important. *Just as you use your own experiences and knowledge to participate in discourse communities, as a writer you must provide ways for readers to use their experiences and knowledge to interact with your writing.*

The technique Gleick uses in this passage is very effective and offers a good model for your own work. He balances the abundance of summary with concrete examples that outsiders can understand. The summary also is balanced with interpretation when it is necessary to explain what certain concepts mean. As a result, this passage nicely illustrates the role interpretation plays in conveying information. Especially effective is the way Gleick uses metaphorical imagery to connect the known and the unknown, as when he states in paragraph 6 that human lungs "pack in a surface area bigger than a tennis court." Few people have seen human lungs, except, perhaps, in pictures, but nearly everyone has seen a tennis court. The image is provocative.

In addition, Gleick periodically shifts from the generalizations of summary to specific facts, as in paragraph 7: "Anatomists are trained to look . . . at the millions of alveoli, microscopic sacs, that end the sequence of branching pipes." When he makes these shifts, however, he is careful to avoid losing readers through unfamiliar technical terminology. The modifying phrase "microscopic sacs" defines "alveoli" for readers so they do not have to search through a dictionary. Overall, the technique builds on what readers already know. It relates new information to commonplace experiences, such as earthquakes, clouds, storms, and tennis courts.

# *Writing Assignment*

SUMMARIZING INFORMATION

The next passage, which comes from the book *Preparing to Teach Writing*, presents information about the relation between language and the way people think. Your task in this assignment is to write a report that summarizes what the passage is about, that identifies its argument, and that discusses how the author supports that argument.

James D. Williams

1   The idea that language influences cognition is very appealing to composition specialists. Known as *linguistic relativism* among linguists and psychologists, this idea emerged around the turn of the century when French anthropologist Lévy-Bruhl published *Les fonctions mentales dans les sociétés inférierures* in 1910. The English translation, *How Natives Think*, was published in 1926. Although successful as a sociologist early in his academic career, Lévy-Bruhl felt that his work was too theoretical, too removed from the realities of the everyday existence of mankind. He began anthropological investigations after questioning the widely accepted view that the human mind functions the same regardless of time or culture. He then set out to study mental operations in the remotest regions of Africa to determine what, if any, differences existed between the cognition of Europeans and tribal peoples.

2   In *How Natives Think*, Lévy-Bruhl argued that his field studies showed great differences between the cognitive operations of the two groups. The tribal subjects he studied proved to be prelogical, which did not mean that they were incapable of logical operations but that they were indifferent to logical contradictions that arose from their failure to identify myths and mystical experiences as unreal. They were, however, incapable of abstract concept formation above a rudimentary type associated with mystical experiences. That is, the primitives in his research might look at a tree and recognize it as a tree without any consideration of the classification of that tree as a member of a broader group of living plants.

3   Lévy-Bruhl was attacked soundly by other scholars for these conclusions. English anthropologists were particularly forceful in their rejection of the idea that different cultures produced different mentalities. Nevertheless, Lévy-Bruhl's work attracted the attention of enough scholars to gain a certain degree of intellectual legitimacy. More significant, his ideas received coverage in the media and led to a popular folk psychology about cross-cultural differences in cognition.

4   This folk psychology was reinforced in the United States through the work of Whorf (1956), an anthropological linguist who did extensive work with American Indian tribal languages during the 1920s and 30s and who was significantly influenced by the work of Lévy-Bruhl. Whorf proposed that linguistics was ideally suited to investigating cognition, owing to his belief that all thought was verbal. Whorf noted that "the Hopi language is seen to contain no words, grammatical forms, constructions, or expressions that refer directly to what we call 'time,' or to past, present or future" (p. 57). On this basis, he proposed that the absence of time gave Hopi speakers a sense of reality far different from "classical Newtonian physics" (p. 58), and he linked this different reality to the sort of observations that Lévy-Bruhl had made earlier about the prelogical quality of tribal cognition. Thus Hopi, and by extrapolation all languages, creates not only a certain model of reality but also a certain way of thinking unique to that language. . . .

5   Although Whorf's work has always been well known among linguists, it never stirred much interest among those working in composition studies. This role fell to Vygotsky, a Russian psychologist and contemporary of Piaget whose observations of child behavior during the late 1920s and early 1930s were unknown in America until the 1960s, when his books were translated into English. These works have provided composition specialists with a significant theoretical framework for the idea that language influences cognition. Especially influential has been *Thought and Language*, the last book Vygotsky wrote before his death in 1934. . . .

6   It was Olson (1977), however, who perhaps most influenced composition specialists. Olson used Vygotsky's theoretical framework to explain the differences in academic achievement he observed among students from diverse linguistic backgrounds. He argued that speech is fundamentally different from writing in several important ways. In his view, they don't use similar mechanisms for conveying meaning: In speech, *meaning* is derived from the shared intentions and context of speaker and hearer, whereas in writing, *meaning* resides in the text itself at the sentence level and has to be extracted by readers. Olson stated that writing has "no recourse to shared context . . . [because] sentences have to be understood in contexts other than those in which they were written" (p. 272). He went on to assert that human history has reflected an evolution from utterance to text that has profoundly affected cultural and psychological development.

7   These observations were consistent with folk theories about language as well as folk psychology. But more significant was Olson's additional argument that writing in general and the essay form in particular account for the development of abstract thought in human beings. Olson asserted that people in nonliterate cultures are incapable of abstract thought; he claimed that writing is the key to developing abstracting ability because it forces people to comprehend events outside their original context, which alters their perception of the world, which in turn leads to cognitive growth. Walters noted in this regard that Olson "is among the most extreme of those who link the conventions of a particular literate form—in his case, the essay—with logical thought as represented in written language" (p. 177). Yet it is difficult to differentiate Olson's claims from those put forward by Goody and Watt. Following Olson's (1977) lead, Ong (1978, 1982) took these ideas a step farther and claimed that "without writing . . . the mind simply cannot engage in [abstract] . . . thinking. . . . Without writing, the mind cannot even generate concepts such as 'history' or analysis" (p. 39).

8   These are powerful claims, and many teachers and scholars in the field have embraced them enthusiastically (see, for example, Dillon, 1981; Hirsch, 1977; Scinto, 1986; Shaughnessy, 1977) because they create an us–them dichotomy that can be used to explain why some students do not succeed in school. Followed to its logical end, this view suggests that children from backgrounds where written discourse is not stressed will have culture-specific cognitive deficiencies that make significant academic achievement essentially impossible. In addition, these claims validate the orientation of most writing teachers. If literacy affects the quality of thought in a positive way, it logically follows that the quality of literacy would bear directly on the quality of thought. Reading great works of literature therefore would have a more beneficial effect on thinking than reading a lab report or a corporate prospectus.

9   In Heath's (1983) research there was evidence of a strong social influence on language development that affected school achievement. To propose that the quality of mind is affected by the quality of language, whether oral or written, is to make a much stronger claim. The educational implications are clear-cut: People who do not read and write, and also probably those who do not read and write very well, must be simpleminded.

10   It is difficult not to find an element of elitism in this position, and some people may even see it as being ethnocentric, especially when writers like Scinto (1986) argue that written language is a "culturally heritable trait" (p. 171). Although there is no

doubt that literacy provides increased opportunities for social mobility in the United States and in most Western nations, there necessarily must be some question as to the specific culture in which written language appears as a heritable trait. In this pluralistic society, it is possible to speak of American culture in the abstract, but the United States simultaneously contains numerous subcultures—black, Hispanic, Asian, and American Indian, as well as the spectrum provided by socioeconomic status and recent, massive immigration—that simply do not place the same weight on writing that mainstream, upper-middle-class, Anglo-European culture does. The task of teaching most likely would be far easier if, indeed, written language were a "culturally heritable trait." In truth, however, children from mainstream and nonmainstream backgrounds alike find much school-sponsored reading and writing to be complex and baffling puzzles.

11   The criticism of linguistic relativism does not rest on such social and educational concerns. It is important to understand that the notion that writing exerts a cultural and psychological influence grew out of anthropological studies that attempted to explain why some cultures have reached a modern stage of development and why some have not (see Finnegan, 1970; Goody, 1968, 1972; Greenfield, 1972; Levi-Strauss, 1966; Lévy-Bruhl, 1975; Luria, 1976). In these studies, researchers gave a group of nonliterate, usually non-Western, subjects a task designed to measure cognitive abilities, then gave the same task to a group of literate, usually Western, subjects and compared the results. Colby and Cole (1976), for example, found that on tests of memory, nonliterate subjects from the Kpelle tribe in Africa performed far below the level of test subjects in the United States who were on average almost five years younger.

12   Similarly, Luria (1976) (who was a student of Vygotsky) found that the nonliterate subjects in his study had more difficulty categorizing and sorting objects than the literate subjects. The nonliterates' method of cognitive processing tended to be more concrete and situation-bound than the literates'. For example, Luria presented his subjects with pictures of a hammer, a saw, an ax, and a piece of lumber, then asked which object did not belong with the others. The literate subjects quickly identified the piece of lumber, because it, unlike the other objects, is not a tool. The nonliterate subjects, on the other hand, seemed unable to understand the question. They insisted that all the objects went together, because there was little use for a hammer, saw, and an ax if there was no lumber to use in making something.

13   From Luria's point of view, that of a psychologist trained in the Western tradition, this functional response was wrong, and he concluded that the nonliterate subjects had difficulty formulating abstract categories. This conclusion is remarkably similar to those proposed by Lévy-Bruhl. It may well be, however, that, as in the case of Piaget and Inhelder's (1969) mountains task, what was actually being tested had little to do with the ability to formulate abstract categories but had very much to do with understanding what the test was about. . . . Thus it is impossible to look at studies like Luria's and determine any causal relations involved because there is no way to know whether the results were influenced by literacy or by schooling. Furthermore, as a consequence of this conflation, the research generally fails to compare similar groups of subjects. In the case of Luria, the groups he compared were not merely literates and nonliterates but literates with schooling and nonliterates without. These factors led Scribner and Cole to state that such studies "fail to support the specific claims made for literacy's effects. . . . No comparisons were ever made between children with and children without a written language" (pp. 11–12). . . .

14   Further evidence against the idea that language influences cognition comes from studies of deaf children who have learned neither speech nor sign language. According to this view, such children either should have no thought at all or should have thought that is profoundly different from what is found in hearing children. Because it is difficult to evaluate cognitive processes without using language in some form,

studies of deaf children's intellectual abilities are often less than definitive. Nevertheless, certain conclusions have been widely accepted. After conducting a series of studies into cognitive development, Furth (1966) reported that "language does not influence development [among deaf children] in any direct, general way" (p. 160). Similarly, Rice and Kemper (1984) report that "deaf children's progress through the early Piagetian stages and structures is roughly parallel to that of hearing children" (p. 37).

15   The weight of the evidence against the idea that language influences cognition—at least the strong version—is so compelling that its most ardent contemporary advocates have quietly retreated somewhat from their earlier positions. Goody (1987), for example, criticized his paper with Watt for placing too much importance on the alphabet as a tool for elevating culture. Olson (1987) suggested that his claim regarding the salutary effects of the essay on cognition may have overstated the case. With both the cognition-influences-language and the language-influences-cognition views discredited among psychologists, what remains?

GROUP ACTIVITIES: SUMMARIZING INFORMATION

1. Pair up with another member of your work group. Review the list of cues on page 133 that writers use to signal what is important in a text. Go through the Williams excerpt together and highlight the cues you find. Use these cues to help you decide what the thesis is.

2. How does Williams support his thesis?

3. After you have finished Activities 1 and 2, share your findings and conclusions with the other members of your group. If there are different points of view, discuss them until you reach agreement on the author's thesis and how he supports it.

4. Produce a full draft of your report to share in class. Rather than teaming with a member of your group, however, you should team with a member of another group. Exchange papers and read the drafts carefully. After you finish, answer the following questions:

- Does the report identify and explain the thesis?
- Does the report analyze any of the ways Williams supports his thesis?
- Is the report accurate?
- What is the most insightful part of the report?

REPORTS OF INFORMATION THAT LEAD TO ACTION

Reports that lead to action commonly are produced in government and business. In government, a report can lead to any number of actions: EPA uses them to develop environmental policies; Congress uses them to set budget priorities; towns use them to determine whether they should annex unincorporated land.

In business, executives often use the information in reports to make decisions. Business reports generally are intended to help solve a problem or answer a question. Although such reports frequently provide a recommendation, not all do. Some merely present the information and explain what it means, which allows management to do what it will with the data. Passage 3 on page 131 was part of a longer report that does not make a recommendation. Passage 7 contains more of this report.

In the early 1980s, the writer worked for a financial consulting firm that helped wealthy investors start savings and loan companies. Part of his job was to produce marketing reports that described the economic and demographic characteristics of towns and communities identified as potential sites for these new S&Ls. The reports examined the cost of housing, the age of residents in the community, their incomes, the proximity of other financial institutions, and so on, without offering any recommendations regarding the suitability of any given site for an S&L. The economists who ran the firm used these reports to interpret the information and make recommendations to investors. The action that resulted from the reports was the decision to open or not to open a savings and loan in a particular community.

Passage 7: The Changing Demographics of San Jose

1   San Jose began shedding its agricultural economic base during the 1950s, and the result was an increase in the number of white-collar workers aged 25–35. The number of inhabitants over the age of 60 began to decline, and the number of inhabitants over 60 with annual incomes greater than $100,000 dropped sharply.

2   By 1965, the shift toward a computer-based economy had accelerated significantly. Donnelly Marketing reports that the median household income had risen from $9,000 a year in 1960 to $15,000 in 1965. Meanwhile, the average age continued to decline: From 1955 to 1965, it fell from 37 to 28.

3   The next 10 years saw a twelve-fold increase in the number of computer and electronics firms in and around San Jose. The population rose from 155,000 to 463,000, although only 36 percent of this increase can be attributed directly to economic growth. The remainder was the result of immigration from Asia and Mexico.

4   Such rapid growth owing to immigration makes it difficult to obtain an accurate picture of the proposed market without describing two distinct populations: The professional class associated with the computer industry and the growing financial center; and the working and welfare classes associated with immigration. (The working class consists of skilled, semiskilled, and unskilled persons who are not employed in an office.)

5   Among the professionals, the number of inhabitants with a college degree increased from 4 percent to 23 percent by 1975. The average age increased to 30. Annual household incomes rose to $23,000, and the number of those making over $100,000 increased by 27 percent. Among the working and welfare classes, the number of persons with some college education decreased by 41 percent. The average age dropped to 21, owing to high birthrates in these groups. Annual household incomes in these groups was $9,500.

This reading selection is interesting for several reasons. For example, it begins the section on demographics, so the first paragraph sets the scene for this part of the report. Look closely at the first sentence, which establishes a cause–effect relation between the shift from an agricultural economic base and the increase in "white-collar workers aged 25–35." This relation underlies the demographic changes that are the focus of the entire section.

In addition, this selection illustrates an important difference between reports of events and reports of information, which was mentioned on page 125. It follows a chronology, and in a very real sense it is about events that occurred in San Jose during the period of the 1950s to the 1970s. Nevertheless, the report is not about individuals but rather about people in general.

Finally, this selection is rich in information. The writer provides specific facts about the demographic changes in San Jose, but he balances these facts with summary. Consider, for example, the last sentence in paragraph 2: "Meanwhile, the average age continued to decline: From 1955 to 1965, it fell from 37 to 28." The first part of this sentence is a summary statement, but it is supported by a factual detail, which is underlined.

The next passage illustrates how to include a recommendation in a report of information. It comes from "The Best Way to Fix Medicare," a *Time* essay written by Michael Kinsley. In this article, Kinsley reports on the financial problems this federally funded health care system faces. He then makes a recommendation for changing the existing system that he believes will reduce Medicare costs enough to keep the program from going bankrupt.

Passage 8: The Best Way to Fix Medicare

1   When the trustees of the Medicare trust fund released their annual report in April, the Republican leaders in Congress were shocked—shocked!—to learn that the fund is projected to run out of money in 2002. . . . This reaction was odd. The trustees issue a report every year, and never before has any leading politician, Republican or Democrat, expressed so much panic. This year's report actually showed an improvement over last year's, which projected that the trust fund would go bust in 2001. . . .

2   The first thing to get straight is this business about a "trust fund." It is an accounting myth. Like the trust fund for Social Security, the Medicare fund is "invested" in special government securities that are not counted as part of the national debt. Medicare's income and outlays are figured into each year's budget as if the trust fund didn't exist. Thus, as the government figures it, each dollar pruned from Medicare magically does double duty: it both saves a dollar for the trust fund *and* reduces the current year's deficit by a dollar. Furthermore, like the Social Security trust fund, the Medicare fund receives money from one group of people (currently workers) and pays out to a different group (retirees). And, like Social Security, Medicare pays current beneficiaries far more than they ever put in.

3   The trust fund covers only half of Medicare: hospitalization insurance, known as Part A. It is financed by a payroll tax—currently 2.9%, split between employee and employer. Part B, for doctor bills, is voluntary, but such a good deal that nearly everyone eligible signs up. Beneficiaries pay a premium—currently $46.10 a month—but this covers only 29% of the cost. The rest comes from general funds. In all, Medicare covers 37 million Americans (33 million senior citizens and 4 million disabled people) at a projected cost this year of $181 billion. . . .

4   [Although several options are being discussed to bring this extremely high expenditure under control, the only one that has any chance of really cutting costs without radically cutting benefits is a version of the "managed care" system.] [Currently,] Medicare is . . . the last bastion of traditional "fee-for-service" insurance, in which you are free to choose any doctor you want and have any treatment he or she recommends. . . . [For about a decade, Medicare] enrollees have had the option of joining an HMO [health maintenance organization], if one is available in their area. [HMOs exemplify what managed care is all about. They reduce the health-care choices enrollees can make, which in turn significantly reduces costs.]

5   It is too late to argue that it would be unfair to "railroad" Medicare patients into managed care against their will. Most of us are already in managed care, and few of

us had any choice about it: our employers put us there. Managed care can be excellent or terrible—it can achieve its savings by efficiency or by skimping on quality—but for almost everybody it is inevitable. The only question is how we get there.

6   The preferred route of many—including the American Medical Association, the conservative Heritage Foundation, the moderate-liberal Progressive Policy Institute and . . . the Republican congressional leadership—is so-called managed competition. Managed care is a type of health insurance; managed competition is a system for choosing *among* types of health insurance, including managed care.

7   In its purest form, managed competition would replace Medicare with a voucher good for the purchase of the health insurance of your choice. The government would lightly supervise the available choices. You could choose an HMO, a PPO, traditional fee-for-service medicine or whatever. If your choice cost more than the value of the voucher, you would pay the difference. If it cost less, you might get a rebate. Competition to sign you up is supposed to restrain prices and guarantee quality. The health-care system for federal employees works roughly like this, and it works well. Last year premiums actually went down. [Kinsley, 1993]

One reason that this excerpt is interesting is that it begins with the report of an event (paragraph 1). Reports of information often are not as engrossing as reports of events, so many writers whose audience—like Kinsley's—consists of outsiders feel that they need some way to hook readers in the first few lines. Starting a report of information with a report of an event can provide such a hook, and it seems to work fairly well in this article. Part of the success lies in the mocking tone that Kinsley adopts when mentioning Republicans, which we have to assume is all in good fun. Consider his statement that the "Republican leaders in Congress were shocked—shocked!—to lean that the fund is projected to run out of money in 2002." The repetition of "shocked" is amusing. Also, as he goes on to explain, this is old news: Everyone who pays attention to such things (and one would hope that members of Congress are in this group) has known for a decade or two that the nation's entire entitlement apparatus, from Social Security to Medicare and Medicaid, is teetering on the verge of collapse as the number of workers paying for the entitlements shrinks and the number of retirees on the dole increases.

Kinsley's catchy first paragraph and the first two sentences of the second also serve another purpose. The style is sharp, converstation-like, and knowledgeable. Kinsley clearly is adopting the role of the insider who is going to divulge the "truth" about Medicare to readers who are outside the bureaucracy that has so much control over their lives. The statement that "this business" about a trust fund is "an accounting myth" is likely to appeal to readers who, if poles are to be believed, increasingly view government as the enemy at worst and at best as an octopus built around myths of one kind or another that prevent politicians from serving the public good. In addition, having captured readers' attention with this tone, Kinsley is able to move into more difficult territory, where he actually starts reporting the information that he must convey if he is to make his recommendation. Readers will be prepared to work their way through the complexities of "Part A," "Part B," "HMOs," "managed care," and so forth to become privy to this insider information. This is very effective writing. We have to admire the skill with which Kinsley uses his rhetorical stance to draw readers into the text by essentially promising them insider secrets, even though we may feel uncomfortable with the fairly obvious manipulation it entails.

Because the factual details associated with Medicare are remarkably complex, Kinsley replies heavily on summary throughout his report. Much of this summary is intended to remind readers of what most of them already know.

READINGS

Patrick L. Courts

Patrick Courts teaches English and has published a number of works about teaching reading and writing. *Literacy and Empowerment*, the book from which the following passage comes, is intended for language arts teachers at various levels. Courts argues that America is not facing the sort of literacy crisis characterized in the ads we see on television for Project Literacy. The difficulty is not so much that large numbers of people cannot read and write but that large numbers are not taught how to use reading and writing to change (and improve) their everyday situations. In his view, the schools teach literacy as a means of maintaining the status quo, not as a way of making life better for those people at the low end of the socioeconomic scale. The passage below reports on teaching writing, and it presents some information about composition that you may find interesting.

PATRICK L. COURTS

LITERACY AND EMPOWERMENT: THE MEANING MAKERS

TEACHING WRITING

1 Possibly one of the least respected jobs in the average English department, including some of the most reputable English departments in the country, is the teaching of writing. Although much is said emphasizing the importance of the teaching of writing—presumably because print literacy is such an important skill for the educated person—one need examine the enterprise only briefly to see that the teaching of writing is not treated as an important endeavor. At large universities, freshman composition is taught by graduate assistants; usually they are students working on advanced degrees in English who must teach these courses in order to pay for their graduate experience and gain the degree that will eventually allow them to escape the drudgery of teaching composition. That these teachers are sometimes excellent is a fortunate accident; and they are, often, still young enough to believe that someone has rewarded them with the chance to teach anything.

2 At smaller universities and colleges, the situation is less easy to characterize. Some institutions believe that the activity is important and they still try to staff these courses with some of the best teachers in the departments. But more often than not, freshman composition courses are staffed either (1) by people who have advanced degrees in English but who are not expected to receive tenure, and who therefore are given enormous student loads in writing courses (guaranteeing that they will never have the time or energy to produce the mandatory publishing record for achieving tenure), or (2) by adjunct faculty—a pleasant-sounding title for people who are radically underpaid to do a difficult, exhausting job. Again, that some of these people work hard and do well has little to do with the message encoded in their treatment or in the treatment of the course.

3 The message is this: Freshman composition is something one tries to escape from teaching; those who cannot escape, teach freshman composition.

In the past, this denigrating outlook resulted almost entirely from the fact that the elite of the profession felt that composition was drudge-work that drudges should teach to drudges so that the elite might eventually teach the high culture bound within the great texts and turn the drudges into well-rounded college graduates. While it would be grossly unfair to suggest that such an attitude characterizes everyone in the profession, this kind of elitism still exists in many English departments.

4 In many cases under the present system, many teachers want to escape the freshman composition courses because they involve so much work. If you are teaching a writing course, especially if you are teaching it well, current research in pedagogy demands that the class be structured more like a workshop than like a traditional classroom. One is expected to create many and varied writing assignments, teach students to peer-edit one another's work, respond to the student writing regularly and clearly, direct students toward constructive change, confer with them individually or in small groups at regular intervals, encourage rewriting and respond to that, and find creative ways to grade so that students will feel free to explore and articulate what they have to say (write). The list goes on, but it is a good list. An enormous amount of fine work has been done over the last twenty years examining the nature of the writing process in young adults and the kinds of activities that assist them in becoming better writers (and, I would argue, better readers).

5 But the result has most often been that those who implement the good ideas suffer the most. Because the task is not shared among most members of a given English department, because the importance of good writing is honored more in the mandate than in the budget, because the literary heritage is more important than teaching students to use language to create the possibility of meaning, those who teach freshman composition well tend to be rewarded with more freshman composition courses, more students, more weekends spent reading and commenting on student papers, less time for conferencing with students, and little expectation for respect and less hope for tenure. The irony in all of this is that a careful examination of freshman composition courses and how they are taught does not reveal that writing is being taught badly—often quite the opposite. When one searches throughout the research and the academy to find out what has actually changed in the teaching of literacy, one finds that writing has received an enormous amount of constructive attention, which has resulted in better teaching. What is startling, however, is that these ideas still have not become a part of the mainstream teaching of literature and literacy in general. What is equally startling is that this single course, freshman composition, still bears the brunt of the responsibility for "fixing" all those illiterate kids who come to college.

6 What elementary school teacher has not heard the high school teachers lament, "If only those elementary school teachers were doing their jobs, we wouldn't have this problem"? What high school teacher has not heard the college professors hiss, "What the hell do they teach them in high school? They certainly don't teach them how to read and write!"? What professor of English has not heard a colleague in some other department contemptuously utter, "If you people were doing your job, these kids would know how to write correctly, and the rest of us wouldn't have to bother with this trivial stuff." (Remember Pat Buchanan and the agenda of not teaching kids to think, but teaching them to think correctly?) Even someone with Harry Truman's knowledge that "the buck stops here" must be amazed at how well educators pass it whenever they can.

7 Of course, one might respond with the apparently obvious comments. With all the good research and good teaching in the area of freshman composition, why hasn't the problem been solved? Ironically, the answer is this: One of the problems has been solved. As good teachers of writing know and have known for some years now, it is possible to teach students to improve their writing to the extent that most of them can produce clear, readable exposition, including a reasonable degree of mastery of the proprieties of usage and punctuation. What it takes to accomplish this radical and much-to-be-desired state of written literacy is simple to describe and possible to implement, but apparently too expensive for the system to bother about.

8 There are ten ingredients:

1. Teachers assist children in the production of their own stories.
2. Students begin to peer-edit and publish their work.
3. Students begin to share their cultural heritage through their stories.

4. Teachers and children establish a community of meaning makers.
5. Students write in a variety of modes for a variety of reasons.
6. Students begin to develop a conscious understanding of their own reasons for reading and writing.
7. Students begin to gain proficiency with the conventions of standard English.
8. Students and teachers transform classrooms.
9. Teachers introduce new and challenging content areas.
10. Steps one through nine create a demand for changes in teacher preparation.

Critical Reading Guide

1. Courts describes two approaches to teaching composition that are linked to the size of a college or university (paragraphs 1 and 2). Which description best fits your school? How does Courts present the description in a way that enables him to characterize all schools?

2. Courts speaks of "the message" (paragraph 3) encoded in the facts he reports. What are two such messages? Are these messages interpretations from fact? If so, are Courts' interpretations reasonable?

3. Find two places where Courts balances summary with a presentation of specific facts. What pattern do you detect in his use of these two forms of presentation?

4. At the end of this passage, Courts offers a list of "10 ingredients." Are the items on this list facts or interpretations? Why?

Journal Entry

Composition has been part of American higher education for more than a century. Reflecting on your own experience, what are some reasons our society asks college students to study composition?

John L. Casti

The next selection comes from John L. Casti's book *Paradigms Lost*. Casti has a PhD in mathematics, and over the years he has written numerous books on science and mathematics. *Paradigms Lost* is a survey of the important scientific questions that scholars and researchers are pursuing today, such as the nature of reality, the possibility of building computers that can think, and the influence of genes on human behavior. The book is intended for a general audience of nonspecialists, although it does require at least a nodding familiarity with the topics in the various fields discussed. The following passage comes from a chapter devoted to the question of life on other planets. In addressing this question, Casti considers the possibility of life-supporting planets in other star systems. Just how do habitable planets come to be?

f_p, The Fraction of Stars Having A Planetary System

1   In the process of stellar formation, a cloud of interstellar gases begins to contract due to gravitational attraction, changing from a slowly revolving amorphous blob into a rapidly spinning, pancake-shaped gaseous disk. Since the rate of spin is too great for the disk to remain stable, one of two things normally occurs: Either the disk flies apart into a few (usually two) more or less equal pieces, each of which then spins at a much slower rate, or the disk throws off a small fraction (1 to 2 percent) of its mass at a distance sufficiently far from the center of rotation that the small mass has a great enough lever arm to slow down the spin of the central disk. The reader will recognize this as the astrophysical equivalent of spinning ice skaters who suddenly throw out their arms to slow their rate of spin. The first case corresponds to the formation of a binary (or multiple) star system of the sort discussed above; the second represents the currently held view as to how planetary systems are formed. It should be noted, however, that these two processes may not be mutually exclusive, since calculations indicate that a habitable planetary system may form if the two stars of a binary system are far enough apart, say over 20 AU (1 AU equals the average distance between the Earth and the Sun). But conventional astronomical wisdom dictates that planetary systems and multiples are like oil and water: They usually don't mix.

2   Our own solar system is an example of the second kind of rotation-slowing process, in which about 1 percent of the original spinning mass was thrown off in the form of the planets (most of it in Jupiter and Saturn). During this process, though, about 99 percent of the angular momentum of the spinning cloud was transferred to the planets (again almost all to Jupiter and Saturn), leaving the central Sun with only a modest rate of spin, low enough to preserve its stability. Since our solar system is the only one of which we have

direct observational evidence, the question of interest for estimating f_p becomes: How typical is our own solar system? In other words, if a star does not form as part of a multiple system, is formation of a planetary system to be expected?

3   One line of attack on the planetary question is just to appeal to the Principle of Mediocrity and say that since our corner of the universe is nothing special, it's likely to be the case that planetary systems are common. Clearly, this is more of a philosophical or a religious argument than a scientific one, so to move beyond it we have two alternatives: direct observational evidence for extrasolar planetary systems, or stronger theoretical evidence to show how the formation of planetary systems fits into the normal process of star formation.

4   The difficulty with direct observation of a planet surrounding a nearby star is graphically described by imagining a birthday cake with a single candle placed next to the beacon atop the Eiffel Tower, and then trying to see the candle being blown out by looking at it from the Postal Tower in London. In short, the minuscule amount of light reflected by even a Jupiter-sized planet is totally buried in the more than billion-times-greater luminosity of the parent star. Thus at the moment the only feasible method of obtaining empirical evidence for planetary systems involves searching for small irregularities in the motion of the star due to the gravitational effects of its hypothetical invisible companions. The best candidate for such indirect detection of a planet appears to be the star 36 Ursae Majoris A, where wobbles in the star's orbit have been attributed to a Jupiter-sized planetary companion. However, these observations have been questioned on various grounds, and at the present time all that can be definitely said about observations of extrasolar planets is summed up in a remark by David Black to the 1984 International Astronomical Union Conference on SETI, noting that "there is currently no observational evidence for the existence of any planetary system other than our own." At the time it was expected

that the Hubble Space Telescope would provide the experimental muscle needed to resolve the matter, but the tragic *Challenger* accident delayed the planned 1986 launch of the telescope, leaving the experimental situation pretty much unchanged.

On the theoretical side, numerous computer simulations of the coalescence of the interstellar gas clouds have rather strongly suggested the likelihood of planetary systems' emerging over a wide range of initial conditions. Figure 6.2 is a simulation by Stephen Dole showing the kinds of planetary systems that emerge out of a homogeneous condensing stellar cloud of the same mass as our solar system, when various quantities of condensation nuclei are injected into the cloud to provide inhomogeneities needed to get the condensation process started. By way of comparison, Figure 6.1 shows our solar system with planetary distances from the Sun measured in astronomical units (AU), while the planetary masses are given relative to the mass of the Earth, taken to be one. Figure 6.2 shows that a variety of hypothetical planetary systems ultimately emerge from such a cloud, with the different quantities of condensation nuclei indicated by the numbers at the left edge of the figure. The vertical "forks" in the figures represent the mean and the extremes of the planetary orbits.

What's striking about these results is the strong similarity of the hypothetical systems to our own solar system, at least in the sense that there appears to be a strong tendency toward the formation of a planetary system consisting of a number of smaller inner planets, together with a few outer "gas giants." Since this general picture persists under a wide range of random condensation nuclei, the results provide strong theoretical support to the case for planetary systems being a common feature of Sun-like stars.

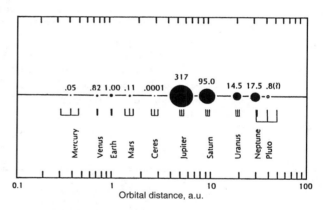

FIGURE 6.1. *The solar system*

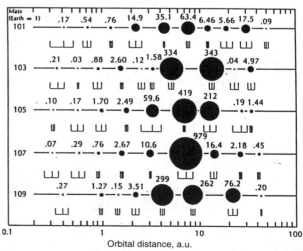

FIGURE 6.2. *Hypothetical planetary systems from computer simulations*

Critical Reading Guide

1. Casti is very careful to explain to readers what the facts mean in his report. On the basis of his explanations, what do you suspect Casti's conclusion is regarding the question of planets around other stars? Are they likely to be common or rare?

2. Casti calls on authorities by name in this passage (paragraphs 4 and 5). What effect does this technique have on readers?

3. Suppose Casti were writing for insiders rather than outsiders. Describe three features of this passage that he would have to change to make it appropriate for the new audience.

4. Refer back to the rhetorical purposes mentioned on page 46. What is the rhetorical purpose of this passage?

5. What purpose do the figures serve? What suggestions could you make to Casti that would enhance the figures' effectiveness?

Deborah Tannen

Deborah Tannen has long been considered one of the nation's top linguists. Her early work focused on the relation between sentence structure and meaning, but over the last several years she has concentrated on gender differences in language. The next passage comes form her book *You Just Don't Understand: Women and Men in Conversation*, which deals with gender differences in language for a general audience. In this book, Tannen describes how males and females interact with one another and the world in strikingly different ways that are reflected in their language. The usual result is miscommunication. The passage deals with interruption—who interrupts whom during a conversation, and why.

DEBORAH TANNEN

YOU JUST DON'T UNDERSTAND: WOMEN AND MEN IN CONVERSATION

Who's Interrupting?
Issues of Dominance and Control

1   Here is a joke that my father likes to tell.

A woman sues her husband for divorce. When the judge asks her why she wants a divorce, she explains that her husband has not spoken to her in two years. The judge asks the husband, "Why haven't you spoken to your wife in two years?" He replies, "I didn't want to interrupt her."

This joke reflects the commonly held stereotype that women talk too much and interrupt men.

In direct contradiction of this stereotype, one of 2 the most widely cited findings to emerge from research on gender and language is that men interrupt women. I have never seen a popular article on the subject that does not cite this finding. It is deeply satisfying because it refutes the misogynistic stereotype that accuses women of talking too much, and it accounts for the experience reported by most women, who feel they are often cut off by men.

Both claims—that men interrupt women and 3 that women interrupt men—reflect and bolster the assumption that an interruption is a hostile act, a kind of conversational bullying. The interrupter is seen as a malevolent aggressor, the interrupted an innocent victim. These assumptions are founded on the premise that interruption is an intrusion, a trampling on someone else's right to the floor, an attempt to dominate.

4   The accusation of interruption is particularly painful in close relationships, where interrupting carries a load of metamessages—that a partner doesn't care enough, doesn't listen, isn't interested. These complaints strike at the core of such a relationship, since that is where most of us seek, above all, to be valued and to be heard. But your feeling interrupted doesn't always mean that someone set out to interrupt you. And being accused of interrupting when you know you didn't intend to is as frustrating as being cut off before you've made your point.

5   Because the complaint "You interrupt me" is so common in intimate relationships, and because it raises issues of dominance and control that are fundamental to the politics of gender, the relationship between interruption and dominance bears closer inspection. For this, it will be necessary to look more closely at what creates and constitutes interruption in conversation.

DO MEN INTERRUPT WOMEN?

6   Researchers who report that men interrupt women come to their conclusion by recording conversation and counting instances of interruption. In identifying interruptions, they do not take into account the substance of the conversations they studied: what was being talked about, speakers' intentions, their reactions to each other, and what effect the "interruption" had on the conversation. Instead, mechanical criteria are used to identify interruptions. Experimental researchers who count things need operational criteria for identifying things to count. But ethnographic researchers—those who go out and observe people doing naturally whatever it is the researchers want to understand—are as wary of operational criteria as experimenters are wedded to them. Identifying interruptions by mechanical criteria is a paradigm case of these differences in points of view.

7   Linguist Adrian Bennett explains that "overlap" is mechanical: Anyone could listen to a conversation, or a tape recording of one, and determine whether or not two voices were going at once. But interruption is inescapably a matter of interpretation regarding individuals' rights and obligations. To determine whether a speaker is violating another speaker's rights, you have to know a lot about both speakers and the situation. For example, what are the speakers saying? How long has each one been talking? What has their past relationship been? How do they feel about being cut off? And, most important, what is the content of the second speaker's comment, relative to the first: Is it a reinforcement, a contradiction, or a change in topic? In other words, what is the second speaker trying to *do*? Apparent support can subtly undercut, and an apparent change of topic can be an indirect means of support—as, for example, when an adolescent boy passes up the opportunity to sympathize with his friend so as not to reinforce the friend's one-down position.

8   All these and other factors influence whether or not anyone's speaking rights have been violated and, if they have been, how significant the violation is. Sometimes you feel interrupted but you don't mind. At other times, you mind very much. Finally, different speakers have different conversational styles, so a speaker might *feel* interrupted even if the other did not *intend* to interrupt.

9   Here is an example that was given by Candace West and Don Zimmerman to show a man interrupting a woman. In this case I think the interruption is justified in terms of interactional rights. (The vertical lines show overlap.)

FEMALE: So uh you really can't bitch when you've got all those on the same day (4.2) but I uh asked my physics professor if I couldn't chan|ge that|
MALE: |Don't |touch that
                     (1.2)
FEMALE: What?
                     (pause)
MALE: I've got everything jus'how I want it in that notebook, you'll screw it up leafin' through it like that.

West and Zimmerman consider this an interruption because the second speaker began while the first speaker was in the middle of a word (*change*). But considering what was being said, the first speaker's rights may not have been violated. Although there are other aspects of this man's talk that make him seem like a conversational bully, interrupting to ask the woman to stop leafing through his notebook does not in itself violate her right to talk. Many people, seeing someone handling their property in a way that was destroying their painstaking organization of it, would feel justified in asking that person to stop immediately, without allowing further damage to be done while waiting for the appropriate syntactic and rhetorical moment to take the floor.

10 Sociologist Stephen Murray gives an example of what he regards as a prototypical case of interruption—where someone cuts in to talk about a different topic when the first speaker has not even made a single point. Here is his example:

H: I think | that
W: | Do you want some more salad?

This simple exchange shows how complex conversation can be. Many people feel that a host has the right, if not the obligation, to offer food to guests, whether or not anyone is talking. Offering food, like asking to have salt or other condiments passed, takes priority, because if the host waited until no one was talking to offer food, and guests waited until no one was talking to ask for platters beyond their reach,

then the better the conversation, the more likely that many guests would go home hungry.

This is not to say that any time is the right time 11 to interrupt to offer food. If a host *habitually* interrupts to offer food *whenever* a partner begins to say something, or interrupts to offer food just when a speaker reaches the climax of a story or the punchline of a joke, it might seem like a violation of rights or the expression of mischievous motives. But the accusation of interrupting cannot be justified on the basis of a single instance like this one.

Conversational style differences muddy the 12 waters. It may be that one person grew up in a home where conversation was constant and all offers of food overlapped ongoing talk, while another grew up in a home where talk was sparse and food was offered only when there was a lull in the conversation. If two such people live together, it is likely that one will overlap to offer food, expecting the other to go on speaking, but the overlap-aversant partner will feel interrupted and maybe even refuse to resume talking. Both would be right, because interruption is not a mechanical category. It is a matter of individual perceptions of rights and obligations, as they grow out of individual habits and expectations.

Writing Assignment

SUMMARIZING WHAT YOU HAVE READ

The purpose of this activity is to give you additional practice in writing a summary of material that you have read, a task that is basic to reporting information. Write a one-page summary of the Deborah Tannen excerpt above. Begin by outlining the content; then go on to report in detail the substance of the passage.

WRITING GUIDE: SUMMARIZING WHAT YOU HAVE READ

Invention

The first task in an assignment like this is to read the topic of the report carefully. You can get a great deal of information about the Tannen passage simply from looking at the title of her book and the title of the chapter from which the passage comes. These two sources will tell you that the book is about how men and women use language in conversations and that interruptions are the topic of the excerpt. Keep in mind that the book as a whole and the passage in particular are reports of information. The last sentence in the first paragraph provides a specific statement of purpose, for it indicates that what follows will report on the perception that "women talk too much and interrupt men."

Because the excerpt provides only a small portion of the chapter, you should not expect to find any answers or conclusions regarding the perception noted in the first paragraph. Instead, you should focus on what information the excerpt *does* offer. You might want to make a list of this information, which will make it easier for you to organize your summary. Remember that the examples Tannen offers are intended to support points she is making, so you will not have to include them as "information." You also should rank the information you extract in terms of its significance. For example, the idea that interruptions are related to "issues of dominance and control" might be more important than the method researchers use to study interruptions. The more significant information should be placed in your first paragraph, which is supposed to outline the content.

Planning

The assignment itself suggests a viable plan. Half of your summary can outline the content, and the other half can report the details of the passage. The list you made during invention will form the substance of your summary.

A danger you face with this assignment is producing a summary that is too brief. A couple of sentences, for example, could summarize the passage in a general way, but they would not satisfy the implicit requirements of the assignment: to show that you can read carefully and comprehend the material. Consequently, you should plan to use summary *and* detail for this report. Your details should consist of specific information taken directly from the passage, and they should appear in the second paragraph.

Drafting

A report on a piece of writing should begin by identifying author and title. Your next step should be to report what the passage is about generally. This information should come primarily from Tannen's first and last two paragraphs.

When reporting the details of the passage, offer a claim, or statement, followed by an example. Here's a typical instance of this organizational pattern:

1. Tannen differentiates between "overlap" and "interruption" by recognizing that in conversations more than one person often talks simultaneously. Following Stephen Murray, a sociologist, Tannen defines "interruption" as being when a speaker "cuts in to talk about a different topic when the first speaker has not even made a single point."

This pattern is very effective because it allows you to make a statement and then to support it with a "fact." The result is coherent writing that strikes readers as reasonable because they can see the substantiating evidence immediately after your claim.

Pausing and Reading

During the pauses you take while writing, read through your draft. Ask yourself whether you have summarized Tannen's passage and whether you have followed each statement with an example. Make notes in the margins to mark those places where you did not follow this pattern. When revising, you can make the necessary adjustments.

Revising

Set your draft aside for 2 or 3 days. When people write, they tend to get so involved with the project that errors in logic, fact, and mechanics elude them. You may want to forget about your first draft of this and any other assignment after you finish it, at least temporarily. When you return to it after some time has passed, you will be able to see things you included that you should have left out and vice versa. At this point, you should begin revising to enhance what you have to say. You may even want to share the draft with a friend to get another point of view.

Editing

If you are working on a computer, spell-check the paper, then print a copy. Count the number of words in each sentence and divide the total by the number of sentences you have, which will give you an average sentence length. If your average sentence length is between 12 and 15 words, take some of the shorter sentences and connect them to make longer ones. Your goal is to have an average of about 20 words per sentence without losing variety in length. That is, you want some long sentences, some medium ones, and some short ones.

You also should examine how you begin your sentences. Many student writers tend to begin sentences with an introductory construction. The majority of your sentences, however, should begin with the subject, not a modifying phrase or clause.

Finally, check your punctuation, using the handbook at the end of this text. Chances are you have some information in quotation marks. Did you remember to put them *outside* commas and periods? If not, study the section on punctuation on page 423 and then make the necessary corrections.

Writing Assignment

REPORTING AND INTERPRETING WHAT YOU HAVE READ

This activity gives you the opportunity to bring together everything that you have studied and practiced in this chapter. It is representative of the kind of task that usually falls under the heading of a report of information. The essay below was written by a journalist named Nat Hentoff. Write a report that tells readers about the essay and that explains what it means. A successful response will be informative and will combine summary and detail. In addition, it will use specific references to support the explanation.

WHEN NICE PEOPLE BURN BOOKS

1 It happened one splendid Sunday morning in a church. Not Jerry Falwell's Baptist sanctuary in Lynchburg, Virginia, but rather the First Unitarian Church in Baltimore. On October 4, 1981, midway through the 11 A.M. service, pernicious ideas were burned at the altar.

2 As reported by Frank P. L. Somerville, religion editor of the *Baltimore Sun*, "Centuries of Jewish, Christian, Islamic, and Hindu writings were 'expurgated'—because of sections described as 'sexist.'

3 "Touched off by a candle and consumed in a pot on a table in front of the altar were slips of paper containing 'patriarchal' excerpts from Martin Luther, Thomas Aquinas, the Koran, St. Augustine, St. Ambrose, St. John Chrysostom, the Hindu Code of Manu V, an anonymous Chinese author, and the Old Testament." Also hurled into the purifying fire were works by Kierkegaard and Karl Barth.

4 The congregation was much exalted: "As the last flame died in the pot, and the organ pealed, there was applause," Somerville wrote.

5 I reported that news of the singed holy spirit to a group of American Civil Liberties Union members in California, and one woman was furious. At me.

6 "We did the same thing at our church two Sundays ago," she said. "And long past time, too. Don't you understand it's just *symbolic*?"

7 I told this ACLU member that when the school board in Drake, North Dakota, threw thirty-four copies of Kurt Vonnegut's *Slaughterhouse Five* into the furnace in 1973, it wasn't because the school was low on fuel. That burning was symbolic, too. Indeed, the two pyres—in North Dakota and in Baltimore—were witnessing to the same lack of faith in the free exchange of ideas.

8 What an inspiring homily for the children attending services at a liberated church: They now know that the way to handle ideas they don't like is to set them on fire.

9 The stirring ceremony in Baltimore is just one more illustration that the spirit of the First Amendment is not being savaged only by malign forces of the Right, whether private or governmental. Campaigns to purge school libraries, for example, have been conducted by feminists as well as by Phyllis Schlafly. Yet most liberal watchdogs of our freedom remain fixed on the Right as *the* enemy of free expression.

10 For a salubrious change, therefore, let us look at what is happening to freedom of speech and press in certain enclaves—some colleges, for instance— where the New Right has no clout at all. Does the pulse of the First Amendment beat more vigorously in these places than where the Yahoos are?

11 Well, consider what happened when Eldridge Cleaver came to Madison, Wisconsin, last October to savor the exhilarating openness of dialogue at the University of Wisconsin. Cleaver's soul is no longer on ice; it's throbbing instead with a religious conviction that is currently connected financially, and presumably theologically, to the Reverend Sun Myung Moon's Unification Church. In Madison, Cleaver never got to talk about his pilgrim's progress from the Black Panthers to the wondrously ecumenical Moonies. In the Humanities Building—*Humanities*—several hundred students and others outraged by Cleaver's apostasy shouted, stamped their feet, chanted "Sieg Heil," and otherwise prevented him from being heard.

12 After ninety minutes of the din, Cleaver wrote on the blackboard, "I regret that the totalitarians have deprived us of our constitutional rights to free assembly and free speech. Down with communism. Long live democracy."

13 And, raising a clenched fist, while blowing kisses with his free hand, Cleaver left. Cleaver says he'll try to speak again but he doesn't know when.

14 The University of Wisconsin administration, through Dean of Students Paul Ginsberg, deplored the behavior of the campus totalitarians of the

Left, and there was a fiercely denunciatory editorial in the Madison *Capital Times*: "These people lack even the most primitive appreciation of the Bill of Rights."

15 It did occur to me, however, that if Eldridge Cleaver had not abandoned his secularist rage at the American Leviathan and had come to Madison as the still burning spear of black radicalism, the result might have been quite different if he had been shouted down that night by young apostles of the New Right. That would have made news around the country, and there would have been collectively signed letters to the *New York Review of Books* and *The Nation* warning of the prowling dangers to free speech in the land. But since Cleaver has long since taken up with bad companions there is not much concern among those who used to raise bail for him as to whether he gets to speak freely or not.

16 A few years ago, William F. Buckley Jr., invited to be commencement speaker at Vassar, was told by student groups that he not only would be shouted down if he came but might also suffer some contusions. All too few liberal members of the Vassar faculty tried to educate their students about the purpose of a university, and indeed a good many faculty members joined in the protests against Buckley's coming. He finally decided not to appear because, he told me, he didn't want to spoil the day for the parents. I saw no letters on behalf of Buckley's free-speech rights in any of the usual liberal forums for such concerns. After all, he had not only taken up with bad companions; he was an original bad companion.

17 During the current academic year, there were dismaying developments concerning freedom for bad ideas in the college press. The managing editor of *The Daily Lobo*, the University of New Mexico's student newspaper, claimed in an editorial that Scholastic Aptitude Test scores show minority students to be academically inferior. Rather than rebut his facile misinterpretation of what those scores actually show—that class, not race, affects the results—black students and their sympathizers invaded the newspaper's office.

18 The managing editor prudently resigned, but the protesters were not satisfied. They wanted the head of the editor. The brave Student Publications Board temporarily suspended her, although the chairman of the journalism department had claimed the suspension was a violation of her First Amendment rights. She was finally given her job back, pending a formal hearing, but she decided to quit. The uproar had not abated, and who knew what would happen at her formal hearing before the Student Publications Board?

19 When it was all over, the chairman of the journalism department observed that the confrontation had actually reinforced respect for First Amendment rights on the University of New Mexico campus because infuriated students now knew they couldn't successfully insist on the firing of an editor because of what had been published.

20 What about the resignations? Oh, they were free-will offerings.

21 I subscribe to most of the journalism reviews around the country, but I saw no offer of support to those two beleaguered student editors in New Mexico from professional journalists who invoke the First Amendment at almost any public opportunity.

22 Then there was a free-speech war at Kent State University, as summarized in the November 12, 1982, issue of *National On-Campus Report*. Five student groups at Kent State are vigorously attempting to get the editor of the student newspaper fired. They are: "gay students, black students, the undergraduate and graduate student governments, and a progressive student alliance."

23 Not a reactionary among them. Most are probably deeply concerned with the savaging of the free press in Chile, Uruguay, Guatemala, South Africa, and other such places.

24 What had this editor at Kent State done to win the enmity of so humanistic a grand alliance? He had written an editorial that said that a gay student group should not have access to student-fee money to sponsor a Halloween dance. Ah, but how had he gone about making his point?

25 "In opening statements," says the *National On-Campus Report*, "he employed words like 'queer' and 'nigger' to show that prejudice against any group is undesirable." Just like Lenny Bruce. Lenny, walking on stage in a club, peering into the audience, and asking, "Any spics here tonight? Any kikes? Any niggers?"

26 Do you think Lenny Bruce could get many college bookings today? Or write a column for a college newspaper?

27 In any case, the rest of the editorial went on to claim that the proper use of student fees was for

educational, not social, activities. The editor was singling out the Kent Gay/Lesbian Foundation. He was opposed to *any* student organization using those fees for dances.

28 Never mind. He had used impermissible words: Queer. Nigger. And those five influential cadres of students are after his head. The editor says that university officials have assured him, however, that he is protected at Kent State by the First Amendment. If that proves to be the case, those five student groups will surely move to terminate, if not defenestrate, those university officials.

29 It is difficult to be a disciple of James Madison on campus these days. Take the case of Phyllis Schlafly and Wabash College. The college is a small, well-regarded liberal arts institution in Crawfordsville, Indiana. In the spring of 1981, the college was riven with discord. Some fifty members of the ninety-odd faculty and staff wrote a stiff letter to the Wabash Lecture Series Committee, which had displayed the exceedingly poor taste to invite Schlafly to speak on campus the next year.

30 The faculty protesters complained that having the sweetheart of the Right near the Wabash River would be "unfortunate and inappropriate." The dread Schlafly is "an ERA opponent . . . a far-right attorney who travels the country, being highly paid to tell women to stay at home fulfilling traditional roles while sending their sons off to war."

31 Furthermore, the authors wrote, "The point of view she represents is that of an ever-decreasing minority of American women and men, and is based in sexist mythology which promulgates beliefs inconsistent with those held by liberally educated persons, and this does not merit a forum at Wabash College under the sponsorship of our Lecture Series."

32 This is an intriguing document by people steeped in the traditions of academic freedom. One of the ways of deciding who gets invited to a campus is the speaker's popularity. If the speaker appeals only to a "decreasing minority of American women and men," she's not worth the fee. So much for Dorothy Day, were she still with us.

33 And heaven [forbid] that anyone be invited whose beliefs are "inconsistent with those held by liberally educated persons." Mirror, mirror on the wall. . . .

34 But do not get the wrong idea about these protesting faculty members: "We subscribe," they emphasized, "to the principles of free speech and free association, of course."

35 All the same, "it does not enhance our image as an all-male college to endorse a well-known sexist by inviting her to speak on our campus." If Phyllis Schlafly is invited nonetheless, "we intend not to participate in any of the activities surrounding Ms. Schlafly's visit and will urge others to do the same."

36 The moral of the story: If you don't like certain ideas, boycott them.

37 The lecture committee responded to the fifty deeply offended faculty members in a most unkind way. The committee told the signers that "William Buckley would endorse your petition. No institution of higher learning, he told us on a visit here, should allow to be heard on its campus any position that it regards as detrimental or 'untrue.'

38 "Apparently," the committee went on, "error is to be refuted not by rational persuasion, but by censorship."

39 Phyllis Schlafly did come to Wabash and she generated a great deal of discussion—most of it against her views—among members of the all-male student body. However, some of the wounded faculty took a long time to recover. One of them, a tenured professor, took aside at a social gathering the wife of a member of the lecture committee that had invited Schlafly. Both were in the same feminist group on campus.

40 The professor cleared her throat, and said to the other woman, "You are going to leave him, aren't you?"

41 "My husband? Why should I leave him?"

42 "Really, how can you stay married to someone who invited Phyllis Schlafly to this campus?"

43 And really, should such a man even be allowed visitation rights with the children?

44 Then there is the Ku Klux Klan. As Klan members have learned in recent months, both in Boston and in Washington, their First Amendment right peaceably to assemble—let alone actually to speak their minds—can only be exercised if they are prepared to be punched in the mouth. Klan members get the same reception that Martin Luther King Jr. and his associates used to receive in Bull Conner's Birmingham.

45 As all right-thinking people knew, however, the First Amendment isn't just for anybody. That presumably is why the administration of the University of Cincinnati has refused this year to allow the

KKK to appear on campus. Bill Wilkerson, the Imperial Wizard of the particular Klan faction that has been barred from the University of Cincinnati, says he's going to sue on First Amendment grounds.

46   Aside from the ACLU's, how many *amicus* briefs do you think the Imperial Wizard is likely to get from liberal organizations devoted to academic freedom?

47   The Klan also figures in a dismaying case from Vancouver, Washington. There, an all-white jury awarded $1,000 to a black high school student after he had charged the Battle Ground School District (including Prairie High School) with discrimination. One of the claims was that the school had discriminated against this young man by permitting white students to wear Ku Klux Klan costumes to a Halloween assembly.

48   Symbolic speech, however, is like spoken or written speech. It is protected under the First Amendment. If the high school administration had originally forbidden the wearing of the Klan costumes to the Halloween assembly, it would have spared itself that part of the black student's lawsuit, but it would have set a precedent for censoring symbolic speech which would have shrunken First Amendment protections at Prairie High School.

49   What should the criteria be for permissible costumes at a Halloween assembly? None that injure the feelings of another student? So a Palestinian kid couldn't wear a PLO outfit. Or a Jewish kid couldn't come as Ariel Sharon, festooned with maps. And watch out for the wise guy who comes dressed as that all-around pain-in-the-ass, Tom Paine.

50   School administrators might say the best approach is to have no costumes at all. That way, there'll be no danger of disruption. But if there were real danger of physical confrontation in the school when a student wears a Klan costume, is the school so powerless that it can't prevent a fight? And indeed, what a compelling opportunity the costumes present to teach about the Klan, to ask those white kids who wore Klan costumes what they know of the history of the Klan. To get black and white kids *talking* about what the Klan represents, in history—and right now.

51   Such teaching is too late for Prairie High School. After that $1,000 award to the black student, the white kids who have been infected by Klan demonology will circulate their poison only among themselves, intensifying their sickness of spirit. There will be no more Klan costumes in that school, and so no more Klan costumes to stimulate class discussion.

52   By the way, in the trial, one offer of proof that the school district had been guilty of discrimination was a photograph of four white boys wearing Klan costumes to that Halloween assembly. It's a rare picture. It was originally printed in the school yearbook but, with the lawsuit and all, the picture was cut out of each yearbook before it was distributed.

53   That's the thing about censorship, whether good liberals or bad companions engage in it. Censorship is like a greased pig. Hard to confine. You start trying to deal with offensive costumes and you wind up with a blank space in the yearbook. Isn't that just like the Klan? Causing decent people to do dumb things.

WRITING GUIDE: REPORTING AND INTERPRETING WHAT YOU HAVE READ

Invention

You may want to read Hentoff's article a couple of times to prepare yourself for writing. A single reading may not reveal the deeper meaning of the article. It might appear to be simply a report of events that lacks any information other than historical, or it might appear to be a misplaced defense of people and groups that liberals commonly label as neo-fascists, such as Eldridge Cleaver, Phillis Schlafly, and the KKK. The real thrust of the article, however, is its argument for free speech.

To get at the second part of the assignment, explaining what the essay means, you should do some exploratory writing. Take 10 or 15 minutes and free write about what free speech and the First Amendment mean to you. Without this sort of reflection, Hentoff's argument cannot mean much.

Planning

The assignment does not specify a length requirement, so you will need to decide in advance how long the paper should be. Hentoff's article deals with some complex questions, so you probably will need at least three pages to provide an adequate report.

You will need an introduction, a body, and a conclusion. You may want to refer to the discussion of introductions and conclusions on pages 88–96. Remember that an effective introduction will set the scene, providing background for the response that allows readers to understand what the issues are. In this case, you might want to open with some remarks about the challenges to free speech throughout the history of our country. Or you might focus on more recent challenges, such as those presented by "political correctness," which would be similar to what Hentoff discusses. In any event, your goal should be to begin with a general discussion of free speech that will allow you to use Hentoff's article as a specific example of the problem or problems introduced in your scene.

If you take this approach, you will have flexibility in how you meet the requirements of the assignment. There are two possible plans. You could interweave your report of the article with your explanation of what it means, or you could separate the paper into two parts. The latter plan seems slightly more effective because it will cause readers to focus on your explanation (interpretation), which is the more rhetorically forceful part of the task.

You should plan to use both summary and detail, and you should identify in advance those details you want to include. You should select details that serve the two parts of the paper—the report and the explanation. When you select details for the explanation, make certain that they clearly support what you intend to say.

Your concluding paragraph should be brief, perhaps no more than three or four sentences. It should take the discussion forward in a way that logically follows the body of your paper. For example, at some point in your report it is likely that you will say something about how Hentoff's article suggests that liberals are more actively engaged in censorship than conservatives. Many college students might be inclined to dismiss the article as a result, considering that large numbers embrace liberal rather than conservative values. They could claim that Hentoff is merely practicing a bit of liberal bashing with this piece. Your conclusion could reasonably suggest, however, that Hentoff's primary concern is for free speech, not political camps. This approach would give you the opportunity to advocate democratic ideals that transcend labels.

An alternative approach might anticipate readers' objections to Hentoff by suggesting that he is in fact advocating democratic ideals that transcend political labels. It might then suggest that Hentoff is simply an idealist who mistakenly assumes that at some point we had more freedom of speech than we currently do. Or it might take an even stronger approach, suggesting that free speech is more appropriately thought about than practiced.

Drafting

You should include the name of the author and the title of the article in your introduction. You have already completed quite a bit of invention and planning, so you should write your first draft of this assignment in a single sitting. Do not worry about neatness or the exact number of details you provide. Concentrate on getting the whole report on paper. Many writers get stuck on the introductory paragraph. If this happens to you, skip over the introduction and go directly to the body. You always can write the introduction after the body and conclusion are in place.

Pausing and Reading

Use the pauses that are part of your writing process effectively. Read the draft and check to make certain that your introduction sets the scene for readers and states your claim. Also check to see whether you are explaining what Hentoff's essay means. Do you deal with free speech? Are you using summary and detail? Do you have details for both parts of the paper? If your answer is no to any of these questions, make notes in the margins so that you can revise later.

You also should read for such factors as rhetorical stance, aim, and tone. If your stance wavers at any point, make a note. The same applies to tone. Remember, however, that during this stage you should simply identify features that need adjustment. Don't begin revising yet.

Revising

A sound recommendation is that you revise at least twice before going on to editing. After you complete your first draft, set it aside for a while, preferably two or three days. Read it through without letting surface errors such as spelling and punctuation interrupt you. Focus on whether the draft communicates what you intended when you composed it. If it does not, begin making corrections. This revision should add and subtract information. Add summary and detail to match the requirements of the assignment. Delete truisms and anything that does not act to inform your readers. You should set the paper aside again after you have finished.

When you return to the paper after at least an hour or two, read it again. This time, you should focus on the clarity of your writing. If you followed our advice about dividing the report into two parts, organization should not be a problem, except, perhaps, at the paragraph level. Check each paragraph to see whether it has a topic sentence. Not all paragraphs have topic sentences, but most do. The sentences that follow should say something about the topic of the paragraph, either directly or indirectly. If you find a sentence that does not say something about the topic, take it out or modify it.

Editing

In addition to performing the standard spell-check on your computer, you may want to look carefully at the words you have used, making certain that they mean exactly what you intend. For example, I often see and hear statements such as "The new policies will have a negative impact on the campus" or "The political changes in the state legislature impacted everyone." The problem in both cases is one of *diction*. When "impact" is used as a noun (the first example), it means the striking of one object against another. When "impact" is used as a verb (the second example), it usually means to pack firmly. Neither of these meanings, however, is possible in the example sentences. Instead of "impact," these sentences should use the words "effect" and "affected," respectively. If you aren't sure about your word choices, check your campus writing center or a good dictionary.

In addition, you will want to examine sentence variety and paragraph length. If any of your paragraphs are more than half a page long, you should break them up into shorter units. Keep in mind that paragraphing is primarily a visual aid for readers.

Finally, check your punctuation, especially comma usage. You may have heard somewhere that the use of commas is determined by the pauses you make when reading a given sentence. Wherever you pause, you place a comma. This advice is not correct. There are about half a dozen easy-to-learn guidelines for commas, and they have nothing to do with pauses. Again, check your campus writing center or your handbook if you have any questions about punctuation.

Interpreting Events

People generally feel compelled to interpret events, to figure out what they mean, even though not all events can be interpreted. In addition, an interpretation is influenced by what one knows about the event. Such knowledge, in turn, is affected by group membership and status.

CHAPTER SIX

Interpreting Events

Reporting is linked to two important skills—interpreting and evaluating. There is no way to interpret an event or information without reporting it first. Moreover, analysis is the critical bridge that writers use to connect reporting to interpreting and evaluating.

People generally feel compelled to interpret events, to figure out what they mean, even though not all events can be interpreted. In addition, an interpretation is influenced by what one knows about the event. Such knowledge, in turn, is affected by group membership and status—what sometimes is thought of as the *ways of knowing* associated with a given group. For example, economists might interpret unstable stock prices in Asia as signaling trouble for the U.S. economy, whereas the man and woman on the street may interpret the event as signaling lower prices for imported goods.

Most people are skilled interpreters of certain events. For example, we interpret the events of daily life with fair success, even when we face the more challenging task of interpreting our own actions from the perspective of others. The kind of interpreting required in college is different insofar as it focuses largely on texts and occasionally demands much more detail, but there are enough similarities to allow you to build on what you already know.

Diverse Voices

Group membership clearly includes language and culture, which leads to differing interpretations of events based on ethnicity and language. We see this regularly when we compare news coverage on local networks with coverage on the Spanish-language channels. For this activity, identify a political event that members of your culture/language group interpret differently from mainstream American views. Compare and contrast the two interpretations. How do you account for the differences and similarities?

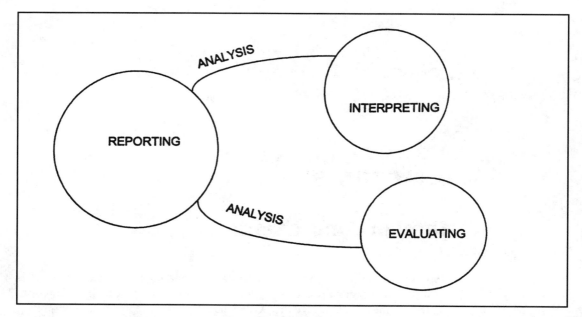

FIG. 6.1.   Analysis is the critical bridge that writers use to connect reporting to interpreting and evaluating.

INTERPRETATIONS OF EVENTS HAVE AIMS

Interpretations require application of three basic rhetorical acts: reporting, summarizing, and analyzing. However, all interpretations are guided by a single aim—to provide explanations. Remember, an interpretation explains what something means. Generally, you can approach this aim from three perspectives, which may exist independently or together in any given text:

1. Explain what an event *is*.
2. Explain the *underlying causes* of the event.
3. Explain how the event will *influence the future*.

Explaining What an Event *Is*

People may understand some events on a literal level but fail to understand them in depth. In such instances, the writer's aim is to explain what the event is. The explanation goes beyond the literal nature of the event itself. For example, Passage 1 is about the 1995 bombing of the federal building in Oklahoma City. On a literal level, no one really needs an explanation of what the event was. It was a bombing. But the quest for meaning requires a deeper understanding, one that places the bombing in a more elaborate and detailed context.

Such explanations do not simply appear. You have to find them in the tapestry of your own experiences and knowledge. You have to make a personal connection

TABLE 6.1

Three Types of Interpretations of Events

Explaining What an Event Is	There are a variety of ways for you to explain what an event is. You may set the event in an appropriate context by comparing and contrasting it with similar, related events. You may analyze the features of the event. Or you may define the event through analysis or metaphor.
Explaining the Underlying Causes of the Event	People commonly assume that all events have identifiable causes and that understanding these causes will allow them to understand the events. Interpretations of this kind focus on identifying the underlying causes and on presenting a reasonable argument for the interpretation. The issue of support is particularly relevant because teachers often ask students to develop a nontraditional interpretation of causality, one that goes beyond what surface appearances may suggest.
Explaining How the Event May Influence the Future	These interpretations serve a teaching function. The goal is twofold: You have to interpret what a given event means and then interpret how it may influence future events. The process involves helping readers learn from the past. Many teachers believe that writing an interpretation that predicts the future is more difficult than writing an interpretation that examines causality.

with the event that in turn makes a connection with readers. In many respects, explaining what an event is resembles a definition. However, successful writers do not turn to a dictionary—they turn inward to their own perceptions and beliefs. As you read the passages below, consider how these writers drew on their own knowledge to develop their explanations.

Journal Entry

Have you ever felt the need to explain the nature of an event to someone? If so, what was the event, and what motivated you to explain it?

Explaining What an Event Is
Through Comparison and Contrast

You have several options when it comes to explaining what an event is, and *comparison and contrast* is one that can be very useful. You may examine the nature of the event by placing it in a larger context of related events, keeping in mind that the audience already must know and understand this larger context to a significant degree. You then would use comparison and contrast to explain how the event is *similar to* and *different from* the known. The following passage illustrates this process. It was written by Miguel, a sophomore in a political science class, and comes from a longer paper he submitted that dealt with worldwide terrorism. This excerpt deals with the 1995 bombing of the federal building in Oklahoma City.

Passage 1: The Growing Distrust of Government

Miguel

1   When 168 people were killed in the Oklahoma City bombing of the Federal Building, Americans were shocked because the act was committed by fellow Americans, not foreign terrorists. They couldn't understand why some citizens would be so angry with the government that they felt compelled to try to destroy it, or at least its symbols. The truth is, however, that the Oklahoma City bombing had something in common with terrorism worldwide—it was perpetuated by people with fundamentalist beliefs and a strong distrust of government.

2   Religious fundamentalism has grown significantly since the early 1970s, and the Christian Coalition, founded by Pat Robertson, is one example of its influence. Democrats as well as social commentators frequently charge that fundamentalists, through the power of the religious right, have taken control of the Republican Party. In every instance, a major goal of fundamentalists—no matter where they live—is to reduce, if not eliminate, the role government plays in the lives of citizens in the arenas of business, personal weapons, and education, while increasing its role in imposing and enforcing fundamentalist views of morality and behavior. As a group's identity becomes more closely aligned with fundamentalism, its distrust of the government increases until it reaches a point of outright hostility. . . .

3   When Republicans took control of the House and Senate in 1994, they spoke of a "revolution." The revolution was just as real, although not as violent, as the revolutions that overturned Iran in the 1970s and that have threatened secular governments worldwide. The link between the Republican and the Islamic "revolutions" is the distrust that followers of both groups have for government, based in large part on their perception that secular government is the enemy of religion, morals, family values, and spirituality.

4   Seen from this perspective, the bombing of the Oklahoma City federal building was as predictable as the overthrow of the Shah in the 1970s. The people of Iran were tired of the abuses against them by the government. They were heavily taxed, and they perceived that the ruling elite benefited at their expense. Living conditions for the majority became worse while they became better for the ruling class. The gap between the have and the have-nots grew every year. Also, the people saw that their leaders did not abide by the laws of the Koran but instead felt protected by their wealth. Members of the ruling elite reportedly went so far as to eat pork regularly, calling it "Teheran chicken."

5   In a similar way, American's distrust of their government has been increasing since President Kennedy's assassination, in part because so many citizens believe that key figures in the government had some role in Kennedy's death. They see the government elite abusing the system for their personal gain. They see the Congress increase Social Security benefits more than 70% while middle-class wages in real dollars fall 20% during the same period. They see tax laws imposed that redistribute wealth from the middle class to the upper and lower classes, and they feel powerless to make things right. They see members of Congress giving speeches about morality one day and newspaper stories the next reporting some Congressman's sexual escapades with an underage boy or girl or another Congressman's blatant acts of sexual harassment.

6   Like the Iranians of the 1970s, Americans have learned to distrust their government. Many have come to view government as the enemy and are acting in their own ways to undermine it. From coast to coast, people run red lights and speed with no regard for the law. Western landowners are engaged in running battles with the Bureau of Land Management over water and grazing rights, and the battles are becoming more intense. Not long ago, Nei County Nevada filed suit against the federal government to get control of land rights from Washington. There have been

instances of shooting, vandalism, and harassment as locals lash out against federal authority.

7   Until recently, actions against the government were so limited that they might be viewed as a form of social protest even though they are dangerous. But as the federal government has intruded more and more into the private lives of citizens, the actions have become more violent. The Unibomer blew people up in an effort to disrupt government and slow the development of technology. A group calling itself the Southwest Freedom Fighters derailed a train. And then there is the Oklahoma City bombing. The escalation of violence is similar to what happened in Iran.

8   Many people are quick to label the Oklahoma City bombing as "mindless" violence, suggesting that there were no motivating factors. The connection, however, between antigovernment actions in America and elsewhere and conservatism and religious fundamentalism suggests that the bombing was a response to complex feelings of powerlessness. For decades, liberal government sought to control and regulate the lives of citizens—just as the Shah's regime sought to "westernize" the people of Iran. The operating premise in both cases is that people are incapable of taking care of themselves, incapable of determining how they want to live their lives. Most people resent paternalism of any kind because it's condescending. Over time this resentment must find an outlet. It seems reasonable to suggest that the Oklahoma City bombing was a reaction to the sense of powerlessness that an intrusive, paternalistic government generates among the people, just as the Islamic revolution in Iran was a reaction to a sense of powerlessness and the perception that the government was attempting to undermine the belief system of the people.

Miguel attempts in this passage to explain the bombing to the Oklahoma City federal building that occurred in 1995. He has determined that the event was more than a criminal action, more than a meaningless act of terrorism. He begins by putting the event in the larger context of religious fundamentalism and antigovernment sentiments. It is the case that fundamentalism has grown worldwide since the 1970s and that this fundamentalism has been linked to conservative social and political trends.

This part of the paper, however, would have been stronger if Miguel had provided more support for putting the Oklahoma City bombing in this context. He does not offer any evidence to support the claim that the bombers, Timothy McVeigh and Terry Nichols, were fundamentalists, nor does he provide any evidence that they distrusted the U.S. government. Instead, Miguel relies on what readers may already know about the case from reading the news. He relies too heavily on what he assumes the audience's knowledge to be. Just a few lines of evidence (or even summary) would have been very useful here.

Having placed the event in a context of governmental distrust, Miguel moves forward. He links the underlying conditions that he has associated with the bombing to what he perceives to have been the distrust and unacceptable social conditions associated with the overthrow of the Shah and the establishment of an Islamic government in Iran. From Miguel's perspective, the bombing was part of a growing escalation of distrust and unlawful behavior on the part of Americans. He suggests through his comparison with Iran that America is on the threshold of a revolution, and he cites a couple of examples in paragraph 7 to substantiate his claim. Paragraph 8, however, crystallizes Miguel's explanation of what the event was. For him, the bombing was a reaction to "the sense of powerlessness" that Americans have come to feel as a result of increasing governmental intrusion into their lives.

There is no question that Miguel's explanation is provocative, in part because he seems to be sanctioning the bombing. But its provocative nature should not blind you to the fact that the writing is pretty good. Miguel put the event in a broader context and used comparison and contrast to explain what it is by moving from the known to the unknown. His interpretation is feasible, even though Miguel assumes too much audience knowledge (he probably wrote the paper shortly after the event occurred, which meant that it was in the news for everyone to see). Nevertheless, Miguel could have improved his explanation by offering more information and evidence to support some of his statements.

Explaining What an Event Is Through Analysis

When you explain what an event is through analysis, you take the whole and divide it into parts, which frequently are themselves events that provide a context for the one you are explaining. The following passage provides a good model of an analysis of the whole in terms of its parts. The writer, Mary, produced it for a political science class that was examining America's legal system. Several weeks earlier, the local newspaper had run a brief article about the events described in the passage. The article was little more than a summary of the events, however, in part because the paper had run numerous articles in the past over a period of about 1 year. Mary followed up on the story by interviewing some of the people involved. As you read, keep in mind that the event Mary wants to explain is identified in the first sentence.

Passage 2: The System Doesn't Work

Mary

1   On January 15, 1996, Dr. Richard Bronkowski pled guilty to the misdemeanor charge of improperly using a company expense account. The event signaled for many the fitting end of a long, drawn-out story of decline. For a handful of others, however, it was graphic evidence that our legal system is broken beyond repair.

2   Bronkowski had been a rising star at Engineered Pharmaceuticals (EP), leading a team of scientists developing protease inhibitors to destroy the ability of the HIV virus to reproduce. His successes put him on the fast track at EP and started attracting attention in the research community. In 1993, a team of university researchers invited Bronkowski to co-author a paper with them. They also were working on protease inhibitors, but of a different kind than those Bronkowski and his team at EP were using. At first, Bronkowski declined, saying that he had too much work to do at EP. The researchers, however, told him that his contribution would be limited to helping with data analysis and writing the conclusion section; he wouldn't be involved in collecting the data, which always is the most time-consuming part of any study. On these conditions, Bronkowski accepted the offer and looked forward to the collaboration.

3   Bronkowski was amazed when he saw the data. They showed that the combination of drugs the research team tested totally blocked the ability of the HIV virus to reproduce, which gave the body's immune system the time necessary to destroy the invader. Bronkowski contacted the university team and questioned the head researcher repeatedly about the results and the procedures used to get them. The team leader was understandably excited about the findings and urged Bronkowski to finish his contribution as soon as possible. Bronkowski worked furiously, and within weeks the paper, under the co-authorship of four university professors, three graduate students, and Bronkowski, was sent out for review.

4   It was accepted immediately because the results were so stunning. Only one reviewer suggested that the findings seemed too good to be true, but he also rec-

ommended publication. Bronkowski was very pleased, seeing the article as another step forward in his career. After the article was published, he began receiving requests to speak at conferences, and there was talk of a promotion. Meanwhile, he had shifted the focus of his own research efforts to include the drugs identified in the paper.

5   Bronkowski told me that he was the first to suspect a problem when he could not duplicate the results. No matter how many times he tried, the drugs failed to reduce HIV reproduction by more than 25%. He contacted the university research team and told them about it, but they reported that they hadn't had any difficulty. Then calls began coming in from other researchers around the country who also had tried duplicating the results, without success. It was clear that something was wrong. Rumors started circulating that the researchers had falsified the data, and it wasn't long before the local press picked up the story. The news articles accused the team members of faking the data to receive the rewards of making a big breakthrough in AIDs research. The university started an investigation.

6   The university's investigation revealed that the data indeed had been falsified, but it wasn't clear who had done it. The evidence pointed at two of the graduate students, who had been primarily responsible for recording data, but the evidence wasn't conclusive. Nevertheless, all three of the students were expelled. The three junior faculty members on the team were fired, and the senior member was forced to resign. Because he had not been involved in data collection, Bronkowski felt that he was outside the process. He was outraged and embarrassed about being associated with the article, but he explained to everyone that he simply had analyzed the data he had received and contributed to the conclusion.

7   As a result, he was surprised when EP announced that it had started its own investigation. Bronkowski reported that at about this time he noticed a distinct change in the way his colleagues and supervisors interacted with him. He found that he was not getting the memos that were routinely circulated to team leaders and that invitations to social events ceased. He was even more surprised a few weeks later when he received a written notice from the president of the company that he was suspended without pay until the investigation was finished.

8   Bronkowski was convinced that he had done nothing wrong, so he decided to challenge the suspension. He hired an attorney who began negotiating with EP. After a few meetings with top executives, the attorney told Bronkowski that the talks were going nowhere. Two days later, EP announced publicly that Bronkowski had been terminated. The president's executive secretary called Bronkowski an hour before the announcement and gave him the news so that he "wouldn't read about it in the morning paper."

9   Bronkowski's attorney advised suing EP for unwarranted termination, and the legal motions began. Without a job, Bronkowski started living off his savings, but within a matter of a few months he had spent $50,000 in legal fees without making any progress. His life savings were entirely depleted. He sold all his assets but still had to borrow from friends and credit cards and suddenly was $30,000 in debt.

10   At this time, EP made another public announcement, stating that it had extended the investigation to include all Bronkowski's research reports, his equipment acquisition records, his assignment of research duties, and his expense account. The newspaper reports that followed suggested not only that Bronkowski had participated in the falsification of the university study but also that he may have falsified other data, including information on his expense account.

11   Outraged, Bronkowski told his attorney to sue the newspapers for libel—only to be informed that winning a libel case against a newspaper is virtually impossible and amazingly expensive, even when the paper prints outright lies. His attorney said that a libel suit would require an attorney who specialized in that kind of case and that costs could run as high as $100,000. Frustrated, Bronkowski called one of the

reporters involved and told him that what he was printing was untrue. The reported told him, "So sue me" and hung up. Bronkowski called his attorney and told him to drop the suit for unwarranted termination—he couldn't afford to continue.

12   However, that was not the end of his difficulties. The publicity made it remarkably difficult to find another job. No major labs would hire him. Finally, he found a part-time job at a small lab in another town where he analyzed blood and urine samples for local hospitals. He barely earned enough to meet his living expenses, and he couldn't pay the debts he owed. He filed for bankruptcy.

13   Eight months later, Bronkowski's attorney called and told him that there was a problem. The district attorney had issued a warrant for his arrest because EP had filed a complaint alleging that he had submitted a receipt for $109 as part of his expense account that actually was a personal expense. Bronkowski had to surrender to police immediately or face the embarrassment of being arrested at his job. Furthermore, the legal fees for fighting the charges would run approximately $12,000, and the attorney needed half of it in advance, plus the $3,000 outstanding on his bill. Trying to ease the devastating effect of this news, the attorney noted that he had reviewed the evidence and that they probably would win the case because it appeared as though the receipt had been submitted by mistake. It was stapled to a dry cleaning bill and a grocery list, suggesting that some personal receipts had gotten mixed in with business receipts.

14   Stunned, Bronkowski asked if there were any options. His attorney told him that there was only one. He could plead guilty to the charge, which was a misdemeanor, and the court would fine him $50. Legal fees in this instance would run about $1,500. Bronkowski told his attorney that he could not plead guilty to something he didn't do and that he needed time to think things through. He didn't have $1,500, so raising $12,000 or $15,000 was out of the question. Then he remembered that public defenders represent people who can't pay for an attorney, so he called the public defender's office to talk to someone about his case. He learned very quickly, however, that he wasn't eligible for such help because he had a job. Public defenders only represent people who are out of work and have no money. They don't represent people who have a job but have no money. For a moment, he thought about representing himself, but he dropped that idea almost immediately. He knew nothing about the law. Reluctantly, he called his attorney and told him he would enter a guilty plea.

15   When Dr. Richard Bronkowski appeared before the court and pled guilty, he was caught in an impossible situation. Charged with a crime he insists he did not commit, he nevertheless had no means of defending himself. His only option was to plead guilty, pay the fine, and leave with a criminal record.

16   When I asked Bronkowski why anyone should believe that he's innocent, he responded with a question of his own, one that I couldn't answer and that convinced me of his innocence. He asked, "Do you really think that I would risk my entire career for $109?" Now the only question I have left is, how many other people each day face a situation like Bronkowski's, charged with a crime they didn't commit but unable to spend tens of thousands of dollars to defend themselves? Bronkowski's case illustrates that our legal system is broken, serving only the rich, who can pay for representation, and the poor, who receive it for free. For the middle class, there is no representation. There is no justice. For Dr. Bronkowski, the guilty plea was an admission of defeat in the face of impossible odds. It was his way of trying, once and for all, to put the whole mess behind him.

Mary's explanation of the event represents one way to apply analysis. She does not analyze the event itself but chose instead to analyze the contributing factors. This analysis allows her and readers to view the event more comprehensively and more intelligently.

Mary is writing for insiders insofar as the original readers were people who might know about Bronkowski and his case. However, Mary provides them with information that few readers had. The newspaper accounts certainly did not offer the kind of detail Mary provides, in part because Bronkowski consistently refused to talk to the press and because the press seemed bent on attacking the man. As a result, readers might know about the external circumstances of the case in general but not the details. This lack of knowledge is important for Mary's analytical explanation of the event. Our impression at the time was that most people believed that Bronkowski was guilty and that he knew he could not win against the overwhelming evidence that the district attorney was prepared to present. It certainly did not occur to many people to think that Bronkowski's plea might be an act of desperation brought on by financial hardship. Thus, Mary's analysis does exactly what it should: It explains the event in such a way that readers have a better understanding of what the event was.

Explaining What an Event Is
Through Definition

Metaphor can be a powerful invention technique that enables people to define something by relating it to something else. In the example "The car was a lemon," the metaphor describes and defines "the car." When an interpretation of events defines what the event is through metaphor, the result is what you may think of as a "metaphoric interpretation."

Few writers push a metaphor beyond a couple of paragraphs because it is hard to do successfully, but there are exceptions. The example passage presented here was written by Sandra Bloom, a psychotherapist who specializes in treating traumatic stress disorders. She wrote this article in response to the 1991 nomination of Clarence Thomas to the U.S. Supreme Court. During the Senate hearings, the press reported that Thomas had sexually harassed former assistant Anita Hill. The Senate Judiciary Committee called Hill to testify, and she accused Thomas of a variety of offensive and perhaps illegal actions. When Thomas testified, he denied all the allegations. He was subsequently appointed to the Court.

In the first part of the article, Bloom argues that U.S. society is traumatized, and she cites our obsession with violence, our mistreatment of children, and our rampant substance abuse as symptomatic evidence. She also argues that our only hope as a nation lies in some sort of "national therapeutic process" that consists of a "self-examination procedure" similar to the sort that individuals undergo during therapy. Healing, in other words, first requires an honest assessment of the problems.

Bloom interprets the hearings by attempting to define metaphorically what they were. Her metaphor is "therapeutic process." That is, what transpired was not a hearing in which the goal was to "establish right and wrong" but rather a process in which the goal was "to heal splits within the individual, within the family, perhaps within a nation." As you read the passage below, you should consider not only how effective the metaphor is but also how Bloom manages to sustain it through 17 paragraphs.

Passage 3: The Case of Clarence Thomas and Anita Hill

Sandra L. Bloom

1   Is such a "national therapeutic process" conceivable or even practical? Is there any precedent, any examples within our own experience, of a nationally experienced self-examination procedure?

2   For a weekend in October, 1991, a significant proportion of Americans were glued to their television screens, much like the winter before. Only this time the

issue at hand was not the thrill of military combat, it was a war of the sexes played out around the issue of sexual harassment. The woman in the case, Anita Hill, claimed that the man in the case, Clarence Thomas, had sexually harassed her in the past, making him potentially unfit to hold an office as important as Justice of the Supreme Court. What made this scenario so important was that these were not just two individuals with a controversial past behind them. It was Republicans vs. Democrats, Conservatives vs. Liberals, Topdog vs. Underdog, Man vs. Woman.

3   Much like what goes on in a dysfunctional family when there is a secret that needs to be told, someone had leaked the information about the case to the press, and suddenly the full glare of public attention was focused on a private hurt, a private lie. Accused and perpetrator sat facing self-styled judges, only no one could figure out who was definitely the accused and who definitely the perpetrator.

4   In the beginning of the hearings, the onlookers were exposed to a graphic portrayal of sexual misconduct in a manner far from titillating. Americans squirmed in their chairs, but listened, as the rawness of human pain was exposed. For that brief time, we were all in the therapist's chair, forced to bear witness to the person's recounting of her own story, her own dread. And then we listened as the distinguished jurist completely denied her allegations and with righteous indignation that most of the audience shared rallied at the panel for exposing their private life to public spectacle.

5   The senators squirmed in their seats, too, because unwittingly they found themselves in the extremely uncomfortable position of needing to be therapists when they do not know how to do anything but be judges in this setting. They tried to ask questions, tried to probe to discover the underlying truth of the experience, some even tried to empathize with the accuser, others with the accused. But given the supposed purpose of the hearings, given the importance of the question—to decide whether Judge Thomas was fit to become a Justice of the Supreme Court—the hearings rapidly degenerated into finger-pointing, character assassination, political polemics, and party politics.

6   All of us were faced with the inevitable dilemma of every therapist—what IS the truth, what IS reality, what DID actually happen? But because this was not therapy, but politics, the onlookers were not able to do what the therapist must do in this situation which is to set aside the need for judgement and allow the process to unfold, allow the truth of each individual's personal experience to be witnessed, understood, and transcended by them.

7   The goal of the judicial process is to establish right and wrong and to mete out punishment for those judged wrongdoers. The goal of the therapeutic process is to heal splits within the individual, within the family, perhaps within a nation. The judicial process requires an assignment of truth. The therapeutic process recognizes that truth is in the eye of the beholder and that Truth is most closely approximated by the summation of all the individual truths.

8   It is no wonder, therefore, that everyone would be extremely uncomfortable with the process, that a judgement would be prematurely rendered, that the process would be terminated without reaching any meaningful conclusions, that all would degenerate into blaming and shame. The main protagonists left the field bruised and probably permanently scarred without an adequate resolution of the issues between them.

9   But was there anything positive that the rest of us can derive from the experience? Was there anything of significance that occurred during those few days that may have far-reaching consequences to the group psyche?

10   Perhaps the most interesting thing about the whole weekend was the fact that so many people switched off football games, movies, and all the usual forms of television entertainment and tuned in to the hearings, transfixed, many even late into the night. Is it because we are a nation of voyeurs? The actual explication of the sexual details of Anita Hill's story were much more clinical than arousing. If anything, people were made more uncomfortable than they were entertained by her

elaboration of her experiences, as was emphasized repeatedly by the press and by individuals.

11   Was it just the public spectacle of two black people recounting or denying details of their sexual life? Or was it that Americans are, at some level, hungry for national and public dialogue on issues of substance? What was unfolding on our television screens was a portrayal of the relationship between American men and American women to which virtually everyone could relate. Viewers were uncomfortable but still drawn to the process, forced to reflect, at least internally, on their own experience with sexual harassment.

12   And while the individual viewer weighed the arguments back and forth, he or she saw our government leaders, all white men of considerable power and influence, openly and publicly listening to the fervent complaints of a woman who was a highly credible accuser. At the same time, the viewer saw our government leaders sympathizing if not empathizing with the accused, a powerful and successful man not unlike many of them, but for the color of his skin.

13   The Senate panel represented every imaginable style of response when confronted with their own discomfort. Some blamed the woman and sided with the man. Some believed the woman with a certainty and condemned the man. Some patronized her, some empathized with her. Some were puzzled, some surprised, some indignant. Some looked guilty, some were angry, some afraid. All appeared embarrassed, confused, and awkward with the entire proceedings. At least briefly, the panel epitomized white male authority attempting at least to begin some strenuous self-examination. And all sat guilty of being part of a body who has excepted themselves from harassment laws the rest of us must follow.

14   When the Senators convened the hearings, they apparently had not fully realized that they were opening up a deep and pus-filled national abscess. Once Anita Hill began to testify, she became an embodiment of the fear and hatred of women and all that is feminine that typifies a large segment of Western and certainly American culture. Anita Hill gave women across the nation the courage to come forth and share their own experiences of sexual harassment with their husbands, their children, their friends and lovers, their co-workers, their bosses, their employees.

15   By their own confusion and befuddlement, and by their willingness to listen, the Senators themselves gave men permission to listen to those women, to weigh their charges, even to empathize with the victims. For each man on that panel who took the opportunity to look at his own lack of awareness, he gave millions of men permission to look at their own. As Clarence Thomas sat there, accused rightly or wrongly, millions of American men sat there with him, knowing in their own hearts the extent of their own culpability, admitted or not.

16   There is no question that the whole thing was handled awkwardly and probably unfairly. As a nation we have not discussed how a process such as this should, in fact, be conducted and few if any people have a clear idea of how to handle this kind of a situation with dignity. It would be unfortunate, however, if the conclusion drawn from all this is that matters of this nature should be kept strictly behind closed doors and let out for the public only when properly washed and sanitized, with all the emotional truth of the experience expunged.

17   Abscesses can only heal when they are lanced, when the pus is allowed to flow out, and the wound cleansed. Sexism is only one of the many American psychic abscesses that are crippling to healthy function. Pus is smelly and disgusting. Lancing an abscess can be an extremely painful process but when an abscess is left to fester, the result is increasing disability and pain. As a nation we must learn to tolerate the discomfort of such psychologically "surgical" procedures in order to achieve healing and recovery.

Bloom already made her argument for a "national therapeutic process" in earlier pages. The metaphor is in place, and the Thomas hearings will provide an example to illustrate the point that Bloom wants to make. Because she is a good writer, Bloom takes the time to remind readers of what the hearings were about. She refreshes the audience's memory in paragraph 2. With the summary out of the way, Bloom can go on to develop her definition. In paragraph 3, for example, she makes a connection between individual (or family) trauma and her idea of national trauma. Paragraph 4 follows up on this connection very skillfully by trying to get readers to identify with the therapeutic process: "For that brief time, we were all in the therapist's chair, forced to bear witness to the person's recounting of her own story, her own dread."

These statements sustain the metaphor quite effectively because they assert that the audience participated in the therapeutic process when watching any part of the hearings. Of course, Bloom has no way of knowing how her readers responded to the event or even if they saw it on TV, but this technique is effective. She is telling those readers who saw the event what their reaction *should* have been, and she is telling those who did not see the event what their reaction *would* have been. Equally important, she is enhancing her definition of the event through her metaphor.

Applying Key Ideas

USING METAPHOR

This activity gives you an opportunity to practice using metaphor to explain what an event is, similar to what you saw Bloom do in her passage.

Major events generally are reported on television and in newspapers and news magazines, but the level of coverage differs considerably. Few TV news programs, for example, can spend more than a couple of minutes (about 300 words) on any one event. Using TV news programs as a source, list some recent events that lend themselves to metaphoric interpretation. Create a single metaphor characterizing what each event is and then jot down several reasons to support each interpretation.

Writing Assignment

EXPLAINING WHAT AN EVENT IS

This writing assignment is intended to let you apply the factors discussed so far with respect to interpreting an event by explaining what it is. Select one of the events from the activity above and write a one- to two-page interpretation that explains what the event is. You should use either comparison and contrast, analysis, or definition.

Diverse Voices

One of the features of American life that puzzles many immigrants is the television talk show, which increasingly is a venue for personal confessions of the most intimate and often vulgar sort. Many cultures simply don't allow this sort of public display.

Some critics of Sandra Bloom's article accuse the writer of being caught up in the talk-show mentality, where every public humiliation is justified as a form of "therapy." In a paper of about three pages, examine your culture's views of public confessions of personal behavior and then interpret the Clarence Thomas hearings from the perspective of those views.

EXPLAINING UNDERLYING CAUSES

When people consider events, they commonly assume that all events have identifiable causes and that understanding these causes will allow them to understand the events. People even demonstrate what might be called a "compulsion" for establishing causality, and the more inscrutable an event is the more opportunities there are for interpretation.

Subject-area expertise is particularly valuable in such situations because it helps keep interpretations grounded in reality. For example, we occasionally hear or read about situations in which someone is being attacked and bystanders do nothing to intervene, and the usual reaction to such stories in incomprehension. One of the more well-known incidents of this kind occurred in 1964, when a woman named Kitty Genovese was murdered as she was returning home from work. Over a 30-minute period, her attacker stabbed her while she cried out for help. This event probably would have received little attention had it not been for the second event: 38 of her neighbors watched and did nothing. Their inaction stunned the nation. Few people could believe that the witnesses to the murder failed to intervene or call the police, and their behavior was generally interpreted as pathological apathy. Nothing else seemed to explain their inaction.

This popular explanation of the underlying cause is challenged, however, among social psychologists. The following reading passage illustrates how subject-area expertise leads to an interpretation of causality quite different from the popular one. The authors, both psychologists, begin their interpretation by referring to the Kitty Genovese case. But because they are interested in the general behavior associated with noninvolvement, the authors mention three similar cases.

Passage 4: When Will People Help?

John Darley and Bibb Latané

1 Kitty Genovese is set upon by a maniac as she returns home from work at 3:00 A.M. Thirty-eight of her neighbors in Kew Gardens come to their windows when she cries out in terror; none comes to her assistance even though her stalker takes over half an hour to murder her. No one even so much as calls the police. She dies.

2 Andrew Mormille is stabbed in the stomach as he rides the A train home to Manhattan. Eleven other riders watch the 17-year-old boy as he bleeds to death; none comes to his assistance even though his attackers have left the car. He dies.

3 An 18-year old switchboard operator, alone in her office in the Bronx, is raped and beaten. Escaping momentarily, she runs naked and bleeding to the street, screaming for help. A crowd of 40 passersby gathers and watches as, in broad daylight, the rapist tries to drag her back upstairs; no one interferes. Finally two policemen happen by and arrest her assailant.

4   Eleanor Bradley trips and breaks her leg while shopping on Fifth Avenue. Dazed and in shock, she calls for help, but the hurrying stream of executives and shoppers simply parts and flows past. After 40 minutes a taxi driver helps her to a doctor.

5   The shocking thing about these cases is that so many people failed to respond. If only one or two had ignored the victim, we might be able to understand their inaction. But when 38 people, or 11 people, or hundreds of people fail to help, we become disturbed. Actually, this fact that shocks us so much is itself the clue to understanding these cases. Although it seems obvious that the more people who watch a victim in distress, the more likely someone will help, what really happens is exactly the opposite. If each member of a group of bystanders is aware that other people are also present, he will be less likely to notice the emergency, less likely to decide that it is an emergency, and less likely to act even if he thinks there is an emergency.

6   This is a surprising assertion—what we are saying is that the victim may actually be less likely to get help, the more people who watch his distress and are available to help. We shall discuss in detail the process through which an individual bystander must go in order to intervene, and we shall present the results of some experiments designed to show the effects of the number of onlookers on the likelihood of intervention.

7   Looking more closely at published descriptions of the behavior of witnesses to these incidents, the people involved begin to look a little less inhuman and a lot more like the rest of us. Although it is unquestionably true that the witnesses in the incidents above did nothing to save the victims, apathy, indifference, and unconcern are not entirely accurate descriptions of their reactions. The 38 witnesses of Kitty Genovese's murder did not merely look at the scene once and then ignore it. They continued to stare out their windows at what was going on. Caught, fascinated, distressed, unwilling to act but unable to turn away, their behavior was neither helpful nor heroic; but it was not indifferent or apathetic.

8   Actually, it was like crowd behavior in many other emergency situations. Car accidents, drownings, fires and attempted suicides all attract substantial numbers of people who watch the drama in helpless fascination without getting directly involved in the action. Are these people alienated and indifferent? Are the rest of us? Obviously not. Why, then, don't we act?

9   The bystander to an emergency has to make a series of decisions about what is happening and what he will do about it. The consequences of these decisions will determine his actions. There are three things he must do if he is to intervene: *notice* that something is happening, *interpret* that event as an emergency, and decide that he has *personal responsibility* for intervention. If he fails to notice the event, if he decides that it is not an emergency, or if he concludes that he is not personally responsible for acting, he will leave the victim unhelped. This state of affairs is shown graphically as a "decision tree." Only one path through this decision tree leads to intervention; all others lead to a failure to help. As we shall show, at each fork of the path in the decision tree, the presence of other bystanders may lead a person down the branch of not helping.

10   Suppose that an emergency is actually taking place; a middle-aged man has a heart attack. He stops short, clutches his chest, and staggers to the nearest building wall, where he slowly slumps to the sidewalk in a sitting position. What is the likelihood that a passerby will come to his assistance? First, the bystander has to *notice* that something is happening. The external event has to break into his thinking and intrude itself on his conscious mind. He must tear himself away from his private thoughts and pay attention to this unusual event.

11   But Americans consider it bad manners to look too closely at other people in public. We are taught to respect the privacy of others, and when among strangers,

we do this by closing our ears and avoiding staring at others—we are embarrassed if caught doing otherwise. In a crowd, then, each person is less likely to notice the first sign of a potential emergency than when alone.

12   Experimental evidence corroborates this everyday observation. Darley and Latané asked college students to an interview about their reactions to urban living. As the students waited to see the interviewer, either by themselves or with two other students, they filled out a preliminary questionnaire. Solitary students often glanced idly about the room while filling out their questionnaires; those in groups, to avoid seeming rudely inquisitive, kept their eyes on their own papers.

13   As part of the study, we staged an emergency: smoke was released into the waiting room through a vent. Two-thirds of the subjects who were alone when the smoke appeared noticed it immediately, but only a quarter of the subjects waiting in groups saw it as quickly. Even after the room had completely filled with smoke one subject from a group of three finally looked up and exclaimed, "God! I must be smoking too much!" Although eventually all the subjects did become aware of the smoke, this study indicates that the more people present, the slower an individual may be to perceive that an emergency does exist and the more likely he is not to see it at all.

14   Once an event is noticed, an onlooker must decide whether or not it is truly an emergency. Emergencies are not always clearly labeled as such; smoke pouring from a building or into a waiting room may be caused by a fire, or it may merely indicate a leak in a steam pipe. Screams in the street may signal an assault or a family quarrel. A man lying in a doorway may be having a coronary or be suffering from diabetic coma—he may simply be sleeping off a drunk. And in any unusual situation, Candid Camera may be watching.

15   A person trying to decide whether or not a given situation is an emergency often refers to the reactions of those around him; he looks at them to see how he should react himself. If everyone else is calm and indifferent, he will tend to remain calm and indifferent; if everyone else is reacting strongly, he will become aroused. This tendency is not merely slavish conformity; ordinarily we derive much valuable information about new situations from how others around us behave. It's a rare traveler who, in picking a roadside restaurant, chooses to stop at one with no other cars in the parking lot.

16   But occasionally the reactions of others provide false information. The studied nonchalance of patients in a dentist's waiting room is a poor indication of the pain awaiting them. In general, it is considered embarrassing to look overly concerned, to seem flustered, to "lose your cool" in public. When we are not alone, most of us try to seem less fearful and anxious than we really are.

17   In a potentially dangerous situation, then, everyone present will appear more unconcerned than they are in fact. Looking at the *apparent* impassivity and lack of reaction of the others, each person is led to believe that nothing really is wrong. Meanwhile the danger may be mounting, to the point where a single person, uninfluenced by the seeming calm of others, would react.

18   A crowd can thus force inaction on its members by implying, through its passivity and apparent indifference, that an event is not an emergency. Any individual in such a crowd is uncomfortably aware that he'll look like a fool if he behaves as though it were—and in these circumstances, until someone acts, no one acts.

19   In the smoke-filled room study, the smoke trickling from the wall constituted an ambiguous but potentially dangerous situation. How did the presence of other people affect a person's response to the situation? Typically, those who were in the waiting room by themselves noticed the smoke at once, gave a slight startled reaction, hesitated, got up and went over to investigate the smoke, hesitated again, and then left the room to find somebody to tell about the smoke. No one showed any signs of panic, but over three-quarters of these people were concerned enough to report the smoke.

20   Others went through an identical experience but in groups of three strangers. Their behavior was radically different. Typically, once someone noticed the smoke, he would look at the other people, see them doing nothing, shrug his shoulders, and then go back to his questionnaire, casting covert glances first at the smoke and then at the others. From these three-person groups, only three out of 24 people reported the smoke. The inhibiting effect of the group was so strong that the other 21 were willing to sit in a room filled with smoke rather than make themselves conspicuous by reacting with alarm and concern—this despite the fact that after three or four minutes the atmosphere in the waiting room grew most unpleasant.

In many respects, Darley and Latané's article is characteristic of interpretations of events. Note that, like Sandra Bloom, the writers begin by offering a summary of the events: in this case, the crime or accident as well as the associated inaction of witnesses. After the initial summary, the authors move quickly to their thesis: that when such events are witnessed by large numbers of people, the victims stand a lower chance of receiving assistance. Thus, the authors' interpretation is that failure to act in a crisis is caused by the number of people present in a given situation, not by some pervasive apathy. The rest of the article goes on to explain and substantiate this interpretation—to argue for its validity, in other words.

You should note that Darley and Latané's success in making this interpretation is significantly influenced by their expertise as psychologists. As they point out in the beginning of the selection, common sense suggests that victims should have greater chances of getting help when large numbers of people are around. Knowledge of psychology allowed the authors to look beyond what common sense suggests, however, and to offer a reasonable interpretation.

Applying Key Ideas

REPORTING EVENTS
AND INTERPRETING CAUSALITY

Events cover a wide range of actions and behaviors. Some lend themselves to interpretation, whereas others do not. For this activity, observe and record an event from campus or the surrounding community. Decide what you believe its cause is. In your work group, report the event orally to your groupmates and then share with them your interpretation of causality. Ask them if they think your interpretation is reasonable and ask for suggestions on how to improve your interpretation. Then write a summary of the event and offer your interpretation of its causes, which you may present to the whole class.

Looking for Fresh Perspectives

Most subject areas are full of events that lend themselves to interpretations of causality. When you study the events and their interpretations, you are gaining valuable insight into how a given discipline views reality. However, most disciplines advocate interpretations that repeat traditional notions of causality, which are part of the core knowledge of a field. A teacher, for example, may describe an event and then inform the class that several underlying causes have been identified by scholars in the field, with one or two causes deemed more effective at explaining the event than the others.

Advances in knowledge often occur when someone in a discipline offers a new view, a new interpretation, that is not entirely congruent with orthodox views. Students can benefit enormously from proposing new interpretations because it asks them not only to know the material exceptionally well but to look at it in new and insightful ways. For this reason, whenever possible, you should draw on your experiences and knowledge to make connections with discourse communities in ways that explore fresh perspectives.

Some historians have said that Patricia N. Limerick has helped advance U.S. history in this way through her writing. Following is an example of her work that illustrates how you might approach a well-known, thoroughly investigated event in a fresh way. Limerick considers herself to be a revisionist historian, which means that she aims to provide a different perspective on commonly accepted historical points of view. For example, books and movies about the West often depict it as a vast empty space waiting to be "civilized" by pioneers from the East. Limerick stresses, however, that the West was already inhabited—by Indians—and in her view westward expansion is largely a story of conquest rather than pioneering.

Passage 5: Innocent Victim or Intolerant Invader?

Patricia N. Limerick

1   The idea of the innocent victim retains extraordinary power, and no situation made a stronger symbolic statement of this than that of the white woman murdered by Indians. Here was surely a clear case of victimization, villainy, and betrayed innocence. But few deaths of this kind occurred in American history with such purity; they were instead embedded in the complex dynamics of race relations, in which neither concept—villain or victim—did much to illuminate history.

2   Narcissa Prentiss Whitman made a very unlikely villain. Deeply moved by the thought of Western Indians living without knowledge of Christianity, Narcissa Prentiss wrote her mission board in 1835, "I now offer myself to the American Board to be employed in their service among the heathen. . . ." In 1836, she left her home in New York to rescue the Indians in Oregon. An unattached female could hardly be a missionary, and before her departure Narcissa Prentiss hastily married another Oregon volunteer, Marcus Whitman. The Whitmans and Henry and Eliza Spalding set off to cross the country. Pioneers on the overland trail, they faced stiff challenges from nature and some from human nature. The fur trappers and traders with whom they traveled resented the delays and sermons that came with missionary companionship. The missionaries themselves presented less than a united front. They had the strong, contentious personalities of self-appointed agents of God. They also had a history; Henry Spalding had courted Narcissa, and lost. Anyone who thinks of the nineteenth-century West as a land of fresh starts and new beginnings might think of Henry Spalding and Narcissa Whitman and the memories they took with them to Oregon.

3   Arrived in the Oregon country, the missionaries—like salesmen dividing up markets—divided up tribes and locations. The Whitmans set to work on the Cayuse Indians. Narcissa Whitman's life in Oregon provides little support for the image of life in the West as free, adventurous, and romantic. Most of the time, she labored. She had one child of her own; she adopted many others—mixed-blood children of fur trappers, and orphans from the overland trail. "My health has been so poor," she wrote her sister in 1846, "and my family has increased so rapidly, that it has been impossible. You will be astonished to know that we have eleven children in our family, and not one of

them our own by birth, but so it is. Seven orphans were brought to our door in Oct., 1844, whose parents both died on the way to this country. Destitute and friendless, there was no other alternative—we must take them in or they must perish."

4 Depending on one's point of view, the Whitman mission had a lucky or an unlucky location—along the Oregon Trail, where exhausted travelers arrived desperate for food, rest, and help. Narcissa Whitman's small home served as kitchen, dining hall, dormitory, and church building, while she longed for privacy and rest. She often cooked three meals a day for twenty people. For five years, she had no stove and cooked in an open fireplace.

5 In the midst of crowds, she was lonely, writing nostalgic letters to friends and family in the East who seemed to answer infrequently; she went as long as two years without a letter from home. Separated by distance and sometimes by quarrels, Narcissa and the other missionary wives in Oregon tried for a time to organize a nineteenth-century version of a woman's support group; at a certain hour every day, they would pause in their work, think of each other, and pray for the strength to be proper mothers to their children in the wilderness.

6 Direct tragedy added to loneliness, overwork, and frustration. The Whitmans' only child, two years old, drowned while playing alone near a stream. Providence was testing Narcissa Whitman's faith in every imaginable way.

7 Then, in November of 1847, after eleven years with the missionaries among them, when the white or mixed-blood mission population had grown to twenty men, ten women, and forty-four children, the Cayuse Indians rose in rebellion and killed fourteen people—including Marcus and Narcissa Whitman.

8 Was Narcissa Whitman an innocent victim of brutality and ingratitude? What possessed the Cayuses?

9 One skill essential to the writing of Western American history is a capacity to deal with multiple points of view. It is as if one were a lawyer at a trial designed on the principle of the Mad Hatter's tea party—as soon as one begins to understand and empathize with the plaintiff's case, it is time to move over and empathize with the defendant. Seldom are there only two parties or only two points of view. Taking into account division within groups—intertribal conflict and factions within tribes and, in Oregon, settlers against missionaries, Protestants against Catholics, British Hudson's Bay Company traders against Americans—it is taxing simply to keep track of the points of view.

10 Why did the Cayuses kill the Whitmans? The chain of events bringing the Whitmans to the Northwest was an odd and arbitrary one. In a recent book, the historian Christopher Miller explains that the Whitman mission was hardly the first crisis to hit the Columbia Plateau and its natives. A "three hundred year cold spell," a "result of the Little Ice Age," had shaken the environment, apparently reducing food sources. Moreover, the effects of European presence in North America began reaching the plateau even before the Europeans themselves arrived. The "conjunction of sickness, with the coming of horses, guns, climatic deterioration, and near constant war" added up to an "eighteenth-century crisis." Punctuated by a disturbing and perplexing ash fall from a volcanic explosion, the changes brought many of the Plateau Indians to the conviction that the world was in trouble. They were thus receptive to a new set of prophecies from religious leaders. A central element of this new worldview came in the reported words of the man known as the Spokan Prophet, words spoken around 1790: "Soon there will come from the rising sun a different kind of man from any you have yet seen, who will bring with them a book and will teach you everything, after that the world will fall to pieces," opening the way to a restored and better world. Groups of Indians therefore began to welcome whites, since learning from these newcomers was to be an essential stage in the route to a new future.

11 In 1831, a small party of Nez Percé and Flathead Indians journeyed to St. Louis, Missouri. For years, Western historians said that these Indians had heard of Jesuits

through contacts with fur traders and had come to ask for their own "Black Robes." That confident claim aside, Christopher Miller has recently written that it is still a "mystery how is all came to pass." Nonetheless, he argues persuasively that the Northwest Indians went to St. Louis pursuing religious fulfillment according to the plateau millennial tradition; it was their unlikely fate to be misunderstood by the equally millennial Christians who heard the story of the visit. A Protestant man named William Walker wrote a letter about the meetings in St. Louis, and the letter was circulated in church newspapers and read at church meetings, leaving the impression that the Indians of Oregon were begging for Christianity.

12   And so, in this chain of circumstances "so bizarre as to seem providential," in Miller's words, the Cayuses got the Whitmans, who had responded to the furor provoked by the letter. Irritations began to pile up. The Whitmans set out to transform the Cayuses from hunters, fishers, and gatherers to farmers, from heathens to Presbyterians. As the place became a way station for the Oregon Trail, the mission began to look like an agency for the service of white people. This was not, in fact, too far from the founder's view of his organization. "It does not concern me so much what is to become of any particular set of Indians," Marcus Whitman wrote his parents, "as to give them the offer of salvation through the gospel and the opportunity of civilization. . . . I have no doubt our greatest work is to be to aid the white settlement of this country and help to found its religious institutions."

13   The Cayuses began to suffer from white people's diseases, to which they had no immunity. Finally, in 1847, they were devastated by measles. While the white people at the mission seldom died from measles, the Indians noticed that an infected Cayuse nearly always died. It was an Indian conviction that disease was "the result of either malevolence or spiritual transgression"; either way, the evidence pointed at the missionaries. When the Cayuses finally turned on the Whitmans, they were giving up "the shared prophetic vision" that these newcomers would teach a lesson essential to reshaping the world. The Cayuses were, in other words, acting in and responding to currents of history of which Narcissa Whitman was not a primary determinant.

14   Descending on the Cayuses, determined to bring light to the "benighted ones" living in "the thick darkness of heathenism," Narcissa Whitman was an intolerant invader. If she was not a villain, neither was she an innocent victim. Her story is melancholy but on the whole predictable, one of many similar stories in Western history that trigger an interventionist's urge. "Watch out, Narcissa," one finds oneself thinking, 140 years too late, "you think you are doing good works, but you are getting yourself—and others—into deep trouble." Given the inability of Cayuses to understand Presbyterians, and the inability of Presbyterians to understand Cayuses, the trouble could only escalate. Narcissa Whitman would not have imagined that there was anything to understand; where the Cayuses had religion, social networks, a thriving trade in horses, and a full culture, Whitman would have seen vacancy or, worse, heathenism.

Because this sample comes from a long work, you reasonably would expect it to be part of a larger argument, and the first paragraph provides some insight into just what the argument is. The selection comes from the first chapter of *The Legacy of Conquest*, in which Limerick is attempting to show that historical understanding is primarily a rhetorical problem historians face in arriving at a viable interpretation of events. She suggests that one of the pervasive "myths" of the West (and perhaps all human experience) is the notion of innocence. The pioneers, from the perspective of this myth, were innocently attempting to strengthen the country, bring civilization to the heathens inhabiting the plains, provide for their families, and so on. They did not set out with the goal of exterminating "red skins." They simply responded to Indian attacks.

Understanding the causes of the nearly total extermination of American Indian culture, if not the American Indians themselves, is made significantly more difficult by the existence of the myth. Limerick, however, suggests that what motivated settlers as well as the indigenous peoples was a complex set of cultural, social, historical, and gender-specific factors that made conflict inevitable, even when, generally, conflict was not a conscious goal on either side. Limerick argues that simple innocence did not really exist in the West, among Native Americans or whites, and she offers the account of Narcissa Whitman as an illustration.

The nature of paragraphs 2 through 7 should be quite familiar by now: a standard narrative report. Paragraph 8 asks the fundamental question that underlies interpretations of causality, but notice that Limerick takes a detour rather than answer the question immediately. She uses paragraph 9 to return to her larger argument: that people are complex and that understanding history requires consideration of multiple perspectives.

Aware that her digression might be a problem for readers, Limerick asks the causality question again at the beginning of paragraph 10. This technique is an effective way of getting readers back on track. Paragraphs 10 through 14 answer the question in a way that makes Narcissa Whitman seem something other than an innocent victim. At best, she was an unwitting participant in the clash of two antithetical world views that were mutually incomprehensible. In the end, the Cayuse killed Narcissa Whitman because she failed to meet their expectations. And she failed to meet their expectations because she did not really understand what those expectations were, or perhaps did not even understand that the Cayuse *had* any expectations.

Linked Assignment

CONSIDERING CAUSES
OF EVENTS

Most subject areas are full of events that lend themselves to interpretations of causality. This activity asks you to consider some of those subject areas and events as a form of invention linked to the following writing assignment.

List several events associated with three of your courses. Some of the events will be significant, of course, but you also should try to include some minor events because they often have not been interpreted as much as the major ones and consequently may be better candidates than major events for interpretation. For each event, jot down as many possible causes as you can think of. You may want to confer with your teachers in these courses to see if you are on the right track.

Writing Assignment

INTERPRETING AN EVENT

This activity gives you an opportunity to apply the techniques you have studied to this point. Select an event from the list you just produced for the linked assignment. In approximately three pages, provide an interpretation of the causes underlying the event. Remember to provide a summary of the event and support for your interpretation.

PREDICTING THE FUTURE

Predictive interpretations serve a teaching function in that they strive to help readers understand an event and learn about how it will affect the future. Many teachers believe that this kind of interpretation is more difficult than writing one that examines causality. The level of knowledge and thought required is deemed to be greater. Because the underlying causes of events that have already happened are in the past, they are easier to identify and easier to link to a given event. The future, on the other hand, is intangible, abstract, in the process of becoming. Writing a successful predictive interpretation involves analyzing and interpreting causality and then extending the identified effects into the future.

The following samples illustrate interpretations that lead to predictions. They concern the 1992 Los Angeles riots, and neither is optimistic. They do, however, have very different stances. When reading, consider the factors that might have led the writers to adopt the stances they do.

The first sample began as a speech by former Senator Bill Bradley, which he gave in the Senate on March 26, 1992, about 1 month before the riots. After the riots, he expanded his remarks and revised the speech for *Harper's Magazine*, which published the essay in July 1992. Bradley was an advocate for civil rights and urban development throughout his political career.

Passage 6: The Crisis of Meaning in American Cities

Bill Bradley

1 America has seen two tragedies this past spring: the horrible injustice of the Rodney King verdict and the deplorable violence that subsequently engulfed Los Angeles.

2 But we will all face a third tragedy if we don't learn the real lesson of this spring. Consider, for example, a teenager who lived in Watts in the 1960s, who saw his neighborhood burned and his friends killed. Politicians came in and said they would restore opportunity, reform the criminal justice system, make the police evenhanded and disciplined, and change the conditions that created the context for the riots.

3 Now jump forward to 1992. The teenager is forty-five years old, and watches his neighborhood burn again and again sees his friends die. What will this man tell his teenage son about the police, the criminal justice system, the need for hard work, and the prospect of a job? What will he say about his personal safety in the neighborhood or the ability of the political system to help him take control of his life and build a better future?

4 The needs of our cities are obvious: more jobs, less violence, and stronger families, all in the context of a growing economy that takes everyone to a higher ground. The federal government must commit significant resources to meet the problems of urban America. It is ludicrous for anyone to pretend otherwise.

5 The fundamental changes, though, won't come from charismatic leaders or from federal bureaucracies. They will come from thousands of "leaders of awareness," in communities across the nation, men and women who will effect lasting change as they champion integrity and humility over self-promotion. But above all, the scapegoating and buck-passing must stop. A sense of urgency must inform our actions. The situation demands a new democratic movement—I call it a conversion, a willingness to convert the outrage of Los Angeles into positive efforts to rebuild our communities.

6 Conversion must start with the acknowledgment that slavery was America's original sin and race remains our unresolved dilemma. The future of American cities is inextricably bound to the issue of race and ethnicity. By the year 2000, only 57 percent of the people entering the work force in America will be native-born whites. That means that the economic future of the children of white Americans will increasingly depend on the talents of non-white Americans. If we allow this group to fail because of our penny-pinching or our timidity about straight talk, America will become a second-rate power. If this country's minorities succeed, America and all Americans will be enriched. If we don't move ahead and find common ground, we will all be diminished.

7 In national politics during the last twenty-five years, the issue of race and urban America has been shaped by distortion and silence. Both political parties have contributed to the problem. Republicans have played the race card in a divisive way in order to win votes—remember Willie Horton—and Democrats have suffocated discussion of the self-destructive behavior among parts of the minority population under a cloak of silence and denial. The result is that yet another generation of our children has been lost. We cannot afford to wait any longer. It is time for candor, time for truth, and time for action.

8 America's cities are poorer, sicker, less educated, and more violent than at any point in my lifetime. The physical problems are obvious: deteriorating schools; aging infrastructure; a diminished manufacturing base; a health care system, short of doctors, that fails to immunize against measles, much less educate about AIDS. The jobs have disappeared. The neighborhoods have been gutted. A genuine depression has hit the cities—unemployment, in some areas, matches the levels of the 1930s.

9 What is less obvious, but equally important, in urban America is the crisis of meaning. Without meaning there can be no hope; without hope there can be no struggle; without struggle there can be no personal betterment. Absence of meaning, influenced by overt and subtle attacks from racist quarters over many years, as well as an increasing pessimism about the possibility of justice, fosters a context for chaos and irresponsibility. Meaning develops from birth. Yet more than 40 percent of all births in the twenty largest cities of America are to women living alone; among black women, more than 65 percent.

10 For kids who have no family outside a gang, no connection to religion, no sense of place outside the territory, and no imagination beyond the violence of TV, our claims that government is on their side ring hollow. To them, government is at best incompetent and at worst corrupt. Instead of being rooted in values such as commitment and community service, their desires, like commodities, become rooted in the shallow ground of immediate gratification. TV bombards these kids with messages of conspicuous consumption. They want it now. They become trapped in the quicksands of American materialism, surfeited with images of sex, violence, and drugs.

11 The physical condition of American cities and the absence of meaning in more and more lives come together at the barrel of a gun. If you were to select one thing that has changed most in cities since the 1960s, it would be fear. Fear covers the streets like a sheet of ice. The number of murders and violent crimes has doubled in the 20 largest cities since 1968. Ninety percent of all violence is committed by males, and they are its predominant victims. Indeed, murder is the leading cause of death for young black males.

12 For African-Americans in cities, violence isn't new. Mothers have sent their children to school through war zones for too many years. What *is* new is the fear among whites of random violence. No place in the city seems safe. Walking the streets seems to be a form of Russian roulette. At its core, this fear is a fear of young black men. Never mind that all black males have to answer for the actions of a few

black males. Never mind that Asian-Americans fear both black and white Americans, or that in Miami and Los Angeles, some of the most feared gangs are Latinos and Chinese. Never mind that the ultimate racism was whites ignoring the violence when it wasn't in their neighborhoods, or that black Americans have always feared certain white neighborhoods.

13   Today many white Americans, whether fairly or unfairly, seem to be saying of some black males, "You litter the street and deface the subway, and no one, white or black, says stop. You cut school, threaten a teacher, 'dis' a social worker, and no one, white or black, says stop. You snatch a purse, you crash a concert, break a telephone booth, and no one, white or black, says stop. You rob a store, rape a jogger, shoot a tourist, and when they catch you—if they catch you—you cry racism. And nobody, white or black, says stop."

14   It makes no difference whether this white rap accurately reflects the reality of our cities. Millions of white Americans believe it's true. In a kind of ironic flip of fate, the fear of brutal white oppression experienced for decades in the black community and the seething anger it generated are now mirrored in the fear whites have of random attack from blacks and the growing anger that fear fuels. The white disdain grows when a frightened white politician convenes a commission to investigate charges of racism, and the anger swells when well-known black spokespersons fill the evening news with threats and bombast.

15   Most politicians don't want to confront the reality that causes the fear. But if politicians don't talk about the reality that everyone knows exists, they cannot lead us out of our current crisis. Because very few people of different races have real conversations with each other—when was the last time you had a conversation about race with a person of a different race?—the white vigilante groups and the black spokespersons who appear on television end up being the ones who educate the uneducated about race. The result is that the divide among races in our cities deepens and white Americans become less and less willing to spend the money to ameliorate the cities' condition or to understand that the absence of meaning in the lives of many urban children ultimately threatens the future of their own children.

16   Yet even in this atmosphere of disintegration, the power of the human spirit abides. Heroic families *do* overcome the odds, sometimes working four jobs to send their kids to college. Churches and mosques are peopled by the faithful who *do* practice the power of love. Neighborhood leaders have turned around local schools, organized health clinics, and rehabilitated blocks of housing. These islands of courage and dedication still offer the possibility of local renewal. And our system of government still offers the possibility of national rebirth.

17   The future of urban America will take one of three paths: abandonment, encirclement, or conversion.

18   Abandonment will occur if people believe that the creation of suburban America, with its corporate parks and malls—along with the increasing availability of communications technology, which reduces the need for urban proximity—means that the city has outlived its usefulness. Like the small town whose industry leaves, the city will wither and disappear. Massive investment in urban America would be throwing money away, the argument would go, and trying to prevent the decline is futile.

19   Encirclement will occur if cities become enclaves of the rich surrounded by the poor. Racial and ethnic walls will rise higher. Class lines will be manned by ever-increasing security forces. Deeper divisions will replace communal life, and politics will be played by dividing up a shrinking economic pie into ever smaller ethnic, racial, and religious slices. It will be a kind of *Clockwork Orange* society in which the rich will pay for their security; the middle class, both black and white, will continue to flee as they confront violence; and the poor will be preyed upon at will or will join the army of violent predators. What will be lost by everyone will be freedom, civility, and the chance to build a common future.

20   Conversion can occur only by winning over all segments of urban life to a new politics of change, empowerment, and common effort. It is as different from the politics of dependency as it is from the politics of greed. Conversion requires listening to the disaffected as well as the powerful. Empowerment requires seizing the moment. It begins with the recognition that all of us advance together or each of us is diminished; that American diversity is not our weakness but our strength; that we will never be able to lead the world by example until we've come to terms with each other and overcome the blight of racial division on our history.

21   The first concrete step toward conversion is to bring an end to violence in the cities, intervene early in a child's life, reduce child abuse, establish some rules, remain unintimidated, and involve the community in its own salvation. That's what community policing, for example, is about.

22   The second step is to bolster families in urban America. That effort begins with the recognition that the most important year in a child's life is the first. Fifteen-month houses must be established for women seven months pregnant who want to live the first year of their lives as mothers in a residential program. We must also provide full funding for Head Start and WIC, more generous tax treatment of children, one-year parental leave, tough child support enforcement, and welfare reform that encourages marriage, work, and personal responsibility.

23   The third step is to create jobs for those who can work—through enterprise zones, the Job Corps, neighborhood reconstruction corps, and investment in the urban infrastructure. It is only through individual empowerment that we can guarantee long-term economic growth. Without economic growth, scapegoats will be sought and racial tensions will heighten. Without growth, hopes will languish.

24   Ultimately, the key to all this is the political process. It has failed to address our urban prospects because politicians feel accountable mainly to those who vote, and urban America has voted in declining numbers—so politicians have ignored them. Voter registration and active participation remain the critical link.

25   Stephen Vincent Benét once said about American diversity: "All of these you are/and each is partly you/and none of them is false/and none is wholly true." For those citizens whose ancestors came generations ago there is a need to reaffirm principles—liberty, equality, democracy—even though these principles have always eluded complete fulfillment. The American city has always been the place where these ideas and cultures clashed—sometimes violently. But all people, even those brought here in chattel slavery, are not African or Italian or Polish or Irish or Japanese. They're American.

26   What we lose when racial or ethnic self-consciousness dominates are tolerance, curiosity, civility—precisely the qualities we need to allow us to live side by side in mutual respect. The fundamental challenge is to understand the suffering of others as well as to share in their joy. To sacrifice that sensitivity on the altar of racial chauvinism is to lose our future. And we *will* lose it unless we move quickly. The American city needs physical rejuvenation, economic opportunity, and moral direction, but above all what it needs is the same thing every small town needs: the willingness to treat a person of any race with the respect you show for a brother or sister, in the belief that together you'll build a better world than you would have ever done alone, a better world in which all Americans stand on common ground.

When Bradley wrote this interpretation, the images of the Los Angeles riots were very strong in readers' minds. The entire country had repeatedly seen the videotape of Los Angeles police officers beating Rodney King, a black motorist stopped for speeding. The officers were charged with brutality, but the jury acquitted them. When the verdict was announced, blacks and Hispanics in Los Angeles rioted. Bradley therefore did not need to provide a summary of the event; he merely needed to refer to it, as he does in the first paragraph.

The second and third paragraphs move directly to his interpretation: that the riots suggest a future characterized by hopelessness and cycles of violence, where personal safety and the ability to build a better tomorrow are nonexistent. An interesting feature of this sample is that Bradley relies a great deal on his reference to the Los Angeles riots of 1965. By comparing the 1992 riots to these earlier ones, Bradley suggests that the cycle of violence already is in place and that the next round may occur in 30 years or 30 months, but nevertheless will occur. Paragraph 4 and those that follow it do not explicitly refer again to this prediction, however. Instead, they present an analysis of prevailing conditions and the argument that Americans must work together to change these conditions. The riots and the prediction of renewed violence remain in the background.

Given the level of awareness most readers probably brought to this essay, and given the strong reaction most people had to the riots, Bradley was able to refrain from any explicit reference for the remainder of the work. Moreover, doing so seems to have served his rhetorical purpose quite well, considering that a goal was to avoid calling attention to the looting and murder while advocating changing the conditions that allowed the riots to occur. It is tempting to conclude that Bradley used his interpretation of the event as an opportunity to analyze current urban conditions and to argue for ways to improve them.

The next example, "Causes, Root Causes, and Cures," takes a very different approach. It was written by Charles Murray, who, at the time of publication, worked at a conservative "think-tank" organized to encourage intellectuals to examine and interpret current events and governmental policies. Although the title suggests that Murray intends to address the underlying causes of the Los Angeles riots, the essay actually focuses on the effect the riots will have on race relations in the future.

Passage 7: Causes, Root Causes, and Cures

Charles Murray

1   THE RODNEY KING verdict seemed as outrageous to me as it did to most Americans. But if it was outrageous, it was also laden with meaning. It opens a new and explosively dangerous period in American race relations. There is every reason to be pessimistic about the outcome. And what we see in response, by white and black leaders alike, is posturing. So let me open by summarizing my interpretation of events as bluntly as possible.

    1. The Rodney King verdict was an expression of white fear about black crime, and this fear is grounded in reality.

    2. The white reaction to the riots will be profoundly different from the reaction in the 1960s, because a consensus of whites no longer accepts that whites are to blame for black problems. This shift in opinion is also grounded in reality.

2   Racism in the United States has metamorphosed since the days of separate drinking fountains for whites and colored. Racism in the 1950s was based on caste relationships and a generalized presumption of white superiority. It was to be combatted by appealing to the best in the American heritage—the belief that to be an American must mean to be free and autonomous, equal under the law. The civil-rights movement seized that moral high ground and succeeded remarkably.

3   On July 3, 1964, the movement achieved its greatest triumph, the passage of the Civil Rights Act. Thirteen days later, a race riot broke out in Harlem, the first of dozens over the next four years. The reaction in white America was some perplexity, some anger, but mostly contrition. It takes a rereading of the newspapers and magazines of that day to realize how very differently whites saw the world then. Whites accepted that they had abused and oppressed blacks for three centuries, and

it was understandable that black rage would come back to haunt them. Whites must do more. This was not the opinion of a few liberal politicians. It was the sentiment of a nation.

4   And so whites did more. The rest of the 1960s saw an outpouring of social programs and reforms. Some of these were openly directed at racial problems, like the Voting Rights Act of 1965. But more broadly, the smorgasbord of programs called the War on Poverty was driven by a desire to make amends.

Shifting Reality

5   IT WAS during that same period that reality began to shift, and with it the meaning of "racism." Two things happened. First, blacks began to behave in ways that scared and angered whites. Some of these ways—inner-city fads and customs and sexual norms—affected whites only at second hand, creating a festering irritation that made whites less sympathetic toward blacks. But the change that quite directly affected whites was skyrocketing black crime, and especially violent crime. Robbery. Assault. Rape. Homicide. White crime climbed too but remained at a much lower absolute level, and much less of it was violent.

6   These changes were not merely statistical. They made a difference in people's lives. After I was mugged at gunpoint in the vestibule of my fiancée's New York apartment building at five o'clock in the afternoon, she could only shake her head in dismay at my carelessness when she found out. Didn't I realize that a favorite target was people returning home after work with their arms full of groceries (as mine had been)? Didn't I know that standard operating procedure was to survey the street before going into the vestibule—even at five o'clock in the afternoon? To live in a big city began to take survival skills that had not been necessary just a few years earlier. This change in reality is captured in a new urban parable, The White Woman's Dilemma. A white woman is walking down an urban street after dark. A block away, two black young men are walking toward her. Does she cross to the other side of the street? If she does, the odds are that she is insulting two innocent young men. If she doesn't, she is putting herself at risk—not a huge risk, but a meaningful one. Given all that, is crossing the street a racist act? Women whom I have heard discuss this dilemma, many of whom are otherwise impeccably liberal, cross the street in such a situation. They feel terrible about it. But they do it anyway.

7   For years, hardly anyone talked about the black crime problem in public, even though it was an absorbing topic at many white social gatherings. Through the 1970s, the standard public rhetoric was that crime really hadn't gotten much worse, it just seemed that way because crime was reported more often. And: How unfair that a poor black stealing a few dollars is thrown in jail while white businessmen steal millions and get a slap on the wrist. And: It is understandable that some blacks lash out against oppression, poverty, and discrimination through crime. It's not their fault.

8   In the 1980s, the public excuses for black crime died out, and America began to prosecute and incarcerate criminals with renewed enthusiasm. But a curious public hypocrisy continued. Thus articles could be published about the disproportionate numbers of blacks in America's prisons, with not a single letter to the editor pointing out that blacks were disproportionately in jail because they had committed a disproportionate number of crimes. Few were prepared to say in public that the reason people were afraid of crime in the cities was not that America was violent, but that from whatever tangled root causes, too many blacks were behaving violently. But if they wouldn't say it in public, whites thought it, and said it to each other. That blacks themselves are most often the victims of black crime is of theoretical interest to whites but is not the pressing point.

9   Not coincidentally, the 1980s also saw a resurgence of sympathy for the police. The generation that in the 1960s called police "pigs" changed its mind. True-to-life cop shows are on prime-time network television almost every night. One of the things that comes across most powerfully in these programs is how capriciously chancy a policeman's life can be and how the most routine arrest can erupt in violence.

10   Superimposing these developments on the Rodney King verdict, it is easy to interpret what is happening. However queasy they may be about what they saw on the videotape, large segments of white America sympathize with the implicit message of the King jury: A thin blue line of police is out there on the perimeter, holding back some very scary people. We rely on them, and we will back them up in just about anything they think they need to do to protect us. I doubt if this message is contingent on the offender's being black. If one imagines the same beating of the white counterpart of Rodney King—straggly-haired and prison-tattooed, let's say, and hopped up on drugs—it is easy to imagine a not-guilty verdict coming back much more quickly than this one did.

Just a Fair Chance?

11   THE SECOND THING that happened to change the nature of racial attitudes among whites was affirmative action. Affirmative action began benignly as an effort to "cast a wider net," as it was said, making sure that blacks got an opportunity to compete for university places and job openings. By the end of the 1960s, affirmative action had become a set of policies whereby blacks were given preference over whites in competition for jobs in universities, law firms, police and fire departments, and most American businesses. Whether the preferences were justified or unjustified is subject to debate, but not that they were preferences. In elite universities, the edge given blacks on admission tests has been in the vicinity of 50 percentiles—that is, a black scoring at the 30th percentile among the applicants to a given college has had about the same chance of admission as a white scoring at the 80th percentile. Racial quotas in the job market are routinely met by what is called "race-norming," whereby the manuals for personnel tests conveniently include conversion tables for adjusting raw scores according to the race of the applicant.

12   As in the case of crime, public rhetoric refused to accommodate the shift in reality. The only acceptable stance to take during the 1970s was that blacks weren't really getting preferential treatment, just a fair chance—if their test scores were lower, it was because the tests were biased against them. So what looked like preferential treatment was really just fair treatment.

13   The final defense was that "everyone we take can do the work"—that is, above a certain threshold of qualifications, everyone could perform about the same. But in practice, the difference in ability between the average black and the average white was often too large to ignore. Face-saving strategies were quietly adopted. In universities, black students who would have failed if they had been white were given passing grades, and doctoral dissertations that would have been rejected were accepted. In businesses, blacks with skills that ordinarily would not have passed muster were shunted into slots where their deficiencies would not be so obvious. All of this was sub rosa, not to be discussed publicly, not to be complained about. But everybody knew.

14   Meanwhile, the 1980s were witnessing the arrival of new waves of Asian immigrants, and another kind of racial discrepancy made its appearance. At the high-school commencement ceremonies, often the valedictorian's speech would be made in halting English by the son or daughter of a Vietnamese farmer who had arrived penniless just a few years earlier. Korean grocery stores became as ubiquitous a feature of the American urban landscape as Irish saloons or Jewish delicatessens had once been. This gave rise to more doublespeak. The rhetoric had always proclaimed

that affirmative action was needed to help minorities who were disadvantaged by the white majority. But Asians refused to exhibit the symptoms of disadvantage. The result, *mirabile dictu*, was that Asians somehow were dropped from the ranks of minorities. By the end of the 1980s, they had after all become subject to quotas: ceilings—of the same variety that Jews had had to face early in this century—to avoid having "too many" Asians in freshman classes.

15   Once again, superimposing these developments on the aftermath of the Rodney King verdict leads naturally to certain expectations. American black leaders are replaying the response to the riots of the 1960s that received so much acceptance then among whites: The rioting and looting are a deplorable but understandable reaction to years of abuse and neglect by the government. But whites watching these scenes are not the whites of the 1960s, and the claims that blacks must receive more assistance will be received with little sympathy. Some of this reaction among whites is mean-spirited and racist in the old sense. But most is not. It is not racism—not racism in the old sense, at any rate—to conclude that blacks have in truth been given a number of advantages for more than twenty years. It is not the old style of racism to conclude that the present problems of the black community owe more to black behavior than to white oppression. And it is above all not the old style of racism to look at the unaided achievements of poor Asian immigrants—and the unaided achievements of poor West Indian immigrants, poor Nigerian immigrants, poor Ethiopian immigrants—and ask, "If they can do it, why can't American blacks?" It is a legitimate question, requiring more than glib answers about the legacy of slavery.

16   But the question is rarely asked—in public. And that is why I began by saying that the Rodney King verdict opens such a dangerous period in American race relations. Those relations have been spiraling downward for many years now without yet provoking American white leaders to confront the sources of the antagonism. There are a few brave exceptions—Senator Bill Bradley has recently grasped the nettle—but certainly none among this year's crop of presidential aspirants, including George Bush. There remains a powerful reticence among whites to ask tough questions of blacks. It is the most tenacious survivor of the old racism: condescension. It should not have to be up to blacks to break this impasse, but I think that's what it may come to. Only when blacks can say at one and the same time that the King verdict was outrageous and that, nonetheless, it's time for blacks and whites to start telling each other publicly what they say among themselves privately, are we likely to see the opening of a dialogue and a hope for reconciliation. The much more likely outcome is that the pieties will continue, and the antagonism deepen.

Given the overall effect of the essay, Murray's opening statement is important. He lets readers know how outrageous he thought the Rodney King verdict was. This statement allows Murray to identify with readers who were upset over the verdict. It signals to readers that the essay does not condone the actions of the police even though it is critical of the riots.

From this point, Murray can move forward quickly. Notice that he offers two interpretations. The first addresses the underlying causes of the verdict, whereas the second predicts the future insofar as it examines "the white reaction to the riots." Although I have separated these two kinds of interpretations for the purposes of this book, a large number of interpretations simultaneously define what an event is, examine causality, and make predictions.

Paragraphs 2 through 10 are designed to support Murray's first interpretation. Notice that Murray does not consider whether the jury's decision to acquit the policemen was just or not. Nor is he concerned about the legal questions associated with the trial. He makes no mention of whether the policemen broke the law, for example. Instead, his analysis of "reality" is designed to support the interpretation that the verdict was the result of white fear of black crime. After presenting evidence for eight paragraphs, his decision to restate the interpretation in paragraph 10 was a good one: It reminds readers of the thesis.

Murray uses the same approach when he moves to the prediction part of the interpretation, starting at paragraph 11. He presents "facts" that are intended to show why white Americans might be unwilling to accept responsibility for the riots. His thesis is that, from the white perspective, black Americans now are a privileged group in many ways, so the riots were an incomprehensible response to the Rodney King verdict. Then, in paragraph 14, he restates his second interpretation, linking the preceding analysis with his claim.

Paragraph 15 is interesting for a couple of reasons. It effectively links the conclusion with the introduction, of course, but it also gets at the real crux of the second interpretation. On the surface, the prediction that whites will not respond to the 1992 riots the way they did to the 1960 riots seems inconsequential. Without further examination, one might be tempted to ask the question that is the death blow to any argument: "So what?" But Murray shifts the ground in paragraph 15 to focus on the decline of race relations in America. Suddenly, the white response to the riots is more meaningful. If black–white antagonism deepens, the future is likely to be punctuated with pervasive racial hostility and outbreaks of violence. This is not a pleasant future at all, but it is what the last paragraph leaves readers thinking about.

Writing Assignment

PROVIDING AN INTERPRETATION
THAT PREDICTS THE FUTURE

Return to the list of events you produced for the linked assignment on page 184. Select one event and provide an interpretation that explains how it will influence the future. Your paper should be approximately three pages long, and you should offer effective support for your interpretation.

GROUP ACTIVITIES: PROVIDING
AN INTERPRETATION THAT
PREDICTS THE FUTURE

1. In a paragraph or less, report the basic features of your event. Exchange your paragraph with at least two groupmates; on separate sheets of paper, each groupmate should provide two possible ways the event could influence the future and two reasons why.

2. Evaluate the input your received from your groupmates. How does it match your interpretation of the event? If your groupmates did not provide you with new perspectives on your event, you should exchange your paragraph again.

3. Use the input you received from your group to develop your first draft. Exchange drafts with a groupmate. Evaluate the draft to determine how effec-

tively the interpretation predicts the future and how reasonably the interpretation is argued. List three things that the writer can do to make the interpretation stronger.

4. Confer with a teacher in the subject area of your event. Describe the nature of this writing assignment, state your event, and summarize your interpretation. Ask the teacher to respond to the effectiveness of your interpretation. Take notes on the teacher's comments and use them to revise your paper.

READINGS

Peter Brown

The following passage appears in *A History of Private Life*, a collection of essays examining how notions of public and private life have changed over the centuries. This particular selection comes from volume one of the series, and it focuses on antiquity. The work received much acclaim when it was published, and it is still viewed as a major achievement in historical writing. In the following passage, Peter Brown describes the rise of Christian morality out of a pagan society, and then he interprets the underlying causes of the event.

PETER BROWN

PERSON AND GROUP IN JUDAISM AND EARLY CHRISTIANITY

1   Paul wrote the community at Corinth, possibly in the spring of A.D. 54: "God is not the author of confusion, but of peace, as in all the churches of the saints." As so often, Paul was writing to impose his own interpretation (in this particular case, to stress the need for prophecy in languages intelligible to all) on a situation of insoluble complexity. As we have seen, the Christian churches in the cities depended on respectable and well-to-do households, members of which might welcome certain rituals of undifferentiated solidarity. But life in an urban environment, unless lived permanently among the totally uprooted and marginal— which was not the case in the Christian urban communities of the first, second, and third centuries— could not be based upon such high moments. If singleness of heart was to survive in the Christian churches and be seen to survive before a suspicious pagan world on the relentlessly public stage of everyday life in the city, it could survive only if caught in the fixative of a group life consciously structured according to habitual and resilient norms.

Hence the paradox of the rise of Christianity as a moral force in the pagan world. The rise of Christianity altered profoundly the moral texture of the late Roman world. Yet in moral matters the Christian leaders made almost no innovations. What they did was more crucial. They created a new group, whose exceptional emphasis on solidarity in the face of its own inner tensions ensured that its members would practice what pagan and Jewish moralists had already begun to preach. That singleness of heart for which a man such as Hermas yearned would be achieved in the successful community of Rome less through the undifferentiated workings of the Spirit than by the intimate discipline of a tight-knit group, whose basic moral attitudes differed from those of their pagan and Jewish neighbors only in the urgency with which such attitudes were adopted and put into practice.

3   It is important to note at the outset the crucial difference between the widespread morality adopted by the Christians and the codes of behavior current among the civic elites. Much of what is claimed as distinctively "Christian" in the morality of the early churches was in reality the distinctive morality of a different segment of Roman society from those we know from the literature of the wellborn.

4   It was a morality of the socially vulnerable. In modestly well-to-do households the mere show of power was not available to control one's slaves or womenfolk. As a result, concern for intimate order, for intimate restraints on behavior, for fidelity between spouses and obedience within the household acted out "in singleness of heart, fearing God," tended to be that much more acute. Obedience on the part of servants, fair dealings between partners, and the fidelity of spouses counted for far more among men more liable to be fatally injured by sexual infidelity, by trickery, and by the insubordination of their few household slaves than were the truly wealthy and powerful. Outside the household a sense of solidarity with a wider range of fellow city-dwellers had developed, in marked contrast to the civic notables, who continued throughout the period to view the world through the narrow slits of their traditional "civic" definition of the urban community. A sense of solidarity was a natural adjunct of a morality of the socially vulnerable. There was, therefore, nothing strange, much less specifically Christian, in the inscription on the undoubtedly pagan tomb of an immigrant Greek pearl merchant on Rome's Via Sacra: "[Here] lie contained the bones of a good man, a man of mercy, a lover of the poor."

5   The difference in the attitudes of the upper classes and the average urban dweller toward giving and sharing affords a sharp contrast. The civic notables "nourished" their city; they were expected to spend large sums maintaining the sense of continued enjoyment and prestige of its regular citizens. If such nourishment happened to relieve some distress among the poor, this was considered an accidental byproduct of relief from which the civic body as a whole, the rich quite as much as the poor, benefited by virtue of being citizens. A large number of the city's inhabitants—most often the truly poor, such as slaves and immigrants—were excluded from such nourishment. These large sums were given to the city and its citizens to enhance the status of the civic body as a whole, not to alleviate any particular state of human affliction among the poor. Individual donations could be magnificent displays of fireworks celebrating great occasions—the power and generosity of the patrons, the splendor of the city. The idea of a steady flow of giving, in the form of alms, to a permanent category of afflicted, the poor, was beyond the horizon of such persons.

6   Among the socially vulnerable it was a matter of daily perception that a relationship did exist between the superfluity enjoyed by the modestly well-to-do and the lack of means experienced by their poorer neighbors. Such an imbalance could be remedied, or at least muted, by the redistribution of very small sums, such as were within the reach of any modest city household or of any comfortable farmer among the rural poor of the countryside. It had long been obvious also to the Jewish communities, as it would be to the Christians, that among small men the maintenance of a margin of financial independence in a hostile world was possible through a small measure of mutual support. By offering alms and the chance of employment to the poorer members of their community, Jews and Christians could protect coreligionists from impoverishment, and hence from outright vulnerability to pagan creditors or pagan employers. It is against this social background that we can begin to understand how the practice of almsgiving to the poor soon became a token of the solidarity of threatened groups of believers. The eventual replacing of a model of urban society that had stressed the duty of the wellborn to nourish *their* city by one based on the notion of the implicit solidarity of the rich in the affliction of the poor remains one of the most clear examples of the shift from a classical to a postclassical Christianized world. This shift was under way by the second century A.D. among the Christian communities.

7   Even without the intervention of the Christian churches, we can detect the slow rise, alongside the civic codes of the notables, of a significantly different morality, based on a different world of social experience. By the early third century, long

before the establishment of the Christian church, aspects of Roman law and of Roman family life were touched by a subtle change in the moral sensibilities of the silent majority of the provincials of the Empire. Respectable wedlock was extended to include even slaves. Emperors posed increasingly as guardians of private morality. Suicide, that proud assertion of the right of the wellborn to dispose, if need be, of his own life, came to be branded as an unnatural "derangement."

8 The Christian church caused this new morality to undergo a subtle process of change by rendering it more universal in its application and far more intimate in its effect of the private life of the believer. Among Christians a somber variant of popular morality facilitated the urgent search for new principles of solidarity that aimed to penetrate the individual ever more deeply with a sense of the gaze of God, with a fear of His Judgment, and with a sharp sense of commitment to the unity of the religious community.

9 To appreciate the extent of the changes in moral ideals brought about within the churches, we need only consider the structures of marriage and sexual discipline that developed in Christian households during the course of the second and third centuries. Galen was struck by the sexual austerity of the Christian communities in the late second century: "Their contempt of death is patent to us every day, and likewise their restraint in cohabitation. For they include not only men but also women who refrain from cohabiting all their lives; and they also number individuals who, in self-discipline and self-control, have attained a pitch not inferior to that of genuine philosophers."[4]

10 On the surface the Christians practiced an austere sexual morality, easily recognizable and acclaimed by outsiders: total sexual renunciation by the few; marital concord between the spouses (such as had begun to permeate the public behavior of the elites, if for very different reasons); strong disapproval of remarriage. This surface was presented openly to outsiders. Lacking the clear ritual boundaries provided in Judaism by circumcision and dietary laws, Christians tended to make their exceptional sexual discipline bear the full burden of expressing the difference between themselves and the pagan world. The message of the Christian apologists was similar to that of later admirers of clerical celibacy, as described by Nie-

tzsche. They appealed to "the faith that a person who is an exception on this point will be an exception in other respects as well."

11 It is important to understand the new inner structures that supported what on the surface seemed no more than a dour morality, readily admired by the average man. The commonplace facts of sexual discipline were supported by a deeper structure of specifically Christian concerns. From Saint Paul onward, the married couple had been expected to bear in their own persons nothing less than an analogue in microcosm of the group's single-hearted solidarity. Even if these might be dangerously confused by the workings of the Holy Spirit, in the undifferentiated "gatherings of the saints" the proper relations of husbands and wives, of masters and slaves, were reasserted in no uncertain manner within the Christian household. These relations were invested with a sense that such fidelity and obedience manifested in a peculiarly transparent manner the prized ideal of unfeigned singleness of heart. With the moral gusto characteristic of a group that courted occasions on which to test its will to cohesion, Christian urban communities even abandoned the normal means which Jewish and pagan males had relied upon to discipline and satisfy their wives. They rejected divorce, and they viewed the remarriage of widows with disapproval. The reasons they came to give, often borrowed from the maxims of the philosophers, would have pleased Plutarch. This exceptional marital morality, practiced by modestly well-to-do men and women, betrayed an exceptional will for order: "A man who divorces his wife admits that he is not even able to govern a woman."

12 It was quite possible for Christian communities to settle down into little more than that. Marital morality could have been presented as a particularly revealing manifestation of the will of the group to singleness of heart. Adultery and sexual scheming among married couples could have been presented as the privileged symptoms of the "zone of negative privacy" associated with doubleness of heart. Without the tolerant space accorded by the ancient city to the upper-class males in which to work off their adolescent urges in relatively free indulgence in sexuality, young people would have married early, as close to puberty as possible, in order to mitigate through lawful wedlock the dis-

ruptive tensions of sexual attraction. Women and, it was occasionally hoped, even men would be disciplined by early marriage and by a sense of the piercing gaze of God penetrating into the recesses of the bedchamber. By avoiding remarriage the community could assure for itself a constant supply of venerable widows and widowers able to devote time and energy to the service of the church. Less exposed than notables to the tensions associated with the exercise of real power—bribery, perjury, hypocrisy, violence, and anger—these quiet citizens "of the middling condition" could show their concern for order and cohesion in the more domestic sphere of sexual self-discipline.

13   The disturbing ease with which the sexes mingled at ritual gatherings of Christians remained distasteful to respectable pagans, and strangers avoided speaking to Christians for that reason. A Christian contemporary of Galen actually petitioned the governor of Alexandria for permission to allow himself to be castrated, for only by such means could he clear himself and his correligionists from the charge of promiscuity! On a more humble level, the difficulties in arranging matches for young people, especially for Christian girls, in a community anxious to avoid marriage with pagans ensured that issues of sexual control would be treated with an intensity greater than that of more settled communities. It also meant that the resulting morality would be much more apparent to outsiders and applied much more rigorously to believers.

14   Such pressures go a long way to explain the moral tone of the average late antique Christian community. What they cannot explain is the further revolution by which sexual renunciation—virginity from birth, or continence vowed at baptism, or continence adopted by married couples or widowers—became the basis of male leadership in the Christian church. In this, Christianity had made *il gran rifiuto* (the great renunciation). In the very centuries when the rabbinate rose to prominence in Judaism by accepting marriage as a near-compulsory criterion of the wise, the leaders of the Christian communities moved in the diametrically opposite direction: access to leadership became identified with near-compulsory celibacy. Seldom has a structure of power risen with such speed and sharpness of outline on the foundation of so intimate an act of renunciation. What Galen had perceived at the end of the second century would distinguish the Christian church in later centuries from both Judaism and Islam.

It is claimed that a disgust for the human body 15 was already prevalent in the pagan world. It is then assumed that when the Christian church moved away from its Jewish roots, where optimistic attitudes toward sexuality and marriage as part of God's good creation had prevailed, Christians took on the bleaker colors of their pagan environment. Such a view is lopsided. The facile contrast between pagan pessimism and Jewish optimism overlooks the importance of sexual renunciation as a means to singleness of heart in the radical Judaism from which Christianity emerged. The possible origins of this renunciation may be diverse in the extreme, but they do not in themselves explain why sexual renunciation rapidly became a badge of specifically male leadership in the Christian communities of the second and third centuries.

We must ask not why the human body could 16 have come to be treated with such disquiet in late antiquity, but the exact opposite. Why is the body singled out by being presented so consistently in sexual terms—as the locus of imagined recesses of sexual motivations and the center of social structures thought of sexually—as being formed originally by a fateful sexual drive to marriage and childbirth? Why was this particular constellation of perceptions about the body allowed to carry so huge a weight in early Christian circles? It is the intensity and the particularity of the charge of significance that counts, not the fact that this significance often was expressed in terms so harshly negative as to rivet the attention of the modern reader, who is understandably bruised by such language.

The division between Christianity and Judaism 17 was sharpest in this. As the rabbis chose to present it, sexuality was an enduring adjunct of the personality. Though potentially unruly, it was amenable to restraint—much as women were both honored as necessary for the existence of Israel, and at the same time were kept from intruding on the serious business of male wisdom. It is a model based on the control and segregation of an irritating but necessary aspect of existence. Among the Christians the exact opposite occurred. Sexuality became a highly charged symbolic marker precisely because its disappearance in the committed individual was considered possible, and because this disappearance was thought to register, more significantly than any other human transformation, the qualities necessary for leadership in the religious community. The removal of sexuality—or, more humbly, removal from sexuality—stood for a state of unhesitating availability to God and one's fellows, associated with the ideal of the single-hearted person.

Critical Reading Guide

1. Paragraph 1 may seem puzzling. It begins with a quotation from St. Paul and ends by suggesting that Christian morality was the product of a calculated plan. What rhetorical function do you see in this paragraph?

2. Brown states that Christian morality was merely a variation of the morality already practiced by the "socially vulnerable," and he contrasts it with the morality described in the "literature of the wellborn." What do you think this "wellborn" morality consisted of?

3. Do you think Brown is writing to insiders or outsiders? If your answer is outsiders, what rhetorical technique would Brown need to use to keep from losing readers unfamiliar with Roman literature?

4. An important part of Brown's interpretation is that Christian morality developed out of an existing pagan morality. Identify three pieces of evidence that Brown uses to support this interpretation.

5. Brown uses sexual behavior as an example to illustrate the differences between Christian and pagan morality, and in paragraph 10 he provides an interpretation to explain why sexual behavior might have been such an important feature among early Christians. What is this interpretation?

6. If you were to summarize Brown's interpretation of the rise of Christian morality, what single cause would you say he considers most important?

Michael Williams

Michael Williams is a senior commentator for the BBC assigned to the Far Eastern Service. The following sample was written in response to events in China in 1989, when student protesters and others marched on Tian An Men Square in Beijing. Between April and June, the students demanded greater freedom and democracy from the government. On May 26, they erected the "Goddess of Democracy" statue that bore a striking resemblance to our own Statue of Liberty. On the evening of June 3, troops who had long been quartered near the protesters moved on the Square with orders to clear the students out. Using tanks, armored vehicles, and automatic weapons, the soldiers broke the protest and cleared the Square. The exact number of casualties remains unknown, but estimates are that as many as 5,000 students were killed. Williams' essay interprets the Tian An Men massacre in an effort to predict its effect on the future.

CHINA AND THE WORLD AFTER TIAN AN MEN

1 Early in July China's Prime Minister, Li Peng, used the occasion of a visit to Peking by the Foreign Minister of the small African state of São Tomé and Principe to denounce unwarranted accusations made against China by Western countries. The African Foreign Minister was the highest-ranking overseas visitor to Peking since the army suppressed the student demonstrations in Tian An Men Square in June. Understandably, since that bloody event the world's statesmen have been in no rush to get to Peking. Indeed, the United States, the European Community and most other Western countries have cancelled all high-level contacts with the Chinese government to mark their disapproval of China's hardline leadership.

2 The brutality of the events in Peking, unparalleled in the communist world in recent years, has laid bare the extraordinary authoritarian nature of the current political regime in China. The most obvious foreign-policy consequence of this has been that relations between China and the West have been placed under considerable strain. And although there have been efforts by the Bush Administration in the United States and other Western governments to prevent a complete breakdown in their relationship with China, the chill in relations between Peking and the West is unlikely to be temporary. Barring a major, and unlikely, reversal of the current policies of repression and clampdown, the cosy intimacy that has prevailed in relations between China and the West over the last decade or more appears to be irretrievably lost.

3 On the contrary, an almost certain consequence of the crushing of the democracy movement is that the close relations that have existed between China and the West for some years have now been brutally terminated. On the Western side, governments will become more responsive to public pressure on human rights and the absence of democracy in China. Hopes that economic reform in China would usher in political reforms have now been dashed, probably for many years to come. Indeed,

on the part of the Chinese leadership, there will probably be an equal desire to distance their country from the West. Although Chinese leaders have made a number of ritual statements stressing that the economic reforms would remain in place, it is clear that they, too, do not wish for the previous closeness in their relationship with the West. Moreover, China's hardline leaders have been ready to blame the West for contaminating students with ideas of 'bourgeois liberalism.'

4 The emergence of a more authoritarian leadership in Peking and the bloody assault on Tian An Men Square on 4 June have raised particular problems for the United States and Britain. The United States and China have shared intelligence facilities in Xinjiang since the late 1970s and have engaged in defence cooperation in many areas. So far the chill in relations between Peking and Washington has not impaired that cooperation, but as pressures for stronger sanctions against China mount both in the House of Representatives and in the Senate, the defence and intelligence relationship could come under greater stress. For Britain the problem is even more acute, because of the Hong Kong situation. The events in Peking in early June have completely eroded what confidence the people of Hong Kong had that they have a secure future once the territory reverts back to China in 1997. The British government is coming under increasing pressure to take measures such as introducing greater democracy in Hong Kong and allowing British passport-holders the right of abode in Britain in order to boost confidence among the territory's 3.5m inhabitants. But the very existence of the Hong Kong problem means that the British government cannot afford to see relations with China irretrievably damaged. A more robust defence of Hong Kong's interests will, however, mean that London's relations with Peking are likely to be more troubled in the years up to 1997.

5 There have been some indications since the June events that China might move closer to the Soviet

Union and the rest of the communist bloc. After all, the suppression of the student movement had been preceded by Mr. Gorbachev's historic visit to Peking, setting the seal on the almost 30-year rift between the two countries. For the most part Soviet and East European media were remarkably restrained in their coverage of the bloody repression in Peking. One article in *Pravda* on 8 June even went so far as to express understanding for the actions taken by the Chinese authorities. In messages to the Soviet leadership since, the Chinese have been unusually fulsome and warm. And in mid-June the Chinese Foreign Minister, Qian Qichen, made an unscheduled stop in East Berlin to thank the East German leadership for their 'internationalist stance' over the events in Peking. At the same time, of course, Mr. Gorbachev's declared commitment to *glasnost* and *perestroika*, and the concern he expressed at a press conference in Bonn on 16 June over events in China, indicate the considerable reservations that the Soviet leadership has over taking advantage of the West's present strained relations with China, to seal a closer relationship with Peking.

6   For other countries, too, the events in Peking are likely to have major implications for their relations with China. This is especially the case for South-East Asia and Japan. Tokyo is coming under increasing pressure to observe the limited sanctions imposed by other industrialised countries, and this was a major issue at the summit meeting of the 'Group of 7' in Paris in mid-July.

7   In the immediate future, the political crisis in China is likely to delay further a settlement of the Cambodia problem. Western governments have been pushing China to abandon its support for the Khmer Rouge once Vietnamese troops are withdrawn in September. But a more repressive China could prove even more intransigent on this issue, especially if Peking becomes markedly estranged from the West. Quite apart from the Cambodia problem, a more hardline regime in China could also mean that Peking's relations with other Asian countries, such as India and the Association of South-East Asian Nations (ASEAN) grouping, could deteriorate. There was widespread dismay among the non-communist members of the ASEAN at the tragic turn of events in Peking in June and fears that a more hardline regime might be an uncomfortable neighbour to live with. Prospects for an early normalisation of relations between China and Indonesia, frozen for more than 20 years, have now suffered a considerable setback.

8   The onset of political instability and repression in China will tarnish the country's image not only in the West but also throughout the third world. But it is with the Western world that the strain will become most obvious. Policies that had been built up over the last 10 years or more by Western countries on the assumption that China after the Cultural Revolution would never revert to a new rigid authoritarianism are now effectively shattered. Moreover, the emergence of a more hardline anti-Western leadership in Peking could well provide Moscow with the opportunity, for the first time since the 1950s, to play the China card against the West.

Critical Reading Guide

1. What is the function of the first paragraph?

2. What is the thesis in the Williams essay? Why do you think Williams decided not to put the thesis in the first paragraph?

3. Identify some "facts" that Williams uses to support his interpretation/predictions. Are they convincing? Why or why not?

4. What is the writer's rhetorical stance in this essay? Insider to outsider? Outsider to outsider? What level of expertise can you imagine Williams might bring to this interpretation that would influence the rhetorical stance? Can we think of journalists as experts?

5. Look carefully at the last paragraph, especially the last sentence. What effect do you believe Williams was trying to produce here? That is, what response do you think he was trying to evoke in readers?

Writing Assignment

JAPANESE-AMERICANS IN U.S. CONCENTRATION CAMPS

A friend in the history department wrote a newspaper article about the forced relocation into concentration camps of Japanese and Japanese-Americans during World War II. He was surprised to discover that many readers were unaware that the United States had ever been at war with Japan. He wrote the following assignment, which he donated for inclusion in this book.

Assignment

On February 19, 1942, President Franklin Roosevelt signed an Executive Order that empowered the U.S. Army to transport everyone in the country of Japanese ancestry to concentration camps and hold them there indefinitely. About 2 months later, approximately 150,000 citizens and immigrants were interned in camps scattered across the nation. The following passage describes the event. It comes from *Concentration Camps USA: Japanese-Americans and World War II*, by Roger Daniels, a professor of history. Read the passage carefully and then write a three- to four-page paper that interprets the event and addresses its underlying causes. Because you might not know a great deal about the war and the role Japanese-Americans played in it, this assignment may require some library work to give you background information.

Japanese-Americans in U.S. Concentration Camps

1   The Bainbridge Island move was administered by Karl R. Bendetsen. He had been promoted to full colonel, transferred to De Witt's staff and made director of the Wartime Civil Control Administration (WCCA), which De Witt had set up on March 11 to handle the Army's part of the evacuation. Tom Clark was loaned to WCCA by the Justice Department to coordinate the activities of civilian agencies helping the Army. It was thus the dress rehearsal for the larger move. A set of "Instructions to All Japanese Living on Bainbridge Island" forbade them to move except to an "approved destination" outside Military Area No. 1 and set up a reception center for them. The government was willing to store some possessions "at the sole risk of the owner" and was willing to allow the evacuees to take only "that which can be carried by the family or the individual" if it was bedding, toilet articles, clothing, and "sufficient knives, forks, spoons, plates, bowls and cups for each member of the family." The fifty-four Japanese families on Bainbridge Island had just six days to get ready, and then were moved to an Assembly Center at the Puyallup (Washington) Fairgrounds. And so it went, all up and down the Coast.

2   With the dress rehearsal a success, 107 other performances were held, as Bendetsen and his staff systematically divided the West Coast into 108 areas for exclusion purposes, with roughly 1000 Japanese in each area. Orders were posted in each locality, setting up a central receiving and information point—usually a public building—to inform the evacuees what to do, what they could take, and when to

report. Interpreters were provided and often friendly Caucasians, usually religious groups like the Friends, did what they could to ease the pain.

WRITING GUIDE: JAPANESE-AMERICANS IN U.S. CONCENTRATION CAMPS

Invention

The most obvious challenge you face with this assignment is getting enough background information to allow you to write a meaningful response. When you go to the library for materials related to the internment, you should examine materials that report what happened to the prisoners after the war ended as well as those that describe the event. Although newspapers might not be a reliable source of information concerning the internment, they nevertheless can provide you with some insight into the national mood at the time. You may want to look at some West Coast papers, such as the *San Francisco Chronicle*, the *Oakland Tribune*, and the *Los Angeles Times*. The editorial pages may be particularly revealing. You might find that producing a time line will help you develop a clearer sense of the event and the details associated with its unfolding.

As you review these materials, let yourself be guided by the assignment. Remember, you are going to interpret the event on the basis of underlying causes, so you should match each stage of the event against one or more hypotheses of causality. As soon as you begin examining materials, however, the first thing you will see is that an official explanation already exists for the internment. Japanese immigrants and Japanese-American citizens were deemed to be a threat to national security. This threat was the underlying cause for the event. You would be wise to assume that the assignment is not merely an exercise in going to the library, collecting information, and then repeating the orthodox view. The goal is to give you the opportunity to develop an alternative interpretation, one that *challenges* the orthodox view or that offers a fresh perspective. As you study each stage of the event and all the related information you have collected, match what you know against the orthodox interpretation and then jot down other potential causes.

Your time line may be a valuable organizing tool, but it may not give you a clear argumentative focus. At this point, you should apply an invention strategy. Although this assignment does not call for a metaphoric interpretation, a metaphor nevertheless could be very useful. A metaphor that comes readily to mind is: "The internment was government-sanctioned robbery." It suggests a clear direction for an interpretation and its associated argument.

Planning

Your time line may be a useful organizing tool, and you may want to use it to block out your paper. For example, your time line can help you write a coherent summary of the event. It also can help you refer easily back to details of the event that you can use to support your argument through fact or illustration.

Early in the planning process, you must decide what your rhetorical stance is going to be. Will you be writing as an outsider to outsiders, an insider to outsiders, an insider to insiders? This decision will influence every facet of your paper. Your introduction, where you summarize the event, will vary by your rhetorical stance.

If you are writing for outsiders, your summary will be longer than it will be if you are writing for insiders.

It is a good idea to maintain a high level of flexibility when you are writing, so that when you are presenting your interpretation of underlying causes you can make adjustments to your text, adding examples or reasons in one place and removing them in another. Nevertheless, the goal of planning is to give yourself a kind of "map" for the paper. With this point in mind, you should note the major features of your essay and the type of support you intend to use. Thus, you might develop an outline that helps you visualize the overall organization of the paper. This outline could be more detailed, if you like, and could include, for example, references to parts of the event you plan to summarize, parts you plan to analyze, and so on.

Drafting

Putting everything you now have into a readable first draft probably is your most demanding challenge. While you were collecting information, generating ideas for you interpretation, and working on organization, you essentially were writing for yourself. Your first draft, however, requires that you begin writing for someone else. One technique that many writers find useful is to assume that this first draft is for a good friend. Writing for a friend will not affect the rhetorical stance you have selected, but it will help you feel more relaxed. Being relaxed at this stage is important because your goal is to get on paper as much as you can of your information, interpretation, and reasons. You want to turn what you have generative so far into a more-or-less coherent whole.

Pausing and Reading

Reread frequently as you write, asking yourself how well the words on the page match the interpretation you planned to make. If you produced a metaphor for the interpretation, ask yourself how well your argument develops that metaphor. As you pause and evaluate the match between your plan and your execution of that plan, do not worry about gaps, holes, or inconsistencies in the writing, and do not try to revise much. Instead, make notes in the margins that will help you recall later what you want to change and how you want to change it.

Revising

You always are better off if you set your first draft aside for a couple of days before attempting a revision. This practice will allow you to approach the paper with a fresh perspective and new ideas. If you followed the advice about writing the first draft for a friend, chances are that you now will want to make the paper more formal, more academic. You will accomplish this task by changing certain words and phrases. For example, you may have used "a lot" in the first draft, but in this second draft you would change it to the more formal "a great deal." Also, you probably will want to reduce the number of contractions a bit, although there is no need to eliminate them completely.

An important revision strategy for making the paper more formal, however, is elaboration. Academic writing is far more elaborate than informal writing. It provides more details, more analysis, more examples. Go through the first draft carefully and begin elaborating. At this stage, you should provide far more elaboration than you believe is necessary. Substance often is associated with elaboration, and your paper should be substantive. This also is a good time to begin using the marginal notes you made as you were writing the first draft.

After you complete the second draft, you should ask someone to read it. Do not ask the reader to look at mechanical features, such as spelling and punctuation. Instead, ask him or her to tell you whether you provided enough background in your introduction for readers to understand the event. Ask whether your interpretation seems reasonable. If not, why not? Ask where your interpretation seems strongest and weakest. Ask whether it is interesting and convincing. Then you should use this information to produce a third draft.

Editing

No one wants to read a paper that has mechanical errors, and you shouldn't expect anyone to read your paper if it has them. By the time you get to the third draft, you probably are working with typed copy, and you probably produced it on a word processor. Take the time to spell check the paper. Then read through it carefully, looking for a range of problems: word choice, punctuation, sentence construction. Your handbook covers these topics in detail, and you should use it. In addition, try to get another reader to look over the paper. Most writers miss errors that are obvious to someone else, and another set of eyes can help you produce a polished paper.

GROUP ACTIVITIES: JAPANESE-AMERICANS IN U.S. CONCENTRATION CAMPS

1. Begin with a brainstorming session on World War II and the U.S. concentration camps. The goal is to generate as much information as possible. Some questions to consider that can get this work started: When did Japan enter the war? What event caused the U.S. to declare war against Japan? What role in U.S. society did those of Japanese ancestry have before the war? What threat could Japanese immigrants and Japanese-Americans have posed? Did German immigrants and German-Americans present a similar threat? What about those of Italian ancestry? Why or why not? If people in this country of German or Italian descent posed a threat, why didn't the government act to intern them?

2. Plan a group library search. Teams of two to three group members will be responsible for collecting information about the war, the social status of Japanese in America prior to the war, the social climate of the time, the assemblage and internment of Japanese, the eventual release from the camps, and so forth. The information should be shared among your group at the next class meeting, when you can discuss and analyze it.

3. Using your notes from the brainstorming session and the information your group collected at the library, make a list of at least three causes that could have influenced the relocation of Japanese immigrants and Japanese-Americans to concentration camps. Use the lists that your group produced for another brainstorming session to reach agreement on the three strongest causes underlying the event.

4. After producing your first draft, exchange papers in your group. Group members should determine whether the introduction provides an adequate summary of the event, whether the thesis is clear and understandable, and whether the paper supports the writer's interpretation. Make notes on how the writer can improve the draft, paying particular attention to ways of strengthening the argumentative features of the interpretation.

5. After revising the first draft, exchange papers with another group and perform the same analysis and provide the same input as outlined in Step 4.

6. After revising the second draft, conduct an editing workshop by exchanging drafts in your group. Check the writing for mechanical errors, sentence construction, and paragraph development. You might, for example, evaluate the number of prepositions in the sentences, aiming to help the writer reduce them where possible. Also check for redundancies.

Interpreting Information

An important key to interpreting information is analysis, a topic already discussed in a limited way. It is your primary tool, serving as a critical bridge that connects reporting with interpreting.

CHAPTER SEVEN

Interpreting Information

Events are tangible, and they tend to follow a recognizable pattern of causality. Even relatively uncommon events—such as the collapse of the Soviet Union or the impact of giant comets on Jupiter—are within the realm of daily experience, allowing outsiders to interpret them reasonably well through analogy. Information, on the other hand, is much more abstract, much less amenable to interpretation. The reason is that information is more than recognizable facts—it also includes intangibles such as the theme of a poem or novel, hidden patterns that lead to conclusions, and subtle motifs that convey attitudes, perceptions, and beliefs. In addition, the ability to interpret a given body of information may require special knowledge or subject-matter expertise.

An important key to interpreting information is analysis, a topic already discussed in a limited way. It is your primary tool, serving as a critical bridge that connects reporting with interpreting. Let's examine analysis more closely and explore how it applies to interpretations of information.

ANALYSIS AND SYNTHESIS

At the most fundamental level, analysis involves breaking wholes into parts. However, analysis is nearly always used in tandem with synthesis, its counterpart, which involves fitting parts into wholes. In addition, analysis rarely stands alone as a particular kind of writing but almost always supports some other rhetorical aim in a paper. With respect to interpreting information, successful analysis involves asking—and then answering—various questions about the information:

- Why is a fact important?
- What is the context for the information?
- How does your information link your topic to the broader subject area?
- What role does your information play in helping you understand your topic or subject area?
- What are the various parts or categories that characterize your information?
- How does your information help you solve the "problem" inherent in your topic?

This last question is important because writing presents several different kinds of problems, some more basic than others. For example, helping readers understand the information you present is a fundamental problem you have to solve. Supporting the claims you make is another problem. Analysis is useful in both instances because it allows you to *describe* the nature of the information, concepts, and ideas that are part of your interpretation. It also offers the opportunity to *define* these same things, which helps readers better understand the information and your interpretation.

Analytical description and definition, of course, involve breaking wholes into parts, and they also are likely to involve fitting parts into wholes, as suggested above. The following example illustrates how analysis works. It comes from *The Good Times*, a collection of essays written by journalist Russell Baker:

Passage 1: Analysis by Classification

1   Inanimate objects are classified into three major categories—those that don't work, those that break down and those that get lost.

2   The goal of all inanimate objects is to resist man and ultimately to defeat him, and the three major classifications are based on the method each object uses to achieve its purpose. As a rule, any object capable of breaking down at the moment when it is most needed will do so. The automobile is typical of the category.

Baker is analyzing "inanimate objects" humorously, and he bases these two paragraphs on the human perception that many of the things in daily life are perverse. The first paragraph is intended to strike a sympathetic chord with readers. Most people, for example, have experienced the frustration of trying to find a set of car keys when they are running late. The point is that Baker's categories are not arbitrary; he is grounding his classification on his audiences' experience. He therefore emphasizes the known.

The second paragraph continues with the same strategy, although these days more readers might respond better had Baker used a computer as his example rather than an automobile. What is particularly important about paragraph 2, however, is that it contains a claim that the analysis and the example support: "The goal of all inanimate objects is to resist man and ultimately to defeat him."

Synthesis, the counterpart to analysis, occurs in the next passage, which comes from "The Western Saddle," an essay written by Verlyn Klinkenborg. It offers an elaborate, extended analysis of the origins of the saddle and in this respect is quite different from Baker's passage.

Passage 2: Fitting a Piece into a Whole

1   Like the cow pony itself, the western saddle descended directly from Spanish colonists in the New World. It may have evolved from some combination of the conquistador's saddle, the estradiota, a massive, thigh-binding combat rig, and the jineta, a light leather pad that was brought to Spain by the Moors. In its early forms, the vaquero's saddle was a homemade rig: just a tree—skeleton of wood and rawhide—and a separate leather covering. Because vaqueros rode in cactus country, they also used tapaderos, stirrup covers now seen mainly on fancy parade saddles, and the heavy leather armor that evolved into cowboy's chaps.

Klinkenborg's approach is serious rather than humorous. One result is that the analysis has more of the unknown than Passage 1. By delving into the unknown,

Klinkenborg provides more information, which makes his analysis richer than Baker's. Klinkenborg bases his analysis on history to give readers a context. He writes about how the western saddle descended from Spanish colonists, and then he traces its evolution from earlier forms, which places it in a larger context. Showing how the western saddle is part of a larger whole is at the core of Klinkenborg's passage, and in this respect it illustrates an important characteristic of analysis.

Organization

Because interpretations of information can be complex, writers need a ready means of organizing their material. An organization that works in a wide range of situations follows a simple structure:

- reporting
- analyzing
- interpreting

That is, you first report your information. Then you analyze and interpret it. In actual writing situations, however, organization is rarely so perfectly linear. Sometimes you will need to include analysis and interpretation while reporting; other times you will need to do some reporting while analyzing.

Thesis and Antithesis

On a more concrete level, organization often centers on the thesis of a given paper. A very common method of organizing consists of what is called *thesis* and *antithesis*. Writers first report information with which they disagree. Frequently, this information is widely accepted by a given group. Then they report new information that contradicts the initial thesis—this is the antithesis. *The antithesis is the real focus of the paper.*

This approach allows for a thorough analysis of the information before delving into the interpretation. Moreover, it allows you to anticipate potential objections to your interpretation by recognizing them early. Such objections appear in the thesis portion of the paper, so you are able to deflate them in the antithesis portion by using analysis. *When you recognize potential objections this way, you enhance the character you are developing for any given piece of writing.* Finally, because thesis–antithesis tends to appear at the beginnings of papers, it has the added advantage of stimulating the audience's interest early, suggesting, as it does, that the writer has something interesting and perhaps even new to discuss.

Passage 3 offers a good example of thesis–antithesis. It comes from *The Wealth Creators*, by Gerald Gunderson, and begins a chapter on merchandising in America.

Passage 3: Overturning a Thesis with an Antithesis

When foreign visitors are given a tour of an American steel mill they might politely say, "That's interesting." But oftentimes this is out of deference to their hosts, since they can see similar operations at home. [However, what causes] . . . foreigners truly [to] marvel at American civilization is [entering] . . . a supermarket for the first time.

The first sentence in this example is important because it establishes a set of expectations regarding the topic. Most of us probably have seen reports of foreign dignitaries visiting a steel mill or an automobile plant, so we are inclined to think the paper will be about such visits. The second sentence deflates those expectations, however. It suggests that a trip to a steel mill is merely part of diplomatic protocol. The third sentence, underlined for emphasis, overturns the thesis of the first sentence and offers a new one: that foreigners are really interested in supermarkets. By the time readers get to the end of this sentence, they have a different set of expectations. They know that the writing is going to examine supermarkets, and perhaps associated enterprises, as an enviable aspect of U.S. society.

Journal Entry

Have you ever had a writing assignment that asked you to compare two very different things? If so, how did you handle it? What were some of the challenges?

THE STRUCTURE
OF INTERPRETATION

Analysis and interpretation require thought and reflection. Passage 4 illustrates this point. It was written by Ako, a sophomore enrolled in a Western civilization course that required a three- to five-page term paper. Here is the topic: "In what ways does Machiavelli's *The Prince* reflect Plato's views on love in *Crito*?" Notice that a casual reading of the assignment may suggest that the teacher was looking for a description. One could imagine, for example, that a simple list might suffice: "*The Prince* reflects Plato's views on love in the following ways." Few teachers, however, are looking for lists when they assign a writing topic, and this teacher was no exception. He gave the assignment to see how well students understood the reading and how well they could explain an elusive point—*elusive because neither work has much to say about love and nothing at all to say about romantic love!*

Understandably, Ako was puzzled by the assignment. She reasoned that a philosopher of Plato's stature probably had quite a lot to say about something as important in life as love and that it most likely was in another work. She did some outside reading and learned that many scholars believe a more thorough discussion of love is in Plato's *Phaedrus*. She then read the relevant section of *Phaedrus*, some 20 pages or so. As a result, she had far more information than she had after reading only *Crito*. She also read some published analyses of *The Prince* that gave her more information than she could get from the book and her teacher alone. This information enabled her to analyze the two works in the assignment more effectively, which in turn enabled her to write a better interpretation. The more information Ako had about the texts, the more she was able to analyze them and develop an interpretation congruent with the assignment. This point is very important for your own work!

As you read Ako's paper, consider the ways in which her analysis is linked to and indeed supports her interpretation.

Passage 4: Political vs. Spiritual Love

Ako

1   Love is important for human beings, and it has been talked and written about since the beginning of civilization. One of the earliest texts ever found by archaeologists, for example, is an Egyptian love poem. Plato also wrote about love, and because his work has in many respects shaped, if not defined, Western culture, we should expect to see his influence in the work of numerous writers throughout history. Sometimes this influence is obvious, as in the "courtly love" tradition of French fabliaux—tales of knights who worshipped women from afar in a "Platonic," or spiritual, relationship rather than a physical one. Other times, the influence is much less obvious. This is the case in Machiavelli's *The Prince*, which does not even talk about love in the usual sense but instead mentions it only in regard to the feelings subjects have for their ruler. Nevertheless, careful analysis shows that *The Prince* does reflect Plato's influence in some important ways.

2   Plato's idealism actually contrasts with Machiavelli's materialism. Plato argues that the fundamental realities in the universe are ideas, the chief of which is "the good." The realities that humans perceive with their senses are imperfect reflections of perfect universal forms. Love also is covered in this analysis, so it isn't surprising that we see Plato valuing spiritual love in *Phaedrus* and elsewhere. That is, the physical beauty that attracts a potential lover is a reflection of a perfect universal form in that beauty is equated with "the good." In *Phaedrus*, Plato says that love is the "best kind of all the kinds of divine possession" and writes: "The man who loves the beautiful is called a lover" (67).

3   Plato recognizes that physical beauty results in desire for physical contact, but he argues that a person must resist such desire. The reason is complex. According to Wheelwright (1962) and other scholars, Plato had a negative view of mankind and life. Wheelwright believes that this view was the result of the Athenian court sentencing Plato's teacher, Socrates, to death. In any event, the rationale of Plato's philosophy is "transcendence." The goal is to rise above earthly concerns, which bring pain and confusion, by concentrating on the spiritual and the intellectual.

4   Plato's transcendentalism is evident in *Phaedrus*, where the spirit is described as consisting of two parts, the emotional and the rational. Plato uses the metaphor of a bad, black horse and a good, white horse to characterize these parts. The two horses represent sexual love and spiritual love, or emotion and reason, respectively. Plato writes: "[When a man] first catches sight of the light of his love . . . , the horse which is obedient [the white one] . . . holds itself back from leaping on the loved one; while the other no longer takes notice [of anything] . . . , but springs powerfully forward [to enjoy] . . . the delights of sex" (77).

5   In Plato's view, a good person will control the emotional, physical side of his nature in order to develop the spiritual or rational side. Emotions are to be feared and distrusted and must be repressed. They reveal our humanity, which Plato equates with everything base and animalistic. When talking about people, for example, he states that when "the better elements of their minds get the upper hand by drawing them to a well-ordered life, and to philosophy, they pass their life in blessedness and harmony" (81). This view, however, actually is in conflict with the Greek notion of harmony—known as the Golden Mean—current during this period and which is expressed in the goal of balancing mind and body. *In concordium, corpus et mentis*, as the Romans said.

6   Several scholars have commented that transcendentalism leads to tyranny. Jackobson (36), for example, argues that Plato's philosophy leads to "cultural and intellectual sterility" because it isolates people from their own humanity, making it easier to rationalize acts of tyranny and cruelty. In other words, Plato denies mankind's biological nature. A person who controls his or her emotions in the way Plato rec-

ommends becomes a robot. If everyone practiced Platonic transcendentalism, there could be no society because the things that bind people together in statehood—pride, family, nationalism, enterprise, and so forth—would cease to exist. Each person would strive to be a nation of one.

7   Statehood can exist in a single person, of course, only in the body of a dictator or king, which is why Machiavelli's prince, in his work of that name, can be viewed as the ultimate product of Plato's transcendentalism and views on love. Machiavelli urges rulers to pursue power single-mindedly, rejecting morals and repressing their emotions. He argues that a prince must be above common behavior, with its emphasis on kindness, truth, and generosity. He states, for example, that "those princes have accomplished most who paid little heed to keeping their promises but who knew how to manipulate the minds of men craftily" (47). Just as Plato argued that a person should abandon normal human pursuits to concentrate on attaining "the good," Machiavelli argues that the ruler should abandon social constraints such as morality and convention to gain power. Although their goals are different, both writers advocate a similar means.

8   Machiavelli's manual for power has no place for love. In *The Prince*, union or marriage is just a matter of expediency; emotions are irrelevant. Reflecting Plato's influence, Machiavelli suggests that human nature is inherently flawed and that people will commit evil more readily than they will perform good. Immediately, Plato's metaphor of the two horses comes to mind. Commenting on love, Machiavelli writes: "Love endures by a bond which men, being scoundrels, may break whenever it serves their advantage to do so" (60). The implication is clear: A ruler who seeks love will be disappointed and ultimately betrayed.

9   The image of the ruler that Machiavelli creates in *The Prince* is of a man who is totally in control. As far as we know, Plato was one of the first writers to advocate such control, claiming that repressing emotion led to "the good." From Machiavelli's perspective in *The Prince*, "the good" is power, not enlightenment, but it requires discipline and sacrifice to attain. It therefore seems that Plato's discussion of love and the goal of repressing emotions may have had a strong influence on Machiavelli.

Ako's paper illustrates a standard approach to interpretation. Notice that she starts with an introductory paragraph that begins with general information and ends with a specific claim, her thesis. "Love is important," she begins and then gives an example to support this observation—the Egyptian love poem. She becomes more focused in the middle of the paragraph when she mentions Plato and his influence. The example of courtly love in French fabliaux increases the focus enough to allow Ako to connect Plato to Machiavelli. After mentioning *The Prince*, Ako is ready to offer her thesis, which appears as the last sentence in the paragraph.

The next step is to report the information that forms the foundation for her interpretation, and Ako begins in paragraph 2 by discussing Plato's idealism and its relation to love as described in *Phaedrus*. Paragraph 3 also reports information, and Ako draws on an authority for additional insight into Plato's work, which, as she says, advocates transcendence. The last sentence in that paragraph, however, contains Ako's first interpretation, her summation of what she believes Plato's work in general and the word "transcendence" in particular mean.

Paragraph 4 is more information, but most of paragraph 5 is interpretation. Plato says nothing directly about repressing emotions, but the metaphor of the horses seems intended to mean that a person should repress them. By the same token, Ako's statement that emotions "reveal our humanity" could be viewed simply as a claim until read in the context of the quotation from Plato that follows it. The claim suddenly seems more like an interpretation. Paragraph 6 begins by presenting information, but the third sentence starts a string of interpretations of Jakobson's analysis.

You probably noticed that Ako has less to say about Machiavelli than she does about Plato—understandable given that Machiavelli really doesn't discuss love in *The Prince*. Paragraph 7 serves several purposes. First, it links Machiavelli with Plato and transcendentalism. Second, it presents a brief summary of *The Prince*, providing the information necessary for later interpretation. Then Ako concludes this paragraph with a different version of her thesis, a useful technique in this paper because the assignment defined its organization. The paper had to consist of two parts, one dealing with *The Prince* and the other with *Crito*, and the repetition keeps readers focused.

Supporting the thesis at this point is important, which is why Ako uses paragraph 8 primarily to validate her claim, showing how the two writers are similar. The one sentence of interpretation in this paragraph comes at the end, where Ako explains the quotation from Machiavelli. The final paragraph shows additional similarities between the two writers and ends by affirming the thesis.

The following list will help you better recognize some of the interpretive statements that appear in Ako's paper:

Paragraph 3:

- The goal is to rise above earthly concerns, which bring pain and confusion, by concentrating on the spiritual and the intellectual.

Paragraph 5:

- In Plato's view, a good person will control the emotional, physical side of his nature in order to develop the spiritual or rational side.
- Emotions are to be feared and distrusted and must be repressed.
- They reveal our humanity, which Plato equates with everything base and animalistic.

Paragraph 6:

- In other words, Plato denies mankind's biological nature.
- A person who controls his or her emotions in the way Plato recommends becomes a robot.
- If everyone practiced Platonic transcendentalism, there could be no society because the things that bind people together—pride, family, nationalism, enterprise, and so forth—would cease to exist. Each person would strive to be a nation of one.

Paragraph 8:

- The implication is clear: A ruler who seeks love will be disappointed and ultimately betrayed.

GROUP ACTIVITIES: ASKING QUESTIONS ABOUT ANALYSIS AND INTERPRETATION

The true value of examining a paper like Ako's lies in considering some of the questions that the writer did and did not ask, questions related to rhetorical stance, membership in a given group, and the aims of a particular assignment. These questions may be implicit or explicit, but they underlie effective analysis and interpretation. The following activities are intended to help you examine some of the questions that underlie the passage so that you can better ask them of yourself when writing your own paper.

1. Decide whether Ako is writing as an insider to an insider, an insider to an outsider, or an outsider to an insider. Then write a brief paragraph that identifies those features of the paper that establish its rhetorical relationship. Share your paragraphs in your work group, discussing your analyses. Finally, pretend that Ako is a member of your group and has asked you for advice about how to improve her paper. What suggestions would you give her?

2. Suppose a teacher asked you to compare two things that seemed entirely unrelated, such as modern religious movements and terrorism. It might help to think of such an assignment as a problem to be solved. You do not see any connection between the two things, but clearly your teacher does, so your first step is to reflect on how your teacher views the material and the subject matter. These views usually will be apparent from your contact with the teacher. As a group, brainstorm to generate a list of approaches you could use to help in the case of modern religious movements and terrorism. (Think about strategies you have used in the past to deal with similar problems.) Did Ako use one of these approaches?

3. Asking why something is important can help you begin interpreting information. What other questions might Ako have asked herself to arrive at a reasonable interpretation? List several of these questions, then share the list with your work group. Did your groupmates find any questions helpful that you had not considered?

Diverse Voices

Different cultures use different techniques for analysis. For example, some cultures analyze the world around them in terms of its properties: Rabbits are soft, long-eared creatures that hop; flowers are colorful, fragrant plants that make great gifts and decoration. Other cultures analyze the world in terms of function: Rabbits are good to eat; flowers can be used to differentiate between types of plants.

For this activity, compare and contrast in about two pages how your home culture analyzes reality with how mainstream American culture appears to analyze it. If your culture uses an approach different from the American mainstream, reflect on how you are influenced by both communities.

Building Your Interpretation

All interpretations of information operate on two levels. That is, your paper will have an interpretive aim, and it also will have a series of minor interpretations that carry your writing forward and, ultimately, build your overall interpretation. Ako's paper offers a good example because it deals with the large issue of love in *The Prince* and *Crito* by addressing a number of smaller issues through specific interpretations. The following excerpt, from paragraph 6, illustrates this technique, which Ako handles very well. She provides information in the first two sentences and states her interpretation of that information in the final one:

> Several scholars have commented that transcendentalism leads to tyranny. Jackobson (36), for example, argues that Plato's philosophy leads to "cultural and intellectual sterility" because it isolates people from their own humanity, making it easier to rationalize acts of tyranny and cruelty. In other words, Plato denies mankind's biological nature.

This sort of organization is fundamental in *all* effective expository writing, not just interpretation. The overall aim of argumentation, for instance, is to make and support a claim, but it does so through a series of minor claims and support.

Writing Assignment

INTERPRETING A TEXT

The following passage comes from "Living Smaller," an article published in *The Atlantic Monthly* by Witold Rybczynski. The article provides a brief history of housing in the United States, and the excerpt describes the shift to larger and larger houses since the 1950s. This assignment gives you an opportunity to apply what you have learned about interpreting information.

Look at the last sentence in paragraph 8: "Expensive housing means that a few people lose but a lot of people gain." This statement seems at odds with the previous two paragraphs. In an essay of two to three pages, interpret the sentence and explain what it means, relating your interpretation to media accounts of homelessness and/or media accounts of the difficulties middle-class people face today in trying to purchase a home.

When Houses Bulked Out

1 A short history of the American house since 1950 would have to include a chapter called "Bigger and Better." The Levittown house had two bedrooms, one small bathroom, and an eat-in kitchen; all its rooms were arranged on a concrete slab whose dimensions were twenty-five by thirty feet (an unfinished attic was often converted into additional living space). William Levitt's strategy becomes apparent if one compares his house with earlier designs for modestly priced houses, such as those included in *Homes of Character*, a pattern book published in 1923 by the Boston architect Robert L. Stevenson. The porches, vestibules, entry halls, and dining rooms (or at least dining alcoves) that were standard domestic amenities in the twenties were absent from the Levittown house, which lacked even a basement. It was bare-bones living.

2   The prosperity of the next two decades was an opportunity to recover some of the lost space. Not surprisingly, new houses increased in size. In 1963 the average new house had 1,450 square feet (the Levittown house had 750 square feet), and over the next decade another 200 square feet, the equivalent of two bedrooms, were added. According to the National Association of Home Builders, the average finished area of a new single-family house in 1989 was about 2,000 square feet, and thousands of houses were even bigger, often 3,000 to 4,000 square feet.

3   Houses became bigger in the sixties and seventies both because rooms were larger and because there were more of them. Kitchen appliances such as dishwashers, food processors, and microwave ovens required larger, more elaborate kitchens with more counter space. Bathrooms proliferated throughout the house: powder rooms, guest bathrooms, private bathrooms attached to bedrooms and equipped with whirlpool baths and separate shower stalls. By 1972 half of all new houses contained two or more bathrooms. Ten years later nearly three quarters did. It became customary for each child to have his or her own bedroom, and for the parents' room to be larger than the others (in Stevenson's plans there were no "master" bedrooms—all bedrooms were roughly the same size). During the sixties most houses augmented the traditional living room with a family room, or rec room. This allowed greater informality in living arrangements—a place for children to play, and a place to put the television. The rec room was also a sign of the growing privatization of family life, which was a reaction to the disintegration of the public realm. The home was becoming the chief locale for family leisure, as it had been in Victorian times.

4   In a consumer society, houses not only shelter people but also are warehouses full of furniture, clothes, toys, sports equipment, and gadgets. It is a measure of the growth of consumerism that one of the things that immediately dates a house of the 1920s is how little storage space it has. In the 1920s a bedroom cupboard three feet wide was considered sufficient; today most bedrooms have a wall-to-wall closet, and master bedrooms are incomplete if they do not have an extended walk-in closet, often grandiloquently called a dressing room. There may be fewer people in the American house of the nineties, but there are a lot more things.

5   There is a price to be paid for this expansion, however. Bigger houses mean more time and money spent on cleaning and maintenance—work traditionally performed by women. Betty Friedan characterized the single-family suburban house as a "domestic trap." The bigger the house, the bigger the trap. Even if one maintains that house-proud homemakers are satisfied to trade their free time for extra housework, what about the many women who now also work outside the home? In *The Second Shift*, Arlie Hochschild studied working couples and found that, on average, women performed three quarters of the housework. She estimated that during the 1960s and 1970s housework and child care accounted for roughly fifteen hours a week of extra work for the working woman. Obviously, working women are ill served by the larger house.

6   The growth in the size of houses is also at odds with the shrinkage in the size of households. Why do families that are, on average, smaller require twice as much space? To some extent the expanding American house reflects a crude, bigger-is-better mentality. Homeownership is a sign of social accomplishment and status, and just as the most prestigious cars were once the Cadillac and the Continental, which served as models for cheaper (but equally bloated) Fords and Chevrolets, the houses of the wealthy—in particular, Hollywood celebrities, whose sprawling Beverly Hills villas were prominently featured in fan magazines—were what the average tract house strove to imitate.

7   The increase in the size of the average new house, and in the level of amenities it contained, naturally cost money, and prices rose accordingly. Of course, the home-building industry was propelled by the same economic imperatives that drove the automobile industry, and found it profitable to furnish the market with more-expen-

sive houses. And like the automobile manufacturers, builders resisted reducing the size of their product dramatically—even when inflation, higher interest rates, and low household incomes (especially those of single-parent families headed by women) suggested that it might be reasonable to do so.

8   When land prices, labor costs, or commercial interest rates rise, the builder passes the increase on to the buyer and raises the selling price of the house. If car prices rise too steeply, a prospective buyer has the choice of spending less and buying secondhand. But houses are not cars. Not only do older houses not depreciate in value but their selling price is affected by the general housing market. If new houses cost more, then so do old houses, even though they were built years before, with less expensive labor, less expensive materials, and cheap money. Hence the higher the cost of new housing the more difficult it is to become a homeowner, and the more beneficial it is to be one already. Expensive housing means that a few people lose but a lot of people gain.

9   Theoretically, prices should eventually drop as a result of reduced demand. However, unlike car prices, over time house prices have so far proved remarkably resistant to declines in demand. (A theory newly gaining prominence holds that house prices will never again be impervious to the rest of the economy.) Many homeowners who are selling a house prefer to wait rather than reduce their asking price significantly. The nature of the home-building industry is also a factor. Large merchant builders have diversified into related fields such as property development and commercial and industrial building. When demand falters, they are more likely to shift the focus of their construction activities than to lower prices. But most builders are small. More than half of all the residential builders in the United States build fewer than ten houses a year. They operate with low overhead and few if any permanent employees; when prices soften, it is easy for them to cut back and wait until things improve, or simply to take a vacation.

10   The American dream of becoming a homeowner is so compelling that for a long time rising prices were slow to discourage demand; and as prices rose, banks and savings-and-loan companies made it easier to borrow money. The rule of thumb traditionally used by lenders to evaluate the financial capabilities of prospective homebuyers was that housing costs (mortgage payments, taxes, and utilities) should not consume more than 25 percent of the household's income. By the 1980s, as house prices began to rise faster than incomes and this trend began to encourage borrowing, the percentage was adjusted upward: to 30 percent, then 35 percent, and sometimes almost as high as 40 percent.

11   The rationale was that higher housing costs were being offset by the appreciation in the resale value of the property. This view had some validity, since houses were rapidly increasing in value, but it was a saving on paper, available only in the future, when the house was sold. In the meantime, the homeowner was obliged to tighten his belt and spend less—on recreation, travel, education, culture, books. Many people simply borrowed more to make up the difference. No wonder that credit cards became so popular, and so widely abused. Homeownership was being maintained, more or less, but at what price?

GROUP ACTIVITIES:
INTERPRETING A TEXT

1. *Preliminary Reflection.* In your group, discuss the conditions that would have to exist for the statement ("Expensive housing means that a few people lose but a lot of people gain") to be true.

2. *Researching.* Write one or two paragraphs that summarize what you know about homelessness and the difficulties the media say that middle-class people face in trying to purchase a home. Each member should share this information

with the group. Use this information as the basis of work that provides you with more details relating to home ownership. Some questions you might ask are: What percentage of the population owns a home? What is the average age of homeowners? How many homeless people are there in the United States? What is the average price of a home in your region today? How much cash must people generally put down to purchase a home? What is the average annual income of people in your region today? What percentage of their monthly income would be required to pay a mortgage? You also should try to determine what age group benefited most from the rapid real estate inflation of the 1970s and 1980s.

3. *Brainstorming.* Share the information your group gathered and brainstorm on the writing assignment. First determine what you will say in response to the assignment; then determine how you will say it. For example, what will constitute the information you present? What will you include in your analysis? Where will you place your interpretation?

4. *Drafting.* Begin drafting your paper. Now that you have greater knowledge of the factors involved, what will be your rhetorical stance, insider or outsider?

5. *Pausing and Reading.* After first drafts are completed, exchange papers and focus on the three parts: presentation of information, analysis, and interpretation. Check your groupmate's essay to determine if it reports the information clearly. Has the writer provided a context for the interpretation? If there is a context, write down some suggestions for ways to improve it. Does the analysis function to support the interpretation? Again, write down some suggestions for ways to enhance the level of support. A well-written paper should provide an analysis that leads reasonably to the interpretation. Has your groupmate succeeded in this respect? Explain why or why not, with suggestions for improvement.

6. *Revising.* Revise your draft on the basis of your groupmate's comments. If possible, schedule a conference with your teacher to talk about the revision. Group Exchange: Your group should work with another group in the class, and you should pair up with a member of the other group. Exchange revised drafts, but before reading, you should tell your partner what you intended to do in this essay and how you think you accomplished that intention. Readers should then read the draft with an eye toward evaluating how well you accomplished your intention. Take notes so that you can use these comments for your next revision. When your partner is finished, switch roles.

7. *Editing.* After you have revised your paper again, exchange with a groupmate. Check sentence lengths (you may have to count words for this). If most of the sentences are about the same length, or if four consecutive sentences are about the same length, make a note that alerts the writer. Return papers and revise to modify sentence length. You may have to make some shorter and some longer, which you can accomplish by joining two short sentences into a single sentence using a semicolon or another technique.

READINGS

Paul E. Peterson

The following passage is an excerpt from Paul E. Peterson's essay "An Immodest Proposal," which analyzes and interprets economic information about children and the elderly in America. He based his title on a famous essay by the 18th-century

British writer Jonathan Swift, which was called "A Modest Proposal." Using satire and irony, Swift criticized the government's treatment of poor people in Ireland by suggesting that they be used as food. Peterson's concluding suggestion is not as radical as Swift's, but it is surprising and certainly would, if implemented, change America's future. Peterson teaches government and is a university professor.

PAUL E. PETERSON

GIVE KIDS THE VOTE

1 Children and the elderly in the United States are linked by a strong dependence on government programs. There is a significant difference between the two groups, though: the elderly are politically powerful, represented in Washington by the Association for the Advancement of Retired People, one of the lobbies most feared by Congress; the young, on the other hand, since they cannot vote, are almost completely without political pull. This political imbalance has a practical effect: the government assistance that elderly Americans receive is both more substantial and easier to obtain than the aid that goes to American children. And because the two groups rely to such a great degree on government largess, the imbalance has a tangible result: poverty among American children is disturbingly high and is increasing, while poverty among the elderly is relatively low and is decreasing. The poverty rate for those over the age of sixty-five fell from 35 percent in 1959 to 25 percent in 1970 to a nadir of 11 percent in 1989; meanwhile, the percentage of children under the age of eighteen who are living in poverty increased from 15 percent in 1970 to 22 percent in 1991.

2 These disparities are not the result of some quirk in the American marketplace; in fact, they are caused by government policies reaching back three decades. The Great Society was "great" most notably for America's growing and increasingly politicized elderly population. Between 1965 and 1975 federal programs serving elderly Americans nearly tripled, from $71.3 billion to $192.9 billion (in constant 1990 dollars). Even with the growth of the elderly population taken into account, the per capita expenditures still more than doubled, from $3,860 to $8,500, over the ten-year period.

3 Although children, too, benefited from a number of the programs that were instituted or expanded during the Great Society era, the dollar amounts they received were less impressive. Together, welfare programs for children—among them Aid to Families with Dependent Children (AFDC), food stamps, and the supplemental food program for women, infants, and children (WIC)—amounted to only $42.3 billion in 1975. This was just 1.2 percent of the GNP, significantly less than the 5.4 percent that went to welfare programs benefiting the elderly.

4 One might have thought that the anomalies created in the rush to construct the Great Society would have been gradually corrected in subsequent years. But what was put in place by 1975 is basically what exists today. The average expenditure for each elderly person who would be poor without those benefits has grown from approximately $20,000 to $30,000 since 1975, while the average expenditure per would-be poor child has climbed from about $1,800 to $2,700.

5 Not only do the dollar amounts for elderly programs greatly exceed those available for children's programs but, perhaps more important, the institutional designs of the programs for the two age groups differ dramatically. Because of the political clout wielded by the nation's seniors, government programs for the elderly have important advantages in their structure and presentation. There are three advantages that are most significant:

6 1. *The elderly receive most of their benefits through two programs rather than from a confus-*

ing array of agencies. The simplicity of programs for the elderly is the envy of children's advocates. Two programs—social security and Medicare—supply 80 percent of the benefits distributed to the elderly. No single program for children accounts for anywhere near as high a percentage of the total. Twenty-four percent of children's benefits are distributed via AFDC, 19 percent via food stamps, 18 percent via Medicaid, 9 percent via housing assistance, 5 percent via WIC, another 5 percent by means of the Earned Income Tax Credit (EITC), and the remaining 20 percent by a host of other programs. The greater the number of programs, the more difficult it is for potential recipients to ascertain their eligibility, to estimate potential benefits, to figure out appropriate procedures, and to locate the place to apply. More programs means more agencies, more application forms, more lines in which to wait, more copies of documents to submit, more variation in the documents that need to be submitted, and so on.

7   Also, because the programs benefiting the elderly are nationally standardized, the elderly can move from New Jersey to Florida (or even overseas) without jeopardizing their social security check or Medicare payment. Families with children find themselves in a quite different situation. Because family welfare programs are decentralized, benefits and eligibility requirements vary widely from state to state. Families may be eligible for assistance in one state or locality but find themselves out of luck elsewhere. The freedom to move that Americans take for granted has much less meaning for families in need of government assistance.

8   2. *The elderly can supplement their benefits with income from their own resources.* If one must sacrifice the resources one has acquired in order to receive government aid, that aid loses much of its attractiveness. In this regard, the elderly have done very well. They keep their savings, retain dividends and interest, and keep their homes while receiving their Medicare and social security benefits. Children's programs, on the other hand, are designed mainly to substitute for independent income, not supplement it. Families are not eligible for AFDC if they have savings of more than $1,000, a car worth more than $1,500, or a home beyond a given value (which varies from state to state). After a four-month transitional period, every dollar earned in

excess of $130 per month by an AFDC family reduces AFDC benefits by a dollar. In general, for every dollar above $2,640 earned by a characteristic poor family, benefits are reduced by about fifty cents. By comparison, a typical retired couple loses about thirty-three cents in benefits for every dollar earned in excess of $10,200.

9   3. *The elderly are more likely to receive their benefits as a matter of "right" than as a "handout."* The elderly receive their benefits as an ostensible reward for past effort rather than as a donation. People contribute to the social security "insurance fund" throughout their working life, and they receive benefits in retirement from the fund to which they have contributed. But, as is well known to policy analysts (though hardly ever mentioned by politicians), designation of social security and Medicare as social insurance is almost a complete fiction. Social security contributions are spent by the government as soon as they are received, and they are spent for purposes that often have nothing to do with retirement. The benefits a retiree receives, moreover, are tied only loosely to the size of his or her contribution. The average retired couple in 1981 contributed only enough to social security during their working years to have earned (by direct contribution and interest on the contribution) four months' worth of medical benefits and three and one-half years of their retirement pension. For the remaining thirteen years of their life span, the couple simply enjoys a gift from working Americans. Yet most Americans believe—and all politicians say—that the elderly have earned their Medicare and social security benefits. No comparable fiction is created for children's programs, which are universally viewed as government handouts.

10   This basic inequality has at its roots a political cause: the 23 million Americans over the age of sixty-five have political power and the 65 million Americans under the age of eighteen do not. There is only one sure cure for this political inequality: all citizens, even our youngest, should be given the right to vote, either by casting their own votes or by having their votes cast for them by their parents or guardians.

11   If children were given the right to vote, fundamental political and public-policy changes would certainly follow. Groups representing children would immediately acquire status and power, they

would demand a larger share of the welfare pie, and they would insist that programs for children be redesigned.

12   If children had had the vote, the 1992 campaign for the presidency would probably have had a distinctly different emphasis. As it was, the positions taken by both George Bush and Bill Clinton testified to the power of the elderly. Neither Bush nor Clinton proposed any significant diminution of the social security system. The only candidate to propose modest reductions, Paul Tsongas, was quickly dispatched by Clinton in the Florida primary. Neither candidate put forward a family-allowance plan or any other program to give children entitlements in any way comparable to those the elderly receive.

13   If the franchise were extended to children, we could anticipate the following changes in public policy:

14   1. Benefits to children would become a matter of right rather than a public benefaction. They would become nationally standardized and administered, and would supplement income as well as offer consumer choice in the selection of a service provider. This would probably mean a substantial program of family allowances (similar to those presently existing in Europe) that would go to all families independent of family earnings.

2. Retirement pensions for the elderly would be scaled back.

3. A system of national health insurance would extend to all households the medical benefits, now enjoyed by those over the age of sixty-five.

15   I'm not necessarily recommending these specific policy innovations, but I'm not especially alarmed by them. What does disturb me is the current imbalance in the structure of the American welfare state. And what is most disturbing is this nation's political incapacity to do anything about it.

Critical Reading Guide

1. Peterson presents and analyzes information about two distinct groups in America—the elderly and the young. His first sentence reports information about these two groups. Which sentences in the first paragraph provide his interpretation of the article's information?

2. What is Peterson's rhetorical purpose? How is that purpose related to his interpretation?

3. The article is divided into three parts. What is the focus of each part?

4. Sometimes Peterson begins a paragraph with an interpretive claim. He then presents information in the paragraph to support that claim. Which paragraphs follow this structure? What advantage is there in this organization?

5. In paragraph 12, Peterson discusses the 1992 presidential elections and states that "The only candidate to propose modest reductions [in the Social Security System], Paul Tsongas, was quickly dispatched by Clinton in the Florida primary." Use your knowledge of U.S. geography, politics, and society, in addition to the information reported in Peterson's article, to write a paragraph that interprets this sentence.

Daniel J. Singal

In the next selection, Daniel Singal reports statistics that indicate that student test scores have declined since the mid-1970s. He asks why scores have fallen, how serious a problem the decline presents for schools and the nation, and what can be done to turn the situation around. Singal is a history professor. His books include *The War Within: From Victorian to Modernist Thought in the South, 1919–1945.*

DANIEL J. SINGAL

THE OTHER CRISIS IN AMERICAN EDUCATION

1 Two crises are stalking American education. Each poses a major threat to the nation's future. The two are very different in character and will require separate strategies if we wish to solve them; yet to date, almost without exception, those concerned with restoring excellence to our schools have lumped them together.

2 The first crisis, which centers on disadvantaged minority children attending inner-city schools, has received considerable attention, as well it should. Put simply, it involves students whose habitat makes it very difficult for them to learn. The key issues are more social than educational. These children clearly need dedicated teachers and a sound curriculum, the two staples of a quality school, but the fact remains that most of them will not make significant progress until they also have decent housing, a better diet, and a safer environment in which to live.

3 The second crisis, in contrast, is far more academic than social and to a surprising extent invisible. It involves approximately half the country's student population—the group that educators refer to as "college-bound." Although the overwhelming majority of these students attend suburban schools, a fair number can be found in big-city or consolidated rural districts, or in independent or parochial schools. Beginning in the mid-1970s these students have been entering college so badly prepared that they have performed far below potential, often to the point of functional disability. We tend to assume that with their high aptitude for learning, they should be able to fend for themselves. However, the experience of the past fifteen years has proved decisively that they can't.

4 For most people, any mention of the problems of American education almost immediately conjures up an image of the wretched conditions in the stereotypical urban ghetto school. But can we really explain the sharp decline in college-entrance-exam scores by pointing to the inner cities, where only a tiny fraction of students even take the Scholastic Aptitude Test, or SAT? Do so many freshmen entering prestigious institutions like Harvard and Berkeley display a limited mastery of basic historical facts, not to mention of their own language, because they come from crime-ridden neighborhoods or school districts with no tax base?

5 If one looks at the aggregate statistics of American education from this perspective, the full dimensions of this other crisis become strikingly apparent. Consider the recent history of the Stanford Achievement Test, which has long served as one of the main instruments for measuring pupil progress in our schools. According to Herbert Rudman, a professor of educational psychology at Michigan State University and a co-author of the test for more than three decades, from the 1920s to the late 1960s American children taking the Stanford made significant gains in their test performance. They made so much progress, in fact, that as the test was revised each decade, the level of difficulty of the questions was increased substantially, reflecting the increasing level of challenge of the instructional materials being used in the schools.

6 From the late 1960s to the early 1980s, however, we managed to squander the better part of that progress, with the greatest losses coming in the high schools. During the past few years the Stanford and other test results have shown some improvement in math and science, and in language skills at the elementary school level. But there has been little or no

movement in the verbal areas among junior high and high school students, and seasoned test interpreters have also seen a tendency for the gains made in the early years of school to wash out as the child becomes older. In effect, the test numbers substantiate what the National Commission on Excellence in Education concluded—quoting the education analyst Paul Copperman—in 1983 in *A Nation at Risk*: "Each generation of Americans has outstripped its parents in education, in literacy, and in economic attainment. For the first time in the history of our country, the educational skills of one generation will not surpass, will not equal, will not even approach, those of their parents."

7   The blame for this wholesale decline in test scores is often put on a throng of underachieving minority students thought to have been pulling down national test averages, but in fact just the opposite is true. To be sure, it is possible to attribute much of the relatively small initial drop in SAT scores, from 1963 to 1970, to the fact that blacks and other minorities began taking the test in larger numbers during those years, but since then the composition of the test population has not changed in any way that would dramatically affect test scores. Most important, blacks have made gradual but significant gains in the past two decades, as measured by school achievement tests like the Stanford and by college-entrance exams. Although their average scores still fall substantially below those of whites, their combined (verbal and math) SAT scores rose by 49 points during the 1980s alone. "Perhaps the most untold story of American education in the past few years is the achievement of black students." Gregory R. Anrig, the president of the Educational Testing Service, declares. "The hard data are encouraging." The sad irony, of course, is that this progress came at a time when the Reagan Administration was proposing drastic cuts in the amount of federal scholarship aid available to students from low-income families, most likely leading many young blacks to believe that a college education was not within their reach.

8   While students in the bottom quartile have shown slow but steady improvement since the 1960s, average test scores have nonetheless gone down, primarily because of the performance of those in the top quartile. This "highest cohort of achievers," Rudman writes, has shown "the great-

est declines across a variety of subjects as well as across age-level groups." Analysts have also found "a substantial drop among those children in the middle range of achievement," he continues, "but less loss and some modest gains at the lower levels." In other words, our brightest youngsters, those most likely to be headed for selective colleges, have suffered the most dramatic setbacks over the past two decades—a fact with grave implications for our ability to compete with other nations in the future. If this is true—and abundant evidence exists to suggest that it is—then we indeed have a second major crisis in our education system.

Sixty Lost Points on the SAT

Look at what has happened on the SAT, a test that   9
retains its well-deserved status as the most important educational measuring device in America. Despite the test's many critics, the number of colleges relying on the SAT keeps increasing, because it provides such an accurate gauge of the basic skills needed for college-level work, among them reading comprehension, vocabulary, and the ability to reason with mathematical concepts. The SAT also has the virtue of having a rock-steady scoring system: it is calibrated, by the College Board, so that a score earned in 1991 will represent almost exactly the same level of performance as it did in, say, 1961. Thus, by tracking the percentage of students coming in above the benchmark of 600 on the College Board scale (which runs from 200 to 800), one can get a good sense of how the country's most capable students have fared over the years.

The news is not encouraging. In 1972, of the   10
high school seniors taking the SAT 11.4 percent had verbal scores over 600; by 1983 the number had dropped to 6.9 percent, and, despite modest gains in the mid-1980s, it remains in that disheart-

ening vicinity. That's a decline of nearly 40 percent. The decline since the mid-1960s has probably been closer to 50 percent, but unfortunately the College Board changed its reporting system in 1972, and earlier data aren't available. The math SAT presents a somewhat different story. Though the percentage scoring over 600 dropped from 17.9 in 1972 to 14.4 by 1981, it has climbed back up to 17.9 in 1991. However, an influx of high-scoring Asian-American students (who now make up eight percent of those taking the test, as compared with two percent in 1972) has apparently had much to do with this recent upsurge.

11   To grasp what these national figures really mean, it helps to approach them from the standpoint of the individual student. How, we should ask, would the drop in SAT scores affect a typical top-quartile senior at a well-regarded suburban high school in 1991? To my knowledge, no published studies have addressed this question, but the available information, including my own research, suggests that our hypothetical senior would come in roughly fifty to sixty points lower on the verbal section and twenty-five points lower on the math than he or she would have in 1970.

12   Consider the trend in average freshman scores at selective colleges. Indeed, perusing a twenty-year-old edition of *Barron's Profiles of American Colleges* is an experience equivalent to entering a different world, with tuitions much lower and SAT scores much higher than at most schools today. In 1970 students arriving at top-ranked institutions like Columbia College, Swarthmore College, the University of Chicago, and Pomona College posted average verbal SATs from 670 to 695; by the mid-1980s the scores ranged from 620 to 640, and they have stayed roughly in that neighborhood ever since. The same pattern appears at colleges a notch or two lower in the academic hierarchy. To take a few examples from different geographic areas, from 1970 to 1987 average verbal scores went from 644 to 570 at Hamilton College, from 607 to 563 at Washington University, from 600 to 560 at the University of Michigan at Ann Arbor, and from 560 to 499 at the University of California at Santa Barbara.

13   The point is *not* that these particular schools have slipped in their relative standings. They all currently receive ratings the same as or higher than those they received twenty years ago from *Bar-*

ron's in terms of competition for admission. One could pick almost any selective institution at random and find the same trend (an exception: the stronger schools in the South, where test scores held steady or rose in the wake of desegregation). Nor can one attribute the drop in scores to a change in the size of the test population or in the percentage of high school seniors taking the SAT (the latter figure has risen significantly only in the past few years, too recently to have affected the 1987 scores). To be sure, an increase in the number of minority students attending these institutions has been a factor, but the basic problem remains: with a 40 percent decline in the proportion of students scoring over 600, there are far fewer high-scoring students to go around.

14   But do these numbers matter? Does a loss of sixty points on the verbal SAT translate into a significant difference in a student's educational experience at college? The testimony of those who teach at the college level suggests that the answer is yes. When a national poll in 1989 asked professors whether they thought undergraduates were "seriously underprepared in basic skills," 75 percent said yes and only 15 percent said no. The same poll asked whether institutions of higher learning were spending "too much time and money teaching students what they should have learned in high school." Sixty-eight percent said yes. Professors feel like this, I should add, not because they are old scolds given to grousing about students but because their work brings them into daily contact with the manifold ways in which the American education system has failed these young people.

15   Those who tend to dismiss those sixty lost SAT points as insignificant haven't seen a college term paper lately. It's not that freshmen in 1991 are unable to read or write. Most of them possess what the National Assessment of Educational Progress calls "satisfactory" skills in this area. But is that enough for college? Do they have sufficient command of the English language to comprehend a college-level text, think through a complex issue, or express a reasonably sophisticated argument on paper? Those of us who were teaching in the early 1970s can attest that the overwhelming majority of freshmen at the more selective colleges arrived with such "advanced" skills. Now only a handful come so equipped.

The Context of Ignorance

16 Take reading, for example. "While the nation's students have the skills to derive a surface understanding of what they read," the NAEP recently reported, "they have difficulty when asked to defend or elaborate upon this surface understanding." That's what most college faculty would say. Emilia da Costa, a Latin America specialist who has taught at Yale for the past eighteen years, estimates that whereas 70 percent of her students can pick out the general theme of an essay or a book, only 25 percent come away with in-depth comprehension of what they read. David Samson, a former lecturer in history and literature at Harvard, likewise observes, "No one reads for nuance. They pay no attention to detail." My own experience confirms this. Countless times I have been amazed at how little students have managed to glean from a book I know they have read, to the point where they are often unable to recall the names of prominently mentioned figures. So much escapes them; even those of above-average ability absorb no more than a dusting of detail from a printed text. And without such detailed information it's impossible for them to gain a real understanding of what the author is saying.

17 Equally distressing is the rate at which today's students read. A friend of mine at the University of Michigan remembers that in the 1960s the normal assignment in his courses was one book a week. Now he allows two to three weeks for each title. He has also reluctantly had to adjust the level of difficulty of his assignments: even a journalist like Walter Lippmann is too hard for most freshmen and sophomores these days, he finds. Again, this is typical. Twelve to fifteen books over a fifteen-week semester used to be the rule of thumb at selective colleges. Today it is six to eight books, and they had better be short texts, written in relatively simple English.

18 As one might expect, students who don't read at an advanced level can't write well either. Their knowledge of grammar is not bad, according to Richard Marius, the director of the expository writing program at Harvard, but "the number of words available to express their thoughts is very, very limited, and the forms by which they express themselves are also very limited." The average incoming Harvard student, he observes, has a "utilitarian command of language" resulting in sentences that follow a simple subject-predicate format with little variation or richness of verbal expression. Harvard, of course, gets the cream of the crop. Those of us teaching at lesser institutions would be happy with utilitarian but serviceable prose from our freshmen. More often we get mangled sentences, essays composed without the slightest sense of paragraphing, and writing that can't sustain a thought for more than half a page.

19 Along with this impoverishment of language comes a downturn in reasoning skills. Da Costa laments that students are no longer trained in logical analysis and consequently have difficulty using evidence to reach a conclusion. R. Jackson Wilson finds this to be the greatest change he has observed during a quarter century of teaching history at Smith College. "Students come to us having sat around for twelve years expressing attitudes toward things rather than analyzing," he says. "They are always ready to tell you how they feel about an issue, but they have never learned how to construct a rational argument to defend their opinions." Again, these complaints are amply substantiated by data from the National Assessment of Educational Progress. On one test of analytic writing measuring "the ability to provide evidence, reason logically, and make a well-developed point," only *four tenths of one percent* of eleventh graders performed at the "elaborated" (what I believe should be considered college-freshman) level.

20 Finally, no account of the present condition of college students would be complete without mention of the extraordinary dearth of factual knowledge they bring to college. Horror stories on this topic abound—and they are probably all true. I will never forget two unusually capable juniors, one of whom was a star political-science major, who came to my

office a few years ago to ask what was this thing called the New Deal. I had made reference to it during a lecture on the assumption that everyone in the class would he well acquainted with Franklin Roosevelt's domestic program, but I was wrong: the two students had checked with their friends, and none of them had heard of the New Deal either. Another junior recently asked me to help him pick a twentieth-century American novelist on whom to write a term paper. He had heard vaguely of F. Scott Fitzgerald and Ernest Hemingway, but did not recognize the names of Sinclair Lewis, John Dos Passos, Norman Mailer, William Styron, and Saul Bellow.

21 Indeed, one can't assume that college students know anything anymore. Paula Fass, a professor of history at the University of California at Berkeley, remains astonished that sophomores and juniors in her upper-level course on American social history are often unable to differentiate between the American Revolution and the Civil War, but rather see them as two big events that happened way back in the past. Alan Heimert, a veteran member of the Harvard English department, encounters the same mushy grasp of historical knowledge and blames it on the "trendy social-studies curriculum" now taught in most high schools which covers broad thematic topics rather than history. "They are aware that someone oppressed someone else," he says with only slight exaggeration, "but they aren't sure exactly what took place and they have no idea of the order in which it happened."

22 Though not always recognized, a direct connection exists between this deficit in factual knowledge and the decline in verbal skills. Most reading, after all, is at bottom a form of information processing in which the mind selects what it wants to know from the printed page and files it away for future use. In conducting that operation of selecting, interpreting, and storing information, the reader constantly relies on his or her previous stock of knowledge as a vital frame of reference. No matter how fascinating or valuable a new detail might be, a person finds it almost impossible to hold in memory and have available for retrieval unless it can be placed in some kind of larger context. Providing that basic intellectual scaffolding used to be a major function of a good high school education. Year-long survey courses in history and literature, covering the United States, Europe, and the world, were designed to ensure that college-bound students would have the necessary background to make sense of the new subject matter they would encounter in college. Yet few high schools today teach that kind of curriculum.

23 Little wonder that so many students experience great difficulty in absorbing detail; since they have no context in which to fit what they read, it quickly flows out of their minds. Unable to retain much, they find little profit in reading, which leads them to read less, which in turn makes it harder for them to improve their reading skills.

24 One often hears this generation accused of laziness. They don't perform well in school or college or later on the job, it is said, because they lack motivation. I don't happen to subscribe to that theory. The percentage of students who are truly lazy—that is, who simply have an aversion to work—is probably no greater today than it has been in the past. The real problem, I'm convinced, is that college-bound youngsters over the past two decades have not received the quality education they deserve. As R. Jackson Wilson observes of his students at Smith, this generation is typically "good-spirited, refreshingly uncowed by teachers' authority, and very willing to work." They enter college with high ambitions, only to find those ambitions dashed in many cases by inadequate skills and knowledge. The normal activities required to earn a bachelor's degree—reading, writing, researching, and reasoning—are so difficult for them that a large number (I would guess a majority at most schools) simply give up in frustration. Some actually leave; the rest go through the motions, learning and contributing little, until it's time to pick up their diplomas. We rightly worry about the nation's high school dropouts. Perhaps we should worry as well about these silent college "dropouts."

How Good Schools Buck the Trend

25 What has caused this great decline in our schools? The multitude of reports that now fill the library shelves tend to designate "social factors" as the prime culprit. Television usually heads the list, followed by rock music, the influence of adolescent peer groups, the increase in both single-parent families and households where both parents work, and even faulty nutrition.

26 Those who attribute the loss of academic performance to social factors don't take account of the small number of high schools around the country

that have managed to escape the downturn. Some are posh private academies; a few are located in blue-collar neighborhoods. What they have in common is a pattern of stable or even rising test scores at a time when virtually all the schools around them experienced sharp declines. There is no indication that the children attending these exceptional schools watched significantly fewer hours of television, listened to less heavy-metal music, were less likely to have working mothers, or ate fewer Big Macs than other children. Rather, they appear to have had the good fortune to go to schools that were intent on steering a steady course in a time of rapid change, thus countering the potentially negative impact of various social factors.

27 It would seem obvious good sense to look closely at this select group of schools to determine what they have been doing right, but as far as I can determine this has been done in only two national studies. The better one was issued by the National Association of Secondary School Principals (NASSP) in 1978, under the somewhat pedestrian title *Guidelines for Improving SAT Scores*. Now out of print and hard to find, it contains one of the most perceptive diagnoses available of the underlying malady in our schools.

28 The report identifies one main characteristic that successful schools have shared—the belief that academics must invariably receive priority over every other activity. "The difference comes," we are told, "from a singular commitment to academic achievement for the college-bound student." These schools did not ignore the other dimensions of student life. By and large, the NASSP found, schools that maintained excellence in academics sought to be excellent in everything else they did; they "proved to be apt jugglers, keeping all important balls in the air." But academic work came first.

Two other factors help account for the prowess 29 of these schools in holding the line against deterioration. The first is a dogged reliance on a traditional liberal-arts curriculum. In an era of minicourses and electives, the tiny group of high schools that kept test scores and achievement high continued to require year-long courses in literature and to encourage enrollment in rigorous math classes, including geometry and advanced algebra. Though the learning environment in those schools was often "broad and imaginative," in the words of the NASSP, fundamentals such as English grammar and vocabulary received heavy stress. The other key factor in preserving academic quality was the practice of grouping students by ability in as many subjects as possible. The contrast was stark: schools that had "severely declining test scores" had "moved determinedly toward heterogeneous grouping" (that is, mixed students of differing ability levels in the same classes), while the "schools who have maintained good SAT scores" tended "to prefer homogeneous grouping."

Critical Reading Guide

1. Singal intertwines reporting, analyzing, and interpreting information throughout his essay. Notice that in paragraph 5 Singal presents one interpretation of the decline in test scores. He then evaluates and discounts this interpretation before presenting his own. Why doesn't he accept the first interpretation? (Or why doesn't he just present his own right away?) What rhetorical device is Singal using (Here's a hint: it is one that has been discussed at other points in this book)?

2. Where in the second section does Singal evaluate an alternative interpretation of facts before presenting his own? Do you find this technique effective? Why or why not?

3. In the third section, Singal claims that college students often cannot interpret what they read. What factor does he cite as the primary cause?

4. Through analysis, Singal links reading skills to other skills deemed fundamental to doing college work. What are these other skills, and what is the relationship that Singal establishes between them?

5. What does Singal mean by a "traditional liberal-arts curriculum" and "mini-courses and electives" in paragraph 27? Does your college offer a traditional liberal arts curriculum? Did your high school? Use your knowledge of such a curriculum in conjunction with the information in Singal's essay to interpret these two terms in one or two paragraphs.

Writing Assignment

INTERPRETING "THE OTHER CRISIS IN AMERICAN EDUCATION"

The goal of this assignment is to give you an opportunity to practice writing an interpretation of information in a text. Daniel Singal presents some information that teachers find staggering: the persistent decline in SAT scores, the inability to differentiate between the American Revolution and the Civil War, and so on. Indeed, the sheer volume of the information in Singal's article might stagger many readers, which would make it hard for them to interpret and thereby understand what the article means.

For this assignment, adopt the stance of an insider writing for outsiders—specifically, parents who have children in high school. Writing an interpretation of Singal's article for them. You paper should be about four pages long.

Lauren B. Resnick

Lauren Resnick is a professor of psychology and has written extensively on theories of reading. As you read the following article, pay particular attention to how Resnick organizes her analysis and her interpretation. Are her theories relevant to your own success as a reader and writer?

LAUREN B. RESNICK

LITERACY IN SCHOOL AND OUT

1   We are told there is a literacy crisis in the United States. Nearing the end of the twentieth century, we have still not succeeded in educating a fully literate citizenry, a goal that was articulated by our founding fathers and that motivated creation of what is probably the most inclusive public education system in the world. As the structure of the economy changes, America's declining ability to compete is attributed to workers' inadequate literacy and numeracy. All of this fuels demands for education-

al reform, mostly calling for tougher standards and higher rates of high school completion. It is assumed that school is the agency responsible for the nation's level of literacy, and that if schools just did their jobs more skillfully and resolutely, the literacy problem would be solved.

I will challenge that assumption in this essay. 2 School is only one of many social forces, institutionalized and not, that determine the nature and extent of the nation's literacy. To understand the literacy crisis and imagine possible solutions, it is essential to examine the nature of literacy practice outside school as well as within. Continuing an earlier analysis of the relationship between mental work as it is performed outside school and the practices of the schools, I examine here several different ways in which people engage with the written word. Since literacy practice outside school has been the object of very little systematic research, my analysis is suggestive rather than definitive. Nevertheless, it is possible to see that there are important discontinuities between school literacy practices and literacy outside school. These discontinuities make it doubtful that schools alone can successfully address the problem.

3   In most discussions of the literacy crisis, it is assumed that literacy is an acquired ability that characterizes individuals; people either possess literacy skills or they do not. The *practice* of literacy, the social conditions under which people actually engage in literate activities, is not examined. Although cognitive scientists and other students of literacy have done much to reveal the invisible mental processes involved in reading and making sense of written texts, most have worked on a widely shared assumption that these processes are, at most, only peripherally affected by the social contexts in which people read and write. It is assumed that individuals carry literacy skills in their heads. As a result, the nature of the situation in which people "do" literacy is not thought to alter the nature of the process.

4   I adopt here, as a heuristic for understanding literacy more deeply, a shift in epistemological perspective. Instead of asking what constitutes literacy *competency* or *ability*, terms that invite efforts to list the skills and knowledge possessed by individuals who are judged literate, I want to examine literacy as a set of cultural practices that people engage in. Taking this perspective does not deny that people engaging in literate activity must be knowledgeable and skillful in particular ways. However, examining literacy as a set of cultural practices rather than as skills or abilities leads to questions that are not often posed in discussions of the literacy crisis. These are questions about the kinds of situations in which literacy is practiced, that is, in which people engage with written texts. *Who* are the actors—both readers and writers—in these situations? How do they define themselves in relation to the texts they

engage with, to each other, to other people who may also engage with those texts? *Why* are they reading and writing? What are they attempting to do with the written word? What kinds of institutional or broadly social invitations, permissions, and constraints influence their activities? *How* do people read and write? What are the processes, cognitive and social, that define literate practices? Finally, *what* do people read and write? What are the texts themselves like, and how do their characteristics facilitate particular forms of literate practice?

5   The shift in perspective from personal skill to cultural practice carries with it implications for a changed view of teaching and instruction. If literacy is viewed as a bundle of skills, then education for literacy is most naturally seen as a matter of organizing effective lessons: that is, diagnosing skill strengths and deficits, providing appropriate exercises in developmentally felicitous sequences, motivating students to engage in these exercises, giving clear explanations and directions. But if literacy is viewed as a set of cultural practices, then education for literacy is more naturally seen as a process of socialization, of induction into a community of literacy practicers. The best model (*metaphor* is perhaps a more accurate term) we have for such induction into communities of practice is the ancient one of apprenticeship. *Apprenticeship* has largely dropped out of our educational vocabulary but warrants revival in new forms.

6   The heart of apprenticeship as a mode of learning is coached practice in actual tasks of production, with decreasing degrees of support from the master or more advanced colleagues. This practice takes place in the context of preparing a product that is socially valued. In traditional craft apprenticeships, there was far less direct instruction than we are used to in schools and relatively little decontextualized practice of component skills. Instead, by working collaboratively, often on tasks they could not yet accomplish entirely on their own, apprentices practiced in a context that both motivated work and gave it meaning. A series of increasingly complex production tasks through which apprentices progressed provided the equivalent of a curriculum. The conditions of work and learning made it possible to rely on considerable self-correction, with apprentices judging their own products against criteria established through extensive observation and discussion of the

group's products. Several recent experimental programs have demonstrated possibilities for adapting elements of traditional apprenticeship forms to education in complex cognitive practices of literacy and mathematics. These programs attempt to establish communities of literate practice in which children can participate under special forms of guidance. Such programs try to make usually hidden mental processes overt, and they encourage student observation and commentary. They also allow skills to build up bit by bit, yet permit participation in meaningful work even for the relatively unskilled, often as a result of sharing the tasks among several participants.

7   In this essay I consider briefly several different kinds of literacy practice and attempt to characterize each in ways that respond to the *who, why, how,* and *what* questions raised earlier. For each, I begin by sketching skilled adult practices as a way of setting a "developmental target"—a possible educational goal. I then try to imagine "beginner" forms of that practice, forms that might characterize the early stages of apprenticeship in literacy. This educational thought experiment provides a template for assessing school literacy practice. How much apprenticeship opportunity does the school typically provide? How might the school be organized to provide more such opportunity? How much of the job of educating a literate citizenry can the school alone be expected to do? In light of this analysis of literacy as situated activity, I then reexamine the nature of the literacy crisis and propose some institutional responses that may be necessary for change.

THREE FORMS
OF LITERACY PRACTICE

8   Literacy is practiced in any situations in which people engage with written texts. The range of literacy situations is vast and varied. In earlier work, we identified, without claiming to be exhaustive, six major categories of literacy activity: the sacred (using print in religious practice and instruction); the useful (using print to mediate practical activities); the informational (using print to convey or acquire knowledge); the pleasurable (reading for the fun of it); the persuasive (using print to influence the behavior or beliefs of others); and the personal-familial (using letters to stay in touch with family and friends). Here I consider three of these categories that are most frequently cited as

literacy objectives of the school—the useful, the informational, and the pleasurable.

Useful Literacy

A common type of literacy practice is the use of   9
written texts to mediate action in the world. Some everyday examples of such practical literacy include reading recipes, following instructions for assembling or manipulating equipment, and consulting bus or airline schedules. These are among the kinds of activities that appear on functional literacy tests such as the recent National Assessment of Educational Progress. The class of useful literacy practices would also include writing letters of inquiry, filling out job applications, and leaving notes for coworkers. Readers come to functional literacy practice of this kind with very immediate goals, usually assuming that the text is authoritative and can successfully guide action. They willingly follow the author's plan of action in order to accomplish a specific task.

   This action-oriented stance shapes the nature of   10
the reading process. Consider, for example, texts that provide instructions for action on physical systems. To engage successfully as a reader of such texts, one must relate each proposition in the text to a specific set of physical objects, infer relationships among those objects, and plan actions on them. In the simplest form of practical literacy, this is done with the objects present. Under these conditions, the physical objects substantially assist the reader in making sense of the text. Research on the processes of following directions shows that readers of such texts shift attention back and forth between the text and the physical display. Furthermore, there is evidence that diagrams, when available, are relied on to a great extent, and that readers often favor the information in diagrams when text and figures conflict. In this kind of literacy activity, the reader needs to construct only a limited mental representation of the situation described by the text, because the elements of the situation are physically present, and it is possible to act directly on them. Furthermore, the physical results of one's actions often provide continuous (if only partial) information about whether one has correctly interpreted the text and diagrams.

   A more cognitively demanding form of practi-   11
cal literacy requires readers to make inferences about the state of a physical system from textual

materials, without being able to see or interact with the physical system directly. In these situations, a more complete mental representation must be constructed by the reader, with less supportive help from the physical environment. This kind of processing is necessary, for example, when texts are read in anticipation of action—that is, preparing to do something without actually doing it. Some simple examples of anticipatory practical reading are using a bus schedule to decide when to go to the busstop, and reading a recipe to determine if a shopping trip is needed before cooking can begin. More complex examples can be found in automated work situations in which the actual physical labor is done by machines, while workers monitor and adjust those machines on the basis of their readings of various indicators. To perform such tasks, workers need a complex mental model of the physical system on which they are operating, a model whose immediate states can be updated on the basis of indicator readings. As such jobs proliferate, a new standard of technical literacy is developing. As in more "hands-on" practical literacy, the reader must be able to act on a physical environment, but a much greater effort of purely mental representation is required.

12   Practical literacy also includes uses of texts to help one act in and on social systems. Tax forms and job applications are of this type. Such forms are used much like instructions for physical systems—that is, in step-by-step fashion, reading a line, then immediately following the instructions given. To participate effectively in this form of literacy, one needs only to understand each line of the instructions and to be willing to persist through many steps. A more general mental model of a situation—of tax rules, for example, or of what a potential employer might be seeking—can help in this step-by-step interpretation but is not strictly necessary. Thus, in this kind of literacy, there is only a limited requirement for mental representation. There are also less formulaic texts that help people act in a social system. Such texts might, for example, guide one in using services of a health care system, initiating grievance proceedings against an employer, or choosing among insurance options. When using these texts, the reader needs to construct a mental model of the system as a whole before it becomes possible to decide how to act.

How do people learn to engage in practical lit- 13 eracy? It is not difficult to imagine an apprenticeship in the functional use of texts occurring within families. With a parent or other older person, a child as young as four or five can participate in an activity in which a text is used to guide physical acts (assembling a game or following a recipe, for example). Very young children cannot yet read the texts themselves, but they can observe important aspects of the practical literacy form such as the ways in which one alternates between reading the text and carrying out a physical act, or the fact that the text is used to verify accuracy of action. By eight or nine years of age, a child participating with an adult might do some or even all of the reading but would not be expected to figure out alone exactly what actions were prescribed. Later, the child might do most of the work alone, calling for occasional help in interpreting certain difficult words or steps. This kind of "scaffolded" learning has been well analyzed and described for a number of typical family activities as well as for learning in traditional craft apprenticeships. Regular engagement in such activities in the family or other extra-school settings probably helps children develop a generalized pattern of interacting with texts ("read-do, read-do") and a broad confidence that enables them to use texts to guide practical activity on their own.

Such practical literacy apprenticeships, howev- 14 er, are largely absent from school. The reading done in school seldom mediates any practical action in the world, and there is hardly ever a chance to work side by side with a more skillful partner toward a shared goal. An exception may be found in the science laboratory. Science educators often complain that too much time is spent setting up experiments and too little on interpreting them. Yet students may learn something about a very basic form of practical literacy from these exercises—to the extent that they get to participate in them. Much elementary-level science instruction proceeds from textbooks rather than laboratories, and the students whose functional literacy is a source of public worry almost never take upper-level science courses. Vocational courses offer another potential site for functional literacy practice in school. Often, however, functional literacy skills are *prerequisite* to entering vocational courses, rather than what can be learned in them. A result is that the students most in need of this form of literacy practice are excluded from the opportunity for practice. Significant opportunities for functional literacy activity also occur in some extracurricular school activities. There is evidence, however, that, with the exception of sports, extracurricular participation in high school is largely limited to the more academically inclined and successful students and does not include those for whom functional literacy development is a concern.

15 These observations suggest that, if school were the only place in which people learned literate practices, we would probably observe far *less* functional literacy in the general population than we do. It seems likely that the many people who become competent at various forms of functional literacy develop their initial competence outside school, through participation with family members and friends. If functional literacy practices are learned mainly outside school, however, certain students—those from families who do not practice much literacy in the home or do not engage their children in such activities—can be expected not to learn them.

Informational Literacy

16 People also read to learn about the world when there is no immediate practical utility for the information acquired. In this kind of literacy activity, the only likely immediate activity after reading is discussion with others. The reader's main task is to build a mental representation of the situation presented in the text and to relate the new information to previously held knowledge. This process of text comprehension has been intensively studied by cognitive scientists. From their research, we know that building mental *situation models* on the basis of a text requires much more than an ability to recognize the words—a level of literacy ability that few people in this country lack. Rather, it depends crucially on the reader's prior knowledge, along with certain general linguistic abilities. It is also highly sensitive to aspects of the text structure, including rhetorical devices, signals about the relationships among sections of the text, and the extent to which suppositions and arguments are laid out explicitly.

17 One aspect of informational reading that has not been much studied is how the reader interprets the author's intention and what knowledge the reader attributes to the author—what we might call building an *author model*. Furthermore, cognitive science has paid almost no attention to what the reader expects to do with the information gained from the text, or to the social context of either the reading or subsequent information use. All of these can be expected to influence reading activity substantially.

18 A wide range of intentions, from personal interest and wanting to know what people are talking about to needing background knowledge for one's profession, can motivate informational reading. Some forms of informational reading can have eventual practical aims, even though immediate action is neither called for nor possible. For example, many advice and "how-to" texts—ranging from household hints and Ann Landers columns to books offering guidance in personal finance or business management—are geared not to individual situations, but to prototypical situations that many people encounter. When reading such texts, people have to imagine themselves in others' situations in order to find useful information for themselves. To do this, they must not only build a mental representation of the situation described in the text but also relate the situation described to their own.

19 In everyday life, probably the most frequent kind of informational literacy activity is newspaper and magazine reading. For most people, reading the news is a matter of "keeping up"—finding out what is going on in the world, updating one's mental accounts of ongoing events. Although such reading appears to be a private activity, it is socially defined in two important senses. First, informational reading is often followed by discussion with others of like interests, and what one chooses to read in a newspaper probably depends to an important degree on what kinds of conversations one anticipates. People may keep up with sports, for example, in order to join the talk at work or follow local news because that is discussed at parties or while attending to business in town. What we find it necessary to "keep up with" is determined partly by the people with whom we associate and the conversational habits of that group. If one is not in a social circle that discusses national and international political events, those parts of the newspaper will probably not receive attention.

Thus, everyday informational reading is a function of the social groups with whom one interacts.

20   A second sense in which reading is socially defined is that the kind of mental representation constructed from the reading depends on the kinds of intentions one ascribes to the authors. American newspaper readers expect journalists to be both knowledgeable and neutral, to convey the facts fully and without bias. Except when reading signed columns and editorials, readers do not devote much attention to determining the newswriters' persuasive intentions, what political positions are represented, or what might have been left out of the communication. In contrast, continental European newspaper readers do not assume neutrality; newspapers and newswriters have known political positions, and readers interpret their articles in this light. People trying to get the whole picture of some important event are likely to read several different news reports because they expect an interpretive slant in each report. In countries with active press censorship, readers must go even further to read between the lines in order to learn what is happening in the world. These different social assumptions can cause differences in the cognitive processes involved in reading. The American assumption of a neutral press, together with a relative absence of political discussion in everyday life, probably has the effect of providing our people with minimal practice in critical textual interpretation. Americans have little experience in looking for authors' intentions or hidden meanings or tracking down missing parts of an argument. Although many become fluent at constructing text and situation models, they have little practice at building author models.

21   Imagined author-reader relations also play a role in the process of writing informational texts. In actual literacy practice, authors writing informational texts have, in the best cases, a lively sense of their audience. They are used to crafting their communications to appeal to imagined readers. Definitions of what constitutes a well-crafted text vary among social communities of readers and writers. Broad distinctions between popular and scholarly writing do not do justice to the variety and distinctiveness of what have come to be called "discourse communities." The readers of different segments of the popular press expect different forms of writing. In recent years a lively

analysis of the varied ways in which different scholarly disciplines shape their written discourse has emerged, and students of literacy have begun to speak of processes of initiation into these discourse communities, referring both to practices of interpretive reading and to those of authoring.

22   Informal, family-based opportunities for apprenticeship in these informational literacy practices are probably less available than are practical literacy apprenticeship opportunities. Not all families regularly read and discuss the information in newspapers or magazines, and most such reading is limited to particular narrow segments of the press. Reading of informational books occurs in only a limited number of families. And even among children growing up in our most literate families, few ever get to observe—much less participate in—the process of actually creating an extended informational text for an interested audience.

23   More than for practical literacy, it seems, we depend on the school as the place in which informational literacy will be cultivated. School is the time and place in most people's lives when they are most intensively engaged in reading for information. Indeed other than newspapers, textbooks provide most Americans' only practice of informational literacy. A populace with the capacity and taste for engaging in informational literacy activities, particularly as they bear on public and civic issues, is part of the Jeffersonian vision of democracy. It is a major reason for treating universal public education as a requirement for a democratic society. But as education has developed, very little literacy practice in school engages students in activities from which they might learn the habits and skills of using texts to understand public issues and participate in public decision making. A consideration of the actual activity of textbook reading in school shows that it is a very different form of literacy practice from the informational reading that might be envisioned as part of the Jeffersonian ideal. Differences can be found in the intentions that people bring to school text reading as opposed to other kinds of informational texts, in the nature of the texts themselves, in the kinds of background knowledge they bring to the reading, and in the rhythm of the activity itself.

24   When texts are assigned in school, they are almost always on topics new to students, for which the students must build initial mental representa-

tions. Textbook reading thus provides little experience in updating mental models, as occurs when keeping up with the news. Worse still, school textbooks are often badly written, a jumble of bits of information without the coherence needed to support this initial building of a representation. Finally, and perhaps most important, students in school read textbooks because of an assignment or a test to be passed, not because they are personally interested in the topic or expect lively conversation about it with others. In many classrooms, there is a catechetical flavor to the way that texts are assigned and used. Small sections are read, and students are expected to give specific, generally noninterpretive answers to questions posed by the teacher. Informational writing experience is, if anything, more restricted. For the most part, if students write informational or analytical texts at all, it is to show teachers that they have done the required reading and absorbed the canonical interpretation. The normal relationship between author (as someone who knows something of interest) and reader (as someone who would like to learn about that something) is absent or seriously attenuated. The typical audience for student writing is only the teacher, who already knows (or is thought to know) all the information conveyed. For the large majority of students, then, no place—neither home nor school—provides an extended opportunity to engage in high levels of authentic informational literacy practice.

Pleasurable Literacy

25 Being literate can also mean reading for pleasure, a form of literacy practice in which reading is its own end. The kinds of texts that people read for the fun of reading are diverse, and the cognitive and social processes engaged are equally different. Narratives—texts with a story line, whether fictional or based in reality—are generally considered to be the material of pleasurable reading, although some people read expository texts that might be classed as information just for the fun of it. Engagement with the text is the primary requisite for pleasurable literacy, and many kinds of texts—from pulp crime stories and Gothic romances to high literature—are capable of providing that engagement. Different kinds of texts, of course, require differing degrees and types of interpretive activity; what is engaging for some may be too difficult or too simple to engage others.

Cognitive scientists have given substantially 26 less attention to the processes involved in pleasurable reading than to the processes of informational and practical literacy, although some psychologists with more interest in motivation and consciousness (including Mihaly Csikszentmihalyi in this volume) have tried to understand the nature of psychological engagement with a story. The nature of fiction reading is also, of course, a major concern of literary theory and criticism. Proponents of a recent literary theory are now exploring the many personal goals served by pleasurable reading—from escape and imagining oneself in more satisfying conditions (as in reading romance stories) to stimulating and resolving curiosity (as in reading mysteries) to penetrating cultures and life situations to which one does not have personal access. Psychologists and literary scholars seem to agree that readers of popular stories—mysteries, romances, and the like—focus all energies on understanding the situation described and perhaps on imagining themselves in that situation. This engagement with the story contrasts with what some would reserve as truly "literary" reading, which involves deliberate attention to language and expressive device. This aspect of literary reading distinguishes it from more popular forms of pleasurable literacy in which language is "transparent," unattended to in its own right, just a vehicle for conveying a story.

At first look, pleasurable literacy seems to fare 27 better than informational literacy in terms of apprenticeship opportunities. For many children, pleasurable literacy practice begins in being read to by parents. The process by which children who are regularly read to gradually "appropriate" the reading act for themselves is often used as a model of how apprenticeship in cultural practice might work for literacy. Encouragement of parents to read to and with their children and extensive reading aloud to children in preschools and kindergartens represent efforts to extend these forms of apprenticeship opportunity to more children.

Similar efforts are made throughout the ele- 28 mentary grades in many schools. Finding pleasure in reading is frequently stressed as a goal of reading instruction. In support of this goal, books of interest to children are made available, and children are encouraged to read them. Time is allowed in the school week for free-choice reading programs and reading for which children are not formally accountable, although they are encouraged to discuss or even write about their reading. Many civic programs aimed at supporting literacy development in schools also stress the pleasurable aspects of literacy. Such programs, which include bookmobiles and other community access programs organized by public libraries, programs that distribute children's books to families at no or low cost, and programs in which volunteers either read to schoolchildren or listen to the children read, focus either implicitly or explicitly on the pleasures of reading.

29   The motivation for such emphasis on reading for pleasure is partly based on sound pedagogy. We know that reading skill develops best when there is massive practice in reading, and children (like adults) are more likely to read a lot when they enjoy the process of reading as well as its possible practical or informational outcomes. But educators and civic organizations also stress reading for pleasure because they recognize it as an authentic form of literacy practice; a more literate nation would engage in more reading for its own sake. With respect to pleasurable literacy, then, more than for the useful or the informational, many schools and surrounding institutions seem to be reaching for authentic forms of practice.

30   Yet the programs that seem to provide some pleasurable literacy apprenticeship opportunities represent a very limited part of the school experience of most students. For most Americans, the only extended discussion of literature they are likely to encounter is in school. But even a brief consideration of the ways in which literature reading is organized in school suggests a fundamental discontinuity with the features of pleasurable reading as we engage in it outside school.

31   A key—perhaps the defining—feature of pleasurable reading is that one picks up and puts down a book or a story at will. There is no need to prove to others that one has read, although sharing opinions about books is not uncommon among those who read for pleasure. In schooling, by contrast, literature is usually doled out in daily assignments. Not only what one is to read, but also the pace of

the reading is imposed. Reading ahead if one is captivated and engaged by the story is not encouraged and may be subtly punished. Proving that one has read the assigned material by answering questions about it or writing book reports is central to school literacy. Not infrequently, literature study is turned into a kind of catechism—a canonic set of readings, standard questions, and expected answers. These activities implicitly carry a message that reading is not a pleasure in its own right. As a result, students who have not acquired a sense of the pleasures of reading elsewhere may not easily acquire it through standard schooling practice, especially after the primary grades.

LITERACY APPRENTICESHIPS

32   The preceding analyses suggest that the schools are not the only—or perhaps even the primary—source of literacy competence. As we have seen, dominant school practice is so mismatched to the ways in which practical, informational, and pleasurable literacy activities take place in everyday life that it seems highly unlikely that schools alone are responsible for the levels of literacy practice we observe in society. We must understand the nation's literacy—or lack of it—in terms of the kinds of literacy apprenticeships that are available to young people. For many, these apprenticeship opportunities are severely limited. In order to substantially change literacy practices in the nation, we cannot simply call for raising school standards. Without a broad cultural shift in the direction of more interpretive literacy activity in all segments of adult society, we cannot expect young people to acquire the skills and habits of literacy practice.

33   Schools could become sites for true literacy apprenticeship, but fundamental shifts in school practice would be required. What is called for are school activities in which students have extensive reason to use written texts in the ways that characterize out-of-school practical, informational, and pleasurable literacy. A number of experimental programs now in use point to the possibilities. These programs share features of apprenticeship environments: children work to produce a product that will be used by others (e.g., they produce a book on a history topic that is then used to teach others, or they collect data that are used to produce

a scientific report); they work collaboratively, but under conditions in which individuals are held responsible for their work; they use tools and apparatus appropriate to the problem; they read and critique each other's writing; they are called upon to elaborate and defend their own work until it reaches a community standard. We know considerably more about how to design and manage such environments than we do about how to get schools to adopt and maintain them. Educational programs are often adopted enthusiastically by a few schools during an experimental phase and then abandoned in favor of conventional school literacy forms, often in the wake of calls for a return to "the basics" and the practices that adult citizens recall from their own school days. Apparently, the school system cannot move far ahead of the general culture.

34   To "bootstrap" ourselves into new levels of literacy participation, I believe we must actively develop other institutions for literacy practice. These can function jointly with schools in the best circumstances or independently when necessary. We need multiple apprenticeship sites where children and youth can spend significant amounts of time working among people who are using the written word for practical, informational, and pleasurable purposes. For younger children, community centers, churches, and other agencies could play this role. Many children now attend after-school and weekend programs at such centers, and there is some evidence that participation in community programs is positively related to school and later work performance. For the most part, however, these agencies offer child care and recreational programs but make no attempt to provide literacy-related activities. When after-school or summer programs are offered with the intention of improving school performance, they usually mimic school conditions rather than provide truly alternative occasions for literacy practice. We need new forms of community programs aimed at developing literacy through apprenticeship. For older students—at least from the beginning of high school—participating (preferably with pay) at real work sites is probably the best way to experience literacy practice, along with training in a variety of social skills and habits that are essential to work performance. Such on-the-job participation would not only provide natural apprenticeships for literacy, but might also solve important motivational problems resulting from some students' belief that even good school performance will not assure them access to jobs and other forms of economic participation.

35   These proposals follow from the shift in perspective with which I began this essay. When we stop thinking about literacy as a collection of skills and begin to view it as a form of cultural practice, we are led to consider the multiple ways in which young people are socialized into the practices of their societies. Although there is room for improvement, schools appear to be doing reasonably well at teaching the basic skills of literacy. But, at least as currently organized, schools are too isolated from everyday ways of using the written word to serve as the only sites for learning literacy practice. For some young people, family, community life, and, eventually, work provide informal apprenticeship opportunities for various literacy practices. For many others, though, these apprenticeship opportunities are unavailable. Unless organized efforts are made to provide literacy apprenticeship environments for these young people, there seems to be little hope of change in our general levels of literacy participation. There is historical precedent for looking outside schools for major changes in literacy levels in a population. Europe's earliest literacy drives took place in homes and churches. Recent literacy campaigns, for example in Cuba and China, have looked to institutions such as citizen armies for literacy education. In past efforts of this kind, only very basic forms of literacy were sought. Today's challenge is greater, and the relatively simple forms of literacy activity that sufficed for basic literacy campaigns cannot be expected to succeed. But with imagination and perseverance, we should be able to develop places and forms for apprenticeship that can effectively reshape literacy practice in our society.

Critical Reading Guide

1. Resnick argues that we should not interpret "literacy" as simply a set of skills. What does her interpretation of "literacy" involve?

2. Resnick organizes this essay in a very straightforward way: She reports her information, analyzes it, then interprets. However, her analysis—the careful examination of three forms of literacy—does contain some interpretation. Try to identify which parts of the three sections (Useful Literacy, Informational Literacy, Pleasurable Literacy) are interpretive. Is there a similar organizational pattern in each section?

3. Which form of literacy do you use most frequently in this class? What about your other classes?

4. The interpretation in paragraph 24 is popular. Much public education demands "noninterpretive answers" from students; however, as noted earlier, college instructors often expect students to go beyond a simple demonstration that they have done the required reading. What are some of the techniques that Resnick later suggests will facilitate learning interpretive skills?

Writing Assignment

INTERPRETING THE LITERACY CRISIS

This writing assignment as a continuation of what you did in the previous one. It is intended to challenge you to see beyond the information in Lauren Resnick's article and to consider what the literacy crisis means to America. What does it mean, for example, when the nation has the highest illiteracy rate of any industrialized country? What does it mean when the average high school senior graduates with an eighth-grade reading level?

In four to five pages, interpret Resnick's article for an audience of your peers.

WRITING GUIDE: INTERPRETING THE LITERACY CRISIS

Invention

Resnick begins her article by challenging the assumption that America's illiteracy is a failure of schools to teach reading and writing. She states in paragraph 2 that "School is only one of many social forces . . . that determine the nature and extent of the nation's literacy." A good starting point for this assignment, therefore, would be to consider some of the other social forces that are at work. You might begin by going back through Resnick's article and identifying those she mentions. The next step would be to reflect on other forces that might be at work. Brainstorming with some of your classmates could prove useful.

Resnick does not devote much space to examining the implications of illiteracy in America. She does not focus on what it means to society to have the rate of illiteracy that currently exists. Instead, she concentrates on ways to improve literacy by shifting responsibility from the schools to society at large. The article does not offer much that can guide your interpretation. Thus, you need to reflect on what illiteracy means. For example, what does it cost, and how does one measure such costs? Is there any connection between illiteracy and welfare? Illiteracy and unemployment? Illiteracy and crime? Illiteracy and social, personal, and technological development? Are there any metaphors that vividly capture any of these connections? You might try freewriting to explore the possibilities.

Resnick writes about the literacy crisis, but she does not provide much solid information about it. As part of your invention, you probably should examine some other sources so that you have more facts on hand before you begin writing. Also, consider whether you will need to define "literacy crisis." If so, you should discuss and/or brainstorm your definition with classmates. Be sure you differentiate between a definition of the literacy crisis and Resnick's definitions of literacy.

Planning

Your plan for this paper must include a report of the information about the literacy crisis, your interpretation, and support for your interpretation. Consider how you will organize parts of the paper. In addition, the assignment asks you to write to your peers, which means that you must decide whether you will adopt the stance of an insider or an outsider. This decision, in turn, will be influenced by the aim of your text. What do you want this paper to do?

Your invention generated quite a bit of information and supporting details for your interpretation. You now need to sort through what you have and begin making decisions on what you will use in your paper. Keep in mind that successful invention activities generate more information and details than you actually can use. Don't try to include everything.

Drafting

Setting the scene for readers is especially important on this assignment because your peers are an audience that is highly literate. Many of them may feel that the problems with reading and writing that others have are not particularly relevant to their lives. Your introduction therefore may need to make literacy relevant.

Once you have drafted your introduction, you should begin organizing your information and developing your interpretation. The hardest part will be moving smoothly between the several parts of the paper, keeping everything coherent. You may need to give particular attention to transitions that connect the parts. The most effective transitions are sentences (rather than phrases and single words like "however" and "on the other hand") that combine new information with old. That is, transitional sentences will include information from a previous paragraph or section and link it to information forthcoming in the next paragraph or section.

Pausing and Reading

During your pauses, read through your draft. Check that the writing is meeting the requirements of the assignment. For example, are you explaining what the literacy crisis means, or are you merely listing instances of illiteracy? Are you writing for an audience of peers, or are you writing for insiders, such as your teacher? Is the draft meeting the aim that you set for the paper? Do you have sufficient support for your interpretation? Make marginal notes to yourself whenever you find a gap in the draft so that you can return to it later.

Revising

Set your draft aside for at least 2 days before you begin revising. You will be able to see your draft more clearly and objectively if you do. Look carefully at the organization of the paper and determine how well it meets the requirements of the assignment. Also consider how effectively you set the scene, how well you supported your interpretation, and how you structured your conclusion. Does the conclusion look forward?

You can benefit from the input of others, especially classmates, during this stage. Ask one or two other people to read your draft and to give you their suggestions for improvement. Match their comments against your own perceptions of the text. Try to get written suggestions from them; if that's not feasible, write down their oral comments. Use the most valuable comments to make the necessary changes to your draft.

Editing

Look at sentence and paragraph structure. The structure of effective paragraphs tends to be well defined, consisting of a topic sentence and a series of sentences that then provide information about the topic. Poorly structured paragraphs, on the other hand, commonly consist of a series of individual assertions. Each assertion potentially could be a topic sentence for a new paragraph. Check sentences for length and pattern variety, and make adjustments as necessary. Check for prepositional phrases; try to have no more than three per sentence. Finally, spell check.

Evaluating Events

Evaluating involves making a judgment. It is an appraisal of the nature, character, quality, status, or worth of an idea, a person, an object, an event, or information. Evaluations of events depend on the ability to see and interpret perceptions.

CHAPTER EIGHT

Evaluating Events

Evaluating involves making a judgment. It is an appraisal of the nature, character, quality, status, or worth of an idea, a person, an object, an event, or information. Evaluations of *events* depend on the ability to see and interpret perceptions.[1] Evaluations, like interpretations, are a form of argument and must be supported with good reasons. When an evaluation lacks support, it is merely an opinion, not a formal appraisal. What is an opinion? It is an evaluation based on personal taste that cannot be supported with evidence. A person may believe that the 1999 Super Bowl was the best ever played, but it would be difficult to find evidence to support that evaluation, and another person may believe that the 1995 Bowl was better.[2]

Writers may wish they had a key to understanding the process of evaluation, but, unfortunately, none exists. We have to use our best judgment and recognize that sometimes that judgment may be wrong. However, a structural analysis of an evaluative paper is possible. Such papers generally involve the following four steps:

1. Provide a background for the event.
2. Analyze and interpret the event.
3. Evaluate the event.
4. Place the event in a broader context.

Providing a background for an event means reporting details so that readers know and understand what the event was. Interpreting the event involves explaining what it means, using analysis, comparison and contrast, definition, and so on, as tools. The evaluation considers the value, but more importantly the *meaningfulness*, of the event. Placing the event in a broader context normally involves fitting it into a social, cultural, or intellectual framework for comparison.

---

[1]Certainly, there is quite a bit of overlap in the rhetorical categories of evaluating, interpreting, and reporting, but for the purposes of learning about writing, these categories are useful.

[2]Opinions can become evaluations under some circumstances. Usually one must step outside his or her own experiences and find evidence to support the opinion, evidence that readers will accept as reasonable.

The sections that follow discuss these parts of an evaluation. First, however, let's look at a sample evaluation to get a better sense of what this kind of writing does. Passage 1 was written by Phuong, a sophomore in an American history class. The class was studying a unit on World War II, and students had been asked to write a brief evaluation of an event associated with the war. Phuong initially appears to have selected Pearl Harbor as his event, but it quickly becomes apparent that he has something else in mind as he focuses on a rumor about President Roosevelt that has circulated persistently since the end of World War II.

Passage 1: Pearl Harbor

Phuong

1   More than 2,500 American soldiers were killed when the Japanese attacked Pearl Harbor on December 7, 1941, in what President Roosevelt described as "a day of infamy." Most of the U.S. Pacific fleet was damaged or sunk, leaving the mainland vulnerable to invasion, and the event galvanized the nation, which until the attack had tried to stay out of the war in spite of Roosevelt's efforts to persuade Congress and the people that America should join the allies in their struggle. After Pearl Harbor, the country threw itself into the war with a fury as it sought to avenge what the President had labeled a "surprise attack." Many years passed before it became clear that the attack was not a surprise but had been engineered by Roosevelt and his closest advisors in a last-ditch effort to draw the country into war (Davis, p. 23). Thus December 7, 1994, is indeed a "day of infamy," not because of the Japanese attack per se but because it represents the lowest point of American politics.

2   President Roosevelt was an "Anglophile" who was determined to support Britain at any cost (Humphries, p. 44). Congress, however, was very reluctant to see America enter the war and passed a series of laws intended to keep the country isolated from the conflict. Fierce political battles waged between Roosevelt's supporters in Congress and those who were determined to remain neutral as the President attempted to provide more and more material aid to England. Roosevelt and his advisors came to realize that nothing short of an all-out attack on this country would move Congress and the people away from their determination to remain "nonparticipants." Germany and Japan, however, refused to cooperate. Neither country had the means to wage war on America because of the great distance involved. In addition, Germany had no great motivation to open yet another front, particularly with a country that was home to so many fellow Germans.

3   Japan, on the other hand, was very angry with the U.S. The Japanese government had been complaining for more than a decade that U.S. trade policies were strangling the island nation. Japanese leaders claimed that Roosevelt was a racist intent upon destroying their country. There was much evidence for this view. For example, during his first administration (1932–36), Roosevelt cut off exports of steel. Because the U.S. was at that time the world's largest steel producer, Japan was forced to purchase inferior scrap metal to meet its needs (Rice, p. 47). In addition, Roosevelt imposed high tariffs on Japanese products, which made it impossible for Japan to conduct trade with America (Rice, p. 48). The Japanese government tried for years to negotiate better trade agreements with the U.S. and failed because Roosevelt's negotiators refused to remove the existing barriers. On more than one occasion, Japanese leaders had declared publicly that war with the United States would be inevitable if America did not end its repressive trade policies. Nevertheless, in late 1940, Roosevelt cut off all export to Japan of raw materials, metal, and petroleum products.

4   Japanese leaders became even more alarmed when they learned that British and U.S. military experts began holding conferences in January 1941 on how to wage

war against Japan. This alarm increased when Roosevelt won a major political victory: Congress approved the Lend-Lease Act that would provide Britain with unlimited war materials. Japanese saw the Act as another step toward the total isolation of their country. By the summer of 1941, matters had deteriorated further. Without provocation, Roosevelt froze all Japanese assets in the U.S., further damaging the Japanese economy. In response, the government began drawing up various war scenarios (Humphries, p. 119), including an attack on the Pearl Harbor Naval Base. The Japanese government began sending coded summaries of these scenarios to its embassy in Washington, DC (Rice, p. 87).

5   Roosevelt was fully apprised of the content of these messages because American intelligence had broken the Japanese secret code about a year earlier (Rice, p. 90). By mid-1941, the President concluded that the Lend-Lease Act would not be enough to save England, and he began making plans for more aggressive action (Humphries, p. 188). He ordered more ships to Pearl Harbor, against the advice of military leaders, until the bulk of the Pacific fleet was anchored there.

6   At the end of November, American intelligence intercepted messages that revealed that a large strike force was on its way to a U.S. target (Rice, p. 211; Humphries, p. 198). All indications were that the target was Pearl Harbor. The President did not respond when he received this information. In fact, he did not reveal it to the nation's military leaders. Over the next few days, there was a frenzy of activity at the Japanese embassy. On December 4, the ambassador received word that the Japanese navy would attack Pearl Harbor. Of course, Roosevelt received the same message. His action was limited to calling the ambassador to the White House, where he asked if the Japanese government was planning any hostilities against the United States. The ambassador assured the President that his government was not (Rice, p. 223). Meanwhile, the embassy staff was destroying documents, getting ready to leave Washington. U.S. intelligence monitored radio transmissions between the strike force and Tokyo until the moment that the attack order was given. The President simply waited.

7   There is no question that the attack on Pearl Harbor was a horrible event. It is made more horrible by the evidence that suggests that it could have been prevented. If President Roosevelt had notified Admiral Kimmel and General Short, the commanders in charge of the base, they could have prepared. The ships could have dispersed, making them less vulnerable to attack. They could have attacked first, which would have surprised the Japanese. But to have done nothing is unconscionable.

8   World War II itself was a horrible event comprised of countless smaller horrible events. Few, however, compare with Roosevelt's actions regarding Pearl Harbor. It seems clear, based on the evidence, that the President offered the Pacific fleet as bait that he knew the Japanese government, under the circumstances, could not resist. It seems clear that he also knew that the attack was underway and did nothing. His involvement in the death of so many is reprehensible.

The first paragraph in this passage works very well to provide a background, or set the scene, for the bombing of Pearl Harbor. It also effectively redefines the event by shifting the focus away from the Japanese attack to the often argued complicity of President Roosevelt. In addition, the last sentence of this paragraph provides a preview of Phuong's evaluation.

What follows in paragraphs 2 through 6 is a sophisticated report–analysis–interpretation of the bombing. Phuong divides the one event into a series of related events not only to report what happened but why. He supports his interpretation through outside sources and a general knowledge of historical events leading up to America's entry into the war, and the analysis is detailed and informed. Finally, notice that the formal evaluation of the event appears in the concluding paragraph.

He labels Roosevelt's supposed complicity "reprehensible." There is an effort to place the event in the broader context of World War II, although in my view, Phuong could have done a bit more in this regard. Nevertheless, the paper overall illustrates very effective writing that can serve as a model for your own work.

The central thesis of Phuong's paper is highly controversial, which may make it difficult for readers to decide whether the interpretation is reasonable. However, if a reader accepts the argument, this part of the paper also provides ample support for Phuong's evaluation. Indeed, if any of the allegations against Roosevelt were true, the event would not be not only "reprehensible" but also criminal. I don't want to get sidetracked on this point. For our purposes, it is enough to note that the support Phuong provides in the analysis and interpretation portion of the paper also serves to support his evaluation.

DISCOURSE COMMUNITIES AND YOUR EVALUATION

Numerous factors influence how people evaluate events. Age, gender, and education are some of the more visible. Discourse communities may exert the most important influence. Groups have collective values that figure significantly in every evaluation. A commonplace example should make this point clear. Several years ago, a number of states determined that insurance companies were charging too much for automobile insurance, and the state insurance commissioners ordered the companies to lower their rates. Insurance executives had a uniformly negative evaluation of the event, declaring that is was unjustified and that it would make insurance harder to get.

Journal Entry

Have you ever believed something or held a particular point of view because it was accepted by those around you? What was it? Do you believe it still?

Diverse Voices

As far as we know, all cultures engage in evaluation. They appear to differ, however, in how they express that evaluation. In cultures that stress formality and politeness, such as the Japanese culture, negative evaluations usually are masked fairly well. For example, an employee's performance would not be characterized as "bad" but might be characterized as "showing good improvement." To an outsider, such expressions might be viewed as softening negative evaluations, but there is a real question regarding how they are interpreted by insiders who know that "showing good improvement" is not a compliment. Other cultures appear to relish hyperbole whether an evaluation is good or bad.

Cultural factors can influence how you respond to evaluation assignments, so it is important for you to understand in what ways, if any, your culture differs from American culture. For this activity, reflect on how your culture is similar to and different from American culture with respect to evaluation; then write a few paragraphs that describe how these similarities and differences have affected you as a student in an American school. Finally, include some evaluation of the advantages and disadvantages you would experience if you were to adopt fully the American culture.

SELECTING AN EVENT FOR EVALUATION

Events can be classified as having occurred in the recent past—something that happened within the last 2 or 3 years—or having occurred later. The two categories present different challenges. Evaluating an event in the recent past has the advantage of immediacy. Readers are more likely to be interested because it will be topical and because they more easily recognize how the event and the evaluation may affect their lives. A disadvantage, however, is that it may be harder to find enough material on the event to make a meaningful and informed evaluation. Consequently, before selecting an event in the recent past, you may want to do some preliminary research to determine whether you can locate enough material.

It is usually easy to find information about events that did not occur in the recent past, provided the event is well known. But some events will have so much material available that you will have to limit your reading; in this case, try to look only at the most recently published works. This way, you will have access to current data and interpretations.[3]

Avoiding the Commonplace

Although people are different in many ways, we do have a tendency to think alike. If you have a good idea for a paper, chances are that someone else will have a similar idea. This human characteristic can cause problems when you are selecting an event for evaluation. For example, in a political science class, the preferred topics are likely to be the Kennedy assassination, the Civil Rights Movement, President Nixon and the Watergate scandal, or Ronald Reagan's election and the rise of conservatism. In an introductory chemistry class, the preferred topics are likely to be global warming, the depletion of the ozone layer, or environmental pollution. When so many people are writing about the same topic, the competition will be greater, not only because everyone will want the same

---

[3]Professionals in many fields recognize the importance of using current materials. In the sciences and social sciences, readers of new publications often skim the references to check the dates of the cited texts. If a large number of the texts are more than 5 years old, readers are likely to dismiss the work as being out of touch with recent developments in the field. You may want to keep this information in mind when you have to write papers for classes in science and social science.

materials but also because the teacher will have many other papers to use as comparative standards.

Recognizing that people tend to select the same topics on any given subject is the first step toward finding a solution. The second step is to spend more time thinking about topics in order to discover one that is less common. An assignment from a political science class for freshmen can help make this point more concrete. The course focused on events that have shaped Western politics during the last half of the century. Although the teacher emphasized events in the United States, she brought in a great deal of material about other countries. The assignment follows:

> For your next paper, describe a political event or movement in detail and then evaluate its significance in shaping the current political climate. For example, you might choose to discuss the Kennedy assassination, the Vietnam War, or the Civil Rights Movement. Papers should be approximately 10 pages, double spaced.

More than three quarters of the students in the class took their cue directly from the assignment sheet, opting to write about one of the events the teacher mentioned. Half of this number wrote about the Civil Rights Movement. Indeed, several of these students thought that their teacher *expected* them to write about one of the events mentioned in the assignment. But the teacher had no such expectations. She had intended the list to do nothing more than provide examples of what students could write about; she did not want it to limit students in any way. A few students did choose different events, which are listed here, and their papers tended to be more successful:

- The rise of Petra Kelly and the Green Party in Germany
- The collapse of the Soviet Union
- The Gulf War
- The War Against Serbia
- President Reagan's initiation of the Strategic Defense (Star Wars) Initiative
- The impeachment proceedings against President Clinton

Linked Assignment

SELECTING AN EVENT FOR EVALUATING

This activity gives you an opportunity to begin preparing for the writing assignment on page 251. Using your campus community as a source of information, identify several events that you can evaluate. In the process, analyze your choices and write down the factors that you believe make them suitable for evaluation. Do they have any features in common? Share your events with other students in your class, comparing and contrasting your choices to theirs. Again, do they have any features in common? Use the feedback from your classmates to select two events that might best serve as the focus of an evaluative paper. You should base your selection in part on your ability to make and then support evaluations of the events. Some questions you may want to pose for yourself are:

- Why do I want to evaluate this event?
- What position will I take?
- Why would others be motivated to read my evaluation?
- What evidence can I use to support my evaluation?
- What do I want my evaluation to do?
- How do I want it to affect readers?

PROVIDE A BACKGROUND FOR THE EVENT

Events occur in a context. They are part of the social and political fabric of a specific time and place. Setting the scene for readers by giving them a background is therefore very important. This background usually consists of a summary of the event, which provides a context for readers. Even when an event is well known, a background is important because it is the only way of ensuring that every reader is familiar with the details of the event.

Background information normally is limited to a paragraph, but sometimes, when the event is linked to one or more other events that also may require some background, the introduction will be longer. Consider the passage below, for example, which comes from an article by Elliot Negin entitled "Why College Tuitions Are So High." It takes Negin three paragraphs to set the scene for readers:

Passage 2: Why College Tuitions Are So High

Elliot Negin

1   Over the past two years numerous articles have appeared in the national press about the "fiscal agony" that American colleges and universities are experiencing. A front-page article in *The New York Times* in February of last year announced, "BAD TIMES FORCE UNIVERSITIES TO RETHINK WHAT THEY ARE." Two months later *Time* magazine ran a cover story warning that administrators are facing a "cost crunch that, recession or no, promises only to grow worse." Other articles have addressed how this crisis affects students. *The Miami Herald*, for example, pointed out last August, "COSTS PUT A DREAM AT RISK."

2   Although it's true that the downturn in the economy forced U.S. colleges to make drastic cutbacks, students began leaving college—or began to choose schools on the basis of cost rather than quality—well before the recession hit. Since the mid-1980s escalating tuition costs have forced low-income students into community colleges or out of school altogether and have either pushed middle-class students into state schools or saddled them with unparalleled debt. Considering that higher education is a primary source of social and economic mobility, this is cause for alarm—especially since tuitions are expected to continue to mount. Tuition and fees now come to more than $20,000 a year at elite private institutions, and the price could jump as high as $40,000 by the year 2000.

3   Most of the recent articles have alluded to the fact that since 1980 colleges and universities have been increasing their tuition and fees at roughly twice the rate of inflation. None of them, however, has explained why.

The first sentence of this passage provides a good framework for what follows. It tells readers that many articles have appeared over the past 2 years that have addressed the financial problems many universities are facing. The reference to "two years" is important because it signals that these problems are not the usual variety that have plagued American higher education for decades but are something new. The rest of the first paragraph is best understood in relation to the passage's title, "Why College Tuitions Are So High." It suggests that many articles have tried to answer the question but that they have not been successful. This passage implicitly promises to do what others have not.

Some of the writers who dealt with this question appear to have focused on economic recession, blaming it for rising tuition. Paragraph 2, however, rejects this connection, noting that tuition increases have been affecting students for some time. In doing so, this paragraph accomplishes two things fairly effectively: It provides more background information, which helps readers understand that the problem extends beyond short-term economic woes, and it stimulates reader expectations by again hinting at the inadequacies of previous articles. Paragraph 2 also suggests that the high cost of tuition has national importance and that it is not merely the problem of college students and their parents. It has social implications because, as Negin writes, "higher education is the primary source of social and economic mobility."

With this background information in place, the writer shifts from tacitly criticizing previous articles to a forthright statement about their failure to explain why college tuitions are increasing at "roughly twice the rate of inflation." The third paragraph signals the end of the introduction. Notice that, in addition to providing a background for the event, these three paragraphs do what any good introduction must do—they let readers know what the article will be about and why the topic is worth discussing.

Linked Assignment

CREATING A BACKGROUND

This activity continues the work you began in the first linked assignment. It is designed to get you started producing information that you can use later for your introduction to the writing assignment on page 251.

Select one of the events you identified on page 246 and write a background for it. You may not want to be overly concerned about your thesis at this point, but you should let readers know why the event is worth writing about, and you should give them some idea of what the paper will be about.

INTERPRETING THE EVENT

Interpreting events is a key part of evaluating them. The best way to illustrate the connection is to continue with the Negin passage. After the introduction, Negin goes on to examine some possible explanations for high tuition costs, but he does not find them convincing. Then, in paragraph 11, he suggests that "tuition inflation" is linked to "the commercialization of campus-based research." This commercialization was achieved "not to attract more students but to attract corporate investment." It becomes clear at this point that rising tuition is not the event that Negin is primarily interested in. He sees it as an outcome of another event, the commercialization of campus-based research. What follows is part of Negin's interpretation of that event:

Passage 3: Why College Tuitions Are So High

1   It is a piece of federal legislation passed in 1980 that is to blame for the tuition increases, according to the coalition. The Bayh-Dole Act, also known as the Unversity-Small Business Patent Act, augmented by a subsequent executive order to include multinational corporations, ceded to universities the ownership of patents developed with federal research funds. This enabled schools to attract foreign and U.S. corporate investment, because they could now sell to companies exclusive licenses on all discoveries made under a company's sponsorship. To sweeten the pot, Congress also altered the federal tax code, giving corporations tax credits for investing in university research.

2   The coalition's theory . . . suggests that universities promptly started to raise tuition—their only source of unrestricted revenue—to cover the exorbitant venture-captial demands of applied research.

3   The higher-education establishment, corporations, and both political parties touted the revised patent law as a solution to the nation's competitiveness problem. It was meant to encourage universities to shift their priorities from pure, or basic, research—which rarely has any immediate practical use—to applied research. For universities to do this, however, they would have had to make an upfront investment to modernize laboratories in order to meet industrial standards and hire industrially qualified scientists at much higher salaries than those they customarily paid. The discoveries resulting from this applied research, so the argument went, would be more easily translated into marketable products, thus making U.S. corporations more competitive. And the universities would recoup their initial investment and earn a profit from royalties on their patent rights.

4   These patent-law changes, Minsky argues, transformed the overriding purpose of the university: "Formerly, universities had only employees and capital. Now they have products to sell. Once universities become a business, the objective is not 'education for the people' but looking for marketable products and selling the institution to corporate investors."

In these paragraphs, Negin begins his interpretation of the Bayh-Dole Act that allowed universities to patent and sell discoveries. The structure is clear and easy to follow. First, there is a brief description of what the Act is about, which is followed by an interpretation of what the Act has meant for the nation's schools. Negin states that it was the Bayh-Dole Act that "enabled schools to attract foreign and U.S. corporate investment." Attracting such investment, however, came at a price—the cost of upfitting university labs so that they could meet industrial standards. In turn, this cost was passed on to students in the form of higher tuition.

This interpretation relies on a causal analysis, which is important to the evaluation that comes later. The intentions that prompted the Bayh-Dole Act probably were good—the goal was to improve the nation's competitive edge—but it had the unexpected outcome of increased tuition. Negin's evaluation is wrapped up in his analysis. He does not simply write that the Act, or high tuition for that matter, is bad. Instead, he explores the consequences of university and corporate collaboration in ways that leave little doubt about his assessment.

The three paragraphs above indicate that Negin's focus in the long central portion of the passage is not tuition but the consequences of the Bayh-Dole Act. You rightly may want to ask yourself, therefore, why Negin gives the impression that his topic is college tuition.

EVALUATING THE EVENT

Very often the actual evaluation of an event comes when readers already know the writer's assessment. They have this knowledge because the interpretation usually makes the writer's position clear. In addition, evaluations do not always take the form of a statement about whether the event was good or bad. Instead, they may be stated in terms of something lost or something gained.

Let's continue examining "Why College Tuitions Are So High" to see how Negin expresses his evaluation of the commercialization of higher education as a loss. As you read the passage below, you may want to reflect on the other portions of this article that you have examined. Has Negin prepared readers for this evaluation? Is it supported?

Passage 4: Why College Tuitions Are So High

1   Over the past forty years federal initiatives have helped open the gates of the academy to women, low-income whites, and racial and ethnic minorities. The commercialization of campus research, however, coupled with the federal government's shift from student-aid grants to loans, has rolled back those gains. Access to higher education is becoming progressively restricted to those students—largely of white, upper-middle-class background—who can pay. The result? Stratification in the college system increasingly mirrors the social stratification that higher education once helped to overcome.

2   Proponents argue that closer university-industry ties will generate new products and enhance U.S. competitiveness, but little has happened since 1980 to justify the huge public subsidies or the end of affordable education for many Americans.

3   The policy has sparked little debate on Capitol Hill, where it still enjoys bipartisan support. Even so, the Coalition for Universities in the Public Interest maintains that he commercialization of publicly funded research is an issue as important to the nation's future as environmental protection.

Most scholars agree that the past 40 years can be characterized as a period in which American higher education has become democratized. This consensus makes Negin's evaluation of the commercialization of higher education particularly damning: In his assessment, the Bayh-Dole Act has reversed the process to such an extent that the nation's colleges are returning to a stratified status in which only students from well-off families can afford higher education. You should note the central role comparison and contrast play here.

If readers accept the argument, then the evaluation is difficult to dispute. Negin's support is, in fact, fairly convincing, which makes his evaluation strong. By stating his evaluation as a loss, Negin adds to its strength. He is, after all, suggesting that in the future higher education will be the exclusive privilege of the upper class, a notion that most readers will find unacceptable. Of course, placing the event in a broader context is the final step in an evaluation. Negin succeeds by linking the event to the broader context of national welfare.

PLACING THE EVENT
IN A BROADER CONTEXT

Effective conclusions either end with the event or they look forward or outward through a generalization. In an evaluation of an event, the conclusion should look outward and should generalize the event to a broader context. Again, "Why College Tuitions Are So High" offers a good example.

By the time Negin gets to the end of his article, he has reported the event (the shift in university priorities) that led to high tuition, and he has evaluated it (it's a bad thing, generally, although it has brought some good). Now, in paragraph 48, Negin looks outward:

Passage 5: Why College Tuitions Are So High

1   "Just as Americans should be concerned about the regulation of the oil under the ground and the timber above it," David Noble says, "they should also be concerned about this precious and irreplaceable asset—what some call intellectual capital. We have no quarrel with universities acting in any way they want so long as they don't take public funds. But when they do—and nearly all do—to ask the question What's in it for the public? is not only legitimate, it's essential democratic behavior."

In this paragraph, Negin sets the commercialization of universities and the resulting increase in tuition in the broader context of what really might be best described as Negin's American dream. He sees higher education as the means to an end—the leveling of society and equal outcomes for all. In the broader context of this dream, the significance of the event, as well as Negin's evaluation of it, take on more meaning.

Writing Assignment

EVALUATING A CAMPUS EVENT

This assignment gives you the opportunity to apply what we have discussed so far. Bring together the work you have completed for the linked assignments dealing with a campus event and write an evaluation of that event. Your paper should be three to four pages long. Keep in mind that your evaluation is a form of argument and that you will have to provide good reasons for your judgment.

READINGS

Stephen Jay Gould

Stephen Jay Gould is a geologist who also is an expert paleontologist. Although the two fields seldom are linked, they are in fact complementary. A geologist studies the earth's crust, specifically the rock formations that form its mountains, valleys, and plains. A paleontologist, on the other hand, studies the fossils embedded in the earth's crust. Gould not only is a world-renowned scientist, he also is one of the country's more popular writers. He has published numerous science books for the general audience, and some of them have been best sellers. In addition, he publishes a nationally syndicated column on science. One of his chief interests is the Burgess Shale, an area rich in fossils located in the Canadian Rockies. The following passage comes from the book *Bully for Brontosaurus*. It is about the Burgess Shale, but the focus is on evaluating the events associated with the discovery of the Shale's fossils. You should know in advance, however, that Gould is not evaluating the events as such but rather the accepted *account* of the discovery.

Literary Bias
on the Slippery Slope

1   EVERY PROFESSION has its version: Some speak of "Sod's law"; others of "Murphy's law." The formulations vary, but all make the same point—if anything bad can happen, it will. Such universality of attribution can only arise for one reason—the principle is true (even though we know that it isn't).

2   The fieldworker's version is simply stated: You always find the most interesting specimens at the very last moment, just when you absolutely must leave. The effect of this phenomenon can easily be quantified. It operates weakly for localities near home and easily revisited and ever more strongly for distant and exotic regions requiring great effort and expense for future expeditions. Everyone has experienced this law of nature. I once spent two weeks on Great Abaco, visiting every nook and cranny of the island and assiduously proving that two supposed species of *Cerion* (my favorite land snail) really belonged to one variable group. On the last morning, as the plane began to load, we drove to the only unexamined place, an isolated corner of the island with the improbable name Hole-in-the-Wall. There we found hundreds of large white snails, members of the second species.

3   Each profession treasures a classic, or canonical, version of the basic story. The paleontological "standard," known to all my colleagues as a favorite campfire tale and anecdote for introductory classes, achieves its top billing by joining the most famous geologist of his era with the most important fossils of any time. The story, I have just discovered, is also entirely false (more than a bit embarrassing since I cited the usual version to begin an earlier essay in this series).

4   Charles Doolittle Walcott (1850–1927) was both the world's leading expert on Cambrian rocks and fossils (the crucial time for the initial flowering of multicellular life) and the most powerful scientific administrator in America. Walcott, who knew every president from Teddy Roosevelt to Calvin Coolidge, and who persuaded Andrew Carnegie to establish the Carnegie Institute of Washington, had little formal education and began his career as a fieldworker for the United States Geological Survey. He rose to chief, and resigned in 1907 to become secretary (their name for boss) of the Smithsonian Institution. Walcott had his finger, more accurately his fist, in every important scientific pot in Washington.

5   Walcott loved the Canadian Rockies and, continuing well into his seventies, spent nearly every summer in tents and on horseback, collecting fossils and indulging his favorite hobby of panoramic photography. In 1909, Walcott made his greatest discovery in Middle Cambrian rocks exposed on the western flank of the ridge connecting Mount Field and Mount Wapta in eastern British Columbia.

6   The fossil record is, almost exclusively, a tale told by the hard parts of organisms. Soft anatomy quickly disaggregates and decays, leaving bones and shells behind. For two basic reasons, we cannot gain an adequate appreciation for the full range of ancient life from these usual remains. First, most organisms contain no hard parts at all, and we miss them entirely. Second, hard parts, especially superficial coverings, often tell us very little about the animal within or underneath. What could you learn about the anatomy of a snail from the shell alone?

7   Paleontologists therefore treasure the exceedingly rare softbodied faunas occasionally preserved when a series of unusual circumstances coincide—rapid burial, oxygen-free environments devoid of bacteria or scavengers, and little subsequent disturbance of sediments.

8   Walcott's 1909 discovery—called the Burgess Shale—surpasses all others in significance because he found an exquisite fauna of soft-bodied organisms from the most crucial of all times. About 570 million years ago, virtually all modern

phyla of animals made their first appearance in an episode called "the Cambrian explosion" to honor its geological rapidity. The Burgess Shale dates from a time just afterward and offers our only insight into the true range of diversity generated by this most prolific of all evolutionary events.

9   Walcott, committed to a conventional view of slow and steady progress in increasing complexity and diversity, completely misinterpreted the Burgess animals. He shoehorned them all into modern groups, interpreting the entire fauna as a set of simpler precursors for later forms. A comprehensive restudy during the past twenty years has inverted Walcott's view and taught us the most surprising thing we know about the history of life: The fossils from this one small quarry in British Columbia exceed, in anatomical diversity, all modern organisms in the world's oceans today. Some fifteen to twenty Burgess creatures cannot be placed into any modern phylum and represent unique forms of life, failed experiments in metazoan design. Within known groups, the Burgess range far exceeds what prevails today. Taxonomists have described almost a million living species of arthropods, but all can be placed into three great groups—insects and their relatives, spiders and their kin, and crustaceans. In Walcott's single Canadian quarry, vastly fewer species include about twenty more basic anatomical designs! The history of life is a tale of decimation and later stabilization of few surviving anatomies, not a story of steady expansion and progress.

10   But this is another story for another time (see my book *Wonderful Life*, 1989). I provide this epitome only to emphasize the context for paleontology's classic instance of Sod's law. These are no ordinary fossils, and their discoverer was no ordinary man.

11   I can provide no better narration for the usual version than the basic source itself—the obituary notice for Walcott published by his longtime friend and former research assistant Charles Schuchert, professor of paleontology at Yale. (Schuchert was, by then, the most powerful paleontologist in America, and Yale became the leading center of training for academic paleontology. The same story is told far and wide in basically similar versions, but I suspect that Schuchert was the primary source for canonization and spread. I first learned the tale from my thesis adviser, Nor-

man D. Newell. He heard it from his adviser, Carl Dunbar, also at Yale, who got it directly from Schuchert.) Schuchert wrote in 1928:

12   One of the most striking of Walcott's faunal discoveries came at the end of the field season of 1909, when Mrs. Walcott's horse slid in going down the trail and turned up a slab that at once attracted her husband's attention. Here was a great treasure—wholly strange Crustacea of Middle Cambrian time—but where in the mountain was the mother rock from which the slab had come? Snow was even then falling, and the solving of the riddle had to be left to another season, but next year the Walcotts were back again on Mount Wapta, and eventually the slab was traced to a layer of shale—later called the Burgess shale—3,000 feet above the town of Field, British Columbia, and 8,000 feet above the sea.

13   Stories are subject to a kind of natural selection. As they propagate in the retelling and mutate by embellishment, most eventually fall by the wayside to extinction from public consciousness. The few survivors hang tough because they speak to deeper themes that stir our souls or tickle our funnybones. The Burgess legend is a particularly good story because it moves from tension to resolution, and enfolds within its basically simple structure two of the greatest themes in conventional narration—serendipity and industry leading to its just reward. We would never have known about the Burgess if Mrs. Walcott's horse hadn't slipped going downslope on the very last day of the field season (as night descended and snow fell, to provide a dramatic backdrop of last-minute chanciness). So Walcott bides his time for a year in considerable anxiety. But he is a good geologist and knows how to find his quarry (literally in this case). He returns the next summer and finally locates the Burgess Shale by hard work and geological skill. He starts with the dislodged block and traces it patiently upslope until he finds the mother lode. Schuchert doesn't mention a time, but most versions state that Walcott spent a week or more trying to locate the source. Walcott's son Sidney, reminiscing sixty years later, wrote in 1971: "We worked our way up, trying to find the bed of rock from which our original find had been dislodged. A week later and some 750 feet higher we decided that we had found the site."

14   I can imagine two basic reasons for the survival and propagation of this canonical story. First, it is simply too good a tale to pass into oblivion. When both good luck and honest labor combine to produce victory, we all feel grateful to discover that fortune occasionally smiles, and uplifted to learn that effort brings reward. Second, the story might be true. And if dramatic and factual value actually coincide, then we have a real winner.

15   I had always grasped the drama and never doubted the veracity (the story is plausible, after all). But in 1988, while spending several days in the Walcott archives at the Smithsonian Institution, I discovered that all key points of the story are false. I found that some of my colleagues had also tracked down the smoking gun before me, for the relevant pages of Walcott's diary had been earmarked and photographed before.

16   Walcott, the great conservative administrator, left a precious gift to future historians by his assiduous recordkeeping. He never missed a day of writing in his diary. Even at the very worst moment of his life, July 11, 1911, he made the following, crisply factual entry about his wife: "Helena killed at Bridgeport Conn. by train being smashed up at 2:30 A.M. Did not hear of it until 3 P.M. Left for Bridgeport 5:35 P.M." (Walcott was meticulous, but please do not think him callous. Overcome with grief the next day, he wrote on July 12: "My love—my wife—my comrade for 24 years. I thank God I had her for that time. Her untimely fate I cannot now understand.")

17   Walcott's diary for the close of the 1909 field season neatly dismisses part one of the canonical tale. Walcott found the first soft-bodied fossils on Burgess ridge either on August 30 or 31. His entry for August 30 reads:

18   Out collecting on the Stephen formation [the unit that includes what Walcott later called the Burgess Shale] all day. Found many interesting fossils on the west slope of the ridge between Mounts Field and Wapta [the right locality for the Burgess Shale]. Helena, Helen, Arthur, and Stuart [his wife, daughter, assistant, and son] came up with remainder of outfit at 4 P.M.

19   On the next day, they had clearly discovered a rich assemblage of soft-bodied fossils. Walcott's quick sketches are so clear that I can identify the three genera he depicts—*Marrella*, the most common Burgess fossil and one of the unique arthropods beyond the range of modern designs; *Waptia*, a bivalved arthropod; and the peculiar trilobite *Naraoia*. Walcott wrote: "Out with Helena and Stuart collecting fossils from the Stephen formation. We found a remarkable group of Phyllopod crustaceans. Took a large number of fine specimens to camp."

20   What about the horse slipping and the snow falling? If this incident occurred at all, we must mark the date as August 30, when Walcott's family came up the slope to meet him in the late afternoon. They might have turned up the slab as they descended for the night, returning the next morning to find the specimens that Walcott drew on August 31. This reconstruction gains some support from a letter that Walcott wrote to Marr (for whom he later named the "lace crab" *Marrella*) in October 1909:

21   When we were collecting from the Middle Cambrian, a stray slab of shale brought down by a snow slide showed a fine Phyllopod crustacean on a broken edge. Mrs. W. and I worked on that slab from 8 in the morning until 6 in the evening and took back with us the finest collection of Phyllopod crustaceans that I have ever seen.

22   (Phyllopod, or "leaf-footed," is an old name for marine arthropods with rows of lacy gills, often used for swimming, on one branch of their legs.)

Transformation can be subtle. A snow slide becomes a snowstorm, and the night before a happy day in the field becomes a forced and hurried end to an entire season. But far more important, Walcott's field season did not finish with the discoveries of August 30 and 31. The party remained on Burgess ridge until September 7! Walcott was thrilled by his discovery and collected with avidity every day thereafter. The diaries breathe not a single word about snow, and Walcott assiduously reported the weather in every entry. His happy week brought nothing but praise for Mother Nature. On September 1 he wrote: "Beautiful warm days."

23   Finally, I strongly suspect that Walcott located the source for his stray block during the last week of his 1909 field season—at least the basic area of outcrop, if not the very richest layers. On September 1, the day after he drew the three arthropods, Walcott wrote: "We continued collecting. Found a fine group of sponges on slope (*in situ*) [meaning undisturbed and in their original position]." Sponges,

containing some hard parts, extend beyond the richest layers of soft-bodied preservation, but the best specimens come from the strata of the Burgess mother lode. On each subsequent day, Walcott found abundant soft-bodied specimens, and his descriptions do not read like the work of a man encountering a lucky stray block here and there. On September 2, he discovers that the supposed shell of an ostracode really houses the body of a Phyllopod: "Working high up on the slope while Helena collected near the trail. Found that the large so-called Leperditia-like test is the shield of a Phyllopod." The Burgess quarry is "high up on the slope," while stray blocks would slide down toward the trail.

24   On September 3, Walcott was even more successful: "Found a fine lot of Phyllopod crustaceans and brought in several slabs of rock to break up at camp." In any event, he continued to collect, and put in a full day for his last hurrah on September 7: "With Stuart and Mr. Rutter went up on fossil beds. Out from 7 A.M. to 6:30 P.M. Our last day in camp for 1909."

25   If I am right about his discovery of the main beds in 1909, then the second part of the canonical tale—the week-long patient tracing of errant block to source in 1910—should be equally false. Walcott's diary for 1910 supports my interpretation. On July 10, champing at the bit, he hiked up to the Burgess Pass campground, but found the area too deep in snow for any excavations. Finally, on July 29, Walcott reports that his party set up "at Burgess Pass campground of 1909." On July 30, they climbed neighboring Mount Field and collected fossils. Walcott indicates that they made their first attempt to locate the Burgess beds on August 1:

26   All out collecting the Burgess formation until 4 P.M. when a cold wind and rain drove us into camp. Measured section of the Burgess formation—420 feet thick. Sidney with me. Stuart with his mother and Helen puttering about camp.

("Measuring a section" is geological jargon for tracing the vertical sequence of strata and noting the rock types and fossils. If you wished to find the source of an errant block dislodged and tumbled below, you would measure the section above, trying to match your block to its most likely layer.)

I think that Charles and Sidney Walcott located the Burgess beds on this very first day, because Walcott writes for his next entry of August 2: "Out 27 collecting with Helena, Stuart, and Sidney. We found a fine lot of 'lace crabs' and various odds and ends of things." "Lace crab" was Walcott's informal field term for *Marrella*, and *Marrella* is the marker of the mother lode—the most common animal in the Burgess Shale. If we wish to give the canonical tale all benefit of doubt, and argue that these lace crabs of August 2 came from dislodged blocks, we still cannot grant a week of strenuous effort for locating the mother lode, for Walcott writes just two days later on August 4: "Helena worked out a lot of Phyllopod crustaceans from 'Lace Crab layer.'" From then on, until the end of summer, they quarried the lace crab layer, now known as the Burgess Shale.

The canonical tale is more romantic and inspiring, but the plain factuality of the diary makes more sense. I have been to the Burgess ridge. The trail lies 28 just a few hundred feet below the main Burgess beds. The slope is simple and steep, with strata well exposed. Tracing an errant block to its source should not have presented a major problem—for Walcott was more than a good geologist; he was a great geologist. He should have located the main beds right away, in 1909, since he had a week to work after first discovering soft-bodied fossils. He was not able to quarry in 1909—the only constraint imposed by limits of time. But he found many fine fossils and probably the main beds themselves. He knew just where to go in 1910 and set up shop in the right place as soon as the snows melted.

Critical Reading Guide 📖

1. What is the rhetorical stance in this passage?

2. What reasons could Gould have for spending two paragraphs talking about the paleontological equivalent of Murphy's Law?

3. What does Gould achieve by stating his evaluation before he says anything about the event he will describe? (Here's a hint: Ask yourself why Gould would mention that the falsehood of the story of the event is "a bit embarrassing.")

4. In the process of narrating the story of Walcott and the Burgess Shale, Gould provides a great deal of information about the Shale, fossils, field work, and geology. Why?

5. How does paragraph 9 fit into the narrative of the event?

6. After Gould states his evaluation in paragraph 3, he states it again in paragraph 15. What is the purpose of paragraphs 16 through 28?

7. Suppose Gould had written this piece for a professional audience. What are some factors that would be different?

Susan Faludi

Susan Faludi is a journalist who has worked for the *New York Times*, the *Miami Herald*, and the *Wall Street Journal*. She has won numerous awards for her reporting, including a Pulitzer Prize in 1991 for a report on the purchase of Safeway Stores that appeared in the *Wall Street Journal*. The passage below comes from Faludi's book, *Backlash: The Undeclared War Against American Women*, published in 1991. This book evaluates the women's movement and society's response to it, arguing that the media, government, and many educational institutions had conspired in a backlash against the advances the women's movement was trying to gain.

In the following passage, Faludi sets the groundwork for her broader assessment of feminism and society. She summarizes the view expressed in some of the popular media that the women's movement has accomplished its goal and that "women now have it all." This is the "event" Faludi intends to evaluate. Her evaluation is that the women's movement has made only marginal progress toward social and economic equality between men and women. She supports this evaluation with statistics as well as references to interviews with and surveys of women who describe their concerns about gender inequality.

SUSAN FALUDI

BACKLASH

1   To be a woman in America at the close of the 20th century—what good fortune. That's what we keep hearing, anyway. The barricades have fallen, politicians assure us. Women have "made it," Madison Avenue cheers. Women's fight for equality has "largely been won," *Time* magazine announces. Enroll at any university, join any law firm, apply for credit at any bank. Women have so many opportunities now, corporate leaders say, that we don't really need equal opportunity policies. Women are so equal now, lawmakers say, that we no longer need an Equal Rights Amendment. Women have "so much," former President Ronald Reagan says, that the White House no longer needs to appoint them to higher office. Even American Express ads are saluting a woman's freedom to charge it. At last, women have received their full citizenship papers.

And yet . . .

2

3   Behind this celebration of the American woman's victory, behind the news, cheerfully and endlessly repeated, that the struggle for women's rights is won, another message flashes. You may be free and equal now, it says to women, but you have never been more miserable.

4   This bulletin of despair is posted everywhere— at the newsstand, on the TV set, at the movies, in advertisements and doctors' offices and academic journals. Professional women are suffering "burnout" and succumbing to an "infertility epidemic." Single women are grieving from a "man shortage." The *New York Times* reports: Childless women are "depressed and confused" and their ranks are swelling. *Newsweek* says: Unwed women are "hysterical" and crumbling under a "profound crisis of confidence." The health advice manuals inform: High-powered career women are stricken with unprecedented outbreaks of "stress-induced disorders," hair loss, bad nerves, alcoholism, and even heart attacks. The psychology books advise: Independent women's loneliness represents "a major mental health problem today." Even founding feminist Betty Friedan has been spreading the word: she warns that women now suffer from a new identity crisis and "new 'problems that have no name.' "

5   How can American women be in so much trouble at the same time that they are supposed to be so blessed? If the status of women has never been higher, why is their emotional state so low? If women got what they asked for, what could possibly be the matter now?

6   The prevailing wisdom of the past decade has supported one, and only one, answer to this riddle: it must be all that equality that's causing all that pain. Women are unhappy precisely *because* they are free. Women are enslaved by their own liberation. They have grabbed at the gold ring of independence, only to miss the one ring that really matters. They have gained control of their fertility, only to destroy it. They have pursued their own professional dreams—and lost out on the greatest female adventure. The women's movement, as we are told time and again, has proved women's own worst enemy.

7   "In dispensing its spoils, women's liberation has given my generation high incomes, our own cigarette, the option of single parenthood, rape crisis centers, personal lines of credit, free love, and female gynecologists," Mona Charen, a young law student, writes in the *National Review*, in an article titled "The Feminist Mistake." "In return it has effectively robbed us of one thing upon which the happiness of most women rests—men." The *National Review* is a conservative publication, but such charges against the women's movement are not confined to its pages. "Our generation was the human sacrifice" to the women's movement, *Los Angeles Times* feature writer Elizabeth Mehren contends in a *Time* cover story. Baby-boom women like her, she says, have been duped by feminism: "We believed the rhetoric." In *Newsweek*, writer Kay Ebeling dubs feminism "the Great Experiment That Failed" and asserts "women in my generation, its perpetrators, are the casualties." Even the beauty magazines are saying it: *Harper's Bazaar* accuses the women's movement of having "lost us [women] ground instead of gaining it."

8   In the last decade, publications from the *New York Times*, to *Vanity Fair* to the *Nation* have issued a steady stream of indictments against the women's movement, with such headlines as WHEN FEMINISM FAILED or THE AWFUL TRUTH ABOUT WOMEN'S LIB. They hold the campaign for women's equality responsible for nearly every woe besetting women, from mental depression to meager savings accounts, from teenage suicides to eating disorders to bad complexions. The "Today" show says women's liberation is to blame for bag ladies. A guest columnist in the *Baltimore Sun* even proposes that feminists produced the rise in slasher movies. By making the "violence" of abortion more acceptable, the author reasons, women's rights activists made it all right to show graphic murders on screen.

9   At the same time, other outlets of popular culture have been forging the same connection: in Hollywood films, of which *Fatal Attraction* is only the most famous, emancipated women with condominiums of their own slink wild-eyed between bare walls, paying for their liberty with an empty bed, a barren womb. "My biological clock is ticking so loud it keeps me awake at night," Sally Field cries in the film *Surrender*, as, in an all too common transformation in the cinema of the '80s, an actress who once played scrappy working heroines is now showcased groveling for a groom. In prime-time television shows, from "Thirtysomething" to "Family Man," single, professional, and

feminist women are humiliated, turned into harpies, or hit by nervous breakdowns; the wise ones recant their independent ways by the closing sequence. In popular novels, from Gail Parent's *A Sign of the Eighties* to Stephen King's *Misery*, unwed women shrink to sniveling spinsters or inflate to fire-breathing she-devils; renouncing all aspirations but marriage, they beg for wedding bands from strangers or swing axes at reluctant bachelors. We "blew it by waiting," a typically remorseful careerist sobs in Freda Bright's *Singular Women*; she and her sister professionals are "condemned to be childless forever." Even Erica Jong's high-flying independent heroine literally crashes by the end of the decade, as the author supplants *Fear of Flying*'s saucy Isadora Wing, a symbol of female sexual emancipation in the '70s, with an embittered careerist-turned-recovering-"co-dependent" in *Any Woman's Blues*—a book that is intended, as the narrator bluntly states, "to demonstrate what a deadend the so-called sexual revolution had become, and how desperate so-called free women were in the last few years of our decadent epoch."

10 Popular psychology manuals peddle the same diagnosis for contemporary female distress. "Feminism, having promised her a stronger sense of her own identity, has given her little more than an identity *crisis*," the best-selling advice manual *Being a Woman* asserts. The authors of the era's self-help classic *Smart Women/Foolish Choices* proclaim that women's distress was "an unfortunate consequence of feminism," because "it created a myth among women that the apex of self-realization could be achieved only through autonomy, independence, and career."

11 In the Reagan and Bush years, government officials have needed no prompting to endorse this thesis. Reagan spokeswoman Faith Whittlesey declared feminism a "straitjacket" for women, in the White House's only policy speech on the status of the American female population—entitled "Radical Feminism in Retreat." Law enforcement officers and judges, too, have pointed a damning finger at feminism, claiming that they can chart a path from rising female independence to rising female pathology. As a California sheriff explained it to the press, "Women are enjoying a lot more freedom now, and as a result, they are committing more crimes." The U.S. Attorney General's Commission on Pornography even proposed that women's professional advancement might be responsible for rising rape rates. With more women in college and at work now, the commission members reasoned in their report, women just have more opportunities to be raped.

12 Some academics have signed on to the consensus, too—and they are the "experts" who have enjoyed the highest profiles on the media circuit. On network news and talk shows, they have advised millions of women that feminism has condemned them to "a lesser life." Legal scholars have railed against "the equality trap." Sociologists have claimed that "feminist-inspired" legislative reforms have stripped women of special "protections." Economists have argued that well-paid working women have created "a less stable American family." And demographers, with greatest fanfare, have legitimated the prevailing wisdom with so-called neutral data on sex ratios and fertility trends; they say they actually have the numbers to prove that equality doesn't mix with marriage and motherhood.

13 Finally, some "liberated" women themselves have joined the lamentations. In confessional accounts, works that invariably receive a hearty greeting from the publishing industry, "recovering Superwomen" tell all. In *The Cost of Loving: Women and the New Fear of Intimacy*, Megan Marshall, a Harvard-pedigreed writer, asserts that the feminist "Myth of Independence" has turned her generation into unloved and unhappy fast-trackers, "dehumanized" by careers and "uncertain of their gender identity." Other diaries of mad Superwomen charge that "the hard-core feminist viewpoint," as one of them puts it, has relegated educated executive achievers to solitary nights of frozen dinners and closet drinking. The triumph of equality, they report, has merely given women hives, stomach cramps, eye-twitching disorders, even comas.

14 But what "equality" are all these authorities talking about?

15 If American women are so equal, why do they represent two-thirds of all poor adults? Why are more than 80 percent of full-time working women making less than $20,000 a year, nearly double the male rate? Why are they still far more likely than men to live in poor housing and receive no health insurance, and twice as likely to draw no pension?

Why does the average working woman's salary still lag as far behind the average man's as it did twenty years ago? Why does the average female college graduate today earn less than a man with no more than a high school diploma (just as she did in the '50s)—and why does the average female high school graduate today earn less than a male high school dropout? Why do American women, in fact, face the worst gender-based pay gap in the developed world?

16   If women have "made it," then why are nearly 80 percent of working women still stuck in traditional "female" jobs—as secretaries, administrative "support" workers and salesclerks? And, conversely, why are they less than 8 percent of all federal and state judges, less than 6 percent of all law partners, and less than one half of 1 percent of top corporate managers? Why are there only three female state governors, two female U.S. senators, and two Fortune 500 chief executives? Why are only nineteen of the four thousand corporate officers and directors women—and why do more than half the boards of Fortune companies still lack even one female member?

17   If women "have it all," then why don't they have the most basic requirements to achieve equality in the work force? Unlike virtually all other industrialized nations, the U.S. government still has no family-leave and child care programs—and more than 99 percent of American private employers don't offer child care either. Though business leaders say they are aware of and deplore sex discrimination, corporate America has yet to make an honest effort toward eradicating it. In a 1990 national poll of chief executives at Fortune 1000 companies, more than 80 percent acknowledged that discrimination impedes female employees' progress—yet less than 1 percent of these same companies regarded *remedying* sex discrimination as a goal that their personnel departments should pursue. In fact, when the companies' human resource officers were asked to rate their department's priorities, women's advancement ranked last.

18   If women are so "free," why are their reproductive freedoms in greater jeopardy today than a decade earlier? Why do women who want to postpone childbearing now have fewer options than ten years ago? The availability of different forms of contraception has declined, research for new birth control has virtually halted, new laws restricting abortion—or even *information* about abortion—for young and poor women have been passed, and the U.S. Supreme Court has shown little ardor in defending the right it granted in 1973.

19   Nor is women's struggle for equal education over; as a 1989 study found, three-fourths of all high schools still violate the federal law banning sex discrimination in education. In colleges, undergraduate women receive only 70 percent of the aid undergraduate men get in grants and work-study jobs—and women's sports programs receive a pittance compared with men's. A review of state equal-education laws in the late '80s found that only thirteen states had adopted the minimum provisions required by the federal Title IX law—and only seven states had anti-discrimination regulations that covered all education levels.

20   Nor do women enjoy equality in their own homes, where they still shoulder 70 percent of the household duties—and the only major change in the last fifteen years is that now middle-class men *think* they do more around the house. (In fact, a national poll finds the ranks of women saying their husbands share equally in child care shrunk to 31 percent in 1987 from 40 percent three years earlier.) Furthermore, in thirty states, it is still generally legal for husbands to rape their wives; and only ten states have laws mandating arrest for domestic violence—even though battering was the leading cause of injury of women in the late '80s. Women who have no other option but to flee find that isn't much of an alternative either. Federal funding for battered women's shelters has been withheld and one-third of the 1 million battered women who seek emergency shelter each year can find none. Blows from men contributed far more to the rising numbers of "bag ladies" than the ill effects of feminism. In the '80s, almost half of all homeless women (the fastest growing segment of the homeless) were refugees of domestic violence.

21   The word may be that women have been "liberated," but women themselves seem to feel otherwise. Repeatedly in national surveys, majorities of women say they are still far from equality. Nearly 70 percent of women polled by the *New York Times* in 1989 said the movement for women's rights had only just begun. Most women in the 1990 Virginia Slims opinion poll agreed with the statement that conditions for their sex in American society had

improved "a little, not a lot." In poll after poll in the decade, overwhelming majorities of women said they needed equal pay and equal job opportunities, they needed an Equal Rights Amendment, they needed the right to an abortion without government interference, they needed a federal law guaranteeing maternity leave, they needed decent child care services. They have none of these. So how exactly have we "won" the war for women's rights?

22   Seen against this background, the much ballyhooed claim that feminism is responsible for making women miserable becomes absurd—and irrelevant. As we shall see in the chapters to follow, the afflictions ascribed to feminism are all myths. From "the man shortage" to "the infertility epidemic" to "female burnout" to "toxic day care," these so-called female crises have had their origins not in the actual conditions of women's lives but rather in a closed system that starts and ends in the media, popular culture, and advertising—an endless feedback loop that perpetuates and exaggerates its own false images of womanhood.

23   Women themselves don't single out the women's movement as the source of their misery. To the contrary, in national surveys 75 to 95 percent of women credit the feminist campaign with *improving* their lives, and a similar proportion say that the women's movement should keep pushing for change. Less than 8 percent think the women's movement might have actually made their lot worse.

• • •

What actually is troubling the American 24 female population, then? If the many ponderers of the Woman Question really wanted to know, they might have asked their subjects. In public opinion surveys, women consistently rank their own inequality, at work and at home, among their most urgent concerns. Over and over, women complain to pollsters about a lack of economic, not marital opportunities; they protest that working men, not working women, fail to spend time in the nursery and the kitchen. The Roper Organization's survey analysts find that men's opposition to equality is "a major cause of resentment and stress" and "a major irritant for most women today." It is justice for their gender, not wedding rings and bassinets, that women believe to be in desperately short supply. When the *New York Times* polled women in 1989 about "the most important problem facing women today," job discrimination was the overwhelming winner; none of the crises the media and popular culture had so assiduously promoted even made the charts. In the 1990 Virginia Slims poll, women were most upset by their lack of money, followed by the refusal of their men to shoulder child care and domestic duties. By contrast, when the women were asked where the quest for a husband or the desire to hold a "less pressured" job or to stay at home ranked on their list of concerns, they placed them at the bottom.

Critical Reading Guide

1. Faludi organizes this passage around sets of contrasts. In paragraph 1, for example, she describes how various segments of society agree that women's fight for equality has been won. Then, in paragraph 4, she describes the supposed cost of this equality. Is this organization effective? Why or why not? Identify another place where Faludi uses this approach.

2. Who do you think is Faludi's primary audience, men or women? Explain how the text supports your decision.

3. Faludi cites many statistics to support her evaluation that women have made only marginal progress toward social and economic equality with men. How could Faludi have made these statistics even more effective as support?

4. Throughout this passage, Faludi uses rhetorical questions. How effective are these questions? How might the rhetorical relationship have influenced Faludi's decision to use them?

5. In paragraph 23, Faludi notes that a survey showed that a large percentage of women credit the women's movement with making their lives better. This information seems to undermine the claims Faludi summarized earlier that link the women's movement with greater unhappiness among women. How does Faludi explain this apparent paradox?

Writing Assignment

EVALUATING AN ABSTRACT EVENT

Below is the full text of Negin's article on college tuition, portions of which appeared earlier. Published in *Atlantic* in 1993, this essay argues that high tuition is the result of a shift in government and educational policy that allowed (indeed, encouraged) universities to own patents for products developed with federal research funds. As owners of these patents, universities are in the position of being able to sell or license them and generate revenues. To attract the first-rate researchers necessary for patentable discoveries, universities had to increase certain faculty salaries significantly, and they had to improve the quality of their research facilities. These factors, Negin claims, have pushed tuition sky-high. It is worth noting that in the case of liberal arts schools that do not usually engage in this sort of research, there has been a collateral effect. When the research universities raised their tuition, the liberal arts schools generally followed their lead.

Assume that Negin's analysis and interpretation are accurate. In this case, the shift universities have undertaken to become capital-intensive businesses is a significant event, although it is a fairly abstract one. Also assume that the editor of your campus newspaper is interested in recent tuition increases at your school. The editor is familiar with Negin's article and has asked you to write an evaluation of tuition increases your school has experienced over the last 5 years. She wants a paper about five pages long.

ELLIOTT NEGIN

WHY COLLEGE TUITIONS ARE SO HIGH

Not inflation, not enrollment decline, but the subsidization of corporate research is largely to blame

1 Over the past two years numerous articles have appeared in the national press about the "fiscal agony" that American colleges and universities are experiencing. A front-page article in *The New York Times* in February of last year announced, "BAD TIMES FORCE UNIVERSITIES TO RETHINK WHAT THEY ARE." Two months later, *Time* magazine ran a cover story warning that administrators are facing a "cost crunch that, recession or no, promises only to grow worse." Other articles have addressed how this crisis affects students. *The Miami Herald*, for example, pointed out last August, "COSTS PUT A DREAM AT RISK."

2   Although it's true that the downturn in the economy forced U.S. colleges to make drastic cutbacks, students began leaving college—or began to choose schools on the basis of cost rather than quality—well before the recession hit. Since the mid-1980s escalating tuition costs have forced low-income students into community colleges or out of school altogether and have either pushed middle-class students into state schools or saddled them with unparalleled debt. Considering that higher education is a primary source of social and economic mobility, this is cause for alarm—especially since tuitions are expected to continue to mount. Tuition and fees now come to more than $20,000 a year at elite private institutions, and the price could jump as high as $40,000 by the year 2000.

3   Most of the recent articles have alluded to the fact that since 1980 colleges and universities have been increasing their tuition and fees at roughly twice the rate of inflation. None of them, however, has explained why.

4   Three years ago the higher-education establishment itself attempted to explain the increases. In the late 1980s the American Council on Education, a premier higher-education umbrella organization, and the College Board, the publisher of the annual listing of college costs and the sponsor of the Scholastic Aptitude Test, commissioned Arthur Hauptman, a consultant to both organizations, to account for the unprecedented tuition increases. In April of 1990, after a two-year investigation, they released the results.

5   The report, a 120-page book called *The College Tuition Spiral*, claims that, essentially, tuitions increased at public colleges because state funding dropped, at private colleges because facilities had been improved and teachers' salaries raised, and at both types of schools because they had to compete for a shrinking pool of college-age youths. "Institutions decided to compete for students through nicer facilities and better services rather than by lowering their prices," Hauptman has said. "That's not a venal decision." A headline in *USA Today* was typical of the largely uncritical press treatment the report received: "TUITION HIKES ARE JUSTIFIED, COLLEGES SAY." Associations and schools affiliated with the American Council on Education embraced the study's conclusions as the official answer. And in November of that year the Department of Education released "The Escalating Costs of Higher Education," a report that included a section supporting Hauptman's core findings. Upon close examination, however, the three major factors that Hauptman identified fail to explain why the price of a college diploma has risen so high so fast.

6   His first assertion, that a downturn in state funding forced public schools to raise tuition, isn't even supported by his own data, which, he states in another section of the report, "do not suggest a slumping in state support for higher education in the 1980s."

7   Hauptman's second assertion is what some critics have called the Chivas Regal argument. It goes like this: An apparently more pervasive desire for a college education, coupled with a shrinking college-age population, convinced administrators that the way to woo prospective students was to raise faculty salaries, upgrade facilities and programs, and offer more student aid, rather than to cut costs and lower tuition.

8   "It's clear that what [colleges] spent this money on was not the quality of instruction," Hauptman says. Colleges decided to keep their most affluent "customers" satisfied by gentrifying their campuses and charging for it. As Hauptman says, it was "a good business decision" in a classic buyer's market. If schools didn't keep up with their competitors, matching them natatorium for natatorium, students wouldn't enroll.

9   Third, Hauptman contends that since private and public schools were faced with a declining pool of eighteen- to twenty-four-year-olds, they could no longer spread their fixed costs over growing numbers of students, as they had in the 1960s and early 1970s. Thus they had to raise tuition. But in the 1980s the number of college students increased at a fairly steady rate. From 1980 to 1990 enrollments rose from 11.4 million to 13.6 million students—a gain of about 20 percent.

10   The flattened-enrollment theory also doesn't explain what amounts to a five-year gap. Enrollments leveled off around 1975, and college officials were aware of demographic trends well before that time, but schools did not raise their tuitions significantly above the rate of inflation until 1980. Tuition actually lagged behind inflation in the late 1970s. Why did colleges and universities wait five years to increase their fees?

11　The National Coalition for Universities in the Public Interest, an organization co-founded by Ralph Nader in 1983, offers a compelling counterargument to Hauptman's report. It blames tuition inflation on the commercialization of campus-based research. Leonard Minsky, another of the coalition's founders, says that universities are raising tuitions "not to attract more students but to attract corporate investment."

12　It is a piece of federal legislation passed in 1980 that is to blame for the tuition increases, according to the coalition. The Bayh-Dole Act, also known as the University–Small Business Patent Act, augmented by a subsequent executive order to include multinational corporations, ceded to universities the ownership of patents developed with federal research funds. This enabled schools to attract foreign and U.S. corporate investment, because they could now sell to companies exclusive licenses on all discoveries made under a company's sponsorship. To sweeten the pot, Congress also altered the federal tax code, giving corporations tax credits for investing in university research.

13　The coalition's theory provides a plausible explanation for Hauptman's mysterious five-year lag time. It suggests that universities promptly started to raise tuition—their only source of unrestricted revenue—to cover the exorbitant venture-capital demands of applied research.

14　The higher-education establishment, corporations, and both political parties touted the revised patent law as a solution to the nation's competitiveness problem. It was meant to encourage universities to shift their priorities from pure, or basic, research—which rarely has any immediate practical use—to applied research. For universities to do this, however, they would have had to make an up-front investment to modernize laboratories in order to meet industrial standards and hire industrially qualified scientists at much higher salaries than those they customarily paid. The discoveries resulting from this applied research, so the argument went, would be more easily translated into marketable products, thus making U.S. corporations more competitive. And the universities would recoup their initial investment and earn a profit from royalties on their patent rights.

15　These patent-law changes, Minsky argues, transformed the overriding purpose of the university: "Formerly, universities had only employees and capital. Now they have products to sell. Once universities become a business, the objective is not 'education for the people' but looking for marketable products and selling the institution to corporate investors."

16　The coalition charges that the strengthening of ties between universities and industry has amounted to an enormous indirect public subsidy, in the form of federal research dollars and tuition revenue, to private corporations—including ones from Japan and Europe.

17　"Corporations sponsor research at universities to use public tax dollars to defray the cost of developing marketable inventions and to spread the risk of failure," says David Noble, a professor of history at York University, in Toronto, and another coalition founder. Corporations fund only about eight percent of university research, Noble says. "They're not building the buildings, or paying for the education of the staff, or supporting the students, or the library, or the land, or the accumulated prestige and knowledge of the university. If they had to replicate these resources in-house, it would cost them orders of magnitude more than what they're paying."

18　The heightened emphasis on capital-intensive applied research has led a number of schools to cut back course offerings and to eliminate entire departments that don't pay for themselves. Columbia University, for example, phased out its geography and linguistics programs in the spring of 1989 and closed its highly regarded graduate school of library service last June. At the same time, the university built the $62 million Morris A. Schapiro Center for Engineering and Physical Science Research.

19　This retrenchment has prompted a debate among administrators about the role of the university. In a 1989 speech the president of Princeton, Harold Shapiro, said, "Some suggest that undergraduate education 'gets in the way' of frontline and increasingly complex research. Others argue that blockbuster grants for research centers, all of which require some type of cost-sharing, siphon internal funds away from teaching. . . . Should we keep the research and education enterprises together?"

20　Arthur Hauptman discusses the research-tuition connection in *The College Tuition Spiral*, but as an afterthought. Even so, his four-page abbreviated description of the link confirms much of the coalition's conclusion. And when I described to him the coalition's hypothesis, he endorsed it. "I don't think it's hypothetical," he said. "I think it's true."

21 Hauptman's study shows that despite laments by many college administrators that federal research funding declined in the 1980s, it actually went up four percent a year. And not all of the increase was associated with Pentagon programs; civilian-sector research budgets grew almost as fast as defense-related activities.

22 Administrators from elite research universities nonetheless complained to Hauptman that federal spending—which represents about 60 percent of all funds spent for campus-based research—did not increase enough to cover research costs adequately. To compete with industry for scientists and engineers, these schools have had to pay six-figure salaries and provide support staff and state-of-the-art laboratories and equipment—which can add up to millions of dollars a year.

23 How do they make up for shortfalls? Raise tuition, Hauptman says.

24 "For many years undergraduate tuitions at many universities have supported research by paying for a substantial portion of the fellowships and assistantships that institutions provide to graduate students," he writes. "But this traditional form of cross-subsidy now appears to have been extended to the use of undergraduate tuitions for the direct support of campus-based research."

25 Erich Bloch, who finished his six-year term as the director of the National Science Foundation in August of 1990, agrees. "No doubt about it," he says, "[research universities] have supported part of their research with tuition funds. . . . Research has become the prime reason for [the university's] existence. At one time it was education."

26 Both Hauptman and Minsky say that the situation at research universities has had a trickle-down effect on less prestigious state and private institutions. More and more schools "want to be considered world-class," as one former higher-education-association president says. And that means research. It's required for tenure, and many find it more lucrative and stimulating than teaching. It also brings prestige, not only to professors but also to their institutions.

27 The trend has pulled faculty members out of the classroom and into the lab. Teaching loads have lightened considerably at most institutions in both the sciences and the humanities, and many highly paid star professors never see an undergraduate—they stipulate it in their contracts. This, too, affects tuition, according to a former official of the Bush Administration. In a report released in November of 1990, Lynne Cheney, then the head of the National Endowment for the Humanities, observed that the emphasis on research over teaching had forced schools to hire more instructors, contributing to tuition increases.

28 Last September a House committee arrived at similar conclusions. In its brief report, "College Education: Paying More and Getting Less," the Select Committee on Children, Youth, and Families laid the blame for tuition inflation on the heightened emphasis on research at schools seeking to emulate Ivy League universities. The recession exacerbated the problem, the report said, by forcing schools to choose between reducing teaching budgets and reducing research budgets. Teaching lost out.

29 Finally, the fact that many of the top research universities are price leaders, to which other schools look when deciding what to charge, also drives up tuition throughout the system. To try to alleviate a related problem, the federal government recently moved to curb interschool collusion in setting tuition rates and financial-aid awards. After a two-year investigation of about sixty prestigious schools, the Justice Department in late May of 1991 charged the eight Ivy League schools and the Massachusetts Institute of Technology with violating the Sherman Antitrust Act by illegally conspiring to limit price competition on financial aid. To avoid a costly legal battle, the Ivies immediately agreed to stop their thirty-five-year practice of offering uniform financial aid awards. They also agreed not to exchange information on planned tuition increases or faculty salaries, even though they were not formally accused of doing so. MIT, however, refused to sign the consent decree and was convicted last September of fixing prices on financial aid packages. Meanwhile, the Justice Department is continuing its investigation of other schools' financial-aid practices.

30 The research-tuition connection has gained in significance as relationships among universities, government, and business have changed over the past twenty years. In the mid-1970s universities began to look to the business community as a potential

ally against "intrusive" federal regulation and as a source of funding to offset flattened federal support. Corporations, sensing an impending return to normalcy on campus after the Vietnam War, warmed to the idea of partnerships. Not only were they interested in rolling back federal regulations, but a marked decline in their ability to compete internationally had them scrambling to find ways to promote productivity and technological innovation. They were also attracted by the growing commercial potential of biotechnology—then the product of campus laboratories. Rather than increase their own in-house research-and-development capacity, which would have reduced their profit margins, they tapped into university research.

31 A major obstacle for corporations, however, was the patent law. At that time the government owned the patents on discoveries made through federally funded research and licensed them nonexclusively, without charge, on an ad hoc basis. The universities wanted ownership, which would allow them both to license patentable inventions directly to corporations for a royalty and to solicit up-front contributions from corporations. But corporations wanted exclusive licenses. If they were going to help pay for specific university research projects, they wanted their initial investment protected. Otherwise, they argued, there was no incentive to support university research.

32 Both sectors claimed that changing the law would facilitate "technology transfer"—the transfer of discoveries and inventions from university labs to corporations and then to the marketplace. The paramount argument for patent-law revision, though, was that it would greatly improve the nation's competitive posture in world markets.

33 Sheldon Steinbach, general counsel for the American Council on Education, began lobbying for the new law in 1974, when he started working closely with Senator Birch Bayh, one of the sponsors of the University–Small Business Patent Act. A few years later Steinbach helped Representative Charles Vanik draft the first research-and-development tax-credit proposal—which Congress eventually passed—to give corporations an additional inducement to support research.

34 ACE's lobbying efforts thus helped create a situation in which the American public now pays for university research four ways: federal tax dollars underwrite most campus-based research; under-

graduate tuitions help pay for labs, scientists, and research assistants; corporations investing in campus research receive tax breaks, which means a loss for the federal treasury; and a corporation with exclusive rights to a patent produced by publicly funded research can sell the product at a monopoly price.

35 Have campus-corporate ventures strengthened U.S. competitiveness or helped our domestic economy? The number of patents issued to universities has grown considerably, nearly doubling from 619 in 1986 to 1,173 in 1990, according to the Association of University Technology Managers. Despite this boom, however, there have been few bona fide commercial successes. Most of the discoveries have been limited and technical.

36 Advocates of university-industry partnerships, however, say that ten years is too brief a time over which to evaluate their success. Even so, a former president of Harvard University—the school that has made some of the biggest corporate deals on record—disputes the idea that they will ever significantly strengthen U.S. competitiveness. In his 1990 book *Universities and the Future of America*, Derek Bok writes that it is a "fallacy" that spending more on university research and promoting university-industry ties will "do much to restore the preeminence of American business."

> Most experts have concluded that the real problems of American competitiveness do not lie early in the product cycle at the stage of making inventions or even starting new companies. The trouble typically begins in later phases when products must be standardized and produced in large quantities at low prices and high quality.

Bok points out that the Japanese did not invent color television, video recorders, or semi-conductors but they are more efficient at designing and manufacturing state-of-the-art versions.

37 Another reason university-industry collaboration will not help U.S. competitiveness, the Coalition for Universities in the Public Interest says, is that Japanese and European corporations have the same access to federally funded campus research that U.S. firms do. A number of major universities, most notably the Massachusetts Institute of Technology, have aggressively courted foreign companies, and their efforts have paid off. According to a 1988 study by the General Accounting Office,

links with U.S. universities helped Toshiba to develop new technology for recording images on disks, Toyota to devise new engineering stress sensors, and the Asahi Chemical Company to computerize its manufacturing processes.

38   In June of 1989 a House subcommittee held hearings on the issue and bluntly criticized universities that were selling research results to foreign corporations. The legislators said that such actions undercut the U.S. economy when, ironically, university officials were asking for more federal support for campus research to help U.S. companies compete internationally.

39   As a follow-up, the subcommittee instructed the GAO to conduct a study of technology transfer from the schools that receive the most federal grant money. The study, published last May, found that twenty-four of the thirty-five universities surveyed had industrial liaison programs with at least one foreign member. In total, 499 foreign corporations were involved, and the programs at MIT, Stanford, and the University of California at Berkeley accounted for 58 percent of them.

40   The GAO study was incorporated into a report by the House Committee on Government Operations, issued last October, which concluded that "the benefits of publicly funded research are being sold at bargain basement prices to foreign corporations and that the very programs that were initiated to increase U.S. competitiveness are benefiting our economic competitors instead." Among other things, it recommended that the federal government require schools to give preference to U.S. corporations when granting patent licenses.

41 David Noble, who was the first to publicize MIT's extensive ties to Japanese corporations, says that such relationships are far from the only problems created by federal patent and tax laws. He argues that these laws are essentially anti-competitive. Exclusive patent licenses give corporations a monopoly on a product for up to seventeen years, but, as Noble points out, "there is no adequate requirement in U.S. patent law that ensures a patent will be worked—that there will be any return to the public." In fact, corporations have sat on patents countless times in the history of science-based industry.

42   When a corporation does decide to work a patent, it can charge the public whatever it wants. Bur-

roughs Wellcome has been roundly criticized for inflating the price of AZT, the anti-AIDS drug that the National Cancer Institute helped develop. In March of 1991 a group of HIV-infected patients sued the British pharmaceutical firm to strip it of its exclusive patent, alleging that the company misleadingly took credit in its patent application for work done by federal scientists. That suit was ultimately dismissed. But the following July the National Institutes of Health granted a nonexclusive license to manufacture AZT to Barr Laboratories "to the extent that NIH is found to have an inventorship interest in the six AZT-related patents issued to Burroughs Wellcome," according to a statement made by Dr. Bernadine Healy, the director of the NIH. Barr Laboratories and Burroughs Wellcome are involved in litigation that will be decided this May.

In a less well known case Michigan State University and NCI developed cisplatin, an anti-cancer drug, with federal research funding, and the government licensed it exclusively to Bristol-Myers (now Bristol-Myers Squibb). Other drug companies have shown interest in producing generic versions, but Bristol-Myers Squibb controls the original patent in the United States and has kept the drug's price artificially high.   43

"The exclusive license is the fulcrum," Leonard   44
Minsky says, "allowing corporations to make excessive profits above and beyond the profits that can be made in a competitive situation. Granting corporations tax breaks for funding their own research, and monopoly control of a product developed with federal research dollars, is corporate welfare. These are public handouts designed to make U.S. companies competitive, but they're counter-competitive devices that reinforce the disability they're designed to cure. We are subsidizing an inefficient system."

Over the past forty years federal initiatives have   45
helped open the gates of the academy to women, low-income whites, and racial and ethnic minorities. The commercialization of campus research, however, coupled with the federal government's shift from student-aid grants to loans, has rolled back those gains. Access to higher education is becoming progressively restricted to those students—largely of white, upper-middle-class background—who can pay. The result? Stratification in the college system increasingly mirrors the social stratification that higher education once helped to overcome.

46 Proponents argue that closer university-industry ties will generate new products and enhance U.S. competitiveness, but little has happened since 1980 to justify the huge public subsidies or the end of affordable education for many Americans.

47 The policy has sparked little debate on Capitol Hill, where it still enjoys bipartisan support. Even so, the Coalition for Universities in the Public Interest maintains that the commercialization of publicly funded research is an issue as important to the nation's future as environmental protection.

"Just as Americans should be concerned about 48 the regulation of the oil under the ground and the timber above it," David Noble says, "they should also be concerned about this precious and irreplaceable asset—what some call intellectual capital. We have no quarrel with universities acting in any way they want so long as they don't take public funds. But when they do—and nearly all do—to ask the question What's in it for the public? is not only legitimate, it's essential democratic behavior."

WRITING GUIDE: EVALUATING AN ABSTRACT EVENT

Invention

The first step in your writing process must be to obtain information on tuition increases at your school. This information usually is available in the registrar's office or university admissions. You also will want to get information about the university's position on the increases. What is the official explanation for the higher rates?

Another important invention step is understanding Negin's argument and identifying its chief points. Without these, providing the necessary background information may be difficult. Much of the early part of the article is not germane to your evaluation, however. For example, paragraphs 1 through 10 examine other explanations for the tuition increase. They are part of Negin's effort to provide a context for his argument, similar to what was discussed with respect to setting the scene. You therefore should focus your attention on paragraph 11 and those that follow. As you read the article, take notes for use later. Highlight important points and write out summaries to enhance your understanding.

Next, what is your evaluation of the tuition increases? Your initial assessment may be limited to "good" or "bad." Think of this as a starting point. You will need to go beyond this simple assessment and provide something more substantive. Negin's essay can serve as a useful example. Consider what motivated your judgment. What are the factors that influenced your evaluation? Write these down. Now, recognizing that your written evaluation has to be expressed as an argument, consider some reasons that readers might have for accepting your evaluation. You may want to identify some of the characteristics of these readers.

Planning

Your planning for this paper should be influenced by the models your studied in this chapter. You know that evaluations begin with a description of the event and that at some point afterward there is an evaluation. You may want to state your evaluation early, after a summary paragraph that outlines the event. This approach allows you to describe the event and analyze it in a way that supports your evaluation. After your analysis is completed, you then restate your evaluation. Or you may want to state your evaluation after the report of the event and follow it with support. In any event, decide on an approach and begin making notes regarding what material will appear in each section of the paper.

During this stage, you might consider other organizational plans. For example, Faludi organized her writing around contrasts. This approach is effective in part because it makes the writer's point seem so much better than the stated alternative. Does your evaluation lend itself to this approach? If so, plan how best to use it in the paper.

Drafting

Don't panic if your evaluation comprises only a small part of the paper. As you are producing the first draft, try to keep in mind the fact that an evaluation paper consists almost entirely of report, analysis, and support. Nevertheless, if you have supported that evaluation adequately, readers will not be confused about your intention. Careful planning helps you in this regard. It helps to have a well mapped-out plan that identifies the various parts of the paper in advance.

If you decided to refer to Negin in your paper, you will need to pay attention to attribution and citation, and you should use your handbook for help in this regard. You will want to be careful to avoid providing simply a summary of Negin's article. Similarly, you will want to make certain that your report of the event is not the focus of your writing. The report is there simply to allow your readers to understand the event you are evaluating.

Pausing and Reading

During pauses in your drafting, read what you have written. Are you realizing your goals? Does the introduction set the scene? Are your analysis and support effective? Is your rhetorical stance clear? Write notes in the margins wherever you will want to make adjustments later.

GROUP ACTIVITIES: EVALUATING AN ABSTRACT EVENT

1. As a group, investigate how much tuition has increased at your school over the last 5 years. Your school may be a teaching, rather than a research, institution, yet tuition may have increased nonetheless in response to increases generally across the country. After you have collected this information, address the following questions in your group: How does your school define itself, as research-oriented or teaching-oriented? If the latter, and if tuition has increased, it suggests that the event Negin describes has a significant effect on all schools. How has your school explained tuition increases? Although it will be easy to find plenty of reasons to offer a negative evaluation of the shift universities have undertaken, it can be valuable to consider some of the benefits. What might they be? After discussing these questions in your group, for about 15 minutes, take the discussion to the entire class to get a range of views.

2. Team up with a groupmate and brainstorm ideas for the various portions of your paper, taking notes throughout. Evaluations often lend themselves to metaphor, so you may want to consider developing metaphors that help you generate ideas for your assessment. Take turns presenting to each other an oral ver-

sion of the paper. The person listening should take notes regarding the effectiveness of each part. Afterward, discuss the presentations, talk about the notes (if necessary), and discuss ways to enhance the overall effectiveness of the evaluation. Use this input to produce your first draft.

3. In your group, take turns reading your drafts aloud. After each person finishes reading, the group should provide input that offers suggestions for improving the draft. The writer should take notes for use during revision.

4. After revising the first draft, exchange papers with a member of another group. Read the draft and focus on three factors: First, does the draft report the event effectively? Write down three things the writer should do to improve this portion of the paper. Second, what is the evaluation? If group members cannot identify it, the paper has a problem, and they should let the writer know and offer suggestions for improvement. Third, circle the three most effective factors that support the evaluation. Write down at least two ideas the writer can use to improve them. Finally, assume the role of the editor in this assignment. After reading the paper, will you publish it? Why or why not? The information you gain from these activities should form the basis for the next revision.

5. Exchange your revised draft with another groupmate. Carefully edit each other's papers, looking for surface errors such as faulty punctuation, misspellings, inaccurate word choice, and so on.

Evaluating Information

Although people make evaluations all the time, evaluations of information can be challenging. The reason is that we have to know quite a bit about a given body of information before we can construct a meaningful evaluation.

CHAPTER NINE

Evaluating Information

Although people make evaluations all the time, evaluations of information can be challenging. The reason is that we have to know quite a bit about a given body of information before we can construct a meaningful evaluation. At the heart of this issue is a question raised in chapter 5 regarding facts. Determining what is a fact can be difficult, yet we all have a tendency to accept published information as factual. One of the more notorious examples comes from research published in the 1960s and 1970s showing that smoking cigarettes was not harmful or unhealthy. Many people accepted this research simply because it was published, but a more critical examination would have revealed that the research was funded by various tobacco companies that clearly had a strong interest in deflecting any concerns about the link between cigarette smoke and cancer. You therefore would be wise to resist uncritical acceptance of information. Keep in mind the old saying: "Statistics are the last refuge of scoundrels." It isn't enough, therefore, to know what the information *is*. To produce a useful evaluation of information a writer must also know something about *who* collected the information as well as *why, how*, and *when* it was collected and distributed. Stated another way, a writer needs information about the information before undertaking an evaluation.

An important first step in this process involves recognizing that those who supply information have an agenda. That is, they are using the information to support a claim or interpretation that they want others to accept. Recognizing this agenda will allow you to understand better the value of the information to you, other readers, and the writer. Perhaps more important, you also will be able to understand better how the writer uses the information to further his or her aims. On result will be that you gain more insight into your own purpose, what you want your evaluation to do.

Evaluations of information take many different forms, but there are two very common types in college classes: evaluations of data and reviews of published articles and books. In this chapter, reviews of books do not include works of literature; such reviews involve a different type of evaluation, which is discussed in chapter 12.

A wide range of evaluations focuses on assessing data of various kinds, but frequently the data are in the form of statistics. Many business and marketing reports fall into this category, as do research reports and surveys. Sometimes the goal is to judge the quality of the data, but more often the goal is to evaluate how effectively the data support some associated claim. In this case, we often find evaluation and interpretation interwoven in a single work. For example, several years ago a book entitled *The Bell Curve* used demographic statistics to argue that people with low incomes have low IQ scores. Critics of the book evaluated the data that the authors presented to support this argument and not only judged it to be inadequate for the argument but also claimed that the authors of the book had misinterpreted the data.

Passage 1, which comes from a book by Francis Fukuyama titled *The Great Disruption*, provides a useful model of an evaluation of information, for it shows clearly how evaluations and interpretations overlap. In the book, Fukuyama argues that modern society went through a drastic change—the great disruption—involving a shift from an industrial to an information-based economy as well as increases in crime, divorce, drug use, and illegitimacy. This passage looks at crime statistics, evaluates them, and then provides an interpretation.

Passage 1: The Great Disruption

Francis Fukuyama

1   Property crime rates are probably a better negative measure of social capital than violent crimes. The latter, and particularly murders, are relatively infrequent, individualistic acts that touch a comparatively small portion of a given population. Property crimes, by contrast, are far more widespread and reflect the behavior of a broader part of the population. In the United States in 1996, for example, there were 632 property crimes committed for every murder. Weighed against this is the fact that violent crimes tend to be more prone to media sensationalism, and hence contribute disproportionately to public perceptions of public safety and thus to social trust. As Figure 2.2 indicates, property crime rates have increased dramatically in England and Wales, and Sweden, as well as the United States. Many other countries saw sharp increases in theft rates, including Scotland, France, New Zealand, Denmark, Norway, Finland, and the Netherlands. Here, the United States is not exceptional: New Zealand, Denmark, the Netherlands, Sweden, and Canada ended up with higher theft rates than the United States over the past generation. Again, Singapore, Korea, and Japan are outliers, with relatively low rates and no discernable increases in property crime rates over the same period.

2   As Figure 2.2 illustrates, property crime rates fell during the 1990s in the United States, England and Wales, and Sweden. Rates also fell in New Zealand, Canada, Finland, France, and Denmark (see Appendix).

3   White-collar crime might seem to be a useful measure of social capital since it is often committed not just by the poor and marginalized but also by the better-off members of society. Unfortunately, data on white-collar crime are far less usable than those on violent and property crime. Definitions vary widely between countries, and data collection and reporting is abysmal. Accordingly, it will not be used here.

4   The data in Figures 2.1 and 2.2 and in the Appendix are based on the self-reporting of national justice or interior ministries. Any criminologist will immediately note that there are many problems in using these data to represent actual levels of crime, much less more amorphous concepts like social capital. The most serious

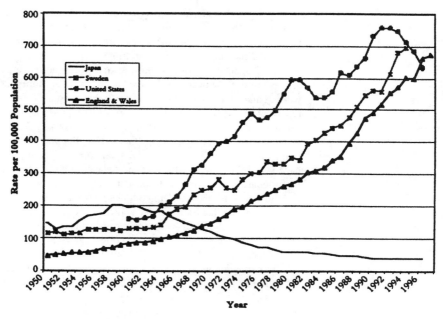

Source: See the Appendix for data.

FIGURE 2.1   Total Violent Crime Rates, 1950–1996

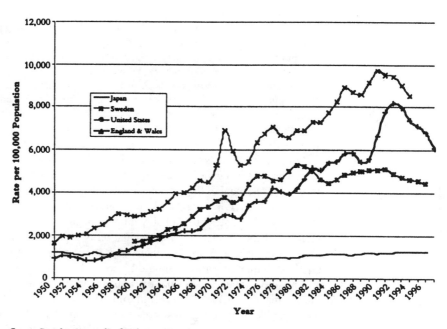

Source: See the Appendix for data.

FIGURE 2.2   Total Theft Crime Rates, 1950–1996

concerns police underreporting (or, in much rarer circumstances, overreporting). That is, only a portion of crimes actually committed are ever reported to the police (by one estimate, reported robberies constituted only 44 to 63 percent of all actual ones), and the number of reported crimes that the police in turn report to national statistical agencies is only a portion of those reported to them. Many reported crimes are dealt with by local police agencies on an informal basis without paperwork or audit trails. Criminologists agree that for most countries, the level of police reporting of crimes has increased as record-keeping systems improved and organizational rules for crime reporting were systematized. Many criminologists have turned to victimization surveys rather than police reports to get at the real level of crime in a society. Such surveys ask a random sample of respondents whether they have ever been victims of crime and hence are not dependent on police agencies. Unfortunately, many countries do not carry out systematic victimization surveys, and those that do (like the United States) have done so only since the 1970s. These surveys indicate that police underreporting of crime in decades past may have been substantial. On the other hand, one recent comparative British study shows victimization rates more or less tracking police reporting rates, rising through the late 1980s in a number of countries and falling thereafter.

5   The methodological problems with existing crime data have led many criminologists to shy away from comparative analysis of crime, or crime trends over long periods of time. But they are missing the forest for the trees. Even if we posit that there have been gradual increases in police reporting rates for most developed countries, the overall rates of increase in reported crime have been extraordinarily dramatic in most cases. It is hard to imagine that the broad upturns in so many different countries over prolonged periods of time are simply a statistical artifact, corresponding as they do to popular perceptions that crime has been on the increase. The crime historian Ted Robert Gurr is skeptical that changes in police reporting practices could have been responsible for increasing numbers after World War II; he notes, for example, that crime rates declined between 1840 and the early twentieth century in most economically advanced countries even as reporting practices were improving. He argues that the real explanation for rising reported crime rates may be the simplest one: that "threatening social behavior . . . began an increase far more rapid than the earlier decline." Indeed, many victimization studies have shown that police reporting corresponds fairly accurately with public perceptions of crime when those crimes are serious. Moreover, it is difficult to explain why the four wealthiest Asian societies appear to be exempt from this trend. Are they the only developed countries that have not improved their crime reporting methods over the past two generations?

Fukuyama presents two different kinds of evaluation of information in this passage. The first is a general assessment of crime data, whereas the second is a more specific assessment of the data presented in figures 1 and 2 of the passage. Sentence 1 of paragraph 1 is an example of a general assessment: Fukuyama states that "Property crime rates are probably a better negative measure of social capital than violent crimes." Notice that this evaluation is promptly followed by interpretation, sentences 2, 3, and 5, that explains what the general assessment means. This is a good technique; you always should try to explain things to readers.

The more specific evaluation appears in paragraph 4, sentence 2, where Fukuyama writes that "Any criminologist will immediately note that there are many problems in using these data to represent actual levels of crime, much less more amorphous concepts like social capital." And as you might expect at this point, Fukuyama follows that evaluation with a series of interpretive sentences.

Applying Key Ideas

WHEN EVALUATION
AND INTERPRETATION OVERLAP

This activity is intended to give you practice in recognizing when evaluation and interpretation are interconnected. Examine one of your textbooks to determine whether it presents any evaluations of information. (Books in the social sciences are especially appropriate for this activity.) Identify several places where evaluation and interpretation overlap. In a couple of paragraphs, offer an explanation of this overlap. Some questions you might consider are: Why does the overlap occur? Is there any underlying pattern? Can you see any specific rhetorical goals that the writer (or writers) is trying to achieve in those places? What determines whether you will classify a passage as interpretation or evaluation?

REVIEWS OF ARTICLES
AND BOOKS

Reviews generally focus on evaluating published articles or books, and they require those who write them to pay careful attention to the details of a text. They also require careful analysis and accurate interpretation. More challenging is the fact that reviewers usually have to know something about the field so they can place the work appropriately in context. Knowledge of the field thus helps reviewers determine whether the work is valuable or not.

In addition, professional reviews are political. Reviewers tend to be in a position to say that a text is congruent with the values of the group or that it is outside those values, which has practical consequences. Books that are criticized by a group or its representative are not likely to sell very well. Failure in the marketplace acts as a disincentive for those who would write outside the mainstream views and values of the group. Reviews therefore can have a significant influence on the development of new ideas and theories at the professional level.

Reviews of articles and books in college may not be significantly concerned with this larger issue but tend to focus instead on the information the work presents. They also may include some mention of the methods the writer used to gather the information and the way the writer interprets it. The following review, which evaluates a composition book, illustrates a typical approach. As you read, consider how the review compares to your own experiences writing reviews.

Passage 2: A Review of *Gaining Ground in College Writing*

Robert Brooke

1   I found this is a startling book: Haswell argues that college students' writing presently matures during the college years, but in ways teachers are unlikely to recognize. His book is thus a challenge to many accepted notions of development. His

data are well worth attention and his arguments for changes in pedagogy may prompt some interior wrestling with pedagogical goals.

2   Haswell's argument is based on an analytic comparison of timed assigned impromptu essays written by three groups: beginning college students, advanced college students, and graduated business employees chosen as competent writers by their supervisors. Hoping to address the profession's concern with the so-called "Kitzhaber effect" (a long-standing myth that claims students' writing ability actually decreases between the first and fourth years of college), Haswell subjected his sample of impromptu essays to a battery of comparisons including syntactic analyses, organizational descriptions, error percentages, production rates, and holistic ratings by local teachers of writing. His results indicate a profound mismatch between teacher *perception* of college students' writing and real, describable *change* in that writing.

3   The mismatch goes like this: According to the holistic ratings that teachers assigned to the essays, there was no statistically significant change in the quality of impromptu essay writing during the college years (though the essays of graduated business writers were rated higher). But according to the analytical comparisons, the advanced undergraduates clearly had begun to approach the competent business writers in three key areas of syntax, organization, and production rate. Essentially, what characterizes the business writers' essays are: (1) organizational strategies that are flexible rather than limiting, with introductions/theses capable of generating discovery during the writing itself, rather than the often inflexible, limiting organizations of first-year college writers; (2) syntactic strategies that increase the modification of nominals and increase the length of sentences by adding more free modifiers at the end of sentences—strategies which, like flexible organization, allow for ongoing clarification and discovery during the writing session; and (3) faster rate of production, quite possibly as a direct result of these more flexible organizational and syntactic strategies. Compared to the impromptu essays of first year students, essays of advanced college students are clearly moving towards these "mature" ways of writing by including more flexible organizations, more nominal clusters and terminal free modifiers, and faster rates of production, even though the teachers gave them holistic ratings that showed no change.

4   Haswell uses these findings to argue that our "ungrounded English teacher vision" of students interferes with our ability to see the growth that's actually occurring and limits our potential for enhancing this growth. He locates our teacherly inability to see the developments in advanced college students' writing in our overattention to errors in student texts and our overemphasis on the airtight organizational strategies emphasized in textbooks. These features of teachers' vision, he says, cause us to be disappointed and dismayed by advanced students' writing, and prevent us from seeing the changes as necessary and fruitful "developmental errors."

5   All of this analysis is compelling and useful, providing college teachers with new ways to look at the syntactic and organizational choices our students make and with good reasons for reexamining our judgments of writing quality. I'd hoped that Haswell's applications of these insights to teaching would prove equally compelling and useful for me, since his clear and good-hearted exposition of his analysis was so provocative. But when he turned to teaching, what I found instead is that his underlying assumptions about teaching were so foreign to me that I ended up wrestling with the last half of the book. (In a way, Haswell prepared me for this struggle. In the long theoretical chapter on development that anchors the middle of his book, Haswell argues that one crucial step in any development is "alienation": an encounter with a way of thinking and acting so foreign to one's own that it is unsettling. For Haswell, when this "alien" way of thinking/acting is also more functional than the ways we already hold, we will then reflect on our past ways and in

time change them by altering the guiding structures they provide. As I worked with Haswell's teaching vision, I felt myself struggling with just such an "alien" vision: his. Though I ended up deciding that his vision isn't finally more functional than the learner-centered pedagogies I use, I certainly felt myself engaged in the sort of struggle he imagines.)

6   Haswell's underlying pedagogical assumptions are that we, as teachers, can be in control of students' progression. By diagnosing what they write, we can identify the near step they need to take in syntax and organization, and then can assign them essays using the features of syntax/organization we think they need. We are in control; we do the assigning; we intervene best at the level of strategy (syntax and organization). As much as I tried, I just couldn't get my mind around these assumptions. In my own experience teaching writing workshops at undergraduate and graduate levels, I operate out of different assumptions. Following well-documented studies of writer's growth in workshop classrooms across grade levels (cf. Calkins *Lessons, From a Child* for elementary, Atwell *In The Middle* for middle school, Rief *Seeking Diversity* for high school, and my own work for college), I assume instead that learners are in control of learning, and we teachers do our best work when we provide supportive environments for that learning. Supportive environments provide writers with ownership, time, response, and reflection; content, community, and motivating purpose guide growth in writing, with strategic elements like style and organization emerging out of these three more primary needs. So I found myself struggling with the pedagogical sections of Haswell's book, largely because I believe in teaching methods that emphasize student choice of genre, tempo, and content for their writing, while he believes in teaching methods that emphasize teacher assignments of specific organizational and syntactic forms.

7   Given the clash between my pedagogical assumptions and his, I found myself wanting to recast Haswell's argument in the last half of the book. Instead of arguing as he did that the organizational and syntactic changes in college students' writing created opportunities for teacher intervention, I wanted to argue that these sorts of changes might be extensions of natural language learning and would occur whether or not we intervened as teachers. Hence, they could be seen as the sort of changes we can expect, watch for, and encourage, but do not need to teach, leaving us free to focus elsewhere.

8   But whether or not I (or any teacher) finally agrees with Haswell's pedagogy seems to be the wrong way of evaluating this book. The right way would emphasize the challenge Haswell presents. Through its analysis of student writing and teacher misperception, Haswell's book will provoke college teachers to rethink and reexamine their judgments and their practice. This makes it an important book, well worth the effort of reading (and arguing with) its four hundred pages.

The first two paragraphs of Brooke's review establish the background for the evaluation. This background orients readers to the material and gives them the information they need to understand the argument. The first paragraphs explain that many college composition teachers believe that students' writing gets worse from the freshman to the senior year in keeping with the "Kitzhaber effect." The paragraphs then establish the major point of comparison: Haswell's book refutes this notion, and it does so on the basis of an empirical study. The study showed that teacher perceptions of students' writing was different from the measurable changes that the writing underwent during four years of college.

Something different—and interesting—about Brooke's introduction is his first statement: "I found this a startling book." In most reviews, we find evaluations toward the end, often in the final paragraph. Brooke's approach therefore represents a degree of risk taking. But notice that there is no way to tell, really, what Brooke means. Is "startling" positive or negative? The word it is ambiguous, and the ambiguity has the effect of enticing readers to continue reading. They want to discover just what Brooke means, so the overall effect is successful. You therefore may want to experiment with this technique in your own writing at some point.

Paragraphs 3 and 4 also are characteristic in that they describe an important part of the book. Space limitations usually make it impossible to provide much detail in a review, so writers have to focus on the most important parts of a text—a point to keep in mind for your own work. In this case, Brooke chose to summarize the major findings of the study described in the book (paragraph 3) and then to summarize Haswell's most important interpretation of those findings (paragraph 4). Providing such information is necessary to give readers more understanding of what the book is about.

After these summaries, Brooke can offer another evaluation, which he does in paragraph 5: "All of this analysis is compelling and useful." You may want to go back to this paragraph and read it again because it illustrates an important technique. Frequently, writing provides the opportunity to bring your own experiences and knowledge to bear on problems. In paragraph 5, Brooke shifts his attention to the second half of Haswell's text, and immediately he is more engaged. He has an opportunity to relate the book to his own experiences. And it is here that readers begin to understand what Brooke meant when he used the word "startling." This part of the review nicely illustrates how you can draw on your experiences to make connections to the audience, the topic, and the broader discourse community.

To his credit, Brooke does not dismiss Haswell's approach to teaching composition, but he does find it "alien." A mean-spirited reviewer probably would have been less kind, perhaps dismissing Haswell's approach rather than seeing in it an opportunity to reassess his or her own ideas and assumptions. In this case, Brooke seems to be providing a model for how he believes others should read Haswell's book, for he certainly knows that most composition specialists share his rather than Haswell's assumptions about teaching. The last paragraph reinforces this perception, suggesting that any evaluation of the book should see it as a challenge. Because teachers and scholars tend to appreciate challenges and being provoked into rethinking ideas, Brooke ultimately believes that the book is "important." This final evaluation is linked to the opening sentence. Now readers understand that Brooke believes Haswell's book is worth examining.

Journal Entry

Have you ever read something and wished the writer were nearby so you could talk to him or her about the text? Have you ever felt frustrated because a writer has buried his or her ideas beneath language that you just can't understand? Have you ever read something so good that you wanted to thank the writer? Make a list of some of the reading that has stimulated or bored you most. Beside each title, write a paragraph or two that tells the writer how the work affected you and why.

Writing Assignment

REVIEWING A TEXTBOOK

This assignment asks you to apply the techniques above to a book review. Text-books are good examples of writing that reports information. Some books succeed, whereas others fail. For this assignment, write a review of one of your text-books. Given the length of most textbooks, you probably will want to limit your review to a chapter or a section of a chapter. Your review should be approximately two pages.

Evaluating Interpretations

People interpret the world around them on a continuing basis. Interpreting gives form and substance to life. Evaluations, of course, can be positive or negative, but the nature of the classroom often seems to encourage the negative. Many teachers view negative assessments as a sign that students are questioning the authority of the texts and the discipline, which many professors encourage as a way of developing independent thought.

It is easy to believe that evaluations should be negative with passion: An interpretation isn't "inadequate," it's "stupid." The problem, however, is that as soon as the vocabulary shifts in this way it violates an important convention of professional writing—objectivity. Tact is a virtue. However, something more is involved: In your writing, using a term like "inadequate" is better than using "bad" or "stupid" because it stimulates you to specify *how* and *in what ways* the interpretation is weak. Labeling something "stupid" does not invite explanation.

The following sample, from an article published in *College Composition and Communication* by Gary Sloan, illustrates the value of careful word choice in evaluations. The title of the article is "Frequency of Errors in Essays by College Freshmen and by Professional Writers." Sloan is talking about results as well as interpretations in Passage 3:

Passage 3: Frequency of Errors

Gary Sloan

A number of studies have shown that the inexperienced and the expert writer do not share the same set of assumptions about the constituents of good writing and that the two approach prewriting, writing, and rewriting in quite different ways (Elbow; Beach; Freedman; Sommers; Flower et al.). While such studies are by no means silent about errors, the treatment is essentially piecemeal and tangential. From the data available, one would have trouble constructing a theory that would even roughly predict the relative distributions of various types of errors in the writing of freshmen and of professionals.

The key words in this passage are *piecemeal* and *tangential*. *Piecemeal* means that something proceeds slowly, by degrees. *Tangential*, on the other hand, means that something is dealt with in an indirect manner. Neither term is particularly negative. Knowledge generally does develop by degrees, and interpretations of data usually build slowly—piecemeal—on earlier ones. Moreover, an interpretation may be "tangential" in regard to a particular line of inquiry simply because the study never intended to explore that line. Sloan's use of language here is skillful. He was able to indicate that, in this context, his evaluation of the interpretations was negative without offending the authors he cited. Remember, Sloan and the authors are members of the same community—English teachers—so he would gain nothing by insulting them. In fact, he would lose because the writers he cites are some of the more influential in the field.

Some people might consider the next example to be even more effective with respect to careful word choice. It was written by two psychologists, Janice Gibson and Mika Haritos-Fatouros. Published in *Psychology Today*, the article examines the psychological mechanisms that allowed ordinary people to obey orders that involved them in acts of cruelty and torture. Their work built on an important study conducted in 1963 by psychologist Stanley Milgram.

Passage 4: The Education of a Torturer

Janice Gibson and Mika Haritos-Fatouros

1   Twenty-five years ago, the late psychologist Stanley Milgram demonstrated convincingly that people unlikely to be cruel in everyday life will administer pain if they are told to by someone in authority. In a famous experiment, Milgram had men wearing laboratory coats direct average American adults to inflict a series of electric shocks on other people. No real shocks were given and the "victims" were acting, but the people didn't know this. They were told that the purpose of the study was to measure the effects of punishment on learning. Obediently, 65 percent of them used what they thought were dangerously high levels of shocks when the experimenter told them to. While they were less likely to administer these supposed shocks as they were moved closer to their victims, almost one-third of them continued to shock when they were close enough to touch.

2   This readiness to torture is not limited to Americans. Following Milgram's lead, other researchers found that people of all ages, from a wide range of countries, were willing to shock others even when they had nothing to gain by complying with the command or nothing to lose by refusing it. So long as someone else, an authority figure, was responsible for the final outcome of the experiment, almost no one absolutely refused to administer shocks. Each study also found, as Milgram had, that some people would give shocks even when the decision was left up to them.

3   Milgram proposed that the reasons people obey or disobey authority fall into three categories. The first is personal history: family or school backgrounds that encourage obedience or defiance. The second, which he called "binding," is made up of ongoing experiences that make people feel comfortable when they obey authority. Strain, the third category, consists of bad feelings from unpleasant experiences connected with obedience. Milgram argued that when the binding factors are more powerful than the strain of cooperating, people will do as they are told. When the strain is greater, they are more likely to disobey.

4   This may explain short-term obedience in the laboratory, but it doesn't explain prolonged patterns of torture during wartime or under some political regimes. Repeatedly, torturers in Argentina and elsewhere performed acts that most of us consider repugnant, and in time this should have placed enough strain on them to prevent their obedience. It didn't. Nor does Milgram's theory explain undirected cruel or violent acts, which occur even when no authority orders them. For this, we have developed a more comprehensive learning model; for torture, we discovered, can be taught.

There is a strong connection between reading and writing, a point this passage reinforces. It is a fine example of the way evaluations of interpretations are typically organized. The first two paragraphs are important because they outline Milgram's study and show briefly how other studies have found similar results. Paragraph 3 presents Milgram's interpretations of the results. Paragraph 4 offers the evaluation of these interpretations. In this case, there is no need to search for tactful adjectives; Milgram's interpretations just do not explain behavior. Gibson and Haritos-Fatouros then give two quick examples to illustrate the failure. In professional communities, the most effective evaluation is one that shows how an interpretation fails to explain what it is intended to explain.

This passage is part of a longer paper, so Gibson and Haritos-Fatouros also address the need for an alternative interpretation. This alternative is not germane here, but at the end of paragraph 4 Gibson and Haritos-Fatouros have organized the text to prepare readers for what will follow. In fact, the final sentence in this paragraph is very effective, not only in terms of organization but also in terms of style. The last clause—"for torture, we discovered, can be taught"—is powerful.

The next passage comes from John Casti's *Paradigms Lost*. Although Casti brings in several topics in this passage—the value of π (pi), the Scopes trial, and so forth—the real focus is on the interpretations that have led "creationists" to reject science and its findings because they conflict with biblical accounts of creation and history. Although Casti's evaluation comes at the end, he gives ample clues to what it will be. In this respect, the passage represents a typical evaluation of information. As your read, take note of the ways Casti signals his evaluation throughout the text.

Passage 5: AND GOD CREATED . . . FROM FISH TO GISH

John L. Casti

1   In an attempt to effect legislative repair to one of the oldest flaws in the fabric of Nature, the state of Indiana in 1897 enacted a law setting the legal value of π at precisely 4, replacing its inconvenient "natural," but irrational, value $\pi = 3.14159265 \ldots$ Later, a Tennessee legislator suggested the value be legally fixed at 3, but this idea was immediately quashed when a British clergyman, in one of those hilarious letters that British clergymen have traditionally sent to *The Times* of London, stuck up for the Indiana value, stating that 3 was inadequate since it wasn't even an even number! But the Tennessee legislature eventually imposed its will on an unruly cosmos anyway by enacting a different law making it illegal to teach evolution in the classroom, an action thrusting the tiny hamlet of Dayton into the international spotlight in 1925 with the celebrated Monkey Trial of John Scopes, a substitute for the local high-school biology teacher, accused of filling the heads of his charges with pernicious Darwinian visions.

2   For most of us, I suppose, the dramatic account of the Scopes trial in the film *Inherit the Wind*, in which a legendary barrister based on Clarence Darrow (played by Spencer Tracy) crushes the fundamentalist arguments of a prosecuting attorney modeled on William Jennings Bryan (played by Fredric March), represented what we thought of as the death knell of legislative tampering with Nature. This despite the fact that Scopes was actually found guilty and assessed a one-hundred-dollar fine (although two years later the Tennessee Supreme Court overturned the conviction on technical grounds). And a death knell it was, at least insofar as brute-force, frontal legislative assaults on Nature by religious fundamentalists are concerned. But in March 1981, not to be outdone by its next-door neighbor, the Arkansas state

legislature revived the spirit of Dayton by resurrecting a fundamentalist interpretation of the origin of life under the new rubric "creation science." With the enactment of the Balanced Treatment for Creation Science and Evolution Science Act (Arkansas Act 590), stating that "public schools in this state shall give balanced treatment to creation science and to evolution science," the battle was rejoined between the fundamentalists and the scientists, only this time it was to be fought on the home ground of science rather than in the pulpits. Let's take a moment to understand why.

3   The essential components of the "creationist" vision of the origin of the Earth and its life forms is contained in the following pledge sworn to by each member of the Creation Research Society:

1. The Bible is the written Word of God, and because we believe it to be inspired throughout, all of its assertions are historically and scientifically true in all the original autographs. To the students of nature, this means that the account of origins in Genesis is a factual presentation of simple historical truths.

2. All basic types of living things, including man, were made by direct creative acts of God during Creation Week as described in Genesis. Whatever biological changes have occurred since Creation have accomplished only changes within the original created kinds.

In addition to swearing this pledge of "allegiance," all prospective members of the society are also required to possess an advanced university degree in some field of science. As a result, members in essence agree to forsake the common practices of their profession in certain areas, and instead accept explanations on the basis of divine authority alone.

4   In 1968 the U.S. Supreme Court outlawed all anti-evolution laws like the Tennessee statute on the grounds that they violated the constitutional prohibition against mixing the state, in the form of the schools, with religion. Since this decision effectively prevented the creationists from having their ideas of religion introduced into the educational curricula, the fundamentalist movement decided to settle for the next best thing and mounted a campaign to push its position into the classrooms, dressing it up as science. The Arkansas bill gives a particularly graphic account of the strategy employed. Arkansas Act 590 lists six principles of "evolution science" side by side with corresponding principles of "creation science," and then goes on to state that both should be given equal time in the classrooms. The two most important principles for our purposes are the following, which I have taken directly from the text of the act: "Creation science means the scientific evidences and related inferences that indicate: (1) Sudden creation of the universe, energy, and life from nothing; . . . (6) A relatively recent inception of the earth and living kinds." Other points of the act involve the occurrence of a global flood, separate ancestry for man and apes, and other similar biblical stipulations. It's clear from the above statements that in order to make their case, the creationists are going to have to attack the conventional scientific views on several aspects of geology, most importantly the matter of the age of the Earth.

5   In speaking of the education of their children, creationists are fond of citing the remark of William Jennings Bryan that "Christians desire that their children shall be taught all the sciences, but they do not want them to lose sight of the Rock of Ages while they study the age of rocks." This well-known remark served for years as a rallying cry for fundamentalists asserting that the rocks of the Earth were only a few thousand years old, just as claimed in Genesis. It doesn't take too much imagination to envision the loathing with which the creationists look upon the increasingly accurate radiocarbon-dating methods developed over the past few decades. With these unassailable methods, used recently, for instance, to demonstrate the medieval origin of the Shroud of Turin, the high levels of uncertainty arising from the old fossil

and sediment dating schemes were eliminated, showing the Earth to be at least 4 billion years old.

6   How did the creationists react to such incontrovertible evidence of an ancient Earth? Well, let me quote Henry Morris, a hydraulics engineer and director of the Creation Research Society: "The only way we can determine the true age of the earth is for God to tell us what it is. And since he *has* told us, very plainly, in the Holy Scriptures that it is several thousand years in age, and no more, that ought to settle all basic questions of chronology." Such an act of faith unfortunately rejects data, methods, experimental equipment, and all of the other paraphernalia of science. In fact, the leading creationists have been even more candid in their rejection of science's traditional methods of inquiry.

7   Duane Gish holds a Ph.D. in biochemistry from the University of California at Berkeley; he is also the vice-director of the Creation Research Society and a regular participant at university debates on the merits of creation science. Since he is trained in the scientific method, especially in an experimental science like biochemistry, it's odd, to say the least, to read in his book *Evolution: The Fossils Say No* that "we do not know how the Creator created, what processes He used, for He used processes which are not now operating anywhere in the natural universe. . . . We cannot discover by scientific investigation anything about the creative processes used by the Creator." With such statements, creation "science" joins the long list of other perverse modern "sciences," such as "fashion science," "dairy science," and "educational science," all of which can be conveniently subsumed under the heading "nonscientific science."

8   Despite the cursory nature of our airing of the creationist views, I think most readers will find no difficulty in understanding the opinion of Judge William Overton in his ruling declaring the Arkansas Act 590 unconstitutional. Citing the creationists' own words in deciding that creation science was not science but religion, the good judge offered one of the most concise, best-thought-out lists of criteria for what constitutes science yet put on the public record. The Overton criteria are:

- It [science] is guided by natural law.
- It has to be explanatory by reference to natural law.
- It is testable against the empirical world.
- Its conclusions are tentative, i.e., are not necessarily the final word.
- It is falsifiable.

Needless to say, creation "science" fails to meet even one of these criteria; ergo, as a *scientific* explanation for the origin of life, it has no real place in our deliberations here.

The first paragraph does not really provide the background for the evaluation that follows, but it does set the tone. The background appears pages earlier in the book this excerpt came from. But setting the tone is important for Casti's evaluation. In this case, he refers to attempts to legislate a natural phenomenon, the value of π, in order to make π conform to preconceived notions of how the world ought to be. Casti probably assumed that most readers would be amused by this story. It happened a hundred years ago, which gives the story a certain quaintness. One can imagine 19th-century politicians believing that they could use their authority to alter reality, and many readers might smile at the foolishness of trying to legislate the ratio between the circumference of a circle and its diameter. This number, π, simply exists, for all circles in all times.

Toward the end of that paragraph, however, Casti shifts the ground significantly, raising the issue of evolution, Darwinism, and the Scopes trial. Chances are that fewer readers will find these topics funny, even though they occurred in 1925, a date sufficiently far in the past as to seem like ancient history to most people. Time does not appear to mitigate people's sensitivity when it comes to evolution and religion. Casti's views begin to emerge when he links efforts to legislate the value of π to censorship of evolution. Clearly, he sees both as attempts to deny natural reality.

> *Diverse Voices*
>
> Some cultures resist negative evaluations of the kind discussed in this chapter. Analyze your home culture and compare it to American culture in this respect. In what ways does evaluation differ? If your home culture resists negative evaluations, how does one communicate displeasure?

READINGS

James D. Williams

The next sample comes from *Preparing to Teach Writing*, a book for prospective English teachers. Most scholars working in the field recognize that there is a strong relation between reading and writing, and numerous efforts have attempted to describe the nature of that relation. One of the more influential descriptions was made by a psycholinguist named Steve Krashen, who formulated what he called "the reading hypothesis." The sample describes and then evaluates the hypothesis.

JAMES D. WILLIAMS

PREPARING TO TEACH WRITING

The Reading Hypothesis

1 Although teachers have only recently become concerned about the effect of reading instruction on writing performance, they have long speculated on the relationship between people's reading habits and their ability to write, perhaps because classroom experience shows us that good writers are usually good readers.

Various scholars have attempted to explain this relationship, and one of the more interesting efforts comes from Steve Krashen (1981b, 1985). He approaches the question from the perspective that composition skill is similar to second language skill: Mastery requires comprehensible input over an extended time. He bases his argument on our present knowledge of language acquisition. 2

3   Let me explain briefly that "acquiring" language is different from "learning" it. Acquisition involves the *unconscious* assimilation *of* language, whereas learning involves the *conscious* mastery of knowledge *about* language (see Chapter 4). In this account, students of a second language acquire that language when surrounded by people who use it daily.

4   We can further distinguish between acquisition and learning by considering that in the early stages of language development children only occasionally repeat sentences they hear; they tend to generate their own expressions. This phenomenon suggests that children do not learn a particularly large set of expressions or phrases that they repeat back under appropriate conditions. Instead, they seem to internalize the grammar of the language, which enables them to produce unique utterances.

5   We can't say that they "learn" this grammar. We can't even say that they are *taught* the grammar; in all but a few cases, parents don't have the linguistic background necessary to describe the complex array of grammatical rules that underlies their children's utterances. But because acquisition is based on unconscious assimilation, no such description is needed. What is required is comprehensible and meaningful input, from which a child makes generalizations regarding form, function, intention, and meaning. By way of illustration, we can consider a scenario in which a parent holds out a ball to a child and asks, "Would you like to play with the ball?" and then rolls the ball to the child.

6   Krashen proposes that writing ability is acquired in a similar manner, through reading rather than through listening. In his view, we gain competence in writing the same way we gain competence in oral language, by comprehending written discourse and by internalizing, after much exposure, the numerous conventions that characterize texts. He states, for example, that "if second language acquisition and the development of writing ability occur in the same way, writing ability is not learned but is acquired via extensive reading in which the focus of the reader is on the message, i.e., reading for genuine interest and/or pleasure" (1985, p. 23).

7   Krashen (1981b, 1985) calls this proposal the *reading hypothesis*, and he argues the following: (1) "all good writers will have done large amounts of pleasure reading" (1981b, p. 3); (2) "good writers, as a group, read and have read more than poor writers" (1981b, p. 3); (3) "reading remains the only way of developing competence in writing" (1981b, p. 9). Drawing on self-report reading surveys, he further argues that good writers are not only active readers, but self-motivated readers who read intensively during adolescence.

8   The reading hypothesis is an elegant way of explaining the differences in writing ability that we see in students, and it seems entirely accurate in proposing that reading allows us to internalize the conventions of written discourse as mental models. Nevertheless, the hypothesis may not be valid.

9   Careful consideration reveals several difficulties. One of the biggest is the notion that writing is the equivalent of a foreign language. This view is quite popular, in part because it reinforces the idea that writing is intrinsically different from speech. Yet we have little or no data to support this position. In fact, a great deal of research indicates that in literate societies writing (at a rudimentary level) and speech manifest themselves at about the same time, which suggests that the two are developmentally linked (Gundlach, 1981, 1982, 1983; Harste, Burke, & Woodward, 1983). If writing is merely another communication mode associated with the primary language and not a separate code, the premise underlying the reading hypothesis is incorrect.

10   Longitudinal studies of language development like those of Walter Loban (1976) also indicate that language proficiency in general and writing ability in particular begin to manifest themselves very early in life—in the case of Loban's subjects, as early as kindergarten. More important, Loban found that the relative proficiency of subjects remains stable over time: Children with skills rated highly in kindergarten were rated highly in twelfth grade. Similarly, those with skills rated low in kindergarten were rated low in twelfth grade. Clearly more factors are at work than simply self-motivated reading during adolescence. Loban's analysis suggests that socioeconomic status was the variable that best accounted for differences in proficiency (which parallels the findings of Heath [1983] who reports significant differences in pragmatic development of language across socioeconomic and ethnic groups).

11   Although Krashen uses empirical data to support the reading hypothesis, we may question the validity of conclusions made on the basis of self-reported data such as he reports. Can we truly say that all good writers were intense, self-motivated readers during adolescence, simply because they say they were? Most researchers recognize that questionnaire surveys are generally subject to an affective dimension difficult to control: They often reflect the image respondents would like to have of themselves, or the image they want investigators to have of them.

12   For example, Irene Clark (1986) conducted a survey at the University of Southern California quite similar to Krashen's, in which she correlated subjects' writing performance with their reading histories. Yet unlike Krashen, Clark found no significant correlation between writing performance and reading history. As she states: "Although students at USC do vary in their writing abilities, at least according to the range of grades given by their instructors and the scores they receive on the [holistically scored] exam, they all claim to have come from remarkably similar home environments . . . and all profess equally similar attitudes and behaviors concerning reading and writing" (p. 9). In attempting to explain these results, she concludes that it is very likely that the subjects "responded not according to what actually occurred [in their reading histories], but according to the way they thought they ought to respond" (p. 11).

13   Krashen formulates the reading hypothesis as merely a correlation between reading and writing, but he seems unable to avoid shifting to a causal relationship when he discusses reading and writing pedagogy. He states, for example, that "reading is the main 'cause' of writing ability" (1981b, p. 12). In other words, not only do good writers tend to be good readers, but good readers tend to be good writers. Evidence from our own experiences, however, suggests that many people are good readers, self-motivated readers, but terrible writers. Most college students, for example, encounter at least one unreadable textbook during their work toward a degree, and chances are it was written by a professor who has read voluminously.

14   There is no question that the reading hypothesis offers an attractive explanation of the connection between reading and writing. Careful analysis indicates, however, that it does not adequately deal with the complexities of the relationship. It fails to account for the psychological and social factors that appear to influence writing proficiency. We should therefore be cautious about accepting the reading hypothesis as a valid representation of the reading/writing relationship.

Critical Reading Guide

1. The first five paragraphs provide background information. Why would such a lengthy "introduction" be necessary in this passage?

2. Paragraph 8 begins by calling Krashen's reading hypothesis "elegant," but it concludes by stating that the hypothesis may not be valid. What kind of organization is the writer using here? What motivation could be influencing the author's decision to use this organization technique?

3. Paragraphs 9 through 13 offer evidence to support the evaluation in paragraph 8. Could the author have provided any additional information that might have made the argument stronger?

4. Compare paragraph 14 with paragraph 8. How are they similar? Does the similarity reinforce your perception of the motivation at work in this evaluation? Why or why not?

Cammie (Student)

Cammie was a first-year student at the time she wrote the following paper. She was enrolled in a history class that examined Western civilization from classical Greece to the Middle Ages. Students read a number of important texts and studied some of the more significant figures in Western civilization, such as Socrates, Plato, Aristotle, and St. Augustine. The first three men were philosophers in ancient Greece whose writings have greatly influenced Western culture. St. Augustine, on the other hand, was an early leader of Christianity. His writings had a profound influence on the development of the Catholic Church and early Christian doctrine. One of his more important books is *The City of God*, which established much of this doctrine. The assignment for this paper asked students to evaluate St. Augustine's treatment of Plato's philosophy in *The City of God*.

CAMMIE

SAINT AUGUSTINE AND PLATONIC THOUGHT

1 Socrates, Plato, and their contemporaries were considered some of the most (if not *the* most) respected and learned men of their time. Their fellow philosophers, including their enemies, held them in high esteem because of their abilities to use logic in an attempt to attain what they referred to as "true knowledge." Their theories were so important and so influential that they are still being taught, discussed, and debated centuries later.

2 St. Augustine, a Christian bishop who lived in North Africa in the fourth century, was an expert rhetorician. In this respect, he was very much like Socrates and Plato. Indeed, St. Augustine was trained in the tradition of Plato; he mastered the same techniques and strategies for writing and speaking that Plato had taught in his school in ancient Athens. It is no wonder, then, that St. Augustine used many of Plato's ideas in his work *The City of God*, which was an attempt to convince many pagans to accept Christian thinking.

3 Even a quick examination of *The City of God* shows Plato's influence. But careful analysis reveals that St. Augustine did not explain or even present Plato's views accurately. In fact, St. Augustine's explanations are consistently distorted. At work seems to be an effort on the part of St. Augustine to enhance his discussion of Christianity by appropriating Platonic philosophy where he could and distorting it when he couldn't appropriate it.

4 One of the Platonic theories St. Augustine discusses at length is the idea that happiness can be obtained only through God. According to St. Augustine, Plato believed not only that there was one God but that man could find happiness only by believing in and living his life for God. However, Plato and his followers actually believed that happiness could be found in true wisdom or in being able to perceive true justice. God isn't even mentioned in regard to happiness. Instead, as in the Allegory of the Cave, Plato says again and again that happiness comes from being able to perceive reality after submitting to the discipline of philosophy, which leads to true wisdom. St. Augustine seems to have misinterpreted the Platonic texts deliberately, perhaps because Plato was so influential that this distortion would make pagans believe there was a strong connection between Platonism and Christianity.

5 Another aspect of Platonic theory that St. Augustine distorted was the idea that Plato believed that everyone should strive to lead an upstanding life. In

The City of God, St. Augustine states that Plato "thought it essential to insist on the need to cleanse one's life by accepting a high moral standard, so that the soul should be relieved by the weight of lust that held it down" (Augustine, 301–2). In reality, Plato stressed taking things in moderation. He felt that happiness came from inside, not through material goods or bodily pleasures.

6   In addition, by referring to "lust" in this passage, St. Augustine alludes to the Christian notions of original sin, atonement, and redemption, which are fundamental parts of Christianity's belief in Christ and God. The implication is that Plato might not have been a Christian, but at least he was a monotheist. Plato, however, was not a monotheist. Also, the idea of original sin and atonement are distinctly Judeo-Christian and have no parallel in ancient Greek culture.

7   This fact presents a serious problem for St. Augustine. Plato, existing as he did in a polytheistic culture, was polytheistic. He could not be anything other than a pagan. Yet everything St. Augustine stands for repudiates paganism. For a thoughtful reader, no amount of distortion and misinterpretation can mask the fundamental incompatibility of the two religious views. St.

Augustine nevertheless ignores this incompatibility. If he didn't, he would have to acknowledge that Plato's views of religion and worship were completely different from those of Christians. As a result, he makes statements such as, "The reputation and prestige they [Socrates and Plato] enjoy above the rest is in proportion to the superiority of their concept of one God, the creator of heaven and earth" (Augustine, 315).

8   It seems hard to believe that someone as smart as St. Augustine could have misinterpreted Plato so much. In fact, it seems entirely unlikely. These interpretations are so flawed and so obvious that they had to have been deliberate. I would suggest that St. Augustine was writing for an audience that had not read Plato and that knew the ancient Greek philosophers only by reputation. Because St. Augustine had been trained as a rhetorician in the Greek tradition, he knew Plato's work very well, and he probably saw an opportunity to use Plato's reputation to enhance the view of Christianity among the pagans. The effect can be compared to today's endorsements by professional athletes. St. Augustine probably knew that few of his readers would ever bother to check Plato's writings to see if his views indeed matched those of Christianity.

Critical Reading Guide

1. Consider Cammie's introduction. How does she go about setting the scene for readers? Is there any information that you wish she had provided? Why do you think Cammie begins the paper by mentioning Socrates and Plato when she is focusing on St. Augustine?

2. What is Cammie's thesis?

3. How would you characterize paragraphs 3 through 6? That is, what is Cammie doing in these paragraphs? Can you describe the paragraphs in terms of the overall structure of the paper?

4. How does Cammie conclude the paper?

5. What is the tone of Cammie's writing? Can you determine what her rhetorical stance is?

6. What features of the paper make Cammie's evaluation convincing?

Writing Assignment

A SHORT EVALUATION
OF AN INTERPRETATION

The short paper presented next was written by Kisha, a student in a political science class. The assignment asked students to examine the accompanying chart and interpret its information using some of the principles and ideas studied in the course. The paper was expected to be approximately three paragraphs. For this assignment, study the chart and read Kisha's interpretation. Then write an evaluation of the interpretation. Your paper should be approximately two pages long. Successful responses will support the evaluation through specific references to the student paper. If your evaluation is negative, be tactful and remember to offer an alternative.

Population Changes in L.A. County

1   Throughout most of its history, Los Angeles has enjoyed a diverse population. It has been one of the few places in the country where Asians, African-Americans, whites, and Hispanics have been able to live together more or less peacefully. The potential for economic advancement has been an important factor in this peaceful coexistence. L.A. has always been a city of opportunity, and those who worked hard were able to advance up the socioeconomic ladder. Another important factor has been the presence of real neighborhoods that have given the various ethnic groups a sense of community. Little Tokyo, Watts, East L.A., Palms, Little Jerusalem (Fairfax District), these neighborhoods are synonymous with high ethnic density, and they reflect the notion of ethnic self-determination that we've discussed in class.

2   The demographic statistics shown in the chart published by the *Times* indicate, however, that the situation in L.A. County is destined to change. The data indicate that L.A.'s historic diversity is going to change drastically in just a few short years. Fifty-five percent of the population already consists of Latinos. The chart shows that they are under 18, which means that in a few years they will be having children. This will increase the Hispanic population dramatically. If you also consider that these people have numerous relatives who are likely to come to the States from Mexico, this will increase the population even more. The effect of the increased Hispanic population will be to reduce the growth and economic influence of the African-American population as the Hispanics develop a socioeconomic hegemony in the city. In class we learned that every hegemony is established at the expense of someone else. Miami is a perfect example. As we learned in class, the Hispanics from Cuba run the city and live in the best neighborhoods while the African-Americans who actually built the city are forced to live in the ghetto and are excluded from the American Dream.

3   A superficial analysis suggests that the Anglo population will experience the greatest impact from this unrestrained growth. Only 23% of the upcoming workforce will be whites in the years ahead. What the chart does not reveal, however, is that the decrease in the Anglo population is probably attributable to the principle of "white flight," which was mentioned in our textbook in connection with socioeconomic mobility. Because of racism, African-Americans lack this mobility, so they cannot leave Watts when the flood of Hispanics takes away their jobs the way the

Los Angeles County: Growing Diversity

While Anglos make up most of Los Angeles County's work force today, the majority of young workers coming into the job market during the next decade will be Latino.

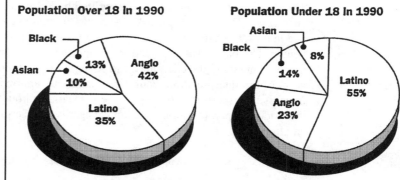

Population Over 18 in 1990

Black
Asian
13%
10%
Anglo 42%
Latino 35%

Population Under 18 in 1990

Asian
Black
14%
8%
Latino 55%
Anglo 23%

The Changing U.S. Labor Force

Anglo men will continue to make up the biggest chunk of the U.S. civilian labor force in 2005, but minorities will register gains.

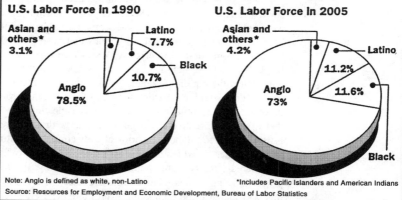

U.S. Labor Force in 1990

Asian and others* 3.1%
Latino 7.7%
Black 10.7%
Anglo 78.5%

U.S. Labor Force in 2005

Asian and others* 4.2%
Latino
11.2%
11.6%
Anglo 73%
Black

Note: Anglo is defined as white, non-Latino
*Includes Pacific Islanders and American Indians
Source: Resources for Employment and Economic Development, Bureau of Labor Statistics

ROBERT BURNS/Los Angeles Times

Anglos can, even though they might want to. They have to stay and compete for jobs with people willing to work for low wages, and that's no contest. African-Americans simply cannot survive on jobs that pay $6 or $7 dollars an hour, but the Hispanics can, which drives wages even lower. Indeed, the statistics on this chart reflect a form of racism. White America has done nothing to stop the flow of illegal immigrants in order to keep African-Americans in poverty. Instead, they have abandoned the cities by fleeing to the suburbs, transforming places like Los Angeles into modern-day plantations. But African-Americans will not tolerate this injustice any longer, and whites and Hispanics alike may see our anger explode into violence if things don't change. As the saying goes, "No justice, no peace."

WRITING GUIDE: A SHORT EVALUATION
OF AN INTERPRETATION

Invention

The first step in responding to this assignment should be to study the charts carefully. They show four different sets of statistics. The top two charts reflect analyses of the Los Angeles County population by age in 1990, and they categorize people into those over 18 and those under 18. The first of these charts shows that the majority of the population over 18 is Anglo, followed closely by Hispanics, who make up 35% of the over 18 group. Blacks and Asians over 18 comprise 13% and 10% of the population, respectively. The second of these charts shows, however, a significant shift in the percentages for the under 18 group. Although the percentages of blacks and Asians are relatively unchanged, the Latino population shows a 20% increase, whereas the Anglo population shows almost a 20% drop.

The bottom two charts are only marginally related to the top two. They reflect projected changes in the composition of the nation's workforce between 1990 and 2005, not demographic changes in Los Angeles. In addition, they show that ethnic groups will experience modest increases as percentages of the overall workforce while Anglos will experience a modest decrease.

The goal of interpretation is to explain what these data mean, and that was Kisha's assignment. The charts, for example, offer no explanation of why the under 18 Hispanic population is 20% larger than the over 18 group. Nor do they offer any explanation of why the Anglo population has experienced the opposite change. You would be wise to spend some time pondering these statistics and jotting down some of your own interpretations before attempting to evaluate Kisha's effort. *Note: If you do not generate your own interpretation of the data, you will not be able to evaluate Kisha's work.*

The next step is to read Kisha's interpretation, comparing her explanation to some of the ideas you generated about the data. What criteria will you use to judge it? After deciding on your criteria, you will need to make your evaluation and begin developing support for it. It is important to draw your support from Kisha's paper, so you should identify those parts of her text that you can use for your evaluation. One way to think about the argumentative nature of your evaluation is to use a metaphor that describes Kisha's paper. For example, is her paper a *light* that illuminates the data, or is it a *fog* that confuses everything? Finally, give some thought to how you will begin your assessment. What kind of background information will readers need? How can you justify the evaluation? What is your rhetorical purpose? Who is your audience? Answers to these questions not only will help you produce an interesting introduction but also will help you write a better paper.

Planning

You might want to look at some of the sample papers discussed earlier in the chapter to get a sense of how you want to organize your response. For example, you will need to decide whether to hold your evaluation until the end of the paper, state it at the beginning, or weave your evaluation into an analysis of Kisha's interpretation. If you already know what you are going to say about Kisha's interpretation, an important part of your planning will involve deciding how to support your view in a way that is reasonable and convincing. In this regard, you might think of using three or four pieces of evidence to support your evaluation. Your planning should include organizing this evidence in the most effective way. Determining what is "the most effective" will depend on your view of Kisha's interpretation, of course; but many good writers build their evidence on the basis of its strength. The idea is to place your strongest reason last, which gives a sense of climax to your argument.

If you produced a metaphor during your invention, at this stage you will need to decide how to make the best use of it. You should be aware that many writers will *overuse* a metaphor in early drafts because the metaphor carries the paper so easily. Try not to worry about this tendency, but do plan on having to go back through your work to make modifications.

Drafting

Many of the papers you write, like this one, are short. In most situations, you should be able to write the first draft of a five-page paper in one sitting. There are certain advantages to this approach, and you may want to try it on this assignment. If you have completed the necessary invention and planning activities, you will have all the information you need to complete the work fairly quickly, and doing it in one sitting will give you a focus that might be missing otherwise.

When you are composing your first draft, do not be overly concerned about the quality of a given sentence or the appropriateness of a particular word. The important thing is to write down everything you can about Kisha's interpretation and about your evaluation.

Pausing and Reading

Read frequently during pauses to keep your plan and direction steady; ask yourself whether the paper is following the plan. If it isn't, you will need to determine why, and your teacher can help. Avoid making extensive revisions at this point. If during rereading you get a new and useful idea, jot it down in the margin or on a separate sheet of paper. This way, you will not forget it and can return to it later.

Revising

Remember that the goal of revision is to adjust larger parts of a paper, such as thesis, evidence, examples, and organization, so that they help the writing match your aim. You may find, for instance, that an example you used in the first draft just does not illustrate what you wanted it to, in which case you will need to find another. Much of your revision for this paper may focus on providing a reasonable evaluation of Kisha's interpretation.

Most writers are close to their work, which makes it hard for them to determine whether certain parts work well. The best way to solve this problem is to have other people read a draft and provide input. Your teacher and classmates are the obvious choices for readers, but sometimes people who are not associated with your class can provide particularly helpful advice. They are not part of the community generating this paper, so they often can see its strengths and weaknesses more clearly than anyone else. After you receive input from other readers, you should match it against your own reading. You cannot feel obligated to make *all* the changes these readers suggest. After all, it is your paper. You have to decide what changes you can make that will improve the paper, and you must understand that not all the advice you receive will be useful.

GROUP ACTIVITIES: A SHORT EVALUATION OF AN INTERPRETATION

1. Take about 10 minutes in your group to discuss what information the charts in this assignment contain. Then spend another 10 to 15 minutes discussing what the data mean. Some questions you might want to consider are: What is the connection between the two top charts? What is the connection between the top charts and the bottom ones? The caption states that the majority of young workers coming into the workforce in the near future will be Latino. What is the basis for this interpretation? How do you account for the great increase in the percentage of Latinos and corresponding decrease in the percentage of Anglos?

2. After you have had a chance to talk about these factors, each member of the group should write a summary of the discussions. Be certain to include any conclusions that your group reached.

3. Write a paragraph that evaluates Kisha's interpretation of the data in the charts. Each group member should read his or her paragraph aloud. Afterward, discuss the evaluations and the evidence that can be used to support them. Some evaluations will be positive, whereas others will be negative. Decide among your group whether this is a problem.

4. Write your first draft and exchange it with a groupmate. Read each draft and provide written comments on ways to make the evaluation more effective. Pay particular attention to the support used for the argument. Does it make the assessment seem reasonable and convincing?

5. Revise the paper on the basis of the above input and then exchange papers with another groupmate. Pretend you are the teacher who gave this writing assignment. Read through the revision and give the writer suggestions on how to improve the paper. Ask the writer what she or he intended to do with the paper, what goals guided it. How can the writer revise the paper to accomplish those goals more effectively? Does the paper meet the requirements of the assignment? This input can be oral, but if so, the writer should take notes to use for a final revision.

Argumentation

Many people think argument involves a quarrel or a disagreement. Among professionals and in classrooms at colleges and universities, however, argument is a way of writing and thinking. It is intended to advance knowledge and understanding and to lay the foundation for decisions and actions.

CHAPTER TEN

Argumentation

Many people think *argument* involves a quarrel or a disagreement. Among professionals and in classrooms at colleges and universities, however, argument is a way of *writing and thinking*. It is intended to advance knowledge and understanding and to lay the foundation for decisions and actions. It is based on agreement rather than disagreement. In a sense, all writing is argumentative because it aims to get readers to accept the writers' perceptions of reality as their own. That is, the essence of an *intellectual argument* is a claim about the world. Successful arguments entail agreement on many levels.

Argumentation is highly rhetorical, which means that it is governed by a range of conventions and specific aims associated with what a writer (or speaker) wants his or her language to accomplish. There are no winners or losers in rhetorical arguments because "winning" is not a goal. The primary goal of intellectual arguments is to get readers or hearers to accept your views, your claims about the world, as *reasonable*.

THE STRUCTURE OF ARGUMENTS

Arguments can be *formal* or *informal*. Formal arguments nearly always are written, whereas informal arguments are usually oral, although some are written. Formal arguments tend to have a more clearly delineated structure than informal ones, and they frequently occur inside a group. Consequently, they are governed by all the conventions associated with that group. Written informal arguments are different in a couple of important respects. They rarely occur inside a group, which means that they lack an insider-to-insider rhetorical stance. In other words, informal arguments generally are aimed at outsiders. In addition, informal arguments often lack the structure and conventions that characterize formal arguments.

Formal arguments, in contrast, occur among insiders, and they vary in the support and standards of proof they use. For example, argumentative papers in English literature will use support taken from a text, whereas those in biology are more likely to use support taken from direct observations. Moreover, formal arguments have higher standards of proof than informal arguments do. Also, support in informal arguments can be anecdotal, coming directly from a person's own experiences. Or it may consist of summarized but undocumented information from authorities. Support in informal arguments frequently is repetitive; the same reason will appear several times with only slight modifications.[1] Support in formal arguments, on the other hand, tends to come from *human* rather than *personal* experience, from research, and from documented information. It is not repetitive, there is more of it, and it is generalizable.

One consequence of these differences is that informal arguments tend to be comfortable and friendly. In many instances, the writer adopts a conversational tone, and readers can identify the writer's voice as reflecting a particular personality. It often seems that the writer is very close to the argument, that the writer has a personal investment in the thesis. *Rhetorical distance* is the term used to describe these features, and in informal arguments there is not much distance at all.

Formal arguments, however, ask writers to develop a rhetorical distance characterized by objectivity and distance. The tone is not conversational, and readers usually cannot recognize a definite voice. In fact, the voice in a formal argument often is described as being an institutional one because readers generally cannot assign any individuality to it. Nevertheless, both types of arguments share some basic features. For example, consider Passage 1. It was recorded in a supermarket between a 5-year-old and his father, who were standing in front of the cereal display.

Passage 1: The Child in the Supermarket

Child: *"I want the cereal with the frog on the front."*
Parent: *"No, that's just junk. We'll get the Cheerios."*
Child: *"But I want the cereal with the frog. It's really good, Daddy."*
Parent: *"No, that's junk. You just want it because it has a toy inside."*
Child: *"Well, they said on TV that it's good for you, Daddy. And it's delicious! Can we get it, Daddy? Please?"*
Parent: *"No. We always get Cheerios. They're good for you, and they don't have so much sugar. The cereal with the frog is all sugar."*
Child: *"But the one with the frog has a flashlight inside, and I need another flashlight." [At this point, the father puts a box of Cheerios in the grocery basket and moves down the aisle. The child follows behind.]*

The first thing to note about this argument is that it presents a *problem*: In this case it is which cereal to buy. Second, there is an underlying *premise*: The father should buy cereal that is "good" or good for the child. There is a proposal that offers a solution to or a better understanding of the problem. The *proposal* is that the father should buy the cereal with the frog on the box. (A *claim* takes the place of a proposal in the majority of academic arguments.) Finally, there are *reasons* to support the proposal. Reasons, along with evidence, fall under the broad heading of *proof.* Although arguments can take many forms, these features, with minor modifications, are always present.[2]

---

[1]In extreme cases, informal arguments won't have *any* support. Consider how many times you've heard someone "support" an argumentation with the expression, "Just because."

[2]The next chapter focuses on a special form of argument called *persuasion.* It is common to differentiate persuasion from argumentation on the basis of its aim and its proofs, but persuasion nevertheless has the same features outlined here for argumentation.

CHAPTER 10

THE BASIC FEATURES OF ARGUMENTATION

Problem   All argumentation is linked to a problem that requires consideration, resolution, or a decision. In Passage 1, the problem was deciding which cereal to buy. In classes, it may be determining the causes of the Civil War or the causes of an economic recession.

Premises   Premises are values and beliefs that people generally agree are true. Consider that there aren't many people who disagree with the suggestion that human life is valuable. In Passage 1, the premise—which you'll remember the child accepted—was that fathers ought to buy cereal that is good for their children. Premises are said to underlie argumentation.

Proposal or Claim   A proposal offers a solution to the problem or issues a call to action. A claim, on the other hand, makes a statement about the problem, offering an interpretation that is useful and reasonable.

Reasons, Evidence, or Proof   Whether you offer a proposal or a claim in an argument, you have to be able to support it. Support can be in the form of reasons, which are grounded in logic, experience, and knowledge. Consider a very simple claim and its support, such as: "We should leave for the airport by 9 a.m., or we may be late." In other situations, you will need evidence in the form of facts, supporting information, and references to authority. Both reasons and evidence often are referred to as *proof*.

Applying Key Ideas

DIFFERENTIATING ARGUMENTS

This activity is designed to help you better understand the features of arguments. The following argument was written by Patricia, a first-year student enrolled in composition. She had been asked to interview at least one composition teacher and then to write a paper about writing. After you read her argument, identify its basic features. If you do not find all the features listed in the box above, offer an explanation of why Patricia may have left them out. Then explain why or why not this argument is well written. Your paper should be about two pages.

1   Every few months, it seems, the news reports the further decline of literacy among American students. Studies show that, after high school and even after college, writing skills, on average, are inadequate. Many companies, for example, have been forced to send their new employees, who join the companies right after college, to training workshops on how to write because they didn't "get it" in college.

The English field is largely responsible for writing instruction in this country, and so far it doesn't seem to be doing a very good job, maybe because English teachers spend too much time studying literature and not enough time studying how to teach people how to read and write. If the country is going to become more productive, it must have a better educated workforce. Consequently, English teachers need to devote more effort to studying how people learn how to write effectively so that they can develop new ways to teach.

2   After conducting interviews with three professors and two public school teachers, it seems that there are at least two major problems that should be addressed immediately. First, most of the people who get a teaching credential in English don't receive any training in composition. Their content courses are in literature. Many of these people don't even take a composition class in college because their high verbal SAT scores exempt them from the requirement. Although studying Chaucer, Milton, and Shakespeare is important, it does not prepare credential candidates for teaching in the public schools. Part of the goal of studying Shakespeare is to enable teachers to pass this important cultural heritage on to students. But in the public schools cultural heritage is irrelevant when a majority of the children can't read a newspaper, much less a Shakespearean play. Of course, students who can't read aren't going to be able to write.

3   A necessary step toward solving the problem of inadequate teacher training involves changing the curriculum of English Education. Many English professors would object because it would reduce enrollments in their literature classes, but can the nation really afford to do nothing to stop the decline of writing skills just to keep a bunch of Ph.D.s happy? I think not. Besides, the needed changes are not particularly radical. English Education majors currently must take a total of ten English/American literature courses for their BA. By reducing this number to eight and requiring two courses in composition theory and methods, students would have the training they need in literature and composition without sacrificing much in terms of the quantity of literature courses they take. In addition, all English Education majors should be required to take two semesters of composition as freshmen.

4   The second problem that needs to be addressed concerns the public school curriculum. All reports of writing in the schools show that teachers just don't assign much writing. According to Professor Cummins in the School of Education, the 1999 National Assessment of Educational Progress, for example, states that students in high school write five to ten minutes a week. This is unacceptable. Writing takes practice, and no one is going to get the necessary practice if they are writing only five to ten minutes a week. And what are the teachers doing? Parents pay their taxes to the schools so that their children can learn how to read and write, but instead students spend their time in driver's ed. and sex education classes. The teachers just aren't teaching students how to write, probably because they never took any classes to learn *how* to teach students how to write. The school curriculum needs to be changed so that teachers are asking students to write a full paper every day. This is the only way that writing skills will improve.

5   The alternative to these changes is continued decline in Americans' ability to write. No real American, however, can sit idly by and watch the country lose to Japan, Korea, and Germany, were reading and writing are taken seriously. It is a fact that we are in competition with people in these and other countries. It is also a fact that we will not be able to compete if workers cannot read and write well. Our level of productivity already has gone down compared to these other countries, and it's because our workers aren't as well educated as the competition. If English teachers don't devote more time to studying how people learn how to write effectively, and if they don't start applying this knowledge to improving students' writing skills, the United States will end up in history's trash heap. No country can maintain superpower status when its citizens have a Third World education.

Starting with a Problem

Arguments begin with a problem. In the public arena, the problem often involves matters of policy or action. For example, the Chapel Hill Town Council decided some years ago to ban all handguns. Before it could implement the policy, however, the Council was required to hold public hearings on the matter. Because public interest was high, the Council planned two meetings to accommodate all those who wanted to speak, one for supporters and one for opponents. At the first meeting, supporters argued that the ban would make Chapel Hill a safer place to live, and they mentioned the significant increase in crime involving handguns over the last few years. At the second meeting, opponents argued not only that the ban would be unconstitutional but also that citizens needed weapons to protect themselves from criminals in an increasingly dangerous environment. Presumably, the Council used these arguments in its decision on handguns.

In college, the problems you have to address in argumentation are not quite as tangible or immediate as those that people face in the public arena. They involve interpretations (and sometimes evaluations) of reading material or class lectures. In some respects, academic problems are more challenging because they often are abstract and hard to grasp fully. In literature, for example, novels are deemed to be interpretive problems. A work like John Steinbeck's *Grapes of Wrath* asks readers to solve the problem of what the text means. All disciplines have a similar orientation, although the nature of the problem differs. In history, the problem of interpretation may lie in texts, but it also may lie in human events; in biology it may lie in cellular events. Regardless of the discipline, however, the focus usually will be on your ability to support your claim for why something happened and what it means—that is, on interpretation of events and information.

Linked Assignment

IDENTIFYING PROBLEMS IN YOUR COMMUNITY

This activity is designed to get you started on planning for an argumentative writing assignment. Make a list of five problems or questions that are being discussed on your campus. After completing your list, state your position on each item. Then write a sentence or two stating your solution.

Premises

As indicated earlier, arguments are based on agreement rather than disagreement. The initial agreement is on *premises*, which are values and beliefs that form the foundation for an argument. If writers and readers do not agree on the values and beliefs that underlie the argument, it cannot move forward. Clearly, however, premises are part of nearly all language. Our lives are full of premises. Some common ones are: life is valuable; good will triumph over evil; those who work hard are rewarded; children should obey their parents. Note that premises do not have to be *true*, only that those who are participating in an argument have to *accept* them as true.[3]

We can find premises all around us if we take the time to look. Consider the following conversation, which I overheard in the school cafeteria; it contains several interesting premises:

Passage 2: The Rock-n-Roll Star

Female Student 1:	"Brad wants me to meet his parents during spring break."
Female Student 2:	"Are you gonna go?"
Female Student 1:	"Well, I'm thinking about it."
Female Student 3:	"You're not getting *serious* about him, are you?"
Female Student 1:	"Maybe. Why?"
Female Student 2:	"I mean, really, Amy. He's in a *band*, for goodness sake. What kind of future do you think you'd have with a drummer?"
Female Student 3:	"Yeah. Use your head for a change. What do you want to do— be 30 years old and having to support this guy while he practices in the garage with his band?"
Female Student 1:	"He's not going to be in a band *forever*. It's just what he likes to do *now*."
Female Student 2:	"Are you kidding? That's all he *thinks* about. He's already on probation because of his poor grades, and I'll be surprised if he doesn't flunk out this semester."
Female Student 1:	"Oh, let's change the subject."

Three premises stand out here: (a) When couples meet each other's parents it means that a relationship is getting serious; (b) a serious relationship is a long-term one that eventually may involve marriage; and (c) stability is highly desirable in a mate. Less visible, perhaps, are the two premises inherent in the friends' suggestion that Amy is making a mistake if she becomes serious about Brad: (a) someone who plays in a band has few prospects for the future; and (b) prospects for the future are highly desirable in a mate, especially in a male.

Consider your own response to the premises in this conversation. As you were reading, did you ever question the idea that stability is desirable in a partner? Did you question the idea that people in bands generally do not offer a stable future? You may question these premises, but the women having this conversation did not. Even Amy accepted them. If she had not, the discussion would have stopped or taken a different direction.

It is important to keep in mind that if readers do not agree with your premises in an argument, there are two likely outcomes. The readers may stop reading, or they may adopt an adversarial stance, finding fault with just about everything you write. Neither outcome is desirable.

Because premises underlie language in general and argumentation in particular, people often assume that their values and beliefs are shared by everyone. Perhaps most are, but many will not be. As a result, part of the revision process for

---

[3]This fact has led to difficulties with rhetoric since the days of the ancient Greeks. One of the world's great philosophers, Plato, criticized rhetoric on the grounds that it did not seek truth but only the appearance of truth, a criticism linked to the understanding that premises do not have to be true for an argument to move forward.

any paper must include an evaluation of premises to make certain that the paper does not advocate personal rather than general values.

People Don't Always Agree on Premises

There are many different kinds of premises, and many different kinds of people, so it is understandable that sometimes premises conflict. During war, for example, the premise that human life is valuable conflicts with the premise that national interests must be protected. Such conflicts often give rise to interesting explorations of life and values.

More common, perhaps, are those situations in which people simply do not agree on premises. When this happens, it is difficult to engage in a formal argument because there is no agreement on values or general principles. The result frequently is human conflict rooted in a reciprocal refusal to accept an argument as reasonable. Some topics have polarized people so much that argumentation has become impossible, leaving room only for conflict. "Abortion," "legalization of marijuana," "euthanasia," and "gun control" are in this category. Pro-life and pro-choice advocates find it difficult to talk together about abortion because there is such a fundamental disagreement on premises. The effect is significant: When people reject your premises, your audience will be limited to people in your group—*those who already agree with you.*

Applying Key Ideas

IDENTIFYING PREMISES

This activity gives you an opportunity to reflect on what premises are about. Identify the premises in Patricia's essay on page 297. In a couple of sentences, explain why you believe readers would or would not accept these premises. Now consider the topics discussed above when talking about disagreement on premises: abortion, legalization of marijuana, euthanasia, and gun control. What premises for each would there be disagreement on?

Diverse Voices

Some premises differ by culture. For example, in the United States, the premise that human life is valuable supersedes most other premises. One result is that suicide is deemed reprehensible under all circumstances. Until fairly recently in Japan, however, a different premise obtained: Honor was deemed more valuable than human life. As a result, suicide was considered to be an acceptable way of preserving one (and one's family) from dishonor. Consider some of the premises that characterize your home culture and then compare them with the premises you perceive to characterize American culture. Write several paragraphs that explain how these premises are similar or different.

Journal Entry

What are some premises that influence your life? Have you ever had an experience in which someone disagreed with those premises? If so, reflect on the experience and explore the nature of the disagreement.

Proposals and Claims

An argumentation will have either a proposal or a claim. Proposals call for actions, whereas claims express views about reality. As a result, arguments structured around proposals have aims that are different from arguments structured around claims. Different kinds of support also may be involved. These observations have led many scholars to suggest that proposals are linked to a special kind of argument, called *persuasion*.

Argumentation and Persuasion

Distinguishing between argumentation and persuasion is important not only because it clarifies proposals and claims but also because these are two major categories of writing. For our purposes here, let's say that they differ along two dimensions—aims and proof. In argumentation, the chief aim is to get the audience to accept your view of reality as being reasonable. The proof you use is weighted toward reason and character, which includes evidence and authority. Emotional appeals may play a part in some types of argumentation, but it usually is a relatively minor part. Persuasion, on the other hand, generally aims to evoke an action of some kind from the audience. The proof you use is weighted toward emotional appeals, authority, and character. Reason may play a part in some persuasion, but it usually is relatively minor.

This simplified analysis, however, does not mean that arguments cannot issue a call to action. They can, and many in fact do. Consider the following proposal, which very easily could be supported without any emotional appeals:

> The United States should provide the former communist nations of eastern Europe $100 billion to help them shift to a market-based economy.

Nevertheless, the simplified analysis does make it much easier to examine argumentation and persuasion as distinct types of writing.

What Makes a Claim Argumentative?

Every argument makes a claim, but not all claims are argumentative. Look at the following statement:

> Michael Jordan was a good basketball player.

Although arguments must begin with agreement on premises, there also must be an element of disagreement, doubt, or uncertainty involved. Without it, you are dealing with a truism or a statement that does not warrant the effort required to get others to accept your perspective. The statement above cannot be considered an argumentative claim because there is no possibility for disagreement or uncertainty. Anyone who would suggest that Michael Jordan was not a good basketball player does not know what he or she is talking about and would be excluded from any further discussion of the matter.

Now consider the next statement:

Michael Jordan was the best basketball player the game has ever known.

This is an argumentative claim because there have been many great basketball players through the years. Some fans might believe that Magic Johnson or Larry Bird was better than Jordan. The task for the writer who makes the above claim is to show readers that Jordan indeed was better than Johnson or Bird or anyone else, and the argument probably would compare respective careers as a way of presenting evidence.

Where Should You Put Your Claim?

The claim, or thesis, usually appears at the beginning of an argumentative paper, preferably at the end of the first paragraph. Readers want to know quickly what a paper is about; they usually are busy people who do not have time to browse through a couple of paragraphs of background material before reaching the claim.

At the same time, it is important to note that a great deal of writing outside the classroom does not provide a claim at the end of the first paragraph. In fact, government reports, financial statements, manuals of all types, and descriptions generally do not have *any* kind of explicit claim, although sometimes it is possible to identify an implicit one. Professional journals as well as popular magazines often publish arguments with claims in various places; some articles have them at the *end*. Most, however, do appear toward the beginning of the argument, although not necessarily in the first paragraph. Passage 3 illustrates this point. It comes from an article by Susan Davis called "Natural Restoration." Note that Davis places her claim, italicized for your convenience, in the third paragraph. Moreover, she states it twice, which isn't common:

Passage 3: A Claim Near the Beginning of an Argumentation

1 By 1953, when South Korea and North Korea signed the Armistice Agreement that ended the Korean War, the 151-mile strip designated as the demilitarized zone had been devastated. Once littered with terraced rice fields, small crop plots and villages, the DMZ was bare of vegetative cover, pockmarked by bomb craters, and crisscrossed by hundreds of artillery roads. Towns and farms had been forsaken. Most of the region's forests had been razed to deny enemy North Koreans cover. Four million lives had been lost. So too had hundreds of acres of farmlands and wildlife habitat.

2 Today, the scarred slopes have been invaded by mixed hardwood forest. Terrace rice paddies have converted to marshland. Grass and shrubs have conquered abandoned farms. The trumpeting cries of the endangered Manchurian cranes replace the sound of gunfire; pheasants, deer, lynx, and occasional tigers roam the still heavily land-mined area. What is a military no-man's land—site of the longest cease-fire in history, only one gunshot from explosive conflict—has become a wildlife sanctuary. And it has become that with no aid from humans—other than removing our presence.

3 *The Korean DMZ illustrates an idea many of us forget: Nature heals itself.* In the midst of warnings of humans' irrevocable impact, news of an irrepressible nature

sounds peculiar. But the DMZ story is not an isolated example. Plants and animals are very stubborn. Given a disturbance, an ecosystem regenerates, even without our helping hands. *Put another way, ecosystems regenerate if we leave them alone.*

Minor Claims

Sometimes teachers talk to students about the need to "develop an argument." When they do, they are referring in part to supporting evidence and examples (discussed in the next sections), but they also have something else in mind. An argument develops or progresses on the basis of *minor claims* that serve to advance the argument and to provide substance to the writing. We can see how minor claims work by looking again at Davis's "Natural Restoration," the full text of which is presented here.

**Natural Restoration:
When Humans Walk Away**
by Susan E. Davis

1   By 1953, when South Korea and North Korea signed the Armistice Agreement that ended the Korean War, the 151-mile-strip designated as the demilitarized zone had been devastated. Once littered with terraced rice fields, small crop plots and villages, the DMZ was bare of vegetative cover, pockmarked by bomb craters, and crisscrossed by hundreds of artillery roads. Towns and farms had been forsaken. Most of the region's forests had been razed to deny enemy North Koreans cover. Four million lives had been lost. So too had hundreds of acres of farmlands and wildlife habitat.

2   Today, the scarred slopes have been invaded by mixed hardwood forest. Terraced rice paddies have converted to marshland. Grass and shrubs have conquered abandoned farms. The trumpeting cries of the endangered Manchurian cranes replace the sound of gunfire; pheasants, deer, lynx, and occasional tigers roam the still heavily land-mined area. What is a military no-man's land—site of the longest cease-fire in history, only one gunshot from explosive conflict—has become a wildlife sanctuary. And it has become that with no aid from humans—other than removing our presence.

3   The Korean DMZ illustrates an idea many of us forget: Nature heals itself. In the midst of warnings of humans' irrevocable impact, news of an irrepressible nature sounds peculiar. But the DMZ story is not an isolated example. Plants and animals are very stubborn. Given a disturbance, an ecosystem regenerates, even without our helping hands. Put another way, ecosystems regenerate if we leave them alone.

4   What's curious is that we've forgotten that.

5   If you ask most people to think of places in the world that "came back" after devastating human impact, you'll stump them. Most pause and say, "What an interesting question." Many look nervous. The idea does not fit environmentalist, or anti-corporate, thinking. It's easier to think of areas that humans ruined than it is to think of areas that nature healed.

6   If you ask a professional ecologist if nature regenerates, you'll get a different answer. Ecologists are different from environmentalists. "Ecology" connotes *study*—generally of ecosystems. "Environmentalism" connotes advocacy—also of ecosystems. But an ecologist won't just agree with the idea that nature comes back. An ecologist will ask "What do you mean by 'come back'?"

7   Good point. Recovery can refer to vegetative cover which differs from pre-disturbance cover. Swordgrass and shrubs, for example, cover much of the 9,000 acres the U.S. bulldozed in Vietnam during the war. But that area used to be hardwood forest. Trees grow on Enewetok, Pacific test site of nearly 50 U.S. nuclear bombs in the

1950s and 1960s. But the few inhabitants living there cannot eat the fruit because it is so highly contaminated with radioactivity. "Nature will always adapt," says Neo Martinez, an ecologist with UC Berkeley's Energy and Resources Department. "The question is with what."

8   In more specific terms, however, recovery refers to an ecosystem returning to its pre-disturbance condition. Korea is a good example of this kind of recovery. The DMZ returned to its condition before the impact of 20th-century human war and before the impact of human agriculture—which began several thousand years ago.

9   Whether or not a devastated area recovers depends on a number of conditions. Most fundamentally, the site needs its original topsoil. That top layer, also called the top, or A horizon, contains the nutrients and microfauna necessary for plants to grow. Its composition may result from thousands of years of geological processes. "When you work in ecology long enough, you become obsessed with soils," says Peter Warshall, an international biological consultant. "I almost think about soils more often than I think about plants."

10   In temperate zones, topsoil often contains seeds, and stem and root fragments, from which new plant life emerges. Some seeds can lie dormant in the topsoil for hundreds of years. But if that A horizon is removed—in the course of strip-mining, or erosion from clear-cutting—there is, literally, no groundwork from which an ecosystem can develop.

11   Similarly, if the top horizon is altered—by adding chemicals, ploughing or planting crops—a different kind of vegetation emerges when the site is abandoned. That's what happened on many now-abandoned farm sites in New England and the Midwest. But if neither fertilizers nor crops are introduced, even heavily used areas can return to the condition of nearby undisturbed areas. Certain grazing lands in Tanzania's Serengeti National Park, for instance, were cordoned off from domesticated animals, and recovered within two or three years.

12   Even when the topsoil of an area is not removed, full recovery will not occur without seeds. Some lie dormant in the soil. Others drift in from nearby vegetated areas. Birds and animals also carry seeds in their feathers, fur or digestive systems. Damaged ecosystems surrounded by undamaged areas have an easier time recovering than those isolated by geographical barriers, such as oceans, mountains, deserts and cities. And once deposited, the seed has to fall into a niche that facilitates germination. Sunlight, moisture, temperature and nutrients all have to be in the right proportions.

13   The process of the subsequent vegetative recovery is called "ecological succession." Its first proponent was naturalist Frederic C. Clements, who claimed that all ecological formations follow an orderly progression from inception to perpetually stable "climax communities," or self-replicating assemblages of plants. "As an organism," he wrote in 1916, "the formation arises, grows, matures, and dies. . . . The climax formation is the adult organism, of which all initial and medial stages are but stages of development."

14   Clements's theory was strongly rooted in Darwinian ideas of biological evolution, and spin-off ideals of social "progress." Today, most ecologists don't believe in "climax communities." Ecosystems change continually, they say. Targeting an ideal, or even stable, formation is next to impossible. The system may pass through a "mature" or "climax" state, but it may be on the way to something else, often to something simpler.

15   Still, most ecologists recognize that succession occurs. Hardy "pioneer" species invade a disturbed site and are then replaced by a series of other plant, insect, and animal associations. The progression, for many modern-day ecologists, is not towards stability but within constantly changing factors.

16   Recovery also depends on the stability of an ecosystem. Stability, according to ecologist C.S. Holling, is a system's ability to absorb change and recover rapidly.

(Another ecological term, "resilience," refers to a system's ability to withstand disturbance in the first place). Arid regions are generally less stable than moist ones. You can still see tank tracks, for instance, in the Southern California desert, where General Patton led his Desert Training Corps—in WWII. Such marks would disappear in the rain, litter and vegetation of a northern forest.

17   No matter what the stability of an ecosystem, however, recovery really depends on time and space. That is, if the time-scale is long enough, and the space-scale is small enough, most areas will revegetate, given the appropriate seed and soil conditions, and an appropriate "hands-off" attitude by humans.

RAINFORESTS

18 For centuries, humans in rainforests in Central and South America, Asia, and Africa have relied on natural restoration in plant cultivation. In slash-and-burn agriculture, forest dwellers chop 1- to 3-acre plots, and then burn the "slash." Unlike temperate forests, 70 percent of a rainforest's calcium, magnesium and potassium are stored in the biomass above ground. Burning releases nutrients into the soil. Farmers cultivate plants for two or three years, until the soil wears out. Then the farmers move to other plots, allowing the original site to grow back.

19   Christopher Uhl, an ecologist at Penn State, studies whether or not rainforests can come back after disturbance. Uhl has found that despite the trauma of slashing and burning forest areas, cultivated plots can return to rainforest within 100 years—if they're left alone. In the first year, seeds for woody pioneer species blow in from plants surrounding the plot. Often they germinate in the safe shade of fallen logs or random pineapple trees, where dead leaves and nutrients nurture the seedling. These pioneers then create the shady micro-climates that then enable slower growing, primary forest species to germinate.

20   Small plots and long fallow periods allow tropical forests to regenerate. But when a plot is too large, it cannot regenerate as easily. Uhl studied a 25-acre site near San Carlos, Panama, which had been cut and bulldozed in 1971 to build a military post. Two years later, the post was abandoned, leaving all 25 acres deprived of regenerating mechanisms. The bulldozing scraped off the topsoil, with its precious seeds, stems and roots. It also removed the felled biomass, thereby stripping the site of nutrients and safe germination sites for seeds from nearby forest.

21   Uhl predicts that the 15-acre central plot will remain totally bare for a millennium, because it is too far from the nearest seed trees. Perimeter acres show some signs of recovery, in the form of grasses and shrubs. But none is taller than 10 feet. This area too will take centuries to revegetate. The danger here is that certain species can be permanently lost if their delicate habitat does not regenerate.

22   That's only 25 acres. One thing that Uhl's studies—and those of others, including Robert Bushchbaker of the Conservation Fund—highlight is that devastated areas need proximity to non-disturbed areas in order to regenerate. Currently, 150 acres of rainforest fall per minute in the Amazon. 3.6 million acres are cleared each year. Fifty-five percent of the original tree cover is already lost. Miles-wide swatches have been stripped of vegetation, burned repeatedly and packed down by cattle hooves. Those areas won't regenerate—and their hot, open spaces will damage remaining stands of forest.

TEMPERATE FORESTS

23 "Trees," wrote Steward H. Holbrook, in the 19th-century *Yankee Loggers*, "merely hide in the soil until the man with the axe or hoe has turned his back for a moment, instantly to send up their first shoots to advance in astonishing numbers and size until all signs of man's efforts have been obliterated."

24   Holbrook may have been exaggerating, but northern temperate forests do heal more easily than rainforests, even after massive clearcutting takes place. Warm, wet

conditions facilitate germination and rapid growth in rainforests. But northern forests have less than one-tenth the number of species per acre than do rainforests. And that—in combination with a deep bed of vegetative litter, and highly resilient seeds—means that northern forests have an easier time returning to their condition pre-disturbance.

25   The Shenandoah National Park is "probably the largest-scale recovery from human abuse we know," says Duncan Morrow, Recreational Resource Assistant of the National Park Service. The Shenandoah had been farmed, grazed, mined, burned and logged for over 200 years before being made a national park in 1935. At that time, one-third of its 195,000 acres was open grazing land. All but 5 percent had been cut over at one time or another.

26   Fifty years later, hardwood deciduous forest covers most of the area. Containing over 108 tree species, the forest is one of the most diverse in the world. Oak and hickory predominate, with sprinklings of American beech, sycamores, and tall tulip poplar. The undergrowth is heavy with mountain laurels, ferns, bushes and shrubs. Deer, bear, fox, bobcat and cougar roam throughout. Roads are crumbling, and abandoned houses are crawling with vegetation. Besides those remnants of human presence, "it's hard to distinguish between these areas and deciduous areas that have not have been clearcut," says Chuck Anibal, chief interpreter for the park. "There is no obvious aesthetic difference to the casual observer."

27   Where there is a difference is between the secondary oak forest and the virgin pockets of densely packed 200-year-old eastern hemlocks. There, thick canopy shades dark, open forest floor. But the qualitative difference, Anibal insists, is due to species composition, not time.

28   In 1976, Congress added 125 square miles to the park, under the Wilderness Preservation System. When the Wilderness Act was passed in 1964 it made the U.S. the first country to legislate a recognition of the value of "wilderness." The act defines "wilderness" as "an area where the earth and its communities of life are untrammeled by man."

29   The crucial elements in the Shenandoah recovery were that it was left alone, and that sufficient seeds sources existed for regeneration. As in the rainforests, when human impact ceased, nature had a chance to heal. But unlike rainforests, the Shenandoah didn't lose its seed sources. Seeds still existed in the soil, and the forest was never completely clearcut. Uncut, diverse segments still existed.

30   The same is true with the demilitarized zone in Korea. The armistice signing ended the shooting phase of what is now called the Forgotten War. It also ended any civilian presence in the area. Entrance into the DMZ is strictly controlled now. Only that has allowed the 2.4 mile-wide zone to regenerate—with some of the tallest patches of wild forest in Korea—and to create feeding grounds for the endangered white-naped and Manchurian cranes.

31   Had the DMZ been "reforested," the tree cover would be a stiff-rowed monocultural forest. Areas in Korea that were reforested after the war still look "scalped," says George Archibald, a biologist with the International Crane Foundation, who has done significant work in creating Korean preserves for endangered cranes. Instead, the DMZ hosts a mixed arboreal regrowth.

32   "It took my breath away," says Bernard Trainor, military correspondent for *The New York Times*, who fought in the war and visited the DMZ last year. "You'd never know it had been turned to sand during the war. I was able to identify all of the terrain features, but it looked completely different. Now it is overgrown with foliage. It was a very emotional experience."

33   Nature often does a better job at restoration than humans do. Take strip mining, for instance. Appalachian sites mined thirty years ago, before reclamation regulations, have begun to regenerate on their own. "Nature has done a remarkable job so far," says Skip Deegan, coordinator of the Sierra Club's Strip Mining Project. "Now

we primarily have nitrogen-fixing trees, like locust, and autumn olive. But as you go further down the mountain, you see little hardwood trees beginning to spring up. Within 20 to 25 years, hardwoods will return."

34   Mining companies today have to reclaim strip sites to their original condition, or "better." Restored areas often contain only "drought-resistant grasses that pop up within a day or two," Deegan says. These are supposed to increase the value of the land. "Basically it's stabilized," Deegan says. "There's some erosion, but nothing too outrageous. But this is a long shot from a good solid growth of trees."

35   Similarly, abandoned, mined-out gravel pits can sometimes regenerate more successfully than those that are "restored." Before mining began, at what is now called the Red River Natural History Area, near Crookston, Minnesota, the area was mostly prairie lands. When the 85-acre site was in operation, it was dusty, barren, and open. When mining ceased in 1960, the pits had filled with groundwater, which eventually created wetlands. Willow and cottonwood seeds floated in on the wind and germinated in the damp soil. Seeds of flower-bearing shrubs like snowberry and raspberry came next. Today, the area is lush with clusters of cottonwood, dogwood, and cattails, honeysuckle, chokecherry, and nannyberry. Red-winged blackbirds, warbling vireos, skunks, foxes, and even moose, use this as habitat.

36   "Many of the areas mined and then left behind could not have been wildlife habitat if they had been reclaimed according to regulations," says Dan Svedarsky, head researcher at the site, which is run through the Northwest Agricultural Experiment Station, at the University of Minnesota. "They would have been used for agriculture or development."

37   For some wildlife, Red River regenerated to a condition better than before mining. Today, nearly twice as many species of birds use the site as habitat than were recorded when mining began in 1900. Thirty-eight of those species are rare or endangered.

38   Both the DMZ and the gravel pit instances raise a "what next?" question. Regenerated areas tend to attract humans. Scientists in Great Britain have understood the habitat value of restored gravel pits since the 1930s and 1940s, when they found that the wetlands attracted rare birds, including the great crested grebe and the little ringed plover. Gravel companies quickly converted habitat value to recreational value. Many sites now offer fishing, swimming and power-boating. One site, operated by Ready Mix Concrete Ltd. even offers a Disney-like theme park. That may not attract wildlife.

39   Unless naturally restored areas are protected, humans will return. Red River and the Shenandoah National Park are both protected. But if North and South Korea ever reunite, human politics could wreak havoc on the present environment of the DMZ, just as it inadvertently allowed a wildlife sanctuary to emerge there 36 years ago.

40   One interesting thing about ecology is that as you learn, you see. When I drive down city streets now, I marvel less at human omnipresence—walls of brick and carpets of concrete—than I do at the sheer persistence of nonhuman life. Weeds struggle through pavement, saplings sway in sidewalk niches, dandelion puffs sail past plate glass windows, seeking soil in which to lodge. Some of these travelers look tenacious, healthy, resilient. Others look neurasthenetic. But they're there.

41   Some human impacts are undeniably irrevocable, especially those that persist in time and space long after the actual activity ceases. DDT disperses through the food web, thereby affecting plants and animals thousands of miles and decades from the original spraying. Plutonium has a radioactive half-life of 24,000 years. Chlorofluorocarbons destroy ozone molecules 150 years after their release in the atmosphere. And every extinction is forever. If anything, understanding nature's ability to heal should drive us to more adamantly regulate persistent activities and substances, to allow damaged areas to recover, and to prevent further losses.

Throughout this article, Davis offers minor claims that are related to and support her major claim: *Nature heals itself.* Consider paragraph 9, where she writes: "Whether or not a devastated area recovers depends on a number of conditions." This sentence is an example of a minor claim. What follows this statement, through paragraph 12, explains and supports the minor claim. Davis repeats this structure at various places in the article, such as paragraph 24. She states that "northern temperate forests do heal more easily than rainforests." The paragraphs that follow paragraph 24 explain and support this minor claim.

A structural outline of Davis's article helps illustrate how the major claim and minor claims work together. A possible outline for the first 17 paragraphs appears here. Some parts of the article were left out (such as the definition of "recovery") to make it easier to focus on the role of minor claims:

I. Thesis (paragraph 3)—Nature heals itself.

    A. Minor claim (paragraph 9)—"Whether or not a devastated area recovers depends on a number of conditions."

        1. Explanation and support (paragraphs 9–12).

    B. Minor claim (paragraph 15)—"Still, most ecologists recognize that succession [recovery] occurs."

        1. Explanation and support follow in that paragraph.

    C. Minor claim (paragraph 16)—"Recovery also depends on the stability of an ecosystem."

        1. Explanation and support follow in that paragraph.

    D. Minor claim (paragraph 17)—"No matter what the stability of an ecosystem, however, recovery really depends on time and space."

    Explanation and support follow in that paragraph.

Minor claims not only advance an argument, they give writing texture and depth. They are a central part of an argument's structure.

Support

Support in an argumentative paper can take several forms, but generally it consists of the *good reasons* that make the claim valid. Drawing on the work of Aristotle, many scholars propose three kinds of proof, based on logos, ethos, and pathos. In modern terms, these kinds of proof are:

- logic or reason (logos)
- character (ethos)
- emotion (pathos)

Logical Proof

Logical proof can consist of data, such as statistics, information from authorities on the subject, direct quotations from authors who share your view, your own reasoning process, and so forth. If we look again at Patricia's essay about English teachers, we can see that she provides logical evidence in several places. In paragraph 3, for example, she writes:

Besides, the needed changes are not particularly radical. English Education majors currently must take a total of ten English/American literature courses for their BA. By reducing this number to eight and requiring two courses in composition theory and methods, students would have the training they need in literature and composition without sacrificing much in terms of the quality of literature courses they take.

Then, in the fourth paragraph, she writes:

The second problem that needs to be addressed concerns the public school curriculum. All reports of writing in the schools show that teachers just don't assign much writing. According to Professor Cummins in the School of Education, the 1999 National Assessment of Educational Progress, for example, states that students in high school write five to ten minutes a week. This is unacceptable.

Each of these examples begins with a minor claim. In the first, it is:

Besides, the needed changes are not particularly radical.

Patricia supports this minor claim by citing the number of courses, 10, that English Education majors must take for an undergraduate degree and by suggesting a reduction to eight to allow for two courses in composition. Using the figures is effective because it demonstrates knowledge of the topic and because a reduction of two courses indeed does not appear to be a radical change. What we have in this example, therefore, is a smooth interweaving of fact and reason, which is characteristic of logical proof.

In the second example, there are two related minor claims:

1. The second problem that needs to be addressed concerns the public school curriculum.
2. All reports of writing in the schools show that teachers just don't assign much writing.

The first minor claim is supported by the second, which in turn requires support. Patricia provides this support when she cites the 1999 report. It is hard to question the validity of the data, and if high school students in fact are writing only 10 minutes a week, Patricia's claim in sentence 2 is reasonable.

In both these examples, Patricia effectively links her proof to her claim. This link is crucial to successful argumentation. It isn't enough simply to include logical support in a paper. Susan Davis' article "Natural Restoration," offers another example of how to make the link. Davis' claim was *Nature heals itself*. Some of the logical support Davis provides for this claim appears in her discussion of rain forests. She writes:

Christopher Uhl, an ecologist at Penn State, studies whether or not rainforests can come back after disturbance. Uhl has found that despite the trauma of slashing and burning forest areas, cultivated plots can return to rainforest within 100 years—if they're left alone. In the first year, seeds for woody pioneer species blow in from plants surrounding the plot. Often they germinate in the safe shade of fallen logs or random pineapple trees, where dead leaves and nutrients nurture the seedling. These pioneers then create the shady micro-climates that then enable slower growing, primary forest species to germinate.

Linking proof to claim makes the argument more effective because readers are reminded of what they should accept. They see more easily how the evidence supports the claim. An additional benefit is that such linking makes the writing more coherent. It helps connect the various parts of a paper into a whole.

Character as Proof

The character a writer projects can be one of the more interesting features of a paper because it is something skillful writers construct. A sense of character can be communicated in various ways, so this type of proof often is linked to the other two types available. The effective use of logical support can help establish a believable character, for example.

A convention in academic and most other types of writing is that anyone who produces an argument must come across to readers as being reasonable, well-informed, and objective. Writers who project these qualities are generally more acceptable to readers than those who do not. The convention is so powerful that some writing teachers have taken extreme measures in trying to help students master the objective tone associated with academic writing. They prohibit students from using, for instance, the personal pronoun "I," even though there is no rule or valid reason for such a prohibition. Personal pronouns aren't directly related to objectivity.

An objective tone avoids sounding emotional, shrill, flippant, or abusive. To establish an objective tone, a writer would, for example, label an idea as "inadequate" rather than "stupid." Moreover, reasonable people tend to recognize that other views may conflict with their own, so successful writers often discuss opposing viewpoints as a way of enhancing their character. Handled properly, such discussion strengthens the argument by making readers judge the writer to be a reasonable person.

Another way writers project a reasonable, well-informed character is to associate themselves with recognized authorities, which can develop their character as insiders. The most common approach is to make references to other writers. Library work and documentation therefore serve not only to help you learn more about a subject but also to help you develop your character. When your views are similar to those of the leading figures in a given field, you elevate yourself and your argument through that association. You support your claim by showing that your views are congruent with those of published scholars. Reason, character, and your own knowledge again are interrelated. Patricia's paper offers a good example. Her interviews with teachers, one of whom she mentions by name, give her writing a level of credibility that it might not have otherwise.

Also, consider that a goal of formal education is to teach students how to reason objectively. Thus, if you develop a reasonable character when responding to a class writing assignment, you signal that you have mastered the ways of thinking that characterize well-educated people and that are endorsed by teachers in particular and by society in general. This observation is what underlies the earlier comment that argumentation is a way of writing and thinking.

Admittedly, the character of an outsider benefits some types of arguments, such as evaluations (of a business or a university, for example) and political questions. Outsiders usually are perceived by audiences as having no personal interests to protect and as being able to see matters more clearly than insiders. However, the majority of student writing requires projecting the character of an insider. The university experience is a kind of apprenticeship, and the character of the insider moves you closer to the necessary familiarity with discipline-specific views.

Emotional Proof

Emotional proof is based on appeals to readers' emotions rather than to their reason. In certain situations, it can be very powerful. For example, consider the efforts in Chapel Hill to ban handguns. Although many speakers on both sides of the question relied on logical evidence to support their positions, some did not. The question is, after all, an emotional one. Those who supported the ban told stories about young children who found a gun in a desk drawer or a closet and accidentally killed themselves when they tried to pick the gun up. If the ban had been in effect, they concluded, these children would be alive today. Those who opposed the ban told stories of families terrorized by thugs who broke into homes and abused women and children until a mother or father managed to grab the family handgun from a desk drawer or a closet and kill the attackers. If the ban had been in effect, they concluded, the family would be dead today.

Although emotional proof is powerful, its most effective use lies in the realm of informal arguments and persuasion. Political discourse is characterized by its emotional appeals, as is advertising. The next chapter examines both in detail. Academic and other types of formal arguments, however, do not make much use of emotional support. When emotional support does appear, it usually is significantly outweighed by logical and ethical support. In many instances, readers of formal arguments will view reliance on emotional evidence as a weakness or a flaw. By the same token, persuasion may make use of logical support, but emotional appeals are what make it most effective.

It is important to stress that the three types of proof can interact in complex ways in argumentation and persuasion. However, it is the case that argumentation will make less use of emotion and more use of reason, whereas persuasion will make less use of reason and more of emotion. These are defining characteristics.

Presenting Evidence

Formal arguments require that sources of evidence be documented, whereas informal arguments do not. Thus, when an assignment calls for including references, it involves a formal argument. The handbook gives detailed information about documentation, so it isn't necessary to discuss it here. However, formal arguments require proper documentation for people who want to know more about the topic.

In an informal argument, simply mentioning the name of an authority usually is sufficient. There is no works cited page, no documentation. This approach makes things easier for writers but harder for readers who want to look more closely at the texts used as references. They would have to do more searching because the publication information would not be included in the paper. This job is so difficult that few readers would take it on. As a result, informal arguments ask readers to accept more willingly the honesty of writers. People generally are willing to do this because when people read informal arguments, they usually have aims that are different from those they have when they read formal arguments. The need to check sources is not as great.

Using Examples

A paper that supports a claim only with proofs, regardless of their type, will not be very interesting. Such a paper lacks what is called *presence*, which is a sense of immediacy and detail. Arguments without presence often seem mechanical, superficial, or amateurish. An important way to give writing presence is by supplying examples. Examples help shift writing from the general to the specific. They help readers relate to a text by making it more concrete. Examples may serve as evidence, but in many instances they are more elaborate than other types of support.

Susan Davis' article on page 304 offers a good illustration of how examples can enrich a paper. She argues that nature recovers from many kinds of damage, provided it is left alone and has not been grievously harmed. Paragraphs 18 through 22 offer evidence related to rain forests, and paragraphs 23 through 40 offer evidence related to temperate forests. In paragraph 24, Davis states that "northern temperate forests do heal more easily than rainforests." To support this assertion, Davis offers the Shenandoah National Park as an example. She writes:

1   The Shenandoah National Park is "probably the largest-scale recovery from human abuse we know," says Duncan Morrow, Recreational Resource Assistant of the National Park Service. The Shenandoah had been farmed, grazed, mined, burned and logged for over 200 years before being made a national park in 1935. At that time, one-third of its 195,000 acres was open grazing land. All but 5 percent had been cut over at one time or another.

2   Fifty years later, hardwood deciduous forest covers most of the area. Containing over 108 tree species, the forest is one of the most diverse in the world. Oak and hickory predominate, with sprinklings of American beech, sycamores, and tall tulip poplar. The undergrowth is heavy with mountain laurels, ferns, bushes and shrubs. Deer, bear, fox, bobcat and cougar roam throughout. Roads are crumbling, and abandoned houses are crawling with vegetation. Besides those remnants of human presence, "it's hard to distinguish between those areas and deciduous areas that have not have [sic] been clearcut," says Chuck Anibal, chief interpreter for the park. "There is no obvious aesthetic difference to the casual observer."

Notice that this example is sandwiched between two pieces of logical support. This organization enhances the texture of the writing in a way that is similar to the discussion of minor claims on page 304. The writing moves from general to specific to general again, as illustrated below:

- General statement by Duncan Morrow
- Example that provides specific information, such as tree and animal species
- General statement by Chuck Anibal

Recognizing Contrary Views

Although the aim of argumentation is to get readers to accept a point of view as reasonable, it is important to stress that argumentation also has secondary aims. For example, an aim of Susan Davis' "Natural Restoration" is to inform readers, to help them know more about the natural processes that restore damaged land when it is left undisturbed. Many writing tasks have multiple aims. One might be to demonstrate level of learning; another might be to demonstrate the ability to use the objective way of thinking that characterizes academic work.

These last two aims are linked to a convention that has an important place in academic arguments. It involves recognizing a view that is *opposed* to the claim of the argument. The goal is not to weaken the argument by pointing out its short-comings, however, but just the opposite. The convention gives writers the chance to show how an opposing view lacks merit. When used correctly, it allows writers to demonstrate that they have a knowledge of the subject matter that includes diverse viewpoints. It allows them to address the complexity of the topic, thereby enhancing their characters. At work is a human tendency to perceive someone who recognizes opposing views and associated complexities as being more objective and reasonable than someone who tries to ignore them.

Although this convention is an important part of argumentation, it is used less regularly in professional writing than it is in college writing. Patricia uses the convention in her essay on page 297, but in "Natural Restoration" Susan Davis does not. Even in college the convention is applied more frequently in humanities courses than in science and social science courses.

Let's return again to Patricia's essay to get a better sense of how the convention works. In paragraph 2, Patricia writes:

> *After conducting interviews with three professors and two public school teachers, it seems that there are at least two major problems that should be addressed immediately. First, most of the people who get a teaching credential in English don't receive any training in composition. Their content courses are in literature. Many of these people don't event take a composition class in college because their high verbal SAT scores exempt them from the requirement. Although studying Chaucer, Milton, and Shakespeare is important, it does not prepare credential candidates for teaching in the public schools. Part of the goal of studying Shakespeare is to enable teachers to pass this important cultural heritage on to students. But in the public schools cultural heritage is irrelevant when a majority of the children can't read a newspaper, much less a Shakespearean play. Of course, students who can't read aren't going to be able to write.*

Patricia suggests that English teachers are trained in literature, not composition, and that such training causes the problem she is addressing in her paper. The implication is that "studying Chaucer, Milton, and Shakespeare" detracts from what would-be teachers need to know. Anticipating some objection to this analysis, Patricia wisely deflects the potential hostility by recognizing the value of such studies. She says that this course work "is important," and she specifies the nature of its importance by linking it to "cultural heritage." Patricia succeeds in acknowledging the value of literary studies, yet she also makes it clear that such studies are irrelevant when students can't read.

This convention helps Patricia establish an effective character for her writing. She does not "trash" literary studies; she recognizes their value. But she implies that anyone who would focus on literature at the sacrifice of reading and writing skills is narrow minded. Rhetorically, Patricia makes anyone seem unreasonable who would argue against changing the existing program for a bachelor's degree in English.

Applying Key Ideas

INCLUDING CONTRARY VIEWS IN AN ARGUMENT

This activity gives you an opportunity to apply the ideas in the section above. The passage below comes from an article that writer Jacob Weisberg published in the *New Republic*. Weisberg argues that lesbians and gays should be permitted to join the military without hiding their sexual orientation. Identify where Weisberg presents material contrary to his argumentation and explain how it strengthens or weakens his claim.

1 The last time the Pentagon elaborated its rules on homosexuals was in 1982, when the office of Secretary of Defense Caspar Weinberger promulgated this rationale:

2 "Homosexuality is incompatible with military service. The presence of such members adversely affects the ability of the Armed Forces to maintain discipline, good order, and morale; to foster mutual trust and confidence among the members; to ensure the integrity of the system of rank and command; to facilitate assignment and worldwide deployment of members who frequently must live and work under close conditions affording minimal privacy; to recruit and retain members of the military services; to maintain the public acceptability of military services; and, in certain circumstances, to prevent breaches of security."

3 Working backward through Weinberger's laundry list, the "public acceptability" argument is probably as close as the DOD [Department of Defense] comes to a legitimate worry. The fear is that some young men would be discouraged from volunteering if they knew they would be serving alongside homosexuals and that parents would object to their boys serving in an unwholesome environment. The same line was taken against racial integration of the services before Harry S. Truman accomplished it by executive order in 1948. In that case fears were largely unrealized, and there is every reason to think they are exaggerated today. Public tolerance for homosexuals is now higher than support for racial integration was 40 years ago. According to a recent Gallup Poll, 60 percent of the public believes that gays should be allowed in the military.

4 The public acceptability argument goes in a particularly vicious circle: gays are unacceptable because they are unacceptable. Straight soldiers will continue to fear and scorn homosexuals until they are forced to become acquainted with them in a routine basis. Of course, the admission of gays will no more eliminate homophobia than the integration of blacks cured racism. But irrational prejudices are bound to diminish over time if the isolation and ignorance they feed upon is ended.

Thesis and Antithesis

Thesis and antithesis is a valuable organizational technique. It is especially useful for argumentation because it offers an effective way to present contrary material. In this approach, writers offer an idea that seems valid, only to drop it a few sentences later for one that is better. It is the second idea that the writers really want to talk about, and they expect readers to attend to it closely. The effect of thesis–antithesis is similar to presenting contrary views: It anticipates opposing arguments, demonstrates knowledge, and establishes character. Because thesis–antithesis usually appears at the beginning of a paper, some important argumentative goals are achieved early. For example, the technique allows writers to capture their readers' attention by establishing a small controversy about the topic. The controversy lies in the opposing views and may be inherently interesting.

The following paragraphs illustrate the technique. They come from a paper on criminal behavior written by Gilberto, a sophomore in college. In this paper, Gilberto argues that the existing criminal-justice system in America is flawed because it is based on the idea that criminals can be rehabilitated:

Passage 4: Genes and Crime

Gilberto

1   Currently, about 1.3 million people are held in America's prisons. They are mostly males between the ages of 18 and 30. The majority is black, and nearly all are repeat offenders. The number would be much higher than 1.3 million if the nation's courts had not decided a decade ago to reduce overcrowding by ordering prisons to release inmates if the population at a given institution rose to 110 percent of capacity. Some estimates suggest that it could be as high as three million.

2   Even at three million, however, the number of convicted criminals is only a small percentage of the overall population. It's also important to note that, although the number of crimes has increased significantly over the last decade or so, the total number of criminals has not, with the exception of homicide. In fact, according to a report issued by the FBI in 1998, the number of crimes reported to police increased almost 1,000 times faster than the prison population. The report also stated that more than 90 percent of the crime in America is committed by the same relatively small group of hardened criminals who are released and then returned to prison after committing additional crimes. The question is *why*.

3   Historically, the mission of America's prison system has been to rehabilitate inmates. The idea is that society has failed these people somehow and that with proper *education*, they can return to society and lead meaningful lives. Thirty years ago, until the ACLU convinced the courts that convict labor was essentially "slave" labor, inmates in many states made license plates or worked on road crews. Prisoners weren't being trained to become brain surgeons, but they were learning basic skills that they could use to earn an honest living after being released. Today, however, all but the blindest supporters of rehabilitation are willing to admit that it hasn't worked. The repeat offenders who fill the prisons are living proof of its failure.

4   Some critics of the prisons argue that eliminating job training was a mistake and that rehabilitation can't work when all inmates do these days is watch television, shoot pool, and lift weights. They argue that returning to traditional notions of rehabilitation would stop the "revolving doors" found in most prisons today by transforming inmates into decent citizens. But a growing amount of evidence in biology and neurophysiology indicates that rehabilitation cannot work because it is fundamentally flawed. The cause of criminal behavior is only marginally related to environment but is largely determined by genetics.

In this excerpt, Gilberto indicates that he will address why most of the crime in America is committed by repeat offenders. In paragraph 3, he suggests that the problem is rooted in the elimination of vocational programs in the nation's prisons, and he seems to blame the ACLU for the existing situation. That is, rehabilitation isn't working because the apparatus of training has been dismantled. In paragraph 4, Gilberto adds support to this thesis when he mentions the "critics of the prisons" who say eliminating job training was a mistake. He even offers a

"I'M SENTENCING YOU TO 25 YEARS IN PRISON WITH NO HOPE OF PAROLE UNTIL AFTER 3 P.M. TOMORROW AFTERNOON!"

touch of emotional evidence when he indicates that all prisoners do is "watch television, shoot pool, and lift weights," which sounds more like a vacation than punishment. Structurally, this portion of the paper has many of the features of an argument. The last two sentences in this paragraph, however, reject the thesis and offer an antithesis. They claim that rehabilitation cannot work because criminal behavior is genetic and is not caused by social factors. The remainder of the paper argues for this claim.

Thesis–antithesis is frequently used when the claims of an argument are contrary to the views of many readers. Gilberto's essay is a case in point. The idea that criminal behavior is genetic has been hotly debated for several years now. In fact, the topic is so controversial that certain groups have made serious efforts, some successful, to get the government to block further research in the area. Gilberto was accurate when he estimated that much of his audience would not accept his thesis. But using thesis–antithesis allows Gilberto to present the commonly accepted view and describe its weaknesses before presenting his own. This approach gets readers to question the dominant view and prepares them for one that challenges it.

Conclusions

Successful writers know that a conclusion should not repeat what they said in the introductions of their papers. In most instances, argumentative conclusions generalize outward. They make a statement about the future or about the status of the problem that motivated the writer's proposal or claim. In this regard, they often are reflective or contemplative; they tell readers what *lesson there is to be learned from the paper*. Let's revisit the Davis passage to see an example of an outward looking, reflective conclusion. (Notice that conclusions are not necessarily limited to a single paragraph.)

Passage 5: An Outward Looking Conclusion

1   One interesting thing about ecology is that as you learn, you see. When I drive down city streets now, I marvel less at human omnipresence—walls of brick and carpets of concrete—than I do at the sheer persistence of nonhuman life. Weeds struggle through pavement, saplings sway in sidewalk niches, dandelion puffs sail past plate glass windows, seeking soil in which to lodge. Some of these travelers look tenacious, healthy, resilient. Others look neurasthenetic. But they're there.

2   Some human impacts are undeniably irrevocable, especially those that persist in time and space long after the actual activity ceases. DDT disperses through the food web, thereby affecting plants and animals thousands of miles and decades from the original spraying. Plutonium has a radioactive half-life of 24,000 years. Chlorofluorocarbons destroy ozone molecules 150 years after their release in the atmosphere. And every extinction is forever. If anything, understanding nature's ability to heal should drive us to more adamantly regulate persistent activities and substances, to allow damaged areas to recover, and to prevent further losses.

In the paragraphs that precede these last two, Davis vividly describes what nature can do to a damaged environment when left alone. She has made her claim, and her evidence is pretty convincing. Throughout, the argument has operated on a fairly detached level because Davis established a rhetorical stance that makes her writing objective. Davis is not writing as an insider to other insiders, however. She is addressing a general audience of outsiders, and she is writing an informal argument. Given this rhetorical stance, a completely objective tone would be off-putting.

In her last paragraphs, Davis shifts the tone, making her argument more personal and more informal. She accomplishes this shift not so much through the use of the personal pronoun but by putting nature and ecology on a *human scale*. She marvels at the "sheer persistence of nonhuman life." This statement motivates readers to reflect on their own experiences with nature. It helps readers relate to nature, the environment, and Davis' argument on a personal level, and we can imagine a reader thinking about trying to control weeds in the backyard or mosquitoes on a summer evening.

Then, having brought ecology from the abstract to the personal, Davis reminds readers of how human activities can have an "irrevocable" effect on nature. The statement that "every extinction is forever" is powerful because it is so obvious and because it comes after a list of toxins that humanity has released into the environment. However, this statement also shifts the focus again, outward this time, toward the future. There is an implicit call to action in the last sentence. Effective conclusions commonly look outward in this way.

Writing Assignment

SCOFFLAWS

Many social commentators today claim that Americans have a growing disdain for law, as evidenced in the number of people who are "scofflaws," those who violate laws regarding such things a littering, speeding, drinking in public, and so on. For this assignment, reflect on your own life experience and write an argumentative essay that supports or refutes this claim. Your paper should be about three pages long, should have an easily identifiable claim, ample support, and examples. In addition, it should recognize the counter view, preferably through thesis–antithesis.

Writing Assignment

PROBLEMS ON CAMPUS

Drawing on the material you generated for the linked assignment on page 299, write an argument that takes a stand on one of the problems you identified that exist on your campus. Your paper should be about four pages long. You should have an identifiable proposal or claim (with minor claims), support, examples, and a conclusion. In addition, you should include contrary views, and this might be a good opportunity to practice using thesis–antithesis for this purpose.

COMMON FLAWS IN ARGUMENTS

An interesting feature of arguments is that they can be flawed even though they may be well written. The structure and organization may be fine, but the argument itself is unacceptable for one reason or another. There are many flaws that can weaken an argument, and books that focus on argumentation analyze them in great detail. Here, however, the aim is more limited—to look at some of the more common flaws so that you can avoid them in your own work and recognize them in the work of others.

Faulty Causality

Many arguments deal with cause–effect relationships. They claim that one event, set of circumstances, or person causes another event or set of circumstances. In the realm of human experience, causality often is described in terms of *responsibility*. A person may not have caused a particular event but is responsible for it.

It is very easy to assume a causal relation where none exists. For example, during presidential campaigns, candidates make all sorts of claims about themselves and their opponents. In the 1996 campaign, challenger Bob Dole stated in his speeches that drug use among teenagers had increased significantly while Bill Clinton was in office. The implicit argumentative claim was that Clinton was responsible. Yet this claim was fatally flawed because it was based on a nonexistent causal relation between drug use among teens and Clinton's position as President. The fact that teen drug use increased was merely a coincidence, just as the increase in personal bankruptcies and the decrease in sunspot activity during this period were coincidences. Moreover, the suggestion (again implicit) that Clinton was responsible for the increase in drug use is indefensible. It denies the fact that, ultimately, parents and teens themselves are responsible for such actions.

When developing an argument that involves causality, it is important to consider the true nature of any cause–effect relation. There usually are many factors that influence events and circumstances, and a valid cause–effect argument will take these factors into account. Causality occurs under certain conditions, which are classified as being of two types, *necessary* and *sufficient*. Necessary conditions must exist or the event cannot occur. For example, a plant cannot grow without water, so the presence of water is a necessary condition for plant growth. But water alone is not sufficient; plants also need nutrients and sunlight. Valid causality therefore requires both necessary and sufficient conditions. In the case of teen drug use, it is difficult to identify necessary and sufficient conditions in ways that legitimately involve President Clinton.

Faulty Generalization

At a dinner party one night, a friend started relating his experience with an expensive new foreign car he had bought a few months earlier. He said that the car was nothing but trouble and had left him stranded three times when it wouldn't start. Another person in the group said that he knew someone with the same kind of car and that it had similar problems. Then he turned to our friend and said: "You should have asked around before you bought that car. They are nothing but junk."

Although people make statements like this one all the time, it is an argumentative flaw call *faulty generalization*. The problem is that the speaker made a generalization on the basis of insufficient information. It is not reasonable (or acceptable) to reach this kind of conclusion from looking at only two examples.

Writers working in science and social science have to be particularly careful not to engage in faulty generalization. In these areas, researchers look at small bodies of data, and they normally limit their conclusions to the object of their investigations. Research examining the study habits of college freshmen at Harvard might not be generalizable to college freshmen at a community college, for example.

Slippery Slope

The slippery slope fallacy may be the most pervasive flaw in argument. It is all around us. What is truly remarkable is that we find so few people who point out this fallacy when it occurs. Consider the following statement from a government anti-drug brochure: "Marijuana use quickly leads to addiction to hard drugs like crack and heroin." The idea is that a single step sends one plummeting down the "slippery slope." In reality, however, people and situations are far more complex than this fallacy admits.

Attacking the Person

Argumentation involves agreement as well as disagreement, and successful arguments often refute contrary positions. The importance character plays in providing support for an argument opens the door to a flaw that sometimes is hard to resist. Contrary positions are held by people with characters every bit as real as your own, and it can be tempting to attack those characters as a way of attacking the positions you disagree with.

Several years ago at UNC Chapel Hill, debate raged regarding whether the university should build a black culture center. There were good reasons presented on both sides, but the arguments often became emotionally charged. The student newspaper printed a letter from a faculty member that mounted an especially forceful argument against construction. It was promptly followed by a rebuttal letter from another faculty member. The rebuttal did not address the argumentative issues raised in the first letter, however. Instead, it attacked the character of the writer, linking him to conservative views and politics and finally dismissing him as a racist.

Successful writers build character; they don't try to destroy it. The best way to refute an argument is to deal with proof, showing that your position is stronger and more reasonable than any contrary position. Attacking someone's character ultimately will reflect negatively on your own.

Journal Entry

Have you ever experienced an argument in which one side or the other used personal attack? How did it make you feel? What was the outcome?

Either/Or Fallacy

Most argumentative topics are complex and defy easy answers. Nevertheless, the appeal of easy answers is strong, and it often finds expression in what is called the *either/or fallacy*. In this fallacy, complex issues are reduced to two simple alternatives. It found perfect expression among campus protesters during the 1960s who were advocating civil rights and opposing the war in Vietnam. They simplified their positions by saying: "If you aren't part of the solution, you are part of the problem." Although the various movements of the 1960s are long past, this statement remains quite powerful. However, there were many people who supported civil rights and who opposed the war but who did not participate in protests. They may not have been part of the solution from the perspective of movement leaders, but it is hard to classify them as part of the problem. To do so is to simplify matters unfairly.

The either/or fallacy often appears when people are advocating causes. Solicitations for donations are typical. People have come to expect visits from solicitors who appear at the door and ask for a donation to help children in Third World countries. If the would-be donor hesitates, these solicitors are trained to ask: "You don't want these children to go hungry, do you?" The implication is that one either makes a donation or wants children to go hungry. Actually, other factors usually are involved. There is no way of knowing whether the solicitor is legitimate and no way of knowing how much of the collected money will go to feed children. Or a person might be out of cash and without a check. The situation can be—and usually is—more complex than the either/or fallacy allows.

READINGS

Albert Shanker

At one time, Albert Shanker was the president of the American Federation of Teachers, one of the largest teachers' unions in the country. For many years he wrote a weekly column for the *New York Times*, where the following passage appeared.

VALUE FREE?

1   It's easy to be in favor of multicultural and global education, in principle. The trouble comes when you try to say exactly what you mean by the term so you can put it into action.

2   If you want to feel convinced about the value of multicultural and global education, all you have to do is to look at the strife that is bred by ethnic, racial, and religious differences. Look at Eastern Europe, at India, at some of our own cities. If only we understood where other people were coming from—if only we had more sensitivity to their cultures—we might not be so wedded to our own points of view. And we might have a better chance of avoiding the conflicts that come from ethnocentrism.

3   However, when we come to apply this principle, there are some serious problems. The New York State Regents' goal for global education, which has also been taken up by multiculturalists, makes some of these problems very clear. According to the goal, "Each student will develop the ability to understand, respect, and accept people of different races; sex; cultural heritage; national origin; religion; and political, economic, and social background, and their values, beliefs, and attitudes."

4   The goal, expressed in a lot of positive words ("understand, respect, and accept"), sounds very broad-minded, very reasonable. And up to a point, it expresses what we'd hope for from a multicultural and global education. An educated person is not narrow-minded or provincial. So of course we don't want students to be prejudiced—to prejudge the correctness or desirability of some idea or action before they know anything about it. We want them to be open to new ideas and ways of doing things.

5   But do we really want them to "respect and accept" the "values, beliefs, and attitudes" of other people, no matter what they are? Is every value, belief, and attitude as good as every other?

6   Do we want them to respect and accept the beliefs that led Chinese leaders to massacre dis-senting students in Tiananmen Square? And what about the values and beliefs that allowed the Ayatollah Khomeini to pronounce a death sentence on Salman Rushdie and the current leaders in Iran to confirm this sentence? Is it okay to condemn an author to death because he wrote something that offends against your religious beliefs?

7   Is exposing unwanted children to the elements and certain death, a custom still widely practiced in some countries in Asia and Africa, to be respected and accepted because it is part of somebody else's culture? Is female circumcision?

8   Must we respect the custom of forcing young children in the Philippines or Thailand to work in conditions of virtual slavery? And must we look respectfully on Hitler's beliefs and actions?

9   Should we teach students to accept the sexism of the Japanese or their racist attitudes toward immigrants just because they're part of the Japanese culture? And should we encourage students, in the name of open-mindedness and cultural sensitivity, to accept Afrikaner values and the racist beliefs that undergird apartheid? (If the United States and other nations had been so "open-minded" over the years, would these values and beliefs now be changing in South Africa?)

10   People who support this kind of approach to multicultural and global education may think they are being objective—even scientific. They may think they're freeing themselves from the limitations of their own culture and its values. But by not taking a position, they are taking one. They are saying that apartheid is okay; that there is nothing wrong with murdering someone who has committed blasphemy.

11   They're also teaching their students not to make moral judgments. If any custom or law of people in any culture is as defensible as any other, what kind of judgment is possible? So, without intending to, they encourage students in prejudice of a different sort: Instead of mindlessly assuming that other ways of doing things have to be wrong, students will mindlessly assume these ways of doing

things have to be right—or at least as good as anyone else's. And by approving practices that would not be tolerated here or in any other democracy, they are saying that some people should be held to lower standards than others—a kind of moral superiority that is hardly consistent with multicultural and global education.

12   It's important that we teach our children about each other's and other people's customs and values. We are unlikely to survive if we don't. But this does not mean teaching students that they need not hold other people's practices—and our own—up to moral scrutiny. If we do this, we confuse objectivity with neutrality. And how can we possibly justify neutrality about the difference between being able to speak and write as we please and having to restrain our tongues and our pens on pain of death?

Critical Reading Guide

1. Shanker makes a subtle but important distinction between a value-laden and a value-free multicultural curriculum. What is that distinction?

2. Shanker suggests that multicultural curricula are value free, although a more accurate description might be that the curricula are very selective in regard to the values they include for study. Using Shanker's article as a basis, what are some values that are ignored in discussions of multiculturalism? What are some that are attended to?

3. What sorts of evidence (logical, ethical, emotional) forms the primary support for Shanker's argument?

4. What is the most important premise in this essay? Is it valid? Can you provide any evidence that suggests it might not be valid?

Henry L. Gates

Henry Gates is a well-known scholar who has written extensively about racism and American society. The following passage appeared in the *New York Times*.

HENRY LOUIS GATES, JR.

WHOSE CULTURE IS IT ANYWAY?

1   I recently asked the dean of a prestigious liberal arts college if his school would ever have, as Berkeley has, a 70 percent nonwhite enrollment. "Never," he replied. "That would completely alter our identity as a center of the liberal arts.

2   The assumption that there is a deep connection between the shape of a college's curriculum and the ethnic composition of its students reflects a disquieting trend in education. Political representation has been confused with the "representation" of various ethnic identities in the curriculum.

3   The cultural right wing, threatened by demographic changes and the ensuing demands for curricular change, has retreated to intellectual protectionism, arguing for a great and inviolable "Western tradition," which contains the seeds, fruit, and flowers of the very best thought or uttered [sic] in history. (Typically, Mortimer Adler has ventured that blacks "wrote no good books.") Meanwhile, the cultural left demands changes to accord with population shifts in gender and ethnicity. Both are wrongheaded.

4   I am just as concerned that so many of my colleagues feel that the rationale for a diverse curriculum depends on the latest Census Bureau report as I am that those opposed see pluralism as forestalling the possibility of a communal "American" identity. To them, the study of our diverse cultures must lead to "tribalism" and "fragmentation."

5   The cultural diversity movement arose partly because of the fragmentation of society by ethnicity, class, and gender. To make it the culprit for this fragmentation is to mistake effect for cause. A curriculum that reflects the achievement of the world's great cultures, not merely the West's, is not "politicized"; rather it situates the West as one of a community of civilizations. After all, culture is always a conversation among different voices.

6   To insist that we "master our own culture" before learning others—as Arthur Schlesinger, Jr., has proposed—only defers the vexed question: What gets to count as "our" culture? What has passed as "common culture" has been an Anglo-American regional culture, masking itself as universal. Significantly different cultures sought refuge underground.

7   Writing in 1903, W. E. B. Du Bois expressed his dream of a high culture that would transcend the color line: "I sit with Shakespeare and he winces not." But the dream was not open to all. "Is this the life you grudge us," he concluded, "O knightly America?" For him, the humanities were a conduit into a republic of letters enabling escape from racism and ethnic chauvinism. Yet no one played a more crucial role than he in excavating the long-buried heritage of Africans and African Americans.

8   The fact of one's ethnicity, for any American of color, is never neutral: One's public treatment, and public behavior, are shaped in large part by one's perceived ethnic identity, just as by one's gender. To demand that Americans shuck their cultural heritages and homogenize themselves into a "universal" WASP culture is to dream of an America in cultural whiteface, and that just won't do.

9   So it's only when we're free to explore the complexities of our hyphenated culture that we can discover what a genuinely common American culture might actually look like.

10   Is multiculturalism un-American? Herman Melville didn't think so. As he wrote: "We are not a narrow tribe, no. . . . We are not a nation, so much as a world." We're all ethnics; the challenge of transcending ethnic chauvinism is one we all face.

11   We've entrusted our schools with the fashioning and refashioning of a democratic polity. That's why schooling has always been a matter of political judgment. But in a nation that has theorized itself as plural from its inception, schools have a very special task.

12   Our society won't survive without the values of tolerance, and cultural tolerance comes to nothing without cultural understanding. The challenge facing America will be the shaping of a truly common public culture, one responsive to the long-silenced cultures of color. If we relinquish the ideal of America as a plural nation, we've abandoned the very experiment America represents. And that is too great a price to pay.

Critical Reading Guide

1. If you haven't read Albert Shanker's essay on page 322, do so. What is the difference between "multiculturalism" and "diversity"?

2. Look carefully at Gates' definition of "culture" in paragraph 5. What exactly does this definition mean, do you think? How does Gates' definition differ from your own?

3. How is Gates' definition of culture linked to the argument of the essay?

4. What is the claim of this essay? What evidence does Gates use to support it?

5. At times, Gates makes "culture" synonymous with "ethnic group." Are there differences between the two? What rhetorical advantage lies in using "culture" in this way?

6. In paragraph 8, Gates speaks to "any American of color," as though he is appealing to the many readers of non-European backgrounds who might make up part of his audience. What features of the essay would you change to make it more effective in this regard?

7. What is the most important premise in Gates' essay?

Writing Assignment

ARGUING DIVERSITY

This writing assignment gives you an opportunity to apply all the ideas about argumentation that you have studied in this chapter. Shanker and Gates present two contrasting views of multiculturalism. Using these samples as background material, investigate the stance your college has in regard to diversity. Does your college, for example, require undergraduates to take a course in multiculturalism? Does it have policies intended to increase ethnic diversity among students and faculty? After completing your investigation, take a position on the question of multiculturalism on your campus. If your college has policies in effect, do you support them or not? If your college doesn't have such policies, should it establish them? Your paper should be about four pages long.

WRITING GUIDE: ARGUING DIVERSITY

Invention

Diversity and multiculturalism mean different things to different people, but in all instances, universities use the terms to mean increasing the presence of minority students and faculty on campus. Different campuses, however, use different criteria for defining "minority." In the South, for example, Hispanics and Asians rarely are defined as minorities, so recruiting efforts focus exclusively on blacks. In California, Asians are not defined as minorities because, according to the state government, they generally succeed economically.

These are some of the considerations you will need to make as you begin thinking about this assignment, and you will need to match your analysis against the questions that the assignment asks. In addition, you will want to look beneath your school's programs and policies. For example, many schools that require undergraduates to complete a course on multiculturalism limit the focus of the course in some interesting ways. On some campuses, these courses deal only with African-American culture. On others they deal only with African-American and Mexican-American cultures. The question of *definition* therefore appears to be a central factor in this assignment.

Planning

Before you begin writing, you must have information about your school's policy on multiculturalism, which means that you probably will need to visit a couple of offices on campus. To obtain information about undergraduate admissions policies, go to the admissions office. To obtain information about graduate admissions, assuming your school has a graduate program, go to the graduate studies office. To obtain information about hiring policies, go to the campus personnel office or to the dean of arts and sciences.

Look closely at the information you receive and ask questions about it. What you receive may not be entirely accurate. Large numbers of colleges have two-tiered admissions and hiring policies that they do not want to make public because they fear public disapproval. For example, during the 1990s, the English Department at UNC Chapel Hill required that applicants to its doctoral program have a minimum score on the Graduate Record Examination (GRE) in the 95th percentile.[4] This requirement was waived for minority applicants, however, who commonly were admitted with GRE scores below the 15th percentile. This information is not readily distributed to the public or even to applicants. The published information addresses only the higher admission standard. The message here is that you need to be prepared to question the information you receive.

In addition, you may learn from personnel that your college is committed to hiring more minority faculty and has been for many years. This commitment may seem suspect if your campus is like many nationwide and has fewer than 10% minority faculty. What are the obstacles to hiring more faculty?

Finally, what do you make of your school's position on diversity? Most people who have considered diversity seriously are fairly evenly divided on the topic. If you support your school's policies, or oppose them, find out why so many others disagree with your stance.

Drafting

Multiculturalism is a topic that appears regularly in campus newspapers, which indicates that arguments for and against it will continue for some time to come. Your first composing task is to set the scene for your argument, providing a background for readers.

After you have presented the problem, you should state your claim or proposal (these will differ depending on whether your school has policies in effect). Because the paper is short, you should present contrary arguments early. You may want to use thesis–antithesis.

This assignment makes emotional support a highly tempting option. After all, diversity has become inextricably linked to racial issues, which offer an endless supply of "hot buttons" that will excite just about any audience. But this assignment should be viewed from the perspective of formal argument. Avoid getting tangled in emotional support. If you have conducted your research thoroughly, you will have more than enough evidence based on reason and character to support your claim, regardless of what your stance is.

Pausing and Reading

During pauses in your writing, read over what you have produced. You do not want to try rewriting anything at this point, but you should make notes for yourself when you see things that need adjustment later. For example, you might read

---

[4]Percentile ranking is a way of comparing scores on a given test. An applicant with a score in the 95th percentile has performed better than 94% of the people taking the test. A score in the 15th percentile, on the other hand, is better than only 14% of the people taking the test.

the first paragraph or two and determine whether you have a claim or proposal. If not, make a note in the margins. Also, consider the types of support you are using, your rhetorical stance, and the amount of information you provide readers about your school. Ask yourself how well your draft is matching the plan you developed earlier. If it is not matching very well, think about some ways to bring the two together. If it is matching, you are on the right track. If you are not sure, ask a friend, a classmate, or your teacher to give you some feedback on the draft.

Revising

Read through your paper several times, thinking about your audience, your claim, your rhetorical stance as insider or outsider, and what additional support would make your claim or proposal stronger. Have you accurately presented the opposition? Have you shown concisely that it is inadequate or flawed? Are you working with acceptable premises? Is your conclusion reflective? Does it prompt readers to generalize your argument to themselves or perhaps to look outward?

After making the changes necessary to answer these questions in the affirmative, reread you paper. What lessons does it convey? If you cannot find any, or if the lessons are mere truisms, revise again.

Persuasion

Because persuasion can be extremely subtle, many people are unaware when they are being manipulated. In persuasion, a proposal more often than not is implicit, conveyed through images (both visual and verbal) that touch the nerves and the hidden workings of the psyche.

CHAPTER ELEVEN

Persuasion

Although the aim of argumentation is to get the audience to accept a claim as reasonable, the aim of persuasion is to cause or influence actions. This distinction is based on the perception that language is an action that works in a performative way. As such, persuasion is a special type of argument. Friends, relatives, and coworkers try to influence one another regularly. For example, your parents may have tried to influence your choice of college and major. Your teachers try to influence you to think independently, and many of them try (unconsciously, perhaps) to influence you to behave as they do. Then there's the TV commercial and the print ad, inescapable forms of persuasion in our society, which advertisers use in an effort to influence behavior and deliver viewers and readers to their clients. Persuasive language is everywhere.

It would be a mistake, however, to see persuasion merely as advertising and personal interactions. TV news programs and documentaries, print journalism, business communications, and many kinds of essays are persuasive. In fact, some people believe that everyone goes through life attempting to manipulate their environment and those who inhabit it. We all want to get our way. This view suggests that everything people do, say, and write has an element of persuasion in it.

Because persuasion can be extremely subtle, many people are unaware when they are being manipulated. In persuasion, a proposal more often than not is *implicit*, conveyed through images (both visual and verbal) that touch the nerves and the hidden workings of the psyche. Automobile dealers who want to sell expensive sports cars know exactly what they are doing when they drape an attractive and largely unclothed woman over the hood in a magazine ad. The men viewing the ad may not understand the psychology involved, and they certainly aren't going to bring reason to bear on their desire for a sports car. They simply feel the sexual promise implicit in ownership. A similar principal is at work in a popular Calvin Kline ad for Obsession perfume. The ad does not show the perfume at all, merely a strikingly attractive nude man and woman standing thigh to thigh in a swing. Women who view this ad are not directly getting the message, "Buy Obsession." Instead, the message is something like, "Look at the type of woman who uses Obsession and the type of man she gets to hang out with." Given the scarcity of people who look like the models in the ad, this message is not particularly reasonable, but it is effective. Indeed, the fact that it circumvents reason illustrates the emotional basis for persuasion.

As these examples suggest, persuasion is linked to self-image and personal needs. People want to feel attractive, desired, stable. Persuasion frequently uses people's perceptions of who they are or, more important, *who they want to be* for its effectiveness. At work is a fundamental principle: The message must appeal to the audience's preferred vision of itself. It is designed to short circuit reason and careful judgment.

These observations have led many people to wonder whether persuasion is ethical, in the moralistic meaning of the term. Sometimes it is, and sometimes it isn't. Unethical persuasion uses distortions and even outright lies to influence people. Ethical persuasion does not rely on distortion or falsehood. The problem lies in being able to tell the difference. Sometimes it is hard to know when information is distorted or untrue. Sometimes, it will not matter. Even people who are smart enough to know better want to believe some things so much that they will. Case in point: Some years ago, millions of dieters embraced the fantasy that grapefruit juice had the ability to consume body fat. They did so contrary to all reason and critical thinking because of the desire for an easy way to lose weight. The position of teachers is clear, however: Persuasion can move people in many ways, but a student's aims should be honest.

PERSUASIVE ESSAYS

Persuasive essays are commonly calls to action. Although we often think of advertising and campaign speeches when we consider examples of persuasion, it is important to recognize that many different kinds of persuasive discourse exist, including the persuasive essay, a form of writing that can be quite powerful. Like advertising and other forms of persuasion, such essays frequently are calls to action, but they do not always strive to bring about prompt, tangible deeds from readers. Instead, they aim to influence more long-term behaviors, attitudes, and ways of thinking. A characteristic technique is to convey a lesson that has the potential to influence readers, often through example. Thus, persuasive essays may draw extensively on the writer's personal experience.

The value of using personal experience to model the call to action cannot be overestimated. It is important, however, to recognize that such personal experience is not limited to the writer. When we think about how we motivate others to act, we realize that there aren't many choices. We can order people to do things, but that seldom works unless we are in a position of authority, and even then the outcome may include a high level of resentment. We can pay people to do things, but certainly not in the context of intellectual life. And yet getting others, especially strangers, to do what we believe they should do is an important part of everyday experience. Sometimes, the motivation to act that you use as a writer will lie in the experiences of those heroes and models that society naturally turns to. At other times, it will lie in general principles or notions that we hold as a society for what it means to "do the right thing." It is the appeal to such models and to what it means to do the right thing that serves as a very compelling motivator. Thus, the available means of persuasion you have as a writer is both rich and potentially noble, which makes persuasive essays among the more interesting and satisfying to produce.

Let's turn now to an example that will help make these generalizations more concrete. The following passage was written by Jane Tompkins, an English teacher who uses a personal anecdote to explain that the values teachers hold seldom find their way into the classroom. She then proposes that teachers should "bring greater sensitivity to the needs of students."

Jane Tompkins

Jane Tompkins' essay was written for fellow teachers, so she speaks as an insider to other insiders. Nevertheless, she makes certain assumptions that many of her readers might not be willing to accept. Consider, for example, the first paragraph, in which she asserts that all teachers "preach some gospel or other." The assumption is that the classroom is unavoidably political, shaped by the politics and ideologies of the teacher.

Passage 1: Teach by the Values You Preach

1 As professors of English we are always, in one way or another, talking about what we think is wrong with the world and, to a lesser extent, about what we'd like to see changed. Whether we seek gender equality, or economic justice, or simply believe in the power and beauty of great literature, we preach some gospel or other. We do this indirectly, but we always do it. Yet our practice in the classroom doesn't often come close to embodying the values we preach.

2 I first became aware of this some four or five years ago when I was teaching at Columbia University. I remember walking to class down an empty hall and thinking to myself, "I should find out what my students want, what they need, and not worry about whether what I've prepared is good enough or ever gets said at all." Up until that day I had always thought that what I was doing was helping my students to understand the material we were studying—Melville or deconstruction or whatever—but at that moment I realized that there were actually three things I was more focused on: a) showing the students how smart I was; b) showing them how knowledgeable I was; and c) showing them how well prepared I was for class. I had been putting on a performance whose true goal was not to help the students learn but to act in such a way that they would have a good opinion of me. More than anything else, this is what we teach our students: how to perform within an institutional academic setting so that they will be thought of highly by their colleagues and instructors.

3 What is behind this model? How did it come to be that our main goal as academicians turned out to be performance? The answer to the question is fairly complicated, but let me offer one partial explanation. Each person comes into a professional situation dragging along with her a large bag full of desires, fears, expectations, needs, resentments—the list goes on. But the main component is fear. Fear is the driving force behind the performance model. Fear of being shown up for what you are: a fraud, stupid, ignorant, a clod, a dolt, a sap, a weakling, someone who can't cut the mustard. And I'm sure that my own fear of being shown up for what I really am was conveyed to my students, and insofar as I was afraid to be exposed, they too would be afraid.

4 Such fear is no doubt fostered by the way our institutions are organized, but it is rooted in childhood. Many, perhaps most, academics are people who as children were good performers at home and in school. That meant that as children we became such expert practitioners at imitating whatever style, stance, or attitude seemed most likely to succeed in the adult world from which we so desperately sought approval that we came to be split into two parts: the real backstage self, who didn't know any-

thing, and the performing self, who got others to believe in its expertise and accomplishments. This pattern of seeking approval has extended itself into our practice as teachers. Still seeking approval from our peers and from our students, we exemplify a model of performance that our students succeed in emulating, thus passing the model down to future generations.

5   One of the odd things about people who teach for a living is how seldom they speak of these matters. This lack of self-awareness may stem from the fact that elite graduate schools teach their students to ignore pedagogy simply by ignoring it themselves. I often wondered by what mysterious process others managed their classes, since no one I knew had been trained to do it and no one ever talked, really talked, about what they did. Oh, there were plenty of success stories and the predictable remarks about a discussion that had been like pulling teeth, but never anything about how it really felt to be up there day after day. In this respect teaching seemed a lot like sex—something you weren't supposed to talk about or focus on but that you nevertheless were supposed to be able to do properly when the time came. People rarely discuss what the experience of teaching—or sex—is really like for them, partly because, at least in whatever subculture it is I belong to, there's no vocabulary for articulating the experience and no institutionalized format for doing so.

6   But there is one thing people do sometimes talk about in relation to teaching, more so now than in the past. They talk about using teaching as a vehicle for social change—to help students detect the manipulations of advertising or to resist the stereotypes of gender, race, and class. But I have come to think that what really matters as far as our own beliefs and projects for change are concerned is not so much what we talk about in class but what we do there. The classroom is a microcosm of the world; it is the chance we have to practice whatever ideals we may cherish. The kind of classroom situation one creates is the acid test of what it is one really stands for. And I wonder if, in the case of college professors, simply performing our competence in front of other people is all that that amounts to in the end.

7   Recently I made an awkward lunge in the direction of creating a different world in the classes I teach. It wasn't virtue or principle that led me to this but brute necessity. A couple of years ago when I realized that I wouldn't have time to prepare my classes in the usual way, I discovered, almost by accident, a way to make teaching more enjoyable and less anxiety-producing.

8   More enjoyment and less anxiety do not sound like very selfless or high-minded goals. But I had discovered that under the guise of serving students, I was being self-centered anyway, always worrying about what people thought of me. So I tried something else for a change.

9   What the method boils down to is this: The students are responsible for presenting the material to the class for most of the semester. I make up the syllabus in advance, explain it in detail at the beginning of the course, and try to give most of my major ideas away. (This is hard; holding on to one's ideas in case one should need them to fill some gap later on is bred in the bone after twenty-five years in the classroom.) The students sign up for two topics that interest them, and they work with whoever else has signed up for their topic. On the first round of reports the groups meet with me outside of class to discuss their ideas and strategies of presentation. I give plenty of feedback in written form but no grades.

10   I find that my classes are better. The students have more to say in every class, more students take part in the discussions, students talk more to one another and less to me, and the intensity and quality of their engagement with the course materials is deeper than usual. Because I don't have the burden of responsibility for how things are going to go every time, I contribute only when I feel I really have something to say. I concentrate better on what is being said, on who is talking, and on how the class is going—how things *feel* in class.

11   The upshot is I do less work and enjoy class more. But I feel guilty about this, partly because somewhere along the way I got the idea that only backbreaking work
should produce results. I struggle not to feel guilty about teaching in a way that is pleasurable and free from fear because part of what I now try to do as a teacher is convey
a sense of the way I think life ought to be. This means, among other things, offering
a course that is not a rat race, either for me or for the students. I no longer believe that
piling on the work is a good in itself or that it proves seriousness and dedication.

12   Still, there is the question of whether, in shifting the burden of performance onto
the students, I'm making them do work I'm too lazy to do myself, sending them off
on a journey with inadequate supplies. It's true that in some cases the students don't
deal with the material as well as I could, but that is exactly why they need to do it.
It's not important for me to polish my skills, but they do need to develop theirs and
to find a voice.

13 Teaching is a service occupation, but it can only work if you discover, at a certain
point, how to make teaching serve you. Staying alive in the classroom and avoiding
burnout means finding out what you need from teaching at any particular time. I've
gone from teaching as performance to teaching as a maternal or coaching activity
because I wanted to remove myself from center stage and get out of the students'
way, to pay more attention to them and less to myself. Ideologically speaking, you
might say I made the move in order to democratize the classroom, but in practice I
did it because I was tired.

14   I'm not suggesting that other teachers should adopt this particular method. There
are a million ways to teach. But what I am saying is that what we do in the classroom *is* our politics. No matter what we may say about Third World-this or feminist-
that, our interactions with our students week in and week out demonstrate what we
are for and what we are against in the long run. The politics of the classroom begins
with the teacher's treatment of and regard for his or her self. A kinder, more sensitive attitude toward one's own needs as a human being, in place of a desperate striving to meet professional and institutional standards of arguable merit, can bring
greater sensitivity to the needs of students and a more sympathetic understanding of
their situations, both as workers in the academy and as people in the wider world.

Tompkins has been teaching for a while, and by all accounts she is really good
at it. Her character as a well-known insider gives her the authority to criticize
teachers and teaching. Those in her audience either know her personally or by
reputation and will value her views, but they may not accept her initial assumption because it is so argumentative. Consequently, Tompkins faces a rhetorical
problem: She wants to insert the assumption to make a point, but she must move
readers away from that assumption quickly or risk losing them.

The solution to this problem is the personal narrative. Tompkins is something of
a star among English teachers, a huge group that does not boast many celebrities,
so her fellow teachers are going to be curious about her—hence the personal anecdote beginning in paragraph 2. It works quite effectively for Tompkins, but keep in
mind that it probably would not work very well for a novice. One way to overcome
the limitation of an outsider status when faced with such a rhetorical problem in a
persuasive essay is to make certain that the anecdote is especially interesting.

Of course, this is not to suggest that Tompkins' anecdote is uninteresting. For
insiders, it is quite interesting, particularly in paragraph 3. Many teachers might
recognize that much of their effort in the classroom is self-centered and designed
to demonstrate their knowledge, but fewer might be willing—unlike Thompson—
to admit that *fear* is what motivates this self-centeredness. It is remarkable that

Tompkins admits her own fears of "being shown up" for what she suggests she sometimes sees herself to be: "a fraud, stupid, ignorant, a clod, a dolt, a sap, a weakling, someone who can't cut the mustard." This admission is bound to touch a nerve among academic readers. For reasons that are not entirely clear, large numbers of overachievers—the very sort of people who get PhDs and become university professors—view themselves as frauds who somehow have managed to fool the world into believing that they actually know something.

Tompkins is demonstrating excellent persuasive technique at this point. Her "confession" has the effect of helping readers identify with her while simultaneously prompting them to sympathize with her. Despite her success and status in academic circles, underneath she is just like everyone else in the audience. This is identification—it bonds readers and writer as insiders.

However, the goal of this essay is not to persuade readers that the author is "just one of the gals." It is to issue a call to action, to persuade readers that they should make changes in the ways they teach so that their classrooms reflect their values, politics, and ideologies. As a result, Tompkins has to return to her initial premise of the classroom as a political arena. Given the bonding that has occurred by this point, she can do so with some safety in paragraph 6, where she states that "the classroom is a microcosm of the world; it is the chance we have to practice whatever ideals we may cherish." Later paragraphs reveal that her own ideals involve democratizing the classroom, a process that makes a course "student-centered" rather than "teacher-centered."

Tompkins' intelligence and sophistication as a writer come through when she recognizes that her audience is not likely to be moved to action simply because she says her approach is good or consistent. They need more motivation, so Tompkins shifts to a persuasive technique that appeals to readers' needs. She tells them that a democratic, student-centered class is *easier to teach because it requires less work*. More leisure time is a powerful need among teachers, and Tompkins explains that she gives students their topics; they go off to do their research and then report back to the class. Perfect. More leisure time for the teacher. This is strong motivation, indeed. The admission of guilt in paragraph 11 is an extremely clever technique. It lets readers know that some feelings of guilt about working less are natural but should be dismissed. The effect is twofold: further writer–reader identification as insiders and an absolution of guilt.

Writing Assignment

YOUR IDEAL CLASSROOM

This assignment gives you the chance to start applying some of the ideas just discussed. You have been a student for many years, and you have probably experienced several different classroom structures and approaches to teaching, but perhaps you have never had a chance to propose what you believe would be an ideal classroom. For this assignment, write a persuasive essay that calls for implementing your ideal classroom structure. You should support your proposal using personal experience as well as reason and references to authority, if appropriate. The paper should be about four pages long.

Whether written for insiders or outsiders, most persuasive essays convey information. Tompkins' example contains a great deal of information about teaching, students, and the writer herself, but the personal nature of this information makes it difficult to generalize to other people and situations. As persuasion and information become more closely interconnected, the persuasive essay undergoes subtle but important changes. Writers start providing minor claims similar to those discussed on page 304. Minor claims are argumentative, not persuasive, so there is a corresponding increase in the weight of reason and character. In persuasive essays that also are highly informative, the balance among emotional, ethical, and logical appeals is almost equal.

Journal Entry

Do you remember the last time you tried to persuade someone to do something? What was it? What happened? What techniques did you use?

The next example of a persuasive essay, written by Katha Pollitt, also supplies a great deal of information, but it comes from reports, government documents, TV programs, and news magazines. Note that Pollitt is an outsider writing for other outsiders. She is a knowledgeable outsider, but an outsider nonetheless. As you read, you should assess how Pollitt's rhetorical stance affects not only the information she offers and how she offers it, but also the persuasiveness of the passage.

Passage 2: Why I Hate "Family Values" (Let Me Count the Ways)

Katha Pollitt

1   Unlike many of the commentators who have made Murphy Brown the most famous unmarried mother since Ingrid Bergman ran off with Roberto Rossellini, I actually watched the notorious childbirth episode. After reading my sleep-resistant 4-year-old her entire collection of Berenstain Bears books, television was all I was fit for. And that is how I know that I belong to the cultural elite: Not only can I spell "potato" correctly, and many other vegetables as well, I thought the show was a veritable riot of family values. First of all, Murph is smart, warm, playful, decent and rich: She'll be a great mom. Second, the dad is her ex-husband: The kid is as close to legitimate as the scriptwriters could manage, given that Murph is divorced. Third, her ex spurned *her*, not, as Dan Quayle implies, the other way around. Fourth, she rejected abortion. On TV, women have abortions only in docudramas, usually after being raped, drugged with birth-defect-inducing chemicals or put into a coma. Finally, what does Murph sing to the newborn? "You make me feel like a natural woman"! Even on the most feminist sitcom in TV history (if you take points off *Kate and Allie* for never so much as mentioning the word "gay"), anatomy is destiny.

2   That a show as fluffy and genial as *Murphy Brown* has touched off a national debate about "family values" speaks volumes—and not just about the apparent

inability of Dan Quayle to distinguish real life from a sitcom. (And since when are TV writers part of the cultural elite, anyway? I thought they were the crowd-pleasing lowbrows, and *intellectuals* were the cultural elite.) The *Murphy Brown* debate, it turns out, isn't really about Murphy Brown; it's about inner-city women, who will be encouraged to produce fatherless babies by Murph's example—the trickle-down theory of values. (Do welfare moms watch *Murphy Brown*? I thought it was supposed to be soap operas, as in "they just sit around all day watching the soaps." Marriage is a major obsession on the soaps—but never mind.) Everybody, it seems, understood this substitution immediately. After all, why get upset about Baby Boy Brown? Is there any doubt that he will be safe, loved, well schooled, taken for checkups, taught to respect the rights and feelings of others and treated to *The Berenstain Bears Visit the Dentist* as often as his little heart desires? Unlike millions of kids who live with both parents, he will never be physically or sexually abused, watch his father beat his mother (domestic assault is the leading cause of injury to women) or cower beneath the blankets while his parents scream at each other. And chances are excellent that he won't sexually assault a retarded girl with a miniature baseball bat, like those high school athletes in posh Glen Ridge, New Jersey; or shoot his lover's spouse, like Amy Fisher; or find himself on trial for rape, like William Kennedy Smith—children of intact and prosperous families every one of them. He'll probably go to Harvard and major in semiotics. Maybe that's the problem. Just think, if Murph were married, like Dan Quayle's mom, he could go to DePauw University and major in golf.

3   That there is something called "the family"—Papa Bear, Mama Bear, Brother Bear and Sister Bear—that is the best setting for raising children, and that it is in trouble because of a decline in "values," are bromides accepted by commentators of all political stripes. The right blames a left-wing cultural conspiracy: obscene rock lyrics, sex ed, abortion, prayerless schools, working mothers, promiscuity, homosexuality, decline of respect for authority and hard work, welfare and, of course, feminism. (On the *Chicago Tribune* Op-Ed page, Allan Carlson, president of the ultraconservative Rockford Institute, found a previously overlooked villain: federal housing subsidies. With all that square footage lying around, singles and unhappy spouses could afford to live on their own.) The left blames the ideology of postindustrial capitalism: consumerism, individualism, selfishness, alienation, lack of social supports for parents and children, atrophied communities, welfare and feminism. The center agonizes over teen sex, welfare moms, crime and divorce, unsure what the causes are beyond some sort of moral failure—probably related to feminism. Interesting how that word keeps coming up.

4   I used to wonder what family values are. As a matter of fact, I still do. If abortion, according to the right, undermines family values, then single motherhood (as the producers of *Murphy Brown* were quick to point out) must be in accord with them, no? No. Over on the left, if gender equality, love and sexual expressivity are desirable features of contemporary marriage, then isn't marriage bound to be unstable, given how hard those things are to achieve and maintain? Not really.

5   Just say no, says the right. Try counseling, says the left. Don't be so lazy, says the center. Indeed, in its guilt-mongering cover story "Legacy of Divorce: How the Fear of Failure Haunts the Children of Broken Marriages," *Newsweek* was unable to come up with any explanation for the high American divorce rate except that people just didn't try hard enough to stay married.

6   When left, right and center agree, watch out. They probably don't know what they're talking about. And so it is with "the family" and "family values." In the first place, these terms lump together distinct social phenomena that in reality have virtually nothing to do with one another. The handful of fortysomething professionals like Murphy Brown who elect to have a child without a male partner have little in

common with the millions of middle- and working-class divorced mothers who find themselves in desperate financial straits because their husbands fail to pay court-awarded child support. And neither category has much in common with inner-city girls like those a teacher friend of mine told me about the other day: a 13-year-old and a 12-year-old, impregnated by boyfriends twice their age and determined to bear and keep the babies—to spite abusive parents, to confirm their parents' low opinion of them, to have someone to love who loves them in return.

7   Beyond that, appeals to "the family" and its "values" frame the discussion as one about morals instead of consequences. In real life, for example, teen sex—the subject of endless sermons—has little relation with teen childbearing. That sounds counterfactual, but it's true. Western European teens have sex about as early and as often as American ones, but are much less likely to have babies. Partly it's because there are far fewer European girls whose lives are as marked by hopelessness and brutality as those of my friend's students. And partly it's because European youth have much better access to sexual information, birth control and abortion. Or consider divorce. In real life, parents divorce for all kinds of reasons, not because they lack moral fiber and are heedless of their children's needs. Indeed, many divorce because they *do* consider their kids, and the poisonous effects of growing up in a household marked by violence, craziness, open verbal warfare or simple lovelessness.

* * *

8   Perhaps this is the place to say that I come to the family-values debate with a personal bias. I am recently separated myself. I think my husband and I would fall under *Newsweek*'s "didn't try harder" rubric, although we thought about splitting up for years, discussed it for almost a whole additional year and consulted no fewer than four therapists, including a marital counselor who advised us that marriage was one of modern mankind's only means of self-transcendence (religion and psychoanalysis were the others, which should have warned me) and admonished us that we risked a future of shallow relationships if we shirked our spiritual mission, not to mention the damage we would "certainly" inflict on our daughter. I thought he was a jackass—shallow relationships? *moi?* But he got to me. Because our marriage wasn't some flaming disaster—with broken dishes and hitting and strange hotel charges showing up on the MasterCard bill. It was just unhappy, in ways that weren't going to change. Still, I think both of us would have been willing to trudge on to spare our child suffering. That's what couples do in women's magazines; that's what the Clintons say they did. But we saw it wouldn't work: As our daughter got older, she would see right through us, the way kids do. And, worse, no matter how hard I tried to put on a happy face, I would wordlessly communicate to her—whose favorite fairy tale is "Cinderella," and whose favorite game is Wedding, complete with bath-towel bridal veil—my resentment and depression and cynicism about relations between the sexes.

9   The family-values types would doubtless say that my husband and I made a selfish choice, which society should have impeded or even prevented. There's a growing sentiment in policy land to make divorce more difficult. In *When the Bough Breaks*, Sylvia Ann Hewlett argues that couples should be forced into therapy (funny how ready people are to believe that counseling, which even when voluntary takes years to modify garden-variety neuroses, can work wonders in months with resistant patients who hate each other). Christopher Lasch briefly supported a constitutional amendment forbidding divorce to couples with minor children, as if lack of a separation agreement would keep people living together (he's backed off that position, he told me recently). The Communitarians, who flood *The Nation*'s mailboxes with self-promoting worryfests, furrow their brows wondering "How can the family be saved without forcing women to stay at home or otherwise violating their

rights?" (Good luck.) But I am still waiting for someone to explain why it would be better for my daughter to grow up in a joyless household than for her to live as she does now, with two reasonably cheerful parents living around the corner from each other, both committed to her support and cooperating, as they say on *Sesame Street*, in her care. We may not love each other, but we both love her. Maybe that's as much as parents can do for their children, and all that should be asked of them.

10   But, of course, civilized cooperation is exactly what many divorced parents find they cannot manage. The statistics on deadbeat and vanishing dads are shocking—less than half pay child support promptly and in full, and around half seldom or never see their kids within a few years of marital breakup. Surely, some of this male abdication can be explained by the very thinness of the traditional paternal role worshiped by the preachers of "values"; it's little more than breadwinning, discipline and fishing trips. How many diapers, after all, has Dan Quayle changed? A large percentage of American fathers have never changed a single one. Maybe the reason so many fathers fade away after divorce is that they were never really there to begin with.

* * *

11   It is true that people's ideas about marriage are not what they were in the 1950s—although those who look back at the fifties nostalgically forget both that many of those marriages were miserable and that the fifties were an atypical decade in more than a century of social change. Married women have been moving steadily into the work force since 1890; beginning even earlier, families have been getting smaller; divorce has been rising; sexual activity has been initiated even earlier and marriage delayed; companionate marriage has been increasingly accepted as desirable by all social classes and both sexes. It may be that these trends have reached a tipping point, at which they come to define a new norm. Few men expect to marry virgins, and children are hardly "stigmatized" by divorce, as they might have been a mere fifteen or twenty years ago. But if people want different things from family life—if women, as Arile Hochschild pointed out in *The Second Shift*, cite as a major reason for separation the failure of their husbands to share domestic labor; if both sexes are less willing to resign themselves to a marriage devoid of sexual pleasure, intimacy or shared goals; if single women decide they want to be mothers; if teenagers want to sleep together—why shouldn't society adapt? Society is, after all, just us. Nor are these developments unique to the United States. All over the industrialized world, divorce rates are high, single women are having babies by choice, homosexuals are coming out of the closet and infidelity, always much more common than anyone wanted to recognize, is on the rise. Indeed, in some ways America is behind the rest of the West: We still go to church, unlike the British, the French and, now that Franco is out of the way, the Spanish. More religious than Spain! Imagine.

12   I'm not saying that these changes are without cost—in poverty, loneliness, insecurity and stress. The reasons for this suffering, however, lie not in moral collapse but in our failure to acknowledge and adjust to changing social relations.

13   We still act as if mothers stayed home with children, wives didn't need to work and men earned a "family wage." We'd rather preach about teenage "promiscuity" than teach young people—especially young women—how to negotiate sexual issues responsibly. If my friend's students had been prepared for puberty by schools and discussion groups and health centers, the way Dutch young people are, they might not have ended up pregnant, victims of what is, after all, statutory rape. And if women earned a dollar for every dollar earned by men, divorce and single parenthood would not mean poverty. Nobody worries about single fathers raising children, after all; indeed, paternal custody is the latest legal fad.

14   What is the point of trying to put the new wine of modern personal relations in the old bottles of the sexual double standard and indissoluble marriage? For that is

what most of the current discourse on "family issues" amounts to. No matter how fallacious, the culture greets moralistic approaches to these subjects with instant agreement. Judith Wallerstein's travesty of social science, *Second Chances*, asserts that children are emotionally traumatized by divorce, and the fact that she had no control group is simply ignored by an ecstatic press. As it happens, a recent study in *Science* did use a control group. By following 17,000 children for four years, and comparing those whose parents split with those whose parents stayed in troubled marriages, the researchers found that the "divorce effect" disappeared entirely for boys and was very small for girls. Not surprisingly, this study attracted absolutely no attention.

15   Similarly, we are quick to blame poor unmarried mothers for all manner of social problems—crime, unemployment, drops in reading scores, teen suicide. The solution? Cut off all welfare for additional children. Force teen mothers to live with their parents. Push women to marry in order to attach them to a male income. (So much for love—talk about marriage as legalized prostitution!)

16   New Jersey's new welfare reform law gives economic coercion a particularly bizarre twist. Welfare moms who marry can keep part of their dole, but only if the man is *not* the father of their children. The logic is that, married or not, Dad has a financial obligation to his kids, but Mr. Just Got Into Town does not. If the law's inventors are right that welfare policy can micromanage marital and reproductive choice, they have just guaranteed that no poor woman will marry her children's father. This is strengthening the family?

17   Charles Murray, of the American Enterprise Institute, thinks New Jersey does not go far enough. Get rid of welfare entirely, he argued in *The New York Times*: Mothers should marry or starve, and if they are foolish enough to prefer the latter, their kids should be put up for adoption or into orphanages. Mickey Kaus, who favors compulsory low-wage employment for the poor, likes orphanages too.

18   None of those punitive approaches will work. There is no evidence that increased poverty decreases family size, and welfare moms aren't likely to meet many men with family-size incomes, or they'd probably be married already, though maybe not for long. The men who impregnated those seventh graders, for example, are much more likely to turn them out as prostitutes than to lead them to the altar. For one thing, those men may well be married themselves.

19   The fact is, the harm connected with the dissolution of "the family" is not a problem of values—at least not individual values—it's a problem of money. When the poor are abandoned to their fates, when there are no jobs, people don't get to display "work ethic," don't feel good about themselves and don't marry or stay married. The girls don't have anything to postpone motherhood for; the boys have no economic prospects that would make them reasonable marriage partners. This was as true in the slums of eighteenth-century London as it is today in the urban slums of Latin America and Africa, as well as the United States. Or take divorce: The real harm of divorce is that it makes lots of women, and their children, poor. One reason, which has got a fair amount of attention recently, is the scandalously low level of child support, plus the tendency of courts to award a disproportionate share of the marital assets to the man. The other reason is that women earn much less than men, thanks to gender discrimination and the failure of the workplace to adapt to the needs of working mothers. Instead of moaning about "family values" we should be thinking about how to provide the poor with decent jobs and social services, and about how to insure economic justice for working women. And let marriage take care of itself.

20   Family values and the cult of the nuclear family is, at bottom, just another way to bash women, especially poor women. If only they would get married and stay married, society's ills would vanish. Inner-city crime would disappear because fathers would communicate manly values to their sons, which would cause jobs to

spring up like mushrooms after rain. Welfare would fade away. Children would do well in school. (Irene Impellizeri, anti-condom vice president of the New York City Board of Education, recently gave a speech attributing inner-city children's poor grades and high dropout rates to the failure of their families to provide "moral models," the way immigrant parents did in the good old days—a dangerous argument for her, in particular, to make; doesn't she know that Italian-American kids have dropout and failure rates only slightly lower than black and Latino teens?)

21   When pundits preach morality, I often find myself thinking of Samuel Johnson, literature's greatest enemy of cant and fatuity. What would the eighteenth-century moralist make of our current obsession with marriage? "Sir," he replied to Boswell, who held that marriage was a natural state, "it is so far from being natural for a man and woman to live in the state of marriage that we find all the motives which they have for remaining in that connection, and the restraints which civilized society imposes to prevent separation, are hardly sufficient to keep them together." Dr. Johnson knew what he was talking about: He and his wife lived apart. And what would he think of our confusion of moral preachments with practical solutions to social problems? Remember his response to Mrs. Thrale's long and flowery speech on the cost of children's clothes. "Nay, madam," he said, "when you are declaiming, declaim; and when you are calculating, calculate."

22   Which is it going to be? Declamation, which feeds no children, employs no jobless and reduces gender relations to an economic bargain? Or calculation, which accepts the fact that the Berenstain Bears, like Murphy Brown, are fiction. The people seem to be voting with their feet on "the family." It's time for our "values" to catch up.

Linked Assignment

VALUES AND PERSUASION

This activity asks you to do some invention for the next writing assignment. Persuasion often deals with values one way or another, as the passages just presented show. For this activity, make a list of five topics that lend themselves to calls to action with respect to values. Perhaps you've seen people littering the campus even though there are ample trash bins, and you want your fellow students to be more conscientious. Perhaps you've been stereotyped on the basis of your race, gender, or native language, and you want others to value you for who you are without interference from a stereotype. For each topic, write a couple of sentences stating what persuasive position you might take if you were to write an essay about it; you also should identify your audience for this essay.

Writing Assignment

CALLING FOR AN ACTION

Select one of the topics you identified for the linked assignment on values and persuasion and write a persuasive essay that calls for some type of action that expresses identifiable values. Be informative as well as persuasive, but keep both your aim (a call for action) and the weight of your support within the parameters of a persuasive essay. That is, you should have more support that comes from emotion and character than from reason. The paper should be approximately five pages long.

ADVERTISING

Many people believe that advertising intends to sell goods and services to an audience. A more accurate perspective is that the *audience itself* is a good that advertising aims to deliver to those who pay for ads. One way to deliver an audience is to increase brand familiarity, usually through repetition. An advertiser may repeat a product name until customers no longer have to think about a purchase; they simply purchase the first brand that comes to mind, which happens to be the one that they have heard about most. Jingles are very effective ways to accomplish this goal because they have a way of sticking in one's thoughts.

Another effective technique involves producing an ad that gets the audience to identify with a good or service. The key is to link the good or service to the self-image of a particular target group. One of the more successful ads in this regard is the Marlboro Man. His tough, rugged image, projecting the individualism associated with the West, made Marlboro cigarettes the best-selling brand in the world. Research indicates that the majority of Marlboro smokers are male and that they identify with the rugged individualism of the cigarette ads that have defined the product.

Most ads combine appeals to self-image with appeals to personal needs. Anything related to losing weight sells well in this country, for example, because more than half of all Americans are overweight and feel unhappy about their appearance. They also may know that being overweight is bad for their health. Consequently, advertising for exercise devices and dieting aids may include both appeals, although the emphasis probably will be on self-image.

Diverse Voices

Advertising often differs significantly from one country to another, but the underlying principles and motivations remain the same. Analyze one or two ads from your home culture and explain how they differ from American ads; then consider what factors they have in common.

 *Applying Key Ideas*

ANALYZING PERSUASIVE APPEALS IN PRINT ADS

This activity is intended to give you some practice analyzing the persuasive elements in print ads. Put together a portfolio of five print ads that combine pictures and text. Write a paragraph for each that analyzes the ad in terms of its persuasive appeals. For example, you might have an ad that appeals to preferred self-image and the personal needs of love and friendship. Your paragraph should state what the appeals are and how they are conveyed in the ad.

Writing Assignment

PRODUCING AN AD

Select a product that you use regularly and produce your own advertisement for it. Your ad should include graphics or a picture as well as text. Moreover, the two elements should work together effectively. If you want to be particularly creative, try creating a video ad after you write a script for it. Successful responses will incorporate personal needs and will be persuasive.

POLITICAL SPEECHES

Political speeches are interesting exercises in persuasion for several reasons. On a basic level, the people making political speeches are trying to persuade their audiences to vote for them rather than for their opponents. The strategies involved in such persuasion often are complex, combining a full range of support that involves reason, character, and emotion. Candidates must take a clear stand on "the issues." They must address the "character issue" by developing and projecting a character that voters find trustworthy, confident, and capable. This character must be part of the "American middle class" but also must have a certain weighty seriousness that sometimes is referred to as *gravitas*. And candidates must wave the flag to demonstrate their love of country.

At the same time, candidates must try to persuade audiences that their opponents *lack* these qualities and so are poor candidates. When the opponent is an incumbent, the goal is to criticize his or her policies as being incompetent, ineffective, and perhaps even un-American.

Ronald Reagan's campaign in 1980 is perhaps one of the clearer examples of these characteristics in recent years. Among the general population, Reagan was the most popular President since Dwight Eisenhower. Some political analysts have attempted to explain his popularity by arguing that Reagan projected a "father image" that the nation found quite appealing. Reagan's opponent in the 1980 election was President Jimmy Carter, who was one of the least popular presidents since Richard Nixon. Part of Carter's unpopularity was probably linked to a speech he gave in which he stated that America was suffering from a "malaise," or sickliness, that had robbed citizens of their sense of ethics and workers of their dedication to productivity. This assessment came back to haunt Carter during the 1980 campaign, because Reagan used it repeatedly to accuse Carter of being weak, ineffective, pessimistic, and perhaps even un-American.

People who enjoy political speeches often admire the way they reflect complex uses of language. It seems that political speeches, particularly those made during campaigns, represent one of the last examples of true oratory, a form of discourse characterized by the careful interplay of form and message. Although few people ever have the need to produce a political speech, the topic is included here because campaign speeches offer some of the best illustrations of extended persuasion that we have in language. When John F. Kennedy stated in his inaugural address, "Ask not what your country can do for you but what you can do for your country," he set a tone that some analysts argue influenced a generation of Americans. In addition, political speeches constitute a form of persuasive discourse that is a crucial part of the American scene and of the social community to which you belong.

John F. Kennedy

When John F. Kennedy announced his candidacy for President, he immediately faced opposition from a variety of sources because of his religion. No Catholic had ever run for the nation's highest office before. Newspaper editorials, political analysts, Republicans running the Nixon campaign, as well as average citizens from one end of the country to the other were concerned that Kennedy, a Catholic, would place his allegiance to the Roman Catholic Church and the Pope before his allegiance to the United States.

The simple-minded argument was that Kennedy's religion would require him to do whatever the Pope told him to do, that he would be little more than a puppet of the Church. Although such notions seem laughable today, in 1960 they were taken quite seriously, so seriously, in fact, that Kennedy decided to challenge this concern head-on by addressing it directly in the campaign speech presented here.

JOHN F. KENNEDY
Campaign Speech
HOUSTON, TEXAS
September 12, 1960

1 I am grateful for your generous invitation to state my views.

2 While the so-called religious issue is necessarily and properly the chief topic here tonight, I want to emphasize from the outset that I believe that we have far more critical issues in the 1960 election: the spread of Communist influence, until it now festers only ninety miles off the coast of Florida—the humiliating treatment of our President and Vice-President by those who no longer respect our power—the hungry children I saw in West Virginia, the old people who cannot pay their doctor's bills, the families forced to give up their farms—an America with too many slums, with too few schools, and too late to the moon and outer space.

3 These are the real issues which should decide this campaign. And they are not religious issues—for war and hunger and ignorance and despair know no religious barrier.

4 But because I am a Catholic, and no Catholic has ever been elected President, the real issues in this campaign have been obscured—perhaps deliberately, in some quarters less responsible than this. So it is apparently necessary for me to state once again—not what kind of church I believe in, for that should be important only to me, but what kind of America I believe in.

5 I believe in an America where the separation of church and state is absolute— where no Catholic prelate would tell the President (should he be a Catholic) how to act and no Protestant minister would tell his parishioners for whom to vote—where no church or church school is granted any public funds or political preference—and where no man is denied public office merely because his religion differs from the President who might appoint him or the people who might elect him.

6 I believe in an America that is officially neither Catholic, Protestant nor Jewish—where no public official either requests or accepts instructions on public policy from the Pope, the National Council of Churches or any other ecclesiastical

source—where no religious body seeks to impose its will directly or indirectly upon the general populace or the public acts of its officials—and where religious liberty is so indivisible that an act against one church is treated as an act against all.

7   For while this year it may be a Catholic against whom the finger of suspicion is pointed, in other years it has been, and may someday be again, a Jew—or a Quaker—or a Unitarian—or a Baptist. It was Virginia's harassment of Baptist preachers, for example, that led to Jefferson's statute of religious freedom. Today, I may be the victim—but tomorrow it may be you—until the whole fabric of our harmonious society is ripped apart at a time of great national peril.

8   Finally, I believe in an America where religious intolerance will someday end—where all men and all churches are treated as equal—where every man has the same right to attend or not to attend the church of his choice—where there is no Catholic vote, no antiCatholic vote, no bloc voting of any kind—and where Catholics, Protestants and Jews, both the lay and the pastoral level, will refrain from those attitudes of disdain and division which have so often marred their works in the past, and promote instead the American ideal of brotherhood.

9   That is the kind of America in which I believe. And it represents the kind of Presidency in which I believe—a great office that must be neither humbled by making it the instrument of any religious group, nor tarnished by arbitrarily withholding it, its occupancy, from the members of any religious group. I believe in a President whose views on religion are his own private affair, neither imposed upon him by the nation or imposed by the nation upon him as a condition to holding that office.

10   I would not look with favor upon a President working to subvert the First Amendment's guarantees of religious liberty (nor would our system of checks and balances permit him to do so). And neither do I look with favor upon those who would work to subvert Article VI of the Constitution by requiring a religious test—even by indirection—for if they disagree with that safeguard, they should be openly working to repeal it.

11   I want a Chief Executive whose public acts are responsible to all and obligated to none—who can attend any ceremony, service or dinner his office may appropriately require him to fulfill and whose fulfillment of his Presidential office is not limited or conditioned by any religious oath, ritual or obligation.

12   This is the kind of America I believe in—and this is the kind of America I fought for in the South Pacific and the kind my brother died for in Europe. No one suggested than [sic] that we might have a "divided loyalty," that we did "not believe in liberty" or that we belonged to a disloyal group that threatened "the freedoms from which our forefathers died."

13   And in fact this is the kind of America for which our forefathers did die when they fled here to escape religious test oaths, that denied office to members of less favored churches, when they fought for the Constitution, the Bill of Rights, the Virginia Statute of Religious Freedom—and when they fought at the shrine I visited today—the Alamo. For side by side with Bowie and Crocket died Fuentes and McCafferty and Bailey and Bedillio and Carey—but no one knows whether they were Catholics or not. For there was no religious test there.

14   I ask you tonight to follow in that tradition, to judge me on the basis of fourteen years in the congress—on my declared stands against an ambassador to the Vatican, against unconstitutional aid to parochial schools, and against any boycott of the public schools (which I attended myself)—instead of judging me on the basis of these pamphlets and publications we have all seen that carefully select quotations out of context from the statements of Catholic Church leaders, usually in other countries, frequently in other centuries, and rarely relevant to any situation here—and always omitting, of course, that statement of the American bishops in 1948 which strongly endorsed church-state separation.

15 I do not consider these other quotations binding upon my public acts—why should you? But let me say, with respect to other countries, that I am wholly opposed to the state being used by any religious group, Catholic or Protestant, to compel, prohibit or persecute the free exercise of any other religion. And that goes for any persecution at any time, by anyone, in any country.

16 And I hope that you and I condemn with equal fervor those nations which deny their Presidency to Protestants and those which deny it to Catholics. And rather than cite the misdeeds of those who differ, I would also cite the record of the Catholic Church in such nations as France and Ireland—and the independence of such statesmen as de Gaulle and Adenauer.

17 But let me stress again that these are my views—for, contrary to common newspaper usage, I am not the Catholic candidate for President. I am the Democratic Party's candidate for President, who happens also to be a Catholic.

18 I do not speak for my church on public matters—and the church does not speak for me.

19 Whatever issues may come before me as President, if I should be elected—on birth control, divorce, censorship, gambling, or any other subject—I will make my decision in accordance with these views, in accordance with what my conscience tells me to be in the national interest, and without regard to outside religious pressure or dictate. And no power or threat of punishment could cause me to decide otherwise.

20 But if the time should ever come—and I do not concede any conflict to be remotely possible—when my office would require me to either violate my conscience, or violate the national interest, then I would resign the office, and I hope any other conscientious public servant would do likewise.

21 But I do not intend to apologize for these views to my critics of either Catholic or Protestant faith, nor do I intend to disavow either my views or my church in order to win this election. If I should lose on the real issues, I shall return to my seat in the Senate, satisfied that I tried my best and was fairly judged.

22 But if this election is decided on the basis that 40,000,000 Americans lost their chance of being President on the day they were baptized, then it is the whole nation that will be the loser in the eyes of Catholics and nonCatholics around the world, in the eyes of history, and in the eyes of our own people.

23 But if, on the other hand, I should win this election, I shall devote every effort of mind and spirit to fulfilling the oath of the Presidency—practically identical, I might add, with the oath I have taken for fourteen years in the Congress. For, without reservation, I can, and I quote, "solemnly swear that I will faithfully execute the office of President of the United States and will to the best of my ability preserve, protect and defend the Constitution, so help me God."

Kennedy begins this speech by setting it in an appropriate context. He wants to make clear that the real issues in the campaign are "war and hunger and ignorance and despair." In doing so, he is appealing to the audience's reason. By implication, the question of his religious beliefs is trivial and is maliciously intended to distract voters' attention away from the real issues. Kennedy therefore does not focus on the religious question directly until paragraph 17. He could have stated at the outset that his religious beliefs have no bearing on the campaign and would have no bearing on his ability to carry out the duties of the President, if he were elected. Such a statement, however, would deny Kennedy the opportunity to develop his character, which is an important function of campaign speeches and persuasion. Kennedy begins to describe America rather than himself. Yet his description, combined with the phrase, "I believe," helps the audience identify Kennedy with America and all that it stands for. The two become linked.

In paragraph 6, Kennedy effectively shifts the focus slightly, portraying himself as a victim of religious intolerance and thereby appealing to the audience's emotions. This shift works well because Americans generally have despised religious intolerance, at least in theory, since the Pilgrims landed at Plymouth Rock. By adopting the role of a victim, Kennedy gains the sympathy of the audience. In addition, it is the case that various religious groups have discriminated against other religious groups. Christians, for example, have persecuted Jews in one way or another for almost 2,000 years. Kennedy reminds the audience that he may be the victim today, but "tomorrow it may be you." This approach helps the audience identify with Kennedy and the difficult situation he is in; it is an effective use of role reversal. Instead of approaching the audience as an insider and then striving to build a stance of insider to insider, Kennedy casts himself as a religious outsider and suggests that the audience—as potential victims—are fellow outsiders.

The speech, however, is not about America; it is about the presidency. Kennedy skillfully shifts the focus again in paragraphs 8 and 9 to talk about the kind of presidency he believes in. This part of the speech is similar to the first part in that Kennedy defines himself and the presidency simultaneously, as though they are one. The goal is to get the audience to think of Kennedy as President. This speech is quite successful because Kennedy's definition of the presidency is congruent with most Americans' views. It combines a "common sense" approach to handling matters of public policy with a decisive, crisp tone that people associate with effective leadership.

Politicians must address audiences on a personal level, as one vulnerable, imperfect human being to another. Kennedy began this process in paragraph 6 when he linked himself and the audience as outsiders. He develops the emotional appeal more fully in paragraph 13 after he has defined himself in ways that the audience can identify with. He asks people "to judge me on the basis of fourteen years in the congress." For any person to ask a group for such judgment is a gamble, but Kennedy has used the process of defining himself and stating his beliefs to become a "member" of the group whose judgment he solicits, so the risk is low. Evidence for this view is in paragraph 15, where Kennedy explicitly links himself and the audience: "I hope that you and I condemn with equal fervor those nations which deny their Presidency to Protestants and those which deny it to Catholics."

Paragraph 17 comprises Kennedy's most direct statement on the issue of religion. The placement near the end of the speech is important. Kennedy has accomplished his major goals and can be more direct. In addition, this simple, straightforward assertion leaves no room for doubt about Kennedy's position: "I do not speak for my church on public matters—and the church does not speak for me." The statement prevents the opposition (in this case the Nixon campaign) from claiming that Kennedy has dodged the question.

Linked Assignment

PREPARING FOR A POLITICAL CAMPAIGN

This activity gives you a chance to engage in some role-playing and generate information and ideas for the writing assignment below. An important part of political success consists of knowing what the issues are that concern voters. In some cases, such knowledge might be intuitive, but in most instances it comes from careful and thoughtful evaluations of current events and voters' reactions to them. Knowledge comes from research, in other words. For this exercise, you must do a bit of role-playing. Pretend that you want to run for an office in either student or local government (you must decide which). Investigate the issues and write a one–two-page paper that describes what they are.

Some suggestions: You may want to begin by brainstorming with classmates to generate ideas and topics; you may want to survey the campus or local newspaper, especially the editorial sections and letters to the editor, to see what people are writing about; or you may want to attend a student or town council meeting.

Writing Assignment

A POLITICAL SPEECH

Using the research you completed for the linked assignment for this task, write a speech that aims to persuade voters to support your campaign. The speech should be 5 to 10 minutes long, and you should be prepare to deliver it—not simply *read it*—to your class.

GROUP ACTIVITIES: A POLITICAL SPEECH

1. Re-examine the issues that arose during your work on the linked assignment. You have generated some ideas; now you should discuss them in detail to determine how useful they are. Have you identified topics that truly are of political interest among your target group of voters?

2. Voter participation has declined nationwide, but it is especially acute on college campuses where large numbers of student body elections engage only about 10% of students. Split your group in half for some library research. One half should investigate the percentage of students who voted in the last two campus elections, and the other half should do the same for the last two local elections. After getting the numbers, investigate the demographic characteristics of the voters. You should be looking for factors such as race, gender, socioeconomic status, year in school, age, membership in campus or community organizations, and so forth.

3. After collecting this information, conduct another brainstorming session in which you examine how voter turnout and demographics might influence your campaign speech.

4. On the basis of the ideas generated in this brainstorming session, write a brief paragraph that summarizes the persuasive strategies and persuasive appeals that will be most effective given your anticipated audience. From this paragraph, produce a short list of the "campaign issues" that you intend to address in your speech.

5. Share the paragraph and the list with your groupmates to get their input on how well you have understood your audience and how well your issues and appeals match that audience.

6. Produce a draft of your speech and share it with your groupmates so they can provide input. After you have revised this draft, begin practicing your delivery alone. Your goal is to deliver a speech, not simply to read a paper. Watching yourself in the mirror will help with your delivery, but the ideal situation is to videotape yourself and play back the tape. If you don't own a video camera or cannot borrow one from a friend or family member, check with your school library or Instructional Development Office. Many schools have cameras that students may borrow.

7. After you have practiced your speech alone, you should meet with your group outside of class so that each member can present his or her speech to the others. This practice will help you feel more comfortable addressing an audience, and it will allow your groupmates to give you useful advice that you can use to polish your delivery.

Interpreting short Fiction

Interpreting literature can be a rewarding experience because it gives writers freedom to explore the universals of the human
condition that characterize literature and
to make those universals relevant to individual reader

CHAPTER TWELVE

Interpreting Short Fiction

Interpreting literature can be a rewarding experience because it gives writers freedom to explore the universals of the human condition that characterize literature and to make those universals relevant to individual readers. Unfortunately, it is not feasible to address the different forms of literature—fiction, poetry, and drama—in one chapter. That task is more appropriate for an entire book. We can, however, examine how to interpret a popular form of literature—short fiction.[1]

Teachers ask students to interpret literature for several reasons, but one of the more important has to do with four basic assumptions about literary texts:

- Literature contains universal truths, or themes, characteristic of the human condition.
- These themes convey some beneficial message.
- The themes and the message generally are hidden in the text, and extracting them is the aim of literary analysis.
- The goal of an intelligent reader, as well as anyone who writes about literature, is not only to discover the themes and the message but also to make them meaningful on an individual level.

On the basis of these assumptions, the fundamental question to answer when interpreting a piece of short fiction is "What does this text mean?" The question of meaning is familiar, but when explaining what a short story means, writers must provide a careful analysis of the elements that make up most works of fiction. These elements are *plot, theme, message, characters, setting, point of view,* and *irony*.[2] In addition, they usually must argue for a particular reading of the story, for an interpretation of the author's message.

To illustrate these key elements, let's consider John Steinbeck's popular short story "The Chrysanthemums."

---

[1]Although this chapter deals specifically with short fiction, much of what you'll learn here can be applied to other types of literature.

[2]Some modern fiction modifies these elements or drops them altogether.

THE CHRYSANTHEMUMS

John Steinbeck

1 The high grey-flannel fog of winter closed off the Salinas Valley from the sky and from all the rest of the world. On every side it sat like a lid on the mountains and made of the great valley a closed pot. On the broad, level land floor the gang plows bit deep and left the black earth shining like metal where the shares had cut. On the foothill ranches across the Salinas River, the yellow stubble fields seemed to be bathed in pale cold sunshine, but there was no sunshine in the valley now in December. The thick willow scrub along the river flamed with sharp and positive yellow leaves.

2 It was a time of quiet and of waiting. The air was cold and tender. A light wind blew up from the southwest so that the farmers were mildly hopeful of a good rain before long; but fog and rain do not go together.

3 Across the river, on Henry Allen's foothill ranch there was little work to be done, for the hay was cut and stored and the orchards were plowed up to receive the rain deeply when it should come. The cattle on the higher slopes were becoming shaggy and rough-coated.

4 Elisa Allen, working in her flower garden, looked down across the yard and saw Henry, her husband, talking to two men in business suits. The three of them stood by the tractor shed, each man with one foot on the side of the little Fordson. They smoked cigarettes and studied the machine as they talked.

5 Elisa watched them for a moment and then went back to her work. She was thirty-five. Her face was lean and strong and her eyes were as clear as water. Her figure looked blocked and heavy in her gardening costume, a man's black hat pulled low down over her eyes, clodhopper shoes, a figured print dress almost completely covered by a big corduroy apron with four big pockets to hold the snips, the trowel and scratcher, the seeds and the knife she worked with. She wore heavy leather gloves to protect her hands while she worked.

6 She was cutting down the old year's chrysanthemum stalks with a pair of short and powerful scissors. She looked down toward the men by the tractor shed now and then. Her face was eager and mature and handsome; even her work with the scissors was over-eager, over-powerful. The chrysanthemum stems seemed too small and easy for her energy.

7 She brushed a cloud of hair out of her eyes with the back of her glove, and left a smudge of earth on her cheek in doing it. Behind her stood the neat white farm house with red geraniums close-banked around it as high as the windows. It was a hard-swept looking little house, with hard-polished windows, and a clean mud-mat on the front steps.

8 Elisa cast another glance toward the tractor shed. The strangers were getting into their Ford coupe. She took off a glove and put her strong fingers down into the forest of new green chrysanthemum sprouts that were growing around the old roots. She spread the leaves and looked down among the close-growing stems. No aphids were there, no sowbugs or snails or cutworms. Her terrier fingers destroyed such pests before they could get started.

9 Elisa started at the sound of her husband's voice. He had come near quietly, and he leaned over the wire fence that protected her flower garden from cattle and dogs and chickens.

10 "At it again," he said. "You've got a strong new crop coming."

11 Elisa straightened her back and pulled on the gardening glove again. "Yes. They'll be strong this coming year." In her tone and on her face there was a little smugness.

12 "You've got a gift with things," Henry observed. "Some of those yellow chrysanthemums you had this year were ten inches across. I wish you'd work out in the orchard and raise some apples that big."

13   Her eyes sharpened. "Maybe I could do it, too. I've a gift with things, all right. My mother had it. She could stick anything in the ground and make it grow. She said it was having planters' hands that knew how to do it."

14   "Well, it sure works with flowers," he said.

15   "Henry, who were those men you were talking to?"

16   "Why, sure, that's what I came to tell you. They were from the Western Meat Company. I sold those thirty head of three-year-old steers. Got nearly my own price, too."

17   "Good," she said. "Good for you."

18   "And I thought," he continued, "I thought how it's Saturday afternoon, and we might go into Salinas for dinner at a restaurant, and then to a picture show—to celebrate, you see."

19   "Good," she repeated. "Oh, yes. That will be good."

20   Henry put on his joking tone. "There's fights tonight. How'd you like to go to the fights?"

21   "Oh, no," she said breathlessly. "No, I wouldn't like fights."

22   "Just fooling, Elisa. We'll go to a movie. Let's see. It's two now. I'm going to take Scotty and bring down those steers from the hill. It'll take us maybe two hours. We'll go in town about five and have dinner at the Cominos Hotel. Like that?"

23   "Of course I'll like it. It's good to eat away from home."

24   "All right, then. I'll go get up a couple of horses."

25   She said, "I'll have plenty of time to transplant some of these sets, I guess."

26   She heard her husband calling Scotty down by the barn. And a little later she saw the two men ride up the pale yellow hillside in search of the steers.

27   There was a little square sandy bed kept for rooting the chrysanthemums. With her trowel she turned the soil over and over, and smoothed it and patted it firm. Then she dug ten parallel trenches to receive the sets. Back at the chrysanthemum bed she pulled out the little crisp shoots, trimmed off the leaves of each one with her scissors and laid it on a small orderly pile.

28   A squeak of wheels and plod of hoofs came from the road. Elisa looked up. The country road ran along the dense bank of willows and cottonwoods that bordered the river, and up this road came a curious vehicle, curiously drawn. It was an old spring-wagon, with a round canvas top on it like the cover of a prairie schooner. It was drawn by an old bay horse and a little grey-and-white burro. A big stubble-bearded man sat between the cover flaps and drove the crawling team. Underneath the wagon, between the hind wheels, a lean and rangy mongrel dog walked sedately. Words were painted on the canvas, in clumsy, crooked letters. "Pots, pans, knives, sisors, lawn mores, Fixed." Two rows of articles, and the triumphantly definitive "Fixed" below. The black paint had run down in little sharp points beneath each letter.

29   Elisa, squatting on the ground, watched to see the crazy, loose-jointed wagon pass by. But it didn't pass. It turned into the farm road in front of her house, crooked old wheels skirling and squeaking. The rangy dog darted from between the wheels and ran ahead. Instantly the two ranch shepherds flew out at him. Then all three stopped, and with stiff and quivering tails, with taut straight legs, with ambassadorial dignity, they slowly circled, sniffing daintily. The caravan pulled up to Elisa's wire fence and stopped. Now the newcomer dog, feeling out-numbered, lowered his tail and retired under the wagon with raised hackles and bared teeth.

30   The man on the wagon seat called out, "That's a bad dog in a fight when he gets started."

31   Elisa laughed. "I see he is. How soon does he generally get started?"

32   The man caught up her laughter and echoed it heartily. "Sometimes not for weeks and weeks," he said. He climbed stiffly down, over the wheel. The horse and the donkey drooped like unwatered flowers.

33   Elisa saw that he was a very big man. Although his hair and beard were greying, he did not look old. His worn black suit was wrinkled and spotted with grease. The

laughter had disappeared from his face and eyes the moment his laughing voice ceased. His eyes were dark, and they were full of the brooding that gets in the eyes of teamsters and of sailors. The calloused hands he rested on the wire fence were cracked, and every crack was a black line. He took off his battered hat.

34   "I'm off my general road, ma'am," he said. "Does this dirt road cut over across the river to the Los Angeles highway?"

35   Elisa stood up and shoved the thick scissors in her apron pocket. "Well, yes, it does, but it winds around and then fords the river. I don't think your team could pull through the sand."

36   He replied with some asperity, "It might surprise you what them beasts can pull through."

37   "When they get started?" she asked.

38   He smiled for a second. "Yes. When they get started."

39   "Well," said Elisa, "I think you'll save time if you go back to the Salinas road and pick up the highway there."

40   He drew a big finger down the chicken wire and made it sing. "I ain't in any hurry, ma'am. I go from Seattle to San Diego and back every year. Takes all my time. About six months each way. I aim to follow nice weather."

41   Elisa took off her gloves and stuffed them in the apron pocket with the scissors. She touched the under edge of her man's hat, searching for fugitive hairs. "That sounds like a nice kind of a way to live," she said.

42   He leaned confidentially over the fence. "Maybe you noticed the writing on my wagon. I mend pots and sharpen knives and scissors. You got any of them things to do?"

43   "Oh, no," she said quickly. "Nothing like that." Her eyes hardened with resistance.

44   "Scissors is the worst thing," he explained. "Most people just ruin scissors trying to sharpen 'em, but I know how. I got a special tool. It's a little bobbit kind of thing, and patented. But it sure does the trick."

45   "No. My scissors are all sharp."

46   "All right, then. Take a pot," he continued earnestly, "a bent pot, or a pot with a hole. I can make it like new so you don't have to buy no new ones. That's a saving for you."

47   "No," she said shortly. "I tell you I have nothing like that for you to do."

48   His face fell to an exaggerated sadness. His voice took on a whining undertone. "I ain't had a thing to do today. Maybe I won't have no supper tonight. You see I'm off my regular road. I know folks on the highway clear from Seattle to San Diego. They save their things for me to sharpen up because they know I do it so good and save them money."

49   "I'm sorry," Elisa said irritably. "I haven't anything for you to do."

50   His eyes left her face and fell to searching the ground. They roamed about until they came to the chrysanthemum bed where she had been working. "What's them plants, ma'am?"

51   The irritation and resistance melted from Elisa's face. "Oh, those are chrysanthemums, giant whites and yellows. I raise them every year, bigger than anybody around here."

52   "Kind of a long-stemmed flower? Looks like a quick puff of colored smoke?" he asked.

53   "That's it. What a nice way to describe them."

54   "They smell kind of nasty till you get used to them," he said.

55   "It's a good bitter smell," she retorted, "not nasty at all."

56   He changed his tone quickly. "I like the smell myself."

57   "I had ten-inch blooms this year," she said.

58   The man leaned farther over the fence. "Look. I know a lady down the road a piece, has got the nicest garden you ever seen. Got nearly every kind of flower but

no chrysantheums. Last time I was mending a copper-bottom washtub for her (that's a hard job but I do it good), she said to me, 'If you ever run acrost some nice chrysantheums I wish you'd try to get me a few seeds.' That's what she told me."

59   Elisa's eyes grew alert and eager. "She couldn't have known much about chrysanthemums. You can raise them from seed, but it's much easier to root the little sprouts you see there."

60   "Oh," he said. "I s'pose I can't take none to her, then."

61   "Why yes you can," Elisa cried. "I can put some in damp sand, and you can carry them right along with you. They'll take root in the pot if you keep them damp. And then she can transplant them."

62   "She'd sure like to have some, ma'am. You say they're nice ones?"

63   "Beautiful," she said. "Oh, beautiful." Her eyes shone. She tore off the battered hat and shook out her dark pretty hair. "I'll put them in a flower pot, and you can take them right with you. Come into the yard."

64   While the man came through the picket gate Elisa ran excitedly along the geranium-bordered path to the back of the house. And she returned carrying a big red flower pot. The gloves were forgotten now. She kneeled on the ground by the starting bed and dug up the sandy soil with her fingers and scooped it into the bright new flower pot. Then she picked up the little pile of shoots she had prepared. With her strong fingers she pressed them into the sand and tamped around them with her knuckles. The man stood over her. "I'll tell you what to do," she said. "You remember so you can tell the lady."

65   "Yes, I'll try to remember."

66   "Well, look. These will take root in about a month. Then she must set them out, about a foot apart in good rich earth like this, see?" She lifted a handful of dark soil for him to look at. "They'll grow fast and tall. Now remember this: In July tell her to cut them down, about eight inches from the ground."

67   "Before they bloom?" he asked.

68   "Yes, before they bloom." Her face was tight with eagerness. "They'll grow right up again. About the last of September the buds will start."

69   She stopped and seemed perplexed. "It's the budding that takes the most care," she said hesitantly. "I don't know how to tell you." She looked deep into his eyes, searchingly. Her mouth opened a little, and she seemed to be listening. "I'll try to tell you," she said. "Did you ever hear of planting hands?"

70   "Can't say I have, ma'am."

71   "Well, I can only tell you what it feels like. It's when you're picking off the buds you don't want. Everything goes right down into your fingertips. You watch your fingers work. They do it themselves. You can feel how it is. They pick and pick the buds. They never make a mistake. They're with the plant. Do you see? Your fingers and the plant. You can feel that, right up your arm. They know. They never make a mistake. You can feel it. When you're like that you can't do anything wrong. Do you see that? Can you understand that?"

72   She was kneeling on the ground looking up at him. Her breast swelled passionately.

73   The man's eyes narrowed. He looked away self-consciously. "Maybe I know," he said. "Sometimes in the night in the wagon there——"

74   Elisa's voice grew husky. She broke in on him, "I've never lived as you do, but I know what you mean. When the night is dark—why, the stars are sharp-pointed, and there's quiet. Why, you rise up and up! Every pointed star gets driven into your body. It's like that. Hot and sharp and—lovely."

75   Kneeling there, her hand went out toward his legs in the greasy black trousers. Her hesitant fingers almost touched the cloth. Then her hand dropped to the ground. She crouched low like a fawning dog.

76   He said, "It's nice, just like you say. Only when you don't have no dinner, it ain't."

77   She stood up then, very straight, and her face was ashamed. She held the flower pot out to him and placed it gently in his arms. "Here. Put it in your wagon, on the seat, where you can watch it. Maybe I can find something for you to do."

78   At the back of the house she dug in the can pile and found two old and battered aluminum saucepans. She carried them back and gave them to him. "Here, maybe you can fix these."

79   His manner changed. He became professional. "Good as new I can fix them." At the back of his wagon he set a little anvil, and out of an oily tool box dug a small machine hammer. Elisa came through the gate to watch him while he pounded out the dents in the kettles. His mouth grew sure and knowing. At a difficult part of the work he sucked his under-lip.

80   "You sleep right in the wagon?" Elisa asked.

81   "Right in the wagon, ma'am. Rain or shine I'm dry as a cow in there."

82   "It must be nice," she said. "It must be very nice. I wish women could do such things."

83   "It ain't the right kind of a life for a woman."

84   Her upper lip raised a little, showing her teeth. "How do you know? How can you tell?" she said.

85   "I don't know, ma'am," he protested. "Of course I don't know. Now here's your kettles, done. You don't have to buy no new ones."

86   "How much?"

87   "Oh, fifty cents'll do. I keep my prices down and my work good. That's why I have all them satisfied customers up and down the highway."

88   Elisa brought him a fifty-cent piece from the house and dropped it in his hand. "You might be surprised to have a rival some time. I can sharpen scissors, too. And I can beat the dents out of little pots. I could show you what a woman might do."

89   He put his hammer back in the oily box and shoved the little anvil out of sight. "It would be a lonely life for a woman, ma'am, and a scarey life, too, with animals creeping under the wagon all night." He climbed over the singletree, steadying himself with a hand on the burro's white rump. He settled himself in the seat, picked up the lines. "Thank you kindly, ma'am," he said. "I'll do like you told me; I'll go back and catch the Salinas road."

90   "Mind," she called, "if you're long in getting there, keep the sand damp."

91   "Sand, ma'am? . . . Sand? Oh, sure. You mean around the chrysantheums. Sure I will." He clucked his tongue. The beasts leaned luxuriously into their collars. The mongrel dog took his place between the back wheels. The wagon turned and crawled out the entrance road and back the way it had come, along the river.

92   Elisa stood in front of her wire fence watching the slow progress of the caravan. Her shoulders were straight, her head thrown back, her eyes half-closed, so that the scene came vaguely into them. Her lips moved silently, forming the words "Good-bye—good-bye." Then she whispered, "That's a bright direction. There's a glowing there." The sound of her whisper startled her. She shook herself free and looked about to see whether anyone had been listening. Only the dogs had heard. They lifted their heads toward her from their sleeping in the dust, and then stretched out their chins and settled asleep again. Elisa turned and ran hurriedly into the house.

93   In the kitchen she reached behind the stove and felt the water tank. It was full of hot water from the noonday cooking. In the bathroom she tore off her soiled clothes and flung them into the corner. And then she scrubbed herself with a little block of pumice, legs and thighs, loins and chest and arms, until her skin was scratched and red. When she had dried herself she stood in front of a mirror in her bedroom and looked at her body. She tightened her stomach and threw out her chest. She turned and looked over her shoulder at her back.

94   After a while she began to dress, slowly. She put on her newest underclothing and her nicest stockings and the dress which was the symbol of her prettiness. She worked carefully on her hair, penciled her eyebrows and rouged her lips.

95   Before she was finished she heard the little thunder of hoofs and the shouts of Henry and his helper as they drove the red steers into the corral. She heard the gate bang shut and set herself for Henry's arrival.

96   His step sounded on the porch. He entered the house calling, "Elisa, where are you?"

97   "In my room, dressing. I'm not ready. There's hot water for your bath. Hurry up. It's getting late."

98   When she heard him splashing in the tub, Elisa laid his dark suit on the bed, and shirt and socks and tie beside it. She stood his polished shoes on the floor beside the bed. Then she went to the porch and sat primly and stiffly down. She looked toward the river road where the willow-line was still yellow with frosted leaves so that under the high grey fog they seemed a thin band of sunshine. This was the only color in the grey afternoon. She sat unmoving for a long time. Her eyes blinked rarely.

99   Henry came banging out of the door, shoving his tie inside his vest as he came. Elisa stiffened and her face grew tight. Henry stopped short and looked at her. "Why—why, Elisa. You look so nice!"

100   "Nice? You think I look nice? What do you mean by 'nice'?"

101   Henry blundered on. "I don't know. I mean you look different, strong and happy."

102   "I am strong? Yes, strong. What do you mean 'strong'?"

103   He looked bewildered. "You're playing some kind of a game," he said helplessly. "It's a kind of a play. You look strong enough to break a calf over your knee, happy enough to eat it like a watermelon."

104   For a second she lost her rigidity. "Henry! Don't talk like that. You didn't know what you said." She grew complete again. "I'm strong," she boasted. "I never knew before how strong."

105   Henry looked down toward the tractor shed, and when he brought his eyes back to her, they were his own again. "I'll get out the car. You can put on your coat while I'm starting."

106   Elisa went into the house. She heard him drive to the gate and idle down his motor, and then she took a long time to put on her hat. She pulled it here and pressed it there. When Henry turned the motor off she slipped into her coat and went out.

107   The little roadster bounced along on the dirt road by the river, raising the birds and driving the rabbits into the brush. Two cranes flapped heavily over the willow-line and dropped into the river-bed.

108   Far ahead on the road Elisa saw a dark speck. She knew.

109   She tried not to look as they passed it, but her eyes would not obey. She whispered to herself sadly, "He might have thrown them off the road. That wouldn't have been much trouble, not very much. But he kept the pot," she explained. "He had to keep the pot. That's why he couldn't get them off the road."

110   The roadster turned a bend and she saw the caravan ahead. She swung full around toward her husband so she could not see the little covered wagon and the mismatched team as the car passed them.

111   In a moment it was over. The thing was done. She did not look back.

112   She said loudly, to be heard above the motor, "It will be good, tonight, a good dinner."

113   "Now you're changed again," Henry complained. He took one hand from the wheel and patted her knee. "I ought to take you in to dinner oftener. It would be good for both of us. We get so heavy out on the ranch."

114   "Henry," she asked, "could we have wine at dinner?"

115   "Sure we could. Say! That will be fine."

116   She was silent for a while; then she said, "Henry, at those prize fights, do the men hurt each other very much?"

117   "Sometimes a little, not often. Why?"

118   "Well, I've read how they break noses, and blood runs down their chests. I've read how the fighting gloves get heavy and soggy with blood."

119   He looked around at her. "What's the matter, Elisa? I didn't know you read things like that." He brought the car to a stop, then turned to the right over the Salinas River bridge.

120   "Do any women ever go to the fights?" she asked.

121   "Oh, sure, some. What's the matter, Elisa? Do you want to go? I don't think you'd like it, but I'll take you if you really want to go."

122   She relaxed limply in the seat. "Oh, no. No. I don't want to go. I'm sure I don't." Her face was turned away from him. "It will be enough if we can have wine. It will be plenty." She turned up her coat collar so he could not see that she was crying weakly—like an old woman.

KEY ELEMENTS OF FICTION

In "The Chrysanthemums," plot, theme, characters, and setting are easy to recognize. At the beginning, Steinbeck sets the scene for readers, introducing characters, location, historical information, and a "problem." The problem unfolds as the plot develops, and then characters, setting, structure, and tone work together to develop the theme of the work. *The theme is that feature of the human condition that a writer conveys in a story.* The key elements also work together to convey the story's *message*, which is *what a writer wants readers to learn about the theme.*

Let's examine these elements in more detail and see how they work in "The Chrysanthemums" and, in the process, how you can use them for an interpretive paper about short fiction (see Table 12.1).

Setting

Setting consists of the place, time, and atmosphere of a story, which often affect characters as well as the theme and message of a work in various ways. The setting for "The Chrysanthemums" is the Salinas Valley in California, which even today is a rich agricultural region. More specifically, the setting is the Allen ranch, where "the hay was cut and stored and the orchards were plowed up to receive the rain deeply when it should come." The time isn't specified, but "The Chrysanthemums" appeared in *The Long Valley*, published in 1938, so it is safe to say that the time of the story is during the mid-1930s.

Atmosphere in short fiction usually is composed of minor details that give readers an overall impression of the setting and consequently the story. These details may be conveyed through simple descriptions, but they can be conveyed in other ways, such as the reactions of characters to the setting and their thoughts about it.

The atmosphere of "The Chrysanthemums" frequently is characterized as oppressive or depressing, and it is easy to understand why. The first paragraph, for example, describes a cold, isolated place. Steinbeck writes that the "high grey-flannel fog of winter closed off the Salinas Valley from the sky and from all the rest of the world." The time is December. But the valley, or at least the Allen ranch, also is a place where certain pressures build, as suggested by the next sentence: "On every

TABLE 12.1
Key Elements of Fiction

Element	Definition	Example From "The Chrysanthemums"
Setting	The place, time, and atmosphere off of a story.	"The high grey-flannel fog of winter closed the Salinas Valley from the sky and from all the rest of the world. On every side it sat like a lid on the mountains and made of the great valley a closed pot. On the broad, level land floor the gang plows bit deep and left the black earth shining like metal where the shares had cut. On the foothill ranches across the Salinas River, the yellow stubble fields seemed to be bathed in the pale cold sunshine, but there was no sunshine in the valley now in December."
Characters	The figures that inhabit fiction; the living beings that stories are about.	Elisa Allen, her husband Hank, and the tinker.
Plot	The sequence of events in a story. Events must be interrelated in ways that involve characters, theme, and message. The actions of characters must develop the theme and convey the message.	Elisa, dressed in work clothes, is tending her flowers when she is approached by a tinker. The tinker offers to repair any household items she may have, but she refuses. The tinker compliments Elisa on her flowers, claiming that a customer has been looking for some plantings for her own garden. The flattery changes Elisa, makes her less harsh. She offers to put some plantings in a pot so that the tinker can take them to the woman. As she is putting the chrysanthemums in the pot, she expresses the wish that women could travel about alone as the tinker does, and then she changes her mind about giving him some work. She offers him two old pots to repair, and so on.
Theme	The universal truth about life that a work of literature conveys.	"The Chrysanthemums" deals with loneliness, repression (both emotional and sexual), and ultimately compromise, themes that are part of everyone's life just as surely as they are part of Elisa Allen's.
Message	The lesson that a writer wants readers to learn from the story. Stated another way, the message is the author's particular interpretation of a theme.	Because a work's message is interpreted by readers, I can offer only possibilities for "The Chrysanthemums." Consider the following: After her encounter with the tinker, Elisa seems ready to overcome the factors that keep her repressed and asexual. She misses the chance, however, when she allows the tinker's betrayal to crush her emotionally. The final scene shows Elisa asking very little from life, simply that she be allowed to have wine with dinner. The message may be that people can't easily free themselves from the social and personal factors that keep them repressed, that freedom requires much more effort than Elisa is able to muster.
Point of View	The narrative relationship between writers and their fiction; the mediating presence of the writer in a given work.	There are four points of view that a writer may adopt: omniscient, limited omniscient, first person, and dramatic. In "The Chrysanthemums," the point of view is dramatic because readers come to know characters on the basis of what they say and do.
Irony	A contrast between appearance and reality.	At the beginning of the story, Steinbeck describes Elisa Allen in a way that makes her seem strong and powerful: "Her face was lean and strong," "her work with the scissors was over-eager, over-powerful." Nevertheless, as the tinker is standing over her, Elisa's "hand went out toward his legs in the greasy black trousers. Her hesitant fingers almost touched the cloth. Then her hand dropped to the ground. She crouched low like a fawning dog."

side it [the fog] sat like a lid on the mountains and made of the great valley a closed pot." This sentence seems to forecast the condition of Elisa Allen.

The atmosphere of a story also can influence the way readers respond to the narrative; it can create a certain *mood*. Many readers, for instance, judge the mood of "The Chrysanthemums" to be one of hopelessness and resignation, whereas "The Descent of Man," which appears later in this chapter, usually is judged to have an ironic mood.

Stories are about people, the *characters* that inhabit fiction. Even those stories, such as *The Hobbit, Animal Farm*, and *Aesop's Fables*, that are about nonhuman creatures or animals give their characters human traits and personalities. Reading fiction therefore involves reading about people and their interactions. The main characters in fiction sometimes are called *protagonists*. They usually are striving to overcome a problem, and in many instances they are striving to overcome the problem established at the beginning of the story. Elisa Allen, for example, is the protagonist of "The Chrysanthemums."

Protagonists are opposed by *antagonists*. Antagonists are not always villains; in many stories they aren't even human. The whale is Captain Ahab's antagonist in Melville's *Moby Dick*; capitalism is one antagonist in Steinbeck's *Grapes of Wrath*; and nature and loneliness are antagonists in Dufoe's *Robinson Crusoe*. In "The Chrysanthemums," there may be several antagonists, depending on a reader's interpretation. Some readers, for example, see Elisa's husband as an antagonist even though he seems to strive to please her. Others see the ranch or ranch life as the antagonist.

Character development is at the heart of an author's artistry. Certain characters simply entertain; others populate the background of a story. More important characters (especially protagonists), however, may serve a teaching function. In a stereotypical way, they often possess negative traits that all readers share to one degree or another. Most people sometimes are meek, passive, proud, arrogant, selfish, romantic, or easily angered, and fictional characters tend to possess these traits to a fault. A character will not just be proud; she will be too proud. A character will not just be romantic; he will be obsessively so.[3]

Fiction generally allows only two options for such characters: They grow and develop, coming to see their shortcomings and striving to overcome them, to be better; or they fail to grow and are punished by life. Many works of fiction portray characters who, at the precise moment that disaster is about to strike and when it is too late to act, recognize that they needed to change to avoid catastrophe. In either case, the goal is to provide readers with a lesson about life. This is the work's message. In many instances, your goal as an interpreter of a work is to help readers understand the nature of the lesson.

Readers have been debating for decades whether Elisa Allen grows and develops or whether she remains unchanged. Certainly there are indications of growth. For example, she sheds her bulky, asexual attire and puts on a pretty dress for the trip into town, and the language that describes this change in clothing suggests that there is a corresponding change in attitude, shifting from repressed emotions that Elisa struggles to control to something more elevated and light. But then the final scene suggests that nothing has changed, for Elisa cannot assert herself beyond asking to have wine with dinner.

A paper that focuses on characters will be concerned largely with how their growth or lack of growth is linked to the lesson of the story. More specifically, it will focus on such questions as:

---

[3]Many characters possess very fine qualities. However, in literature negative traits frequently define a character's humanity—and thus our own.

- What problem traits do the characters possess?
- What other factors define the nature of the characters?
- How are these traits linked to the message of the story? To other characters?
- Do the characters change? If so, at what point in the story does the change occur?
- What events or mental/emotional states are associated with the change?
- If the characters don't change, why not? What does their failure to change teach readers?

Answering these questions and determining whether Elisa Allen's character undergoes growth and development may hinge on the interpretation of the message that Steinbeck conveys. However, "The Chrysanthemums" is a popular story rich in interpretive possibilities because the message is not clear or obvious. In fact, large numbers of readers are willing to confess that they are not sure what the story means even after studying it for many years.

Linked Assignment

ANALYZING CHARACTER

The list of questions above provides a good starting point for character analysis. This activity will give you a chance to apply the ideas discussed so far and to begin generating your own ideas about the characters in Steinbeck's story. Try to answer each question for the character of Elisa Allen.

Plot

Most stories have a *plot*, which is the sequence of events in a story. This sequence is different from the simple chronology of a narrative report, however. Events must be interrelated in complex ways that involve characters and events. The actions of characters must convey both the theme and the message.

The events in a story generally are driven by some conflict or tension that motivates actions. Conflicts can be internal or external. Internal conflicts occur in the minds and hearts of characters, whereas external conflicts occur between characters, between characters and society, or between characters and nature. Authors of better works use both types of conflict rather than one or the other. In such cases, external conflict is linked to internal conflict, which in turn is associated with the growth and development of a character.

Events in fiction tend to be linked in a causal way such that each one intensifies the tension or conflict in the plot. Most stories have a *climax*, where the tension and conflict reach their highest level. After the climax comes what is called "the falling action," a series of events that leads to resolution of the original problem that caused the tension or conflict. Generally, the climax comes toward the end, and the falling action is brief. Readers of "The Chrysanthemums," for example, tend to identify the climax as the moment when Elisa sees that the tinker has thrown away her plantings.

Not all fiction provides a resolution. Modern short stories (and some novels) frequently have a climax that does not lead to resolution but rather to a further complication of the problem. Such stories refuse to answer the questions they raise about characters and life, which may make some readers feel dissatisfied because they are "left hanging" at the end. "The Chrysanthemums," as well as "The Descent of Man," on page 368, illustrates this characteristic. Some readers of "The Chrysanthemums" are frustrated because they want to know what happens to Elisa, but Steinbeck gives them few clues.

Writing about the plot of a story generally involves addressing a range of questions that that focus on "what," "how," and "why." A few of the more common of these questions appear here:

- What is the main conflict or tension? Is it internal or external?
- What are the minor conflicts or tensions? Are they internal or external?
- What characters are involved?
- How are the conflicts and tensions connected?
- What is the author's position on the conflict?
- What is the climax?
- How does the author resolve the conflict?
- If the author does not resolve the conflict, what conclusions can you draw about the future of the characters, particularly the protagonist? What does this future tell you about life? About yourself?

Theme and Message

Determining what a text means involves dealing with the universal truth a work of literature addresses, which is called the *theme*. Common themes in fiction are *love, sacrifice, the importance of family, ambition*, and so on. *Message* is closely linked to the lesson that the author wants readers to learn from the story. Stated another way, the message is the author's particular interpretation of a theme.

Complex works usually contain several, sometimes conflicting, themes and messages, which creates problems for analysis and interpretation. Before writing an interpretation, one may have to decide which theme is most important, why the author's message is not clear, or even what the message is.

Group Membership and Meaning

Language has multiple layers of meaning, which increases the likelihood of finding more than one theme or message in a single work. Different readers may respond to different layers as a result of such factors as group membership, personal background, and knowledge. For example, an expert on John Steinbeck is likely to find connections in "The Chrysanthemums" to other works by Steinbeck that someone with less training and experience simply will not see, just as someone experienced with gardening (and/or chrysanthemums) might see something in the story that a strictly literary expert might not see.

Beneath this fairly straightforward principle is an important idea: Determining the meaning of a text is a *constructive process*. Meaning does not reside in words themselves but is something readers construct on the basis of the interactions among what they know about a subject, their knowledge of how the world operates, and their membership in specific groups. The words on the page act as cues to evoke this knowledge, but the knowledge itself is shaped by the communities to which people belong and by their experiences.

In this constructive view, determining what a literary text means consists of passing the author's language through the filter of one's own understanding and experience to reconstruct it as meaning on a personal level. Consequently, any work can be interpreted in many different ways because each person's knowledge and experience are different. This view doesn't suggest that anything goes, however. It would be pretty difficult to argue successfully that "The Chrysanthemums" is the story of a woman possessed by the devil, for example. Interpretations are inherently limited by the text and have to be based on and supported by the text. As a result, most people tend to agree, at least in a general way, on what works of literature mean. Nevertheless, some readings are going to be more revealing and more meaningful than others because some readers will bring more knowledge, imagination, and experience to the text.

Interpreting Literature for Your Place and Time

Most literary texts strive to help readers gain a better understanding of what life is about; they encourage readers to reflect on life's problems in ways that can enhance daily living. For example, "The Chrysanthemums" deals with loneliness, repression, and resignation, themes that are part of everyone's life just as surely as they are part of Elisa Allen's. Effective interpretations of literature must address these themes—what the author William Faulkner once called the "eternal verities."

But an interpretation must do something more. Themes may be universal, but the message that an author conveys is his or her interpretation of those themes and consequently is tied to the author's particular time and place. As a result, readers have to take possession of a text by making the author's message meaningful to their *own* time and place. Anyone who writes about literature acts to facilitate the process and implicitly recognizes that each generation must reinterpret the lessons of literature. Personal experience and knowledge, as well as the spirit of the times, are especially relevant during this process.

For example, interpretations of "The Chrysanthemums" that were written 40 years ago dealt with Elisa's loneliness and sexual and emotional repression, but these themes were linked to the harshness of ranch life and Elisa's lack of children. The chrysanthemums in the story were viewed as surrogate children. Elisa's apparent dissatisfaction, as well as her "strength" in the beginning of the story and her teary "weakness" at the end, was deemed to be a reflection of her inability to have children and thereby reach fulfillment as a woman. The message commonly was deemed to be that women without children lead unhappy lives. More recent interpretations also deal with Elisa's loneliness and repression of emotion, but the themes are linked to a stereotypical repression of women by a male-dominated society. Elisa is surrounded by men and is ultimately betrayed by them, as exemplified by her husband's inadequate response to her metamorphosis and by the tinker's lie. Such interpretations argue that Elisa is a victim of patriarchal society who longs for but cannot have the freedom of men. The message commonly is deemed to be that women cannot find fulfillment until they escape the domination of men. These views just would not have occurred to many people four decades ago.

THEME AND MESSAGE

So far, this chapter has considered several themes and a couple of messages for "The Chrysanthemums." In two or three paragraphs, discuss whether you perceive these themes to be legitimate and then examine what you believe is the message of the story. What are some good reasons for readers to accept your argument as reasonable?

Point of View

Writing good fiction is remarkably difficult. Justifiably, we call it an art. One reason lies in the problem of telling a story in a way that immerses readers in the action, that makes them a part of the narrative, without making them too aware of the mediating presence of the writer. Few readers want to be reminded that someone is telling them a story and is in fact a part of it, even though the artificial nature of the experience is implicit. Some commentators have argued that film has become the narrative medium of choice for most people in the world partly because it so effectively reduces the presence of the story teller. Viewers are like peeping-toms looking into the private lives of characters on the screen. The perspective is unmediated.

The situation is quite different in fiction, where a narrative relationship between writers and their fiction mediates everything that readers know about the fictional world. In fact, not only is the narrative relationship defined in terms of the point of view but in many instances the story is *understood* through that point of view. Moreover, because the narrator who tells a story may be a "voice," or persona, assumed by a writer, point of view often is described with respect to the narrator rather than the real person who wrote the work.

There are four points of view that writers use most often in fiction: *omniscient, limited omniscient, first person*, and *dramatic*. Let's take up each one in turn.

Omniscient

This point of view gives the narrator unlimited access to the thoughts of all characters and complete knowledge of their past, present, and future actions. In addition, this sort of narrator often addresses readers directly, making comments about the characters or the plot.

Limited Omniscient

As the name suggests, this point of view is more restricted than the first category. Authors who employ this approach limit their omniscience to a single character. If they make comments about other characters or the plot, they do so in the context of the single character. Often, actions and other characters are viewed only through this character's perspective. Extreme forms of this point of view consist of "stream of consciousness" narratives, in which the author attempts to tell a story from inside the thoughts of a single character.

First Person

The author's presence usually is reduced in the first person point of view. In stories written with this approach, the narrator is a character, and readers experience the plot and other characters through what the narrator/character says and thinks. Sometimes the thought processes of such narrators/characters are flawed in revealing ways so that readers can have more awareness than the narrator of what is happening in a story. In such cases, the writer deliberately creates a narrative voice different from his or her own. The narrator/character may, for example, be an innocent and may see value where there is none.

Dramatic

Finally, the dramatic point of view provides a narrator who cannot enter the minds of characters and knows them only through their actions. This approach comes closest to a narrative report because the narrator serves as a reporter or as the lens of a camera. Readers come to know characters solely on the basis of what they say and on the basis of what other characters say about them. In many respects, reading the story is similar to watching a play or a movie. Any messages or lessons are implicit in the words and actions of the characters and have to be interpreted by readers because the author does not address readers directly.

Point of view often provides an important focus for writing about fiction. It offers insight into how the author conceptualized the story, and it also says something about how the author wanted readers to interact with the narrative. As the narrative voice becomes less noticeable, the writing tends to shift from telling to showing; that is, the author stops telling readers what is going on in a story and asks them to figure it out for themselves on the basis of the character interactions. One result is that readers have to do more interpretation to figure out what the story means.

Linked Assignment

POINT OF VIEW

The point of view of "The Chrysanthemums" is dramatic. Use examples from the story that illustrate this point of view. Next, take a section of the story, such as Elisa's encounter with the tinker, and rewrite it using another point of view. In one or two paragraphs, discuss how your shift in point of view affected the story.

Irony

Irony involves creating a contrast between appearance and reality. If you asked a friend after a test how she did and she rolled her eyes and said, "Oh, *great*," dropping her tone in the process, you would understand that she really did not do well. Her statement would be ironic.

People use irony in many situations, so it is not surprising that works of fiction employ irony regularly. Authors use two main types, verbal irony and situational irony. Verbal irony consists of stating the opposite of reality. The illustration above is an example of verbal irony.

In many different kinds of works, irony is a major source of comedy, particularly when authors engage in irony by understating reality or by overstating it. For instance, in a special collection of Donald Duck cartoons commemorating Donald's 50th birthday, the narrator asks Donald why his friends so often try to avoid him. Hanging his head, Donald responds hesitantly: "Well, I do have a little bit of a temper." Of course, Donald's hot temper is one of his defining characteristics, so the line is funny. Film maker Woody Allen, on the other hand, often uses overstatement to make people laugh.

Situational irony relies on unexpected events to highlight contrasts that can be humorous or thought provoking. Boyle's short story "The Descent of Man" uses this technique. The janitor not only seems to know the work of Noam Chomsky and Fredrich Nietzsche—two intellectuals renowned for the difficulty of their ideas—but he also seems to read German. Boyle makes the situation more ironic, and more humorous, by having the janitor speak a very strong black English vernacular. The contrast is unexpected and funny.

Diverse Voices

The idea of a response paper is strange to many students from other cultures where sharing feelings with others is discouraged. Response papers—or their equivalent—in these cultures are expected merely to provide summaries of plot, character, and other key elements. Can you identify ways in which the American response paper may be unlike expectations in your home culture? Can you explain the American emphasis on personal response?

Writing Assignment

INTERPRETING
"THE CHRYSANTHEMUMS"

The previous sections have looked fairly closely at "The Chrysanthemums" and have proposed themes as well as messages for the story. The linked assignments gave you opportunities to apply certain analytical tools to the story and to generate some ideas about it. In addition, the discussion created a model of how to approach analysis and interpretation of the story. The goal of this writing assignment is to allow you to put these various parts together into an interpretive paper. In three to five pages, examine the themes in the story, then argue for your interpretation of its message. Although you may decide to turn to published sources to support your argument, remember that your support should come primarily from the text.

WRITING GUIDE: INTERPRETING
"THE CHRYSANTHEMUMS"

Invention

You already have completed much of the invention for this assignment in the linked assignments that preceded it. Before you begin writing, you should review each of those exercises, asking yourself in the process how you can use them to gain insight in to the themes and message of the story. You have worked with the story's message, and now you should consider more carefully the support you have that will get readers to accept your argument as reasonable.

Keep in mind the discussion of insider and outsider at various points earlier in this text. Will you be writing as an insider or outsider? And your audience? Will it be insiders or outsiders? How will your rhetorical stance influence what you write and the support you use?

Planning

The introduction will set the scene for the paper by supplying background information and stating the "problem" that the paper will address. Next comes the claim. You have several options from this point: You can move immediately into the textual evidence that supports your claim; you can introduce views different from your own, using the technique of thesis–antithesis; you can introduce expert views from published sources that support your own; and so forth. Your analysis and discussion of the work's themes must come before your discussion of message, so you should determine which themes you will use and develop a general plan for linking them to your interpretation of message.

You also should consider how you will use examples from the text as evidence to support your claim. Marking page numbers and paragraphs is helpful at this stage. Keep in mind, however, that arguments move from minor claims to examples and evidence. You don't want to find yourself with these features reversed.

Drafting

If you completed any of the linked assignments, you have quite a bit of writing about "The Chrysanthemums." You may want to use it as a starting point, especially if you have it on computer. You can add and delete material until your draft begins to match the plan you worked out above.

Consider how you are using the key elements in your interpretation. For example, many readers agree that the atmosphere of "The Chrysanthemums" is important in identifying the themes of repression and isolation. If you deal with these themes in your paper, you probably will want to include some analysis of atmosphere.

Many writers during the drafting stage will use quotations from the story that are too long for the finished product. This is not a problem as long as you understand that you should keep your quotations relatively short. Long, block quotations are not really appropriate for a paper like this one. At this point, however, it is most important that you get all your information and arguments in order. You can reduce long quotations during revision.

Pausing and Reading

Use the pauses you take during drafting to read what you have produced. You are dealing with several parts of the whole paper—theme, setting, atmosphere, character, and so on—which can make it difficult to tie everything together. As you read, ask yourself how the parts are working to communicate your interpretation. If some of the parts are not fitting together well, make a note so you can return to those sections later. Also consider how much or how little of the plot you are summarizing for readers. Too much and your paper loses focus. Too little and readers will have a hard time understanding your interpretation.

Revising

When your first draft is finished, read through it quickly to see how well it flows. Does the introduction set the scene for the argument? Does it state your claim clearly and directly? Does your discussion of themes move easily to your discussion of message? Does your evidence from the text support your claim? If your answer to any of these questions is "no," you'll need to go back and adjust the draft.

After making the necessary changes, read the paper again, more slowly. Does the introduction lead to expectations that are met in the body? Is the rhetorical stance consistent? That is, are you addressing the audience as an insider or as an outsider? Which role is the audience in? Have you provided textured details? That is, does the paper shift smoothly between generalities and rich details? Does the conclusion look outward?

Model 1: Repression in "The Chrysanthemums"

The following paper was written by Maria, a sophomore in an introduction to literature class. She was responding to an assignment similar to the one above and had to explore theme in the short story. As you read, pay particular attention to how Maria uses excerpts from the story to support her claims.

Sexual Repression in "The Chrysanthemums"

Maria

1   John Steinbeck begins "The Chrysanthemums" by describing the Salinas Valley and the Allen ranch it contains in ways that emphasize the fact that both are cut off from mainstream society. The "high grey-flannel fog of winter closed off the Salinas Valley from the sky and from all the rest of the world. On every side it sat like a lid on the mountains and made of the great valley a closed pot." These images set the atmosphere of the story, but they also reveal a great deal about the theme, which is sexual repression.

2   We see the beginnings of this repression early, in the way that Steinbeck describes Elisa. Her figure "looked blocked and heavy," and she is wearing a "man's hat pulled low down over her eyes, clodhopper shoes, . . . a big corduroy apron with four big pockets . . . and heavy leather gloves to protect her hands." In other words, she looks like a man. In addition, Steinbeck does not describe Elisa as a pretty woman—instead, he states that she is "handsome." This word choice strengthens the image of Elisa as a woman whose sexuality is so repressed that she has the physical appearance of a man.

3   For all her appearance of strength, however, Elisa is a very fragile person whose femininity lies beneath a thin veneer of masculinity. Initially, it seems as though this veneer has been imposed by a hard life on the ranch and a passionless marriage to an insensitive man. This perception, however, is off the mark.

4   We begin to understand why when the tinker arrives and we witness the first signs of Elisa's repressed femininity emerge. After exchanging small talk, Elisa removes her gloves and "touched the under edge of her man's hat, searching for fugitive hairs." This latter action is clearly that of a woman; men generally don't try to recapture under their hats hairs that have fallen loose. What follows this subtle action is even more revealing of Elisa's repression, and it can be described as a pathological seduction.

5   The tinker asks to mend her damaged pots, and Elisa quickly says "no," she doesn't need anything mended. Her eyes harden "with resistance," as though the tinker has asked her for sex. Compelled by her socialized role as woman, Elisa says

"no" even though she really wants to say "yes." The tinker understands this and tries another approach, offering to sharpen scissors, which are clear phallic symbols. Elisa tells him that all her scissors are "sharp," suggesting that her husband's tool is sufficient for her needs, again brushing off the tinker's advances. The tinker's offer to mend a pot with a hole is erotically suggestive.

6   Rebuffed, the tinker takes yet another approach that is characteristic of the seduction ritual: He falls into "an exaggerated sadness." This is the equivalent in the nonfiction world of the male feigning sadness after hearing "no" and claiming that if the woman really cared for him she would submit. The aim is to appeal to the female's maternal instincts. His approach is unsuccessful, however, because middle-aged, childless Elisa has repressed those instincts to such an extent that they, as well as her sexual energy, are invested in her chrysanthemums. Dumb luck, as well as tenaciousness, brings flowers into the focus of the tinker's attention, and then his success is assured.

7   As soon as he mentions them, Elisa's "irritation and resistance" melt away. She is excited as she invites the tinker into her yard, which is the equivalent of inviting him into her bedroom. She assumes a submissive position, on her knees on the ground before the tinker, and her explanation of how to tend the young shoots has the tone and connotations of foreplay that leaves Elisa's breasts swelling "passionately." Her voice grows husky and the symbolic intercourse begins, cast in terms of a dark night and "sharp-pointed" stars that get "driven into your body." The experience, she says, is "Hot and sharp and—lovely." But the symbolic sex is not enough; perhaps if she truly were a man rather than a repressed woman, it would have been, but she needs something more—an emotional connection, a sign of tenderness. Thus, she reaches out to the tinker while still on the ground, reaches out to him "like a fawning dog." Of course, the tinker, like a typical man, rejects her, and suddenly she feels ashamed that she allowed herself to be seduced. She realizes that her "no" had meant "yes" all along, and she becomes brusque.

8   Quickly, Elisa cloaks herself in masculinity, repressing her femininity once again. Bringing a couple of pots to the tinker for repair is a way of asserting a superior position toward him, but it is easy to miss the deeper significance of the action. Elisa is not merely providing make-work to reduce him to the level of hired help—she is paying him as a man would pay a prostitute for services rendered. The effect is significant: Not only does it heighten the contemptible character of the tinker, but it also heightens our awareness of the degree to which Elisa is willing to repress her femininity. She engages in that most masculine of activities, paying for sex. And at 50 cents, what cheap sex it was.

9   Interestingly, Elisa reinforces the repression of her femininity and the cloak of masculinity through her banter, in which she asserts that she can mend a pot as well as a man and could weather the hardships of life on the road just as easily. These statements raise an important question: To what extent is Elisa responsible for her own repression? There are indications here that she may be almost totally responsible, which suggests that the hints throughout the story that ranch life or even her husband may be to blame, somehow, are false clues intended to mask the fact that Elisa's hell is one of her own making. It is difficult to argue that her actions are in any way influenced by her husband or by life on the ranch. They come from some inner source, some inner conflict raging in Elisa's heart.

10   Like any woman guilty of illicit sex, Elisa's first desire is to cleanse herself, so she runs a hot bath and scrubs her skin with a pumice stone in an act of masochism and penance. Also characteristically, she dresses for another seduction, of her husband this time, stirred into guilt-driven lust for her husband by her encounter with the tinker as well as into a desire to try to expatiate her guilt by having licit sex with her husband. It is clear, however, that neither her guilt nor the eroticism of having sex with two men in one day is sufficient to overcome the alienation—or perhaps outright hostility—Elisa feels for her husband. We don't know why she has these

feelings, and there is nothing in the story to shed light on them. We only know that when he enters her presence after getting dressed for dinner, she "stiffened and her face grew tight." When he tells her that she looks "nice," she implicitly rebukes him for not offering some other comment, perhaps a higher form of praise: "Nice? You think I look nice? What do you mean by 'nice'?" It seems that Elisa cannot help but betray herself; in spite of her good intentions, she always does and says the wrong thing and thereby increases her isolation and her repression.

11   The final scene, in which she and her husband overtake the tinker and she sees that he threw away the plantings she had given him, is anticlimactic. It serves simply to highlight her confusion and despair over being wracked by conflicting emotions and desires. On the one hand, she wants to go to the fights, whereas on the other she is repelled by them. Her husband, always trying to accommodate, is caught in a losing situation. Nothing he ever can say or do will resolve his wife's inner conflict, her sexual repression, and in the end Elisa turns away from him again, literally and symbolically, so that he "could not see that she was crying weakly—like an old woman."

THE RESPONSE PAPER

Many different classes may require a response paper, but they are most common in literature classes. When teachers assign a response paper, they generally want to give students an occasion not only to describe their reaction to a given literary work but also to think about the key elements of the text that prompted that reaction. In addition, they want to give students an opportunity to explore some ideas linked to a text that can be developed into a longer paper.

These goals significantly influence what you can do in a response paper. For example, after reading Tom Boyle's short story "The Descent of Man," your response might be that the story is funny. That's an honest response and one that many readers have. But obviously a successful paper will not consist of a single line: "I laughed when I read Boyle's story." The teacher will have the tacit expectation that you will explain *why* you thought "The Descent of Man" was funny. In other words, a successful response paper will consist of a *statement* of your reaction to a work followed by an *analysis* that *explains* why you reacted the way you did.

The sample response paper below was written by Connie, a sophomore, after she read Boyle's story. As you read her paper, notice how she uses analysis and concrete examples to explain her response. In a sense, a response paper is a kind of argument with a thesis and supporting evidence, and you will see some of the structure of the argument in Connie's writing.

Journal Entry

Consider some of the works of literature that you've read. What were some of the more memorable features of these works? Characters? Theme? Message?

THE DESCENT OF MAN

T. C. Boyle

1   I was living with a woman who suddenly began to stink. It was very difficult. The first time I confronted her she merely smiled. "Occupational hazard," she said. The next time she curled her lip. There were other problems too. Hairs, for instance.

Hairs that began to appear on her clothing, sharp and black and brutal. Invariably I would awake to find these hairs in my mouth, or I would glance into the mirror to see them slashing like razor edges across the collars of my white shirts. Then too there was the fruit. I began to discover moldering bits of it about the house—apple and banana most characteristically—but plum and tangelo or even passion fruit and yim-yim were not at all anomalous. These fruit fragments occurred principally in the bedroom, on the pillow, surrounded by darkening spots. It was not long before I located their source: they lay hidden like gems in the long wild hanks of her hair. Another occupational hazard.

2   Jane was in the habit of sitting before the air conditioner when she came home from work, fingering out her hair, drying the sweat from her face and neck in the cool hum of the machine, fruit bits sifting silently to the carpet, black hairs drifting like feathers. On these occasions the room would fill with the stink of her, bestial and fetid. And I would find my eyes watering, my mind imaging the dark rotting trunks of the rain forest, stained sienna and mandalay and Hooker's green with the excrements dropped from above. My ears would keen with the whistling and crawk-ing of the jungle birds, the screechings of the snot-nosed apes in the branches. And then, slack-faced and tight-boweled, I would step into the bathroom and retch, the sweetness of my own intestinal secrets a balm against the potent hairy stench of her.

3   One evening, just after her bath (the faintest odor lingered, yet still it was so tren-chant I had to fight the impulse to get up and urinate on a tree or a post or some-thing), I lay my hand casually across her belly and was suddenly startled to see an insect flit from its cover, skate up the swell of her abdomen, and bury itself in her navel. "Good Christ," I said.

4   "Hm?" she returned, peering over the cover of her Yerkish[1] reader.

5   "That," I said. "That bug, that insect, that vermin."

6   She sat up, plucked the thing from its cachette, raised it to her lips and popped it between her front teeth. "Louse," she said, sucking. "Went down to the old-age home on Thirteenth Street to pick them up."

7   I anticipated her: "Not for—?"

8   "Why certainly, potpie—so Konrad can experience a tangible gratification of his social impulses during the grooming ritual. You know: you scratch my back, I scratch yours."

9   I lay in bed that night sweating, thinking about Jane and those slippery-fingered monkeys poking away at her, and listening for the lice crawling across her scalp or nestling their bloody little siphons in the tufts under her arms. Finally, about four, I got up and took three Doriden. I woke at two in the afternoon, an insect in my ear. It was only an earwig. I had missed my train, failed to call in at the office. There was a note from Jane: Pick me up at four. Konrad sends love.

10   The Primate Center stood in the midst of a macadamized acre or two, looking very much like a school building: faded brick, fluted columns, high mesh fences. Finger paintings and mobiles hung in the windows, misshapen ceramics crouched along the sills. A flag raggled at the top of a whitewashed flagpole. I found myself bending to examine the cornerstone: Asa Priff Grammar School, 1939. Inside it was dark and cool, the halls were lined with lockers and curling watercolors, the linoleum gleamed like a shy smile. I stepped into the BOYS' ROOM. The urinals were a foot and a half from the floor. Designed for little people, I mused. Young-sters. Hardly big enough to hold their little peters without the teacher's help. I smiled, and situated myself over one of the urinals, the strong honest scent of Pine-Sol in my nostrils. At that moment the door wheezed open and a chimpanzee shuf-fled in. He was dressed in shorts, shirt and bow tie. He nodded to me, it seemed, and

---

[1]From work of Robert Hearns Yerkes (1875–1956), American psychologist who found-ed Yale Labs of primate biology.

made a few odd gestures with his hands as he moved up to the urinal beside mine. Then he opened his fly and pulled out an enormous slick red organ like a peeled banana. I looked away, embarrassed, but could hear him urinating mightily. The stream hissed against the porcelain like a thunderstorm, rattled the drain as it went down. My own water wouldn't come. I began to feel foolish. The chimp shook himself daintily, zippered up, pulled the plunger, crossed to the sink, washed and dried his hands, and left. I found I no longer had to go.

11   Out in the hallway the janitor was leaning on his flathead broom. The chimp stood before him gesticulating with manic dexterity: brushing his forehead and tugging his chin, slapping his hands under his armpits, tapping his wrists, his tongue, his ear, his lip. The janitor watched intently. Suddenly—after a particularly virulent flurry—the man burst into laughter, rich braying globes of it. The chimp folded his lip and joined in, adding his weird nasal snickering to the janitor's barrel laugh. I stood by the door to the BOYS' ROOM in a quandary. I began to feel that it might be wiser to wait in the car—but then I didn't want to call attention to myself, darting in and out like that. The janitor might think I was stealing paper towels or something. So I stood there, thinking to have a word with him after the chimp moved on—with the expectation that he could give me some grassroots insight into the nature of Jane's job. But the chimp didn't move on. The two continued laughing, now harder than ever. The janitor's face was tear-streaked. Each time he looked up the chimp produced a gesticular flurry that would stagger him again. Finally the janitor wound down a bit, and still chuckling, held out his hands, palms up. The chimp flung his arms up over his head and then heaved them down again, rhythmically slapping the big palms with his own. "Right on! Mastuh Konrad," the janitor said, "Right on!" The chimp grinned, then hitched up his shorts and sauntered off down the hall. The janitor turned back to his broom, still chuckling.

12   I cleared my throat. The broom began a geometrically precise course up the hall toward me. It stopped at my toes, the ridge of detritus flush with the pinions of my wingtips. The janitor looked up. The pupil of his right eye was fixed in the corner, beneath the lid, and the white was red. There was an ironic gap between his front teeth. "Kin ah do sumfin fo yo, mah good man?" he said.

13   "I'm waiting for Miss Good."

14   "Ohhh, Miz *Good*," he said, nodding his head. "Fust ah tought yo was thievin paypuh tow-els outen de Boys' Room but den when ah sees yo standin dere rigid as de Venus de Milo ah thinks to mahsef: he is some kinda new sculpture de stoodents done made is what he is." He was squinting up at me and grinning like we'd just come back from sailing around the world together.

15   "That's a nice broom," I said.

16   He looked at me steadily, grinning still. "Yo's wonderin what me and Mastuh Konrad was jivin bout up dere, isn't yo? Well, ah tells yo: he was relatin a hoomerous anecdote, de punch line ob which has deep cosmic implications in dat it establishes a common groun between monks and Ho-mo sapiens despite dere divergent ancestries." He shook his head, chortled. "Yes in-deed, dat Mastuh Konrad is quite de wit."

17   "You mean to tell me you actually understand all that lip-pulling and finger-waving?" I was beginning to feel a nameless sense of outrage.

18   "Oh sartinly, mah good man. Dat ASL."

19   "What?"

20   "ASL is what we was talkin. A-merican Sign Language. Developed for de deef n dumb. Yo sees, Mastuh Konrad is sumfin ob a genius round here. He can commoonicate de mos esoteric i-deas in bof ASL and Yerkish, re-spond to and translate English, French, German and Chinese. Fack, it was Miz Good was tellin me dat Konrad is workin right now on a Yerkish translation ob Darwin's *De-scent o Man*. He is mainly into anthro-pology, yo knows, but he has cultivated a in-teress in udder

fields too. Dis lass fall he done undertook a Yerkish translation ob Chomsky's *Language and Mind* and Nietzsche's *Jenseits von Gut und Böse*.[2] And dat's some pretty heavy shit, Jackson."

21 I was hot with outrage. "Stuff," I said. "Stuff and nonsense."

22 "No sense in feelin personally treatened by Mastuh Konrad's chievements, mah good fellow—yo's got to ree-lize dat he is a genius."

23 A word came to me: "Bullhonk," I said. And turned to leave.

24 The janitor caught me by the shirtsleeve. "He is now scorin his turd opera," he whispered. I tore away from him and stamped out of the building.

25 Jane was waiting in the car. I climbed in, cranked down the sunroof and opened the air vents.

26 At home I poured a water glass of gin, held it to my nostrils and inhaled. Jane sat before the air conditioner, her hair like a urinal mop, stinking. Black hairs cut the atmosphere, fruit bits whispered to the carpet. Occasionally the tip of my tongue entered the gin. I sniffed and tasted, thinking of plastic factories and turpentine distilleries and rich sulfurous smoke. On my way to the bedroom I poured a second glass.

27 In the bedroom I sniffed gin and dressed for dinner. "Jane?" I called, "shouldn't you be getting ready?" She appeared in the doorway. She was dressed in her work clothes: jeans and sweatshirt. The sweatshirt was gray and hooded. There were yellow stains on the sleeves. I thought of the lower depths of animal cages, beneath the floor meshing. "I figured I'd go like this," she said. I was knotting my tie. "And I wish you'd stop insisting on baths every night—I'm getting tired of smelling like a coupon in a detergent box. It's unnatural. Unhealthy."

28 In the car on the way to the restaurant I lit a cigar, a cheap twisted black thing like half a pepperoni. Jane sat hunched against her door, unwashed. I had never before smoked a cigar. I tried to start a conversation but Jane said she didn't feel like talking: talk seemed so useless, such an anachronism. We drove on in silence. And I reflected that this was not the Jane I knew and loved. Where, I wondered, was the girl who changed wigs three or four times a day and sported nails like a Chinese emperor?—and where was the girl who dressed like an Arabian bazaar and smelled like the trade winds?

29 She was committed. The project, the study, grants. I could read the signs: she was growing away from me.

30 The restaurant was dark, a maze of rocky gardens, pancake-leafed vegetation, black fountains. We stood squinting just inside the door. Birds whistled, carp hissed through the pools. Somewhere a monkey screeched. Jane put her hand on my shoulder and whispered in my ear. "Siamang," she said. At that moment the leaves parted beside us: a rubbery little fellow emerged and motioned us to sit on a bench beneath a wicker birdcage. He was wearing a soiled loincloth and eight or ten necklaces of yellowed teeth. His hair flamed out like a brushfire. In the dim light from the braziers I noticed his nostrils—both shrunken and pinched, as if once pierced straight through. His face was of course inscrutable. As soon as we were seated he removed my socks and shoes, Jane's sneakers, and wrapped our feet in what I later learned were plantain leaves. I started to object—I bitterly resent anyone looking at my feet—but Jane shushed me. We had waited three months for reservations.

31 The maitre d' signed for us to follow and led us through a dripping stone-walled tunnel to an outdoor garden where the flagstones gave way to dirt and we found ourselves on a narrow plant-choked path. He licked along like an iguana and we hurried to keep up. Wet fronds slapped back in my face, creepers snatched at my ankles, mud sucked at the plantain leaves on my feet. The scents of mold and damp and

---

[2]"Beyond good and evil."

long-lying urine hung in the air, and I thought of the men's room at the subway station. It was dark as a womb. I offered Jane my hand, but she refused it. Her breathing was fast. The monkey chatter was loud as a zoo afire. "Far out," she said. I slapped a mosquito on my neck.

32   A moment later we found ourselves seated at a bamboo table overhung with branch and vine. Across from us sat Dr. and Mrs. U-Hwak-Lo, director of the Primate Center and wife. A candle guttered between them. I cleared my throat, and then began idly tracing my finger around the circular hole cut in the table's center. The Doctor's ears were the size of peanuts. "Glad you two could make it," he said. "I've long been urging Jane to sample some of our humble island fare." I smiled, crushed a spider against the back of my chair. The Doctor's English was perfect, pure Martha's Vineyard—he sounded like Ted Kennedy's insurance salesman. His wife's was weak: "Yes," she said, "nussing cook here, all roar." "How exciting!" said Jane. And then the conversation turned to primates, and the Center.

33   Mrs. U-Hwak-Lo and I smiled at one another. Jane and the Doctor were already deeply absorbed in a dialogue concerning the incidence of anal retention in chimps deprived of Frisbee coordination during the sensorimotor period. I gestured toward them with my head and arched my eyebrows wittily. Mrs. U-Hwak-Lo giggled. It was then that Jane's proximity began to affect me. The close wet air seemed to concentrate her essence, distill its potency. The U-Hwak-Los seemed unaffected. I began to feel queasy. I reached for the fingerbowl and drank down its contents. Mrs. U-Hwak-Lo smiled. It was coconut oil. Just then the waiter appeared carrying a wooden bowl the size of a truck tire. A single string of teeth slapped against his breastbone as he set the bowl down and slipped off into the shadows. The Doctor and Jane were oblivious—they were talking excitedly, occasionally lapsing into what I took to be ASL, ear- and nose- and lip-picking like a manager and his third-base coach. I peered into the bowl: it was filled to the rim with clean-picked chicken bones. Mrs. U-Hwak-Lo nodded, grinning: "No on-tray," she said. "Appeticer." At that moment a simian screamed somewhere close, screamed like death itself. Jane looked up. "Rhesus," she said.

34   On my return from the men's room I had some difficulty locating the table in the dark. I had already waded through two murky fountains and was preparing to plunge through my third when I heard Mrs. U-Hwak-Lo's voice behind me. "Here," she said. "Make quick, repass now serve." She took my hand and led me back to the table. "Oh, they're enormously resourceful," the Doctor was saying as I stumbled into my chair, pants wet to the knees. "They first employ a general anesthetic—a distillation of the chu-bok root—and then the chef (who logically doubles as village surgeon) makes a circular incision about the macaque's cranium, carefully peeling back the already-shaven scalp, and staunching the blood flow quite effectively with maura-ro, a highly absorbent powder derived from the tamana leaf. He then removes both the frontal and parietal plates to expose the brain . . ." I looked at Jane: she was rapt. I wasn't really listening. My attention was directed toward what I took to be the main course, which had appeared in my absence. An unsteady pinkish mound now occupied the center of the table, completely obscuring the circular hole—it looked like cherry vanilla yogurt, a carton and a half, perhaps two. On closer inspection, I noticed several black hairs peeping out from around its flaccid edges. And thought immediately of the bush-headed maitre d'. I pointed to one of the hairs, remarking to Mrs. U-Hwak-Lo that the rudiments of culinary hygiene could be a little more rigorously observed among the staff. She smiled. Encouraged, I asked her what exactly the dish was. "Much delicacy," she said. "Very rare find in land of Lincoln." At that moment the waiter appeared and handed each of us a bamboo stick beaten flat and sharpened at one end.

35   ". . . then the tribal elders or visiting dignitaries are seated around the table," the Doctor was saying. "The chef has previously of course located the macaque beneath the table, the exposed part of the creature's brain protruding from the hole in its cen-

ter. After the feast, the lower ranks of the village population divide up the remnants. It's really quiet efficient."

36   "How fascinating!" said Jane. "Shall we try some?"

37   "By all means . . . but tell me, how has Konrad been coming with that Yerkish epic he's been working up?"

38   Jane turned to answer, bamboo stick poised: "Oh I'm so glad you asked—I'd almost forgotten. He's finished his tenth book and tells me he'll be doing two more—out of deference to the Miltonic tradition. Isn't that a groove?"

39   "Yes," said the Doctor, gesturing toward the rosy lump in the center of the table. "Yes it is. He's certainly—and I hope you won't mind the pun—a brainy fellow. Ho-ho."

40   "Oh, Doctor," Jane laughed, and plunged her stick into the pink. Beneath the table, in the dark, a tiny fist clutched at my pantleg.

41   I missed work again the following day. This time it took five Doriden to put me under. I had lain in bed sweating and tossing, listening to Jane's quiet breathing, inhaling her fumes. At dawn I dozed off, dreamed briefly of elementary school cafe-terias swarming with knickered chimps and weltered with trays of cherry vanilla yogurt, and woke stale-mouthed. Then I took the pills. It was three-thirty when I woke again. There was a note from Jane: Bringing Konrad home for dinner. Vacu-um rug and clean toilet.

42   Konrad was impeccably dressed—long pants, platform wedgies, cufflinks. He smelled of eau de cologne, Jane of used litter. They arrived during the seven o'clock news. I opened the door for them.

43   "Hello Jane," I said. We stood at the door, awkward, silent.

44   "Well?" she said. "Aren't you going to greet our guest?" "Hello, Konrad," I said. And then: "I believe we met in the boys' room at the Center the other day?" He bowed deeply, straight-faced, his upper lip like a halved cantaloupe. Then he broke into a snicker, turned to Jane and juggled out an impossible series of gestures. Jane laughed. Something caught in my throat. "Is he trying to say something?" I asked. "Oh potpie," she said, "it was nothing—just a little quote from Yeats."

45   "Yeats?"

46   "Yes, you know: 'An aged man is but a paltry thing.' "[3]

47   Jane served watercress sandwiches and animal crackers as hors d'oeuvres. She brought them into the living room on a cut-glass serving tray and set them down before Konrad and me, where we sat on the sofa, watching the news. Then she returned to the kitchen. Konrad plucked up a tiny sandwich and swallowed it like a communion wafer, sucking the tips of his fingers. Then he lifted the tray and offered it to me. I declined. "No, thank you," I said. Konrad shrugged, set the plate down in his lap, and carefully stacked all the sandwiches in its center. I pretended to be absorbed with the news: actually I studied him, half-face. He was filling the gaps in his sandwich-construction with animal crackers. His lower lip protruded, his ears were rubbery, he was balding. With both hands he crushed the heap of crackers and sandwiches together and began kneading it until it took on the consistency of raw dough. Then he lifted the whole thing to his mouth and swallowed it without chew-ing. There were no whites to his eyes.

48   Konrad's only reaction to the newscast was a burst of excitement over a war story—the reporter stood against the wasteland of treadless tanks and recoilless guns in Thailand or Syria or Chile; huts were burning, old women weeping. "Wow-wow! Eeeeeeee! Er-er-er-er," Konrad said. Jane appeared in the kitchen doorway, hands dripping. "What is it, Konrad?" she said. He made a series of vio-lent gestures. "Well?" I asked. She translated: 'Konrad says that 'the pig oppres-sors' genocidal tactics will lead to their mutual extermination and usher in a new

---

[3]From "Sailing to Byzantium" by William Butler Yeats (1856–1939), Irish poet.

golden age . . .' "—here she hesitated, looked up at him to continue (he was springing up and down on the couch, flailing his fists as though they held whips and scourges)—" '. . . of freedom and equality for all, regardless of race, creed, color—or genus.' I wouldn't worry," she added, "it's just his daily slice of revolutionary rhetoric. He'll calm down in a minute—he likes to play Che,[4] but he's basically nonviolent."

49   Ten minutes later Jane served dinner. Konrad, with remarkable speed and coordination, consumed four cans of fruit cocktail, thirty-two spareribs, half a dozen each of oranges, apples, and pomegranates, two cheeseburgers and three quarts of chocolate malted. In the kitchen, clearing up, I commented to Jane about our guest's prodigious appetite. He was sitting in the other room, listening to *Don Giovanni*,[5] sipping brandy. Jane said that he was a big, active male and that she could attest to his need for so many calories. "How much does he weigh?" I asked. "Stripped," she said, "one eighty-one. When he stands up straight he's four eight and three quarters." I mulled over this information while I scraped away at the dishes, filed them in the dishwasher, neat ranks of blue china. A few moments later I stepped into the living room to observe Jane stroking Konrad's ears, his head in her lap. I stand five seven, one forty-three.

50   When I returned from work the following day, Jane was gone. Her dresser drawers were bare, the closet empty. There were white rectangles on the wall where her Rousseau[6] reproductions had hung. The top plank of the bookcase was ribbed with the dust-prints of her Edgar Rice Burroughs[7] collection. Her girls' softball trophy, her natural foods cookbook, her oaken cudgel, her moog, her wok: all gone. There were no notes. A pain jabbed at my sternum, tears started in my eyes. I was alone, deserted, friendless. I began to long even for the stink of her. On the pillow in the bedroom I found a fermenting chunk of pineapple. And sobbed.

51   By the time I thought of the Primate Center the sun was already on the wane. It was dark when I got there. Loose gravel grated beneath my shoes in the parking lot; the flag snapped at the top of its pole; the lights grinned lickerishly from the Center's windows. Inside the lighting was subdued, the building hushed. I began searching through the rooms, opening and slamming doors. The linoleum glowed all the way up the long corridor. At the far end I heard someone whistling "My Old Kentucky Home." It was the janitor. "Howdedo," he said. "Wut kin ah do fo yo at such a inauspicious hour ob de night?"

52   I was candid with him. "I'm looking for Miss Good."

53   "Ohhh, she leave bout fo-turdy evy day—sartinly yo should be well apprised ob dat fack."

54   "I thought she might be working late tonight."

55   "Noooo, no chance ob dat." He was staring at the floor.

56   "Mind if I look for myself?"

57   "Mah good man, ah trusts yo is not intimatin dat ah would diskise de troof . . . far be it fum me to pre-varicate just to proteck a young lady wut run off fum a man dat doan unnerstan her needs nor 'low her to spress de natchrul inclination ob her soul."

58   At that moment a girlish giggle sounded from down the hall. Jane's girlish giggle. The janitor's right hand spread itself across my chest. 'Ah wooden insinooate mahself in de middle ob a highly sinificant speriment if ah was yo, Jackson," he said, hissing through the gap in his teeth. I pushed by him and started down the corridor. Jane's laugh leaped out again. From the last door on my left. I hurried. Suddenly the Doctor and his wife stepped from the shadows to block the doorway. "Mr.

---

[4]Che Guevara (1928–1967), Cuban revolutionary killed in Bolivia.
[5]Opera (1787) by Mozart.
[6]Henri Rousseau (1844–1910), French painter.
[7]Popular American novelist (1875–1950), author of the Tarzan books.

Horne," said the Doctor, arms folded against his chest, "take hold of yourself. We are conducting a series of experiments here that I simply cannot allow you to—"

59   "A fig for your experiments," I shouted. "I want to speak to my, my—roommate." I could hear the janitor's footsteps behind me. "Get out of my way, Doctor," I said. Mrs. U-Hwak-Lo smiled. I felt panicky. Thought of the Tong Wars. "Is dey a problem here, Doc?" the janitor said, his breath hot on the back of my neck. I broke. Grabbed the Doctor by his elbows, wheeled around and shoved him into the janitor. They went down on the linoleum like spastic skaters. I applied my shoulder to the door and battered my way in, Mrs. U-Hwak-Lo's shrill in my ear: "You make big missake, Misser!" Inside I found Jane, legs and arms bare, pinching a lab smock across her chest. She looked puzzled at first, then annoyed. She stepped up to me, made some rude gestures in my face. I could hear scrambling in the hallway behind me. Then I saw Konrad—in a pair of baggy BVDs. I grabbed Jane. But Konrad was there in an instant—he hit me like a grill of a Cadillac and I spun across the room, tumbling desks and chairs as I went. I slumped against the chalkboard. The door slammed: Jane was gone. Konrad swelled his chest, swayed toward me, the fluorescent lights hissing overhead, the chalkboard cold against the back of my neck. And I looked up into the black eyes, teeth, fur, rock-ribbed arms.

Response Paper

Connie

1   When I first read "The Descent of Man," I found it funny and laughed. Boyle's writing is vivid, and I could visualize the settings and actions easily. When I read the story a second time, however, I realized that the reason why it is so funny is that Boyle manipulates readers by connecting ideas in ways we've never thought of before. They are absurd and sad at the same time, a combination that underlies most comedy.

2   Perhaps the best example of this combination is the conversation between the janitor and Jane's husband. The husband saw the janitor and the chimp, Konrad, conversing in sign language and wanted to know what they were saying. The janitor says that Konrad "was relatin a hoomerous anecdote, de punch line ob which has deep cosmic implications in dat it establishes a common groun between monks and Ho-mo sapiens despite dere divergent ancestries" (58) The janitor goes on to explain, in his strong black dialect, that Konrad, "is mainly into anthro-pology, yo knows, but he has cultivated a in-teress in udder fields too. Dis lass fall he done undertook a Yerkish translation of Chomsky's *Language and Mind* and Nietzsche's *Jenseits von Gut and Böse*. And dat's some pretty heavy shit, Jackson" (58). The contrasts and connections here are unexpected and wild. No one would expect a janitor to talk about Chomsky and Nietzsche. The fact that this janitor talks like Amos of the famous *Amos & Andy* show makes the situation more absurd because we expect people who use this ascent to be dumb. But Boyle takes the absurdity and the humor one step farther by implying that the janitor also reads German.

3   Another good example is found in the conversation between Jane and Doctor U-Hawk-Lo. "Jane and the doctor were already deeply absorbed in a dialogue concerning the incidence of anal retention in chimps deprived of Frisbee coordination during the sensorimotor period" (60). I see the humor here as being threefold. First, Boyle proposes that chimps and humans have the same mechanism of psychological development. Second, Boyle mixes up Freud's psychoanalysis and Piaget's theory of childhood cognitive development. Third, Boyle deflates these "elevated" ideas by linking them to playing with a Frisbee.

4   But the most striking connection is Konrad, the chimp who is "sumfin ob a genius round here" (58), who has "finished his tenth book and tells me [Jane] he'll be doing two more—out of deference to the Miltonic tradition" (61).

5   The reason why it's funny is linked to the title, "The Descent of Man." In *The Descent of Man*, Darwin proposes that humans evolved from lower species. Thus,

mankind would have chimps somewhere in its ancestry, a fact that puts people higher than apes on the evolutionary tree. In this story, however, Boyle reverses the hierarchy and thereby uses the word "descent" in a way different from how Darwin used it. Man is no longer higher than chimps. Konrad is so intelligent that he is superior to men, particularly to the husband. But there also is another "descent" when Jane has sex with the chimp. We end up in a situation in which the title of Darwin's scientific treatise become a metaphor for bestiality. It occurred to me that given the sexual nature of the last scene, maybe Boyle could have increased the humor by calling the story not "The Descent of Man" but "The Descent of Woman."

Connie states her reaction to "The Descent of Man" in the first sentence. This is a good approach because reaction papers do not require an introductory paragraph that lays the foundation for the essay, that moves from general to specific information. Connie sensed, however, that saying simply that she laughed when she read the story does not meet the assignment, so she supplied additional information. She states that she read the story a second time and analyzed the reason why she laughed. Her thesis for this paper is "Boyle manipulates readers by connecting ideas in ways we've never thought of before." Connie's teacher had not talked about irony, so this term is not in the paper, but Connie nevertheless understands the concept of irony.

Paragraphs 2 through 4 offer examples of situational irony from the story, and they also explain why the irony may strike readers as funny. The level of detail that Connie provides is important because it supports her argument and it shows that she has read the story attentively. Connie effectively uses her personal experience and knowledge in the argument. She goes beyond the text and the class for additional information, such as the details from the *Amos & Andy* show in paragraph 2 and Freud and Piaget in paragraph 3. Supplying this information shows that Connie has thought enough about the story and the assignment to relate it to other areas, which teachers usually appreciate.

Putting the strongest point toward the end of a paper is a good strategy, and Connie's essay illustrates how to do it effectively. She notes that the most "striking connection," or irony, lies in Konrad and the title of the story. For Connie, the verbal irony implicit in the title is funnier than the situational irony, and she explains why. Readers may disagree with her assessment, but they must allow that her assessment is well reasoned.

Finally, Connie's ending is satisfying because she engages in a bit of her own verbal irony. The last sentence indicates that Connie is sufficiently self-confident as a writer to suggest a way of improving the story and making it funnier. It also indicates, again, that she has thought deeply about the story. Her teachers concluded that Connie had done more than just react to "The Descent of Man"—she had *inter*acted with it.

READINGS

Shirley Jackson

Shirley Jackson was born in California but spent most of her life in New England. According to some accounts, she developed a passion for writing early, producing poems and short stories even as a child. Her interest blossomed when she began attending Syracuse University, where she edited a literary magazine. After graduating, she became a prolific writer, publishing short stories, novels, and children's books. Today Jackson is probably best known for "The Lottery," which was published in 1948 and which continues to intrigue readers who wrestle with what it means.

SHIRLEY JACKSON

THE LOTTERY

1   The morning of June 27th was clear and sunny, with the fresh warmth of a full-summer day; the flowers were blossoming profusely and the grass was richly green. The people of the village began to gather in the square, between the post office and the bank, around ten o'clock; in some towns there were so many people that the lottery took two days and had to be started on June 26th, but in this village, where there were only about three hundred people, the whole lottery took less than two hours, so it could begin at ten o'clock in the morning and still be through in time to allow the villagers to get home for noon dinner.

2   The children assembled first, of course. School was recently over for the summer, and the feeling of liberty sat uneasily on most of them; they tended to gather together quietly for a while before they broke into boisterous play, and their talk was still of the classroom and the teacher, of books and reprimands. Bobby Martin had already stuffed his pockets full of stones, and the other boys soon followed his example, selecting the smoothest and roundest stones; Bobby and Harry Jones and Dickie Delacroix—the villagers pronounced this name "Dellacroy"—eventually made a great pile of stones in one corner of the square and guarded it against the raids of the other boys. The girls stood aside, talking among themselves, looking over their shoulders at the boys, and the very small children rolled in the dust or clung to the hands of their older brothers or sisters.

3   Soon the men began to gather, surveying their own children, speaking of planting and rain, tractors and taxes. They stood together, away from the pile of stones in the corner, and their jokes were quiet and they smiled rather than laughed. The women, wearing faded house dresses and sweaters, came shortly after their menfolk. They greeted one another and exchanged bits of gossip as they went to join their husbands. Soon the women, standing by their husbands, began to call to their children, and the children came reluctantly, having to be called four or five times. Bobby Martin ducked under his mother's grasping hand and ran, laughing, back to the pile of stones. His father spoke up sharply, and Bobby came quickly and took his place between his father and his oldest brother.

4   The lottery was conducted—as were the square dances, the teen-age club, the Halloween program—by Mr. Summers, who had time and energy to devote to civic activities. He was a round-faced, jovial man and he ran the coal business, and people were sorry for him, because he had no children and his wife was a scold. When he arrived in the square, carrying the black wooden box, there was a murmur of conversation among the villagers, and he waved and called. "Little late today, folks." The postmaster, Mr. Graves, followed him, carrying a three-legged stool, and the stool was put in the center of the square and Mr. Summers set the black box down on it. The villagers kept their distance, leaving a space between themselves and the stool, and when Mr. Summers said, "Some of you fellows want to give me a hand?" there was a hesitation before two men, Mr. Martin and his oldest son, Baxter, came forward to hold the box steady on the stool while Mr. Summers stirred up the papers inside it.

5   The original paraphernalia for the lottery had been lost long ago, and the black box now resting on the stool had been put into use even before Old Man Warner, the oldest man in town, was born. Mr. Summers spoke frequently to the villagers about making a new box, but no one liked to upset even as much tradition as was represented by the

black box. There was a story that the present box had been made with some pieces of the box that had preceded it, the one that had been constructed when the first people settled down to make a village here. Every year, after the lottery, Mr. Summers began talking again about a new box, but every year the subject was allowed to fade off without anything's being done. The black box grew shabbier each year; by now it was no longer completely black but splintered badly along one side to show the original wood color, and in some places faded or stained.

6 Mr. Martin and his oldest son, Baxter, held the black box securely on the stool until Mr. Summers had stirred the papers thoroughly with his hand. Because so much of the ritual had been forgotten or discarded, Mr. Summers had been successful in having slips of paper substituted for the chips of wood that had been used for generations. Chips of wood, Mr. Summers had argued, had been all very well when the village was tiny, but now that the population was more than three hundred and likely to keep on growing, it was necessary to use something that would fit more easily into the black box. The night before the lottery, Mr. Summers and Mr. Graves made up the slips of paper and put them in the box, and it was then taken to the safe of Mr. Summers' coal company and locked up until Mr. Summers was ready to take it to the square next morning. The rest of the year, the box was put way, sometimes one place, sometimes another; it had spent one year in Mr. Graves's barn and another year underfoot in the post office, and sometimes it was set on a shelf in the Martin grocery and left there.

7 There was a great deal of fussing to be done before Mr. Summers declared the lottery open. There were the lists to make up—of heads of families, heads of households in each family, members of each household in each family. There was the proper swearing-in of Mr. Summers by the postmaster, as the official of the lottery; at one time, some people remembered, there had been a recital of some sort, performed by the official of the lottery, a perfunctory, tuneless chant that had been rattled off duly each year; some people believed that the official of the lottery used to stand just so when he said or sang it, others believed that he was supposed to walk among the people, but years and years ago this part of the ritual had been allowed

to lapse. There had been, also, a ritual salute, which the official of the lottery had had to use in addressing each person who came up to draw from the box, but this also had changed with time, until now it was felt necessary only for the official to speak to each person approaching. Mr. Summers was very good at all this; in his clean white shirt and blue jeans, with one hand resting carelessly on the black box, he seemed very proper and important as he talked interminably to Mr. Graves and the Martins.

8 Just as Mr. Summers finally left off talking and turned to the assembled villagers, Mrs. Hutchinson came hurriedly along the path to the square, her sweater thrown over her shoulders, and slid into place in the back of the crowd. "Clean forgot what day it was," she said to Mrs. Delacroix, who stood next to her, and they both laughed softly. "Thought my old man was out back stacking wood," Mrs. Hutchinson went on, "and then I looked out the window and the kids was gone, and then I remembered it was the twenty-seventh and came a-running." She dried her hands on her apron, and Mrs. Delacroix said, "You're in time, though. They're still talking away up there."

9 Mrs. Hutchinson craned her neck to see through the crowd and found her husband and children standing near the front. She tapped Mrs. Delacroix on the arm as a farewell and began to make her way through the crowd. The people separated good-humoredly to let her through: two or three people said, in voices just loud enough to be heard across the crowd, "Here comes your, Missus, Hutchinson," and "Bill, she made it after all." Mrs. Hutchinson reached her husband, and Mr. Summers, who had been waiting, said cheerfully, "Thought we were going to have to get on without you, Tessie." Mrs. Hutchinson said, grinning, "Wouldn't have me leave m'dishes in the sink, now, would you, Joe?," and soft laughter ran through the crowd as the people stirred back into position after Mrs. Hutchinson's arrival.

10 "Well, now," Mr. Summers said soberly, "guess we better get started, get this over with, so's we can go back to work. Anybody ain't here?"

11 "Dunbar," several people said. "Dunbar, Dunbar."

12 Mr. Summers consulted his list. "Clyde Dunbar," he said. "That's right. He's broke his leg, hasn't he? Who's drawing for him?"

13 "Me, I guess," a woman said, and Mr. Summers turned to look at her. "Wife draws for her hus-

band," Mr. Summers said. "Don't you have a grown boy to do it for you, Janey?" Although Mr. Summers and everyone else in the village knew the answer perfectly well, it was the business of the official of the lottery to ask such questions formally. Mr. Summers waited with an expression of polite interest while Mrs. Dunbar answered. "Horace's not but sixteen yet," Mrs. Dunbar said regretfully. "Guess I gotta fill in for the old man this year."

14 "Right," Mr. Summers said. He made a note on the list he was holding. Then he asked, "Watson boy drawing this year?"

15 A tall boy in the crowd raised his hand. "Here," he said. "I'm drawing for my mother and me." He blinked his eyes nervously and ducked his head as several voices in the crowd said things like "Good fellow, Jack," and "Glad to see your mother's got a man to do it."

16 "Well," Mr. Summers said, "guess that's everyone. Old Man Warner make it?"

17 "Here," a voice said, and Mr. Summers nodded.

18 A sudden hush fell on the crowd as Mr. Summers cleared his throat and looked at the list. "All ready?" he called. "Now, I'll read the names—heads of families first—and the men come up and take a paper out of the box. Keep the paper folded in your hand without looking at it until everyone has had a turn. Everything clear?"

19 The people had done it so many times that they only half listened to the directions: most of them were quiet, wetting their lips, not looking around. Then Mr. Summers raised one hand high and said, "Adams." A man disengaged himself from the crowd and came forward. "Hi, Steve," Mr. Summers said, and Mr. Adams said, "Hi, Joe." They grinned at one another humorlessly and nervously. Then Mr. Adams reached into the black box and took out a folded paper. He held it firmly by one corner as he turned and went hastily back to his place in the crowd, where he stood a little apart from his family, not looking down at his hand.

20 "Allen," Mr. Summers said. "Anderson. . . . Bentham."

21 "Seems like there's no time at all between lotteries any more," Mrs. Delacroix said to Mrs. Graves in the back row.

22 "Seems like we got through with the last one only last week."

23 "Time sure goes fast," Mrs. Graves said.

"Clark. . . . Delacroix" 24

"There goes my old man," Mrs. Delacroix said. 25 She held her breath while her husband went forward.

"Dunbar," Mr. Summers said, and Mrs. Dunbar 26 went steadily to the box while one of the women said. "Go on, Janey," and another said, "There she goes."

"We're next," Mrs. Graves said. She watched 27 while Mr. Graves came around from the side of the box, greeted Mr. Summers gravely and selected a slip of paper from the box. By now, all through the crowd there were men holding the small folded papers in their large hands, turning them over and over nervously. Mrs. Dunbar and her two sons stood together, Mrs. Dunbar holding the slip of paper.

"Harburt. . . . Hutchinson." 28

"Get up there, Bill," Mrs. Hutchinson said, and 29 the people near her laughed.

"Jones." 30

"They do say," Mr. Adams said to Old Man 31 Warner, who stood next to him, "that over in the north village they're talking of giving up the lottery."

Old Man Warner snorted. "Pack of crazy 32 fools," he said. "Listening to the young folks, nothing's good enough for them. Next thing you know, they'll be wanting to go back to living in caves, nobody work any more, live *that* way for a while. Used to be a saying about 'Lottery in June, corn be heavy soon.' First thing you know, we'd all be eating stewed chickweed and acorns. There's *always* been a lottery," he added petulantly. "Bad enough to see young Joe Summers up there joking with everybody."

"Some places have already quit lotteries," Mrs. 33 Adams said.

"Nothing but trouble in that," Old Man Warner 34 said stoutly. "Pack of young fools."

"Martin." And Bobby Martin watched his 35 father go forward. "Overdyke. . . . Percy."

"I wish they'd hurry," Mrs. Dunbar said to her 36 older son. "I wish they'd hurry."

"They're almost through," her son said. 37

"You get ready to run tell Dad," Mrs. Dunbar 38 said.

Mr. Summers called his own name and then 39 stepped forward precisely and selected a slip from the box. Then he called, "Warner."

40   "Seventy-seventh year I been in the lottery," Old Man Warner said as he went through the crowd. "Seventy-seventh time."

41   "Watson" The tall boy came awkwardly through the crowd. Someone said, "Don't be nervous, Jack," and Mr. Summers said, "Take your time, son."

42   "Zanini."

43   After that, there was a long pause, a breathless pause, until Mr. Summers, holding his slip of paper in the air, said, "All right, fellows." For a minute, no one moved, and then all the slips of paper were opened. Suddenly, all the women began to speak at once, saying, "Who is it?," "Who's got it?," "Is it the Dunbars?," "Is it the Watsons?" Then the voices began to say, "It's Hutchinson. It's Bill," "Bill Hutchinson's got it."

44   "Go tell your father," Mrs. Dunbar said to her older son.

45   People began to look around to see the Hutchinsons. Bill Hutchinson was standing quiet, staring down at the paper in his hand. Suddenly, Tessie Hutchinson shouted to Mr. Summers. "You didn't give him time enough to take any paper he wanted. I saw you. It wasn't fair!"

46   "Be a good sport, Tessie," Mrs. Delacroix called, and Mrs. Graves said, "All of us took the same chance."

47   "Shut up, Tessie," Bill Hutchinson said.

48   "Well, everyone," Mr. Summers said, "that was done pretty fast, and now we've got to be hurrying a little more to get done in time." He consulted his next list. "Bill," he said, "you draw for the Hutchinson family. You got any other households in the Hutchinsons?"

49   "There's Don and Eva," Mrs. Hutchinson yelled. "Make them take their chance!"

50   "Daughters draw with their husbands' families, Tessie," Mr. Summers said gently. "You know that as well as anyone else."

51   "It wasn't fair," Tessie said.

52   "I guess not, Joe," Bill Hutchinson said regretfully. "My daughter draws with her husband's family; that's only fair. And I've got no other family except the kids."

53   "Then, as far as drawing for families is concerned, it's you," Mr. Summers said in explanation, "and as far as drawing for households is concerned, that's you, too. Right?"

54   "Right," Bill Hutchinson said.

55   "How many kids, Bill?" Mr. Summers asked formally.

56   "Three," Bill Hutchinson said.

57   "There's Bill, Jr., and Nancy, and little Dave. And Tessie and me."

58   "All right, then," Mr. Summers said. "Harry, you got their tickets back?"

59   Mr. Graves nodded and held up the slips of paper. "Put them in the box, then," Mr. Summers directed. "Take Bill's and put it in."

60   "I think we ought to start over," Mrs. Hutchinson said, as quietly as she could. "I tell you it wasn't fair. You didn't give him time enough to choose. Everybody saw that."

61   Mr. Graves had selected the five slips and put them in the box, and he dropped all the papers but those onto the ground, where the breeze caught them and lifted them off.

62   "Listen, everybody," Mrs. Hutchinson was saying to the people around her.

63   "Ready, Bill?" Mr. Summers asked, and Bill Hutchinson, with one quick glance around at his wife and children, nodded.

64   "Remember," Mr. Summers said, "take the slips and keep them folded until each person has taken one. Harry, you help little Dave." Mr. Graves took the hand of the little boy, who came willingly with him up to the box. "Take a paper out of the box, Davy," Mr. Summers said. Davy put his hand into the box and laughed. "Take just one paper," Mr. Summers said. "Harry, you hold it for him." Mr. Graves took the child's hand and removed the folded paper from the tight fist and held it while little Dave stood next to him and looked up at him wonderingly.

65   "Nancy next," Mr. Summers said. Nancy was twelve, and her school friends breathed heavily as she went forward switching her skirt, and took a slip daintily from the box. "Bill, Jr.," Mr. Summers said, and Billy, his face red and his feet overlarge, near knocked the box over as he got a paper out. "Tessie," Mr. Summers said. She hesitated for a minute, looking around defiantly, and then set her lips and went up to the box. She snatched a paper out and held it behind her.

66   "Bill," Mr. Summers said, and Bill Hutchinson reached into the box and felt around, bringing his hand out at last with the slip of paper in it.

67   The crowd was quiet. A girl whispered, "I hope it's not Nancy," and the sound of the whisper reached the edges of the crowd.

68   "It's not the way it used to be," Old Man Warner said clearly. "People ain't the way they used to be."

69   "All right," Mr. Summers said. "Open the papers. Harry, you open little Dave's."

70   Mr. Graves opened the slip of paper and there was a general sigh through the crowd as he held it up and everyone could see that it was blank. Nancy and Bill, Jr., opened theirs at the same time, and both beamed and laughed, turning around to the crowd and holding their slips of paper above their heads.

71   "Tessie," Mr. Summers said. There was a pause, and then Mr. Summers looked at Bill Hutchinson, and Bill unfolded his paper and showed it. It was blank.

72   "It's Tessie," Mr. Summers said, and his voice was hushed. "Show us her paper, Bill."

73   Bill Hutchinson went over to his wife and forced the slip of paper out of her hand. It had a black spot on it, the black spot Mr. Summers had made the night before with the heavy pencil in the coal company office. Bill Hutchinson held it up, and there was a stir in the crowd.

74   "All right, folks," Mr. Summers said. "Let's finish quickly."

75   Although the villagers had forgotten the ritual and lost the original black box, they still remembered to use stones. The pile of stones the boys had made earlier was ready; there were stones on the ground with the blowing scraps of paper that had come out of the box. Mrs. Delacroix selected a stone so large she had to pick it up with both hands and turned to Mrs. Dunbar. "Come on," she said. "Hurry up."

76   Mrs. Dunbar had small stones in both hands, and she said, gasping for breath, "I can't run at all. You'll have to go ahead and I'll catch up with you."

77   The children had stones already. And someone gave little Davy Hutchinson a few pebbles.

78   Tessie Hutchinson was in the center of a cleared space by now, and she held her hands out desperately as the villagers moved in on her. "It isn't fair," she said. A stone hit her on the side of the head. Old Man Warner was saying, "Come on, come on, everyone." Steve Adams was in the front of the crowd of villagers, with Mrs. Graves beside him.

79   "It isn't fair, it isn't right," Mrs. Hutchinson screamed, and then they were upon her.

Critical Reading Guide

1. "The Lottery" begins fairly simply, with no hint that something dark is about to happen. When does the mood shift? How does Jackson create the change of mood?

2. A central element of the story is the value the villagers place on tradition. What role does tradition play in the story? How is it related to the story's theme?

3. How does the point of view influence the impact the story has on readers?

4. Stories like "The Lottery" have to be believable if they are to work. How does Jackson make this story believable?

5. At the end of the story, Mrs. Hutchinson screams, "It isn't fair." How might these words be linked to the theme of the story?

Writing Assignment

THE LOTTERY

Assume that you are in a literature course that asks you to write an argumentative essay examining the theme of "The Lottery." Identify and then examine the theme in this story, giving special attention to the lesson it conveys. Be sure to support your argument by using evidence and examples from the text. Your paper should be approximately five pages long.

GROUP ACTIVITIES: THE LOTTERY

1. Complex works usually have several themes. Part of the challenge you face in writing about literature lies in deciding what theme is the most important in a work. To help in this regard, spend about 5 minutes jotting down what you believe is the primary theme and message of "The Lottery." Also write down two or three secondary themes. When your list is completed, spend 10 to 15 minutes justifying your choices and briefly identifying some evidence from the text to support them.

2. Each group member should share his or her choices and support. Afterward, discuss the themes and message. You might being by considering such questions as: Have some groupmates reversed the order of primary and secondary themes? Have other identified themes that are insupportable? Are there more complex themes that the group may sense are in the story but that they can't quite identify?

3. A real danger whenever you write about the theme of a work is that everyone else in class will identify the same theme and the same message. As a result, the papers end up sounding alike. Discuss among your group how you may be able to avoid this problem.

4. Begin writing your first draft in class but finish at home.

5. At your next workshop, exchange drafts and look carefully at the introductions. Do they set the scene by providing the necessary background information? Is the thesis stated clearly and concisely? Provide notes in the margins for how the write can improve these features. Next look at supporting evidence. Does it support the writer's discussion of the theme? After making these written comments, talk to the writer about them.

Handbook

Effective writers always have a variety of tools at hand to help them produce texts that are clear, concise, well constructed, and easy to read.

Form and Function

Writers use a handbook as a resource for answering questions and solving problems associated with composing. The answers are congruent with the features of what is known as formal Standard English, the dialect of English that is most widely accepted (and expected) in writing.

PART ONE

Form and Function

Effective writers always have a variety of tools at hand to help them produce texts that are clear, concise, well constructed, and easy to read. A good dictionary is one such tool, a thesaurus another. A handbook, however, is one of the more useful tools for writers because it provides answers to a wide range of questions associated with the *form* of writing. Writers use a handbook as a resource for answering questions and solving problems associated with composing. The answers are congruent with the features of what is known as *formal Standard English*, the dialect of English that is most widely accepted (and expected) in writing.

This handbook examines major features of formal Standard English and is divided into two parts. The first discusses selected structural features: sentence structure, punctuation, word choice, paragraph development, and so forth. The second part discusses some of the conventions and expectations associated with writing in specific academic areas.

Although there may be some benefit in reading the handbook from end to end, it really is not designed with that approach in mind. Instead, it should be used as a resource for answering questions about writing on an "as needed" basis. Because it is relatively brief, it cannot answer all questions, but certainly it will be able to answer many of them. For more detailed information, a comprehensive handbook is preferable.

Many features of form are so well fixed that there can be no deviation from them. For example, in formal Standard English, singular subjects work with singular verbs—thus, we can have sentence 1 but not sentence 2:

1. The number of problems is bigger than we thought.
2. *The number of problems are bigger than we thought.[1]

In these sentences, the subject is *number*, which is singular, so the verb connected to it also must be singular. Because *are* is plural, it is unacceptable.

Many other features of form, however, are not so well fixed. One result is that there are significant differences between the way people use spoken English and

---

[1]The asterisk is used to identify ungrammatical sentences.

the way they use written English. These differences often are described in terms of language *conventions*, which means that they are a matter of general agreement, not a matter of rule. For example, in speech, even well-educated people use the expression *I feel real tired*, even though standard usage calls for *I feel really tired*. Differences of this sort generally do not cause problems during conversations. Problems arise, however, when people transport features of speech to their writing, in part because writing is more formal than most speech and readers generally expect writers to use the conventions of Standard English.

Inexperienced writers commonly violate such conventions, and it takes some time and effort to master the various forms of written English. For instance, many inexperienced writers use the expression *a lot*—which they usually spell incorrectly as one word—to communicate a large quantity or frequency. Although there is no rule that prevents one from using *a lot* in writing, there is a convention against it. The preferred expression is *a great deal* or *many*. Consider the contrasting sentences that follow:

3. Many people refuse to vote as a way of showing their displeasure with government.
4. ?A lot of people refuse to vote as a way of showing their displeasure with government.[2]
5. Phenomenologists devote a great deal of time to reflecting on mental states.
6. ?Phenomenologists devote a lot of time to reflecting on mental states.

One consequence of considering form as a matter of convention is that many of the questions associated with form and good writing can be understood as questions of *style* and *usage*. This handbook emphasizes the connection between style and usage throughout, almost as a necessity—not merely to differentiate between standard and nonstandard features but also to differentiate among the conventions that govern writing in the academic disciplines. Different groups of writers—social scientists and humanists, for instance—use different conventions of form and style, and the ability to apply these conventions is often seen as a measure of writing skill.

SENTENCE STRUCTURE

Sentences are made up of individual words that have a certain *form*. Whenever these individual words are put into a sentence, however, they also take on a certain *function*. Understanding sentence structure requires knowing how the form and function of words work together to convey meaning.

The most simple sentences have only two words, as in sentence 7:

7. Dogs bark.

The form of these two words is *noun* and *verb*, respectively. Although many people define a noun as a person, place, or thing, this is not entirely accurate. A better definition is that *a noun is any word that serves as a label*. This definition is

---

[2]A question mark in front of a sentence is used to indicate that it is questionable or unacceptable in formal Standard English, although it is grammatical.

convenient because it allows us to identify words like *Monday* as a noun, even though it is not a person, place, or thing. A verb, on the other hand, describes an action or helps identify a state of being or existence. In sentence 7, *bark* is an action, whereas in the sentence *Buggsy felt tired*, the verb *felt* links the noun *Buggsy* to the word *tired*. Together, *felt* and *tired* identify the state of being of *Buggsy*.

Subjects and Predicates

On the basis of sentence 7, we can conclude that sentences have at least one noun and one verb. The noun and verb have a functional relation described as *subject* and *predicate*. The subject is what the sentence is about, and the predicate expresses an action performed by the subject or is a statement of the subject's status. Thus, in sentence 7, *Dogs* is the subject and *bark* is the predicate. In the sentence *Buggsy felt tired*, *Buggsy* is the subject and *felt tired* is the predicate.

Clauses and Phrases

A subject and a predicate make up a sentence, but they also make up a *clause*. Every sentence has at least one clause. However, clauses can be combined into a single sentence, as in the following:

• Macarena ordered a burger, and Fritz ordered a hot dog.

English has two major types of clauses—*independent* and *dependent*. An independent clause can exist and be punctuated as a sentence, whereas a dependent clause cannot. In fact, the term *dependent* reflects the character of this type of clause; it must be attached to an independent clause.

There are two categories of dependent clause—the *subordinate clause* and the *relative clause*. (Relative clauses are discussed on pages 403–405; subordinate clauses on pages 416–417.) Subordinate clauses always begin with a *subordinating conjunction*, samples of which are shown here:

because	if	as
until	since	whereas
although	though	while

Nouns and verbs are the building blocks of clauses and of sentences, but they rarely work as isolated units. Instead, they work with other types of words to form larger units that may be thought of as noun constructions and verb constructions. For example, we have already seen that the word *dog* is a noun; now consider *a hot dog* in the example sentence above. The words *a* and *hot* work with *dog* to make a single construction dominated by the noun. The name for this construction is a *noun phrase*. In the next example sentence, the italicized portion illustrates a *verb phrase* (the dominant part is the verb):

• Raul *is sleeping*.

A phrase is a group of words functioning together in a sentence as a single construction. Phrases generally are not deemed to be the same as clauses because they lack a subject and a predicate. They cannot be punctuated as a sentence. Later in this handbook we examine other types of phrases.

SUMMARY

- ➤ There are two major types of clauses—*independent* and *dependent*.
- ➤ Independent clauses can exist as sentences, whereas dependent clauses cannot but must be connected to an independent clause.
- ➤ There are two types of dependent clauses—*relative* clauses and *subordinate* clauses.
- ➤ Phrases cannot be punctuated as a sentence and do not have a subject/predicate combination. Instead, they are characterized by the word that dominates their structure, such as a noun or verb, which gives us noun phrases and verb phrases.

Applying Key Ideas

Part 1

Directions: This activity is designed to give you some practice in recognizing and differentiating subjects and predicates. In each of the following sentences, underline the subject and predicate.

Example: <u>Macarena and Fritz</u> <u>spread their towels on the sand at Santa Monica Beach.</u>

1. The sea gulls were squawking overhead.
2. Macarena tossed up a crust of bread.
3. Meanwhile, Fritz opened the cooler and took out a bottle of wine.
4. He smacked his lips in anticipation of the fruity Chardonnay.
5. A few clouds began to cluster out over the ocean.
6. Slowly, Fritz began pouring the wine.
7. A sudden flush colored Macarena's face.
8. Several gulls landed nearby and started begging for food.
9. The popping of the cork as Fritz pulled it from the bottle startled the birds.
10. They flew up, screeching and angry.

Part 2

Directions: In the following sentences, underline the independent clauses and put brackets around the dependent clauses.

Example: [As Fritz poured the wine,] <u>a gull swooped down and grabbed a sandwich.</u>

1. The bird flew up and away until it was struck by another bird.
2. While the first thief lay dazed on the sand, the second thief and its friends gobbled the sandwich.

3. Fritz was angry now because the picnic was being spoiled.

4. Before he could say anything, another bird dove at the picnic basket.

5. Fritz swung his shoe at the diving bird, even though he generally liked animals.

6. Macarena tried sipping her wine as the bird came around for another pass.

7. Although Fritz had wisely closed the picnic basket, the gull dove again, going at Fritz this time.

8. The bird began flapping its wings furiously, until it was in a power dive straight for Fritz's head.

9. Fritz screamed when the bird hit him full on, exploding in a burst of feathers.

10. As consciousness dimmed, Fritz thought he heard the circling gulls laughing.

Part 3

Directions: Select a paragraph of your own writing and identify the independent and dependent clauses.

Objects

Nouns can function as subjects in sentences, and when they do they often are agents; that is, they perform the action expressed in the verb. However, nouns also can receive the action of the verb, and when they do, they function as *objects*. Sentences 8 and 9 illustrate this principle:

8. Fred kissed Macarena.

9. Fritz bumped his head.

In sentence 8, *Macarena* is the object; in sentence 59, *head* is the object.

Nouns

Nouns are of different types. Some label particulars in the world, such as the *Sears Tower, Michael Jordan, Toni Braxton, Lake Tahoe,* and *Porsche 911*. These we call *proper nouns*. Other nouns label the world more generally, as in *friend, apple, car, horse, computer,* and *shirt*. These we call *common nouns*. In addition to differing with respect to being particular or general, common nouns can be counted, whereas proper nouns usually cannot. There is only one Sears Tower, only one Michael Jordan, and so forth, but there are many friends, apples, cars, and horses. A third type of noun that cannot be counted in most situations is called a *mass noun. Water, air, knowledge,* and *justice* are all mass nouns.

Nouns and Number

Most common nouns are made plural (indicating that there is more than one) by adding the suffix *-s*. There are several exceptions, however.

Nouns Ending in -*ch*, -*s*, -*sh*, -*ss*, -*tch*, -*x*, or -*z*

Nouns ending with these forms usually are made plural by adding -*es*, as in *glasses, churches,* and *boxes.*

Nouns Ending in -*y*

Nouns ending in -*y* have two forms. If the -*y* is preceded by a vowel, the plural form is made simply by adding -*s*, as in *boys, toys,* and *joys.* However, if the -*y* is not preceded by a vowel, the plural form is made by changing the -*y* to -*i* and adding -*es,* as in *candies, yummies,* and *dairies.*

Nouns Ending in -*f*

Nouns ending if -*f* have two forms, but unlike those ending in -*y*, there is no consistent rule or convention governing which form to use. Some nouns ending in -*f* are made plural by adding -*s*, as in *briefs, chiefs,* and *roofs,* whereas others are made plural by changing the -*f* to -*v* and adding -*es*, as in *wives, calves,* and *thieves.*

Nouns Ending in -*o*

Most nouns ending in *o* are made plural by adding -*s*, as in *videos, patios,* and *tacos.* When the -*o* is preceded by a consonant, the plural is made by adding -*es*, as in *potatoes, tomatoes,* and *heroes.*

Mass Nouns

We generally do not pluralize mass nouns; their singular and plural form are the same.

Irregular Nouns

English has several irregular nouns—from Old English—that do not become plural through adding -*s* or -*es*; the change is more significant. Consider the following singular/plural forms:

child/children	foot/feet	goose/geese
man/men	mouse/mice	woman/women

Compound Nouns and Measurement

Compound nouns are formed by adding two or more words together, as in *attorney general* and *father-in-law.* The plural form is made by adding -*s* to the first word, as in *attorneys general* and *fathers-in-law.* This principle does not apply to measurements, as in *1 cupful of sugar.* To pluralize *cupful*, we add -*s* to the end of the word, not to the unit of measurement, giving *3 cupfuls*, not *3 cupsful.*

Greek and Latin Terms

Some nouns derived from Greek or Latin have retained their original forms for singular and plural, which are different from English. Furthermore, a few nouns differ in form according to gender. The following examples illustrate those nouns that often give writers difficulty:

Criterion (singular)/**Criteria** (plural)

Datum (singular)/**Data** (plural)

Memorandum (singular)/**Memoranda** (plural)

Phenomenon (singular)/**Phenomena** (plural)

Schema (singular)/**Schemata** (plural)

Stratum (singular)/**Strata** (plural)

Alumni (plural)

Alumnus (singular, male)

Alumna (singular, female)

Articles

Articles are words that work with nouns to signal certain features. The English articles are:

a   an   the

To understand how we use articles, it is necessary to consider that utterances or written statements have an audience and a context. Even individual sentences such as those used as examples in this book have a context consisting of the world at large and how that world operates. Consider sentence 10, for example:

10. Macarena stopped the car.

The context for this sentence is a world in which people drive cars, in which they stop cars by taking the right foot off the accelerator and pressing the brake pedal, and so forth. Given this context, few people would read sentence 10 and understand that, like some super hero, Macarena stopped the car by jumping in front of it and holding up her hands.

On this account, *a* and *an* are called *indefinite articles* because they are used when a noun is not tangible or within sensory range of the speaker or writer and the audience; they also are used when a noun is not known to a speaker or writer or has not been specifically referenced in the given context. *The* is called a *definite article* because it is used when a noun *is* tangible or within sensory range and when it is known to a speaker or writer and has been specifically referenced. Consider the following sentences:

11. The cat was stuck in the tree.
12. A cat was stuck in the tree.
13. The question came up at our last meeting.
14. ?A question came up at our last meeting.

In sentence 11, the definite articles in front of *cat* and *tree* indicate that both are known or perhaps visible. The cat and the tree are specific entities. In sentence 12, however, the cat is not known—it is generic. Thus, if my cat were stuck in the tree that grows in my backyard, I might use sentence 11 to inform my wife of the situation. If a cat known neither to me nor my wife were stuck in that tree, and if I saw it but my wife did not, I might use sentence 12. The cat is unknown, but the tree is known.

Problems occur with articles in two situations. The most common among native speakers is when an article is used incorrectly—a definite article when the noun is not specific or known or an indefinite article when it is. This problem usually occurs when a writer fails to identify an idea, event, or person in an early part of a paper and then makes reference to it as though it existed in the given context when it does not. The second problem occurs among nonnative speakers, especially those from Asia, when they leave out the article. Japanese, for example, has no articles, so it is difficult for Japanese speakers learning English to remember to include them. Sentence 15 illustrates a typical result:

15. *Fritz bought apple.

Pronouns

English, like other languages, resists the duplication of nouns in sentences, so it replaces duplicated nouns with what are called *pronouns*. The nouns that get replaced are called *antecedents*. Consider sentence 16:

16. ?Fritz liked ice cream, so Fritz ate ice cream every day.

The duplication of the nouns *Fritz* and *ice cream* just does not sound right to most people because English generally does not allow it. Acceptable alternatives are sentences 16a and 16b:

16a. Fritz liked ice cream, so he ate it every day.
16b. He liked ice cream, so Fritz ate it every day.

In this instance, however, 16b is not quite as appropriate as 16a because the sentence lacks a clear context. Sentences are part of a context that includes the complexities of human relationships, prior knowledge related to past, present, and future events, and, of course, prior conversations. The pronoun *he* in sentence 16b suggests that *Fritz* already has been identified or is known, which is contrary to fact. This point becomes even more visible if we put both pronouns in the beginning of the sentence—?*He liked it, so Fritz ate ice cream every day*. We cannot know with certainty that *it* refers to *ice cream*. By definition, antecedents come before their pronouns, but in this illustration they do not. In sentence 16a, on the other hand, *Fritz* and *ice cream* appear in the first part of the sentence, so the pronouns are linked to these antecedents without any doubt or confusion about which nouns the pronouns have replaced.

SUMMARY

➤ Pronouns should follow their antecedents.

Personal Pronouns

Pronouns that replace a duplicated noun are referred to as *personal* or *common* pronouns. The common pronouns are listed here:

Singular: I, me, you, he, him, she, her, it
Plural: we, us, you, they, them

In addition, there are several other types of pronouns: *demonstrative, reciprocal, possessive, indefinite, reflexive,* and *relative.*

Usage Note: ## Personal Pronouns

When personal pronouns appear with common and proper nouns, their order is governed by convention. Specifically, the pronouns should follow the nouns, as shown in the following sentences:

17. Fred, Fritz, and *I* drove to Malibu.
18. Macarena gave Buggsy and *her* a mean look.

Case

The functional role of nouns in English—whether subject or object—does not cause them to change their form, but it does cause most pronouns to change. These changes are described in terms of *case*, which is a way of expressing the relation between form and function. Thus, when a word is functioning as a subject, it is in the *nominative* case; when a word is functioning as an object, it is in the *objective* case. The following lists show the nominative and objective case forms of those pronouns that change depending on function:

Nominative Case
I, he, she, they, we, who

Objective Case
me, him, her, they, us, whom

Sentences 19 and 20 illustrate the proper usage for the personal pronoun *I* in nominative and objective cases:

19. Buggsy and *I* went to the movies.
20. Macarena kissed Fred and *me*.

Usage Note: ## Case Forms

Nonstandard usage commonly reverses nominative case and objective case pronouns, resulting in sentences like 21 and 22:

21. ?Fritz and *me* gave the flowers to Macarena.

22. ?Buggsy asked Fred, Raul, and *I* to drive to Las Vegas.

The standard equivalents are shown in sentences 21a and 22a:

21a. Fritz and *I* gave the flowers to Macarena.

22a. Buggsy asked Fred, Raul, and *me* to drive to Las Vegas.

When participating in a conversation, most people do not react too negatively to the sort of usage error illustrated in sentences 21 and 22. However, they generally react very negatively when they see such usage in writing.

Applying Key Ideas

Part 1

Directions: Some of the following sentences violate conventions governing pronoun usage. In each case, correct the usage error.

Example: Macarena and ~~Me~~ ^I drove to Las Vegas for the weekend.

1. Fred and her loved camping in the desert, even when it was hot.
2. Buggsy had a cabin at Big Bear Lake, and he let Macarena, Rita, and I stay there for a week.
3. Buggsy knew that her and I would keep the place neat.
4. The fish were jumping, so I rented poles for Macarena, Rita, and me.
5. As Rita and her got into the fishing boat, it tipped over.
6. Rita and I knew how to swim, but Macarena didn't, so she started to go down.
7. Macarena was a big woman, and Macarena was strong, so when I grabbed her she started to pull I down with her.
8. Fortunately, Rita helped us both by grabbing I by the shoulder and pulling we two up to the surface.
9. Us three then scrambled into the boat, feeling more than a little foolish.
10. After all that, the fish weren't biting, and Macarena was the only one of us who caught a fish, which she gave to Rita and me.

Part 2

Directions: Select a page of your own writing and scan it for pronoun usage. If you detect any misapplications of the conventions, correct them.

Demonstrative Pronouns

There are four demonstrative pronouns:

this, that, these, those

They serve to single out, highlight, or draw attention to a noun, as in sentences 23, 24, and 25:

23. *That* car is a wreck.
24. *Those* peaches don't look very ripe.
25. *This* book is really interesting.

Usage Note: **Indefinite Demonstrative Pronoun**

The demonstrative pronoun *this* does not always work to draw attention to a noun. In certain situations, it replaces an entire sentence, as in the following:

Fritz cleaned his apartment. *This* amazed Macarena.

Here, *this* refers to the fact that Fritz cleaned his apartment, and in this kind of construction it usually is referred to as an *indefinite demonstrative* pronoun because there is no definite antecedent. In this particular instance, with the two sentences side by side, the relation between them is clear. However, it is easy to forget that the indefinite demonstrative makes sense only when the referenced sentence is immediately before the pronoun. As a result, many writers often will have several sentences separating the indefinite demonstrative *this* and the fact or action it refers to. Readers do not have an easy time figuring out the connection, as in the following example:

Steinbeck's <u>The Red Pony</u> *is usually published as a single novella, even though it originally appeared as four separate (though related) short stories in 1934. Only the first of these stories, "The Gift," has anything to do with a red pony. The others deal with the general hardship of life on a ranch and the pervasive mean-spiritedness of Jody's parents, whose oppressive treatment of the boy has caused him to be so timid that he is afraid to speak. This can be confusing to young readers.*

The word *this* in the last sentence should refer to the idea in the previous sentence, but it doesn't. Instead, it is related to the second sentence, but the relation is not clear, and it certainly is not strong, because of the intervening sentence. Using the indefinite demonstrative in this instance is not appropriate because it negatively affects clarity and understanding. The sentence would have to be moved upward to be successful.

Note, however, that many professional writers and teachers object to any use of *this* in such a broad way, arguing that an alternative, more precise structure is better. They recommend replacing the indefinite demonstrative pronoun with an appropriate noun. This injunction may be overly severe because legitimate uses of the indefinite demonstrative pronoun do exist. A wiser approach is to use it sparingly and to make certain that it immediately follows the referenced sentence.

SUMMARY

➢ Use the indefinite demonstrative pronoun sparingly.

Reciprocal Pronouns

English has two reciprocal pronouns—*each other* and *one another*—which are used to refer to the individual parts of a plural noun. Consider sentences 26 and 27:

26. The girls sent notes to *each other*.
27. The boys smiled at *one another*.

Each Other and One Another

Each other and *one another* do not mean the same thing, so they are not interchangeable. *Each other* signifies two people or things, whereas *one another* signifies more than two. Thus, sentence 26 refers to two girls; sentence 27 refers to more than two boys.

Possessive Pronouns

Possessive pronouns indicate possession, as in sentences 28 and 29:

28. *My* son loves baseball.
29. The shoes were *mine*.

The possessive pronouns are listed here:

Singular: my, mine, your, yours, her, hers, his, its
Plural: our, ours, your, yours, their, theirs

Usage Note: Its and Your

Possessive pronouns are fixed forms; that is, they exist independently of their corresponding personal pronouns. For example, *I, me, my,* and *mine* are independent lexical items. The possessive of common and proper nouns, on the other hand, is formed by adding *apostrophe* plus *s*, as in *Fred's*. The possessive form thus is not independent of the common or proper noun.

For unknown reasons, large numbers of writers confuse the possessive form of *its* with the contracted form of *it is*—*it's*. Writing *it's* as the possessive *its* is deemed a major error of form.

A similar problem occurs with the possessive *your* and the contraction of *you are*—*you're*. In this case, however, the confusion results in using the possessive for the contraction, as in the following example:

I know your a good swimmer.

Using the possessive instead of the contraction in such instances is also deemed a major error of form. Normally, both errors can be eliminated through careful editing.

SUMMARY

> It's = it is
> Its = possessive
> You're = you are
> Your = possessive

Indefinite Pronouns

Indefinite pronouns have general rather than specific antecedents, which means that they refer to general entities or concepts, as in sentence 30:

30. *Everyone* arrived very tired.

The indefinite pronoun *everyone* does not refer to any specific individual but rather to individuals in a group, hence its indefinite status.

The following list shows the indefinite pronouns in English:

all	any	anybody
anything	anyone	another
both	each	every
everybody	everyone	everything
either	few	fewer
many	neither	nobody
no one	none	one
several	some	somebody
something		

A common problem people have with indefinite pronouns involves number. Some indefinite pronouns always are singular, others are always plural, and a few can be both, depending on the construction. Table 1.1 offers some representative examples.

Usage Note: ## Indefinite Pronouns

Indefinite pronouns are the source of various usage problems, and being able to solve them is a significant step toward becoming a better writer. Although we cannot cover all the problems here owing to space limitations, we can examine the more common ones.

Everyone/Everybody

The indefinite pronouns *everyone* and *everybody* create difficulties because we commonly use them to signify more than one person—nevertheless, they are generally *singular*, *not plural* forms. Consequently, sentence 31 is grammatical, but sentence 32 is ungrammatical:

31. Everyone is a winner.
32. *Everyone are a winner.

TABLE 1.1
Indefinite Pronouns and Number. Indefinite pronouns usually
are either singular or plural in number, but some can be both.

Pronoun	Number	Example
all	singular and plural	*All* I wanted *is* all I got.
		All of the people *are* hungry.
		All babies are sweet.
any	singular and plural	*Any* of the offers *was* acceptable.
		The kids arrived, and Fritz wanted to know
		whether *any were* going to the movie.
anybody, anything, anyone	singular	If *anybody is* going to scream, it will be me.
both	plural	*Both* of the boys *were* in trouble.
each	singular	*Each is* very handsome.
every, everybody, everyone, everything	usually singular; plural in special circumstances	*Everyone has* an equal chance of success.
either	usually singular; plural in special circumstances	*Either* Fred or Fritz *is* responsible.
few, fewer	plural	*Few* of our troubles *are* caused by nature.
many	plural	Increasing numbers of people are disenchanted with city life, and *many are* buying homes in small towns.
most	plural	Cars are expensive, yet *most depreciate* 40% as soon as *they are* driven off the lot.
neither	usually singular; plural in special circumstances	*Neither* Macarena nor Buggsy *knows* anything about cars.
nobody, no one	singular	*Nobody is* home, and *no one answers* the phone.
none	singular	*None* of his books *sells* very well.
		None of the people *is* in good shape.
one	singular	*One is* certain to experience regret by age 40.
several	plural	Rita saw dogs digging up her flowers, and *several were* chasing her cat.
		Several of the books *need* repair.
some	singular and plural	The forest fire damage many tress, but *some* actually *were* destroyed.
somebody, something	singular	*Something is* rotten in Denmark.

Few people make this mistake, however. A far more common error occurs when *everyone* or *everybody* serves as an antecedent for another pronoun, as in the following sentences:

33. *Everyone* reached into the hat and pulled out *his or her* number.

33a. *Everyone reached into the hat and pulled out *their* number.

34. *Everybody* had decided to put on *his or her* bathing suit and take a swim.

34a. *Everybody had decided to put on *their* bathing suit and take a swim.

Some constructions, however, are problematic, such as the following:

35. *?Everybody* loved the casino, and *he or she* gambled the night away.

35a. *?Everybody* loved the casino, and *they* gambled the night away.

The difficulty is that *everybody* in sentences 35 and 35a signifies an entire group of people, as opposed to sentences 33 and 34, in which the indefinite pronoun signifies each individual in a group. Sentence 35a, therefore, would seem more acceptable than sentence 35, even though grammatically *everybody* is singular. The verb tense in sentence 35a masks the problem. Notice what happens when we change the verb tense to present:

35b. *Everybody* love the casino, and *they* gamble the night away.

However, sentence 34 can shift from being ungrammatical to being questionable if we pluralize *suit*:

34b. ?*Everybody* had decided to put on *their* bathing *suits* and take a swim.

There is no real solution to these difficulties, although using *everyone* or *everybody* to signify individuals rather than groups of people helps somewhat.

SUMMARY

➤ Generally, use *everyone* and *everybody* to signify individuals in a group rather than an entire group.

Applying Key Ideas 🔑

Directions: Some of the following sentences violate conventions governing pronoun usage. In each case, correct the usage error.

Example: Buggsy took the cigar out of ~~it's~~ its silver case.

1. Fritz, Macarena, and Rita decided to give each other money rather than gifts for Christmas.
2. None of the boys were particularly successful, even though they worked hard.
3. Everyone at the party left their coats in the master bedroom.
4. Macarena saw the pool and determined that if anyone was going to get wet that night it would be her.
5. Neither the host nor the guests knows much about politics, Fritz thought.
6. Fritz turned to Macarena and said, "Your only going to dance with me tonight!"
7. Both of Buggsy's goons was out of sight near the ferns, but Rita saw them anyway.
8. When everyone raised their glasses to toast Buggsy, Rita could see the guns inside the goon's jackets.
9. Meanwhile, the dog was barking inside its little house, demanding that the guests quiet down.
10. Rita looked closely at the goons and realized that each were a little tipsy from the champagne.

He and She—His and Her

Having raised the issue of pronouns and number, it is important to consider a usage question that was debated hotly during the 1970s. Note that many languages change the form of nouns and pronouns to mark them for gender. Spanish, for example, marks masculine nouns with the suffix *-o* and feminine nouns with the suffix *-a*. Pronouns follow a similar pattern. Languages that make these kinds of distinctions are known as *inflected* languages.

Although English was at one time a highly inflected language, it has dropped most, but not all, of the inflections over the last several centuries. Pronouns and some nouns, however, continue to be inflected. Well-known examples of inflected nouns are *actor* and *actress, steward* and *stewardess*. Less well-known are words such as *blond*, which changes its spelling but not its pronunciation depending on gender; males are *blond*, whereas females are *blonde*. Until the 1970s, the convention held that when using a pronoun to refer to people in general the masculine pronoun (e.g., *he* or *his*) was appropriate. Heightened concern over gender equality prompted a change in the convention, which now holds that both masculine and feminine pronouns should be used in such instances, as sentence 33 illustrates.

The change in the usage convention was accompanied by a great deal of controversy. Although the new convention is fairly well established today, the controversy has not died completely. Many people continue to object to the new convention, arguing that there is nothing sexist in using masculine pronouns generically. Others argue that the new convention is patronizing and that masculine pronouns should not be used at all but should be replaced by feminine pronouns—or that writers should alternate, using all masculine pronouns in one paragraph and all feminine pronouns in another.

Recognizing that such political issues are not likely to be resolved readily, large numbers of people suggest that the best approach is to avoid writing sentences that force a decision regarding generic signification. One way to do this is to use plural constructions rather than singular indefinite pronouns; another way is to drop the indefinite pronouns when possible. These recommendations are sensible and are therefore endorsed here. Note, however, that it is not always possible to pluralize a construction. In such instances, this handbook recommends using *he and she* or *his and her*. Always avoid using a slash in these constructions (*he/she* or *his/her*).

SUMMARY

> Pluralize constructions whenever possible to avoid having to use generic signification, or drop the indefinite pronouns.
> Never use slash (he/she or his/her) constructions.

If we apply this convention to the earlier sentences, we have the following:

36. *Everyone* reached into the hat and pulled out a number.

37. *They* had decided to put on *their* bathing suits and take a swim.

38. *They* loved the casino and gambled the night away.

Notice that pluralizing requires pluralizing throughout. Thus, it was necessary to change *suit* to *suits* in sentence 37.

Either

The word *either* can be used in more than one way. For example, it commonly functions as a noun modifier. Sentence 39 provides an illustration:

39. Either team was a good contender for the championship.

Few writers have any difficulty with this kind of construction. However, *either* also works with the word *or* to express a choice between two options, and when it does so with nouns, deciding on the right number can be a problem. Consider the following sentences:

40. Either Buggsy or Rita de Luna is going to win the contest.
41. Either towels or dishes is an appropriate gift.
42. *Either Raul or the goons are headed for trouble.

In sentence 42, the verb's number must be singular, even though the second noun in the subject—*the goons*—is plural. The only exception to this convention appears to be constructions similar to sentence 43:

43. Either the policemen or the firemen are getting a raise.

Few and Less

In formal Standard English, *few* and *less* do not mean the same thing. Although both are related to quantity, *few* (and *fewer*) is used when referring to a countable quantity, whereas *less* is used when referring to volume or any uncountable quantity. The following sentences illustrate the difference:

44. Few people know the difference between right and wrong.
45. Her glass held less beer than mine.

A usage difficulty arises for many when they make comparisons:

46.   There were fewer friends at the reunion than I had hoped for.
46a. *There were less friends at the reunion than I had hoped for.
47.   The team's leading slugger had fewer hits this year than last.
47a. *The team's leading slugger had less hits this year than last.
48.   *Raul had fewer air in his tank than Maria did.
48a. Raul and less air in his tank than Maria did.

SUMMARY

➢ Always use *few* or *fewer* with countable quantities; use *less* with volume or uncountable quantities.

Neither

The word *neither* functions in much the same way as *either*, the difference being that it expresses negation. In terms of number, it always is singular, as in the following examples:

49. Neither of the accused was guilty.
50. Buggsy and Rita de Luna loved ballroom dancing, but neither was found of the crowds.

Just as *either* often functions with *or*, so *neither* often functions with *nor*. When it does, the number generally is singular:

51. Neither Macarena nor Fritz was very hungry.

Notice, however, that an apparent exception occurs when the two nouns of the subject are plural:

52. Neither mothers nor fathers have an exclusive right to their children.

None

The word *none* is always singular. Usage problems generally occur when *none* is part of a construction that includes a plural noun. Consider the following sentences:

53. None of the goons was shorter than six feet.
53a. *None of the goons were shorter than six feet.
54. None of the problems of three little people like us amounts to a hill of beans considering what's going on in the world.
54a. *None of the problems of three little people like us amount to a hill of beans considering what's going on in the world.

SUMMARY

> ➤ *None* is always singular.

Reflexive Pronouns

When subjects perform actions on themselves, we need a special way to signify the reflexive nature of the action. We do so through the use of *reflexive pronouns*. Consider the act of shaving, as in sentence 55, in which *Macarena*, the subject, performs a reflexive action:

55. *Macarena shaved Macarena.

This duplication is not allowed, but we cannot use a personal pronoun for the object, *Macarena*. Doing so results in a different meaning, as in sentence 55a:

55a. Macarena shaved her.

In 55a, the pronoun *her* cannot refer to *Macarena* but must refer to someone else. To avoid this problem, English provides a set of special *reflexive pronouns* that signify a reflexive action:

Singular: myself, yourself, himself, herself, itself
Plural: ourselves, yourselves, themselves

Thus, to express the idea that Macarena shaved Macarena, we would have 55b:

55b. Macarena shaved *herself*.

Usage Note: ## Reflexive Pronouns

Sometimes reflexive pronouns work as *intensifiers*, as in sentences 56 and 57:

56. They *themselves* lost the case.
57. We *ourselves* must take appropriate action.

Many people are not sure how to use the pronouns *I* and *me*, so they use a reflexive pronoun to escape the problem of having to make a decision. The result, however, is equally incorrect, as in the following sentences:

58. *Macarena, Fritz, and *myself* stopped at Farmers Market for fresh strawberries.
59. *Buggsy took Fred, Macarena, and *myself* to his casino in Las Vegas.

Using a reflexive pronoun to replace a personal pronoun creates a problem in such sentences because there is no reflexive action. Replacing a personal pronoun with a reflexive is a violation of standard usage.

SUMMARY

➤ Reflexive pronouns must signify a reflexive action, or they must work as intensifiers.

Relative Pronouns

A clause consists of a subject and a predicate, but sentences commonly have more than one clause. There are several ways to join clauses together in a sentence, and one of the more interesting involves the use of a *relative pronoun*. The following list shows the major relative pronouns in English:

who	whom	that
which	whose	where
when	why	

Relative Clauses

When we use a relative pronoun to join two clauses, the pronoun generally replaces a duplicated noun or noun construction. This process turns the construction with the relative pronoun into a *relative clause*. Consider the following sentences:

> 60. Fritz knew a boy *who had red hair*.
>
> 61. The book *that Fritz bought* was a best seller.

Sentence 60 is composed of the clauses *Fritz knew a boy* and *A boy had red hair*. Sentence 61 is composed of *The book was a best seller* and *Fritz bought the book*. In sentence 60, the relative pronoun *who* replaced the duplicated noun construction *a boy*; that is, *a boy* is the antecedent. In sentence 61, the relative pronoun *that* replaced the duplicated noun construction *the book*.

Sometimes, however, a relative pronoun replaces an idea rather than a word or construction. Sentences 62 and 63 illustrate this principle:

> 62. Macarena spent the weekend in Las Vegas, *which surprised her friends*.
>
> 63. The show started early, *which caused some problems*.

In sentence 62, the relative pronoun *which* represents *the fact that Macarena spent the weekend in Las Vegas,* whereas in 63 it represents *the fact that the show started early.*

Note also that the relative clauses in sentences 62 and 63 are set off with commas. This point is examined in detail later, but here it is useful to understand that some relative clauses can be set off whereas other cannot. We cannot, for example, put commas around the relative clause in sentence 61.

Usage Note: Relative Pronouns

That and Which

Most people treat the relative pronouns *that* and *which* as being identical. Formal standard usage, however, differentiates them along a very clear line. *That* is used exclusively to introduce relative clauses that cannot be set off with commas. *Which*, on the other hand, is used to introduce relative clauses that *must be* set off with commas.

This convention illuminates the following sentences:

> 64.   ?The car which I like has fat tires and a good stereo.
>
> 64a. *The car, that I like, has fat tires and a good stereo.
>
> 64b. The car that I like has fat tires and a good stereo.
>
> 64c. The car, which I like, has fat tires and a good stereo.

SUMMARY

> ➢ *Which* always introduces a relative clause set off with commas.

Who and Whom

Another difficulty for many people involves the pronouns *who* and *whom*. Even those who use Standard English fairly consistently have dropped *whom* from most of their speech, and increasingly it is being dropped from writing as well. In speech, most people use *who* or *that*, and even in much journalistic writing we find *who* being used rather than *whom*.

The difference between *who* and *whom* is related to case, which we examined earlier. *Who* always functions as the subject of a relative clause, so it is in the nominative case. *Whom*, on the other hand, always functions as an object, so it is in the objective case. As with other pronouns in English, the form of these relative pronouns is determined by their case—*whom* is the objective form of *who*. Consider these sentences:

- The man *who* owned the horse worked at a bank.
- The man *whom* I knew loved to fly.

Because one can never know in advance how an audience will respond to writing that does not apply the *who/whom* distinction, this handbook recommends a conservative approach—use *whom* as the objective-case form of the pronoun.

SUMMARY

➢ *Who* is always a subject.
➢ *Whom* is always an object.
➢ Use *who* for the nominative case; use *whom* for the objective case.

That and Who

Another feature of formal standard usage involves differentiating between *that* and *who*. As in the case of *that* and *which*, many people mistakenly believe that these words are interchangeable:

- ?The boy *that* found the wallet turned it in at the police station.
- The boy *who* found the wallet turned it in at the police station.

These pronouns are not interchangeable in formal Standard English; they are quite different. Standard usage provides that *who* is used for people and *that* is used for everything else. Use *who* as a relative pronoun for people and use *that* for everything else.

 *Applying Key Ideas*

Part 1

Directions: Some of the following sentences violate conventions governing pronoun usage. In each case, correct the usage error.

Example: The decline in social capital is often measured by the increase in the
                                    who
number of people ~~that~~ refuse to abide by laws that regulate civil behavior, such as traffic regulations.

1. Buggsy invited Macarena, Fritz, and myself to his casino in Vegas.
2. Macarena, who Fritz loved beyond all measure, was infatuated with Buggsy.
3. Whomever leaves the party early will not be invited to another.
4. Fritz began reading a new book about civil society, which was something that he thought he knew about just a little.
5. The book which he was reading seemed to be very popular among the cafe crowd.
6. There were three goons at Buggsy's party that looked cross and eager for an argument.
7. Macarena became a bit upset when she had to pour herself a glass of champagne.
8. Suddenly, Fritz was by her side with an apologetic smile which made Macarena feel better at once, and she knew that whoever else came into her life, Fritz always would be special.
9. Meanwhile, the woman who Buggsy was dancing with tripped near the pool and almost fell in.
10. When the band took a break, Buggsy told Fritz, Macarena, and myself that we seemed to lack ambition, which could be a serious character flaw.

Part 2

Directions: Examine a page or two of a paper you wrote in the past for pronoun usage. Look particularly at your use of relative and reflexive pronouns. If you find instances of correct or incorrect usage, circle them and compare that usage with the previous discussions about pronouns.

Verbs

Understanding more complex sentence patterns requires knowing a few things about verbs. First, they come in different varieties. A verb like *bark* in *Dogs bark* is fairly simple because it works only with the subject of the sentence. Other verbs, however, must work with both a subject and an object. Consider sentence 65:

65. Fritz kissed Macarena.

Notice that *kissed*, unlike *bark*, cannot work with a subject alone. Sentence 66, therefore, is ungrammatical:

66. *Fritz kissed.

Transitive and Intransitive Verbs

Verbs like *bark* that do not require an object are called *intransitive* verbs; verbs like *kiss* that do require an object are called *transitive* verbs. On this basis, we can identify two important sentence patterns in English based on functional relations:

- SV (subject/verb)

- SVO (subject/verb/object)

SVO is the most common pattern in English.

Usage Note: *Lie and Lay*

The verbs *lie* and *lay* are similar in many respects, but they have one fundamental difference. *Lie* is intransitive and *lay* is transitive. Widespread nonstandard usage, however, treats *lay* as an intransitive verb, as in sentence 67:

    67. ?Fritz wanted to *lay* down.

This usage is nonstandard because *lay* requires an object, as in sentence 68:

    68. Buggsy *lay the book* on the table.

To make sentence 67 conform to Standard English, we would have to change the verb *lay* to *lie*, as in sentence 67a:

    67a. Fritz wanted to *lie* down.

The past-tense forms of these verbs can easily cause confusion, and they often demand special consideration before use:

Intransitive
    lie (present)   lay (past)

Transitive
    lay (present)   laid (past)

Using sentences 68 and 67a to illustrate the past-tense forms would give us the following:

    68a. Buggsy *laid* the book on the table.
    67b. Fritz *lay* down.

Linking Verbs

In the sentence *Buggsy felt tired*, the verb *felt* works with the word *tired* to identify the status or state of being of the subject, *Buggsy*. We can say that *felt* links the word *tired* to *Buggsy* because it describes his status. We might even say that the word *tired* completes the predicate because without it we would have an ungrammatical sentence (for this reason, words and constructions that complete a predicate are called *complements*):

- *Buggsy felt.

Felt is an example of a special category of verbs called *linking verbs*. They generally connect the subject to a word that describes the status of the subject or that renames the subject, as the following sentences illustrate:

69. Fred *was* a winner.
70. Macarena *remained* president.
71. The flowers *smelled* good.
71. Buggsy *seemed* lonely.
73. The cheese *tasted* sour.

Linking verbs are all forms of *be* (*is, was, were, am, are*) and the verbs listed here:

become	*feel*	*grow*
look	*prove*	*seems*
smell	*sound*	*taste*

Got also can function as a linking verb when it is used in the sense of *become*, as in *Fred got tired*. Note, however, that some of these verbs, specifically *smell, feel, sound, prove*, and *grow*, also can function as regular verbs, as in *Fred smelled the flowers*.

Tense

Verbs describe an action or express a state of being, but they also indicate the time of the action. *Tense* is the term we use to describe *the change in the form of a verb* to signal when an action occurred. Although there are three possible tenses—past, present, and future—English has only two tenses—past and present. We signal the future in English in various ways, most commonly by adding the word *will* to the verb construction.

Number

All verbs must agree in number with their subjects; that is, they are either singular or plural. Standard English signals a singular verb with an *s* suffix. Consider sentences 74 and 75:

74. Macarena and Fritz love dancing.
75. Fred loves swimming.

In sentence 74, the subject is plural because it is made up of *Macarena and Fritz*; in sentence 75, however, the subject is singular.

Usage Note: Number

Some dialects do not match the number of the subject and its verb, as illustrated in the following sentence:

• ?I goes to the market and gets some milk.

Although such forms are acceptable in certain dialects, they are not acceptable in formal Standard English.

Subject–Verb Agreement

When the verb of a predicate does not agree in number with the subject, we say that there is an error of *subject–verb agreement*. This error is one of the more common in writing and usually occurs when the subject is followed by a construction with another noun. The proximity of the nonsubject noun causes the writer unconsciously to match the number of the verb to it. Consider sentences 76 and 77:

76. *The number of problems baffle us.
77. *Our team of volunteers are working hard to raise money.

The subject of sentence 76 is *number*, a singular noun, not *problems*; thus, the number of the verb should be singular, giving us *baffles*. Sentence 77 illustrates a similar situation. The subject is *team*, not *volunteers*, so the verb should be singular, giving us *is*.

Usage Note: *There* and *Here*

Sometimes sentences begin with the word *there* or *here*. These words are not subjects; they just fill the subject position in the sentence. The true subject comes after the verb, as in sentences 78 and 79:

78. There are *five people* in the room.
79. Here is *the sandwich*.

In such sentences, the number of the verb must agree with the number of the subject; thus, sentence 78a is ungrammatical:

78a. *There is five people in the room.

Verb Forms

In Standard English, verbs have tense; that is, they generally indicate the time of an action as being either past or present. English also provides the option of signaling the duration or ongoing nature of an action—what is known as *aspect*—through three verb forms, the *progressive*, the *perfect,* and a combination of the two known as the *perfect progressive*.[3]

Progressive Verb Form

The progressive verb form is used to communicate that an action is ongoing, as illustrated in the following sentences:

80. Macarena was dancing the night away.
81. Fritz is going to do well on the test.
82. Fred will be leaving soon.

---

[3]Black English Vernacular reverses this situation: Tense is optional, whereas aspect is required.

From these examples, we see that the progressive is composed of a form of the verb *be* and a verb that has the suffix *-ing* attached.

Perfect Verb Form

The perfect verb form is used to communicate that an action has been fully completed, as illustrated in these three sentences:

83. Buggsy had invested a great deal of money in the casino.
84. Rita has stopped her acting lessons.
85. Mrs. DeMarco will have eaten by now.

These examples show that the perfect is composed of a form of *have* and a verb that has the suffix *-ed* or *-en* attached.

Perfect Progressive Verb Form

The perfect progressive is a combination of perfect and progressive verb forms. It indicates that an action that was ongoing at some point is now completed, as the following sentences illustrate:

86. Buggsy had been drinking that night.
87. Rita de Luna has been thinking about Buggsy's offer.
88. Macarena will have been driving for two days before she reaches her destination.

Perfect progressive is composed of a form of *have*, *be* plus the suffix *-en*, and a verb with the *-ing* suffix attached.

Applying Key Ideas

Directions: Some of the following sentences violate conventions governing verb usage. In each case, correct the usage error.

were
Example: Macarena and Fritz ~~was~~ invited to Buggsy's party.

1. There was at least 200 people at Buggsy's party, all of them elegantly dressed.
2. When Fritz thought about the future, he realized that a wide range of options were open to him, but he also recognized that the sheer number of them was the problem.
3. Several of the guests at the party was celebrities, and many more held political office.
4. At a table near the pool, a team of rowdy rugby players were drinking champagne like sailors, until finally one could not hold up and had to lay down in a guest room.

5. One of the goons was afraid that the bed might become soiled, so he lay a towel beside the drunken rugby player for safety's sake.

6. Several Brazilians arrived late, and as they entered, the band broke out into a hot samba to celebrate them.

7. There were a couple of good dancers in that group, and they started moving to the beat.

8. A goon turned to one of the Brazilians and said, "I see that you guys likes the music. Don't feel bad about dancing all you want—this is a party!"

9. With the music and the champagne, many in the crowd was getting dizzy, and before long people started jumping into the pool without even bothering to put on swimming suits.

10. Buggsy laughed and said to Macarena, "There's the people I want to invite to all my parties!"

Modifiers: Adjectivals and Adverbials

Although nouns and verbs are the principal parts of sentences, other constructions play important supporting roles. Perhaps the most important of these is the category of *modifiers*, words and phrases that provide information about nouns and verbs (and sometimes to entire clauses or sentences). Indeed, there is a sense in which everything in a sentence other than the nouns and verbs is a modifier. This handbook is too brief to explore this proposition in detail, but understanding its general principles is fairly straightforward.

Given that nouns and verbs are the building blocks of sentences, we can predict that modifiers must be of two types—those that supply information to nouns and those that supply information to verbs. This prediction is essentially correct, with the exception noted above of modifiers that supply information to clauses and sentences. Noun modifiers are called *adjectivals,* and verb modifiers are called *adverbials*. Note, however, that *modifier* is a function category, as is adjectival and adverbial (thus, these terms are subcategories of the broader category). Most words can function as modifiers, but their form does not necessarily change; a noun functioning as an adjectival is still a noun.

Adjectivals

Adjectival modifiers supply information, usually sensory, to nouns and noun phrases. The most common type of adjectival modifier is the *simple adjective*. Consider the following sentences:

89. Macarena drove a *red* Porsche.

90. Buggsy would not eat the *cold* macaroni.

91. His *best* shirt had a stain on the collar.

Each of these simple adjectives supplies information to its associated noun: The Porsche was *red*; the macaroni was *cold*; the shirt was his *best*.

As just indicated, other types of words, such and nouns and verbs, can function as adverbials, as the following sentences illustrate:

92. We often curl up by the fire on a *winter* evening.

93. The *running* brook sparkled in the sunlight.

Simple adjectives come before the nouns they modify. However, there are two special adjectives that do not. The first kind appears in sentences like *Buggsy felt tired*. The word *tired* is an adjective, and it supplies information to *Buggsy,* but it follows the linking verb *felt*. Because adjectives of this type have a special relation with linking verbs, they have a specific name: *predicate adjective*. Predicate adjectives always follow linking verbs.

The second type of special adjective is called an *adjective complement*, illustrated in sentence 94:

94. Fred and Fritz painted the town *red*.

Notice that the adjective *red* completes the predicate, but it doesn't immediately follow the verb. Moreover, *painted* is not a linking verb.

Adverbials

Adverbial modifiers supply information to verbs, to adjectivals, to other adverbials, to clauses, and to sentences. The information is not sensory but instead deals with the following:

time, place, manner, degree, cause, concession

Like adjectivals, adverbials consist of *simple adverbs* and words of varying forms and entire constructions that function adverbially. The following examples illustrate adverbials that provide information about time, place, manner, and degree. (The other two types of modification are examined under the heading of subordination.)

Time: They arrived *late*.

Place: We stopped *there* for a rest.

Manner: Fred opened the box *slowly*.

Degree: Macarena felt *very* tired. Rita opened the box *quite* rapidly.

More on Linking Verbs

Linking verbs generally connect the subject to a word that describes the status of the subject or that renames the subject. Thus, a linking verb is followed by either a noun (or noun phrase) or an adjective. Consider the sentence *Buggsy felt tired*; *felt* is a linking verb, and *tired* is an adjective.

Usage Note: ## Adjectives and Adverbs

Good and Well

Many people have difficulty with the modifiers *good* and *well*. The problem is that *good* always is an adjective, whereas *well* can function as either an adjective or an adverb. In nonstandard usage *good* appears as both an adjective and an adverb, and *well* appears only in limited ways. The example sentences here illustrate the most common nonstandard usage of *good*:

95. ?I did *good* on the test.
96. ?You played *good*.

Standard usage is quite clear on this point—*well* is called for in these instances, as in 95a and 96a:

95a. I did *well* on the test.
96a. You played *well*.

Another situation arises with the linking verb *feel*. When describing how they are feeling, most people say that they feel *good*, as in sentence 97:

97. I feel *good*.

Formal standard usage differentiates between *I feel good* and *I feel well*. *Well* nearly always refers to one's state of health; only in most unusual circumstances would *feel* appear as a regular verb signifying that one has a sense of touch that is working properly. Thus, *I feel well* indicates that one is healthy. More to the point, it indicates that, after some particular illness or disease, one has regained previous health. A person recovered from the flu, for example, might say *I feel well*. *I feel good*, on the other hand, can refer to one's general state of well-being, which can be physiological, psychological, or both. With respect to one's health, however, *I feel good* does not mean, in formal standard usage, that one has regained previous health. It means that one is feeling better at the moment of the utterance than in the past but that the illness or disease is still present. On this account, one might say, after a few days in bed with the flu, *I feel good today*, meaning that one feels relatively better than the day before.

Equally problematic is the situation associated with the question, *How are you today?* If one responds in a way that signifies general well-being, then the appropriate response is *I am good*, although the inherent ambiguity here is interesting. It could mean that one is virtuous, which certainly is a state of being, but perhaps one more often desired than attained. If, however, one responds in a way that signifies health, the appropriate response is *I am well*.

Bad and Badly

The linking verb *feel* is associated with a common usage problem. In the face of hardship or accident, people naturally want to express their sadness or remorse, but doing so often leads to an unacceptable form. There are two possibilities:

98. I heard about the accident. ?I feel *badly*.
98a. I heard about the accident. I feel *bad*.

Feel is a linking verb when referring to one's state of being, so it must be followed by an adjective. *Bad* is an adjective, but *badly* is not—it's an adverb. Consequently, *badly* does not make any sense, really, because it does not refer to a state of being. In fact, if we took sentence 98 literally, it would mean that the speaker has lost his or her tactile perception: Upon touching something, the speaker simply cannot *feel* it. This is not a state or condition that people experience very often, and it certainly is not related to remorse. Thus, *I feel bad* reflects standard usage.

SUMMARY

> ➤ With a linking verb, use *bad* rather than *badly* to express remorse.

Part 1

Directions: Identify the simple adjectives and adverbs in the following sentences.

Example: The band took a short break and somehow managed to drink two cases of champagne.

1. They returned to the bandstand excited and ready to whip the party guests into a wild frenzy.
2. Swing jazz was the latest craze in Hollywood, so the band started with an old Benny Goodman number that sent a dozen couples into a hot jitterbug.
3. The summer evening suddenly got warmer, and the band increase the tempo.
4. Couples started doing lifts and throws at a crazy pace, and sweat began to pour down the flushed faces of the musicians.
5. They really stated to work now, and the music became louder.
6. Most people were out of the pool when one dancer lost his balance during a difficult lift and toppled into the water.
7. People laughed, and the band played on.
8. Macarena grabbed Fritz and pulled him out into the jumping crowd.
9. They were great dancers, having practiced for months, and they began to jump and jive like professionals, using the most intricate steps anyone had ever seen.
10. The horn players were by now blowing out their lungs, and the drummer, a slim, dark young girl from the Bronx, seemed as though she would faint at any time.

Conjunctions

There are two types of conjunctions—*coordinating* and *subordinating*. The coordinating conjunctions connect equal elements, such as two or more nouns, two or more verbs, and so forth. The subordinating conjunctions connect a dependent clause to an independent clause.

Coordinating Conjunctions

and, but, for, nor, or, yet

Subordinating Conjunctions

because	if	as
until	since	whereas
although	though	while
unless	so that	once
after	before	when
whenever	as if	even if
in order that	as soon as	even though
insofar as	as though	inasmuch as
so that		

Coordination

The term *coordination* signifies equal elements working together. This condition is accomplished in English with coordinating conjunctions. Coordinating conjunctions can join individual words or phrases, such as nouns and verbs, and they can join clauses. Consider the following examples:

99. Maria *and* Raul went to a dance.	(two nouns)
100. The boy with the dark hair *and* the girl with the green eyes could really dance.	(two noun phrases)
101. Raul ate *and* drank all night.	(two verbs)
102. Rita tripped on the rug *but* didn't fall.	(two verb phrases)
103. Macarena needed milk, *but* she didn't want to go to the market.	(two clauses)
104. The sun was shinning, *and* the day was warm.	(two clauses)

Sentences 103 and 104 illustrate the conjoining of two independent clauses. Each clause could be and independent sentence, as shown here:

103a. Macarena needed milk. But she didn't want to go to the market.

104a. The sun was shinning. And the day was warm.

Usage Note: ## Coordination and Punctuation

Coordination is fairly straightforward, but the conventions of punctuating coordinated elements often causes difficulties. First, there are two distinct conventions associated with a list of items. The most widely used convention dictates that each item in the list be separated with a comma, even the item that comes before the coordinating conjunction. Sentence 105 illustrates this convention:

105. Buggsy loved gambling, women, and cheap cigars.

The second convention is used almost exclusively among journalists. It does not provide for a comma in front of the conjunction, as shown in sentence 105a:

105a. Buggsy loved gambling, women and cheap cigars.

Unless you are writing for a journalism class or a newspaper, avoid the second convention.

SUMMARY

> Separate each item in a list with a comma.

Convention also requires a comma when two independent clauses are joined with a coordination conjunction. The comma must come before the conjunction, as in sentences 103 and 104:

103. Macarena needed milk, *but* she didn't want to go to the market.
104. The sun was shinning, *and* the day was warm.

Failure to provide a comma in such instances is usually deemed a major error.

Usage Note: ## Beginning a Sentence with a Conjunction

Many students are told incorrectly that they cannot begin a sentence with a word like *and, but,* or *for*. Although most sentences in English begin with the subject, there is absolutely nothing incorrect or inappropriate about starting sentences with a coordinating conjunction.

SUMMARY

> Sentences may begin with a coordinating conjunction, but do so sparingly.

Subordination

There are two major types of clauses—independent and dependent. Independent clauses can function as sentences, whereas dependent clauses cannot but must be connected to an independent clause. The most frequent connection is made with a *subordinating conjunction* (see the list on page 415), as the following sentences illustrate:

106. Fritz went to the market *because he needed bread.*
107. Macarena loved fine wine, *whereas Fred loved beer.*
108. *Although Rita de Luna was an experienced performer,* she became nervous before every show.

Subordinate clauses function as adverbials, supplying information to a verb phrase (as in the case of sentence 106) or to an entire clause (as in the case of sentences 107 and 108). Adverbials generally provide information about *time, place, manner, degree, cause, contrast,* and *concession*; subordinate clauses, however, provide information about time, cause, contrast, and concession. The examples that follow illustrate these three types.

Time:	*When Raul walked into the house,* he could smell the cake baking.
	Fritz washed the dishes *while Macarena put on the new CD by Rita de Luna.*
Cause:	We ate *because we were hungry*.
Contrast:	Buggsy loved Las Vegas, *whereas his wife hated it.*
Concession:	*Although she didn't like broccoli,* she ate it.

Because

The subordinating conjunction *because* appears with a linking verb in nonstandard usage. Consider the following:

• Fred got a second job. *The reason was *because he needed more money*.

The second sentence has the linking verb *was* and the subordinate clause *because he needed more money*. Linking verbs, however, cannot be followed by a subordinate clause; they must be followed by a noun (or noun phrase) or an adjective. Thus, this example sentence is ungrammatical. Formal standard usage requires a complex noun phrase beginning with the word *that* in this sentence, as illustrated below:

• Fred got a second job. The reason was that he needed more money.

Usage Note:

Since, While, Because, and Whereas

The subordinating conjunctions *since* and *while* are related to time, as the following sentences show:

• Since Maria started working at the jewelry store, business has increased 20%.
• Buggsy smoked a cigar while he watched the couples dance.

In common usage, however, these conjunctions are used to signify cause and contrast, as in the following:

• ?Since he needed milk, Fred went to the market.
• ?The police suspected Buggy's goons, while the DA suspected no one.

Formal standard usage does not allow such sentences; *since* and *while* should be used only when signifying a temporal relationship. To signify cause or contrast, formal standard usage calls for *because* and *whereas*.

➤ *Since* and *while* signify time.

➤ *Because* signifies cause, and *whereas* signifies contrast.

Applying Key Ideas

Part 1

Directions: Use coordinating and subordinating conjunctions to combine the sets sentences into single sentences.

Example: a. A civil society is based on respect for others.
  b. A civil society considers the common good to be more important than individual rights.

  Because a civil society is based on respect for others, it considers the common good to be more important than individual rights.

1. a. The decrease in civic-organization membership is one indicator that the nation's social capital is declining.
   b. Without social capital, a civil society is very difficult.

2. a. Many political scientists now argue that America's focus on extreme individualism is out of hand.
   b. They do not offer many suggestions on how the nation might move away from extreme individualism toward greater community.

3. a. One problem is that individualism is fueled by isolation.
   b. Technology, whether it be television, cell phones, or video games, is a powerful force in the further isolation of people.
   c. It disengages them from civic organizations, the community, and each other.

4. a. The world is overcrowded.
   b. Most people see technology's power to isolate as a good thing.
   c. They have a hard time looking farther into the future and understanding that, actually, it is a bad thing.

5. a. Advertising makes matters worse.
   b. Advertising promotes technology by linking such devices as cell phones to social status.

Part 2

Directions: Some of the following sentences violate punctuation conventions governing coordination. In each case, correct the error.

Example: Macarena and Fritz drove to Las Vegas and they stayed at the Luxor Hotel and Casino.

1. Macarena immediately called room service and ordered champagne, lobster and cracked crab.

2. Fritz was eager to try the Jacuzzi so he began filling the tub.

3. Macarena was eager to get to the casino but she nevertheless lingered over her dinner.

4. She decided to eat, and drink slowly.

5. Fritz soaked in the tub thinking about the evening ahead, and then began fantasizing about winning a jackpot.

6. Fritz knew that he should call Buggsy and arrange to visit his casino, but was reluctant.

7. The bathroom had a huge window that looked out over the Strip and Fritz could see the many lights from the hotels twinkling in the growing dusk.

8. Suddenly, a shooting star streaked passed and Fritz knew that he would be lucky that night.

9. He stepped out of the Jacuzzi, slipped on his rob and went to tell Macarena that he felt very lucky.

10. Macarena had put on some Tony Bennett so Fritz took her in his arms and they started to dance.

Prepositional Phrases

A *preposition* generally works with a noun phrase, and together they compose a *prepositional phrase*. The preposition links its noun phrase to either a verb phrase or another noun phrase, which means that the prepositional phrase functions either *adverbially or adjectivally*.

109.	The woman *with the red hair* drove a Porsche.	(adjectival)
110.	Fritz walked *down the street*.	(adverbial)
111.	*In the morning*, Fred always has wild hair.	(adverbial)

The list of English prepositions is quite long, but some of the more common are shown in the following list, including some multiple-word prepositions:

about	above	across
after	against	along
among	around	as
at	before	behind
below	beneath	beyond
by	concerning	despite
down	during	except
for	from	in
into	like	near
of	off	on
out	outside	over
past	through	to
toward	under	until
up	upon	with

| within | without | due to |
| according to | in spite of | in keeping with |

Usage Note: Prepositions

Number of Prepositions

When writing a formal or semiformal paper, many people produce sentences that have too many prepositions, which has the effect of making their writing hard to read. Consider the following example sentence:

The determination of the causes of the accident through the use of modern investigative techniques and the application of proper protocols was rendered impossible and raised numerous questions related to the skill of the team and their commitment to following proper procedures.

Although it is difficult to figure out exactly what this sentence means, a rough translation might be:

The investigative team failed to follow proper procedures and thus could not determine the cause of the accident, which makes us question their skill.

Perhaps the biggest difference between these two versions is that the second has far fewer prepositions. As the number of prepositions in a given sentence increases, its readability decreases. Thus, a useful rule thumb is to have as few prepositions as possible in your writing. More specifically, try to have no more than three prepositions per sentence.

At the End of Sentences

Large numbers of people mistakenly believe that they must not end a sentence with a preposition, having encountered this prohibition at some point in school. The prohibition has absolutely no foundation. Certain types of sentences can quite easily *and quite correctly* end with a preposition. Consider the following examples:

112. Won't you come in?
113. I liked the box that the gift came in.

Like

The word *like* is a preposition, and in standard usage it introduces a prepositional phrase, as shown in sentence 114:

114. There was no one quite *like Rita de Luna*.

In conversation, however, many people use *like* as a subordinating conjunction, as in sentences 115 and 116:

115. ?Fred acted *like he knew something about art*.
116. ?If Fred had taken the money to Buggsy *like he should have*, he wouldn't have to hide from Buggsy's goons.

This usage is nonstandard. In formal standard usage, only a subordinating conjunction is appropriate in such constructions, as in sentences 115a and 116a:

115a. Fred acted *as though* he knew something about art.

116a. If Fred had taken the money to Buggsy *as* he should have, he wouldn't have to hide from Buggsy's goons.

SUMMARY

> ➤ Always use *like* as a preposition, never as a subordinating conjunction.

Applying Key Ideas

Part 1

Directions: Circle the prepositions in the following sentences.

1. Fritz put his tuxedo on while Macarena slipped into a long black evening gown.
2. They rode the glass-enclosed elevator down from the 30th floor to the casino, which was already crowded and noisy.
3. They watched the crap tables for a while before they moved to the roulette wheels.
4. With a smile on his face, Fritz watched the fast action, remembering the shooting star he saw from his window.
5. He pulled a tight roll of 100 dollar bills from his pocket and bought $5,000 worth of chips.
6. Macarena looked at him and nodded her head, so Fritz put all the chips on number 31 and watched the wheel spin.
7. Until that moment, Fritz had never been so focused, but now all of his attention was on the little white ball as it made its way around the wheel, ready to fall.
8. The sound of the crowd fell away, and all he could hear was the faint whirl of the wheel and the ball, with its shinning white lacquer.
9. Then the ball dropped and bounced and then bounced again, landing with a note of finality on number 31.
10. Suddenly, the noise of the crowd swelled up around him, and Fritz remember to breath, all the while realizing that now he and Macarena had a huge pile of cash.

Part 2

Directions: Select a page of a paper you wrote at some point in the past and analyze each sentence for prepositions. Circle each preposition, and wherever a sentence has more than three prepositions, rewrite the sentence to reduce their number.

Dependent clauses provide modifying information to either phrases or clauses, and they can do so in two ways. Consider the following sentences:

117. Macarena liked the dress *that had the dropped shoulders*. (relative clause)

118. Fritz, *who never had enough money*, had holes in the soles of his shoes. (relative clause)

119. Buggsy had been bored *since he stopped going to the races*. (subordinate clause)

120. *Because he was a bit plump*, he decided to diet. (subordinate clause)

Sentences 117 and 118 have relative clauses, but they are functioning in different ways; the same is true for the subordinate clauses in sentences 119 and 120. The clauses in 117 and 119 provide what may be thought of as essential or identifying information. Notice also that they lack punctuation, whereas sentences 119 and 120 are set off with a comma. Clauses that supply essential or identifying information are called *restrictive clauses*. The clauses in sentences 118 and 120, on the other hand, provide additional information that is incidental. Such clauses are called *nonrestrictive clauses*.

SUMMARY

➤ Restrictive clauses provide essential or identifying information and are not set off with punctuation.
➤ Nonrestrictive clauses provide incidental information and are set off with punctuation.

Usage Note: Relative Clauses and Relative Pronouns

The relative pronouns *that* and *which* connect relative clauses to independent clauses, but they do so in different ways. Although in conversation people commonly use these pronouns interchangeably, in formal standard usage they are different. *That* always introduces a restrictive relative clause; *which,* however, usually introduces a nonrestrictive relative clause. Consider the following examples:

121. The book that Rita bought was a first edition.

121a. ?The book which Rita bought was a first edition.

121b. *The book, that Rita bought, was a first edition.

121c. The book, which Rita bought, was a first edition.

Sentences 121 and 121c are especially interesting because they illustrate how the nature of the dependent clause affects the meaning of a sentence. In sentence

121, *the book* is identified as the one Rita bought. In sentence 121c, on the other hand, the fact that Rita bought the book is incidental to the fact that the book was a first edition.

SUMMARY

> *That* connects a restrictive relative clause to an independent clause and has no punctuation.
> *Which* connects a nonrestrictive relative clause to an independent clause and is set off with punctuation.

PUNCTUATION

Punctuation is largely a matter of convention rather than rule, but some of the conventions are strict. Along with misspelling, punctuation problems are deemed major errors. Fortunately, the conventions governing punctuation are fairly straightforward.

Periods

All sentences end with a period. Note, however, that putting a period at the end of a string of words does not make the string a sentence. Subordinate clauses, for example, cannot exist without a dependent clause. Putting a period at the end of an orphaned subordinate clause creates what is known as a *sentence fragment*. Consider the following examples:

122. *Because it was important to the effort.

123. *While the politicians debated the bill.

124. *Although Buggsy loved to gamble.

Commas

The guidelines for commas are very strict and should be followed carefully. Some people mistakenly believe that commas represent pausing places in a sentence or that they mark where anyone reading a sentence aloud might take a breath. Both notions are completely false. Comma use is related to the structure of sentences, not to reading or pauses. *Do not use commas in any way that is not specified below:*

> Separate each item in a series with a comma.
>
> Example: Rita, Rod, and Macarena danced the pachanga.

> Always use a comma when joining two independent clauses with a coordinating conjunction.
>
> Example: Buggsy hired the best entertainers for his casino in Las Vegas, and he paid them well.

➢ Always use a comma to set off nonrestrictive clauses.

Example: Rita de Luna signed the new contract, which surprised her agent.
Example: Buggsy, because he liked Fritz, ordered more champagne.

➢ Always use a comma to set off an introductory prepositional phrase or subordinate clause.

Example: In the morning, Rita couldn't remember the name of the champagne,
Example: Although he was tired, Fritz cleaned his apartment.

The conventions above regulate all legitimate uses of commas. Nevertheless, some errors with commas are so common that they deserve special treatment here. The following are some prohibitions regarding commas:

➢ Never join two independent clauses with a comma only. (Doing so creates what is known as a *comma splice*.)

Example: ?The police suspected that Buggsy was involved in illegal gambling, they decided to put a tap on his phone to gather information.

➢ Never use a comma to separate two verb phrases joined by a coordinating conjunction.

Example: ?The court approved a search warrant for Buggy's Bel Air mansion, and also approved the phone tap.

➢ Never put a comma behind a coordinating conjunction unless the conjunction is followed immediately by a nonrestrictive phrase or clause.

Example: ?And, he also asked for more money.
Example: ?Yet, he knew that she was innocent.
Example: But, in the morning, he changed his mind.
Example: And, because he needed a job, he accepted.

Semicolon

The semicolon has two uses. The most common is to join two independent clauses without a coordinating conjunction, as illustrated in the following examples:

125. Macarena drove to the Beverly Center to meet Fred; she was supposed to meet him at 3 p.m.

126. Fred, meanwhile, was stuck in traffic on the Santa Monica freeway; he hadn't moved more than 50 feet in the past 20 minutes.

The semicolon also is used to separate items in a list when one of the items contains a phrase or a clause that is set off with commas (or dashes). Consider the following examples:

127. Buggsy was a suspect for several reasons: 1) he owned a casino in Las Vegas that barely showed a profit last year; 2) two of his goons, Scarface

and Slim Jim, had left town without a trace; and 3) he had bragged in the past about what he would do to anyone who snitched on him.

128. The recipe called for the following items: sugar from Madagascar; saffron, preferably unprocessed, from Celon; and mint picked with dew still on the leaves.

Colon

The colon, like the semicolon, has two uses. The most common is to signify that something, such as a list, an example, or a quotation, is to follow. Sentence 129 illustrates the use of a colon with a list.

129. The guests at Buggsy's party included the following: Major Bardberry, Mayor Jenkins, Chief Justice Warmer, and District Attorney Brown.

The colon also is used to connect two independent clauses when the second clause functions to explain the first. Consider the following example:

130. Buggsy leaned forward to kiss Rita de Luna but stopped suddenly: Out of the corner of his eye he spotted his wife peeping from behind a fern.

Parentheses and the Dash

Parentheses are used to set off additional or extra information inside a sentence. This usage is so common, in fact, that the information is referred to as a parenthetical construction. The following sentence illustrates this principle:

131. Macarena took Fritz (the man of the hour) by the hand and led him to the dance floor.

The dash also is used to set off such information, but it often is used to connect two independent clauses, as shown in the following example:

132. Fred straightened his bow tie and checked himself in the mirror—he wanted to make a good impression on his host.

Usage Note: ## Conjunctions, Semicolons, Colons, and Dashes

The previous sections show that writers have four ways to connect independent clauses. Understanding how these ways differ involves knowing something about style. For example, the choice between using a coordinating conjunction and a comma or a semicolon depends on what the writer wants to do with such a sentence. The conjunction and comma slow the pace of reading more than the semicolon, which, stylistically, suggests that the relation between the two clauses is not as strong as when a writer uses a semicolon. Most handbooks therefore recommend using the semicolon when a writer wants to signal that the clauses are closely connected. The colon, on the other hand, signals that the second clause will explain the first. The dash, although used to link equal clauses, also signifies that the second clause should receive more emphasis. From this perspective, the study of punctuation is a study of style.

Salutations

Letters normally begin with a salutation—*Dear Buggsy* or *Dear Mr. Smith*. The person addressed may not be dear to the writer at all, but convention requires us to have such a salutation. The punctuation that follows the salutation also is a matter of convention. When writing a familiar letter and using the addressee's first name, the salutation ends with a comma. When writing a more formal letter and using the addressee's last name, the salutation ends with a colon. Consider the following examples:

- Dear Rita,
- Dear Fritz,
- Dear Dr. Razzle-dazzle:
- Dear Senator Milton:

Quotation Marks

Quotation marks are used to identify quoted material. Although such material includes oral statements, in academic writing it usually is limited to excerpts of previously published works. Consider the following example:

> *This premise makes it reasonable to propose, then, that any relation between intelligence and bilingualism can be evaluated within a group. Although the design of these studies was sound, the results were inconclusive. Nevertheless, Hakuta (1986, p. 40) asserted that "bilingualism . . . bears little relationship to performance on [intelligence tests]."*

Usage Note: Quotation Marks

There are two important features of quotation marks that merit close attention. The first has to do with placement. *Quotation marks go outside commas and periods.* For reasons that remain opaque, many people put quotation marks inside commas and periods, but this is an error in American English.

There is one exception to this convention, but it is a fairly simple one. When a quotation is followed by the parenthetical citation, the quotation mark appears at the end of the quotation whereas the period appears at the end of the sentence. The following example illustrates this convention:

> *The discretionary funds available for the next fiscal year have decreased by 22% as a result of what MacMillian (1998) termed, "the erosion of the public sector tax base following the shrinking of the middle class" (p. 317).*

Applying Key Ideas 🔑

Directions: Some of the following sentences violate punctuation conventions governing coordination. In each case, correct the error.

Example: As Smithers noted, "The quality of life is not determined by the amount of money one has but rather by the quality of one's friends."

1. Men and women differ in many ways, but none more visible than their different experiences with friends

2. Women for example tend to maintain friendships throughout their lives and they also are able to make new friends after they are married and start families.

3. Men on the other hand tend to shed their friends after marriage moreover, they tend not to make new friends as they grow older.

4. According to Smithers "Only 3% of married men over 40 have more than one person other than their wives whom they consider a good friend and 92% have no one at all.

5. Men in Smithers' study ranked the following as the five most important factors in their lives, family, job, financial security, health, religion.

6. Indeed friends did not even appear in the list of top 10 factors.

7. Women however had a different list, family, friends, financial security, health, job, religion.

8. Smithers argued on this basis that "many of the health problems men experience between 50 and 60 may be exacerbated by their lack of friends", and he went on to suggest that when men rely solely on their families for support during illnesses they are automatically at higher risk.

9. Part of the explanation for men shedding themselves of friends as they grow older may be related to the pervasive competition that governs most male relationships but another important part appears to be tied to the male tendency to feel that their lives are made complete by marriage and children.

10. If this is the case and the evidence is compelling it suggests that we need to reevaluate popular notions of the romantic predisposition of males and females

WORD CHOICE

One of the great challenges of producing good writing is finding the right words to express thoughts, feelings, attitudes, knowledge, and hopes. The search is difficult. The words don't come easily. As a result, many writers abandon the search and settle on pedestrian words that may convey a message of sorts but that fail to enrich or inspire.

Equally problematic is the tendency to draw on the lexicon of words used for conversation. This lexicon works well when we talk to others—even though it is relatively small, consisting, on average, of about 3,000 words. When this lexicon is applied to writing, it is insufficient. Thus, a question that writers must ask repeatedly as they work is not only whether they have chosen the right word but also whether they have chosen the *best* word.

The following examples illustrate what is involved in word choice. In each case, the word or words that need reevaluation are underlined; a suggested revision and analysis accompany the original.

Example 1

The change in our understanding of the core curriculum during the 1970s <u>impacted</u> schools nationwide as they sought to shift to more relevant offerings.

Revision

The change in our understanding of the core curriculum during the 1970s <u>affected</u> schools nationwide as they sought to shift to more relevant offerings.

Analysis

When *impact* is used as a verb, it means to drive or strike something. It does not mean "to influence" or "to change."

Example 2

The trouble with America's legal system is that most judges <u>could care less</u> about justice; they are interested only in expediency.

Revision

The trouble with America's legal system is that most judges <u>could not care less</u> about justice; they are interested only in expediency.

Analysis

The intended meaning of the underlined expression is that judges care very little about justice. However, the actual meaning of *could care less* is just the opposite: Judges have some level of caring that could be less than it is. The correct word choice, *could not care less,* means that the level of caring is zero; hence, it cannot go any lower.

Example 3

The violence in the movie was so graphic that it made me <u>nauseous</u>.

Revision

The violence in the movie was so graphic that it made me <u>nauseated</u>.

Analysis

Nauseous means "vomit inducing," so the writer in this example is actually stating that she made people sick to their stomachs. What the writer wants to say, however, is that the movie violence made her sick to her stomach. When one is sick in this way, he or she is *nauseated,* not *nauseous.*

These examples illustrate how some words are commonly confused and mis-used. The following list shows a number of words that people confuse regularly; it can provide a resource for deciding on correct word choice.

Commonly Confused Words

A–B

a while: usually part of a prepositional phrase, as in *I will see you in a while* and *We stopped for a while.*

awhile: an adverb, used in expressions such as *We drove awhile before talking.*

accept: means to receive something
except: means to exclude something

act: a single event
action: an event made up of more than one act

adherence: one's support for something
adherents: those who lend their support

advice: a noun meaning the counsel we receive from others
advise: a verb meaning to give counsel

affect: a verb meaning to influence or bring about a change, except when used in a psychological sense as a noun to mean emotion
effect: when used as a noun, it means the result of an action; when used as a verb it means to bring about or cause

anxious: means worried, fearful, and nervous
eager: signifies desire marked by enthusiasm and excitement

apposed: means to set two things side by side
opposed: means to set two (or more) things against each other

assume: means to hold a hypothesis without proof
presume: means to hold a belief without proof

avocation: means hobby
vocation: means job or profession

bazaar: means a marketplace, often outdoors
bizarre: means odd or strange

beside: means next to or at the side of something
besides: means in addition to

boy: means a young male
buoy: means a floating marker or to lift up; note, however, that *boy* and *buoy* are pronounced exactly the same, even though in common speech *buoy* is pronounced incorrectly as /boo-ie/

brake: means to stop or that part of a vehicle used for stopping
break: means to shatter or render inoperable

bring: means to carry something forward
take: means to carry something away

brunet: a male with brown hair
brunette: a female with brown hair

burger: short for hamburger
burgher: term for a person who lives in a town (seldom used today)

burglary: the act of entering a building with the intent of stealing something
robbery: the act of stealing using violence or the threat of violence
theft: the act of stealing without violence or the threat to violence, usually committed surreptitiously

C–D

callous: emotional hardness
callus: area of dead, hardened skin as a result of friction

celibate: means that one abstains from sexual intercourse
chaste: means that one is morally pure and abstains from sexual intercourse

cement: as a noun, it is a powdery combination of clay and lime used as an adhesive when mixed with water; as a verb, it means to bond together
concrete: the hard, rocklike substance used in construction (made from cement and gravel; also means the opposite of abstract

cite: the act of using a quotation to support a point
site: a location

classic: used to signify something that has been recognized as being of the highest quality for many years
classical: used to refer to a historical period, usually that of ancient Greece and Rome

client: a person who employs the services of a professional
customer: a person who purchases something

compare to: the act of describing similarities
compare with: the act of describing similarities and differences
contrast: the act of describing differences

complement: the act of completing something by adding to it
compliment: the act of bestowing praise

compose: the act of putting things together, as in *The whole is compose of several parts*
comprise: means contains, as in *The whole comprises the parts*
constitute: the act of forming or creating, as in *The parts constitute the whole*

concerned about: means to be worried or preoccupied
concerned with: means to be involved with or engaged in something

conscience: one's sense of morality
conscious: means to be awake and aware

council: a group that provides advice
counsel: as a noun it means advice or one who provides legal advice; as a verb it means to advise

contagious: used to signify a disease transmitted by contact, usually with another person
infectious: used to signify a disease transmitted through a medium, usually air, water, or a bodily fluid

contempt: a feeling of scorn for something or someone

contemptible: signifies that something or someone deserves scorn

contemptuous: signifies what one expresses when feeling scorn for something or someone

continual: signifies that an act or action is repeated periodically

continuous: signifies that an act or action is repeated without interruption

damaged: signifies not only that harm has been done to someone or something but that the harm is partial rather than complete; thus, *completely damaged* is inappropriate and *partially damaged* is redundant

destroyed: signifies that the harm done to someone or something is complete; thus, *partially destroyed* is inappropriate and *completely destroyed* is redundant

desert: as a noun it signifies a largely barren area of land that has little rainfall; as a verb it means to abandon

dessert: a sweet, such as cake, ice cream, or pie, usually eaten at the end of a meal

discreet: means to be prudent or secretive

discrete: means that something or someone is separate or individual

disinterested: means that one is impartial or neutral regarding a given subject

uninterested: means that one lacks any interest

drier: signifies that something is comparatively less moist

dryer: a machine used for drying clothes

E–F

egoistic: means that one is self-centered

egotistic: means that one is prideful and boastful

elicit: means to evoke or bring out

illicit: means that an act or action is illegal

emerge: the act of coming into view

immerse: the act of plunging into something

emigrant: a person who leaves his or her country for a foreign land

immigrant: a person who enters a foreign country

engine: large vehicles are powered by engines

motor: small vehicles and appliances are powered by motors; note, however, that cars may be said to be powered by either and engine or a motor

farther: used with measurable distance, as in *We drove five miles farther than we should have*

further: the equivalent of *more* or *additional,* as in *He would not tolerate further argument*; also used with figurative distance, as in *The scientists moved one step further in their search for a solution*

feat: means a remarkable accomplishment

feet: appendages used for walking

fete: means a lavish party

feel: used to signify one's emotional or physical state, as in *I feel dizzy*

believe: used to signify what one accepts to be true, as in *I believe that Social Security is an unfair redistribution of wealth*

think: used to signify mental operations, as in *I think I'll have another beer*

flaunt: means to show off or provide an unseemly display
flout: means to defy rules or authority

forego: means to come before, precede
forgo: means to relinquish or to give up something

G–H

gibe: means to taunt or verbally harass
jibe: means to fit or conform

gourmand: signifies someone who eats a great deal
gourmet: signifies someone who has a refined appreciation for food

guarantee: a promise, usually written, to perform a certain action
warranty: a promise, usually written, that a statement is true

hangar: a place for storing aircraft
hanger: a device for hanging clothes

hanged: means to kill someone by hanging, as in *The horse thieves were hanged at noon*
hung: means that something has been put up, as in *She hung the picture in the den*

hardy: means that something or someone is strong
hearty: means that a person is healthy or jovial; can also mean that something is nourishing

heroin: a highly addictive narcotic
heroine: a female hero

I

imply: means to convey meaning indirectly
infer: means to grasp indirect meaning

impracticable: means that something, usually a plan or suggestion, is unworkable
impractical: means that something, usually a plan or suggestion, is incongruent with the demands of reality, that it is unsound or even foolish

incidence: the frequency with which something occurs
incidents: things that occur

incredible: signifies that something is unbelievable
incredulous: signifies that one doubts or is skeptical

insistent: means that one is demanding
persistent: means that one stays focused firmly on a task

instinct: automatic behavior not based on reason but on biology
intuition: term used to describe a largely unconscious reasoning process that leads to some conclusion

L

lend: this verb means to give someone something for a period, at the end of which the item must be returned; note that in formal Standard English, the past-tense form of *lend* is *lent*, not *loaned,* even though the latter has become predominant in nearly all usage situations except for the very formal
loan: a noun signifying money (to be repaid with interest) or some other item lent for a period

lessee: a tenant who rents property from an owner
lessor: an owner to rents property

lightening: the act of going from dark to light or of going from heavy to light
lightning: a flash of electricity in the sky associated with thunder storms

loose: means not tight, usually, but also can mean to unfasten
lose: means the opposite of win; or also means to misplace or fail to keep

M

manikin: a model of the human body that has detachable parts, often used in studying anatomy
mannequin: model of the human body used to display clothing

mask: a disguise used to hide the face
masque: a masquerade

moot: open to discussion, debatable
mute: speechless

more than: always used with figures, as in *She made more than $100,000 last year*
over: traditionally, this word was used to designate a location, as in *He is somewhere over the rainbow*; increasingly, *over* is used (and accepted) with figures, as in *She made over $100,000 last year,* but in formal situations, use *more than* in such constructions

P

parity: means the same as equality
parody: means to imitate in a mocking or comic fashion

parlay: means to increase
parley: means to discuss

patience: emotional tolerance in the face of distress
patients: people who are ill and receiving treatment

precede: means to go before something else
proceed: means to move forward or continue

prescribe: means to order or to establish by rule
proscribe: means to prohibit

principal: a person, idea, or thing of the first order, as in *She was the school principal*
principle: an idea or ethical code of conduct that influences behavior

R–S

real: an adjective used to characterize the existence of a person or thing as authentic or actual, as in *He was a real athlete*
really: an adverb used as an intensifier for a verb, as in *She danced really well*

replica: a copy of a piece of art that is produced by or under the direction of the original artist
reproduction: a copy of a piece of art produce by someone who has not association with the original artist

right: means correct; also means to fix or remedy, as in *She set things right*
rite: means a religious ritual

sac: a pouch in an animal or plant used for carrying eggs or offspring
sack: a bag people use for carrying items; also used as a verb meaning to fire from a job

soluble: means that something can be dissolved
solvable: signifies a problem that can be solved

stanch: means to stop the flow of a liquid
staunch: means to be firm in one's beliefs

stationary: means to be immobile
stationery: refers to paper used specifically for writing

stimulant: a drug that temporarily increases heart rate and other bodily functions; often increases alertness (note that alcohol is a *depressant,* not a stimulant)
stimulus: something that rouses or incites to activity, such as an incentive

straight: means that something is not crooked (also refers to heterosexual, as opposed to homosexual orientation)
strait: a narrow body of water that flows between two land masses

sure: an adjective, as in *He brought in the trout with a sure hand*
surely: an adverb, as in *She surely understands the difference*

T–Z

toxic: an adjective meaning poisonous
toxin: a noun signifying a poisonous substance (note that the plural of *toxin* is *toxins*; *toxics,* although found in much scientific literature, such as EPA documents, is unacceptable)

toe: an appendage of the foot (note that the expression *Toe the line* means to adhere to a strict standard)
tow: means to pull, usually with a rope or chain

tort: the legal name given to law suits alleging wrongful or negligent actions
torte: a pastry that usually contains fruit

tortuous: means twisting and complex
torturous: signifies something related to torture

troop: a company of soldiers
troupe: a company of actors

SENTENCE VARIETY

The most common sentence structure in English follows the pattern *SVO*—subject, verb, object. Consequently, the majority of all sentences will begin with the subject. However, if the sentences in a paper do not display some variety, the writing quickly becomes monotonous. Most readers, in fact, will stop reading a paper that does not reflect appropriate sentence variety.

Such variety can be achieved in two ways. The first involves sentence length. The average length of sentences in professional writing—which seems to offer a pretty good model to imitate—is about 22 words. The average length of sentences in undergraduate writing, in contrast, is only about 12 words. Thus, an important first step toward better writing is to increase sentence length. Combining short sentences into longer ones is the most common method of increasing length, as the example below illustrates:

Most people think that they know something about the history of the early Christian church. They know that early Christians were poor. These Christians were persecuted by the Romans. They were fed to lions in the Coliseum. They were denied the freedom to worship God and read the Bible. This knowledge, however, is based largely on movie and TV programs. It has little basis in historical fact. The early Christians, for example, actually were members of the upper class. They were tolerated for many years until their own intolerance of pagans led to reprisals. In Rome, the Christians become notorious for their destruction of temples and beating of pagan worshipers.

If we use sentence combining to adjust the sentence length in this passage, it becomes smoother and arguably more readable. The revised version follows:

Most people think that they know something about the history of the early Christian church. They know that early Christians were poor, were persecuted by the Romans, who frequently fed them to lions in the Coliseum, and they know that the Christians were denied the freedom to worship God and read the Bible. This knowledge, however, is based largely on movie and TV programs and has little basis in historical fact. The early Christians, for example, actually were members of the upper class and were tolerated for many years—until their own intolerance of pagans led to reprisals. In Rome, the Christians became notorious for their destruction of temples and beating of pagan worshipers.

In most instances, sentence combining involves joining shorter sentences into longer ones using *coordinating conjunctions* (*and, but, for, nor, or, yet, so*). Note, however, that sentence combining also involves *subordinating conjunctions* (such as *although, because, as, if, until,* and so forth). The next to the last sentence in the example above, for instance, uses *until*.

Achieving variety in sentence length requires some conscious effort early on, and you may find that you have to count the number of words from time to time to help yourself make the necessary adjustments. Eventually, the process becomes more automatic, and such counting is no longer needed.

The second approach to achieving sentence variety involves modifying the SVO pattern by using modifying clauses and phrases placed in three positions: in front of the subject, between the subject and predicate, and after the predicate. These modifiers often are described in terms of their position vis-à-vis the independent clause: initial, medial, final. Consider these examples:

1. *Although fields such as sociology and anthropology are classified as social sciences,* Wilson argued that there is little "science" in them at all.
   Initial modifier

2. Wilson, *an expert on ants,* achieved popular recognition in the late 1970s.
   Medial modifier

3. He proposed that human behavior is largely determined by biological factors, *as it is in virtually all other animals on the planet.*   **Final modifier**

As in the case of sentence length, adjusting your sentence patterns may require conscious effort initially. You may need to examine your sentences and add or delete modifiers. (Many student writers, for example, use too many initial modifiers.) Keep in mind, however, that about 80% of your sentences still should begin with the subject.

PARAGRAPH DEVELOPMENT

It is fairly common for people to think of a paragraph as a series of related sentences that develop a single idea. The common perception is that each paragraph must have a topic sentence—a sentence that announces what the paragraph is about. These notions of paragraphs, however, are off the mark. There is no question that readers expect sentences in a paragraph (and in a paper, for that matter) to be related; nevertheless, paragraphs do not always develop a single idea. In addition, not all paragraphs have a topic sentence (this paragraph offers an interesting example.) For these reasons, we can gain a better understanding of paragraphs by recognizing that they are primarily a visual aid for readers. Paragraphs, in other words, are breaks in a text that make it easier to read. In this respect, they have much in common with headings and subheadings.

With this notion in mind, you can focus most of your attention on the visual aspect of paragraphing when you write. Here's a hint: *Most paragraphs are about 100 words long.* Thus, if you have a paragraph that goes on for a page or two, a quick glance will tell you that it is too long, and you also will see about where to make the paragraph should break. If, on the other hand, your paragraphs are two or three sentences (resembling paragraphs in newspapers), then you can combine them into longer units.

Coherence and Unity

Having established the paragraph as primarily a visual aid to reading, it nevertheless is important to stress that the sentences in a paragraph must work together as a unit. Achieving this sort of coherence and unity involves understanding something about the structure of paragraphs, which in some respects is similar to the structure of sentences.

Paragraphs are about assertions. They often begin with one major assertion and then shift to one or more minor assertions, which sometimes are supported through example, illustration, analysis, and reason. Consider the first paragraph of this section:

> *It is fairly common for people to think of a paragraph as a series of related sentences that develop a single idea. The common perception is that each paragraph must have a topic sentence—a sentence that announces what the paragraph is about. These notions of paragraphs, however, are off the mark. There is no question that readers expect sentences in a paragraph (and in a paper, for that matter) to be related; nevertheless, paragraphs do not always develop a single idea. In addition, not all paragraphs have a topic sentence (this paragraph offers an interesting example.) For these reasons, we can gain a better understanding of paragraphs by recognizing that they are essentially a visual aid for readers—and a recent development in writing. Paragraphs, in other words, are visual breaks in a text that make it*

easier to read. In this respect, they have much in common with headings and sub-heading.

Every sentence in this paragraph is an assertion, but what is important is how the assertions are linked. For example, the first two sentences are assertions about common notions of paragraphs. The third sentence, however, offers another assertion in opposition to the first two, and it moves the discussion forward: The common perception is not entirely accurate, and sentences 4 and 5 provide examples of why. But what is the right perception of paragraphs? The answer is in the remaining sentences. Although this paragraph lacks a topic sentence, its structure is tight because all the sentences work together. The following outline may help illustrate this point:

I. First assertions (sentences 1 and 2)

II. Transition (sentence 3)

III. Examples (sentences 4 and 5)

IV. Second assertions (remaining sentences)

Although it is difficult to talk about a general structure for paragraphs because each one is unique, we can say that all paragraphs build assertions, one upon another. Examining another sample paragraph illustrates this point. The following passage comes from *Feeling the Spirit*, by Frances Kostarelos:

> *Before and after the Civil War, black dreams, visions, hopes, and strategies for social justice and equality were kept alive in black churches in the South and in the urban North. Between 1850 and 1930 Chicago's black population increased from 323 to 233,903 (Spear 1967:12). Black immigrants moved North to escape rural economic destitution, Jim Crow laws, and white brutality. They hoped for steady work, an improved standard of living, and social mobility. In Chicago, black aspirations for equality were cut short by white racism and economic and political power (Spear 1967:29–49). Blacks encountered economic subordination, job discrimination, and de facto segregation in the city. Hostile and powerful whites forced blacks to settle in enclaves apart from white residential areas. White racists demanded segregated schools, neighborhoods, recreational facilities, and public accommodations (Spear 1967; Anderson and Pickering 1986).*

Like our first example, this paragraph consists of a series of related assertions. The first is in sentence 1. Understanding the link between sentence 1 and sentence 2 requires some reflection on the irony that blacks experienced similar levels of racism in the North and South, but sentence 2 also provides a context for that racism—almost an eightfold increase in black residents in Chicago over an 80-year period. Sentences 3 and 4 explain the reason for such a huge increase. The remaining sentences explain the conditions these internal immigrants faced upon arriving in the Windy City. Again, however, it is important to consider how each assertion builds on those that come before.

The final sample paragraph further illustrates the interconnected nature of sentences in a paragraph. It comes from *Literacy and Bilingualism* by James Williams and Grace Snipper. The first sentence makes an assertion, but it also introduces the concept of "academic literacy." The sentences that follow function to explain (or define) what academic literacy is, with the final sentence actually providing an illustrative example. This paragraph may seem more tightly structured than the other samples, but this appearance is largely the result of the aim of the paragraph, which is definition.

> *We would argue that too many people confuse cultural literacy with what we call "academic literacy," the ability to process and interact with a body of artifacts and ideas preserved with the specific domains of educational institutions. It is a set of behaviors peculiar to the formally educated. Academic literacy reflects the notions that literate people are those who read literature, philosophy, history, and contemporary essays, the very sort of texts college students face during their first two years of undergraduate work. It reflects the notion that they can also write about these texts in some fashion. And it reflects the belief that they can comprehend such texts within the large context of Western cultural traditions that reach back to ancient Greece. For example, someone who is academically literate could be expected to read and article about marathons and associate this modern sporting event with the Battle of Marathon, in which the Greeks fought against the Persians in 490 B.C.*

Many writers do not pay much attention to paragraphs, even though they may give a great deal of attention to sentences and words. Nevertheless, effective paragraph development—which involves ensuring that sentences work together closely—is crucial to good writing. As in the case of sentence variety, paragraph development is likely to require conscious attention for some time. That is, you may have to look carefully at the paragraphs you write and question how one sentence works with the one before and so on.

Academic Writing

Academic writing is a genre, or type, of writing with many unique characteristics. Student academic writing is more peculiar still, owing to the nature of the audience and the underlying reasons teachers have for asking students to complete writing assignments.

PART TWO

Academic Writing

INTRODUCTION

Academic writing is a genre, or type, of writing with many unique characteristics. Student academic writing is more peculiar still, owing to the nature of the audience and the underlying reasons teachers have for asking students to complete writing assignments. One of the more important characteristics of academic writing is the emphasis on *analysis* and *interpretation*. In academic writing, papers commonly examine facts to determine their nature and then explain the results to readers. They also follow certain conventions associated with standards of proof. Interpretations must be supported with good reasons, and such support follows discipline-specific formats, such as the *MLA Handbook for Writers of Research Papers* for those writing for a humanities audience and the *Publication Manual of the American Psychological Association* (APA) for those writing for a social sciences audience. The details of these formats are discussed in the sections that follow.

Perhaps the most common type of writing assignment in college is the research paper, but other common types include essay exams and lab reports. *Undergraduate research papers, however, are not true research papers.*

This point requires some elaboration. There are two major types of true research papers. In the first, a writer collects existing information and summarizes it for an audience that needs or wants it. In the second, a writer generates (usually through an experiment or study) and then reports new information. The typical research paper students produce is quite different because it summarizes information that the reader (the professor) usually already has. Thus, academic research papers represent an exercise with goals somewhat removed from the actual reporting of researched information. The same is true of lab reports, at least at the lower division level. Such writing typically reports on experiments that are merely replications of old experiments. In fact, such lab reports commonly are reiterations of the procedures specified in a lab manual for a given procedure.

What, then, are teachers looking for when they assign a paper? What are their aims? Although the answers will vary slightly from professor to professor, we can identify four major aims:

- To determine that students understand the material and can write about it intelligently.
- To introduce students to the ways of knowing and standards of proof in a discipline.
- To get students to look at key questions in a discipline from different perspectives through reading outside the required textbooks.
- To expand students' knowledge of key topics through intensive outside reading.

Academic writing in general examines and interprets facts, but there are certain measurable differences based on discipline. The following sections examine some of these differences and offer examples of the various types of writing that faculty require in their courses.

DOCUMENTATION

Documentation consists of providing references for ideas and words that you obtain from sources and then use in your writing. In academic writing, you always have to acknowledge any use you make of other people's work. Failure to provide such credit constitutes *plagiarism*, which is an intentional attempt to pass someone else's words and ideas off as your own.

Many writers assume that they need to provide proper documentation *only* when they provide a direct quotation from another work, but this assumption is false. Documentation is necessary under three circumstances:[4]

- When providing a direct quotation.
- When using another writer's ideas in your text.
- When paraphrasing the words or ideas of another writer.

Proper documentation includes both *attribution* and *citation*. Attribution means providing the name of the source, whereas citation involves providing identifying information. Consider the following paragraph:

For several centuries, the kingdoms of the upper and lower Nile existed in a state of competitive tension. Matters became more complicated around 5,000 B.C. because the Lower Kingdom made several technological advances that the Upper Kingdom could not match. Orson (1997) argued, for example, that these advances ranged from weapons to pottery and that the archeological finds in the delta from 1984 clearly show the failed attempts of Upper Kingdom artisans to duplicate the work of their Lower-Kingdom counterparts.

---

[4]The majority of plagiarism occurs because of carelessness or lack of adequate knowledge, but some occurs because time constraints make it easier to meet a deadline by taking shortcuts. The most extreme form of plagiarism consists of taking an entire paper that was written by someone else and representing it as one's own. Because teachers read extensively and are very familiar with the sort of texts that lend themselves to this form of plagiarism, perpetrators nearly always are found out. The penalties can be severe: Some schools expel students, and many fail them in the course.

The third sentence illustrates proper attribution, for it names the author. It also illustrates proper citation, in this case by parenthetical reference using the date of publication (1997). Note that reference is necessary even though the material is not quoted directly but is paraphrased.

Paraphrasing

Producing an acceptable paraphrase is one of the more difficult tasks writers face when it comes to using sources. The problem is at least twofold. First, the original wording usually sounds so good that writers are reluctant to sully an idea by putting it into their own words. Second, producing an acceptable paraphrase requires a pretty thorough understanding of the material, which takes time and effort that too often are in short supply. One solution is to use sources only to support your own ideas; do not use them as the basis of a paper. When you must incorporate other writers' ideas into your work, the best approach is to ask yourself how you would express a given idea to someone you know. This approach will help you put the source material into your own words, provided you do not look at the original as you construct the paraphrase. A good way to practice paraphrasing is to read a passage, set it aside for several minutes, and then restate the passage in your own words, speaking into a tape recorder. You then can play back the recording and compare it to the original.

Because no one can justify writing a paper that is composed largely of direct quotations, paraphrasing is a very important tool. Outsiders often just do not have enough information about a topic, so much of their writing reflects research they conducted to become more knowledgeable. Such information should appear as paraphrasing, with appropriate references.

The following examples are intended to provide a better understanding of unacceptable and acceptable paraphrases:

Original

Americans universally loath lawyers, consistently ranking them dead last—even below used car salesmen—in surveys that measure the relative prestige and respect accorded certain jobs. There is no question that this loathing is well deserved: As a group, attorneys are ignorant, anti-intellectual, totally without morals or ethics, and arrogant. What a profound irony, then, that we have put lawyers in charge of every nuance of our lives by electing them to public office. Fully 98% of all politicians are attorneys. Thus, we are faced with an absurd fact: We have put people we wouldn't offer table scraps to if we knew they were starving in control of our lives, the education of our children, the quality of our roads, water, and air, and, increasingly, what we do in the bedroom.

—Wolfgang Martin, *Society on the Brink,* 1998

Unacceptable Paraphrase

The distaste Americans have for lawyers is incongruent with political realities, for about 98% of politicians are attorneys. This fact raises the question of why voters put a group of people they dislike into office.

This paraphrase is unacceptable because it conveys the substance of the original passage without attributing the information to the original author and without indicating a source. It gives the impression that the information came from the writer, not from Wolfgang Martin. Notice also that the writer's phrase, *98% of politicians are attorneys*, is almost identical to the original, *98% of all politicians are attorneys*. Changing a single word is not paraphrasing. The writer simply should have kept the original and placed it in quotation marks.

Acceptable Paraphrase

One of the biggest contradictions of American life is the strange relationship we have with lawyers. For example, Martin (1998) pointed out that even though Americans generally despise attorneys, we nevertheless elect them to public office more often than members of any other group. Indeed, Martin noted that the overwhelming majority of politicians are lawyers. This fact does not bode well for quality of life or democracy.

Rhetorical Factors

The ethical considerations of documentation are complemented by rhetorical ones. Proper documentation says something about you as a writer, and it also says something about your paper. For example, documentation enhances one's ethos, or character, through association. When you cite well-known, reputable sources accurately, you align yourself with leaders in a given field and simultaneously signify your respect for readers. Thus, there are three important reasons for providing careful documentation:

- Serves as an element of proof for an argument.
- Serves to enhance the writer's ethos, or character.
- Allows readers to follow up on the writer's topic.

With regard to research papers, it is common to view documentation as the substance of one's work. As a result, many college papers consist primarily of the words and ideas of published authors. This approach is defeating from a number of perspectives. For example, any paper that consists primarily of someone else's words and ideas runs a high risk of plagiarizing. Also, there just aren't many teachers who want you to turn in a paper that does not reflect your thoughts and ideas. This approach also requires both a great deal of reading and the ability to create a patchwork of references from several texts. It is a lot of work. A more successful approach consists of writing an initial draft based on your knowledge and what you want to say. During subsequent revisions, you should add references that support your position.

Common Knowledge

When working on a paper, many student writers fear that they must provide documentation for every statement or piece of information in the text. A great deal of what every writer brings to a paper is based on common knowledge, not on information obtained from a source. Common knowledge does not require documentation.

The next example illustrates the difference between common knowledge and information obtained from a source:

> *A significant portion of modern civilization is based on ideas and principles that originated in ancient Greece. For example, the Greeks developed the alphabet, geometry, logic, and the precursors of modern science. Smith (1998) recently noted that even our concept of matter—composed of atoms—is based on an understanding of the world that was proposed by ancient Greek philosophers.*

The first two sentences express common knowledge, whereas the third sentence provides information from a source, so it must be referenced, as indicated. Common knowledge often comes from books that one no longer remembers; perhaps an equal share comes from teachers whose lessons—but not selected nuggets of information—are but faint memory traces; some also comes from conversations, news programs, and the like. In a world slightly more neurotic than our own, writers would have to document lessons from an eighth-grade class or a book read during the summer before the start of Grade 10 if they used that information in their work. But for our purposes, when a given piece of information is known to huge numbers of people—as in the case of the Greeks and the alphabet, for example— we do not have to document it. Nevertheless, what we can label common knowledge varies from person to person. Some people know nothing about the ancient Greeks and their influence on modern society; consequently, if they were to write a paper on this topic, they would have to acquire that knowledge *for the paper*, probably through reading, in which case they would have to provide references. This situation highlights an important guideline for all writing:

➢ You should not try to write on topics you know nothing about.

Using Quotations

Some simple but important conventions govern how you use quotations in writing. Quotations do not merely appear in the text; they support claims, provide examples, and offer support. Thus, there must be an identifiable connection between the quotation and the text where it is located.

The most effective way to make this connection is by naming the source author and indicating that he or she "suggests," "recommends," "states," "reports," and so on. The next example illustrates this technique:

> *The political response to President Clinton's affair was mitigated by the public's awareness that it was profoundly hypocritical. As Robertson (1998) reported, "Congress was ready to punish Clinton for doing what many of them had done in the past, were doing in the present, and would do in the future." Not surprisingly, public support of the President remained strong.*

In some instances, it is appropriate to make the quotation part of a sentence in the paper, essentially using the source material to finish your sentence. Consider this example:

> *In addition, the actions of Congress raised the important question of "the role government would attempt to play in regulating the sexual behavior of consenting adults" (McBurney, 1998).*

Ellipses

Sometimes the source you want to quote contains information that is not relevant to the point you want to make. In this situation, you may remove the irrelevant portion of the quotation. When you do, however, you must note that part of the quoted material is missing, and the tools you use are *ellipses*. Ellipses consist of three periods with a space separating each, as illustrated here:

> *McBurney (1998) argued that the "success of Congress in elevating . . . sexual misconduct to the level of impeachable offense" will quickly lead to the erosion of the most personal of personal freedoms—whom we decide to have sex with, where, and when.*

Occasionally, the deleted material will be followed by a comma or some other type of punctuation. When this occurs, simply put the punctuation after the ellipses. Thus, if the ellipsis occurs at the end of a sentence, you will have four periods. *Note, however, that you should not begin a quotation with ellipses.*

WRITING IN THE HUMANITIES

The facts in humanistic writing tend to consist of or reside in texts—poems, plays, novels, historical records, and so on—and works of art. Unlike writing in the sciences and social sciences, writing in the humanities seldom engages in direct observation of experience; instead it focuses on a personal experience between the writer and the artifact under analysis. Thus, the method of inquiry in humanistic writing is *nonempirical*.

One of the chief differences between writing in the humanities and writing in science and social science is that humanists generally believe that the artifacts they write about convey some universal truth. Scientists and social scientists, on the other hand, operate under the assumption that their observations are generalizable only to the subjects or objects being studied. The conventions of these disciplines require a great deal of caution with regard to generalizing from specific findings to larger populations or events.

This difference has clear consequences for anyone writing in the humanities. For example, the facts deemed appropriate for interpretation in a paper necessarily differ in kind as well as in nature. In the humanities, it is taken as a given that a literary work or a piece of art reflects the human condition. This point is rarely the focus of any analysis or interpretation. Instead, writing in the humanities strives to describe the human condition conveyed in the work of art and then to explain what it means (or should mean) to an audience. Both the description and the explanation are interpretations. In other words, writing in the humanities presumes that the subjects of discussion convey a meaningful, universal statement about life and that the role of the writer is to interpret that statement for others. Necessarily, the interpretations deal with emotional, personal, and social values.

Another consequence is that writing in the humanities focuses on the individual; it operates under the assumption that different people bring their unique experiences to a document or a work of art and that their interpretations are colored by those experiences. Thus, in theory, any given work can be interpreted an unlimited number of times. Shakespeare's plays, for example, have been interpreted countless times over the last 300 years, and, again in theory, each of those interpretations is unique. In practice, however, we probably would find that a large number of such interpretations are repetitive or derivative.

It is important to understand that interpretations in the humanities are rarely deemed "right" or "wrong." They are deemed "reasonable" or "unreasonable," based on a range of factors, particularly acceptable standards of proof. On the most significant level, these standards of proof involve an understanding of and familiarity with the work being discussed, but this understanding and familiarity must also include the *context* of the work. For example, a reasonable interpretation of *Hamlet* requires not only knowledge of the play but also some knowledge of Shakespeare's other tragedies and the genre of tragedy in the Western tradition. A student may not have such knowledge prior to writing the research paper, but it is assumed that he or she will afterward.

The humanities are composed of several disciplines, and each has a different way of looking at the human experience. Thus, writing in literature and the visual arts tends to focus on questions of meaning, whereas writing in history tends to focus on questions of cause and effect, and so forth. Nevertheless, these disciplines share identifiable conventions of form. Each uses the MLA Style Guide, and each tends to expect papers to be organized into three major parts:

- An introduction that identifies the topic or subject under discussion.
- A section that describes and analyzes the topic or subject.
- A section that presents and supports the writer's interpretation.

THE MLA DOCUMENTATION STYLE

The *MLA Handbook for Writers of Research Papers* is published by the Modern Language Association and governs documentation conventions in English literature and several other disciplines in the humanities, such as art, drama, and film. It also provides guidelines for organizing a paper, such as the following:

- Double space all text, even long quotations and bibliography.
- Set 1-inch margins on all sides of the paper.
- Place page numbers either in the upper right-hand corner or centered at the bottom of the page.
- Although optional in the *MLA Handbook*, this text recommends a cover page that includes the title of the paper, your name, followed by the professor's name, the name of the course, and the date; this information should be centered on the page; double space each line, but use triple space between each entry.
- Use present tense when referring to the contents of a published work.
- Write out numbers below 10; use Arabic numerals for all numbers greater than 10; write out all numbers when they begin a sentence.

Proper documentation in the MLA style includes in-text references to works used as resources and a bibliography that lists these works in alphabetical order. The bibliography is titled *Works Cited* and appears at the end of the paper on one or more separate pages. The title should be centered on the first page of the bibliography and entered on the first line.

In-Text Citation

In-text attribution and citation take different forms under the MLA conventions, depending on how you use the source material. There are five options, each of which is illustrated here:

1. A direct quotation incorporated as part of a sentence you write.
2. A direct quotation that supports a point you make or that is congruent with your interpretation of the author's position.
3. A long quotation.
4. A paraphrase.
5. Reference to an entire work.

Option 1: Direct Quotation as Part of a Sentence

Several studies have linked the failure of fathers to pay child support and mothers' interference with, and in many cases outright obstruction of, visitation rights, even when those rights are delineated in a court order. One recent study, for example, determined that fully 90% of the fathers who had not paid child support during a 6-month period had stopped "making payments after their ex-wives refused to comply with court-ordered visitation and after the courts failed to take adequate action to enforce the fathers' parental rights" (Reisbach 134–135).

Notice that by incorporating the quotation directly into the text the writer provides a continuation of his own sentence. The effect is to link the writer's ideas closely to those in the quotation.

Option 2: Direct Quotation as Support

In the next example, the writer provides attribution in the text and does not use the quotation to continue a thought. Instead, the writer reports what is stated in the source document. The effect is twofold—it stresses the writer's interpretation of the quoted material and it more clearly uses the quotation as argumentative support:

Courts in virtually every state in the nation have considered the link between child support and visitation, and in each instance they have ruled that the refusal of the mother to abide by court orders enforcing fathers' parental rights does not constitute grounds for withholding support payments. Commenting on this situation, Anderson notes that such rulings have "removed the only leverage fathers might have for persuading their ex-wives to cooperate on visitation" (19).

Option 3: A Long Quotation

Sometimes, you will have a direct quotation that is longer than two or three lines. In such cases, set the material in a *block quotation*, which is separated from the body of the text by indenting on both sides. Please note that, years ago, block quotations were single-spaced; today, however, they are double-spaced. Also note that an introductory statement normally precedes the quotation and that the statement ends with a colon. The block quotation should begin with a capital letter, even if it is not the actual beginning of a sentence in the original:

The reality of divorce in America is that the courts award custody to mothers about 90% of the time, even when it clearly is in the best interests of the children to be in the custody of their fathers. Furthermore, between 60 and 70% of all custodial mothers deny or interfere with court-ordered visitation. Commenting on this situation, Roberts and Fitzgerald argue that:

> *Only 3% of the support payments ex-wives receive goes toward the actual expenses of minor children, leading us to conclude that fathers quite rightly view child support as ransom; when visitation does not occur, fathers feel justified in withholding all ransom payments. The courts, however, refuse to recognize the inequity involved and have consistently used child support (as well as alimony) as a means of punishing fathers and redistributing income to mothers, even in those increasingly frequent cases in which the mother earns more than the father (136).*

Option 4: Paraphrase

A paraphrase requires attribution and the page number of where the paraphrased material appears, as illustrated here:

> *The position of the courts is that parental rights and support are separate issues and that fathers must pursue legal options through the courts. However, as Daniel Orstein points out, most fathers are paying so much in child support that they cannot afford legal remedies; moreover, the courts generally rule against those who can, making the legal-options argument patently absurd (98).*

Option 5: Reference to an Entire Work

If you are making reference to an entire work, you need only provide the name of the author and the work, without parenthetical information, as illustrated next:

> *In <u>Fathers and Divorce</u>, Hector Dominguez argues convincingly that, statistically, we should expect custody awards to split evenly between mothers and fathers; however, the huge disparity in such awards in favor of mothers leads to the inevitable conclusion that the courts exercise a double standard with respect to the law. The question is why. It is unreasonable to claim that only 10% of fathers can provide a wholesome, nurturing home for their children. Drawing on evolutionary biology, Dominguez goes on to argue that the only rational explanation is that family law judges—more than 90% of whom are male—use the bench as an opportunity to bully and intimidate other men in classic alpha-male fashion.*

WORKS CITED

How references appear in the works cited section depends on the nature of the material. For example, the format for listing books is different from the format for articles. The following examples illustrate the various possibilities. Note that it is important to follow the format exactly when preparing your Works Cited page. Indeed, it is recommended that you have these examples handy while working.

Books

A Book with One Author

Martinez, Laura. *Making Meaning in a Postmodern World.* New York: Harper, 1998.

Sanderson, John D. *Philosophy for the 21st Century.* Berkeley: U California P, 1999.

Waldenstein, Mark. *Art During the Middle Ages: Religious Icons and the Church*. Princeton: Princeton U P, 1998.

More than One Book by the Same Author

Chomsky, Noam. *Syntactic Structures*. The Hague, The Netherlands: Mouton, 1957.

---. *Rules and Representations*. New York: Columbia U P, 1980.

---. *Lectures on Government and Binding*. Dordrecht, The Netherlands: Foris, 1981.

Note that the first entry provides the author's full name; subsequent entries use three hyphens rather than the name. Also note that the works are listed by date of publication, with the earliest work appearing first. In the event that the works cited have two or more authors, the hyphen serves as a substitute for all the names, provided that they are identical for all the works.

A Book with Two or Three Authors

Blakesley, Roger S., and Jing Hua Zhou. *A Short History of Film Music, 1940–1960*. New York: Scribners, 1998.

Cunningham, Mary A., Frances Montalvo, and Robert Kryznsky. *Shakespeare's Dramaturgy in a New Light*, Stanford: Stanford U P, 1999.

A Book with More than Three Authors

Gulliani-Philo, Elvira C., et al. *Wine-Making in the Cucamonga Valley, 1830-1930*. New York: Oxford U P, 1996.

Patterson, Edward J., et al. *Lighting in Miloz Milozovic's Theatrical Productions*. Cambridge: Harvard U P, 1999.

A Book with a Title in the Title

Gunderson, Milly. *A Feminist's Interpretation of MacBeth*. Oxford: Oxford U P, 1997.

Kilpatrick, Jonathan. *Steinbeck's The Grapes of Wrath Refigured*. Baltimore: Johns-Hopkins U P, 1998.

Miller, Steven P. *Leitmotifs in "The Love Song of J. Alfred Prufrock."* Berkeley: U of California P, 1987.

Titles of plays and books are underlined or set in italics, whereas titles of articles and poems appear in quotation marks. Thus, when the title of a play or book appears in the title of a book you are referencing—as in the case of *MacBeth* and *The Grapes of Wrath* above—the embedded title is not underlined. The title of poems and articles, however, are still set in quotation marks.

An Edited Book

Simpson, French M., ed. *Romance in the Courtly Tradition*. New York: Viking. 1997.

A Book with More than One Editor

Martin, Wolfgang, Maria Gomez, and Edward Johns, eds. *The Effects of Gender on Child Development in Custody Cases*. Oxford: Oxford U P, 1996.

A Work in an Edited Volume

Shimada, Katsuyo. "Kabuki Theater Before World War II." Ed. Robert Fukuyama, *The Effect of the Second World War on Japanese Art*. Iowa City, U Iowa P, 1998.

Wilson, Francis J. "The Moral Bankruptcy of the American Judiciary." Ed. Betty S. Edwards, *Legal Ethics: The Failure to Enforce Professional Standards*. New York: Horn, 1998.

A Multivolume Work

Bush, Douglas. *British Literature*. 5 vols. Cambridge: Cambridge U P, 1947.

Note that the entry above is appropriate if you are referencing the entire set of books. If you are referencing one book in a multivolume set, the format differs slightly, as shown below:

Lee, Kim Sung. *A History of American Involvement in Southeast Asia*. Vol. 2. Cambridge: Harvard U P, 1985. 3 vols.

A Book in Translation

Gunterstrasse, Karl. *A Postmodern Interpretation of Thomas Mann's Work*. Trans. Freda Bunderstadt and Robert Heissenberg. New York: Avon, 1988.

Samaniego, Raffey. *Post-Neo-Marxist Literature of Latin American: The New Beginning*. Trans. Gilberto Gonzales. Baltimore: Johns-Hopkins U P, 1999.

A Book in a New Edition

Williams, James D. *Preparing to Teach Writing*. 2nd ed. Mahwah, New Jersey: Lawrence Erlbaum, 1998.

A Book in Reprint

Kinneavy, James. *A Theory of Discourse*. 1971. New York: Norton, 1980.

For a reprinted book, the original publication date follows the title. It is not necessary to provide the name of the original publisher in this format. The name of the second (reprint) publisher appears after the original publication date; the date of the reprint then appears at the end of the entry.

Conference Proceedings

Campuzano, Phillipe. "Neo-Marxism and the Decline of the American Middle Class." *Socioeconomic Trends at the End of the Century*. Proc. of the Society for Independent Thought, 5–8 Jan. 1998. San Francisco, Jossey-Bass, 1998.

Note that when using a particular paper from the proceeding, the reference should be listed according to the author's name. The title of the referenced paper follows the author's name. The name of the conference appears after the name of the paper. The date of the proceeding follows the name of the conference organizers, which in turn is followed by the publisher of the proceedings and the publication date. When referring to an entire proceeding, the reference should be listed according to the proceeding title, as shown here:

Postmodernism in Film and Literature. Proc. of the Film Society of America, 15 June 1997. Los Angeles: Sage, 1998.

Dissertations

Dissertations are book-length treatises that are required of students completing a doctoral degree. Most dissertations are not published, but some are. The formats differ insofar as the title of an unpublished dissertation appears in quotation marks, whereas the title of a published dissertation is underlined or set in italics. In addition, the entry for the published dissertation must include the name of the granting university as well as the name of the publisher, as the examples below illustrate:

Unpublished

O'Brien, Maureen K. "A Study of Kinship Relations Among the Vai of West Africa." Diss. U Pennsylvania, 1999.

Published

Leong, Xia Kai. *Landscape Painting in Ancient China: 1200–250 B.C.* Diss. U Chicago, 1994. Princeton: Princeton U P, 1996.

Articles

In academic writing, articles that appear in academic journals are treated differently from those that appear in popular magazines, or periodicals. For academic journals, it is necessary to provide the volume and issue numbers, whereas for periodicals it is necessary simply to provide the date. The following examples illustrate the distinction.

Journals

Zador, Michael. "The Modern Masters: A Study of Suspense Film as a Genre." *Cinematique* 10 (1997): 110–119.

Note that the volume number appears after the name of the journal. The date of the issue is set in parentheses and is followed by the inclusive page numbers of the article. Pagination in journals is either by volume or by issue. In the example above, pagination is by volume, whereas in the example below it is by issue (volume 8, issue 2):

Weisenheimer, Joshua J. "Composition Instruction and the 'Kitzhaber Affect.'" *Journal of English Studies* 8.2 (1978): 45–54.

Periodicals

Some periodicals appear weekly, whereas others appear monthly. The format for referencing differs depending on the frequency of publication. The first example below illustrates the format for a weekly periodical, whereas the second illustrates the format for a monthly:

Richardson, Storm. "Synthetic Drums and the Death of Rock 'n' Roll." *Rolling Stone* 30 Sept. 1990: 7–15.

Kimpowsky, Helena. "The Real Thing: Feminism's Return to the Victorian Woman." *Harper's Magazine* Dec. 1996: 23–35.

Some articles do not appear on continuous pages in periodicals. Whenever the page numbers are not continuous, give only the first page number followed by a plus sign, as in 17+.

Newspapers

The format for newspaper articles is similar to the format for weekly periodicals, but you also must include the section number and page number of the referenced article. Note that the words *A* and *The* are omitted in the names of the newspapers:

Henderson, Rita. "Zippergate: What the Lewinski Tapes Reveal." *San Francisco Chronicle* 18 June 1998: B15.

Smith, Roger H. "LA Cops: Bad to the Bone." *Los Angeles Times* 17 Oct. 1992: A1.

Electronic Sources

The Internet and the World Wide Web offer new sources of information that you may find useful when writing an academic paper. The appropriate format for referencing these sources using the MLA style is fairly straightforward.

Please note that you should use such sources with caution. Although the Internet and the Web frequently are touted as the future of research and scholarship, that future is not here yet and probably will not be for many years to come. The reality is that the overwhelming majority of the information available on the Internet and the Web is of very poor quality, and it also is at an amazingly low entry level. It may be useful for elementary school students, but it rarely attains the level of depth and sophistication required for university-level work. The obvious exception occurs when publishers make journals available online, but access to these journals commonly requires a subscription fee. Some university libraries—but certainly not all—pay this fee so that students will have online access, but the number of journals published online remains relatively small.

The format for electronic references provides for the author's name, as shown here. Following the author's name is the name of the referenced article, in quotation marks, followed by the name of the journal or periodical, the issue number and the date of publication. The full URL address appears in angle brackets (< >). Finally, in parentheses, is the date on which you accessed the information.

Witherspoon, Charles M. "Spielberg: From Iconoclast to Traditionalist." *Cinematique* 12 (1998): <http://cine.phy.ulaval.ca/1885> (10 Nov. 1998).

Film and Television Programs

The formats for film and television programs are very similar. Both require the name of the director, although the TV program also requires the name of the person who created the program. Also, film titles are underlined or placed in italics, whereas the titles of TV programs are set in quotation marks. In addition, TV programs require the date of broadcast:

Escape from Moscow. Dir. Douglas Weiskopf. With Feather Tippetts, Nikki Koloshnokoff, and Victoria Kessler. Crown. 1966.

"Starlight." *The Universe.* Created by Robert Oppenheimenn. Dir. Judy Smith. PBS, KCET, Los Angeles. 31 May 1989.

King Lear

James

English 154
Dr. Grant
2-22-98

In writing *King Lear*, Shakespeare varied little from the basic story of the ancient king as presented in his principal sources, Holinshed's *Chronicles* and Higgins' *The Mirror for Magistrates*. The fact that Shakespeare's version of the story is several times as long as either of his sources is a result of the dramatization of the historical outline provided in Holinshed and Higgins.

The similarity between Shakespeare's play and the historical sources is most evident at the beginning of King Lear. For example, Shakespeare writes, "Know that we have divided in three our kingdom; and 'tis our fast intent to shake all cares and business from our age, conferring them on younger strengths while we unburdened crawl toward death" (1065). This line is very similar to what appears in Holinshed:

> It is written that he had by his wife, three daughters without other issue, whose names were Gonorilla, Regan, and Cordeilla, which daughters he greatly loued, but specially Cordeilla the yoongest farre aboue the two elder. When Leir therefore was come to great yeres, & began to waxe unweldie through age, he thought to understand the affections of his daughters towards him, and preferred hir whome he best loued, to the succession ouer the kingdome. (531)

The similarity between Shakespeare's Lear and the one described in Holinshed is further illustrated in the dialogue between Lear and his daughters when he asks them how much they love him. In Shakespeare, Goneril says, "Sir, I love you more than word can wield the matter; dearer than eyesight, space, and liberty; beyond what can be valued, rich or rare; no less than life" (1066). These words reflect the strong influence of Holinshed, as can be seen by comparing the corresponding event as recorded in the Chronicles: "Gonorilla, who calling hir gods to record, protested that she loued him more than hir owne life, which by right and reason should be most deare vnto hir" (531).

It is during the above scene of the play that Cordelia enrages her father by telling him that she loves him only as a daughter should love her father. The anger her words spark in Lear seems too great in terms of what Cordelia said, but in *The Mirror*, Cordelia's response makes Lear's anger seem more appropriate: "I will at once my loue declare and tell: I loude you euer as my father well, no otherwise, if more to know you eraue: we loue you chiefly for the goodes you haue" (148).

It is important to note that, although Shakespeare follows his sources very closely at the beginning of the play, he diverges from them significantly after the opening scenes. The sources and Shakespeare deal with Lear's mistreatment at the hands of his daughters, but there are no secret letters telling of the French invasion and no pleasant-natured Albany to rail against his wife. The entire subplot of Glouchester and Edmund does not exist at all in Higgins or Holinshed, although it is an important part of the play. Instead, the sources outline the story in broad strokes, as we see in *The Mirror*, in which Higgins records Cordelia as stating:

> But while I these ioyes enioyed, at home in Fraunce my father Leire in Britayne waxed aged olde, my sisters yet themselues the more aloft t'aduaunce, thought well they might be by his leaue, or sans so bolde: to take the realme & rule it as they wold. They rose as rebels voyde of reason quite, and they depriude his of his crowne and might. (150)

1

Likewise, in the Chronicles, Holinshed summarizes the situation after the revolt by writing:

> In the end, such was the unkindnesse, or (as I maie saie) the unnaturalnesse which he found in his two daughters, notwithstanding their faire and pleasant words uttered in time past, that being constrained of necessitie, he fled the land, & sailed into Gallia, there to seeke some comfort of his yongest daughter Cordeilla, whome before time he hated. (534).

We can see from these passages that Shakespeare made some significant changes in his version of the Lear story. In the sources, Lear sailed to France to ask his youngest daughter for aid. Several other changes will be discussed later. But it is important to note that here the motives for Shakespeare's alterations begin to become apparent. A key to many of Shakespeare's changes is found in the excerpt above. The "unnaturalnesse" Holinshed speaks of is what Shakespeare strives to emphasize in *King Lear*. The unnatural acts of Lear's daughters is stressed throughout the play. To strengthen the atmosphere of the unnatural, the poet uses various devil images when describing Regan and Goneril. For example, Goneril's husband, Albany, says to his wife, "See thyself, devil: proper deformity seems not in the fiend so horrid as in woman" (1091). Lear also portrays his eldest daughters as monsters when he says, "Down from the waist they are Centaurs, though women all above" (1095).

The sense of the unnatural is also increased by the tempest and Lear's slow decent into madness. There is a mysterious quality about the storm that seems to match the "unkindness" of Regan and Goneril. As Kent says:

> Things that love night love not such nights as these. The wrathful skies gallow the very wanderers of the dark and make them keep their caves. Since I was man, such sheets of fire, such bursts of horrid thunder, such groans of roaring wind and rain, I never remember to have heard. Man's nature cannot carry th' affliction nor the fear. (1083)

Although the desire to address the theme of the unnatural is one of the major motives for Shakespeare's departure from his sources, it is important to recognized that he had to make certain changes in the original story to make a tragedy. The struggle of changing the fairly straightforward accounts of Lear found in Holinshed and Higgns is best illustrated in the last few scenes of the play. In neither source does Cordeilla or Lear die directly after the battle with France. Of course, such an ending does not produce the emotional impact (or the sense of tragedy) achieved in Shakespeare's version. For example, Holinshed's account is as follows:

> Hereupon, when this armie and nauie of ships was readie, Leir and his daughter Cordeilla with hir husband tooke the sea, and arriuing in Britaine, fought with their enimies, and discomfited them in battell, in the which Maglanus and Henninus were slaine: and then was Leir restored to this king dome, which he ruled after this by the space of two yeeres, and then died, fortied yeeres after he first began to reigne. His bodie was buried at Leicester in a vaut vunder the chanell of the riuer of Sore beneth the towne. (535)

2

This account is echoed in Higgins, who writes: "The Britishe kinges were fayne to yelde our right, and so my father well this realme did guide, three yeares in peace and after that he dide" (153).

Thus, we can see two motives for the changes Shakespeare made in his source material. On the one hand, there was the desire to build up the unnaturalness of Lear's daughters. This in turn helps build the emotional climate that reaches its climax in the reconciliation of Lear and Cordelia. Were Shakespeare to neglect the undaughterly actions of Goneril and Regan, the agony and suffering that Lear undergoes on their account would make his end seem pointless. In this sense, the strong development of the unnatural fiend in Regan and Goneril is directly related to the second motive of making the Lear story a tragedy. The flight of Lear into the tempest and the storming agony he has raging through his mind serve to make the play what it is—a tragedy. The murder of Cordelia and the resulting death of Lear serve to make the play what it is—a tragedy. And as Lear dies, we can truly say that he is a man "more sinned against than sinning."

3

WORKS CITED

Higgins, John. *The Mirror for Magistrates*. Ed. Lily Campbell. London: Cambridge U P, 1946.
Holinshed, Richard. *The British Chronicles*, Vol. 1. London: Cambridge U P, 1801. 3 vols.
Shakespeare, William. *King Lear*. Ed. Alfred Harbage. Baltimore: Penguin, 1969.

4

WRITING IN THE SOCIAL SCIENCES

Writing in the humanities can be characterized as focusing on the individual. That is, interpreting a work of art commonly involves translating the universal experience of the artwork into an individual experience. Writing in the social sciences is different in that it usually deals with groups of people rather than with individuals. The social sciences themselves tend to focus on differentiating between knowledge of how people in general behave and knowledge of how a single person behaves. Statistics, because they offer insight into aggregate data and help depersonalize findings, are one of the principal tools in social science. Be that as it may, few undergraduate courses in the social sciences require any knowledge of statistics. Most such courses focus, instead, on training students to be more accurate observers of the world around them; as a result, the majority of papers you may be asked to write will call upon your powers of observation and your ability to differentiate qualitatively rather than quantitatively.

Social scientists tend to fall into two camps—those who engage in theoretical activities and those who engage in empirical ones. Theoretical activities involve building models of human behavior. For example, Freud, the father of modern psychology, theorized that all young boys suffer from what he termed the "Oedipus complex," a suppressed desire to have sex with their mothers. With this incest model, he attempted to explain certain features of the human experience, even though he had no data, really, to substantiate the theory. Westermark, on the other hand, collected incest data from hundreds of societies around the world and found that sexual contact and/or desire among parents and offspring, as well as among siblings, is extremely rare. These empirical data not only refuted Freud's theory but led to a new one involving incest aversion. So here we see two different approaches to the same question that produce quite different results.

The conventions that govern writing in the social sciences are more strictly defined than those in the humanities; as a result, the expectations among teachers are high that you follow these conventions closely. Some of the conventions deal with global features of organizing a paper. For example, papers normally begin with the outline of a theoretical framework; then they go on to ask a question about human behavior that can be answered in terms of that framework. This first step is known as "formulating a hypothesis." Answering the question may involve testing, measuring, observation, and so forth, but the approach usually is empirical, involving the collection of data (or facts) that one then interprets through the filter of the theoretical framework. An empirical focus is congruent with the ways of knowing that characterize the social sciences.

Also note that the scope of writing in the social sciences is tightly controlled. The more questions one tries to answer in any given situation, the more variables there are that can lead to confusing or misleading interpretations. Consequently, writing in the social sciences tends to be very focused—writers work with small data sets. Another convention restricts how the information is interpreted, limiting interpretations to the data at hand. Generalizing beyond the data is viewed as a major error. In addition, the data in social science writing may "suggest" or "indicate," but it never "proves." This convention is very important to your work, because the temptation to make a claim of proof can be quite strong. Having said that, it is important to note that social science writing is argumentative. Argumentative proof therefore is a fundamental requirement for any paper you write.

At work in such papers are assumptions and standards of proof that those working in the humanities commonly do not accept. Emotions often play a significant role in humanistic writing, but it does not in social science writing. Thus, papers in the humanities reveal personal involvement in the topic, whereas those in the social sciences do not. The assumption in the social sciences is that personal involvement creates unacceptable biases. (One practical consequence is that social science writing values the use of passive constructions, whereas humanities writing does not.)

The argumentative proofs that dominate social science writing focus on good reasons that serve to substantiate any interpretive claims about the data under discussion. In advanced work, many of these good reasons normally are inherent in the design of the study that produced the data. For example, a study that collected data from, say, 1,000 people is likely to be viewed as more credible than one that collected data from a single person. By the same token, interpretations of data that rely on statistical analysis are likely to be viewed as more credible than interpretations based on, say, intuition. The writing undergraduates must produce, however, seldom reaches such levels. The usual standard of proof therefore will be how effectively you can interpret facts through the filter of the theoretical model you have selected for your paper. Stated another way, your success will depend, in large part, on how well you can interpret information based on what you have learned in class.

THE APA DOCUMENTATION STYLE

Writing in social science is governed by the conventions of the *Publication Manual of the American Psychological Association*. The APA guide provides information about documentation, but it also offers instructions associated with organizing a paper, such as the following:

- Double space all text, even long quotations and bibliography.
- Set 1-inch margins on all sides of the paper.
- Place page numbers in the upper right-hand corner of the page.
- Provide a cover page that includes the title of the paper, your name, the name of your professor, the title of the course, and the date; below this information provide a running head that is a shortened version of the title (under 50 characters); set the running head as a continuing header in the upper left-hand corner of each page of text; all lines should be double spaced, with triple space between entries.
- Use the past tense when referring to previously published materials.
- Write out all numbers under 10 and use Arabic numerals for all numbers greater than nine, except when the number is used to identify data, in which case always use the Arabic numeral; write out all numbers at the beginning of a sentence.

Proper documentation in the APA style includes in-text references to works used as resources and a bibliography that lists these works in alphabetical order. The bibliography is titled *References* and appears at the end of the paper on one or more separate pages. The title should be centered on the first page of the bibliography and should be placed on the first line.

In-Text Citation

In-text attribution and citation takes different forms under the APA conventions, depending on how you use the source material. There are five options, each of which is illustrated here:

1. A direct quotation incorporated as part of a sentence you write.
2. A direct quotation that supports a point you make or that is congruent with your interpretation of the author's position.
3. A long quotation.
4. A paraphrase.
5. Reference to an entire work.

Option 1: Direct Quotation as Part of a Sentence

Initially, research that linked biology with psychology was suspect. For many decades, mainstream thought in psychology held that human behavior was influenced primarily by environment, with biology playing only the "minor" role of establishing structure, such as neurological pathways. This position led to numerous farfetched proposals that today seem quaint. For example, as a discipline, psychology proposed that something as fundamental as gender-specific behavior was governed by environment rather than biology, even though the biological differences between males and females in all primate species—as well as behavioral differences—are significant and one might even say defining. Many psychologists did not trust biology "to provide meaningful insights into behaviors that were deemed to be social in origin" (Westin, 1989, p. 43).

Notice that by incorporating the quotation directly into the text the writer provides a continuation of his own sentence. The effect is to link the writer's ideas closely to those in the quotation.

Option 2: Direct Quotation as Support

In the next example, the writer provides attribution in the text and does not use the quotation to continue a thought. Instead, the writer reports what is stated in the source document. The effect is twofold—it stresses the writer's interpretation of the quoted material and it more clearly uses the quotation as argumentative support:

The environmental argument continues to be popular as a kind of "folk psychology" among those who lack professional training, as well as among a shrinking number of professionals who either do not understand the new data or have a vested interest in preserving outdated ideas. On the whole, however, the argument has been rejected in light of the significant amount of research compiled since the late 1980s, most of which involved studies of twins reared apart from birth. As Lincoln and Krum (1998) noted in their comprehensive review of the literature, "Researchers' ability to match manifested behaviors in twins reared apart has forced a complete rethinking of the nature/nurture argument" (p.23).

Option 3: A Long Quotation

If you have a direct quotation that is longer than two or three lines, set the material in a *block quotation*, which is separated from the body of the text by indenting on both sides. Please note that, years ago, block quotations were single-spaced; today, however, they are double-spaced. Also note that an introductory statement normally precedes the quotation and that the statement ends with a colon. The block quotation should begin with a capital letter, even if it is not the actual beginning of a sentence in the original:

> *In most instances, the findings from studies of twins are compelling. Cathcart, Jones, and Okada (1999), for example, studied 100 sets of twins from 7 different countries in a cross-cultural assessment of behavior between twins reared apart. Their findings are representative:*
>
> > *In more than 80 percent of the subjects, matched behaviors reached a robust level of significance. As noted in Chapter 1, Mariel and Lupe, for example, wore their hair in the same style, wore a similar style of clothing, enjoyed the same kind of music and the same movies, and married men in similar professions. (pp. 179–180)*

Option 4: Paraphrase

A paraphrase requires attribution and the page number of where the paraphrased material appears, as illustrated here:

> *Understanding the persistence of the environmental model requires an assessment of the role it plays in the human psyche. Argyle and Robertson (1998) suggested that many people derive comfort from the model because the alternative strikes many as restricting opportunities for growth and development. The biological model is mistakenly viewed as deterministic (pp. 89–95).*

Option 5: Reference to an Entire Work

If you are making reference to an entire work, you need only provide the name of the author and the work and the date of publication, as illustrated here:

> *In <u>Genes and Primate Behavior</u>, Cathcart (1998) argued that this view is rooted in notions of social inequality and the worthwhile effort to eradicate social barriers. From his perspective, the question of intelligence is at the heart of the matter. Those with low levels of intelligence can point to social inequalities as the cause of any deficiencies, which allows them to feel good about themselves even in light of obvious shortcomings. Thus, in Cathcart's view, the environmental model allows people to adopt the role of victim.*

REFERENCES

How information appears in the references section depends on the nature of the material. For example, the format for listing books is different from the format for articles. One of the more significant differences is that the titles of books appear in lower case (with the exception of the first word in the title), whereas the titles of journals is in upper and lower case. The following examples illustrate the various possibilities for the APA style. Note that it is important to follow the format exactly when preparing your Reference page. Indeed, it is recommended that you have these examples handy while working.

Books

A Book with One Author

Anderson, A. (1997). *Tax structures and corporate profits*. New York: Oxford.

Rodriguez, M. (1999). *Social structures among the pre-Columbian Mayans of southern Mexico*. Norwood, NJ: Ablex.

Zhou, Z. H. (1998). *Hemisphericity and abnormalities in the corpus callosum: Three case studies*. Los Angeles: Sage.

More than One Book by the Same Author

When referencing more than one book by the same author, list the books chronologically, with the most recent book last, as illustrated here:

Eliade, M. (1957). *Social structures among the west African tribal people*. Princeton, NJ: Princeton University Press.

Eliade, M. (1959). *Shamanism and its origins: Magical realism*. Cambridge: Cambridge University Press.

A Book with Two or More Authors

Baker, J., & Robertson, A. (1998). *Statistical analyses of cellular dimorphism in stasis*. Norwood, NJ: Ablex.

Britton, J., Burgess, T., Martin, N., McLeod, A., & Rosen, H. (1975). *The development of writing abilities*. London: Macmillian Education Ltd.

A Book with a Title in the Title

Montgomery, F. A. (1990). *Topological questions in "Parallel Distributed Processing": The case for neural networks*. Cambridge, MA: Harvard University Press.

An Edited Book

Irwin, F. (Ed.). (1985). *Psychobiology and human behavior*. Stanford: Stanford University Press.

A Book with More than One Editor

Martin, W., Gomez, M., & Johns, E. (Eds.). (1996). *The effects of gender on child development in custody cases*. Oxford: Oxford University Press.

A Work in an Edited Volume

Scardamalia, M., & Bereiter, C. (1983). The development of evaluative, diagnostic, and remedial capabilities in children's composing. In M. Martlew (Ed.), *The psychology of written language: A developmental approach*. London: Wiley.

Smith, W. (1993). Assessing the reliability and adequacy of using holistic scoring of essays as a college composition placement program technique. In M.

Williams & B. Huot (Eds.), *Validating holistic scoring for writing assessment.* Cresskill, NJ: Hampton.

A Multivolume Work

A multivolume work often is an edited edition that is published over a period of years. The following entry illustrates that you must provide the inclusive publication dates of the volumes. Note also that, following the title, you must provide reference only to those volumes you actually used in your writing.

Walpol, E. A. (Ed.). (1989–1993). *The collected works of Sigmund Freud* (Vols. 2–4). London: Heinmann.

A Book in Translation

Lévy-Bruhl, L. (1926). *How natives think* (L. Clare, Trans.). New York: Knopf.

Sokolov, A. (1975). *Inner speech and thought* (A. Koskolnikoff, Trans.). Cambridge, MA: MIT Press.

A Book in a New Edition

Williams, J. D. (1998). *Preparing to teach writing* (2nd ed.). Mahwah, NJ: Erlbaum.

A Book in Reprint

Ebrahim, E. (1997). *Stochastic processes in postmodern archaeology.* Cambridge, MA: Harvard University Press. (Original work published 1988)

Conference Proceedings

Campuzano, P. (1998). Neo-marxism and the decline of the American middle class. *Proceedings of the Society for Independent Thought* (January 5–8, 1998). San Francisco: Jossey-Bass.

An Unpublished Paper Presented at a Conference

Jackson, M. (1998, June). *Writing performance and gender differences: A longitudinal study of 6th graders.* Paper presented at the regional meeting of the National Council of Teachers of English, Seattle.

Dissertations

Dissertations are book-length treatises that are required of students completing a doctoral degree. Most dissertations are not published, but some are. The formats differ insofar as an unpublished dissertation must be identified as such; a published dissertation, on the other hand, follows the same format as a published book.

Moore, M. (1989). *Territoriality among beta splendens: Implications for further research.* Unpublished doctoral dissertation, University of Southern California, Los Angeles, CA.

Articles

In academic writing, articles that appear in academic journals are treated differently from those that appear in popular magazines, or periodicals. For academic journals, it is necessary to provide the volume and issue numbers, whereas for periodicals it is necessary simply to provide the date. The examples below illustrated the distinction. Notice that the APA documentation style does not use quotation marks around the titles of articles and that the volume number, which appears after the name of the journal, is italicized.

Journals

Russell, D. (1987). Writing across the curriculum and the communications movement: Some lessons from the past. *College Composition and Communication, 38,* 184–194.

Journals are paginated either by volume or by issue. The previous example illustrates pagination by volume, whereas the next one illustrates pagination by issue. Note that the volume number is italicized in both instances:

Harris, J., Owen, W., & Kzyrzyrzki, A. (1997). The development of logic in preoperational children. *Journal of Brain and Language, 58*(3), 432–446.

Periodicals

Some periodicals appear weekly, whereas others appear monthly. The format for referencing differs depending on the frequency of publication. The first example below illustrates the format for a weekly periodical, whereas the second illustrates the format for a monthly:

Nixon, J., Kamakura, H., & Vaughn, A. (1995, September 15). Social unrest in the former Soviet Union. *US News & World Report, 118,* 18–20, 34–37.

Note the page numbers in the previous entry. This format indicates that the article did not run continuously but appeared on separated pages. In such an event, list all the various continuous page numbers.

Lee, K., & Wong, J. (1997, December). The new social science. *Atlantic, 74,* 31–36.

Newspapers

The format for newspaper articles is similar to the format for weekly periodicals, but you also must include the section number and page number of the referenced article. Also, use *p.* (page) or *pp.* (pages) to identify the section and page numbers.

Henderson, R. (1998, June 18). Zippergate: What the Lewinski tapes reveal. *The San Francisco Chronicle,* p. 15B.

Smith, R. H. (1992, October 17). LA cops: Bad to the bone. *The Los Angeles Times,* p. 1A.

Electronic Sources

The Internet and the World Wide Web offer new sources of information that you may find useful when writing an academic paper. The appropriate format for referencing these sources using the APA style is fairly straightforward.

Please note that you should use such sources with caution. Although the Internet and the Web frequently are touted as the future of research and scholarship, that future is not here yet and probably will not be for many years to come. The reality is that the overwhelming majority of the information available on the Internet and the Web is of very poor quality, and it also is at an amazingly low entry level. It may be useful for elementary school students, but it rarely attains the level of depth and sophistication required for university-level work. The obvious exception occurs when publishers make journals available online, but access to these journals commonly requires a subscription fee. Some university libraries—but certainly not all—pay this fee so that students will have online access, but the number of journals published online remains relatively small.

In the case of journals published online, the format follows what was listed above for journals and periodicals, with the exception of the URL address, which should appear following the name of the journal, and the date you visited the site, which should appear at the end of the entry. The format for sources other than published journals includes the author's name, the date of publication, the title of the article, which should appear in italics, identification that the sources is a Web document, which should appear in brackets, the full URL address, and, in parentheses, the date you accessed the information.

Witherspoon, V. (1998, September). Natural restoration of the Korean demilitarized zone. *Nature, 45*, 23–28. URL http://www.nature.com (visited 1998, November 30).

Zador, T., & Antonelli, B. (1998, October 10). The problems with Clinton's presidency [Web document]. URLhtt://www.clinton.lewinsky.talltales.usc.edu/politicalcomedy (visited 1998, November 28).

Film and Television Programs

The formats for film and television programs are very similar. Both require the name of the director, although the TV program also requires the name of the person who created the program. Also, film titles are underlined or placed in italics, whereas the titles of TV programs are set in quotation marks. In addition, TV programs require the date of broadcast:

Smith, J. (Director) & Oppenheimenn, R. (Producer). (1989). Starlight. Los Angeles, KCET.

Weiskopf, D. (Director), & Prucha, L. (Producer). (1966). *Escape from Moscow*. [Film]. Los Angeles: Crown International Pictures.

Observations of the Locomotion, Grooming,
and Reproductive Behavior of *Acheta domesticus*

Craig

Dr. Scott
Psychobiology 10
10-2-96

Running head: Acheta domesticus

Head: Acheta domesticus

Introduction

The laboratory exercise dealt with the locomotion, grooming, and reproduction of the common house cricket, *Acheta domesticus*. Cheng and Leonnelli (1989) reported that Acheta domesticus uses its antennae as appendages in social interactions. These interactions, according to Smith, Fennell, and McIntyre (1988) include greetings, communications about food, danger, and sex. The lab team attempted to observe the method of walking, jumping, grooming, and interactions used by the cricket. Various aspects of reproduction were observed, including activities of the male and female before, during, and after copulation.

Methods

The crickets used in this study were grown on a Tennessee "cricket ranch" and belong to the species Acheta domesticus, also known as Gryllus domesticus (Henderson, 1987). The cricket used for the locomotion and grooming exercise was a large female that had been removed from the breeder just prior to being observed. The male used for the reproduction exercise had been isolated for 24 hours in half of the terrarium. The females in the reproduction observation had been isolated in a coffee can for 24 hours.

The equipment included a terrarium, a length of string, and liquid paper in various colors. The string was used as a leash in the grooming and locomotion observations. The liquid paper was used to mark the female crickets used in the reproduction exercise. The terrarium also was used in the reproduction observation. Its bottom was covered with sand, and there was a water dispenser. A cricket "home," made from a piece of egg carton, was in one corner. Finally, the terrarium was divided in half with dividers.

A female cricket was leashed with a piece of string tied behind the first two pairs of legs. She then was induced to jump by lightly prodding her posterior. The approximate length and height of each of her jumps were recorded. She was then suspended over the table and lowered to the table top.

The cricket was then used for observation of walking. To slow her movements she was induced to walk up a screen. The cricket was observed to determine which legs moved when, how fast she moved, how far and how long was a stride interval.

To test grooming behavior, alcohol was dabbed with a Q-tip on the antennae of the female used in the previous observations. This was repeated on the other antennae and on the cricket legs.

Finally, the reproductive behavior was observed in a male isolated in half of the terrarium and with four of the females that had been isolated in coffee cans. The females were marked on the dorsal side of their thoraxes with small dabs of liquid paper in various colors.

The female crickets were added to one side of the terrarium. The behavior of the crickets was then observed with marked females being added or removed from one side to induce mating.

1

Results

Just before the cricket jumped, it got into a characteristic posture. She stood still with her body low and her legs close to her body. The cricket's rear jumping legs were pulled close to where they meet the body. During the jump these legs were extended behind the abdomen.

The results of making the cricket take 10 consecutive jumps led to various measurements. The height of each jump was difficult to measure but was approximately 4 inches.

When the cricket was suspended over the table, it showed two types of behavior. The cricket either froze in a position that resembled a jumping position or attempted to fly. When the cricket in the jumping position hit the table, it started to jump, whereas the flying cricket stopped all movement.

The cricket moved at about 2 inches a second on a flat, porous surface and at about .5 inch every second on a nearly vertical screen. The stride interval, movement of all 6 legs, varied considerably depending on where the cricket was walking, and no accurate measure of its length or duration was recorded.

The cricket was very cooperative during the grooming observation; she cleaned herself constantly. The cricket pulled the alcohol treated antennae down to its jaws with its pro-thoracic legs. The antennae was always groomed from the part closest to the head towards the tip. Grooming of the legs was similar to antenna grooming. The leg was moved up to the jaws, and the cricket worked from the part closest to the body outwards towards the claw.

When the two marked females were introduced into the male's territory, they exhibited a great deal of activity. The females ran around the cage for approximately 3 minutes before settling down. The male also was very active during this time; he moved when he was run over by one of the females as she ran around the tank.

The male made contact with one of the females with his antennae against her antennae. The male then turned to face away from the female's head. He then raised his body high on his hind legs with his wings buzzing quickly and making a soft quick chirping sound. The female made an attempt to mount the male, but another female jostled them and knocked the mounting female away. The male chirped loudly in response and pivoted back and forth quickly, with his body raised in the air. He then groomed his antennae and waved them around quickly. Then he started to prowl the tank.

When the male made contact with either of the females in the tank, he quickly turned around and chirped softly and quickly. The females seemed uninterested in this display and wandered off. The remaining two females were added to the tank in the hope that they might mate with the male, even though he constantly would put on a display for any of the females that he came into contact with.

2

Discussion

The jumping behavior in crickets appears to be a standard flight mechanism. The crickets jump to get away from perceived danger. The motionlessness before the jump is what Broom (1981) called "exaggerating primary defense, e.g., a camouflaged animal remaining motionless" (p. 73). Broom also noted that the jump is another kind of defense.

Walking in the cricket follows a stride pattern that gives the animal good footing on most surfaces. The cricket always has most of his legs supporting him. Furthermore, the legs on one side or the legs of a pair are not moved directly after each other because it might reduce traction.

The crickets in this study seemed to rely on their antennae for most of their sensory information. This might explain why they groomed themselves thoroughly after the alcohol application. In addition, as describe by Poole and Wilson (1988), crickets use their antennae for social interactions. This behavior was clear during the male cricket's courtship efforts. The lack of response on the part of the females (except for the one attempt at copulation) probably was the result of the handling they had received during the study.

All of the behaviors studied seem to have survival value. Jumping allows the cricket to escape from danger. Grooming keeps the cricket in working order and is necessary for social interaction.

3

REFERENCES

Broom, D. M. (1981). *Biology of behavior*. New York: Cambridge University Press.

Cheng, X., & Leonnelli, C. (1989). Social interactions in *Acheta domesticus*. *Science, 42*, 221–226.

Henderson, W. (1987). Typology of *Acheta domesticus*. *Journal of Entomology, 57*, 176–181.

Poole, R., & Wilson, E. F. (1988). Communication in *Acheta domesticus*. *Journal of Entomology, 58*, 23–29.

Smith, F. R., Fennel, A., & McIntrye, J. (1988). Properties of the communicative behavior of the common house cricket, Acheta domesticus. *Natural Science Quarterly, 15*(2), 76–82.

4

WRITING IN SCIENCE

Many people automatically believe that scientific writing is full of jargon and hard to understand. Certainly, a great deal of writing in science is demanding, but when it is, the audience is composed of scientists. When the audience is composed of general readers, the writing usually is clear and straightforward. Nearly all of the scientific writing you may do as an undergraduate will be targeted toward an audience of general readers. Your professors understand the differences associated with audience very well and only occasionally will ask for a paper targeted toward professionals.

Scientific writing necessarily reflects the general goals and conventions of science, such as exploring the nature of the world in an objective manner. Because personal biases and emotions can cloud the accurate observation and interpretation of natural phenomena, scientific writing strives to eliminate these factors as much as possible. One way is through the design of studies, which not only must follow accepted procedures but which also must be reproducible. That is, if a scientist conducts a study that others cannot reproduce, the findings are immediately suspect. Double-blind experiments, often conducted in medical research, are a very effective means of reducing personal biases. In drug trials, for example, neither the subjects nor the people administering the drugs knows who receives the experimental medication and who receives a placebo.

Language is one of the more significant factors in bias, so science has developed conventions that aim to reduce the amount of bias in writing. For example, scientific writing regularly uses passive constructions rather than active because it allows writers to explain procedures without mentioning themselves. Conventions also govern the form of scientific papers. They commonly begin with an abstract that summarizes the report in under 200 words. They are divided into sections with headings labeled *introduction, methods, results,* and *conclusion*. These conventions standardize papers and reduce the effects of personal, individual styles. The content of these sections is straightforward: The introduction reviews the relevant literature and establishes a theoretical framework; the methods section describes the methods used to collect data; the results section presents the findings; and the conclusion interprets the findings.

The lab report is a common type of scientific writing that students must produce, and it is tempting to think of such reports as being purely descriptive. The goal seems to be merely describing the procedures and results of an experiment. There are other, more important, goals, however. Lab activities are intended to provide training in careful observation, procedures, and logical interpretation of findings. In addition, lab reports are fundamentally argumentative and require evidence to support claims. Typical lab activities involve replication of well-known experiments, and most of the time the results of the replication match those in the lab book. It is important to note that teachers often are most interested in experiments that go awry because students then are forced to explain what went wrong, forced into skillful interpretation and argumentation.

SCIENTIFIC DOCUMENTATION STYLE

The life and applied sciences differ from the humanities and social sciences insofar as there is no one documentation style that every writer uses. Instead, most writers use a documentation style particular to a given journal. They get information about the style from journal guidelines. Thus, there are individual formats for physics, math, chemistry, and biology, and within each discipline there often are additional formats. In chemistry, for example, there are two fairly popular publication guides, the *Handbook for Authors of Papers in American Chemical Society Publications* and the *Style Guide for Chemists*. In biology, some writers use the CBE (Council of Biology Editors) Style Manual, which comments on the wide variety of formats used and then presents two very different approaches for documentation.

This lack of standardization creates a problem: Putting together a documentation guide becomes an exercise that may not have much application. Having said that, the goal here is to offer a guide that can be used in the most situations, and the numeric format meets that goal. This format uses a numbering system in the text to refer readers to a list of sources in the "References" section at the end of the paper. The numbers appear consecutively, so the sources are listed by order of appearance rather than alphabetically or chronologically by date of publication. Like other documentation formats, this one requires that all text and entries be double spaced. The paper should have a title page that shows the title, your name, the name of the class and teacher, and the date. The paper also should have 1-inch margins on all sides.

In-Text Citation

In-text citation takes four forms under the numeric format, which are listed here:

1. A direct quotation that supports a point you make or that is congruent with your interpretation of the author's position.
2. A long quotation.
3. A paraphrase.
4. Reference to an entire work.

Option 1: Direct Quotation as Support

Note that the reference number as well as the page number for the direct quotation appear in parentheses following the authors' names.

> *Theophyline is an alkaloid of the xanthine group and has been used for some time as a smooth muscle relaxant of bronchi constriction, making it an effective drug in treating asthma. Garcia and Edelman (1, p. 46) reviewed the work of various researchers involved in forming the purines that underlie synthesis of theophyline and called such work "a significant breakthrough in treating asthma."*

Option 2: A Long Quotation

> *Theophyline, in fact, is the drug of choice for treating asthma because it acts rapidly and has few side effects. Describing this drug, Watson and Greig noted that:*
>> *Theophyline is present in small quantities in the leaves of the tea plant, and it was from this source that Kossei first isolated the drug in 1888. The original synthesis was performed by Traube in 1900. Truabe's work involved the general use of 4, 5-diaminopyrimidines to form purines. Within a few years, however, formic acid, ethyl chloroformate, urea, and thiourea were employed for the preparation of 8-oxo- and 8-thiopurine. (2, p. 79)*

Option 3: A Paraphrase

The general synthesis of 8-oxo- and 8-thiopurine initially involved a lengthy process of hydration and secretion, but within a few years the process was accelerated (3). In fact, the original time was reduced from two weeks to three hours, which was necessary if theophylline was to be commercially viable (4).

Option 4: Reference to an Entire Work

More recent work in asthma drugs offers promising results. Rogers and Kimura reported, for example, that k-primaphylline, synthesized from 6, 8-oxo-purine, is nearly twice as effective as theophylline at reducing bronchial constriction (5).

REFERENCES

How information appears in the references section depends on the nature of the material. For example, the format for listing books is different from the format for articles. When listing articles, you must provide the inclusive page numbers, but this is not necessary for a book. In addition, references are listed by order of appearance in the text rather than alphabetically. Note that in the numeric format, titles do not appear in italics or quotation marks. The examples below illustrate the various possibilities of the numeric style. Because it is important to follow the format exactly when preparing your Reference page, you should have these examples handy while working.

Books

A Book with One Author

1. Bradbury, J. Analysis of holons and CFCs in real time. Washington, DC: US Government Printing Office; 1998.
2. McCarthy, T. The synthesis of 2, 4, 5-oxy-benzene-probutinate. Berkeley, CA: University of California Press; 1978.
3. Sanchez, M. Chaos theory and cardio irregularities. Baltimore, MD: Johns-Hopkins University Press; 1999.

More than One Book by the Same Author

When referencing more than one book by the same author, list the books by order of appearance:

4. Wolff, K. Electromagnetic interference. New York: Academic Press; 1990.
5. Wolff, K. Nonlinear dynamic systems. New York: Academic Press; 1991.

A Book with Two or More Authors

6. Cheng, X.; Shu, L. Holons and the formation of ozone-depleting precursors. Cambridge, MA: MIT Press.
7. Franklin, J.; Montgomery, W.; Okada, K. Household sinks for toxins and other pollutants. Washington, DC: US Government Printing Office; 1993.

A Book with a Title in the Title

> 8. Montgomery, F. A. Topological questions in "Parallel Distributed Processing": the case for neural networks. Cambridge, MA: Harvard University Press; 1990.

An Edited Book

When referencing an edited book, list the work by the editor's name and use parentheses to identify the editor.

> 9. Chang, J. (Ed.). Fractal functions in mathematical topology. Los Angeles: Scientific Press; 1992.

A Book with More than One Editor

> 10. Wittrock, J.; Berliner, I. A. (Eds.). Quasar formation as a function of gravimetric pressures in n-dimensions. New York: Academic Press; 1989.

A Work in an Edited Volume

Note that when referencing a work in an edited volume, it is necessary to provide the page numbers of the selection. The listing appears with the author of the selection first, then the title of the selection. Following the title is the name of the editor or editors and the title of the volume. Note that inclusive page numbers must appear at the end of the entry.

> 11. Somlinarski, K. Self-organized systems in galaxy formation. Mondragon, B. Biological perspectives on the cosmos. Chicago: University of Chicago Press; 1998: 111–129.

A Multivolume Work

> 12. Feigenbaum, M. Strange attractors: the mathematics of phase space arrays. 2 vols. Sante Fe: Los Alamos Press; 1985.

A Book in Translation

> 13. Ornstein, P.; Willey, J. A.; Leong, R. String theory and the Planck constant. Trans. Grassberger, M. Princeton: Princeton University Press; 1996.

A Book in a New Edition

> 14. Garcia-Medina, J. Calculating vibrations of Planck units in 10-dimensional space. 2nd ed. Palo Alto: Stanford University Press; 1991.

A Book in Reprint

> 15. Ebrahim, E. Stochastic processes in bypass operations. Rpt. Baltimore, MD: Johns-Hopkins University Press; 1997.

Conference Proceedings

16. Sunstein, B. (Ed.). Protease inhibitors and the suppression of HIV. Proceedings of the CDC conference on AIDS prevention; 1994 September 15–17; Atlanta, GA. Washington, DC: US Government Printing Office; 1995.

An Unpublished Paper Presented at a Conference

17. Johnson, M.; Shu, R.; Zhou, T. The release of VOCs in municipal incinerators. Paper presented at the EPA conference on urban pollutants; Durham, NC; June 3–4 1997.

Technical Report

18. Environmental Protection Agency. Chemical analysis of VOCs. Technical Report 977-00933. Washington, DC: US Government Printing Office; 1989.

Dissertations

Dissertations are book-length treatises that are required of students completing a doctoral degree. Most dissertations are not published, but some are. The formats differ insofar as an unpublished dissertation must be identified as such; a published dissertation, on the other hand, follows the same format as a published book.

19. Moore, M. Territoriality among beta splendens: Implications for further research. Unpublished doctoral dissertation; University of Southern California, Los Angeles, CA; 1989.

Articles

In academic writing, articles that appear in academic journals are treated differently from those that appear in popular magazines, or periodicals. For academic journals, it is necessary to provide the volume and issue numbers, whereas for periodicals it is necessary simply to provide the date. The following examples illustrate the distinction. Note that the names of journals are abbreviated in the numeric format.

Journals

20. Miller, L.; Rudder, C. Reduction of NO_x and SO_2 emissions through a dry-spray injection process. J. Envir. Tech. 17: 189–211.

Journals are paginated either by volume or by issue. The previous example illustrates pagination by volume, whereas the one that follows illustrates pagination by issue.

21. Simpson, F. Climatic change and ozone depletion. Atm. Sci. 15(3): 17–25; 1989.

Periodicals

Some periodicals appear weekly, whereas others appear monthly. The format for referencing depends on the frequency of publication. The first example illustrates the format for a weekly periodical, whereas the second illustrates the format for a monthly:

22. Smith, C. The debate about cloning. US News & World Rpt. June 3, 1998: 34–37.

23. Villa, J.; Hernandez, J. PET and MRI techniques for measuring cortical functions. Sci. Amer. December 1997: 15–18.

Electronic Sources

The Internet and the World Wide Web offer new sources of information that you may find useful when writing an academic paper. The appropriate format for referencing these sources using the numeric style is fairly straightforward.

Please note that you should use such sources with caution. Although the Internet and the Web frequently are touted as the future of research and scholarship, that future is not here yet and probably will not be for many years to come. The reality is that the overwhelming majority of the information available on the Internet and the Web is of very poor quality, and it also is at an amazingly low entry level. It may be useful for elementary school students, but it rarely attains the level of depth and sophistication required for university-level work. The obvious exception occurs when publishers make journals available online, but access to these journals commonly requires a subscription fee. Some university libraries—but certainly not all—pay this fee so that students will have online access, but the number of journals published online remains relatively small.

In the case of journals published online, the format follows what was listed above for journals and periodicals, with the exception of the URL address, which should appear following the name of the journal, and the date you visited the site, which should appear at the end of the entry, as illustrated in the first example below. The format for sources other than published journals includes the author's name, the title of the article, the full URL address, and, in parentheses, the date you accessed the information, as illustrated in the second example below:

24. Klangenbush, O.; y de Spain, S. Metastasis of cancer cells in the presence of t-cell inhibitors. Sci. 1997; 86: 41–47. <http://science.com/112.233.83/html> (January 5, 1998).

25. Bell, D. Planck units as a gravitimetric function. <http://gravity.units.physics.caltec.edu> (April 15, 1997).

Perpetual Motion

Nancy

Dr. Xao
Physics 11
4-15-98

When one mentions the term "perpetual motion," most people envision a machine that will run forever. For the physics student, however, a perpetual motion machine is one that does useful work without drawing on an external force. In other words, it is a machine in which the output is greater than the input, ultimately leading to a machine that can create energy. Historically, perpetual motion arose in connection with the search for a machine or mechanism that would continue to do useful work once set in motion or would give more energy than it used in a cycle of operation.

The early perpetual motionists saw what they perceived to be perpetual motion on a large scale every day—the sun rising and setting, the moon waxing and waning, and the tides ebbing and flowing. Nature's forces surrounded the perpetual motionists, and harnessing these ever-present forces in order to make work easier was seen as a natural and necessary thing to do. To these people, who concentrated on supplying everyone with the basic necessities, automatic machinery was not a goal to be achieved but rather another aspect of the work to be done. It is not surprising, then, to discover that all of the early perpetual motion machines concerned the craft of the miller, who used either water or wind to grind his corn. However, efforts to create perpetual motion machines were not limited to wind and water propulsion, and, for the most part, the perpetual motionists kept up with the technological advances of the times, such that a sort of perpetuity was established between the perpetual motionists and technology itself—any advance in technology seeming to spark a new idea for perpetual motion in the mind of some inventor. It seemed that perpetual motion was always close, but the ineluctable laws of motion and energy conservation, of which these early inventors had no knowledge, thwarted their success every time. Looking back on them with the knowledge we have today, it would be easy to judge these people as foolish or to place them among the alchemists in the sense that they were seeking the impossible. But to look at them in this manner would be to sell them short, because it was their failure in many cases that became the foundation from which theories were developed—theories that still stand today and that have become the basis of our laws of thermodynamics.

To fully appreciate what the perpetual motionists were attempting to create, it is perhaps helpful to know the odds that they were up against. Simon Stevinus, a great mathematician of the 16th century, proved the law of equilibrium on an inclined plane by showing that perpetual motion could not exist. This is one of the earliest examples of a theory still in use today that came about, in part, as an attempt to disprove the notion that a perpetual motion machine could be made. Stevinus proved his theory of equilibrium on an inclined plane by taking a cord of uniform density on which were strung 14 balls of equal mass set an equal distance apart. He then hung the connected balls on a triangular-shaped support made up of two unequally inclined planes with a common horizontal base.

In determining the conditions for equilibrium, one of two things must be true: Either the balls are in equilibrium when so arranged, or they are not. If they are not in equilibrium and motion ensues, the motion cannot change the condition of the system because there will always be 8 balls on one plane, 4 on another plane, and two on the third. Therefore, once the system starts to move, it must continue, or more specifically, it must

1

demonstrate perpetual motion. Because the system does not move, the law for equilibrium on an inclined plane is proved.[1]

While their quest ensued, physicists continued to turn their attention toward finding relationships between heat and other forms of energy. These relationships were experimented with and theorized about until finally, in 1842, the German physicist Julius Robert Mayer (1814–1878) formally stated that "Once in existence, force cannot be annihilated; it can only change its form."[2] This statement, known as the foundation of the First Law of Thermodynamics, has been expanded, such that the law now states, in simplified terms, that "a fixed amount of mechanical work always produces the equivalent amount of heat, and thus energy can be converted from work into heat, but it can neither be created nor can it be destroyed."[3]

This latter part of the First Law, concerning the creation and destruction of energy, is referred to as the Principle of the Conservation of Energy. This principle is the primary reason why it is now believed that a perpetual motion machine cannot exist. If, as stated earlier, a perpetual motion machine is one whose efficiency exceeds 100%, then energy would have to be created somewhere during the cycle of operation, and it is this fact that violates the Principle. Just from a practical point of view, if one chose to invalidate the First Law of Thermodynamics (as many perpetual motionists did), creating a perpetual motion machine would still be impossible because in the world of man, all motion involves some rubbing of one material over another. At the point to rubbing, opposing forces, called friction, tend to stop the machine, requiring energy to keep the machine moving. Even if friction could be reduced, as with a pendulum hanging in a vacuum, not all friction is lost because at the string, where the fibers rub against one another, friction still exists. Even if hung on a string of quartz glass, one of the best materials for reducing internal rubbing friction, the pendulum would swing for a long time but not forever.

Despite this argument, some perpetual motionists say that friction does not destroy the energy of motion; it merely converts some mechanical kinetic energy into heat energy. In this regard they are correct, but if these inventors go one step further to suggest that the heat energy can be converted back into mechanical energy to be returned to the machine, then they lack understanding of one of the fundamental laws of heat engines, which states that no heat engine can ever exceed 100% efficiency.

Interestingly enough, an experiment was done with heat engines by Nicolas Leonard Sadi Carnot (1796–1832), a French physicist and theoretician, on the steam engine that proved the law about 100% efficiency. The First Law states that a fixed amount of mechanical work can be converted into an equal amount of heat, but based on experience, Carnot did not feel that this held true for a heat engine as a "closed circuit," in which water was heated until it changed into steam, the steam moved a piston, was exhausted, condensed back into water, and fell back into the boiler. From his experiment, Carnot concluded that there was an unavoidable loss of thermal energy in the process of condensation. Therefore, the transformation of heat into useful power was "fixed solely by the temperature of the bodies between which was effected . . . The transfer of the caloric."[4]

Later, Carnot's findings were formally presented by Rudolf Clausisu (1822–1888) in the form of the Second Law of Thermodynamics. This law states that to do work, heat

2

acts like a water mill: It must run "downhill" to do the work, and the more it goes downhill, the more work it will do. In other words, heat goes from a higher temperature to a lower temperature to do work and cannot be increased without the expenditure of more work. If a hot body is placed with a colder one, the tendency is to equalize their temperatures—not to increase their difference.

Coincidentally, designs for perpetual motion machines were presented in which neither friction nor electrical resistance was a significant problem in the design of the machine, but a problem arose in that these machines were, in effect, trying to circumvent the Second Law. For example, it was proposed that an ocean liner could extract the heat from the ocean and use it for propulsion. This idea violates the Second Law in that heat will not of its own accord flow from a cooler body to a warmer body.

The First and Second Laws of Thermodynamics and the Principle of the Conservation of Energy were firmly established in the scientific community by the middle 19th century. Unfortunately, these scientific advancements seemed to remain within the scientific community, falling on deaf ears whenever announced to the public, such that many people went on searching for the miracle machine that would provide them with a constant source of energy and make them wealthy.

References

1. Blackwood, O. General physics. London: Wiley & Sons, 1955.
2. Cajori, F. A history of physics. London: Macmillan, 1899.
3. Chase, C. T. The evolution of modern physics. New York: van Nostrand, 1947.
4. Fraser, C. Half-hours with great scientists: The story of an obsession. New York: Reinhold, 1948.

4

Index

INDEX

A

Adjectivals, 411–412
Adjective complement, 412
Adjectives and adverbs
    bad and *badly*, 413–414
    good and *well*, 412–413
Adverbials, 412, 417
Advertising, 341–342
    and audience, 341
Analysis
    of information, 207–209
    interpretation of events by, 170–173
Analysis of writing, elements of, 31
Anderson, Bonnie, 50–54
Antagonists, role in fiction, 358
Antecedents, and pronouns, 392
Antithesis, interpretation of information, 209–210
Argument
    conclusion of, 317–318
    evidence in, 296, 297, 312
    examples in, 313
    examples of, 321–325
    features of, 296–297
    formal arguments, 295–296, 312
    informal arguments, 295, 296, 312
    intellectual argument, 295
    and interpretation, 32, 35–36
    compared to persuasion, 302, 329
    premises of, 296, 297, 299–301
    problem of, 296, 297, 299
    proposals and claims, 296, 297, 302–309
    recognition of opposing views, 313–315
    steps in writing, 325–327
    structure of, 295–296
    support in, 296, 297, 309–312
    thesis-antithesis in, 315–317
Argument, flaws of
    attack of the person, 320–321
    either/or fallacy, 321
    faulty causality, 319–320
    faulty generalization, 320
    slippery slope, 320

Aries, Philippe, 194–198
Articles, 391–392
    definite article, 391–392
    indefinite article, 391
Atmosphere, short fiction, 356–357
Audience
    and advertising, 341
    and conventions, 34
    general audience, meaning of, 91
    insider-to-insider writing, 37, 38, 100–101
    insider/outsider-to-outsider writing, 37, 38, 90–92
    and interpretive report, 98–101
    and premises, 44
    and rhetorical stance, 33–34
    and subject matter, 34–35
    teacher as, 39

B

Backlash: The Undeclared War Against American Women (Faludi), 256–260
Bad and *badly*, 413–414
Baker, Russell, 208
Battle Cry of Freedom (McPherson), 91–92, 94–95, 109–111
"Best Way to Fix Medicare, The" (Kinsley), 145–146
Bishop, Morris, 46–50
Bloom, Sandra, 173–176
Body of report, 92–93
    details in, 92–93
    elements of, 93
Book reviews, 275–278
Boorstin, Daniel, 90–91, 92–93, 102–103, 115–116
Boyle, T. C., 368–375
Bradley, Bill, 185–189
Brooke, Robert, 275–278
Brown, Peter, 194–198
Bully for Brontosaurus: Reflections in Natural History (Gould), 251–255

C

Case
  nominative case, 393
  objective case, 393
Casti, John L., 149–151, 281–284
Cause and effect
  faulty causality, 319–320
  as support, 102
"Causes, Root Causes, and Cures" (Murray),
    189–193
Chaos: Making a New Science (Gleick),
    136–139
Character
  analysis of, 358–359
  antagonists, 358
  defined, 103
  protagonists, 358
  in short fiction, 358–359
Character-based support, 103
  character as proof, 311–312
  combined with reason-based support, 104–
    106
"Chrysanthemums, The" (Steinbeck), 350–381
Claims. *See* Proposals and claims
Clauses
  comma with, 424–425
  dependent clause, 387, 416, 422
  independent clauses, 387, 416
  nonrestrictive clauses, 422
  relative clauses, 387, 403–404
  restrictive clauses, 422
  semicolon with, 424
  subordinate clause, 387
Climax, in fiction, 359
Colon, uses of, 425
Comma splice, 424
Commas, uses of, 423–424
Common nouns, 389
Communities
  diversity of. *See* Culture and diversity
  professional communities, 40
Comparison and contrast
  interpretation of events by, 167–170
  as support, 102–103
Complements, predicate, 407
Compound nouns, 390
Computers, for drafting, 68
*Concentration Camps USA: Japanese-Americans
    and World War II* (Daniels), 201
Conclusions, 93–96
  of argument, 317–318
  generalization in, 95–96
  linked to end of event, 94
Conflict, in fiction, 359–360
Confrontational rhetorical purpose
  defined, 46
  example of, 54–56
Conjunctions
  coordinating conjunctions, 414–415
  subordinating conjunctions, 387, 414–415,
    416–417
Conventional reality, meaning of, 30
Conventions
  and audience, 34
  purposes of, 1–2
Coordinating conjunctions, 414–415
Coordination, and punctuation, 415–416
Courts, Patrick L., 147–148
Culture and diversity
  and advertising, 341
  and analysis of information, 214
  and evaluation of events, 244–245
  facts and culture, 128
  insiders/outsiders and language, 29
  insiders/outsiders and writing, 30–31, 33,
    37–38
  and interpretation of events, 165
  and metaphorical language, 67
  personal behavior, 176–177
  and personal voice, 132–133
  premises in, 301
  and response papers, 364
  second-language learning, 106
  and successful writing, 89
  and writing ability, 4

D

Daniels, Roger, 201
Darley, John, 177–180
Dash, uses of, 425
Davis, Susan E., 303–309, 313–314, 317–318
Definite article, 391–392
Definition
  interpretation of events by, 173–176
  as support, 102
Demonstrative pronouns, 394–395
  indefinite demonstrative pronouns, 395
Dependent clause, 387, 416, 422
"Descent of Man, The" (Boyle), 368–375
Details
  in body of report, 93
  factual details, 130–132
  in personal writing, 9
Dictionary, as writing tool, 102
Direct method, personal writing, 4, 9–10
Discourse communities, 29, 30
  and evaluation of events, 244
*Discoverers: A History of Man's Search to Know
    His World and Himself* (Boorstin), 90,
    92–93, 115–118
Discussion, invention stage, 61
Diversity. *See* Culture and diversity
Drafting stage, 60, 68
  aspects of, 68
  revising drafts, examples of, 69–81
Dramatic point of view, 363
Duby, George, 194–198

E

Editing
    editing stage, 60, 82–86
    meaning of, 68
    for sentence variety, 82–83
Either/or fallacy, 321
Emotional proof, 312
Evaluation, nature of, 241
Evaluation of data
    evaluation of interpretations, 279–284
    examples of, 272–289
    negative evaluations, 279–280
    organization of, 280–281
    reviews of books/articles, 275–278
    setting tone for, 283–284
    statistical, 272–274, 289–291
    steps in writing, 291–293
Evaluation of events
    background information, 247–248
    conclusion, 250–251
    and discourse communities, 244
    examples of, 251–267
    interpretation of event, 248–249
    selection of event, 245–247
    steps in writing, 267–268
Events. *See* Evaluation of events; Interpretation
    of events
Evidence, in argument, 296, 297, 312
Examples, in argument, 313

F

Facts, 126–130
    and group membership, 127–128
    nature of facts, 126–127
    sources of, 129–130
Faludi, Susan, 256–260
Faulty causality, 319–320
Faulty generalization, 320
Fiction. *See* Literature interpretation (short fiction)
First person, point of view, 363
Formal arguments, 295–296, 312
*Fourth Estate: A History of Women in the Middle
    Ages* (Shahar), 54–56
*Freedom Bound: A History of America's Civil
    Rights Movement* (Weisbrot), 95–96,
    112–114
Freewriting, 62–63
    and looping, 63
"Frequency of Errors in Essays by College
    Freshmen and by Professional Writers"
    (Sloan), 279–280
Fukuyama, Francis, 272–274
Future predictions, 185–193

G

Gaining Ground in College Writing (Haswell),
    review of, 275–278

Gates, Henry Louis, Jr., 323–324
Generalization
    in conclusion, 95–96
    faulty, 320
Gibson, Janice, 280–281
Gleick, James, 136–139
Goldhammer, Arthur, 194
Good Times, The (Baker), 208
Good and *well*, 412–413
Gould, Stephen Jay, 251–255
Great Disruption, The (Fukuyama), 272–274
Gunderson, Gerald, 209–210

H

Hakuta, Kenji, 104–105
Haritos-Fatouros, Mika, 280–281
Hentoff, Nat, 157–160
History of Private Life, A (Goldhammer), 194
*History of Their Own: Women in Europe from
    Prehistory to the Present* (Anderson and
    Zinsser), 50–54

I

"Immodest Proposal, An" (Peterson), 218–221
Indefinite article, 391
Indefinite demonstrative pronouns, 395
Indefinite pronouns, 397–399
Independent clause, 387, 416
Indirect method, personal writing, 4, 16, 27–28
Informal arguments, 295, 296, 312
Information
    in persuasive essay, 335–340
    See also Evaluation of data; Interpretation of
        information; Reporting information
Innovative rhetorical purpose
    defined, 46
    example of, 50–54
Intellectual argument, 295
Interpretation
    and argument, 32, 35–36
    purposes of, 32–33
Interpretation of events
    aims of, 166
    by analysis, 170–173
    by comparison and contrast, 167–170
    by definition, 173–176
    examples of, 168–176, 177–180, 181–182,
        185–188, 189–192, 194–201
    explanation of event, 166–167
    future predictions, 185–193
    metaphor in, 173–176
    steps in writing, 202–204
    underlying cause, interpretation of, 177–180
    unique perspective on, 180–184
Interpretation of information
    analysis of information, 207–209
    antithesis, 209–210

Interpretation of information (*Cont.*)
    examples of, 215–217, 218–236
    levels of, 215
    steps in writing, 217–218, 237–239
    structure of writing, 210–213
    thesis, 209
Interpretations, evaluation of, 279–284
Interpretive reports, 87, 97–106
    and audience, 98–99
    character-based support, 103
    as insider-to-insider writing, 100–101
    nature of, 97
    reason-based support, 102–103
    reason/character-based support, 104–106
    seeing versus looking in, 97–98
    steps in writing, 122–124
Intransitive verbs, 406–407
Introduction, 88–92
    elements of, 93
    familiarity in, 89
    writing for outsiders, 90–92
Invention stage, 42, 60, 61–67
    discussion, 61
    freewriting, 62–63
    journals, 64
    metaphor, 65–67
    outlining, 62
    talk-write, 65
Irony, 363–364
    situational irony, 364
    verbal irony, 363–364
Irregular nouns, 390

J

Jackson, Shirley, 376–381
Jargon, 29
Journalists' questions, 87–88
Journals, usefulness of, 64

K

Kennedy, John F., 343–345
Kinsley, Michael, 145–146
Klinkenborg, Verlyn, 208–209

L

Language
    and diverse groups, 29, 360–361
    form, 385–386
    formal Standard English, 385
Latané, Bibb, 177–180
Legacy of Conquest, The (Limerick), 181–184
Lie and *lay*, 407
Limerick, Patricia N., 181–184

Limited omniscient point of view, 362
Linking verbs, 407–408, 412
Literacy and Empowerment: The Meaning Makers (Courts), 147–148
"Literacy In School and Out" (Resnick), 228–236
Literature
    basic assumptions about, 349
    examples of (short fiction), 350–356, 377–381
Literature interpretation (short fiction)
    characters, 358–359
    example of, 366–368
    irony, 363
    plot, 359–360
    point of view, 362–363
    response paper, 368–376
    setting, 356–357
    steps in writing, 364–366
    theme, 360–362
    writing guide, 364–366
"Living Smaller" (Rybczynski), 215–217
Logical proof, 309–311
Looping, and freewriting, 63
"Lottery, The" (Jackson), 377–381

M

McPherson, James M., 91–92, 94–95, 109–111
Mass nouns, 389, 390
Metaphor, 65–67
    defined, 65
    in interpretation of events, 173–176
    metaphorical language, 66, 67
    writing of, 66–67
Minor claims, 304–309, 310
    examples of, 304–309
    relationship to major claim, 309
Mirror of Language (Hakuta), 104–105
Mission statement, of school, 38, 58
Modern Language Association (MLA) Handbook for Writers of Research Papers, 2
Modifiers
    adjectivals, 411–412
    adverbials, 412
Mood, short fiction, 357
Murray, Charles, 189–193

N

"Natural Restoration" (Davis), 303–309, 313–314, 317–318
Nava, Michael, 4–10
Negin, Elliott, 247–251, 261–267
Nominative case, 393
Nonrestrictive clauses, 422
Noun phrase, 387

Nouns, 389–391
  common nouns, 389
  compound nouns, 390
  Greek and Latin derived, 390–391
  mass nouns, 389, 390
  plurals, construction of, 389–391
  proper nouns, 389

O

Object of sentence, 389
Objective case, 393
Objective reports, meaning of, 87
Omniscient point of view, 362
Outlining, usefulness of, 62

P

Paradigms Lost (Casti), 149–151, 281–284
Paragraph development, 436–438
  coherence and unity, 437–438
Paraphrase, usefulness of, 103
Parentheses, uses of, 425
Perfect progressive verb form, 410
Perfect verb form, 410
Period, use of, 423
"Person and Group in Judaism and Early Chris-
    tianity" (Aries, Duby, and Veyne),
    194–198
Personal pronouns, 393
Personal writing
  direct method, 4, 9–10
  examples of, 4–10, 16–24, 25–26
  functions of, 2–3
  indirect method, 4, 16, 27–28
  personal experience in persuasive essay,
    330–334
  relationship to public writing, 81
  writing assignment, 10–15
Persuasion
  advertising, 341–342
  compared to argument, 302, 329
  ethical issues, 330
  examples of, 331–333, 335–340, 343–346
  information conveyed in, 335–340
  personal experience in, 330–334
  political speeches, 342–348
Peterson, Paul E., 218–221
Phrases
  noun phrase, 387
  prepositional phrases, 419
  verb phrase, 387
Planning stage, 60
  aspects of, 67
Plot, analysis of, 360
Plurals
  of indefinite pronouns, 398–399
  of nouns, 389–391

of possessive pronouns, 396
  subject-verb agreement, 408–409
Point of view, 362–363
  dramatic, 363
  first person, 363
  limited omniscient, 362
  omniscient, 362
Political speeches, 342–348
  example of, 343–346
  language of, 342–343
  persuasive elements, 342–343
Pollitt, Katha, 335–340
Possessive pronouns, 396
Predicate adjectives, 412
Predicate of sentence, 387
Premises, 43–44
  of argument, 296, 297, 299–301
  audience acceptance of, 44
  definition of, 299
  evaluation of, 45
  identification of, 301
  nature of, 43–44
Preparing to Teach Writing (Williams), 140–143,
    284–286
Prepositional phrases, 419
Prepositions
  at end of sentences, 420
  like, 420–421
  listing of, 419
  number in sentences, 420
Problem, of argument, 296, 297
Problem solving, writing as, 81
Progressive verb form, 409–410
Pronouns
  and antecedents, 392
  case, 393
  demonstrative pronouns, 394–395
  gender usage issue, 400
  indefinite pronouns, 397–399
  personal pronouns, 393
  possessive pronouns, 396
  reciprocal pronouns, 396
  reflexive pronouns, 402–403
  relative pronouns, 403–405
Proof of argument, 296, 297
Proper nouns, 389
Proposals and claims
  of argument, 296, 297, 302–309
  minor claims, 304–309
  placement in writing, 303–304
Protagonists, role in fiction, 358
*Publication Manual of the American Psychologi-
    cal Association*, 2
Punctuation
  colon, 425
  commas, 423–424
  and coordination, 415–416
  dash, 425
  parentheses, 425

Punctuation (*Cont.*)
period, 423
quotation marks, 426
semicolon, 424–425

Q

Quotation marks, use of, 426

R

Radetsky, Peter, 91, 106–108
Reason-based support, 102–103
cause and effect, 102
combined with character-based support,
104–106
comparison and contrast, 102–103
definition, 102
Reciprocal pronouns, 396
Reflection, and writing, 2, 59
Reflexive pronouns, 402–403
Relative clauses, 387, 403–404, 422
Relative pronouns, 403–405, 422
Reporting events
body of report, 92–93
conclusions, 93–96
examples of, 106–118
interpretive reports, 87, 97–106
introduction, 88–92
objective and subjective reports, 87
title of report, 88
See also Interpretive reports
Reporting information
aim of report, 130, 133, 143–144
examples of, 147–154, 157–160
facts in, 126–130
reports leading to action, 143–147
steps in writing, 160–163
summarizing information, 130–133
summary report, 133–139
Resnick, Lauren B., 228–236
Response paper, 368–376
example of, 375–376
Restrictive clauses, 422
Reviews, of books/articles, 275–278
Revising stage, 60, 68–81
elements of, 69
example of, 69–81
versus editing, 68
Rhetorical distance, meaning of, 296
Rhetorical purpose
confrontational type, 46, 54–59
definition of, 46
innovative type, 46, 50–54
traditional type, 46–50
Rhetorical stance, and audience, 33–34
Role-playing, 39, 100, 346–347
Rybczynski, Witold, 215–217

S

Salutation of letter, punctuation, 425
Scannell, Kate, 25–27
Seltzer, Richard, 16–24
Semicolon, uses of, 424–425
Sentence fragment, 423
Sentence variety
editing for, 82–83
writing varied sentences, 434–436
Sentences
clauses and phrases, 387
objects, 389
simple sentence, 386–387
subject and predicate, 387
Setting, short fiction, 356–357
Shahar, Shalamith, 54–56
Shanker, Albert, 321–323
Singal, Daniel J., 221–227
Situational irony, 364
Slippery slope, 320
Sloan, Gary, 279–280
Standards of proof, 35–36
Statistics, data evaluation, 272–274, 289–291
Steinbeck, John, 349–381
Subject areas, nature of, 40
Subject matter, and audience, 34–35
Subject of sentence, 387
Subject-verb agreement, 409
Subjective reports, meaning of, 87
Subjects, academic, nature of, 40
Subordinate clauses, 387, 416–417, 423
Subordinating conjunctions, 387, 414–415,
416–417
Summarizing information, 130–133
factual details in, 130–132
shifts in, 132
signals of important information in, 133
Summary report, 133–139
and audience, 133–134, 136
examples of, 134–135
features of, 134
on literature assignments, 135–136
on specialized information, 136–139
Support
of argument, 296, 297, 309–312
character as proof, 311–312
emotional proof, 312
logical proof, 309–311
Synthesis, examples of, 208

T

Talk-write, 65
Tannen, Deborah, 152–154
"Teach by the Values You Preach" (Tompkins),
331–334
Teacher, as audience, 39
Tense, 408

That and *which*, 422–423
That and *who*, 405
Theme
   defined, 356, 360
   in fiction, 360–362
   and place/time, 361
There and *here*, 409
Thesis
   nature of, 41
   premises of, 43–44
   compared to topics, 41–42
Thesis-antithesis
   in argument, 315–317
   in interpretation of information, 209–210
Title of report, 88
   working title, 88
Tompkins, Jane, 331–334
Tone
   in evaluation of data, 283–284
   objective tone, 311
Topics
   nature of, 41
   compared to thesis, 41–42
Traditional rhetorical purpose
   defined, 46
   example of, 47–50
Transitive verbs, 406–407

V

"Value Free?" (Shanker), 321–323
Verb forms
   perfect progressive verb form, 410
   perfect verb form, 410
   progressive verb form, 409–410
Verb phrase, 387
Verbal irony, 363–364
Verbs
   intransitive verbs, 406–407
   lie and *lay*, 407
   linking verbs, 407–408, 412
   number, 408
   subject-verb agreement, 408–409

tense, 408
   transitive verbs, 406–407
Veyne, Paul, 194–198
Viruses (Radetsky), 91, 106–108

W

Wealth Creators, The (Gunderson), 209–210
Weisberg, Jacob, 315
Weisbrot, Robert, 95–96, 112–114
"Western Saddle, The" (Klinkenborg), 208–209
"When Nice People Burn Books" (Hentoff),
   157–160
Who and *whom*, 404–405
"Whose Culture Is It Anyway?" (Gates), 323–324
"Why College Tuitions Are So High" (Negin),
   247–251, 261–267
"Why I Hate 'Family Values' (Let Me Count the
   Ways)" (Pollitt), 335–340
Williams, James D., 140–143, 284–286
Williams, Michael, 199–201
Word choice, 427–429
   commonly confused words, 429–434
   examples of, 428
Working title, 88
Writing process
   drafting, 68
   editing, 82–86
   invention, 61–67
   planning, 67
   publishing stage, 60, 86
   revising, 68–81
   stages of writing (table), 60

Y

*You Just Don't Understand: Women and Men in
   Conversation* (Tannen), 152–154

Z

Zinsser, Judith, 50–54

selection credits

SELECTION CREDITS

GARDENLAND, SACRAMENTO, CALIFORNIA, *5*

From *Hometowns: Gay Men Write About Where They Belong*, pp. 21–29, by Michael Nava, John Preston ed. Published by the Penguin Group, NY. Copyright (c) 1991. Reprinted by permission of the author.

IMELDA, *16*

From *Letters to a Young Doctor*, by Richard Selzer. Published by Simon & Schuster, New York, 1982. Copyright (c) 1982. David Goldman and Janet Selzer, Trustees. Used with permission of the Trustees.

SKILLS AND PILLS, *25*

Excerpt from *Death of the Good Doctor*, pp. 7–15, by Kate Scannell. Published by Cleis Press, San Francisco. Used with permission.

THE MIDDLE AGES, *47*

Reprinted by permission of *American Heritage Magazine* by Morris Bishop, a division of Forbes, Inc. Copyright (c) Forbes, Inc.

THE TOWNSWOMAN'S DAILY LIFE, *51*

From *A History of Their Own, Volume II*, pp. 353–357, by Bonnie Anderson and Judith Zinsser. Copyright (c) 1988. Bonnie Anderson and Judith Zinsser. Reprinted by permission of the publisher HarperCollins Publishers, Inc.

TOWNSWOMEN, *54*

From *The Fourth Estate: A History of Women in the Middle Ages*, pp. 174–177, by Dr. Shulamith Shahar. Published by Routledge, a division of Taylor & Francis Books Ltd. Used with permission of the publisher.

SHOE, *69*

Image by Jeff McNally. (c) Tribune Media Services, Inc. All rights reserved. Reprinted with permission.

A JAPANESE CHILD LEARNS ENGLISH, *104*

From *Mirror of Language* by Kenji Hakuta. Copyright (c) 1986 by Basic Books, Inc. Reprinted by permission of Basic Books, a member of Perseus Books, L.L.C.

VIRUSES, *107*

Excerpt from *The Invisible Invaders*, pp. 51–54, by Peter Radetsky. Copyright (c) 1995 Peter Radetsky. Reprinted by permission of Little, Brown and Company, Inc.

FAREWELL TO THE NINETY DAYS' WAR, *109*

From *Battle Cry of Freedom: The Era of the Civil War*, pp. 339–344, by James M. McPherson. Copyright (c) 1988 by Oxford University Press, Inc. Used by permission of Oxford University Press, Inc.

ed by Arthur Goldhammer, Cambridge, Mass.: The Belknap Press of Harvard University Press, Copyright (c) 1987 by the President and Fellows of Harvard College.

THE WORLD TODAY, *199*

Reprinted from *China and the World After Tian An Men*, p. 127+, by Michael Williams, *The World Today*, Aug/Sept 1989. Used with permission of the publisher.

JAPANESE-AMERICANS IN U.S. CONCENTRATION CAMPS, *201*

Reprinted from *Concentration Camps, USA* by Roger Nelson. Copyright (c) 1971 by Roger Nelson. Used with permission of the author.

WHEN HOUSES BULKED OUT, *215*

The Atlantic Monthly, Volume 267, pp. 64–69+. Copyright (c) 1991 Witold Rybczynski. First published in *The Atlantic Monthly*, February 1991. Reprinted with permission.

GIVE KIDS THE VOTE, *219*

Excerpted from *An Immodest Proposal* by Paul E. Peterson. Published by *Daedalus, Journal of the American Academy of Arts and Sciences*, Fall 1992, Vol. 212, No. 4, entitled *Immobile Democracy*. Used with permission of the publisher.

THE OTHER CRISIS IN AMERICAN EDUCATION, *222*

The Atlantic Monthly, Volume 268, pp. 69–62. Copyright (c) 1991 Daniel J. Singal. First published in *The Atlantic Monthly*, November 1991. Reprinted with permission.

LITERACY IN SCHOOL AND OUT, *228*

Excerpted from *Literacy In School and Out* by Lauren B. Resnick. Published by *Daedalus, Journal of the American Academy of Arts and Sciences*, Spring 1990, Vol. 119, No. 2, entitled *Literacy in America*. Used with permission of the publisher.

LITERARY BIAS ON THE SLIPPERY SLOPE, *252*

From *Bully for Brontosaurus: Reflections in Natural History*, pp. 241–249, by Stephen Jay Gould. Copyright (c) 1991 Stephen Jay Gould. Reprinted by permission of W. W. Norton & Company, Inc.

BACKLASH, *256*

From *Backlash* by Susan Faludi. Copyright (c) 1991 by Susan Faludi. Reprinted by permission of Crown Publishers, Inc.

WHY COLLEGE TUITIONS ARE SO HIGH, *261*

The Atlantic Monthly, Volume 271. Copyright (c) 1993 Elliott Negin. First published in *The Atlantic Monthly*, March 1993. Reprinted with permission of the author.

THE GREAT DISRUPTION, *272*

Reprinted with permission of The Free Press, a Division of Simon & Schuster, from *The Great Disruption: Human Nature and the Reconstitution of Social Order*, figs. 2.1, 2.2, pp. 32–36, by Francis Fukuyama. Copyright (c) 1999 by Francis Fukuyama. Reprinted by permission of the publisher.

GAINING GROUND IN COLLEGE WRITINGS, *275*

Excerpted from *The Journal of College Composition and Communication* by Robert Brooke. Copyright (c) 1993 by the National Council of Teachers of English. Reprinted with permission.

THE EDUCATION OF A TORTURER, *280*

Excerpted from *Psychology Today*, November 1986, by J. T. Gibson and M. Haritos-Fatouros. Copyright (c) 1986 Sussex Publishers, Inc. Reprinted with permission from *Psychology Today Magazine*.

PREPARING TO TEACH WRITING, *284*

From *Preparing to Teach Writing*, pp. 62–65, by James Williams. Published by Lawrence Erlbaum Associates, New Jersey. Used with permission.

LOS ANGELES COUNTY: GROWING DIVERSITY, *290*

First published by *The Los Angeles Times*, Los Angeles Times Syndicate, June 1994 by Robert Burns. Reprinted with permission.

NATURAL RESTORATION: WHEN HUMANS WALK AWAY, *304*

Excerpted from *Whole Earth Review*, No. 66, March 23, 1996, pp. 102–104 by Susan E. Davis. Reprinted with permission from the publisher.

GAYS IN ARMS: TIME FOR A FAIR FIGHT, *315*

From *Gays in Arms: Time for a Fair Fight* by Jacob Weisberg, *The New Republic*, February 1990. Used with permission of the publisher.

CARTOON, *317*

Image reproduced from the *Tampa Tribune* 1988 by Wayne Stayskal. Used with permission of Wayne Stayskal.

VALUE FREE? *322*

Reprinted from *The New York Times*, January 6, 1991, by Albert Shanker. Copyright (c) 1991 by the New York Times Co. Reprinted with permission of the American Federation of Teachers.

WHOSE CULTURE IS IT ANYWAY? *323*

Reprinted from *The New York Times*, May 4, 1991, by Henry L. Gates, Jr. Copyright (c) 1991 by the New York Times Co. Reprinted with permission.

TEACH BY THE VALUES YOU PREACH, *331*

From *Pedagogy of the Distressed*, by Jane Tompkins. Excerpted from *College English*, *Volume 52*, No. 6. Copyright (c) 1990 by the National Council of Teachers of English. Reprinted with permission.

WHY I HATE "FAMILY VALUES" (LET ME COUNT THE WAYS), *335*

From "Why I Hate 'Family Values' (Let Me Count the Ways)" by Katha Pollitt. Reprinted from *The Nation*, July 20, 1993. Used with permission.

JOHN F. KENNEDY, Campaign Speech, *343*

Delivered in Houston, Texas, September 12, 1960.

THE CHRYSANTHEMUMS, *350*

From *The Long Valley*, pp. 9–23, by John Steinbeck. Copyright 1937, renewed (c) 1965 by John Steinbeck. Used by permission of Viking Penguin, a division of Penguin Putnam Inc.

DESCENT OF MAN, *368*

From *Descent of Man* by T. Coraghessan Boyle (Boston: An Atlantic Monthly Press/Little Brown book) Copyright (c) 1974, 1976, 1979 T. Coraghessan Boyle. First appeared in *The Paris Review*. Reprinted by permission of Georges Borchardt Inc. for the author.

THE LOTTERY, *377*

From *The Lottery* by Shirley Jackson. Copyright (c) 1948, 1949 Shirley Jackson. Copyright renewed 1976, 1977 by Laurence Hyman, Barry Hyman, Mrs. Sarah Webster, and Mrs. Joanne Schnurer. Reprinted by permission of Farrar, Straus and Giroux, L.L.C.

STUDENT PAPERS

The following titles were all written by students and permission to reprint has been granted to the author: *My First Job, Freewriting, Journal, Deciding to Go to College, Bookshop Fire, Campus Attack, Mall Survey, Acheta Domesticus, Summary & Detail in a Sentence, Summary Report of a Book, Growing Distrust of Government, The System Doesn't Work, Political vs. Spiritual Love, Response Paper (Boyle), Pearl Harbor, St. Augustine & Platonic Thought, Population Changes in L.A. County, Untitled, Genes & Crime, King Lear, Perpetual Motion.*